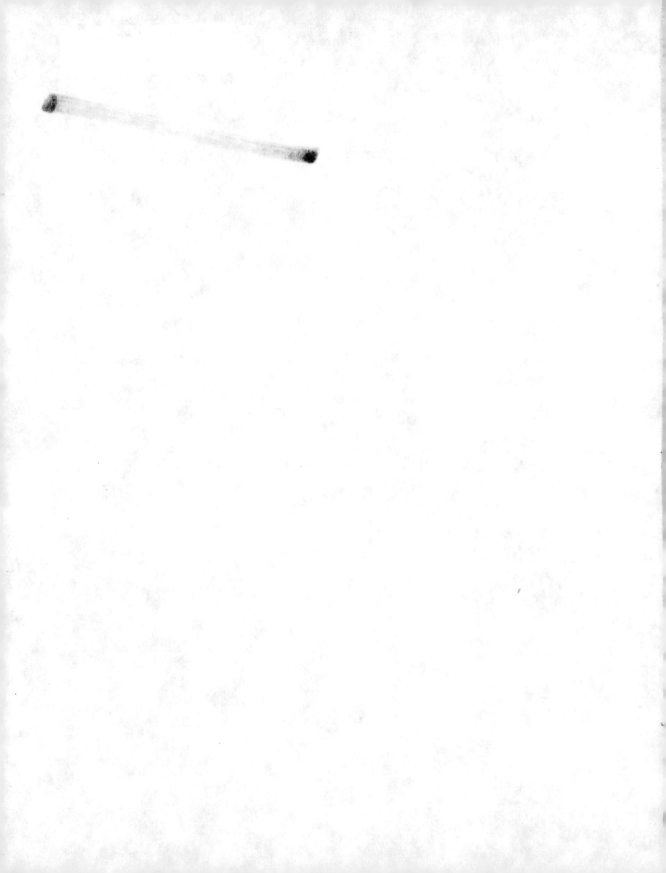

Measuring and Evaluating School Learning

Measuring and Evaluating School Learning

SECOND EDITION

Lou M. Carey
University of South Florida

ALLYN AND BACON
Boston London Toronto Sydney Tokyo Singapore

Editor-in-Chief, Education: Nancy Forsyth
Series Editorial Assistant: Christine R. Nelson
Editorial-Production Administrator: Annette Joseph
Composition Buyer: Linda Cox
Manufacturing Buyer: Louise Richardson
Cover Administrator: Linda K. Dickinson
Cover Designer: Studio Nine

Library of Congress Cataloging-in-Publication Data

Carey, Lou.
  Measuring and evaluating school learning / Lou M. Carey. — 2nd ed.
      p. cm.
  Includes bibliographical references and index.
  ISBN 0–205–12865–3
  1. Educational tests and measurements—United States. I. Title.
LB3051.C36   1994
371.2′6′0973—dc20   93–35571
                                                                                  CIP

Printed in the United States of America

10 9 8 7 6 5 4 3 2 1   99 98 97 96 95 94 93

Permissions Credits: Materials from *ParTEST User's Manual* (1991) and *ParGRADE/ParSCORE User's Manual* (1992) (including Figures 2.1, 6.13, 6.14, 7.2, 8.1, 8.2, 8.3, 14.9, and 14.10), © Economic Research, Inc., Reprinted by permission. Figures 15.9, 15.10, 15.11, 15.12, and 15.13, Copyright © 1992 by Macmillan/McGraw-Hill School Publishing Company. All rights reserved. Reprinted by permission.

BRIEF CONTENTS

CONTENTS

PART II DESIGNING, DEVELOPING, AND USING OBJECTIVE TESTS

PART III DESIGNING, DEVELOPING, AND USING ALTERNATIVE ASSESSMENTS

PART IV   COMMUNICATING STUDENT PROGRESS

APPENDICES

PREFACE

Measuring and Evaluating School Learning focuses on the information and skills teachers need to design, develop, analyze, and interpret tests; to use test results in planning, monitoring, and evaluating instruction; and to evaluate student progress. It is directed to undergraduate education students who are preparing to teach and to graduate students who want to improve their teaching and testing skills. It can also serve as a reference for educators in schools, universities, businesses, and government agencies.

The book assumes that readers have had little, if any, instruction in educational measurement, evaluation, or statistics. The Practice Exercises require readers to be familiar with the curriculum and skills in their fields, with basic learning principles, and with the application of these principles to their disciplines.

Testing is an integral part of the teaching and learning process, and it provides teachers with vital information. When tests are anchored to the instructional goals in the curriculum guide, readiness tests help teachers determine whether students have the knowledge and skills necessary to begin a unit of instruction. Pretests help teachers identify skills that need to be emphasized during instruction. With practice tests, teachers can monitor skill development, identify instructional needs, and pace instruction. Finally, post-tests help teachers evaluate student progress and locate inadequacies in instruction.

PLAN FOR THE TEXT

Measuring and Evaluating School Learning presents the following four-part process for constructing and using tests:

- Part I—Linking Testing and Instruction
- Part II—Designing, Developing, and Using Objective Tests
- Part III—Designing, Developing, and Using Alternative Assessments
- Part IV—Communicating Student Progress

Part I, Linking Testing and Instruction, includes locating and sequencing instructional goals, describing the achievement characteristics of new groups of students, analyzing state and school district instructional goals, and writing behavioral objectives. Part II, Designing, Developing, and Using Objective Tests, includes designing test and item specifications to help ensure validity and reliability; writing test items and constructing tests; and using data generated from tests to evaluate group performance, evaluate objective test items and tests, evaluate an individual student's achievement from a criterion-referenced and norm-referenced perspective, and evaluate instruction. Part III, Designing, Developing, and Using Alternative Assessments, includes constructing and using essay, product development, and active performance tests; constructing and using behavior observation forms and attitude questionnaires; developing and administering tests for nonreaders; as well as analyzing and evaluating student progress using portfolios and mastery charts. Part IV, Communicating Student Progress, includes procedures for grading and reporting student progress and for interpreting students' performance on standardized tests.

This text is constructed using sound principles of learning. First, chapters are sequenced in the natural order that tasks are undertaken by teachers in the classroom. For example, early chapters describe procedures for beginning a school year, including analyzing the assigned curriculum guide and achievement characteristics of new students. These chapters are not intended to substitute for courses in curriculum or educational psychology; instead, they serve to remind readers of relevant prerequisite information and tasks and provide the critical context for a course in classroom testing. These chapters also provide the foundation for linking curriculum, instruction, and testing. From these curriculum-learner anchors, the text illustrates, in order, design, development, analysis, evaluation, and reporting procedures.

Second, each chapter begins with a list of learning outcomes (Objectives) to focus readers' attention. Third, applicable concepts, principles, and procedures are introduced for each phase of the process and accompanied by an array of examples and illustrations. For the novice, these examples and illustrations serve to facilitate learning new capabilities and promote transfer of these capabilities to students' disciplines and teaching areas. Fourth, a single concrete example, based on the instructional goal of writing a paragraph, is used throughout the text to demonstrate procedures and to illustrate the linkages among the phases of design, development, analysis, evaluation, and communication.

Fifth, beginning with Chapter 2, the discussion in each chapter concludes with the following sections: Computer Technology, a presentation of technological advances in the testing field; Summary, an overview of key concepts and procedures; Practice Exercises, problems and activities that facilitate learning and transfer; and Feedback, responses to exercises to aid in understanding. The final unit within the Practice Exercises, called Enrichment, is especially useful in facilitating transfer of newly acquired skills and information. Because learners' responses to many of the exercises and Enrichment activities will vary, these sections can serve as a basis for classroom discussion and further elaboration. Finally, each chapter presents References, citing sources used in preparing the chapter, and Suggested Readings, providing additional sources for readers who may wish to pursue further given topics.

USE OF COMPUTER DEMONSTRATION PROGRAMS

The preparation of preservice and inservice teachers should include experience with the emerging technologies that are shaping the "best practices" models of professionalism. As computers and computer applications become commonplace fixtures in the classroom, it is critical that both new and experienced teachers develop the skills and dispositions for using technological support. The value of integrating computer technology with effective classroom testing and management of student progress has been demonstrated in schools nationwide.

To provide preservice and inservice teachers with the opportunity to learn about these technological advances, the second edition of *Measuring and Evaluating School Learning* has added several features. A section called Computer Technology has been added in each chapter (except 15), offering guidance and examples of computer applications for the principles and procedures introduced in that chapter. In addition, to give readers real experience with computer applications in classroom measurement and evaluation, two computer programs are provided with the text: ParTEST Demo and ParGRADE Demo (Economics Research, Inc., 1988). These two demonstration programs provide students with a medium in which they can experience actual computer applications.

Students may use the ParTEST Demo program (Economics Research, Inc., 1988) to gain technical experience through reviewing the example item bank and tests included on the disk, designing and developing their own computerized test item banks, assembling a variety of tests from their item banks, printing tests they have created, and printing student feedback reports for their tests. The example item bank on writing paragraphs in the ParTEST Demo was taken directly from the test design and development examples provided in this text.

Students may use the ParGRADE Demo program (Economics Research, Inc., 1988) to review the example pupil test data included on the disk, enter pupil performance data, enter grading criteria, enter weighting factors to tailor composite scores according to a plan, and convert raw scores to a variety of derived scores. Students can become familiar with all the features and operations of this electronic gradebook, but they cannot print pupil performance reports using the demonstration version of the program.

The ParTEST Demo and ParGRADE Demo programs are easy to open on an IBM or compatible computer by inserting the disk in drive A and typing PT or PG. The programs are menu driven, and operation is made easy with HELP features and onscreen prompts. Additional information on operating the ParTEST and ParGRADE programs is provided in the *Student Manual* and the *Instructor's Manual* that accompany this text. Learning to operate these item bank and gradebook programs during this course on measurement and evaluation of pupil progress will help teachers integrate these technological advancements into both their perspectives on testing and their routine work as classroom teachers.

APPROACH TO LEARNING AND TEACHING

Measuring and Evaluating School Learning is intended for all students enrolled in an introductory measurement course for teachers. Such students typically are from a variety of disciplines, such as language arts, mathematics, science, social studies, physical education, business education, elementary education, and special education. Because these students have diverse backgrounds, they do not have the discipline expertise required to analyze correctly the instructional goals in secondary school curricula for disciplines other than their own. For example, students who are expert in American government, chemistry, or music can be expected to understand illustrations and apply skills in these disciplines. However, students lacking expertise in these areas will be at a disadvantage. Because similar problems surface, regardless of the discipline, areas chosen for illustration and exercises were purposefully selected from common knowledge disciplines. All students, regardless of their majors, will be able to analyze such goals correctly and find such analyses quite challenging.

Students must be able to look beyond the content of the goals used as examples in this text in order to concentrate on the learning, measurement, and evaluation principles and procedures involved. After applying these skills using basic examples, students will be prepared to transfer them to their own disciplines for class projects or for their own work. Completing the activities prescribed in the Enrichment section of the Practice Exercises for each chapter will also help students transfer the skills to their own disciplines.

These common knowledge examples also have an advantage for teachers of this course. Like students, our areas of expertise beyond measurement and evaluation are diverse. Using basic skills examples enables us to provide many illustrations, adequate guidance, and corrective feedback to students as they perform the tasks.

ACKNOWLEDGMENTS

Many individuals participated in the formative evaluation of this book. I would like to acknowledge my colleagues—Roger Wilk, Constance Hines, and James Carey—who field tested versions of the text with their classes and provided valuable criticism on content, organization, presentation, and effectiveness.

Students in my classes also used field-tested versions and provided valuable guidance. The following students deserve special mention: Sue Beck, elementary education; Mark Lange, English education; John Myrick, physics education; Allison Salisbury, biology education; and Katie Winterhalter, mathematics education. Working as a small field-test group, these individuals applied each chapter to their majors and substantially influenced the final version of the text. Their contributions have undoubtedly increased its relevance for other students who want to learn testing principles and procedures.

Additional thanks go to Ralph F. Lewis of Economics Research, Inc., for his assistance in integrating the ParTEST illustrations and examples as well as his permission to use these materials.

The preparation of this second edition was guided by comments received from those individuals who reviewed the book for Allyn and Bacon: James M. Applefield, University of North Carolina at Wilmington; Robert M. Brashear, Western Michigan University; William L. Deaton, Auburn University at Montgomery; Louise Fleming, Ashland University; and James R. MacCluskie, Edinboro University of Pennsylvania.

And once again, thanks go to those individuals who reviewed the first edition: Tony Allen, University of Rhode Island; James Applefield, University of North Carolina at Wilmington; Steve Dunbar, University of Iowa; Richard Jaeger, University of North Carolina at Charlotte; Don Mizokawa, University of Washington; Bruce Rogers, University of Northern Iowa; John Sanderston, University of Virginia; Landa Trentham, Auburn University; and Gaylen Wallace, University of Missouri at St. Louis.

REFERENCES

Economics Research, Inc. (1988). *Tutorials for ParTEST and ParSCORE/ParGRADE* [Computer programs]. Costa Mesa, CA: Author.

Economics Research, Inc. (1991). *ParTEST user's manual*. Costa Mesa, CA: Author.

Economics Research, Inc. (1992). *ParSCORE andParGRADE user's manual*. Costa Mesa, CA: Author.

Measuring and Evaluating School Learning

CHAPTER 1

Introduction

Teachers choose their careers in the classroom for a variety of reasons. Some enjoy a particular subject, some have been inspired by teachers they had when they were students, and others enjoy helping people learn. Few, if any, enter the profession because they want to design and develop tests or interpret test results. Testing, however, plays a vital role in teaching. It also can help you refine your teaching skills throughout your career.

Effective teachers must also be proficient in testing, and proficiency in testing requires the synthesis of many different skills. Teachers must know about their discipline; about the nature of learning; and about their students' language skills, interests, and experiences. They must be able to write clearly, summarize and analyze data, and make comparisons and inferences to interpret test results. In applying testing principles and procedures, they must use their professional judgment and make informed decisions about their methods and instruction. Because teaching is a decision-based activity, the quality of instruction will depend on teachers' ability to gather, interpret, and use relevant information.

This text discusses all aspects of test development, use, and interpretation. Each chapter begins with a list of objectives that should help direct your study. The objectives are followed by relevant concepts, principles, and procedures. Many tables and figures illustrate the concepts and procedures, and a Summary section concludes each chapter. To help you develop your testing skills, each chapter ends with a comprehensive set of Practice Exercises. Many of these exercises require judgment and interpretation; thus, they should help you formulate questions you may want to ask during class discussions. Each set of Practice Exercises also includes suggestions for enrichment activities. These suggestions should help you transfer the skills to your discipline and classroom. As you read the text and complete the exercises, you will learn how to plan for new classes, create and use classroom tests, and report on students' overall progress.

The first phase, planning, consists of four activities: identifying and sequencing instructional goals, describing student achievement characteristics, analyzing instructional goals, and writing behavioral objectives. The information you gather and the decisions you make during this first phase become the basis for all subsequent activities.

In the second and third phases of the process, you must design and develop tests and evaluate your students' performances. The information you gather during these phases will help you improve both your tests and your instruction. The last phase is communication. You will need to grade and report your students' progress and to interpret their performance on standardized tests. Figure 1.1 illustrates these four phases and indicates the chap-

FIGURE 1.1
Using Tests in the Classroom

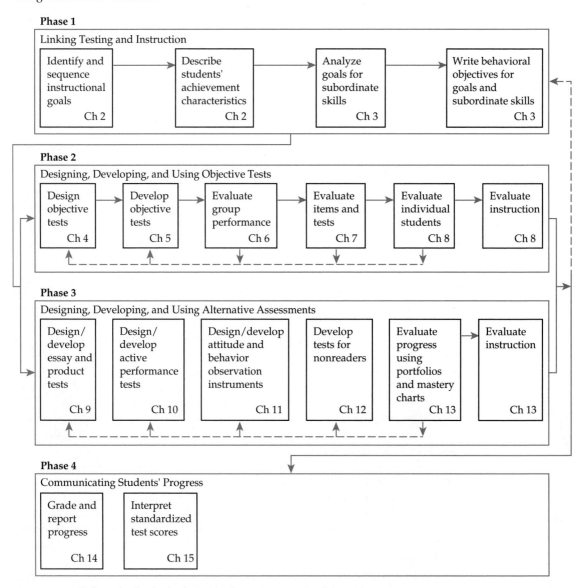

– – – – Reflects feedback of information for revisions and refinements

ters that describe each activity. The remaining sections of this chapter present an overview of each phase.

PLANNING FOR INSTRUCTION AND TESTS

The planning phase begins with two questions: What am I expected to teach in this course? and Whom am I expected to teach? To answer the first question, consult your curriculum guide, recommended lists of goals and objectives, and the manuals for standardized tests adopted by your district. After you have identified and compared instructional goals and objectives from these different sources, sort the goals by topic and then sequence the ones you will use. The list of sequenced instructional goals will guide your test design and development activities for each unit of instruction.

The best sources of information about your students' achievement characteristics are the students' permanent school records. These records contain standardized test scores, grades, and other pertinent information. After you decide which information you need, prepare a form on which you summarize the group's achievement characteristics. This group summary will help you design appropriate tests, establish minimum standards for performance, and interpret test results.

With the instructional goals in hand and the characteristics of students in mind, you are ready to analyze the goals to identify the skills students will need in order to demonstrate mastery of your instructional goals. You should separate each goal into subordinate tasks and then sequence the tasks in some logical order. This activity, which is called *goal analysis* or *task analysis*, produces a framework of tasks that becomes the foundation for both your lessons and tests.

Finally, you will need to develop a list of behavioral objectives that are based on each goal and its framework of skills. These objectives should specify the conditions or the circumstances under which the students will demonstrate their mastery of the skills. To create appropriate behavioral objectives, consider the achievement characteristics of the group, the task's content and specified behavior, the classroom environment, and available resources. In certain instances, you may also need to include criteria for judging the quality of a group's performance.

DESIGNING, DEVELOPING, AND USING OBJECTIVE TESTS

Designing Tests

The types of tests you design will depend on the kinds of decisions you want to make. You may decide to use readiness tests and pretests, which will provide information about your students before you plan instruction. You may want to administer practice tests to enable students to rehearse the skills and to monitor their progress during instruction. Regardless of whether you use these types of tests, you will probably need to design posttests to evaluate both the students' progress and the quality of instruction. Your purpose and the decisions you wish to make should guide your design activities.

Test designs are called *tables of test specifications* or *test blueprints*. To develop a table of test specifications, you should consider not only the purpose for the test but also the objectives for the unit, student characteristics, the classroom environment, resources available for testing and scoring, the time available for the test, and ways to produce valid and reliable scores. You can then use this information to select the specific objectives from the goal framework to be measured, prescribe the best test and item format, and determine the number of test items to include for each skill.

In prescribing the best test and item format for each objective, consider the conditions, behavior, and content specified in the objective. Different objectives will require different test formats. Some objectives can best be measured using objective tests, some using essay tests, some using product development tests, and others using performance tests. Within the objective-test category, some objectives are best measured using completion questions and others are best measured using selected-response items. Some objectives can be measured adequately using only 1 question; others may require a minimum of 10 to 15 items. Decisions about objectives selected, test formats, item formats, and the number of items required are recorded on the table of test specifications.

Developing Tests

With the table of test specifications complete, you are ready to develop tests. Factors to consider when writing test items include (1) the conditions, behavior, and content specified in the selected objectives; (2) the achievement characteristics of the group, including the students' vocabulary and reading levels; (3) the contexts and situations familiar to group members; and (4) the clarity and accuracy of grammar and punctuation used to write the items. In addition to these major factors, consider recommendations for formatting objective test items and for writing instructions for product development and performance tests.

Using Tests

Test results can be used to describe and evaluate the group's overall performance, the test, an individual student's test performance, and instruction, in that order. To make judgments about quality, you will need some standard or criterion against which to compare results. These criteria are developed using your interpretation of the complexity of the skills measured and the achievement characteristics of the students tested. When measures indicate that students have performed as well as or better than anticipated, you can conclude that instruction and the test were effective. However, if students' performance falls short of anticipated levels, then you have evidence that the instruction, and perhaps the test, should be questioned.

Indicators you will use to evaluate a group's overall test performance include the shape and location of the raw score distribution; measures of central tendency, including the mean and median; and measures of variability, including the range and standard deviation. As before, the complexity of skills measured and the achievement characteristics of the group are used to set standards for performance. The actual measures are compared with the anticipated ones to determine the quality of the group's performance.

When evaluating the quality of an objective test, the performance indicators used include each item's difficulty index and discrimination index. Items found questionable using these indices are reviewed further using a distractor analysis. Items judged defective following this review are eliminated, and test scores are adjusted accordingly before evaluating instruction or an individual's performance. The overall quality of a test is judged using indices of the test's internal consistency, which provide a general indication of test score reliability.

The third type of analysis involves evaluating each student's test performance. Describe each student's performance by comparing it to the overall group's performance and by determining the number of skills mastered. Before you make your final judgment, compare each student's performance with her or his previous achievement to determine whether students have equaled or surpassed their previous records. By combining students' mastery performances into a group composite, you will be able to identify quickly the particular students who need enrichment and those who need review or remediation on specific skills. Finally, you can locate skill areas in which instruction was good, acceptable, and inadequate.

When evaluating the quality of instruction, sort items by objective or goal and then compare difficulty and discrimination indices for sets of items. When students' performance does not meet anticipated levels for all or most items within a skill set, then instruction related to the skill is questioned.

DESIGNING, DEVELOPING, AND USING ALTERNATIVE ASSESSMENTS

Designing Alternative Assessments

Many instructional goals included in the curriculum guide are best assessed using alternative assessment procedures rather than objective tests. Alternative assessments include essay tests, product exams, active performance exams, and often ratings of students' attitudes and behaviors as well. Alternative testing procedures are also required for nonreaders since these students cannot complete tests constructed in traditional test formats. Similar to objective tests, tables of test specifications are used to describe the specifics of each type of alternative assessment instrument.

Developing Alternative Assessments

Creating alternative assessments typically includes writing questions or directions to guide students' work and constructing either checklists or rating scales to help you reduce subjectivity in scoring. Besides providing better scoring objectivity, checklists and rating scales help you pinpoint the strengths and weaknesses in students' original work and provide them with specific, corrective feedback.

Using Alternative Assessments

Information from alternative assessments can be used to evaluate the progress of individual students and groups of students and to evaluate the quality of instruction. In addition to students' achievement status at any one time, alternative assessments can be used to monitor students' growth and development. Teachers often collect students' work into portfolios to enable achievement progress reviews by teachers, students themselves, and parents.

Besides individual portfolios, many teachers use mastery charts to monitor a student's progress in the instructional goals taught during a course or grade level. Once mastery charts are completed for all members of a class, teachers can evaluate the quality of their instruction by determining the percentage of students who mastered each main component of a product or performance. Group performance information can be used to monitor and improve the quality of instruction for each instructional goal in the curriculum guide.

COMMUNICATING STUDENTS' PROGRESS

Grading and Reporting Progress

Your students' grades should accurately summarize and reflect their performances during each term, semester, and year. To ensure this accuracy, you will need to consider the instructional goals and objectives covered during a term, those measured by each posttest, each student's posttest scores, the district's grading policies, and the proportion each test will contribute to the final grade. In addition, you may need to synthesize individual scores into a composite score and either establish or locate standards for converting composite scores into term grades. Design your gradebook to accommodate all of this information and aid your work.

Interpreting Standardized Test Performances

Every teacher should be able to interpret students' scores on standardized tests. Chapter 15 describes (1) the nature, the purpose, and the construction of standardized tests; (2) the purpose for the norm group; (3) the normal distribution and its relationship to standardized test scores; (4) the relationship of the scores to each other; and (5) how each score on a student's profile is interpreted.

COMPUTER TECHNOLOGY

Today, more and more teachers use computer-based test item banks, test scoring programs, and gradebook programs to aid in their testing and information management tasks. Although the user's manuals that accompany these programs provide invaluable information for operating the programs, they do not provide, nor do they intend to provide, the information necessary to learn to design and develop a quality testing program. Once you understand the basics of designing and developing a quality testing program, however, these computer-based programs and manuals will prove invaluable for easily implementing your designs, developing your items, assembling your tests, scoring the tests, obtaining achievement summaries for a class, and producing reports of an individual's or group's progress.

The manner in which computer-based testing and grading programs are used by teachers to aid in their testing and information management tasks is described in each chapter of this text. Although there are several commercial test item bank, scoring, and gradebook programs available today, demonstration programs for ParTEST (Economics Research, Inc., 1991) and ParGRADE (Economics Research, Inc., 1992) are included with this text to provide hands-on experience in using computer-based programs. The Computer Technology sections in each chapter link the testing, scoring, and grading procedures introduced in the chapter to the ParTEST and ParGRADE programs, and your *Student Manual* contains instructions for using the programs.

Many teachers ask what considerations are important when choosing a computer-based testing program for themselves. Table 1.1 lists some general criteria you can use to evaluate the suitability of available programs. After you have studied this text and used the ParTEST and ParGRADE programs to design and develop your own tests, you will undoubtedly be able to develop a more sophisticated list of selection criteria for yourself.

If the school system in which you work does not provide computer support for classroom testing, scoring, grading, and record keeping, you may want to take advantage of the low cost and availability of personal computers. The ParTEST and ParGRADE programs are one example of a number of programs from a variety of publishers that are designed for use on a personal computer. You will be able to review programs that cover a wide range of

TABLE 1.1
General Considerations for Selecting a Computer-Based Testing and Information Management System

I. General Considerations
  A. What types of computer-based testing, scoring, and gradebook programs are provided by your school district for use by teachers?
  B. What type of technical assistance is available for users of a given system?
  C. What types of computer, storage, disk configuration, and printer are required to operate the system?
  D. What types of test scanning and scoring programs are available in the school or school district, and are they compatible with gradebook programs you may be considering? (Scanning and scoring programs usually link directly with gradebook programs from the same publisher.)
  E. What item banking assembly programs are available for the scanning and scoring services available to you?
II. Linking Testing and Instruction
  A. In the item banking program, are there multiple ways to classify and store items that will enable you to track your items by instructional goal, behavioral objective, learning level, text chapter, reading level, test purpose, and so on?
  B. Is there a way you can use a test plan or blueprint to retrieve items from your test item bank?
III. Creating Items
  A. Does the program support the development of objective-style test items?
  B. Does the program support the development of essay and problem-style test items?
  C. Does the program support the development of alternative-style tests, including product tests, live performance tests, attitude and behavior rating scales, and checklists?
IV. Scoring Tests and Updating the Item Bank
  A. Is there a scoring program linked to the item bank program?
  B. Can you automatically update item data in your item bank each time you score tests?
  C. Does the scoring program support the development of student progress reports and a gradebook?
V. Test Performance Analysis
  A. Does the scoring program provide indices of group performances, including score distributions, measures of central tendency, and measures of variability?
  B. Does the scoring program provide information about the norm-referenced and criterion-referenced performance of individual students on a test?
  C. Does the program provide indices of item quality, including difficulty, discrimination, and distractor quality?
  D. Does the program provide indices of overall test quality?
VI. Gradebook
  A. Does the program link the scoring program to a gradebook program to enable automatic entry of students' scores into a gradebook?
  B. Does the program enable you to convert students' raw scores to common scale scores for weighting?

    C. Does the program enable you to weight scores and calculate cumulative scores for a term?

    D. Does the program enable you to use various marks for communicating students' progress (e.g., A–D, Credit/No Credit, Mastery/Nonmastery)?

    E. Does the program assign grades according to your weighting plan and grading criteria?

    F. Does the program produce a variety of reports of students' performance and progress?

---

capability, complexity, and cost, and choose the programs that best suit your needs and your budget. Teachers with sufficient levels of interest and skill in computers sometimes choose to develop their own test management programs and use any of the popular spreadsheet programs for record keeping and grading. Whatever your level of computer skills and however you choose to use technology in your classroom, you will find that computer support can be a valuable time saver in your testing program.

DOCUMENTING THE PROCESS

The documents related to planning, designing, developing, summarizing, analyzing, and evaluating tests presented in this text are closely related and they build one on the other. Although each chapter provides many examples and illustrations, the book uses one instructional goal to illustrate how the decisions you make at any stage in the process influence your decisions at other stages. Thus, you will undoubtedly want to compare the documents developed at different stages. The primary documents for each phase of activity for the sample instructional goal are repeated in Appendices A through K to help you avoid flipping through the chapters to make your comparisons. For example, if you want to compare the table of test specifications described in Chapter 4 (Table 4.2) with the documents on which it is based, turn to the Appendices. Appendix A contains the instructional goal framework (Figure 3.6) and Appendix B contains the behavioral objectives (Table 3.6) developed from the goal framework. If you want to see samples of tests developed from the table of specifications in Chapter 4, see Appendices D through G. Appendices I through K contain the analysis and evaluation documents that are based on the planning, design, and development documents.

SUMMARY

In its narrowest applications, this book is about designing, developing, and using classroom measures of students' progress. In this text, however, testing and alternative assessment are viewed in a broader sense, as an integral part of the teaching and learning process. Testing and alternative assessment must flow directly from sound curriculum design and can even help sharpen our thinking about curriculum and focus our efforts in planning instructional methods, materials, and activities. Testing and alternative assessment are more than just tools for grading. They are methods for collecting information that improves our professional judgments about the quality of our instruction and the needs of our students. In its broadest applications, this book is about one of the foundations of the teaching profession: the systematic collection and use of information for guiding our decisions about our teaching and our students.

REFERENCES

Economics Research, Inc. (1991). *ParTEST user's manual*. Costa Mesa, CA: Author.

Economics Research, Inc. (1992). *ParSCORE & ParGRADE user's manual*. Costa Mesa, CA: Author.

CHAPTER 2

Planning for New Classes

OBJECTIVES

- Identify sources of instructional goals for a course.
- Determine the congruence among instructional goals found in various sources.
- Describe how to sequence instructional goals for a course.
- Describe how class groups are formed.
- Define the terms *heterogeneous* and *homogeneous* and relate them to group achievement levels.
- Determine which information to use in assessing the achievement characteristics of a class group.
- Design a form for summarizing group achievement.
- Use student achievement data to describe previous performance levels of newly assigned class groups.

Two of a teacher's first tasks at the beginning of a new school year are to determine what he or she is expected to teach and to whom. Although these tasks might at first appear to be unrelated to testing activities, they provide the foundation necessary for determining what skills to test and for interpreting the test scores obtained. This chapter describes these two planning activities. The first activity is to identify and sequence instructional goals for a course, and the second is to assess the achievement characteristics of assigned class groups.

IDENTIFYING INSTRUCTIONAL GOALS

Education is a highly complex system that requires curriculum planning and coordination. Curriculum plans are communicated through curriculum guides listing instructional goals that students in a given grade level and subject are expected to achieve. These guides are produced by a team that usually includes classroom teachers, curriculum specialists, and university-level content experts. Teams developing curriculum guides in vocational subjects commonly include experts from business and industry as well.

Curriculum guides serve as a foundation to plan and coordinate two main activities at the state, district, and school levels: instruction and testing. At the state level, the guides are used to coordinate instruction across school districts, to adopt the most relevant instructional texts, and to provide a foundation for statewide achievement tests. School administrators at the district level use the state guides as one resource for developing their own more comprehensive curriculum guides. The district guides are then used to coordinate instruction across schools and grade levels and to select instructional texts for each subject and grade. Related to testing, the guides are used to select the most appropriate standardized tests and to develop districtwide achievement tests. Classroom teachers use the district's curriculum guide to identify and sequence the instructional goals assigned for their subject and grade level, to plan instructional units and lessons, and to develop achievement tests that measure students' progress. Curriculum guides help ensure that important instructional goals are not inadvertently omitted, that unintended repetition is avoided, and that a direct match exists between the instruction provided and the tests used to measure students' progress.

Most school districts publish curriculum guides, at least in the basic skills subjects; if one is provided for your subject, it will define your primary teaching responsibilities. Sometimes, however, guides either are not provided or are not as complete as you would like. If a curriculum guide is not provided for your subject, you should prepare one yourself. If the one provided is sketchy and incomplete, you will need to expand or clarify the instructional goals included. In either situation, you can turn to a variety of resources for help.

Sources of Instructional Goals

Instructional goals can be located in various places. As noted, some state departments of education provide curriculum guides for specific subjects, particularly subjects dealing with basic skills. These guides are one valuable source of instructional goals. The publications of professional associations that describe goals and standards for your discipline may be useful as well. You can also turn to textbooks and other instructional materials adopted for your subject. Scanning several adopted texts should give you an overview of the goals different authors consider important.

The teacher's and administrator's manuals for standardized achievement tests that will be administered to your students are another good source of instructional goals. These documents often describe not only goals but related instructional objectives as well. They describe the specific form of the test and the grade in which each objective is tested. They also key each objective to published instructional materials.

Elements of an Instructional Goal   *action students w/ do.*

The instructional goals listed in curriculum guides are broad statements of learning outcomes that indicate both the behavior and the instructional content students are to acquire. The behaviors included in an instructional goal should be observable and measurable. They describe overt student behaviors that demonstrate whether students acquired the desired knowledge or skill. Words typically used to describe overt behaviors include *list, select, define, recite, sequence, summarize, classify, predict, solve,* and *explain.* Terms such as *understand, appreciate,* and *comprehend* are not used in instructional goals because they do not clearly indicate how students will demonstrate that they have acquired the desired skill or information. Although the underlying purpose of instruction is to produce understanding and comprehension, instructional goals are written to communicate how students will visibly demonstrate these internal processes.

The second part of an instructional goal identifies the content of the instruction. This content may be a topic, such as punctuation, capitalization, mixed fractions, or the Constitution. The content part of the goal identifies the topic and the particular portion of the topic to be studied.

The sample instructional goals listed in Tables 2.1, 2.2, and 2.3 were selected from elementary and secondary school curriculum guides in language arts, mathematics, and special education, respectively. Notice that regardless of the subject area considered, each goal listed in the three tables includes both the desired student behavior and the instructional content to be learned. Note also that the behaviors included describe overt actions rather than such terms as *comprehends* and *understands.*

Comparing Instructional Goals from Different Sources

Comparing the instructional goals in the school district's curriculum guide with those found in other sources can often be useful. You may compare the guide with (1) the state guide, if one is available; (2) the text and instructional materials for the class; (3) recommended goal lists of professional associations; and (4) goals and objectives measured on mandated, standardized achievement tests. In making such an analysis, you may find some instructional goals recommended in all your resources. You may also discover that some goals in the curriculum guide are included in only a few, or none, of the

TABLE 2.1
Sample Instructional Goals for Language Arts at Various Grade Levels

1. Sequence a group of four pictures.
2. Arrange four sentences into a meaningful paragraph.
3. Alphabetize any given list of words.
4. Use guide words to locate specified words in a dictionary.
5. Write a story using a logical organizational pattern.
6. Paraphrase a written passage.
7. Distinguish between fact and opinion.
8. Determine the cause and effect of an event or action.
9. Infer tone and mood from a written passage.
10. Use regular plural forms of nouns.
11. Capitalize proper nouns.
12. Capitalize appropriate words in titles.
13. Match nouns and pronouns.
14. Select the appropriate tense of regular verbs in context.
15. Make subjects and verbs agree.
16. Write declarative sentences.
17. Write interrogative sentences.
18. Write compound sentences using a comma, semicolon, and colon.
19. Use a comma to separate words in a series.
20. Use an apostrophe to form contractions.
21. Associate words that are the same or opposite in meaning.
22. Form derived words using prefixes and suffixes.
23. Determine the meaning of a word in context.
24. Identify metaphors and similes.

TABLE 2.2
Sample Instructional Goals for Mathematics at Various Grade Levels

1. Add whole numbers with regrouping.
2. Subtract whole numbers with regrouping.
3. Multiply whole numbers with regrouping.
4. Divide whole numbers with regrouping.
5. Add proper fractions having like denominators.
6. Subtract proper fractions having unlike denominators.
7. Multiply proper and improper fractions.
8. Read and write mixed decimal numbers through hundredths.
9. Add, subtract, multiply, and divide mixed decimal numbers.
10. Round a number having two decimal places to the nearest whole number.
11. Write equations to solve word problems.
12. Solve word problems involving money.
13. Solve word problems involving time.
14. Solve word problems involving temperature.
15. Solve word problems involving length.
16. Solve word problems involving liquid capacity.
17. Solve word problems involving mass.
18. Solve word problems involving percentages.
19. Calculate probabilities.
20. Calculate the mean.
21. Find the perimeters of given objects.
22. Find the areas of given objects.
23. Read graphs including ordered pairs and coordinates.

TABLE 2.3
Sample Instructional Goals for Exceptional Students at Various Grade Levels

A. Goals for Students Who Are Educable	B. Goals for Students Who Are Trainable
1. Match identical symbols (letters and numerals).	1. Distinguish basic sensory qualities (hot-cold, wet-dry, burning smell, hard-soft, spoiled-fresh).
2. Discriminate colors.	2. Name and locate body parts.
3. Discriminate sounds.	3. Demonstrate self-help in safety situations.
4. Copy upper-case and lower-case letters.	4. Demonstrate self-help in dressing.
5. Write own name and address.	5. Demonstrate general work skills.
6. Compare objects by size, dimensions, quantity, position, or sequence.	Demonstrate appropriate work
7. Write letters of the alphabet when named.	6. relations.
8. Demonstrate self-care skills in personal hygiene.	
9. Demonstrate self-care skills in health and safety.	
10. Demonstrate appropriate peer group interactions.	

other sources. The other documents may also recommend goals that the assigned curriculum guide does not. When the same instructional goal appears in multiple sources, it is undoubtedly one that content experts consider very important. When a goal appears only in the district's curriculum guide, it is one that local curriculum specialists and teachers consider important for the district. If the district's curriculum guide and the adopted text exclude goals appearing on mandated, standardized tests, you may want to insert these goals in your curriculum guide as an addendum.

If goals from various sources are worded differently but imply the same behavior and content, you may consider them the same. The language arts instructional goals for the fifth grade in Table 2.4 were taken from three different sources. Notice that, although the wording is different, their intent is the same. Because the goals prescribed in the state guide and the test manual are more complete than the one in the district guide, they could be used to clarify and expand the district's goal statement.

To help you remember the sources of similar goals, assign symbols to your sources and key them to your curriculum guide. When an instructional goal from another source matches one in the district guide, place the symbol for that source in the margin beside the goal. You may also want to edit the district's goal to include any clarifying information found in other sources. If you decide to add goals to the curriculum guide, note the source in the margin

TABLE 2.4
Language Arts Instructional Goals

Goal Source	Goal
District curriculum guide	Uses context clues to supply the meanings of words
State-level curriculum guide	Infers the meanings of words in context using: (a) example clues, (b) direct explanation clues, (c) synonym clues, and (d) compare and contrast clues
Teacher's manual for a standardized test	Selects the definitions for multimeaning words in context and uses context clues to identify word meanings

beside each one. Referencing other sources in your curriculum guide will help you evaluate the completeness of the curriculum guide, determine the guide's congruence with adopted instructional materials and standardized tests, and perhaps sequence goals for your new class.

Table 2.5 provides an example of the congruence between a school district's curriculum guide and three other goal sources. Goals similar to Goal 1, "Sequence a group of four pictures," appear on the standardized test and in the state curriculum guide. The adopted text does not include instruction for this goal. The second goal is included in the text, the standardized test manual, and the state curriculum guide. The third goal appears in the text and the state curriculum guide but not on the standardized test. A teacher reviewing this analysis should recognize that Goal 1 presents an instructional problem to be solved. Because the adopted text does not include instruction for this goal, the teacher will undoubtedly need to develop all instruction related to it.

TABLE 2.5
A Comparison of Instructional Goals from Different Sources

Goals in Curriculum Guide	Other Sources
1. Sequence a group of four pictures.	T(5), S
2. Arrange four sentences into a meaningful paragraph.	I, T(5), S
3. Write a friendly letter.	I, S

Note: T(5) = Standardized test (month usually administered)
      S = State curriculum guide
      I = Adopted instructional materials

Sequencing Instructional Goals

Once you have a list of instructional goals for the course, cluster them by topic and sequence them. This planning activity can help you decide where to begin instruction and how to proceed during the year. When you have finished, your curriculum guide will have all your instructional goals ordered in the sequence you plan to present them. The guide can direct your instructional activities throughout the year and help you develop records to monitor students' mastery of your instructional goals.

The several strategies you can use to sequence instructional goals differ in importance. Three of the most important considerations in selecting a sequence are the relationships among the goals, the dates when standardized tests are administered, and the sequence of topics in the textbook. The most important consideration is the relationship among the goals. Some goals are hierarchically related, meaning that certain skills must be learned before others. For example, the goal "Recognize nouns" is a prerequisite to the goal "Differentiate between common nouns and proper nouns." In another hierarchical relationship, the goal "Add without regrouping" must precede the goal "Add with regrouping." The first sequencing strategy is to identify and sequence all goals in the guide that are hierarchically related.

Once goals are ordered according to their hierarchical relationships, the next important consideration is the timing of any standardized tests that all your students are required to take. Your goal sequence should permit you to teach the skills these tests measure before the tests are administered. The third consideration, text order, is one of convenience. To the degree possible, goals should be ordered to correspond to their presentation sequence in the textbook.

Even after sequencing goals in the curriculum guide using these three strategies, some goals may remain to be sequenced. These remaining goals can be sequenced using such factors as complexity, familiarity, chronology, or potential motivation. When you have completed your goal analysis and sequencing, you will be ready to consider the students who have been assigned to your class.

ASSESSING GROUP CHARACTERISTICS

Most teachers are assigned new class groups at the beginning of each school year. The achievement characteristics of the students in each group will affect all instructional activities, including the analysis of the instructional goals, lesson development, the selection of resource material, the delivery of instruction, the writing of test items, and the interpretation of test performance. Because each class will be different, you should assess the achievement levels of each group and tailor your instructional activities accordingly.

Assignment of Class Groups

In forming class groups, school administrators consider several factors in addition to previous achievement. They usually try to balance the number of students in each class, the number of males and females in a group, and the cultural and racial mix at each grade level. They must also consider scheduling for such elective subjects as art, band, chorus, and special programs. All of these factors affect administrative decisions concerning class groups, but none of these factors is as important to the teacher as the students' previous achievement levels.

The school district's philosophy influences how classes are grouped. Some districts attempt to tailor instruction to the needs of students who are similar in previous achievement. Such districts form separate class groups of high, medium, and low achievers. In other districts, each class group has a representative number of students from each achievement level. Some districts use a combination of the two methods, depending on the subject and grade level. Given all the philosophical and practical trades that administrators made in forming your classes, it is important for you to identify the achievement characteristics of each group.

Homogeneous and Heterogeneous Groups

Information about a group's previous achievement will help you establish expectations for group performance. As you observe students' progress, compare these expectations with their actual performance and then refine your judgments about their work.

In analyzing student characteristics, you should first determine whether a group is homogeneous or heterogeneous in achievement. A *homogeneous* group contains students who are similar in a given characteristic. For example, a group that is homogeneous in previous achievement contains students with similar histories of either high, average, or low achievement. A *heterogeneous* group contains students who are dissimilar in a given characteristic. A group that is heterogeneous in achievement contains students with a wide range of previous performances.

Homogeneous and *heterogeneous* are not absolute descriptors. They are relative terms, much like such adjectives as *tall* and *average*. We might ask, How tall is tall, how average is average, and how homogeneous is homogeneous? A class group with only high-achieving students is easily classified as homogeneous. When compared to the first group, a class containing average and above-average students would be heterogeneous. On the other hand, this class would be more homogeneous than a group whose scores ranged from very low to very high.

Throughout the school year, teachers continuously ask themselves, How are my students doing? You can usually answer this question by comparing students' current achievement with their previous work. For example, if you have been assigned a group that is heterogeneous in previous work, you may expect a wide range of scores on your first test. For a homogeneous group of high achievers, you might anticipate a narrow range of high test scores, and for a homogeneous group of low achievers, a narrow range of lower test scores.

After you administer your first test, you can compare the students' scores with your expectations. If the two fall within the same range, you can tentatively conclude that the group is performing normally. If the students did not perform as expected, note the incongruity, seek reasons, and wait for more information on subsequent tests.

Class Summary Forms

The availability of computers for producing current records has enabled many school districts to provide teachers with a summary of each newly formed group's previous achievement. These performance summaries usually contain the grades each student in the class received on semester exams and final course grades in the same or closely related courses. They also frequently contain students' standardized test scores in such basic subjects as mathematics and language. These forms will help you determine whether each group is heterogeneous or homogeneous in previous achievement.

Although interpreting grades previously earned on semester exams and in courses is rather straightforward, some information about interpreting the commonly reported standardized test scores will be useful. The standardized test scores included on the permanent record indicate how well the student performed relative to a comparable norm group of students. Note the particular standardized test scores used to indicate the student's performance levels. Undoubtedly, either stanine or percentile scores will be reported, and sometimes both scores are included in the record. If stanine scores are used, they can be interpreted as follows:

1. Stanines range from a low score of 1 to a high score of 9.
2. Stanines of 1, 2, and 3 reflect below-average achievement in the subject compared to the norm group.
3. Stanines 4, 5, and 6 reflect average-level achievement compared to the norm group.
4. Stanines 7, 8, and 9 reflect above-average achievement compared to the norm group.

If percentile scores are reported, they can be interpreted as follows:

1. Percentile scores range from a low score of 1 to a high score of 99.
2. Any given score indicates that the student scored better on the test than that percentage of students in the norm group. For example, a percentile

score of 86 means that the student who earned this score surpassed 86 percent of the students in the norm group.

3. Generally, percentile scores below 25 are considered to indicate below-average achievement compared to the norm group.
4. Percentile scores between 25 and 75 are considered to reflect average achievement.
5. Percentile scores above 75 are considered to signify above-average achievement compared to students in the norm group.

Using either the stanine or the percentile score, each student's performance can be classified as below average, average, or above average in the basic skills measured by the test.

Table 2.6 contains two abbreviated summary forms that a science teacher might have developed for two classes. A complete form would include data for many more students. In addition to science grades, the teacher summarized the students' English and math grades from the previous year, their most recent standardized test scores, and their grades on the previous year's semester exams in science.

Describing Class Groups

Given a summary form for a group of students, you are ready to interpret the information and describe the class. You will want to determine whether the class is heterogeneous or homogeneous, and if homogeneous, whether it is above average, average, or below average in previous achievement. You can then use this information to establish your initial expectations for the group's performance. Differences in assigned groups will influence how you analyze instructional goals, plan lessons, and write test items.

In analyzing a class group, consider their performance levels in each category of data, such as previous grades, standardized test scores, and semester exam scores. Then, with their performance within a category described, compare their performance across categories to determine whether the information across categories is similar or incongruent. If the performance levels across all categories indicate the same range of performance, then you can be relatively sure you have an accurate description of the class. However, if you note incongruent performance across categories, consider this in establishing your initial expectations.

Consider how a science teacher might interpret the data in Table 2.6. The first clue about Group I's makeup comes from their grades in English, math, and science. Most students earned grades of C, along with an occasional B and D. This similarity of performance suggests a homogeneous, average group. The group's standardized test (stanine) scores range from 6 to 4 in language and reading, and all but one score in mathematics fall into the average range. Semester exam grades in science also indicate a homogeneous group of aver-

TABLE 2.6
Class Summary Forms

Group I

| Students | Previous Grades | | | Standardized Achievement Test Stanine Scores[a] | | | Districtwide Semester Sci. Exams | |
	Eng.	Math	Sci.	Lang. Mech.	Read.	Math	S1[b]	S2
• Abrams	C	C	C	5	5	6	C	C
• Brown	C	C	C	5	4	5	C	C
Crown	C	B	C	6	5	6	C	B
Davis	C	C	C	5	5	5	C	C
• Evans	B	B	B	6	6	7	C	B
Flynn	C	B	C	6	6	6	B	C
Good	C	C	B	5	5	5	C	C
Hayes	B	C	C	5	6	5	C	C
Jones	C	C	C	4	5	5	C	D
Kelly	D	C	D	4	4	4	D	C

Group II

| Students | Previous Grades | | | Standardized Achievement Test Stanine Scores[a] | | | Districtwide Semester Sci. Exams | |
	Eng.	Math	Sci.	Lang. Mech.	Read.	Math	S1[b]	S2
Allen	A	B	B	9	9	7	B	A
Boyd	C	B	C	6	6	7	B	C
Carter	C	C	C	4	5	5	C	C
• Doyle	A	A	A	9	9	9	A	A
Egan	B	A	B	6	7	8	B	B
• Fowler	C	C	B	6	6	6	C	B
Graham	B	B	C	7	6	7	B	C
• Howe	D	D	C	3	3	4	D	C
Johnson	F	D	D	2	3	3	F	D
Keller	C	B	B	7	7	6	B	B

[a]Stanine scores range from 1 to 9. Compared to norm group:
  Scores 1, 2, and 3 indicate below-average achievement.
  Scores 4, 5, and 6 indicate average achievement.
  Scores 7, 8, and 9 indicate above-average achievement.
[b]S1 = Semester one of previous year; S2 = Semester two of previous year.

age performance. All three categories of performance reflect the same range of achievement for the group; thus, a teacher looking at these data may reasonably expect Group I to be a homogeneous class that will continue to achieve at an average level.

The data for Group II, however, indicate a different pattern of previous achievement. Grades range from A to F, stanine scores range from 9 to 2, and semester exam grades range from A to F. All three categories of performance reflect consistent, heterogeneous achievement for the group. The teacher might thus anticipate a wide range of achievement from this class group.

Unfortunately, in some school districts, the teacher is given only a list of students' names for each new class. It is very difficult to begin planning for a group without any information about the students' achievement characteristics. Should you find yourself in this situation, request that the school provide the necessary information. If your request is not honored, review your students' permanent records to obtain the background information. At a minimum, summarize the standardized achievement test scores in language and mathematics to determine whether the group is homogeneous or heterogeneous in these basic skills. Once you have decided on the information you want, find out where and how it is recorded on one student's record. Using this record as an example, you can design a form that will help you summarize and interpret the rest of your data.

In interpreting students' records, be careful not to develop inflexible expectations for the group. Previous performance is not a sure indicator of how individuals will perform in a new situation. A year's maturation, a new group of students, and a new teacher are all factors that can affect individual performances. In turn, these changes can produce different results for a portion, if not for all, of the class.

COMPUTER TECHNOLOGY

At the beginning of a school term, create a computer-based list of students, often called a *class roster*, for your class or classes. A class roster includes students' names, identification numbers, telephone numbers, grading codes, and special comments. In addition to the identification information, the class roster includes spaces for students' test scores.

Why should teachers create a class roster? The class roster enables them to record automatically their students' scores on each examination, to create quickly interim or midterm reports of individual students' progress for parents, and to determine rapidly either students' grades or the particular instructional goals they have mastered, partially mastered, or not mastered during a term. Performing these tasks for each student without a computer requires many hours of work. With a computer, recording, grading, and reporting can be accomplished in a fraction of the time required to perform these tasks by hand.

There are three ways to enter new student information into a class roster. You can have your students mark the information about themselves on computer-readable scan sheets, and then have the computer read the information directly into the program. Using a computer keyboard, you can type the necessary information into the class roster yourself. A third method is to enter data into the roster from a computer disk. Many schools today provide teachers with computer files that list pertinent information about new students in each of their classes. Once your roster is created for a class, you may enter new students or delete students who have dropped your class at any time during a grading term.

Figure 2.1 contains a sample ParGRADE (Economics Research, Inc., 1992) class roster for a new group of students. The top of the form identifies the class, the time and days the class meets, the teacher's name, the term and year, and the total number of students in the class. The first column contains the record number, the second includes the students' identification numbers, the third column lists the students in alphabetical order, the fourth contains the telephone numbers, the fifth column contains the grade codes for each student, and the last column includes any special comments the teacher wants to note for each student. This particular record is for sev-

FIGURE 2.1
A Sample Student Roster from the ParGRADE Program

Course:	4023	Instructor:	Karen Hauser		
Course:	LANG 7	Term/Year:	Spring 94		
Day/Time:	M-F 10:00				
	28	students in this roster			

	ID#	Student Name	Phone	Code	Comments
1	432-34-3233	Augustine, Katy	813 974 3220		
2	544-25-6564	Bailey, Brooke	813 988 9209		Special Diet
3	436-26-7783	Carey, Edward	813 968 9592		
4	246-35-7811	Cromer, Cindy	813 989 4255		Entered 10/30
5	590-22-5619	Deddens, Robert	813 974 3400		
Etc.					

Source: Adapted from Figure 41 (p. 96). Economics Research, Inc. (1992). *ParSCORE & ParGRADE User's Manual.* Costa Mesa, CA.

enth-grade language arts with the assigned course number 4023. The class meets Monday through Friday at 10:00 A.M. The teacher's name is Karen Hauser, the record is for spring term, 1994, and there are 28 students in the language arts class. You should examine the instructions in the ParGRADE program (Economic Research, Inc., 1992) and in your *Student Manual* for creating a class roster.

SUMMARY

Two planning activities can help a teacher prepare for new classes. The first is to establish the instructional goals for a course, and the second is to assess the achievement characteristics of assigned classes.

Instructional goals are general statements of intended learning outcomes that describe the behavior the student is to demonstrate and the content to be learned. Sources of instructional goals include the school district's curriculum guide, the state's curriculum guide, professional associations' recommended lists of instructional goals and objectives, adopted instructional texts, and the teacher's or administrator's manual for required, standardized achievement tests. You should compare the instructional goals in all these sources and add goals and objectives from state guides and standardized tests that are not found in the district's curriculum guide. You may then cluster the goals by topic, sequence them by logical order, and assign each goal to specific terms and semesters, depending on when students will be tested on each goal.

Knowing the previous achievement levels of a new class can help you set initial expectations for class performance, analyze instructional goals, develop and pace lessons, write test items, and interpret group performance.

Many school districts provide teachers with class summary forms that can be used to describe the achievement characteristics of a new group. Using the data in these forms, you can determine whether each assigned group is homogeneous or heterogeneous in previous achievement. This determination will aid in planning instruction, designing tests, and interpreting students' performance. You should be cautious in forming opinions about new class groups, however, and should be willing to reinterpret students' progress depending on your own experiences with the group.

Today, computers aid teachers in performing record-keeping tasks. At the beginning of the school year, you can create a computer-based student roster for each class that contains students' names and other information such as student identification numbers, telephone numbers, and special grading information. With the roster it is easy to manage students' mastery records and to produce interim and term summary reports of achievement for individual students and class groups.

PRACTICE EXERCISES

I. **Identifying Instructional Goals**
   A. Who usually decides what skills will be taught in a given subject and grade level?
   B. List the types of people usually included on a school district's curriculum team.
   C. List potential resources you can use to identify the instructional goals for a course
   D. List three reasons for matching district curriculum guides with state guides, goals and objectives for standardized tests, and adopted textbooks.

II. **Identifying Elements of an Instructional Goal**
   A. Name the two parts of an instructional goal and describe the function of each part
   B. Identify the behavior and content in the following instructional goals by underlining the behavior with two lines and the content with one line.
      1. Name synonyms for given words.
      2. Name antonyms for given words.
      3. Alphabetize any given list of words.
      4. Retell a story in own words.
      5. Recite a paragraph verbatim.
      6. Add three-digit numbers with regrouping.
      7. Solve story problems using addition.
      8. Name the capital city for each state.
   C. Analyze the following instructional goals and revise those that need clarification or improvement. (There is no one correct way to revise these goals. Revised goals should include both observable behavior and content.)
      1. Understands currency of different denominations.
      2. Punctuate.
      3. Identify one-half, one-third, and one-fourth of a given area.
      4. Understand how to measure the length, width, and height of a given object.
      5. Identify the main idea in a paragraph.
      6. The mean and median.

III. **Determining Congruence among Goals from Different Sources**
   Column A lists six mathematics goals taken from district curriculum guides. Column B lists mathematics goals from state curriculum guides. Although the state goals are worded differently, some match the goals in the district guides. Indicate matching goals by placing the letter of the state goal in the space preceding the number of the district goal.

Column A	*Column B*
_____ **1.** Determine equivalent amounts of money.	a. Given a fraction, identify an equal decimal number.
_____ **2.** Write fractions as decimal numbers.	b. Determine the correct change for a given purchase.
_____ **3.** Calculate the lowest form of given fractions.	c. Multiply mixed fractions.
_____ **4.** Add fractions.	d. Equate coins and dollar bills of different denominations.
_____ **5.** Subtract fractions.	e. Reduce fractions.
_____ **6.** Use multiplication to solve mixed-fraction problems.	f. Select the money required to equal a given amount.

IV. Sequencing Goals

A. List four strategies for sequencing instructional goals.

B. Use the following procedure to cluster and sequence the set of instructional goals listed in Table 2.7.

1. Divide the goals into three categories of similar goals and title each category.
2. Write the names of the categories in the order you would present them to students.
3. Sequence the goals within each category in the order you would present them to students.

V. Describing Groups

A. List four factors that school administrators usually consider when they form class groups.

B. Which of the four factors listed in item A (above) will have the most influence on teachers when they plan instruction and interpret student performance?

C. What do the terms *heterogeneous* and *homogeneous* mean when applied to group achievement?

D. List the four types of information that would help you determine if a class were heterogeneous or homogeneous in achievement.

E. If you were designing a form to summarize a group's previous achievement, what would the rows and columns on your form indicate? Show how you might design your form.

F. Table 2.8 presents achievement data for a newly formed English class. Use the information in the table to describe the class.

1. Previous English grades
2. Standardized achievement test in language skills
3. Districtwide English exam
4. Congruence among indicators

TABLE 2.7
Exercise for Sequencing Instructional Goals

Goals

1. Locate the subject of a simple sentence.
2. Select verbs to show future tense.
3. Match singular subjects with singular verbs.
4. Locate the predicate of a simple sentence.
5. Match plural subjects with plural verbs.
6. Select verbs to show present tense.
7. Identify simple sentences.
8. Select verbs to show past tense.

Goal Categories (Topics)   *Goal Sequence (by Number)*

TABLE 2.8
Data Summary Form for an English Class

Students	Previous Year's English Grades	Standardized Achievement Test (Stanines[a])	Districtwide English Exam[b] (% Correct)
1. Allen, B.	C	3	72
2. Bonito, B	C	2	60
3. Brown, L.	D	3	75
4. Carter, D.	C	3	78
5. Donovan, T.	D	1	43
6. Evans, R.	C	3	64
7. Fischer, A.	C	2	74
8. Garcia, J.	C	2	62
9. Good, T.	B	3	68
10. Graham, N.	B	3	76
11. Hanson, A.	C	3	75
12. Howe, R.	C	2	70
13. Kelley, N.	D	3	73
14. Miller, C.	C	2	64
15. Otto, J.	C	2	60
16. Potter, G.	D	1	53
17. Scott, H.	C	2	68
18. Smith, J.	C	2	72
19. Taylor, B.	B	3	78
20. Washburn, M.	D	1	46

Average
Score   = 67%

Range   =
78 − 43 = 35

[a] Stanine scores range from 1 to 9. Scores of 1, 2, and 3 are considered below average; 4, 5, and 6 average; and 7, 8, and 9 above average.
[b] The district has set a minimum passing score for the exam of 70 percent.

    G. If you were the teacher for the class in Table 2.8, how might you expect the group to perform during the coming year?

VI. Enrichment
    A. Obtain a school district curriculum guide for the subject and grade level you teach or plan to teach. Review the types and sequencing of instructional goals and the scope of the subject the goals define.
    B. Ask teachers and administrators in a school how class groups are formed there.
    C. If you can obtain permission to review a district's class summary form for a newly formed class in your subject, analyze the data provided on the form, describe the group in terms of its achievement characteristics, and predict the general level of achievement you would expect for the class.

FEEDBACK

I. **Identifying Instructional Goals**

   A. District curriculum teams write curriculum guides that describe the instructional goals and objectives for a given subject and grade level. When guides are not provided by the district, teachers create their own.

   B. Curriculum teams usually include classroom teachers, curriculum supervisors, university-level content experts, and representatives from business and industry.

   C. Resources include district curriculum guides, state curriculum guides, assigned textbooks and other instructional resources, professional societies' recommendations for instructional goals, and teachers' or administrators' manuals for mandated standardized tests.

   D. Matching goals in a school district's curriculum guide with other sources will permit you to:

      1. Identify matching goals and objectives.

      2. Identify goals and objectives that are unique to the district.

      3. Identify important goals and objectives not found in the district guide.

II. **Identifying Elements of an Instructional Goal**

   A. Instructional goals contain the desired student behavior and the content of the topic that students will learn.

   B. Behavior and content are underlined with two lines and one line, respectively, in the following instructional goals:

      1. Name synonyms for given words.

      2. Name antonyms for given words.

      3. Alphabetize any given list of words.

      4. Retell a story in own words.

      5. Recite a paragraph verbatim.

      6. Add three-digit numbers with regrouping.

      7. Solve story problems using addition.

      8. Name the capital city for each state.

   C. The instructional goals may be clarified as follows:

      1. Equates coins and bills with their defined values.

      2. Some possible clarifications include:

         a. Selects the correct punctuation to end a sentence.

         b. Uses quotation marks, commas, and ending punctuation to punctuate direct quotations correctly.

         c. Punctuates the greeting and closing of a letter.

         d. Uses commas to separate items in a series.

      3. This goal includes both the behavior and content.

      4. Measures the length, width, and height of an object using metric and English scales.

      5. This goal includes both the behavior and content.

      6. Possible goals include:

         a. Define the mean and median of a set of scores.

         b. Calculate the mean and median of a set of scores.

         c. Interpret the mean and median of a set of scores.

         d. Plot the mean and median of a set of scores.

III. **Determining Congruence among Goals from Different Sources**
The district and state curriculum guides contain these matching goals:

1. d	**4.** no match
2. a	**5.** no match
3. e	**6.** c

IV. **Sequencing Goals**
A. The four strategies for sequencing instructional goals include:
1. Group goals according to topics.
2. Once you have grouped goals by topic, identify any hierarchical relationships among the goals in each set. If a hierarchy of goals exists, place prerequisite goals first.
3. If the goals show no hierarchical relationship within a set, sequence each set according to either their order in the textbook or the dates the standardized tests will be administered.
4. Other logical factors, such as chronology, complexity, concreteness, familiarity, or motivation potential, can be used to sequence goals not organized using the preceding strategies.
B. The instructional goals listed in Table 2.7 may be categorized and sequenced in this manner:

Goal Category	*Goal Sequence*
1. Identify complete sentences.	$1 \rightarrow 4 \rightarrow 7$
2. Match subjects and verbs.	$3 \rightarrow 5$
3. Select verb tense.*	$6 \rightarrow 8 \rightarrow 2$

* The goals in this category are not hierarchically related and may be presented in any order.

V. **Describing Groups**
A. Factors in class assignments include sexual balance, racial or cultural balance, the scheduling of elective subjects, and previous achievement levels.
B. The previous achievement levels of students will have the most influence on teachers.
C. Heterogeneous groups contain students who vary or are dissimilar in achievement. Homogeneous groups contain students who are similar in achievement.
D. You might want to collect:
1. Previously earned grades in the same subject.
2. Previously earned grades in language and math skills if these subjects are important for the subject to be taught.
3. The most recent standardized test scores.
4. Grades on previous semester exams in the same subject.
E. Your form should be tailored to the types of information you decide to collect. Your form should have a row for each student in the group and a column for each type of information you plan to record.
F. The information in Table 2.8 shows that:
1. Students' grades ranged from *D* to *B*, with most students receiving a *C*'s; 5 students received *D*'s; 12 students *C*'s, and 3 students *B*'s. Based on grades alone, the group appears to be relatively homogeneous and average in achievement.
2. Students' scores on the standardized achievement test in language ranged from 1 to 3; 9 students received a score of 3, 8 received a score of 2, and 3 a score of 1. Their performance was homogeneous and below average.

3. Students' scores on the districtwide English exam were low. The average score earned by the class was 67 percent; the scores ranged from 43 to 78 percent. Half the students passed the exam at a relatively low level, and half failed.
4. The three indicators of performance are relatively congruent, although the assigned grades appear to be somewhat higher than would be predicted by the test scores.

This information should lead you to conclude that the group is relatively homogeneous and below average in previous English achievement.

G. You might expect the group's test performances to be limited in range and toward the low end of the scale.

REFERENCE

Economics Research, Inc. (1992). *ParSCORE & ParGRADE user's manual* (pp. 29–50). Costa Mesa, CA: Author.

SUGGESTED READINGS

Consult the following materials for further information on planning for new classes:

— The curriculum guides from a local school district for the grades and subjects you plan to teach

— The instructor's manual for the standardized test adopted for the school district in which you teach or plan to teach
— Sample permanent records for students in a local school district

CHAPTER 3

Analyzing Instructional Goals for Instruction and Tests

OBJECTIVES

- Define the following six levels of learning commonly found in curriculum guides: knowledge, comprehension, application, analysis, synthesis, and evaluation.
- Given a list of instructional goals, classify each goal by the level of learning required.
- Define the following five types of learning commonly included in curriculum guides: intellectual skills, verbal information, cognitive strategies, motor skills, and attitudes.
- Given a list of instructional goals, classify each goal by the type of learning required.
- Given an instructional goal, identify the framework of subordinate skills required to perform the goal and sequence of skills.
- Convert subordinate skills into behavioral objectives by adding performance conditions and, when needed, criteria for acceptable performance.

Chapter 2 presents procedures for identifying and sequencing instructional goals and suggests methods for describing assigned groups of students. This chapter reviews goal analysis techniques that are essential prerequisites to effective instruction and evaluation. Goal analysis provides a foundation for developing and interpreting classroom achievement tests that should be directly related to the instructional goals for the course. Goal analysis identifies the type of learning involved, the subordinate skills required to achieve the goal, and the relationship among the subordinate skills. Such an analysis will help you relate the subordinate skills to your instruction and achievement tests. You can also use a goal framework to evaluate adopted textbooks and to select supplementary instructional materials. This chapter includes three sections. The first section summarizes the six levels of learning defined by Bloom, Madaus, and Hastings (1981) and the five types of learning described by Gagné (1985). The second section describes common instructional goal analysis procedures. The third section suggests ways to write behavioral objectives for goals and their subordinate skills. If this is your first exposure to learning analysis, you may want to obtain the texts listed at the end of the chapter. They will provide more detailed information about the classification and analysis of instructional goals.

LEVELS OF LEARNING

Bloom, Madaus, and Hastings (1981) have identified six learning levels that educators often use in writing instructional goals and objectives. These levels help clarify the depth of skills students are to acquire and the kinds of responses that will demonstrate students' skills and knowledge. The six levels of learning appear in Table 3.1.

The first level, *knowledge,* involves the recall or recognition of information that has been learned. This level is sometimes referred to as rote memory or repetition. For example, a student who memorizes and repeats the statement, "In 1492, Columbus sailed the ocean blue," would be participating in a knowledge task. Other examples include memorizing and repeating poems or lines from a play; recalling dates and persons associated with important events;

TABLE 3.1
Six Levels of Learning Defined by Bloom, Madaus, and Hastings

Level of Learning	Definition
Knowledge	Recalling or recognizing specific elements in a subject area
Comprehension	*Translation:* putting a concept or message into different words or changing from one symbolic system to another
	Interpretation: seeing the relationships among the separate parts of a communication
	Extrapolation: going beyond a literal communication and making inferences about consequences
Application	Using rules, principles, procedures, generalizations, and formulas to solve problems
Analysis	Separating a unit into its component parts so the relationship among the parts is made clear
Synthesis	Arranging and combining separate elements to form a whole
Evaluation	Using criteria and standards to make judgments about the value of ideas, products, and procedures

and recalling formulas, rules, procedures, facts, and definitions. No mental process other than remembering is involved.

The second level, *comprehension,* involves paraphrasing information or translating a given message into one's own words. Students participating in a comprehension task might explain the meaning of the sentence, "In 1492, Columbus sailed the ocean blue," with such statements as "Columbus began exploring in 1492" or "Columbus discovered America in 1492." Converting a story problem into a formula, converting a formula into words, inferring the main idea from a paragraph or story, and paraphrasing a definition are other comprehension tasks. Any translation, interpretation, or inference that demonstrates a student's understanding of a communication falls into this learning category.

At the *application* level, students solve problems by applying rules, principles, generalizations, or procedures. Using formulas to solve numerical problems, following rules of grammar and spelling, and constructing an object according to a plan are application tasks. At this level, students are expected to demonstrate their understanding of a rule, a principle, or a procedure by applying it to a task or problem.

The fourth level of learning, *analysis,* involves dividing a concept or unit into smaller parts so the parts and the relationship among them is clear. Dividing a story into the components of plot, characterization, and setting and then describing the relationship of these components is one example of analysis. Conducting a literature search for a term paper or a research project is another. In this chapter, you will learn how to divide an instructional goal into its subordinate skills and how to sequence the skills according to their relationship. These activities also represent the analysis level of learning.

At the fifth level, *synthesis,* the learner combines and integrates separate elements according to their relationship. This reassessment of components permits the learner to organize, summarize, and explain information and to make predictions. Assembling information for an essay or a position paper is one example of synthesis. The person writing the document must consider the ideas to be expressed, the interest and skills of the intended readers, the desired mood, and the appropriate writing style. The final product should reflect the writer's synthesis and interpretation of these elements. Original research also involves synthesis-level learning. The researcher analyzes the literature, identifies the variables, and synthesizes the relationships among the variables through statements of hypotheses. The procedures and instruments used to conduct the study constitute the researcher's interpretative summary of the context, the variables, and the relationships among the variables. The literature, the current hypotheses, the procedures used, and the research results are synthesized to make up the discussion and conclusions.

The sixth level of learning, *evaluation,* involves using criteria and standards to judge the quality and the value of ideas, products, or procedures. Criteria used to judge quality include such factors as accuracy, precision, economy, consistency, assumptions, evidence, and organization. In turn, these criteria become the basis for standards of work quality.

Teachers often expect students to judge the quality or worth of their own and others' work. Students can learn to evaluate many types of work, including their own essays, papers, artwork, and term projects; other people's articles, artwork, and term projects; speeches, plays, books, and movies; commercial products; events they have planned or sponsored; and instruction and tests.

Teachers use the six levels of learning to clarify and interpret the behavior specified in instructional goals and to write their own goals and objectives. Considering the level of learning ensures that the desired behavior in the goal or objective clearly communicates the level of learning intended. The levels can also be used to ensure that achievement tests include items that measure student performance relevant to instructional goals.

TYPES OF LEARNING

Robert Gagné (1985) has identified five types of learning: intellectual skills, verbal information, cognitive strategies, motor skills, and attitudes. A summary and examples of each type of learning appear in Table 3.2. The following sections of the text explain intellectual skills and verbal information and describe methods you can use to identify subordinate skills for instructional goals of each type. Many goals used as examples reflect basic skills because the content is obvious. Focus thus can be placed on definitions and procedures used in goal analysis. After reading about each type of learning, you should be able to apply the procedures to goals in your own subject area.

Cognitive strategies are mentioned here and included in Table 3.2 to provide a complete summary of Gagné's types of learning; however, cognitive strategies are not described in detail because they are analyzed for instruction and testing in much the same way as are the higher levels of intellectual skills, with the notable exception being that the performance of cognitive strategies normally implies independent thinking and original solutions to novel problems. Motor skills and attitudes are also included here, but both are described in more detail in Chapter 10 in the Alternative Assessments section of this text.

Intellectual Skills

When we use symbols to interact with our environment, we are applying intellectual skills (Gagné 1985). To understand or make sense of phenomena we encounter, we *differentiate* among objects and ideas, generalize our learning by *classifying,* and *solve problems* that perplex us. Intellectual skills also enable us to *explain* why things happen and to *predict* what will happen under

TABLE 3.2
Gagné's Five Types of Learning

Type of Learning	Definition	Example
Intellectual Skills	The use of symbols to interact with the environment. Often called *procedural knowledge*, intellectual skills are used to interpret phenomena and solve problems. Subcategories are: 1. Discriminations—differentiating among objects as similar or different 2. Concrete concepts—using physical characteristics to classify objects into categories 3. Defined concepts—using a definition to classify objects, events, or conditions into categories 4. Rules—following a mental procedure to solve a problem or create a product 5. Principles—combining two or more concepts and describing the relationships among them to explain observed phenomena or to predict an outcome	1. Learning that rectangles are not the same as squares 2. Learning that an object is a square because it has four equal sides that are closed and form right angles 3. Learning that the founder of an organization is the person primarily responsible for the existence of the organization 4. Learning to calculate the circumference of a circle, punctuate sentences, write a short story 5. Explain erosion or predict the weather
Verbal Information	1. Associating objects, events, symbols, or conditions with their names 2. Remembering facts and repeating or recounting information	1. Learning that the symbol + means to add, the symbol 2 is two, a particular person is called John, and the word *fever* indicates an abnormally high body temperature 2. Recalling that John had a fever on Saturday, the words to a particular song, and that given authors wrote fiction
Cognitive Strategies	Managing one's own internal mental processes of learning, remembering, and thinking, often toward the development of unique solutions to new problems	1. Planning a group activity in such a way that all group members feel they are making important contributions 2. Devising a strategy in chess to counter a novel sequence of moves 3. Inventing a mnemonic to help remember new terms for a biology exam 4. Applying physical principles of inertia to explain patterns of social change

(continued)

TABLE 3.2 Continued

Type of Learning	Definition	Example
Motor Skills	Physical procedures that require movement, precision, and timing, and that include simultaneous or sequential steps. Learning complex motor skills requires both knowledge of the steps and practice.	Playing the piano, riding a bicycle, operating machinery and equipment, tying knots and buttoning buttons, sewing, and painting
Attitudes	Mental states that govern our choices and behavior. An attitude has three main elements: 1. Affective—a person's positive or negative feelings toward something 2. Behavioral—the way a person acts or behaves 3. Cognitive—knowing about or how to do something. This component may include intellectual skills, verbal information, and motor skills. It usually includes information about cultural expectations, rewards, and consequences for behaving in a prescribed manner	Respecting the property of others 1. Having a positive feeling about oneself and other people who show respect for the property of others 2. Obtaining permission to use another's property; exercising care and following directions when using borrowed property; returning property undamaged and quickly 3. Learning expectations for behavior with borrowed property; learning the rewards of and consequences for acceptable and unacceptable behavior; and learning how to use the borrowed property correctly

given circumstances. Our use of intellectual skills produces visible results, but the mental processes we use are not observable. Intellectual skills are also referred to as *procedural knowledge* or learning how to do something. The procedures involved, however, are mental rather than physical. Intellectual skills include the reading, language, and arithmetic goals commonly referred to as basic skills. They thus make up a large portion of school learning.

Intellectual skills are divided into four subcategories that form a hierarchy of simple to complex skills. The most basic skill is *discrimination* learning, which serves as a foundation for the development of *concrete concepts*. In turn, concrete concepts permit the formation of *defined concepts*, and both types of concepts are required for the development of *rules*. The following paragraphs explain each of these subcategories.

Discrimination   In discrimination learning, a student compares objects on the basis of their physical properties. At its simplest level, discrimination is the ability to recognize that two objects are the same or different. For example, a child learning to tell the difference between nickels and dimes must use the physical characteristics of the coins to determine whether they are the same or different. Being able to tell the difference between letters of the alphabet and between numbers are other examples of discrimination learning.

Concepts   Two types of concepts make up this category: concrete concepts and defined concepts. A *concrete concept* refers to objects whose physical properties permit us to recognize, classify, and generalize. Learning a concrete concept involves distinguishing the physical characteristics that make an object a member of a class. For example, children learn to classify neighborhood animals as dogs by first learning to recognize the distinguishing characteristics of dogs. Once they recognize these unique characteristics, they can correctly classify a dog when they see one. They learn to distinguish bottles, boxes, cans, and numerous other objects by their physical properties.

A *defined concept* includes more than physical properties in its definition. It may have physical characteristics as a component, but the definition will also describe a relationship between or among objects. For example, *teacher* and *father* are defined concepts. We cannot classify people as teachers or fathers if we know only their physical characteristics. We also need to know what they do and how they relate to other people. To determine whether someone fits into the category of teacher or father, we must know how these terms are defined.

Vase is another example of a defined concept. We can define a vase as an object that holds cut flowers or cut plants. This definition permits us to relate a vase to a class of objects (containers) and to discriminate cut flowers or cut plants from their growing counterparts. The word *holds* tells us what the vase does or is used for and thus describes the relationship between the objects. Using this definition, we can identify as vases all sorts of different containers, including tin cans, wine bottles, crystal containers, pitchers, and baskets. We can also discriminate between containers that are vases and those that are flower pots. For example, if we see a pitcher being used as a vase, we would not say to ourselves, "That is not a vase." Instead, we would probably think, "That is an interesting vase." We recognize the pitcher's change in function because it now matches our definition of vase.

Other examples of defined concepts include *leader, honesty, fairness, principle*, and *dangerous*. To classify examples of these concepts, a person must know how each concept is defined. Some definitions will be brief and straightforward; others will be complex statements of related features, uses, relationships, and characteristics. The clearer and more precise a definition, the more accurately a person will be able to classify examples of the concept.

Rules   Rules are propositions that govern our behavior toward stimuli and cause us to respond in a given or expected way. We follow rules to perform skills correctly (Gagné 1985). Language and mathematics are two examples of rule-governed skills. If we want to use language correctly, we must follow rules of spelling, sentence construction, punctuation, subject and verb agreement, capitalization, and so forth. The rules for addition enable us to add numbers correctly, regardless of their nature, quantity, and size.

A rule may be brief, as in "Capitalize proper nouns," or it may be a long procedure, like the ones needed to do long division and to calculate a standard deviation. Rules are composed of two or more concepts. For example, the rule, "Capitalize proper nouns," is made up of three concepts: capitalize, proper nouns, and nouns. Before students can follow this rule, they must learn all three concepts. They must be able to follow the rules for capitalizing words, for classifying words as nouns, and for classifying the subset of nouns called *proper nouns.* To classify nouns and proper nouns correctly, students must know how these concepts are defined. Once they know the concepts involved, they are ready to learn and apply the rule for capitalizing proper nouns.

Principles are rules used to explain and interpret phenomena and to predict what will happen in given circumstances. They explain why events happen by combining two or more concepts and their relationships. The relationships of the concepts may be causal (one concept causes another concept) or correlational (one concept is positively or negatively related to another). "Poor eating habits usually result in digestive problems" exemplifies a commonly accepted principle that has a causal relationship between the named concepts. "Cigarette smoking is positively related to various health disorders" is an example of a correlational principle. We use these principles to predict what will happen if someone consistently overeats, eats the wrong foods, or smokes cigarettes. When individuals who have poor eating habits or who smoke cigarettes develop health problems, we then explain their condition using the commonly believed principles. Like rules, principles may be brief and straightforward or they may be lengthy with many concepts and their relationships. For example, you might use a principle to explain how a group of students performed on a test or to predict how one would perform. The concepts included in your principle might be (1) student's ability, (2) student's motivation and effort, (3) the quality of the instruction provided, and (4) the quality of the test administered. The principle might be expressed as follows:

$$\text{High Test Achievement} = \text{High Student Ability} + \text{High Motivation and Effort} + \text{Quality Instruction} + \text{Quality Measure of Achievement}$$

With this principle in mind, you would explain observed high test achievement as resulting from or as caused by the presence of this combination of factors. If you believed these factors to be present before administering an achievement test, you would undoubtedly predict high achievement on the test.

Verbal Information

Gagné (1985) identified a second type of learning as verbal information. Verbal information involves learning names or labels, facts, and collections of information that are sometimes called bodies of knowledge. Unlike intellectual skills, which represent procedural knowledge, verbal information represents declarative knowledge. Much of what is taught in school is verbal information. When students learn to name the parts of the body, repeat historical facts, or memorize poems, they are learning verbal information.

Names and Labels   Learning the names for objects, events, ideas, and symbols involves consistently associating the name with a given object, event, idea, or symbol. For example, the symbol *9* is always called nine, the symbol + means to add, a particular teacher is Mr. Jones, the word *red* refers to a particular color, and $\overline{X}$ is the symbol for an average score. We often learn the name for an object at the same time as we learn its distinguishing characteristics. A person who learns the name for an object, however, may not be able to generalize the properties of the object and to recognize other examples of the same concept. Thus, to name or label something, a person must simply remember the name of a given object, event, idea, or symbol when it is encountered.

Facts   Verbal information also includes facts, such as knowing that a particular building is the library, that the library is the newest building in town, that it contains more books than any other library in the state, and that it is open from eight o'clock in the morning until nine o'clock at night.

Verbal information and intellectual skills appear to work in a symbiotic way. Verbal information helps us communicate our intellectual skills, and intellectual skills help us organize and structure our verbal information. Although verbal information appears to be a simpler form of knowledge than do intellectual skills, it is not necessarily subordinate. For example, students could more easily communicate or verbalize the concrete concept *boat* if they knew the name of a floating vehicle that carries cargo or people. At the same time, they do not have to know the name *boat* to classify examples. Likewise, they can learn that the name of a particular object is *boat* without being able to classify other examples of the concept.

PROCEDURES FOR ANALYZING INSTRUCTIONAL GOALS

Based on Bloom's (1956) definition, *analysis* is the intellectual process of separating a unit into its component parts so the relationship among the parts is made clear. In instructional goal analysis, the unit is the instructional goal, and the purpose for the analysis is to identify the information and tasks, often called *subordinate skills*, required to perform the goal. In addition, the subordinate skills should be sequenced to illustrate the relationships among them.

Instructional goal analysis can be relatively complex, even for experts in a discipline; however, it can be made easier by using common analytical procedures.

There are a variety of analysis procedures that teachers can use to analyze instructional goals in their curriculum guides. Three of the most commonly employed procedures are the matrix diagram, tree diagram, and flowchart. No one of these procedures works best for every instructional goal within a discipline, and some teachers prefer to work with one strategy rather than another. The following sections describe each of these procedures.

The Matrix Diagram

The matrix diagram is two-dimensional structure of rows, columns, and intersecting cells. The basic structure of the matrix diagram is illustrated in Figure 3.1. The columns, labeled A through D, can be used to analyze the sequence one dimension in the analysis. The rows, labeled I through IV, can be used to analyze and sequence a second dimension. The intersecting cells, labeled I.A through IV.D, can be used to note relationships between each row-by-column set. A matrix diagram can have any number of rows and cells, and the appropriate number is determined during the analysis process.

The Tree Diagram

The second analysis procedure is the tree diagram, and its structure is illustrated in Figure 3.2. The trunk on the far left side of the diagram (I) usually contains the behavior and content in the instructional goal. The branches in the second level (I.A and I.B) are typically used to name the key subordinate skills in the goal. The third level of branches (I.A.1 through I.B.2) is used to break down each of the key subordinate skills named in the second level. Each successive level is used to break down further the identified subordinate skills.

The Flowchart

The third analysis procedure is the flowchart. Flowcharts are similar to tree diagrams but they differ in two key ways: orientation and flexibility. A tree

FIGURE 3.1
A Matrix
Diagram

	A	B	C	D
I	I.A	I.B	I.C	I.D
II	II.A	II.B	II.C	II.D
III	III.A	III.B	III.C	III.D
IV	IV.A	IV.B	IV.C	IV.D

FIGURE 3.2
The Tree Diagram

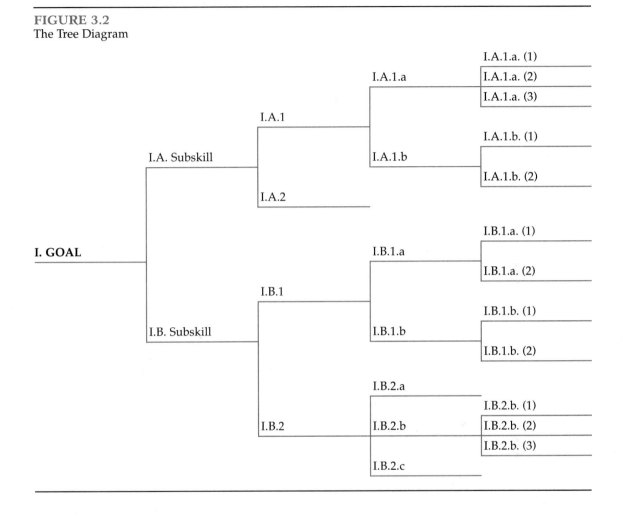

diagram is oriented horizontally on the page, whereas the flowchart is organized vertically, with the instructional goal at the top of the page and the most basic subordinate skills at the bottom. The flowchart is more flexible than the tree diagram in that it can be constructed to illustrate single and simultaneous operations, decision points, and iterations. A flowchart diagram is illustrated in Figure 3.3.

The structure of the flowchart implies the type of instructional goal best suited to this analysis format: physical or mental procedures such as sports, operating equipment, performing mathematical operations, or solving problems (e.g., scientific method). The placement of tasks in the diagram, the shape of the boxes, and the direction of the arrows all communicate the relationships among the tasks. For example, A.1 and A.2 are hierarchically related to A in Figure 3.3. The hierarchical relationship is indicated by the

FIGURE 3.3

The Flowchart Goal Analysis Procedure

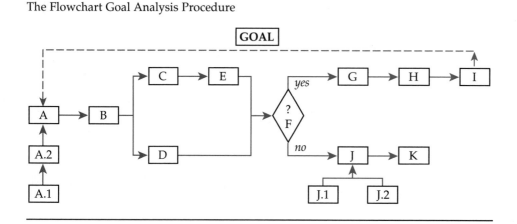

vertical placement of the tasks and the upward direction of the arrow connecting the tasks. Tasks A and B are chronologically related, with A being performed before B. The chronological relationship is indicated by the horizontal placement of the tasks and the direction of the arrows. Tasks C and D occur simultaneously, and this is indicated by their vertical placement on parallel, horizontal lines. Task F is diamond shaped, and the diamond indicates a decision point in the procedure. If the decision is yes, then the performer advances to steps G, H, and I. If the decision is no, the performer takes a different path through steps J and K. The broken line connecting tasks I and A and the direction of the arrow indicates an iteration or return to the previous step.

An Example

The instructional goal, "Write a paragraph," is used to illustrate goal analysis using a matrix diagram, tree diagram, and flowchart. This particular goal was chosen for the example because it appears in curriculum guides from primary grades through graduate school; thus, it can be used to exemplify the educational mandate or *continuous quality improvement*. It is also interdisciplinary since teachers, regardless of their subject area, are concerned with students' ability to express ideas within a discipline. In addition, students' progress on this goal can be assessed using both objective tests and alternative assessments. Finally, it is an example with which all teachers are familiar, regardless of whether their area of expertise is in physics, art, special education, or any of the myriad of specialties that comprise education. Analyzing instructional goals in an unfamiliar content area makes the analysis process more difficult than necessary, so the instructional goal of writing a paragraph is used in the examples that follow.

USING A MATRIX DIAGRAM TO
ANALYZE INTELLECTUAL SKILLS

The two-dimensional matrix analysis procedure is particularly useful for classroom teachers since instruction is comprised of both learning and content. One dimension can be used to analyze and sequence learning tasks, and the other can be used to identify and sequence the main concepts in any given domain. The intersecting learning-by-content cells can be used to note interrelationships between particular levels of learning and areas of content. The following steps can be used to analyze an instructional goal using a matrix analysis procedure:

1. Identify the levels of learning appropriate for the instructional goal, and sequence them in the columns from most basic (left) to most complex (right).
2. Identify the concepts (content) contained in the instructional goal, and sequence them in the rows.
3. Integrate the learning and content elements by noting particular relationships in the intersecting row-by-column cells.

Each of these steps is described in the following sections.

Analyze Levels of Learning

Since the instructional goal, write a paragraph, is an intellectual skill, the elements of an intellectual skill can be used to create the column headings in the matrix. Translating Bloom's and Gagné's categories into useful goal analysis categories requires some analysis and interpretation. The categories included and their sequence are a matter of professional judgment, and they are often modified to suit both a particular instructional goal and the teacher's "sense of sequence."

Both Bloom's and Gagné's categories of intellectual skills have a defined order from simple to complex, and the column headings should generally reflect this order. Their categories are quite broad, however, and further analysis is usually required to create the most useful matrix. For example, Bloom's knowledge category and Gagné's concepts category can be further broken down using the basic informational questions, Who? What? Where? When? and Why? For the paragraph goal, the questions What? and Where? can be equated to the *physical characteristics* of a paragraph (concrete concepts). The question Why? can be equated to the *functional characteristics* of a paragraph (defined concepts), and How? can be equated to the *quality characteristics* of a paragraph (defined concepts). For other instructional goals, you might need different basic categories of information or concepts, and you should choose those that are, in your professional judgment, best suited to the goal you are analyzing.

Figure 3.4 contains two sample matrix diagrams with sequenced levels of learning for intellectual skill goals. The top matrix contains columns that are based on Bloom's categories. They are reconfigured, however, to suit better the task of analyzing instructional goals. Knowledge and comprehension are clustered together, and the categories of state/recall physical (A), functional (B), and quality (C) characteristics are included within these two categories. The application category is next and, following rules based on characteristic combinations, students are to discriminate between examples and nonexamples (D) of a concept. Column (E) is the evaluation of given examples, which requires both analysis and synthesis of the physical, functional, and quality characteristics for making judgments about the quality of a paragraph. The last column, (F), is also listed under analysis and synthesis since these skills are also required for the production of a paragraph.

The bottom matrix is based on Gagné's levels of intellectual skills. The first column (A) contains concrete concepts, or the physical characteristics of the concept to be learned. Both the second and third columns contain defined concepts. The particular defined concepts considered appropriate for the production of a paragraph are the functional and quality characteristics. The three columns on the right (D, E, and F) are all under the rules heading since students must synthesize concrete and defined concepts into rules for discriminating examples and nonexamples, evaluating given examples, and producing examples.

Notice the double line between columns C and D in both sample matrices. This line signals the difference between recall-type tasks and higher-order

Comparisons

FIGURE 3.4

Sample Column Headings Based on Bloom's and Gagné's Levels of Intellectual Skills

Bloom's Levels: Knowledge, Comprehension, Application, Analysis, Synthesis, Evaluation

	KNOWLEDGE AND COMPREHENSION			APPLICATION	ANALYSIS AND SYNTHESIS	
	A State/Recall Physical Characteristic	**B** State/Recall Functional Charactertistic	**C** State/Recall Quality Characteristic	**D** Discriminate Examples & Nonexamples	**E** Evaluate Given Examples	**F** Produce Examples
CONCEPTS/ CONTENT						

Gagné's Levels of Intellectual Skills: Concrete and Defined Concepts, Rules, Principles

	CONCRETE CONCEPTS	DEFINED CONCEPTS		RULES		
	A State/Recall Physical Characteristic	**B** State/Recall Functional Charactertistic	**C** State/Recall Quality Characteristic	**D** Discriminate Examples & Nonexamples	**E** Evaluate Given Examples	**F** Produce Examples
CONCEPTS/ CONTENT						

tasks that require intellectual processing such as analysis and synthesis. Notice also that evaluation is located before production in both matrices. This is due to the fact that teachers want students to recognize the quality characteristics of paragraphs and use them in evaluating given paragraphs as practice for integrating them into their plans for producing original paragraphs.

Some teachers prefer using Bloom's categories for analyzing instructional goals, whereas others are more successful using Gagné's categories. In your work, use the system you find most comfortable. Further, you should not hesitate to alter the content or order of the categories for given instructional goals. These categories are to be used as guides, and they can be tailored to fit a particular goal or group of students.

Analyze Content

The second dimension in the matrix is content, and main areas of content are placed in the row headings. The procedure for identifying the row headings is to analyze the intellectual skill instructional goal in order to identify its concepts, rules, or principles. The steps in analyzing the goal for the matrix rows are the following:

1. State (or locate) the rule for a paragraph.
2. Underline the key concepts in the rule.
3. Determine the relationship among the key concepts.
4. Sequence the concepts based on the identified relationships.

Rule and Key Concepts   The rule for writing a paragraph with key concepts underlined could be stated as follows:

> A <u>paragraph</u> is a series of sentences on one topic. It typically contains a <u>topic sentence, supporting sentences,</u> and a <u>concluding sentence.</u> The first sentence of a paragraph is usually indented.

The concepts in the paragraph rule that are not underlined describe either physical or functional characteristics of a paragraph, and they can be addressed during the analysis of the key concepts.

Relationship   The next step in the analysis process is to determine the relationships among the key concepts selected. In this example, topic sentences, supporting sentences, and concluding sentences all name types of sentences contained in paragraphs. Further, they typically have a chronological relationship with topic sentences placed first, supporting sentences placed in the center, and concluding sentences located at the end of the paragraph.

Sequence   The final step is to sequence the key concepts in the matrix rows based on their identified relationships. Among the three types of sentences, they would be placed in the rows from top to bottom based on their natural sequence. The teacher has some leeway, however, in whether to place the concept paragraph first or last in the sequence. For this example, it is placed first in order to form a foundation for the three types of sentences contained in it. Figure 3.5 contains the matrix diagram with the levels of learning inserted in the column headings and the discipline-based content inserted in the row headings. The concept and rule labels have been omitted in the column headings for convenience.

Integrate Learning and Content

The third step in the analysis is to integrate the learning levels and content. You could list the major learning outcomes for the paragraph instructional unit by simply integrating the row and column headings. For example, combining all the column headings with the first row heading in Figure 3.5 produces the following learning outcomes:

> I.A State/Recall the physical characteristics of a paragraph
> I.B State/Recall the functional characteristics of a paragraph
> I.C State/Recall the quality characteristics of a paragraph
> I.D Discriminate between examples and nonexamples of paragraphs
> I.E Evaluate given paragraphs
> I.F Produce paragraphs

Notice that learning outcome I.F is the instructional goal, "Write a paragraph." Combining all column headings with all row headings in the matrix

FIGURE 3.5
Sample Matrix Diagram for the Intellectual Skill "Write a Paragraph"

CONCEPTS/ CONTENT	A State/Recall Physical Characteristics of:	B State/Recall Functional Charactertistics of:	C State/Recall Quality Characteristics of:	D Discriminate Between Examples & Nonexamples	E Evaluate Given Examples	F Produce Examples of:
I. Paragraph						
II. Topic Sentence						
III. Supporting Sentences						
IV. Concluding Sentences						

(I.A through IV.F) automatically produces a comprehensive list of the general student learning outcomes (behavior and content) for the instructional unit on paragraphs. This is an important list of outcomes since it forms the foundation for the unit's behavioral objectives, which will be discussed in a later section of this chapter.

With the matrix diagram completed to this point, you have the foundation for analyzing the relationships between each row and column heading. Any relationships identified, that are judged reasonable for the target learners, can be paraphrased in the intersecting cells. During the integration process, teachers often find that some cells contain several interconnecting relationships while others are scant or blank. You may find that some of the cells are no more than a summary of other cells. You may also decide to add another column or row or to delete an existing one. These findings should not be disconcerting, however, since the matrix is simply a guide for the goal analysis.

Figure 3.6 contains the complete matrix diagram for the paragraph instructional goal. Notice that the cells I.C and I.E are left blank. They are blank because the paragraph quality characteristics are elaborated in cells II, III, and

FIGURE 3.6
Sample Matrix Diagram Analysis for the Instructional Goal "Write a Paragraph"

CONCEPTS/ CONTENT	A State/Recall Physical Characteristics	B State/Recall Functional Charactertistics	C State/Recall Quality Characteristics	D Discriminate Examples & Nonexamples	E Evaluate Given Examples	F Produce Examples
I. Paragraph	Series of sentences Indented	Express ideas on one topic		Correct vs. not indented Many topics		Time Series Feelings Procedure Description
II. Topic Sentence	Typically first Indented	Introduce topic	Relevance Scope Interest	Topic vs. Supporting Concluding	Correct vs. flawed by: Relevance Scope Interest	Time Series Feelings Procedure Description
III. Supporting Sentences	Middle sentences	Elaborate topic	Relevance Sequence Transition	Supporting vs. Topic Concluding	Correct vs. flawed by: Relevance Sequence Transition	Time Series Feelings Procedure Description
IV. Concluding Sentences	Typically last	Conclude/ summarize topic	Transition Relevance Sums up Scope	Concluding vs. Topic Supporting	Correct vs. flawed by: Transition Relevance Conclusion Scope	Time Series Feelings Procedure Description

IV.C, and the evaluation skills are elaborated in cells II, III, and IV.E. If you had chosen to repeat these quality characteristics and evaluation tasks in row I, it would not have been incorrect, just redundant. The particular criteria listed in column C, the particular judgments listed in column E, and the specific types of paragraphs listed in column F reflect the unique choices of the teacher. Other teachers might have stressed different types of paragraphs to be written or emphasized different criteria.

USING A TREE DIAGRAM TO ANALYZE INTELLECTUAL SKILLS

Similar to the matrix analysis procedure, the product resulting from the tree diagram analysis should be a list of the subordinate tasks required to perform the instructional goal. The task statements should contain both the behavior (learning) and the content.

The tree diagram procedure is somewhat more difficult for teachers to use because it provides less guidance during the analysis process. Without guidance, teachers are tempted to include prerequisite skills, such as writing a complete sentence or punctuating sentences. Although you could correctly argue that such tasks are subordinate to writing paragraphs, they are prerequisites that should be mastered before entering a unit of instruction on paragraph construction.

Some teachers find the tree diagram procedure more complex to use; others prefer it because of the freedom and lack of structure. Suggested steps for using a tree diagram are the following:

1. In the far left margin, and centered between the top and bottom of the diagram, write the instructional goal.
2. State clearly the main rule or principle that is required to perform the goal and underline the key concepts in the rule (or rules in the principle).
3. Analyze the relationships (e.g., hierarchical, chronological, importance, abstractness, etc.) among the key concepts and sequence them in the next column according to the identified relationships.
4. Transform each key concept into a learning task by adding an appropriate level of learning required to perform the task. Anchor the key learning tasks to the instructional goal using the tree branches.
5. Analyze each of the key learning tasks by asking yourself, What must a learner know or be able to do in order to perform this task? Subordinate tasks identified should be listed in the next column and connected using the tree structure.
6. Keep identifying subordinate skills for each level until you reach a level you believe all students in your target group have mastered.

A sample tree diagram is illustrated in Figure 3.7. Notice that the contents are similar to those included in the matrix diagram.

FIGURE 3.7

Sample Tree Diagram for the Instructional Goal "Write a Paragraph"

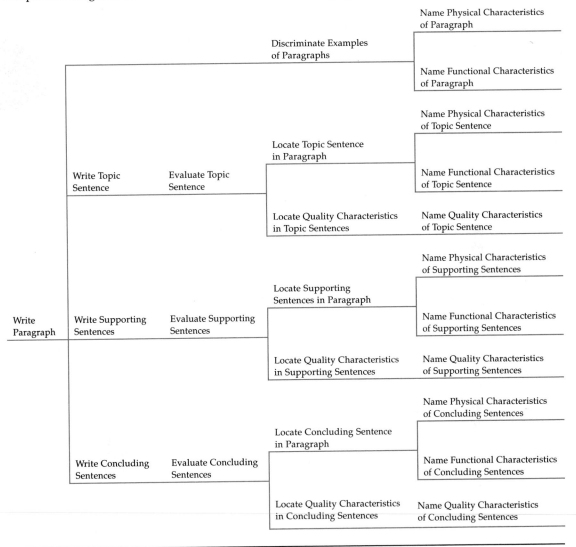

USING A FLOWCHART TO
ANALYZE INTELLECTUAL SKILLS

The flowchart procedure can also be used to analyze the paragraph instructional goal. As noted previously, one main difference between tree diagrams and flowcharts is the orientation of the diagram on the page and the use of arrows to indicate relationships among learning tasks. Figure 3.8 contains the paragraph instructional goal analyzed using a flowchart. The goal, write a paragraph (I), appears at the top of the chart, and the four key subordinate skills are to discriminate between paragraphs and nonparagraphs (I.A), write topic sentences (I.B), write supporting sentences (I.C), and write concluding sentences (I.D). The upward arrows from these four skills to the instructional goal indicate that they are hierarchically related to the goal. The relationship among these four tasks is chronological rather than hierarchical, and the structure of the flowchart illustrates their sequential nature. The remaining tasks in the flowchart are all hierarchically related to these four main subordinate skills, and the hierarchical nature is again illustrated using the upward arrows.

Notice the similarities between the subordinate skills identified using the matrix, tree diagram, and flowchart procedures. They are similar because the content of the goal and the intellectual skills required to perform the goal were integrated during the analysis process.

ANALYZING INSTRUCTIONAL GOALS THAT ARE VERBAL INFORMATION

Students will learn and remember verbal information more easily if it is organized in a meaningful way and presented as interrelated or connected facts and names. Gagné has recommended creating frameworks (*schemata*), which cluster similar facts and information, and providing a meaningful context for learning labels and names. For example, instead of presenting important historical figures in chronological order, a teacher might group them according to the nature of their accomplishments. Notable writers, inventors, politicians, and explorers could all be presented in their turn. In introducing new vocabulary, a teacher could present groups of related words, such as those associated with food and eating, work, recreation, and travel. Two schemata for presenting verbal information related to geography and biology appear in Table 3.3. Each diagram separates information into categories, and columns and rows provide space for related information and examples.

Although the goal analysis procedure is time consuming, it is a necessary prerequisite to writing behavioral objectives, developing lesson plans, evaluating instructional materials, developing relevant tests, and diagnosing students' problems. If you have difficulty analyzing and sequencing subordinate skills for instructional goals, the skills probably have become automatic for you. This state of automatic performance enables you to perform efficiently with little conscious thought about what you are doing. Although automatic performance makes routine tasks easier, it also makes the analysis of subordinate skills for an instructional goal more difficult. New teachers often comment that they really had not understood their subject

FIGURE 3.8
Sample Flowchart Analysis of the Instructional Goal "Write a Paragraph"

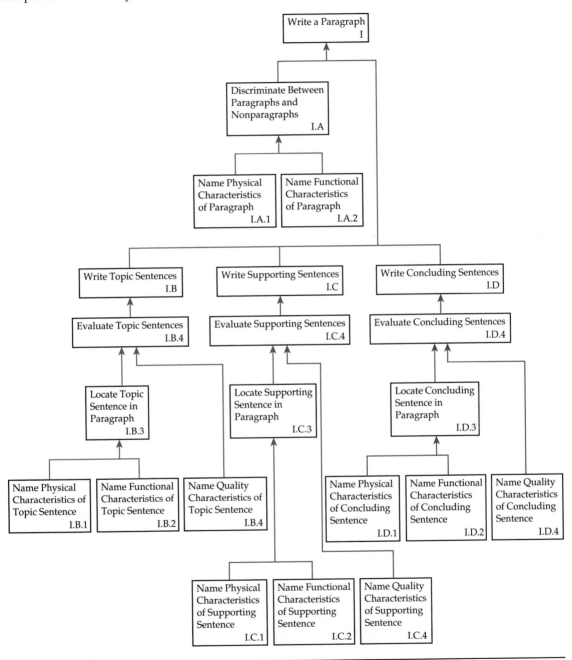

TABLE 3.3
Matrix Diagram for Organizing Verbal Information Related to Geography
and Biology

A. Geography: Countries Located in the Americas

MAIN CONTENT AREAS	A Name	B Capital city	C Size in sq. miles	D Location on map	E Population	F Climate
I. Countries in North America	I.A	I.B	I.C	I.D	I.E	I.F
II. Countries in Central America	II.A	II.B	II.C	II.D	II.E	II.F
III. Countries in South America	III.A	III.B	III.C	III.D	III.E	III.F

B. Biology: Human Body System

MAIN CONTENT AREAS	A Name/Recall Physical Characteristics	B Name/Recall Functional Characteristics	C Name/Location of System in Body
I. Circulatory	I.A	I.B	I.C
II. Respiratory	II.A	II.B	II.C
III. Digestive	III.A	III.B	III.C
IV. Nervous	IV.A	IV.B	IV.C
IV. Muscular	V.A	V.B	V.C
VI. Skeletal	VI.A	VI.B	VI.C

until they tried to teach it to someone else. This and similar comments
indicate the automatic nature of the skills these teachers are trying to communicate. Before they can effectively convey these skills to other people, they
must mentally relearn each skill by breaking it down into all of its component
skills.

Personally, you may prefer either the flowchart, the tree diagram, or the
matrix analysis method for analyzing the intellectual skill instructional goals
in your curriculum guide. If you are using one method and experiencing
difficulty with your analysis, try another. Procedurally oriented goals, such as
those for performing long division, seem easier to analyze using the flowchart
procedure, whereas creation-oriented goals, such as writing a sentence, paragraph, essay, or research report, seem easier to analyze using the matrix
analysis method.

WRITING BEHAVIORAL OBJECTIVES

A behavioral objective is a statement of intended learning outcomes that includes the subordinate skill from the instructional goal framework, the conditions under which the skill will be performed, and the criteria for acceptable performance. The subordinate skills in the goal framework, whether they are formatted in a matrix, a tree diagram, or a flowchart, should already contain the behavior and content. Adding conditions helps define the nature and complexity of the task, and criteria specify the limits of an acceptable answer. Behavioral objectives (sometimes called *performance objectives* and *instructional objectives*) that include the conditions and criteria for performance are valuable guides for developing lessons and for writing test items that measure the intended performance.

Conditions

Conditions is a term used to indicate the information, tools, equipment, or other resources students will be given when they are asked to perform the skill. Conditions are used to prescribe the stimulus that will be provided for the task and to limit the task's scope and complexity so that it is reasonable for given students.

To prescribe the stimulus for a subordinate skill, you need to consider the behavior in the skill and what students will need in order to demonstrate that behavior. Consider how the conditions in the following examples prescribe the stimuli students will be given to perform the subordinate skills.

Conditions	*Subordinate Skills*
1. Given the name of a concrete concept, . . .	1. . . . list the distinguishing properties of the concept.
2. Given a prototype of a concrete concept, . . .	2. . . . list the distinguishing properties of the concept.
3. Given a list of the distinguishing properties of a concrete concept, . . .	3. . . . name the concept.
4. Given several examples and nonexamples of a concept, . . .	4. . . . classify examples of the concept.
5. Given several examples of a concrete concept, . . .	5. . . . analyze the examples and list their common characteristics.

Although, at first glance, the stimuli appear to be obvious, this is not always the case. Notice, for example, that subordinate skills 1 and 2 are the same, yet the conditions are different. In example 1, students will be given the name as a stimulus, whereas in example 2, they will be given an actual object with which to work. The differences in these stimuli will change the nature of the task. When given the name as a stimulus, students will need to search their memories to recall the distinguishing characteristics they have learned, with no clues provided. On the other hand, the actual object will provide clues but it may also cause unskilled students to confuse "unique" characteristics with others not used to define the class. For example, birds, dogs, and fish all have two eyes. Being precise in prescribing the stimulus helps ensure that written test items measure the intended behavior.

In setting performance conditions, you should also consider the sophistication and achievement levels of students in the group. You can vary the conditions in a behavioral objective so that the required performance matches the skill level of your students. Consider the subordinate skill, "Locate specified places on a state map." The conditions you specify will determine the complexity of this task. Notice how the following three conditions affect the difficulty of the task:

Conditions	*Subordinate Skill*
1. Given a simplified state map with no more than 10 identified points, . . .	. . . locate specified places on the map.
2. Given a simplified state map with 20 to 30 identified points, . . .	
3. Given a commercially prepared state map, . . .	

Notice that the basic stimulus remains the same: given a state map. However, qualifiers are added to each condition to limit the complexity of the stimulus and the behavior. The first condition would be most appropriate for lower elementary grades; the second for upper elementary grades; and the third for junior high, senior high, or adult students. Although the basic skill of locating specified places on a state map remains the same, the conditions have an important effect on the complexity of the task.

Performance Criteria

Behavioral objectives sometimes include performance criteria, which indicate how well the subordinate skill is to be performed. They should be added only when student responses are expected to vary. For example, you could expect a range of answers for a test question based on the behavioral objective, "Given no measurement tool, estimate the length of a specified object." By adding the criterion, "correct to within one foot," you could set the boundaries for an acceptable answer.

The behavioral objective, "Type, from handwritten copy, an average of 50 words per minute," specifies an acceptable speed for students' work. Adding another criterion, "with no more than two typing errors," establishes the number of acceptable errors. The speed and error criteria help communicate exactly what the student is expected to do.

If only one correct response is possible, criteria are not needed. Consider, for example, the behavioral objective, "Calculate the average score for a set of test scores." A criterion such as "correctly" or "80 percent of the time" is not necessary. If the student calculates the scores correctly, then only one answer is possible. For the criterion, "80 percent of the time," students would have to calculate average scores on five different test items. Although some teachers might require this, most would consider it impractical.

Table 3.4 lists three learning tasks and five related behavioral objectives. The two behavioral objectives for the task, "Capitalize proper nouns," specify different conditions. For the first objective, students are given sentences without proper nouns capitalized. For the second, they are given a list of words containing common nouns and proper nouns. The behavioral objectives do not include criteria because none are needed to judge the accuracy of students' work.

The behavioral objective for the second task, "Estimate the distance between specified places on a map," includes three conditions and the criterion for performance. The "givens" are a simplified map, a ruler, and a simplified mileage scale. To be considered accurate, the students' answers must be within 2 miles of the teacher's calculations.

TABLE 3.4
Behavioral Objectives for Three Learning Tasks

Task: Capitalize proper nouns

Conditions	Performance	Criteria
1. Given sentences without proper nouns capitalized, . . .	. . . locate and capitalize the proper nouns.	
2. Given a list of words containing common and proper nouns, . . .	. . . locate and capitalize the proper nouns.	

Task: Estimate the distance between specified places on a map

Conditions	Performance	Criteria
1. Given a simplified map with 10 to 12 identified places, a ruler, and a scale with one inch equal to 10 miles, . . .	. . . estimate the distance between specified places, . . .	. . . with the distance accurate to within 2 miles.

Task: Add numbers

Conditions	Performance	Criteria
1. Given two whole numbers of two digits that do not require regrouping, . . .	. . . add the numbers.	
2. Given two whole numbers of two digits that require regrouping, . . .	. . . add the numbers.	

The behavioral objectives for the third task, "Add numbers," has conditions that limit the digits in each number, the numbers in each problem, and whether regrouping is required. Criteria for judging answers are not needed because correct answers are not expected to vary.

USING AN INSTRUCTIONAL GOAL FRAMEWORK TO GENERATE BEHAVIORAL OBJECTIVES

The instructional goal framework is the foundation for creating the behavioral objectives for a unit of instruction. The procedure for developing objectives is illustrated using the hypothetical instructional goal framework in Table 3.5. This table could represent either an intellectual skill or a verbal information goal, depending on the behaviors listed in the column headings at the top of the table. Every cell in a goal framework that contains paraphrased information connecting a content-by-learning task pair should have at least one corresponding behavioral objective. Therefore, in Table 3.5, there would be one or more behavioral objectives constructed for the cells I.A, I.B, I.C, and so forth for every cell. Synthesizing the information from the goal framework and adding realistic conditions and criteria to this information should produce the appropriate behavioral objectives for the instructional goal.

In addition to contructing one or more behavioral objectives for individual cells within the framework, you may combine cells to make more complex objectives when appropriate. It is often unnecessary to combine cells when the instructional goal is an intellectual skill, since such cells are naturally combined due to the hierarchical nature of skills in the framework. For in-

TABLE 3.5
Hypothetical Instructional Goal Framework for Identifying Behavior Objectives

CONTENT AREAS	LEARNING TASKS					
	A	B	C	D	E	F
I.	I.A	I.B	I.C	I.D	I.E	I.F
II.	II.A	II.B	II.C	II.D	II.E	II.F
III.	III.A	III.B	III.C	III.D	III.E	III.F
IV.	IV.A	IV.B	IV.C	IV.D	IV.E	IV.F

stance, writing topic sentences requires the synthesis of many subordinate skills. When the goal matrix represents a schemata of verbal information, however, you may want to combine cells when deriving objectives. Combination objectives typically form the basis for essay test questions that require the analysis skills of comparing and contrasting or the synthesis skills of describing and discussing.

In combining matrix cells, it is best to combine cells within a single row or within a single column of the framework to create these "supra-objectives." For example, you might want to create a synthesis-style behavioral objective from Table 3.5 by combining cells I.A, I.B, and I.C within content area I. An objective for such a combination of cells might require students to describe or discuss a concept by synthesizing information about its physical characteristics, uses, and qualities. Such a combination objective might prescribe discussing one country by location, climate, population, and government system, or prescribe discussing the circulatory system by physical, functional, and location characteristics.

Besides combining cells within a row for deriving objectives, cells may be combined within columns. A combination of cells from a column in the matrix will integrate information within one level of learning but across interrelated concepts in the content rows. An objective might be created that combines cells in the first column of Table 3.5, or cells I.A, II.A, III.A, and IV.A. If these cells were each related to naming the form of government in various countries, then the behavioral objective would relate to comparing the countries by their forms of government. Combining cells on the diagonal in the goal framework (e.g., cells I.A, II.B, III.C, and IV.D) typically does not make sense because such a combination would mix both learning task levels and main content areas, which is an illogical integration.

In summary, behavioral objectives are written based on the cells in the instructional goal framework. Every cell that contains information that interconnects concepts and learning tasks should have at least one objective, and each cell may have more than one objective. Instructional objectives may be created by combining relevant cells within a concept area (e.g., describe, discuss) or across content within a learning task area (e.g., compare, contrast). When the learning tasks are intellectual skills, however, their hierarchical nature creates supra-objectives for the single cell because higher-order skills cannot be performed without the previous acquisition of lower skills in the hierarchy.

An Example

The completed instructional goal framework in Figure 3.6 was used to derive the behavioral objectives listed in Table 3.6 for the paragraph instructional goal. The first column of the table identifies the particular enabling skill from the goal framework, and the second column contains the objective codes. These codes identify both the enabling skill and the specific objective within the skill. For example, there are four objectives for the enabling skills I.A and

I.B and only two objectives for enabling skill I.D. Notice that the conditions included in each objective vary the stimulus material students will have for performing the task and that the behaviors reflect how students are to respond to demonstrate their mastery. Notice also that enabling skill I.F, "Write a paragraph," is included at the end of the table. This was done to illustrate that skill I.F is the highest-level skill included in the unit. The placement of skills within the table is a matter of preference, and the order of objectives in this table reflects the sequence the teacher plans to use in teaching and testing the skills.

At this point in the development process, test items could be written for the behavioral objectives derived from the instructional goal framework, but before writing tests, it makes sense to learn some guidelines for designing tests that will provide valid, reliable test results. It will also be useful to look at the different types of tests that are used in the classroom and to learn to specify items for each type of test. After these topics are addressed in Chapter 4, techniques will be introduced in Chapter 5 for writing test items.

COMPUTER TECHNOLOGY

With the instructional goal analyzed and the behavioral objectives written, you are ready to create a test item bank and to name the categories (user descriptor fields) you will use to organize the test items your bank.

Creating an Item Bank

An item bank is a computer-based file of test items. Many classroom teachers commonly use computer-based item bank programs to create a large file of test items for each of the instructional goals in their curriculum guide. Then, rather than creating and typing a new test each time they need to administer an exam, they can assemble a variety of classroom tests from the item bank based on test purpose. Computer-based item banks are popular with teachers because once the items are typed into the bank and edited for clarity, they can be retrieved from the bank in any combination for any number of tests without retyping or reediting the items. This flexibility is particularly helpful for teachers who need to create five or six different exams in the same subject for different classes or for teachers who need to create a variety of test forms for one class in order to eliminate copying behavior among students during the exam. It is also useful for creating entirely new make-up tests for students who missed an examination.

Creating an item bank is really very simple. First, choose a name for your bank. The item bank name in ParTEST (Economics Research, Inc., 1991) is limited to eight characters. A good name for an item bank for the paragraph instructional goal would be PARAGRPH. Item banks should be given names that indicate the content of the items included. When you follow this strategy,

TABLE 3.6
Table of Behavioral Objectives for the Instructional Goal, "Write a Paragraph"

Enabling Skill	Objective Code	Behavioral Objective
I.A	I.A.1	Given the term *paragraph*, recall its physical characteristics.
	I.A.2	Given the physical characteristics of a paragraph, recall its name.
	I.A.3	Given the term *paragraph* <u>and</u> a list of possible physical characteristics related to the concept, choose those for a paragraph.
	I.A.4	Given a description of the physical characteristics of a paragraph and a list of terms related to paragraphs, select the term *paragraph* as the concept being described.
I.B	I.B.1	Given the term *paragraph*, recall its functional characteristics.
	I.B.2	Given the functional characteristics of a paragraph, recall its name.
	I.B.3	Given the term *paragraph* <u>and</u> a list of possible functional characteristics related to the concept, choose those for a paragraph.
	I.B.4	Given a description of the functional characteristics of a paragraph and a list of terms related to paragraphs, select the term *paragraph* as the concept being described.
I.D	I.D.1	Given a correctly indented and not indented paragraphs, distinguish the correctly formatted paragraph.
	I.D.2	Given paragraphs on one topic and nonparagraphs containing two or more topics, discriminate between them.
II.A	II.A.1	Given the term *topic sentence*, recall its physical characteristics.
	II.A.2	Given the physical characteristics of a topic sentence, recall its name.
	II.A.3	Given the term *topic sentence* <u>and</u> a list of possible physical characteristics related to the concept, choose those for a topic sentence.
	II.A.4	Given a description of the physical characteristics of a topic sentence and a list of terms related to paragraphs, select the term *topic sentence* as the concept being described.
II.B	II.B.1	Given the term *topic sentence*, recall its functional characteristics.
	II.B.2	Given the functional characteristics of a topic sentence, recall its name.
	II.B.3	Given the term *topic sentence* <u>and</u> a list of possible functional characteristics related to the concept, choose those for a topic sentence.
	II.B.4	Given a description of the functional characteristics of a topic sentence and a list of terms related to paragraphs, select the term *topic sentence* as the concept being described.

(continued)

TABLE 3.6 Continued

Enabling Skill	Objective Code	Behavioral Objective
II.C	II.C.1	Given the term *topic sentence*, recall its quality characteristics.
	II.C.2	Given the quality characteristics of a topic sentence, recall its name.
	II.C.3	Given the term *topic sentence* <u>and</u> a list of possible quality characteristics related to the concept, choose those for a topic sentence.
	II.C.4	Given a description of the quality characteristics of a topic sentence and a list of terms related to paragraphs, select the term *topic sentence* as the concept being described.
II.D	II.D.1	Given a complete paragraph, correctly indented, locate the topic sentence.
II.E	II.E.1	Given an incomplete paragraph with the topic sentence omitted and three to four optional topic sentences, choose the best topic sentence.
	II.E.2	Given a complete paragraph with the topic sentence flawed by relevance and a list of possible judgments about the topic sentence that includes "no flaw present," as well as the quality criteria for topic sentences, choose the problem with the topic sentence.
	II.E.3	Given a complete paragraph with the topic sentence flawed by scope and a list of possible judgments about the topic sentence that includes "no flaw present," as well as the criteria for quality topic sentences, choose the problem with the topic sentence.
	II.E.4	Given a complete paragraph with the topic sentence flawed by interest, a list of possible judgments about the topic sentence that includes "no flaw present," as well as the criteria for quality topic sentences, choose the problem with the topic sentence.
	II.E.5	Given complete paragraphs with the topic sentence flawed by either relevance, scope, or interest value, rewrite the given topic sentence to meet quality criteria.
II.F	II.F.1	Given an incomplete paragraph (time series, feelings, procedure, or description), write a topic sentence to introduce the given paragraph.
III.A	III.A.1	Given the term *supporting sentence*, recall its physical characteristics.
	III.A.2	Given the physical characteristics of a supporting sentence, recall its name.
	III.A.3	Given the term *supporting sentence* <u>and</u> a list of possible physical characteristics related to the concept, choose those for a supporting sentence.

Enabling Skill	Objective Code	Behavioral Objective
	III.A.4	Given a description of the physical characteristics of a supporting sentence and a list of terms related to paragraphs, select the term *supporting sentence* as the concept being described.
III.B	III.B.1	Given the term *supporting sentence*, recall its functional characteristics.
	III.B.2	Given the functional characteristics of a supporting sentence, recall its name.
	III.B.3	Given the term *supporting sentence* <u>and</u> a list of possible functional characteristics related to the concept, choose those for a supporting sentence.
	III.B.4	Given a description of the functional characteristics of a supporting sentence and a list of terms related to paragraphs, select the term *supporting sentence* as the concept being described.
III.C	III.C.1	Given the term *supporting sentence*, recall its quality characteristics.
	III.C.2	Given the quality characteristics of a supporting sentence, recall its name.
	III.C.3	Given the term *supporting sentence* <u>and</u> a list of possible quality characteristics related to the concept, choose those for a supporting sentence.
	III.C.4	Given a description of the quality characteristics of a supporting sentence and a list of terms related to paragraphs, select the term *supporting sentence* as the concept being described.
III.D	III.D.1	Given a complete paragraph, correctly indented, locate the supporting sentences.
III.E	III.E.1	Given an incomplete paragraph with the supporting sentences omitted and three to four optional supporting sentences to be used for completing the paragraph, choose the best set of sentences.
	III.E.2	Given a complete paragraph with the supporting sentences flawed by relevance and a list of possible judgments about the supporting sentences that includes "no flaw present," as well as the quality criteria for supporting sentences, choose the problem with the sentences.
	III.E.3	Given a complete paragraph with the supporting sentences flawed by sequence of information and a list of possible judgments about the supporting sentences that includes "no flaw present," as well as the criteria for quality supporting sentences, identify the problem with the sentence.

(continued)

TABLE 3.6 Continued

Enabling Skill	Objective Code	Behavioral Objective
	III.E.4	Given a complete paragraph with the supporting sentences out of natural chronological/procedural order, reorder the supporting sentences.
	III.E.5	Given a complete paragraph with the supporting sentences flawed by transition, a list of possible judgments about the supporting sentences that includes "no flaw present," as well as the criteria for quality supporting sentences, identify the problem with the sentences.
	III.E.6	Given complete paragraphs with the supporting sentence flawed by either relevance, sequence, or transition, rewrite the highlighted sentence to meet quality criteria.
III.F	III.F.1	Given an incomplete paragraph (time series, feelings, procedure, or description), with one or more supporting sentences missing, write supporting sentences to elaborate the topic introduced.
IV.A	IV.A.1	Given the term *concluding sentence,* recall its physical characteristics.
	IV.A.2	Given the physical characteristics of a concluding sentence, recall its name.
	IV.A.3	Given the term *concluding sentence* <u>and</u> a list of possible physical characteristics related to the concept, choose those for a concluding sentence.
	IV.A.4	Given a description of the physical characteristics of a concluding sentence and a list of terms related to paragraphs, select the term *concluding sentence* as the concept being described.
IV.B	IV.B.1	Given the term *concluding sentence,* recall its functional characteristics.
	IV.B.2	Given the functional characteristics of a concluding sentence, recall its name.
	IV.B.3	Given the term *concluding sentence* <u>and</u> a list of possible functional characteristics related to the concept, choose those for a concluding sentence.
	IV.B.4	Given a description of the functional characteristics of a concluding sentence and a list of terms related to paragraphs, select the term *concluding sentence* as the concept being described.
IV.C	IV.C.1	Given the term *concluding sentence,* recall its quality characteristics.
	IV.C.2	Given the quality characteristics of a concluding sentence, recall its name.

Enabling Skill	Objective Code	Behavioral Objective
	IV.C.3	Given the term *concluding sentence* <u>and</u> a list of possible quality characteristics related to the concept, choose those for a concluding sentence.
	IV.C.4	Given a description of the quality characteristics of a concluding sentence and a list of terms related to paragraphs, select the term *concluding sentence* as the concept being described.
IV.D	IV.D.1	Given a complete paragraph, correctly indented, locate the concluding sentence.
IV.E	IV.E.1	Given an incomplete paragraph with the concluding sentence omitted and three to four optional concluding sentences, choose the best sentence.
	IV.E.2	Given a complete paragraph with the concluding sentence flawed by relevance and a list of possible judgments about the concluding sentence that includes "no flaw present," as well as the quality criteria for concluding sentences, choose the problem with the sentence.
	IV.E.3	Given a complete paragraph with the concluding sentence flawed by redundancy with topic sentence, a list of possible judgments about the concluding sentence that includes "no flaw present," as well as the criteria for quality concluding sentences, identify the problem with the sentence.
	IV.E.4	Given a complete paragraph with the concluding sentence flawed by scope and a list of possible judgments about the concluding sentence that includes "no flaw present," as well as the criteria for quality concluding sentences, identify the problem with the sentence.
	IV.E.5	Given complete paragraphs with the concluding sentence flawed by either relevance, redundancy, or scope, rewrite the given concluding sentence to meet quality criteria.
IV.F	IV.F.1	Given an incomplete paragraph (time series, feelings, procedure, or description), write a concluding sentence to summarize the ideas presented.
I.F	I.F.1	Given a topic requiring a description of something, write a 4- to 6-sentence paragraph.
	I.F.2	Given a topic requiring time series (chronology), write a 4- to 6-sentence paragraph.
	I.F.3	Given a topic that is a procedure for doing something, write a 4- to 6-sentence paragraph.
	I.F.4	Given a topic that is an expression of feelings or attitude, write a 4- to 6-sentence paragraph.

you can easily use the name to locate a particular test item bank for a specific instructional goal. Once you have your name selected, simply type it into the program and your new test item bank is created. At this point, the item bank named PARAGRPH is only a shell in which you would enter test items as you write them (see Chapter 5), but now is the time to give the item bank form and structure for organizing the test items that you will write.

Defining User Descriptor Fields

After naming and creating your item bank, name the user descriptor fields. User descriptor fields are categories teachers use to organize test items for storage in the item bank and for retrieval of items from the bank when they are needed for particular tests. The ParTEST (Economics Research, Inc., 1991) program has six user descriptor fields that teachers can use as they are or rename to suit their specific designs. The names of the six categories that come with the program are:

1. Subject
2. Topic
3. Objective
4. Chapter
5. Source
6. Cognitive Type

These categories are used to classify your test items as you write them and enter them into the bank. Each descriptor category name and subcategory you assign can have only 15 characters, so you may need to abbreviate some of the names you choose.

Using the paragraph instructional goal as an example, the subject (category 1) entered for all test items as they are typed into the bank would most likely be PARAGRAPH to identify the overall subject area of the instructional goal, "Write a paragraph."

There are four logical topic descriptors (category 2) for the paragraph instructional goal, and they are: PARAGRAPH, TOPIC SENTENCE, SUPPORTING SENT, and CONCLUDING SENT. Notice that the topic descriptors are abbreviated to the required 15 characters and that you may readily identify the topic of an item stored using these topic abbreviations. Notice also the relationship among these four topic descriptors and the row headings in the instructional goal framework in Figure 3.6.

The category 3 descriptor, OBJECTIVE, is an extremely critical descriptor since it enables you to identify the particular behavioral objective that is measured by each of the test items that you include in your bank. Suppose you were creating test items for each of the paragraph behavioral objectives included in Table 3.6. You would simply record the code of the objective in the objective category as you created the item. For example, test items for the first behavioral objective in Table 3.6 would be assigned the code I.A.1 in the objective category, test items for the second objective would be assigned the code I.A.2, and those for the last objective in the unit would be assigned the code I.F.4 in the objective category. When you classify the items you create in your item bank using the behavioral objective codes, you can quickly locate and retrieve all the items you have for the behavioral objective of interest.

The fourth descriptor category, CHAPTER, and the fifth, SOURCE, enable you to link the items in the bank to reference and study materials. The chapter category enables you to link each item in your item bank to the particular textbook chapter that students use to study the skills. For example, if the information on writing paragraphs were located in Chapter 6 of the students' textbook, all items entered into the item bank would be assigned to the category CHAPTER 6. The fifth descriptor category is SOURCE, and this category enables you to identify whether a particular question is based on the textbook, class notes, a particular reference assigned from the library, a video, a CD–ROM, or any other source of information you use in your class.

The sixth category, COGNITIVE TYPE, is used to indicate the type or level of learning required for the test item. It is usually a good idea to include the particular learning categories that you used during your analysis of the instructional goal. From the paragraph instructional goal framework in Figure 3.6, you could identify six different levels of an intellectual skill from the column headings, including: PHYSICAL CHAR, FUNCTIONAL CHAR, QUALITY CHAR, CLASSIFICATION, EVALUATION, AND PRODUCTION. Notice that logical abbreviations are used to keep the category names within the 15-character limit. Besides these intellectual skill categories, you might use Bloom's descriptors of knowledge: comprehension, application, analysis, synthesis, and evaluation. You might also use the categories of verbal information, intellectual skills, motor skills, and attitudes.

The following list summarizes the user descriptors appropriate for a test item bank for the instructional unit on writing a paragraph:

1. Subject: PARAGRAPH
2. Topic: PARAGRAPH, TOPIC SENTENCE, SUPPORTING SENT, CONCLUDING SENT (Topics taken from row headings in Figure 3.6)
3. Objective: I.A.1–I.F.4; II.A.1–II.F.1; III.A.1–III.F.1; IV.A.1–IV.F.1 (Objective codes taken from the behavioral objectives in Table 3.6)
4. Chapter: 6 (chapter taken from hypothetical students' textbook)
5. Source: Textbook, Lecture, Ref Material (from teacher's plans)
6. Cognitive Type: PHYSICAL CHAR, FUNCTIONAL CHAR, QUALITY CHAR, CLASSIFICATION, EVALUATION, PRODUCTION (from column headings in Figure 3.6)

The utility of these user descriptors will become more evident in the next chapter on designing and assembling tests for particular purposes. You should examine the six user descriptors provided in the EXAMPLES item bank in your ParTEST demonstration program (Economics Research, Inc., 1991). Follow directions in your *Student Manual*, to rename the item bank PROJECT to suit the instructional goal you have chosen, and rename the six

SUMMARY

Instructional goals provide a focus for instruction and describe the learning outcomes for units and lessons. To develop lessons and tests, you should first clarify each instructional goal for a course according to the level of learning (Bloom, Madaus, & Hastings, 1981) and the types of learning involved (Gagné, 1985). Using the Bloom, Madaus, and Hastings classification strategy, cognitive goals can be identified as being either knowledge, comprehension, application, analysis, synthesis, or evaluation. Knowledge is the most basic level, and evaluation is the most complex. Using the Gagné classification strategy, goals can be classified as intellectual skills, verbal information, cognitive strategies, motor skills, or attitudes.

Gagné suggests procedures for analyzing each instructional goal based on its classification. Intellectual skill goals that are rules or principles should be separated into their discrete concepts and the relationships among the concepts. Defined concepts can be separated into their subordinate concepts and the relationships among them. Concrete concepts are separated into the unique physical properties that define the class. Dividing each intellectual skill into its subordinate tasks and sequencing the tasks according to their relationship result in a learning hierarchy, or task analysis. These analyses can be performed using either a matrix, tree diagram, or flowchart.

Gagné makes the following suggestions for analyzing verbal information:

1. Names and labels should be placed in a meaningful context.
2. Facts should be organized into bodies of knowledge or schemata of related facts using tables that help clarify the relationships among the facts.

His suggestion for organizing names and labels so they are placed in a meaningful context would result in placing these tasks, when possible, on the task analyses beside or near the named concepts. This means that verbal information will appear on the frameworks for intellectual skills, cognitive strategies, motor skills, and attitudes.

The instructional goals and their subordinate skills, identified through task analysis, should be converted into behavioral objectives. Behavioral objectives include the subordinate skill, the conditions, and sometimes the criteria for acceptable performance. The stimulus required for the prescribed behavior and the skill level of target students help determine the conditions a teacher decides to include in behavioral objectives. When students' responses can vary, criteria are included to define an acceptable answer. Appropriately written behavioral objectives provide valuable guidelines for lesson planning and the development of test items.

Computer-based item banks contain many test items that teachers create to measure students' mastery of the enabling skills and instructional goals in the curriculum guide. You can create a computer-based item bank by simply choosing a logical name for an instructional goal and then following the program instructions for recording the name in the program. To maximize the utility of the item bank, choose user descriptors that help you organize and readily retrieve items from the bank. Most commercially available programs have prenamed user descriptors that include categories such as subject, topic, enabling skills, objectives, test type, chapter, and cognitive type. After completing your instructional goal framework and writing congruent behavioral objectives, choose six user descriptors that seem most appropriate for classifying the skills in your goal framework. Preestablished user descriptors in the item bank program can then be modified to suit the nature of your instructional goal and used to classify test items as they are entered into the item bank. Carefully naming user descriptors and using them to classify the items you place in the bank will ensure easy retrieval of items when you create tests from the bank.

PRACTICE EXERCISES

I. Levels of Learning

Match each task listed in Column A with the appropriate level of learning listed in Column B. You may refer to Table 3.1 for definitions of each term in Column B.

Column A

_____ **1.** Calculate the average score for a set of test scores.

_____ **2.** Break a rule or principle into its separate elements and describe the relationships among them.

_____ **3.** Use specified criteria to judge the quality of a product.

_____ **4.** Use the relationships among a variety of elements to combine them into a whole.

_____ **5.** Paraphrase a fact, a definition, or a procedure.

_____ **6.** Recall the verbatim definitions for a given list of concepts.

_____ **7.** Write the formula for calculating a standard deviation.

_____ **8.** Write a technical report for a given target audience.

Column B

a. Knowledge

b. Comprehension

c. Application

d. Analysis

e. Synthesis

f. Evaluation

II. Types of Learning

A. In your own words, define Gagné's five types of learning and write at least one instructional goal or behavioral objective from your content area that fits each type of learning: intellectual skills, verbal information, cognitive strategies, motor skills, and attitudes.

B. Read the following list of instructional goals in Column A and classify the type of learning each represents from Column B.

Column A

_____ **1.** Write a persuasive essay with a unique line of reasoning.

_____ **2.** Recite a short poem.

_____ **3.** Choose to work independently on school assignments.

_____ **4.** Name common traffic signs.

_____ **5.** Choose to be punctual.

_____ **6.** Bounce a ball.

_____ **7.** Name the capital city for each state.

_____ **8.** Write a paragraph containing a topic sentence, supporting facts, and a concluding sentence.

_____ **9.** Button a shirt.

_____ **10.** Alphabetize any given list of words.

_____ **11.** Select the correct coins to make any given amount of money up to 99 cents.

_____ **12.** On a map, name and locate all fifty states in the United States.

_____ **13.** Interpret a state map.

_____ **14.** Organize homework, projects, and study time to ensure adequate preparation for final exams.

Column B

a. Intellectual skills
b. Verbal information
c. Cognitive strategies
d. Motor skills
e. Attitudes

III. Instructional Goal Analysis

A. For the instructional goal, "Write compound sentences," perform the following:

1. Create an intellectual skills analysis matrix using column headings similar to those in Figure 3.4.

2. Determine the row headings you will need.

3. Analyze the goal by determining what information should be included in intersecting cells. Check your goal matrix with the one in Table 3.7.

Note: Do not worry if your frameworks do not include enough detail or are different from those of other students. A sketchy framework is better than none at all, and your ability to analyze goals will improve with practice. Creating good frameworks takes time and experience. After developing and using a framework, you will want to make changes that reflect your classroom experiences with students.

B. **Verbal Information.** Develop a table that includes information students will need to "Name common traffic signs." Your table should include sign colors, sign shapes, and sign names. (See Table 3.8 for feedback.)

IV. **Behavioral Objectives**

Write behavioral objectives based on the coordinating conjunction (III) and compound sentence (IV) rows of the instructional goal matrix in Table 3.7. Recall that when using the matrix analysis procedure, subordinate skills are created by synthesizing the information from row and column headings and from intersecting row-by-column cells. Compare your list of behavioral objectives with those included in Table 3.9.

V. **Enrichment**

A. Choose an instructional goal for a subject you know well. Identify the analysis procedure for the type of goal you choose and develop a framework of the subordinate skills required to achieve the goal. Ask another person who is familiar with the subject to critique your work. When you are satisfied that the framework is adequate, convert each subordinate skill into a behavioral objective by adding conditions and necessary criteria.

B. Create a computer-based test item bank for your instructional goal, and select six user descriptors for the bank based on your instructional goal framework and behavioral objectives.

FEEDBACK

I. **Levels of Learning**

1. c		5. b	
2. d		6. a	
3. f		7. a	
4. e		8. e	

II. **Types of Learning**

A. Definitions (If you are unsure about the appropriateness of your instructional goals or objectives, you may want to discuss your examples with classmates or with the professor.)

Intellectual skills involve the use of symbols to interact with the environment. Intellectual skills are mental procedures used to interpret phenomena and solve problems. They include discrimination, concrete concepts, defined concepts, and rules.

Verbal information, often called *declarative knowledge,* involves associating objects, symbols, events, or conditions with their names. It also includes remembering facts and repeating or recounting information.

Cognitive strategies are the mental processes by which we control thinking and construct or choose solutions to problems.

TABLE 3.7

Goal Analysis Framework for the Intellectual Skill "Write a Compound Sentence" (Problem III.A)

MAIN CONTENT AREAS	RECALL			PERFORM		
	A Name/Recall Physical Characteristics	**B** Name/Recall Functional Characteristics	**C** Name/Recall Quality Characteristics	**D** Discriminate Examples/ Nonexamples	**E** Evaluate Good vs. Poor Examples	**F** Produce Examples
I. Comma	Period with tail I.A	Alert reader I.B	 I.C	Comma vs. 1. period 2. semi-colon I.D	 I.E	Comma I.F
II. Simple Sentence	Subject, predicate II.A	Communicate simply, clearly II.B	Complete II.C	Simple vs. 1. compound 2. complex II.D	Complete vs. incomplete II.E	Simple sentence II.F
III. Coordinating Conjunction	Word between two simple sentences III.A	Combine two simple sentences III.B	Imply relationship between two sentences III.C	Conjunction vs. 1. subject 2. verb 3. comma III.D	Match relationship vs. mismatch relationship III.E	Best for given pair of sentences III.F

IV. Compound Sentence	Two simple sentences joined with comma, coordinating conjunction
	
	IV.A
		Combine simple sentences to smooth message, reduce jerkiness
		
		IV.B
			1. Two interrelated simple sentences (e.g., first introduces idea and second elaborates, explains qualifies, refutes)
			2. When needed, proper noun of second sentence changed to pronoun
			3. Relevant coordinating conjunction
			IV.C
				1. Compound vs.
				  a. simple
				  b. complex
				  c. simple with dual subjects
				  d. simple with dual objects
				2. Comma vs. no comma
				3. Conjunction vs. no conjunction
				IV.D
					1. Related vs. unrelated simple sentences
					2. Proper nouns converted vs. unconverted
					3. Coordinating conjunction relevant vs. irrelevant
					IV.E.
						1. Convert two simple to one compound
						2. Elaborate given simple sentence into compound by adding second simple sentence
						IV.F

Motor skills are physical tasks that require movement, precision, and timing. They often take the form of physical procedures having a series of steps to be performed either simultaneously or in a prescribed sequence.

Attitudes are mental states that govern our choices and behavior. Attitudes have three main components: affective, behavioral, and cognitive.

B. Classification

1. c	5. e	9. d	13. a
2. b	6. d	10. a	14. c
3. e	7. b	11. a	
4. b	8. a	12. b	

III. Instructional Goal Analysis

A. The steps in identifying the content are to: (1) state clearly the rule for compound sentences, (2) underline the key concepts in the rule, and (3) sequence these concepts from the least to most complex in the left column of the goal analysis matrix. The rule is: A *compound sentence* contains two *simple sentences* connected using a *comma* preceding a *coordinating conjunction*. The goal analysis matrix is in Table 3.7.

B. The verbal information for naming common traffic signs is in Table 3.8.

IV. Behavioral Objectives

Table 3.9 contains behavioral objectives for skills in rows III and IV of Table 3.7.

TABLE 3.8
Analysis of the Instructional Goal: Name Common Traffic Signs

Name of Sign	Shape of Sign	Colors of Sign
Stop	Octagon	Red with white
Yield	Triangle, tip down	
Do not enter	Circle within square	
Action prohibited		
Warning, road conditions	Diamond	Yellow with black
Warning, railroad	X within circle	
Warning, no passing	Triangle with tip pointing to right	
Warning, school zone	Triangle top, rectangle bottom	
Warning, construction	Diamond	Orange with black
Warning, maintenance		
Regulatory sign	Rectangle or square	White with black
Information sign		
Railroad crossing	Crossbuck	
Public recreation	Rectangle	Brown with white
Park signs		
Motorist service signs	Rectangle	Blue with white
Directional information	Rectangle	Green with white

TABLE 3.9
Subordinate Skills and Behavioral Objectives for the Goal,
"Write Compound Sentences"

Subordinate Skills	Objective Codes	Behavioral Objectives
III.A	III.A.1.	Given the term *coordinating conjunction*, name its physical characteristics.
	III.A.2.	Given the term *coordinating conjunction* and a list of alternative physical characteristics, select the correct characteristics.
III.B	III.B.1.	Given the term *coordinating conjunction*, state its role or function.
	III.B.2.	Given a description of the function of the coordinating conjunction, name it as the word described.
	III.B.3.	Given the term *coordinating conjunction* and a list of alternative purposes, select the correct purpose.
	III.B.4.	Given a statement of the purpose for a coordinating conjunction and a list of the names and types of words found in a typical sentence, select the correct term.
III.C	III.C.1.	Given the term *coordinating conjunction*, name its quality characteristics.
	III.C.2.	Given a description of the quality characteristic of a coordinating conjunction, name the described term.
	III.C.3.	Given the term *coordinating conjunction* and a list of possible quality characteristics, select the appropriate criterion.
	III.C.4.	Given the criterion for selecting coordinating conjunctions and a list of possible word types found in a sentence, select the correct term.
III.D	III.D.1.	Given a compound sentence, locate the coordinating conjunction (underline, circle, etc.).
	III.D.2.	Given a compound sentence with various elements of the sentence underlined and numbered (e.g., subject, verb, comma, and coordinating conjunction), locate the coordinating conjunction.
III.E	III.E.1.	Given two simple sentences and a coordinating conjunction, judge whether the conjunction is logical.
	III.E.2.	Given: (a) two simple sentences joined by a comma and a blank space and (b) a list of alternative coordinating conjunctions, choose the most logical conjunction.
III.F	III.F.1.	Given two simple sentences separated by a comma and a blank space, write an appropriate coordinating conjunction in the space.

Subordinate Skills	Objective Codes	Behavioral Objectives
IV.A	IV.A.1.	Given the term *compound sentence,* name the physical characteristics.
	IV.A.2.	Given a description of the physical characteristics of compound sentences, name the type of sentence.
	IV.A.3.	Given the term *compound sentence* and a list of alternative physical characteristics, choose its description.
	IV.A.4.	Given a description of the physical characteristics of compound sentences and a list of possible names of the sentence type, choose its name.
IV.B	IV.B.1.	Given the term *compound sentence,* name the functional characteristics.
	IV.B.2.	Given the term *compound sentence* and a list of alternative purposes for this sentence type, choose its purpose.
IV.C	IV.C.1.	Given the term *compound sentences,* name three quality characteristics.
	IV.C.2.	Given the term *compound sentence* and a list of potential quality characteristics, select those characteristics for compound sentences.
IV.D	IV.D.1.	Given a list of sentences—including compound, simple, complex, simple with dual subjects, and simple with dual verbs or objects—select the compound sentences.
IV.E	IV.E.1.	Given a set of quality compound sentences—along with some that are flawed by unrelated simple sentences, repeated proper nouns in second simple sentence, missing commas or coordinating conjunctions, or illogical coordinating conjunctions—locate the proper compound sentences.
	IV.E.2.	Given compound sentences that are correctly and incorrectly constructed with selected parts of the sentences underlined and numbered, locate any flaws contained in the sentences.
IV.F	IV.F.1.	Given two complete simple sentences, convert them to one compound sentence by changing punctuation, adding the conjunction, and, if necessary, converting a proper noun subject to a pronoun.
	IV.F.2.	Given a simple sentence, convert it to a compound sentence by adding an appropriate simple sentence and logical coordinating conjunction.

REFERENCES

Bloom, B. S. (1956). *Taxonomy of educational objectives: The classification of educational goals, Handbook I: Cognitive domain.* New York: David McKay.

Bloom, B. S., Madaus, G. F., & Hastings, J. T. (1981). *Evaluation to improve learning.* New York: McGraw-Hill.

Economics Research, Inc. (1991). *ParTEST user's manual.* Costa Mesa, CA: Author.

Gagné, R. M. (1985). *The conditions of learning and theory of instruction.* New York: Holt, Rinehart and Winston.

SUGGESTED READINGS

Dick, W., & Carey, L. M. (1994). *The systematic design of instruction* (4th ed.). Glenview, IL: Harper Collins.

Ebel, R. L., & Frisbie, D. A. (1991). *Essentials of educational measurement* (5th ed.) (pp. 41–54). Englewood Cliffs, NJ: Prentice Hall.

Gagné, R. M., & Driscol, M. P. (1988). *Essentials of learning for instruction* (2nd ed.) (pp. 43–61). Englewood Cliffs, NJ: Prentice Hall.

Gearheart, C., & Gearheart, B. (1990). *Introduction to special education assessment* (pp. 81–92). Denver, CO: Love.

Gronlund, N. E., & Linn, R. L. (1990). *Measurement and evaluation in teaching* (6th ed.) (pp. 23–46). New York: Macmillan.

Hopkins, C. D., & Antes, R. L. (1990). *Classroom measurement and evaluation* (3rd ed.) (pp. 39–68). Itasca, IL: F. E. Peacock.

Hopkins, K. D., Stanley, J. C., & Hopkins, B. R. (1990). *Educational and psychological measurement and evaluation* (3rd ed.) (pp. 165–192). Englewood Cliffs, NJ: Prentice Hall.

Kubiszyn, T., & Borich, G. (1990). *Educational testing and measurement* (3rd ed.) (pp. 31–60). Glenview, IL: Scott, Foresman/Little, Brown.

Mehrens, W. A., and Lehmann, I. J. (1991). *Measurement and evaluation in education and psychology* (4th ed.) (pp. 27–48). New York: CBS College Publishing.

Nitko, A. J. (1989). Designing tests that are integrated with instruction. In R. L. Linn (Ed.), *Educational measurement* (3rd ed.) (pp. 447–474). New York: Macmillan.

Oosterhof, A. (1990). *Classroom applications of educational measurement* (pp. 12–30). Columbus, OH: Merrill.

Sax, G. (1989). *Principles of educational and psychological measurement and evaluation* (3rd ed.) (pp. 59–89). Belmont, CA: Wadsworth.

Wittrock, M. C., & Baker, E. L. (Eds.). (1991). *Testing and cognition.* Englewood Cliffs, NJ: Prentice Hall.

CHAPTER 4

Designing Test and Item Specifications to Help Ensure Validity and Reliability

MEASUREMENT, TESTS, AND EVALUATION

Three terms frequently used in this text are *measurement, test,* and *evaluation.* Although these terms are related, there are important differences among them. The term *measurement* refers to quantifying or assigning a number to express the degree to which a characteristic is present. Some common characteristics measured for people include height, weight, and skill attainment. The number or measure used to express height is based on a scale of feet and inches; the measure for weight is expressed as pounds; and the measure of skill attainment is a score that reflects the number of items answered correctly or points earned on some type of achievement test. Using any of these measures, people can be ranked on scales that reflect the degree to which they possess the characteristic.

Measures of a characteristic are obtained using measuring instruments. A yardstick is the instrument used to obtain a measure of height; a weight scale is the instrument used to obtain a measure of weight; and an assigned set of tasks to be performed, called a test, is the instrument used to obtain a skill measure. The quality or stability of the instrument used to obtain a measure will influence the accuracy of the measure.

Evaluation is the procedure used to determine the quality of something. Decisions about quality require criteria or standards that can be applied to judge worth. Once you have a measure of some characteristic, you can compare the measure against established criteria or standards to determine whether it reflects an excellent, good, adequate, poor, or unacceptable level of the characteristic. Both the measures and the tests, or instruments, can be evaluated. For example, some criteria for evaluating a measure of height are based on group norms (e.g., he is quite tall compared to other boys his age); some on cultural expectations (e.g., he is too short to be considered for that role in the play); and others on health (e.g., her growth rate and height reflect physiological problems). Standards for judging a measure of weight are also based on group comparisons, cultural expectations, and health. Likewise, standards for evaluating a skill measure are based on group comparisons (e.g., above average, average, or below average compared to other people with similar experience and training) or on a level set to reflect high accomplishment of the skill itself (e.g., typing 60 words a minute with no mistakes).

Instruments used to obtain measures are also evaluated. One criterion for judging the quality of an instrument is the consistency with which it produces the same measure under the same conditions. For example, a weight scale that produced three different weight measures for the same person at 10-minute intervals would be an inadequate instrument, whereas one that indicated the same weight each time would be considered good. Likewise, a skill test that resulted in very different scores for the same person on the same day would be judged an inadequate test.

A second criterion for evaluating a test or instrument is whether it actually measures the characteristic it is supposed to measure. A yardstick would be an inadequate instrument to measure weight, and a test focused on tennis rules would not provide an adequate measure of a student's ability to play the game. Other less important criteria used to evaluate a test include costs and practicality. Tests that consistently measure what they are supposed to measure, yet are either too expensive or too cumbersome for a given situation, would be judged inadequate for the circumstances.

Teachers use measures of student achievement to evaluate: (1) students' progress throughout a term or year, (2) the quality of their tests, and (3) the quality of their instruction. Schools use measures of students' achievement, behavior, and attitudes to evaluate the quality of the curriculum and the overall program. Because measures of an individual's performance are the building blocks of evaluation, accurate evaluation at the classroom, school, and district levels cannot be accomplished without accurate measures. Likewise, accurate measures cannot be obtained without quality tests. This chapter presents methods you can use to design tests most likely to produce accurate measures of students' achievement.

CRITERION-REFERENCED TESTS

Chapter 3 described procedures you can use to analyze your instructional goals and to write behavioral objectives for the subordinate skills identified in the goal frameworks. A goal framework of subordinate skills, sometimes called a *domain,* provides the foundation you need to design both your instruction and your classroom tests. Three names are generally used for tests based on the carefully identified and sequenced set of skills in a goal framework: *criterion-referenced tests, domain-referenced tests,* and *objective-referenced tests.* The set of skills in the framework is the criterion, or standard, used to judge students' progress on an instructional goal. The term *criterion-referenced test* simply means that the items on the test are referenced to or drawn from a carefully specified set of subordinate skills that make up the goal. On a *domain-referenced test,* the test items are referenced to or drawn from a carefully delineated domain of tasks. Thus, students' performance on such tests is referenced to the criterion set of skills or domain. For *objective-referenced tests,* the subordinate skills in the goal framework are converted to measurable behavioral objectives before test construction.

Whether an objective-referenced test is also criterion referenced depends on the foundation for the objectives used. Objective-referenced tests based on a loosely connected set of objectives are not criterion-referenced tests. They do not become true criterion-referenced tests by simply specifying a cut-off score or criterion for passing or by selecting the number of items that must be answered correctly for each objective measured. Because the objectives developed in Chapter 3 are based on carefully specified goal frameworks, objective-referenced tests based on those objectives would be criterion-referenced tests. Although these terms might be interchangeable under these circumstances, the terms *test* and *criterion-referenced test* are used for convenience in the following chapters on test design, development, and analysis.

Four major factors need to be considered in the test design process. The first factor is to design tests most likely to yield valid results for the decisions you need to make. The second is to design tests most likely to provide reliable, or consistent, results. The third factor is the main purpose for the test, and the fourth is the type of test that best suits the prescribed purpose. This chapter describes each factor and how it influences design considerations. Decisions made during the design stage are recorded in matrices called *tables of test specifications*. These tables are used to record the sample of objectives to be included on each test, the best item format to use for each objective selected, and the number of items to be selected for each objective. Procedures for developing tables of test specifications are described.

VALIDITY AND TEST DESIGN

The term *validity* refers to the appropriateness of inferences made from students' test results. If a test adequately measures the behavioral objectives it is intended to measure, the students' test scores should be valid for the inferences based on these scores. The tests you administer are more likely to result in valid decisions if you consider validity as you design the test. To help ensure that your tests provide valid measures of student progress, consider the following five questions during the design process.

1. *How well do the behavioral objectives selected for the test represent the instructional goal framework?* Ensuring that the skills measured accurately reflect the goal framework or domain involves a particular form of validity called *content validity*. A goal framework usually includes behavioral objectives that represent different, but related, content areas and different levels of skill. For example, the instructional goal on writing paragraphs includes objectives related to four content areas: paragraphs, topic sentences, supporting sentences, and concluding sentences. Different levels of learning are also commonly found among the objectives in a goal framework. Some objectives require students to recall names, facts, characteristics, rules, or principles. Other objectives require students to apply this information in order to classify, analyze, synthesize, solve, or create something. For example, both recall- and application-level skills are included in the goal on writing a paragraph. Students need to recall the rule for writing paragraphs and the rules for writing each type of sentence within a paragraph. They also need to be able to apply these rules and definitions for discriminating among the types of sentences, evaluating sentences, and writing paragraphs. In designing a test that will have good content validity, objectives should be selected to represent each main content area and level of learning included in the goal framework. Inferences made about students' achievement of an instructional goal that are

based on a test that is not representative of the instructional goal framework are likely to be invalid or incorrect.

2. *How will test results be used?* You are more likely to obtain valid test results if, during the design process, you consider the planning and evaluation decisions you need to make. Related to planning instruction, you may want to determine whether you will need to develop remedial instruction, whether you need to develop lessons for all the behavioral objectives in the framework or only a subset of them, or whether you need to develop review or enrichment lessons for the unit. Evaluation decisions will be necessary regarding the appropriateness of the instructional goal for a given group of students, the quality of your lessons, or students' achievement in order to assign grades. Considering the use of test results during the design stage will help you select, for each test, the most appropriate objectives from the goal framework and the best item formats for each objective chosen.

3. *Which test item format will best measure achievement of each objective?* A variety of item formats can be selected, and some types measure the behaviors prescribed in objectives better than other types. The more closely students' responses match the behavior specified in the objectives, the more likely their scores will validly reflect their achievement of the objectives. Objective item formats that require students to select an answer from among a set of alternatives may be best for measuring student performance on some objectives. Other objectives in the goal framework may be measured best by requiring students to supply a missing word or complete a sentence. Still others may be measured best by essay questions, product development, or some type of active performance. In designing a test, the behavior specified in the objective should be considered carefully when selecting the most appropriate item.

4. *How many test items will be required to measure performance adequately on each objective?* Objectives that require students to recall names, facts, characteristics, or definitions usually require only one item to determine whether the student can recall the required information. However, if students are to apply this information to classify examples or solve a problem, then several items will be needed for them to demonstrate their application skills. For example, only one item would be needed to test whether students can recall the definition for a common noun; several items would be needed to determine whether students can discriminate consistently between common nouns and other parts of speech. When designing tests, you should consider the complexity of each objective selected and then prescribe an adequate number of items to measure the objective.

5. *When and how will the test be administered?* Considering the purpose for the test will help you design a test schedule and administration procedure most likely to result in scores that are valid for the decisions to be made. Tests used for planning decisions, such as whether remedial instruction is needed for a group and which behavioral objectives need to be emphasized during a unit, should be scheduled and administered before planning lessons for the unit. These preliminary tests need not be announced in advance because students

are not expected to prepare for them; they can be administered informally during a class session or as a homework exercise.

Tests used to provide students with an opportunity to practice skills after instruction, to evaluate the quality of lessons, or to determine whether review or enrichment is needed should be administered following initial instruction. They can be administered informally as a class exercise, as a small group activity, or as individual tests. They also can be administered during a class period or as a homework assignment. Tests used to evaluate students' overall achievement and grade their progress should be administered following all instruction and review, and they should be announced in advance to enable students to prepare for them. They also should be administered during a class period, whenever possible, to ensure that each student's score reflects only his or her efforts. Tests used for the purpose of assigning students' grades that are administered unannounced, before the conclusion of instruction, or in an unsupervised setting may not accurately reflect students' achievement. Thus, decisions based on these scores may be invalid.

RELIABILITY AND TEST DESIGN

Reliability refers to the consistency or stability of the test scores obtained. For example, if a student received a low score on a test taken in the morning, the teacher should be able to expect similar results if the student were to take the same or an equivalent test in the afternoon. Similar test scores would suggest that the test was reliable. If the student received a substantially higher or lower score the second time, the test would be unreliable. Valid inferences about students' performance cannot be made when test scores are unreliable.

Because students' test performances are influenced by many factors—including variations in memory, motivation, attention, and fatigue—absolute reliability (i.e., obtaining the exact same score twice) is unlikely. Test scores should be stable enough, however, to permit accurate judgments about students' mastery of the objectives.

Although you will not be able to eliminate fluctuations in test scores, you can help ensure that your tests will produce the most reliable scores possible. When designing a test, follow these five steps.

1. *Select a representative sample of objectives from the goal framework.* The better your objectives represent the entire framework, the more reliable the scores will be. For example, a test covering a goal framework that has 10 objectives ranging from easy to difficult should include test items that reflect each objective. If two different forms of the test are to be used, the second form should also contain items for every objective. The two test forms should produce relatively consistent scores because both cover the entire framework of objectives. On the other hand, one test containing items for the 5 easiest

objectives and a second test reflecting the 5 most difficult objectives would produce very different scores. If time is available to measure only a subset of objectives from the framework, then objectives should be selected to represent both the easy and difficult objectives.

2. *Select enough items to represent adequately the skills required in each objective.* Enough test items should be included for an objective to cover all the possible situations implied in the objective. For example, if students are to select common nouns from among a list of words that includes nouns and other parts of speech, enough items should be prescribed to include all categories of nouns that students will encounter. One or two items that relate to only one category, such as persons, would not adequately measure students' mastery of the objective. A test that included only one or two items in one category of nouns and one that included several items from all four categories are likely to produce very different scores.

3. *Select item formats that reduce the likelihood of guessing.* Students who do not know an answer may guess. If they guess correctly on one form of a test and incorrectly on the second, their scores will not be stable. When guessing is possible, the reliability of test scores will be lower than if guessing were not possible.

4. *Prescribe only the number of items that students can complete in the time available.* Test scores will be more reliable when students are given enough time to complete the test. Students' emotional states during a test can influence their performance, and hurrying causes some students to become careless. To increase the reliability of scores, adjust the length of the test to match the time available for its completion.

5. *Determine ways to maintain positive student attitudes toward testing.* Students' attitudes about a test can affect their motivation and effort, and test planning should identify ways to ensure positive attitudes. For example, you should plan to inform students of a test's date and time, the purpose for the test, and how the results will be used. Never plan to use tests as a punishment or as a substitute for unplanned lessons. Such misuses produce poor motivation and may result in unreliable scores.

TYPES OF SUBORDINATE SKILLS

The subordinate skills in the instructional goal framework can be divided into two categories: skills students should have mastered during a previous unit or year and skills that should be the primary focus for current instruction. Subordinate skills in the goal framework that should have been previously mastered are commonly called *prerequisite skills*. Subordinate skills that constitute the primary focus for current instruction are called *enabling skills*.

Before beginning to design tests for a unit of instruction, divide the subordinate skills in the goal framework into prerequisite and enabling skills. This division is based on your best judgment about whether a particular skill or set of skills in the framework was mastered by students during previous instruction. For example, students may already know the physical and functional characteristics of paragraphs and know how to apply these characteristics for discriminating between examples and nonexamples. They may not have mastered the quality characteristics for evaluating paragraphs and for producing good examples. In this case, skills related to physical and functional characteristics and to discrimination of examples would be classified as prerequisite skills. Enabling skills would be those for quality characteristics, evaluation, and production of paragraphs. The existence of prerequisite skills in a goal framework has implications for the type of achievement tests you design.

TYPES OF TESTS

Teachers develop and administer four types of achievement tests: entry behaviors tests, pretests, practice tests, and posttests. Each type is administered for a different purpose, and the purpose helps determine which subordinate skills will be selected for the test and when the test is administered.

Entry Behaviors Tests

Teachers use entry behaviors tests (also known as *readiness tests*) to determine whether students have mastered the prerequisite skills they need to begin a unit of instruction. The skills selected from the goal framework for an entry behaviors test include only those classified as prerequisite skills. Entry behaviors tests are administered before planning any unit lessons. Teachers use results from entry behaviors tests in three ways:

1. They determine whether the instructional goal is appropriate for a given group of students. If none or few of the students in a class have mastered the prerequisite skills, then the goal is probably too complex for the class.
2. They determine whether remedial instruction is necessary. If several students in the class have not mastered the prerequisite skills, then these students will need remedial instruction.
3. They group students in the class for instruction in the unit. Students can be grouped according to whether they have or have not mastered prerequisite skills. Thus, instruction can be tailored to students' needs.

It is not always necessary to design an entry behaviors test. If none of the subordinate skills in the goal framework are classified as prerequisites, or if you have recently taught the prerequisites and are familiar with students' mastery of them, then no entry behaviors test is needed. Additionally, if you have a homogeneous group of high-achieving students, you may safely assume that they have mastered the subordinate skills classified as prerequisite. However, if you have a heterogeneous group and are unfamiliar with their skills in the area, then consider designing an entry behaviors test to determine whether remedial instruction is warranted. Students may struggle with the enabling skills in a unit of instruction, not because the materials or instruction are poor, but because they do not possess essential prerequisite skills. Without testing the group on these skills before instruction begins, a teacher may not detect the real cause of students' problems until it is too late.

Pretests

Pretests are also administered before instruction, and results are used to plan lessons for the unit. When adequately designed, they include all the subordinate skills classified as enabling skills in the goal framework and thus provide an overview of students' skills for the entire unit. The teacher can use this information to plan review for any skills previously mastered and to develop lessons emphasizing skills that remain to be learned. Pretest data can also be used to group students who already have mastered most of the enabling skills and students who have not.

Pretests are not always necessary. If the enabling skills in a goal framework are not likely to have been encountered during previous instruction at school or at home, then it is reasonable to assume that instruction should be developed for each skill. However, if students are likely to have encountered previous instruction on any of the enabling skills, then a pretest will help you identify these skills and develop efficient instruction by focusing lessons on skills that remain to be learned. Sometimes students benefit from a pretest even if the teacher does not. Pretests can help students identify important skills to be learned, guide their study, and help them review for posttests.

If you decide that both an entry behaviors test and a pretest would be useful for a particular unit, you can combine them into one test because both need to be administered before planning instruction. However, items for each test should be scored separately because each serves a different purpose. A total score on the entire test will not help you determine who is ready for the instruction or how the lessons should be designed.

Practice Tests

Teachers often administer informal practice tests immediately following instruction on a limited set of enabling skills. These tests are completed either in class or as homework. Data from these tests may be used in at least four ways. First, the teacher may determine the effectiveness of the instruction, identify skills that most students have not mastered, and seek new ways to present additional instruction. Second, students may be regrouped according to their mastery of the objectives. Third, the data may help the teacher diagnose misconceptions and problems that students may have developed during instruction. Fourth, practice test results may be used for developing review materials and posttests. Students can also use these tests to determine whether they have learned required skills, to help them formulate questions, and to guide their study for exams.

To make adequate judgments, both teachers and students need detailed information; thus, practice tests should be designed to cover only a limited number of the enabling skills and their corresponding behavioral objectives. Because these tests are meant to provide practice for students and to help teachers plan, they should not be used to determine course grades.

Posttests

Posttests are given after instruction is completed; they help a teacher determine the effectiveness of instruction, evaluate student progress, and assign grades. The teacher can use posttest data to identify ineffective elements of the instruction and to improve the lessons for subsequent classes.

Any test used to assign term grades—whether a short quiz, an exam covering an entire unit, or a comprehensive exam over several units—is a posttest. Quizzes usually include the enabling skills for one or two lessons; unit exams cover a representative sample of all the enabling skills in a unit; and comprehensive exams contain a few of the most important enabling skills for each of several units. The enabling skills selected for a comprehensive exam are usually at the highest level of learning for each unit and should encompass all other enabling skills in the goal frameworks.

Because posttests are used to assign term grades, they should represent students' best efforts. The teacher should inform students of test dates and content to be covered. Unannounced tests, including pop quizzes, are inappropriate because they may not be valid reflections of students' learning. Unannounced quizzes fall into the category of practice tests.

DESIGNING TESTS USING
TABLES OF TEST SPECIFICATIONS

Once you have determined the types of tests you will administer, you need to write a prescription for each type. Developing tables of test specifications will help you construct tests most likely to produce reliable scores that are valid for the decisions to be made. The process involves the following five steps:

1. Prescribe the types of tests needed to support your decisions during a unit of instruction.
2. Select the most representative subordinate skills from the instructional goal framework for each type of test prescribed.
3. Select one or more behavioral objectives for each subordinate skill chosen.

4. Specify the number of items required to measure students' performance as accurately as possible on each objective.
5. Estimate the time required for students to answer the total number of items specified for each objective and for the test.

Specify the Types of Tests for an Instructional Unit

Usually, there is a fixed amount of time available for instruction in a given course and for units of instruction within the course. Teachers must balance this fixed time between class time devoted to instruction and learning and class time devoted to testing students' skills. Some teachers administer only posttests because they believe that the amount of instructional time should be maximized and testing time should be minimized. Although such a rationale appears at first to be prudent, it might be a naive approach leading to ineffective instruction and inadequate learner achievement. For example, providing even the best-quality instruction for enabling skills will result in inadequate posttest performance by students who do not possess the mandatory prerequisite skills for entering the instruction (e.g., instruction on writing paragraphs when they cannot write simple sentences). Likewise, devoting time to introducing and rehearsing enabling skills that were mastered in a previous class is inefficient for teachers and often boring for students. The balance between teaching and testing time should be carefully considered if instruction is to be maximally efficient. In fact, many educators argue that good tests are an integral part of instruction and an important learning aid for students; thus, time spent on testing is also time spent on learning.

There are several criteria for helping you to decide whether you will need readiness tests, pretests, and/or practice tests in addition to posttests. They include (1) the complexity of the instructional goal, (2) the characteristics of the target learners, and (3) the school-based considerations of time and curriculum.

Goal Complexity Instructional goals that are judged to be complex and hierarchical may require a variety of types of tests if teachers are to maximize students' potential for achieving the goal. Readiness tests support judgments about appropriate levels of goal complexity for given student groups and judgments about grouping students for instructional effectiveness. Helping students acquire complex skills may necessitate several practice tests in a variety of formats to enable students to store the skills in memory and to retrieve them when needed. These tests also enable teachers to detect and correct students' misconceptions and errors in applying the skills. When instructional goals are complex intellectual skills, teachers will undoubtedly prescribe multiple types of tests for efficient management of the instructional unit.

Learners' Characteristics The characteristics of target students should also figure into determining the number and types of tests needed. If a group is homogeneous and consists of high, average, or low achievers, the teacher may be able to predict accurately the learners' status on prerequisite and enabling skills. On the other hand, if the group is rather heterogeneous, the teacher may increase instructional efficiency by testing students' achievement of subordinate skills and then grouping by achievement levels on the skills. Estimating students' achievement of prerequisite skills might be risky when students come to the classroom from a variety of previous classes and teachers.

School-Based Considerations School-based considerations for determining the types of tests for a particular instructional unit include the importance of the goal in the curriculum, the number of class periods available for a unit, and the length of individual class periods. Related to the curriculum, if the same goal (e.g., writing a sentence) were considered a basic life skill and included across several years of the curriculum, then teachers would undoubtedly prescribe tests for prerequisites and enabling skills to identify students' current skill levels and to aid their lesson planning and evaluation activities. The time available for the total unit will also enter into the decision. If you have only three class periods to devote to a particular goal, then the notion of including readiness tests, pretests, practice tests, and posttests becomes absurd. Considering the time available during a single class session and the possible need for changing learners' focus and activity in order to maintain their attention may help you determine whether to include some form of practice test as a routine part of the daily lesson structure.

Select Prerequisite and Enabling Skills

Both the purpose for the test and the interrelationship among the prerequisite and enabling skills in the goal framework must be considered when designing tests to help ensure validity and reliability. The following paragraphs illustrate the design process used to specify subordinate skills for a table of test specifications for each of the four types of tests.

Readiness Tests Since the purpose for readiness tests is to measure learners' mastery of prerequisite skills for a given instructional goal, the *most* representative set of objectives for a readiness test would include every subordinate, prerequisite skill in the instructional goal framework. Table 4.1 contains a skeletal replication of a hypothetical instructional goal matrix.

1. The first three columns in each row (A, B, and C) reflect recall-level skills related to identifying physical, functional, and quality characteristics.

TABLE 4.1
Hypothetical Instructional Goal Analysis Matrix

MAIN CONTENT AREAS	RECALL LEVEL			PERFORM LEVEL		
	A Name/Recall Physical Characteristics	**B** Name/Recall Functional Characteristics	**C** Name/Recall Quality Charactics	**D** Discriminate Examples/ Nonexamples	**E** Evaluate Examples	**F** Produce Examples
I. Prerequisite Skills	I.A	I.B	I.C	I.D	I.E	I.F
II. Prerequisite Skills	II.A	II.B	II.C	II.D	II.E	II.F
III. Enabling Skills	III.A	III.B	III.C	III.D	III.E	III.F
IV. Enabling Skills	IV.A	IV.B	IV.C	IV.D	IV.E	IV.F

2. The last three columns in each row (D, E, and F) reflect performance-level skills related to classifying examples and nonexamples, evaluating the quality of given examples, and producing acceptable examples.
3. Skills within each row progress hierarchically from left to right in one area of content, with left-side skills subordinate to right-side skills within a row. Skills also tend to progress hierarchically in the last column from skill I.F, lowest level, through skill IV.F, highest level.

Since the most representative set of prerequisite skills for a readiness test would include all prerequisite skills, then the table of specifications for this hypothetical unit should prescribe the prerequisite skills represented by cells I.A through II.F in Table 4.1. A readiness test that measures all these prerequisite skills should yield scores that have very good potential for aiding valid decisions about who is and who is not ready for the unit. These scores should also be reliable since all prerequisites are included; students could reasonably be expected to earn a similar score regardless of the particular items used to represent each of these prerequisite skills.

Sometimes, due to management constraints, you cannot prescribe that every prerequisite skill in the goal framework is included on a readiness test. However, you should still try to prescribe the most representative subset of prerequisite skills possible in order to maximize the potential for obtaining reliable test scores and for making valid decisions about who is prepared to begin instruction on the enabling skills. Some subsets of prerequisite skills from the goal matrix have more potential for yielding reliable scores and valid decisions than others. Two rules to follow in sampling among all prerequisite skills in the framework include:

1. Select skills from all relevant rows in the goal framework, ensuring that all content areas are represented in the test.
2. Select skills from the right-hand side (performance-level skills) since these performance-level skills are likely to encompass the subordinate recall-level skills.

Using these two rules for sampling among the two rows of prerequisite skills in Table 4.1, you could reduce the number of objectives included on the readiness test from 12 to 6 and specify only the prerequisite skills from cells I.D through I.F and II.D through II.F. You can see in Table 4.1 that these are the highest-level skills in each content row and that both content rows are represented; thus, this prescription would more than likely yield reliable test scores and enable valid decisions about who is ready for instruction on the enabling skills.

Assuming that selecting any other 6 of the 12 prerequisite skills would result in the same level of representation would be inaccurate. Suppose that the 6 skills were instead selected from cells I.A through I.F in Table 4.1. Selecting these 6 prerequisites would totally eliminate the second, and possibly more complex, strand of skills, which would very likely reduce the validity of decisions about who was prepared to enter the unit. Likewise, specifying skills I.A through I.C and II.A through II.C, or the first three cells in each content row, would also be an inferior representation of skills that would yield very questionable test scores for determining students' readiness.

Suppose you could only include two skills in the readiness test rather than six skills. You could help ensure the best representation of skills by selecting one skill cell from each content area and by selecting that cell from the far right side of the goal framework. In Table 4.1, the most ideal skills to select for this circumstance would be skills I.F and II.F. If learners could produce examples or solve problems in each content area, then you could validly conclude they were ready for the unit. In summary, a test that measures prerequisite skills from all content areas and that contains higher-order skills has more potential for yielding reliable test scores and for supporting valid judgments about learners' readiness than tests representing only some content strands or lower level skills.

Pretests   The purpose for pretests is to determine which ones of the enabling skills have been previously mastered. This information is used to plan lessons efficiently in that enabling skills previously mastered by all students can simply be reviewed, whereas skills that most students fail to perform adequately must be introduced, elaborated, and rehearsed during the unit. This purpose for the pretest implies that the individual student and group status on every enabling skill in the goal framework should be measured.

Related to the example skills in Table 4.1, then, the pretest would ideally include skills A through F in Row III and skills A through F in Row IV.

Recall the manner in which the number of skills measured on the readiness test was reduced and the representativeness of the skills measured for determining pupils' readiness for the unit was maintained. Could you reduce the enabling skills measured on the pretest to only skills III.F and IV.F in Table 4.1 and still have pretest scores valid for lesson planning decisions? No. Measuring only these 2 skills would indicate who had and who had not mastered the instructional goal, but it would not reveal which of the other 10 skills were mastered. For those students who could not perform skills III.F and IV.F, you could not efficiently develop lesson plans to aid their acquisition of the instructional goal. In designing pretests, you might want to follow the strategy of including all the enabling skills on the test that time will allow. When you must compromise, again follow the strategy of sampling from all major content areas and from all higher-level skills in those areas.

Practice Tests   The purposes for practice tests are to enable learners to rehearse and transfer new skills learned in a lesson and to help students and teachers monitor learning progress during instruction. Based on these purposes, a single practice test typically measures fewer enabling skills than the other three types of tests. It is often focused on a single lesson or two and administered during or immediately following instruction. A unit of instruction may have only one pretest or posttest, but it typically has several practice tests that measure different portions of the enabling skills.

Determining exactly how to select enabling skills for practice tests requires knowledge of the enabling skills in a unit and their interrelationships. For illustration purposes, suppose you decide to design four practice tests for the hypothetical unit in Table 4.1. The first practice test might include enabling skills III.A through III.F, and the second one might focus only on enabling skills III.E and III.F for additional rehearsal and transfer. Likewise for the enabling skills in Row IV, perhaps the third practice would encompass the recall skills in cells IV.A through IV.C, and the final practice test might measure the performance skills in cells IV.D through IV.F. In designing actual practice tests, you must consider the complexity of enabling skills, how they are divided for lessons within the unit, and the amount of class time that is available for rehearsal and feedback.

Posttests   The purpose for posttests is to describe students' achievement of the enabling skills and instructional goals. Most teachers have latitude in how unit-level examinations are designed, which means that one can observe many different styles of posttests. Some teachers prefer administering a series of smaller examinations, each of which covers a portion of the enabling skills in the unit. Such small, focused examinations are often called *quizzes*. Other teachers prefer a combination of focused quizzes and a comprehensive unit examination that measures performance on all enabling skills. Yet others administer no posttests besides a comprehensive unit-level exam. Regardless of the strategy you prefer, unit posttests should either collectively or singly measure all the enabling skills in a unit.

A comprehensive posttest for a unit would resemble a comprehensive pretest in that it measures all the enabling skills in the unit. In fact, if you were asked to discriminate between a pretest and posttest for a unit, you should not be able to tell which is which. The only difference would be in how the students' scores from the two tests were used. Similar to the pretest, a comprehensive posttest design from the hypothetical unit in Table 4.1 would include as many of the enabling skills as time allowed, and ideally all skills, III.A through IV.F, would be represented on the test. Should you need to sample among them, the same rule of prescribing skills from each content area and from the higher-level skills would be followed. A teacher who chose to administer two posttests might include only skills from content row III on one exam and only skills from content row IV on the other. Another strategy might be to administer three posttests with the following enabling skill prescriptions:

Test 1: Row III, skills A through F
Test 2: Row IV, skills A through F
Test 3: Skills III.F and IV.F

Term and Semester Posttests   When designing comprehensive term and semester examinations that measure enabling skills and goals from across many units of instruction, the same rule of representativeness should be followed. Suppose that the hypothetical unit of instruction in Table 4.1 was to be combined with 22 other instructional units for the semester examination. Following the rule of representativeness, which enabling skills would you select to represent this unit in the comprehensive exam? Hopefully, you would choose skills III.F and IV.F or simply IV.F if III.F is hierarchically subordinate. Should these skills not be measurable on the semester exam because of test format policies in the school (e.g., only objective-style tests), you might choose instead skills III.E and IV.E or singly IV.E if III.E is hierarchically subordinate. With the subordinate skills prescribed for an examination, you are ready to select the particular objectives that will be used to guide the process of teaching and measuring each skill.

Select Behavioral Objectives for Each Subordinate Skill Prescribed

For each prerequisite and enabling skill in an instructional goal framework, there is one or more behavioral objectives, and test designers should choose among the options to specify the particular objectives for a given test. Recall that behavioral objectives differ from subordinate skills in that they include conditions under which students are expected to perform the prescribed skill. The function of these conditions is to set the difficulty level of the subordinate skill and to prescribe the stimulus material that learners will have for performing the skill. Behavioral objectives in most school subjects will prescribe that students either write an answer, select an answer from among alternatives, produce a product of some type, or actively perform, as in delivering an oral speech.

The ideal criterion for selecting behavioral objectives for specified subordinate skills is the *congruence* between the behavior specified in the enabling skill and the conditions and behaviors included in its behavioral objectives. For example, if the subordinate skill specifies that students state the physical characteristics of a given concrete concept or name the quality characteristics of a given defined concept, the most ideal behavioral objectives for these skills would require learners to state these characteristics from memory. Depending on the scope of a test, however, requiring students to write lengthy definitions of concrete and defined concepts may seriously restrict the number of subordinate skills that can be tested in a typical class period. From another practical perspective, many lengthy definitions written by 40 or more students may require more time to score than the teacher has available, especially if the purpose for the test is to determine learners' readiness or to plan lessons. Classroom teachers who prescribe and administer cumbersome tests that do not help, but instead hinder, their work rarely maintain any kind of testing strategy besides administering posttests.

In choosing the most appropriate behavioral objectives for prerequisite and enabling skills, you will need to balance several different criteria related to ideals and utility. The most ideal test can be perfectly useless when you cannot possibly obtain the data in the time available. Some of the factors you will need to balance against the congruence of behaviors in subordinate skills and objectives are the following:

1. The purpose for the test and how you plan to use the data
2. The time available for obtaining the test performance data versus the time required to administer and score the test as well as summarize and interpret the data
3. The breadth of the goal framework prescribed for a given test
4. Whether learners' performance is to be described for planning purposes or for determining grades
5. The compatibility of objectives within a single test format

Specifying objectives for enabling skills typically involves designing the best test to meet a myriad of test design criteria rather than designing the perfect test for any one criterion.

Specify the Number of Items for Each Objective Chosen

A test should include enough items for each objective to ensure that the skill is measured adequately. There are several criteria to use in determining how many items should be prescribed for a behavioral objective. They include:

1. The complexity of the skill described in the objective
2. The possibility of correctly guessing an answer given the item format
3. The possibility of committing inadvertent errors in answering an item

Basically, ask yourself, How many times must students correctly perform a skill for me to be reasonably sure that they have mastered it?

Consider first the issue of objective complexity. You would not need to administer many test items to be sure that students remember the name of something. This is a very simple recall-level skill, and you would undoubtedly specify only one or possibly two items. On the other hand, classifying examples of concepts in several categories is quite a bit more complex, and you would undoubtedly specify several items to ensure that students could accurately and consistently perform this skill across all categories.

The ease of correctly guessing an answer is a second factor to consider in determining the number of test items to prescribe. When learners have a 50-50 chance of correctly guessing the answer to an item, then you will need to prescribe more items. For example, students have a 50 percent chance of guessing correctly whether the term *Coca Cola* is a proper noun. If only this single item is presented and the student answers it correctly, then you really do not know whether the student possesses the skill or simply guessed correctly. Increasing the number of instances presented for classification reduces students' ability to appear skilled when they are not.

On the other hand, suppose you present students with only one item related to a skill they have thoroughly mastered. There are any number of circumstances, such as misreading the directions or not understanding an irrelevant term in the item, that might cause students to miss the single item presented. Should the students miss the item, your test data will not help determine whether students do not have the skill or inadvertently missed the item due to some other factor.

This discussion might lead you to conclude that more is always better when prescribing the number of items for each objective, but this is not the case. Considering the time available for the total test and the potential for tiring students during the test, you will need to compromise and specify only the number of items you believe will help ensure that students' scores on the total test validly reflect their true achievement status on the skills measured.

Estimate the Time Required for the Overall Test

Approximating the time required for students to complete a test always constitutes a best-guess situation. However, with knowledge of students' typical work speed, the format of an item, and the number of items per objective, you will be able to obtain a ball-park figure for the total time a test will require. This last step in developing the table of test specifications is important because it can illustrate whether you have prescribed more items from an ideal perspective than your students can possibly answer in the allotted time. When students earn low scores on exams related to fatigue or inadequate time to complete the test, you will be compromising the reliability of your scores and the validity of your decisions.

The table of test specifications should include time estimates for answering all items prescribed for each objective and for the total test. These items can be estimated by using the following process:

1. Consider the complexity of the behavioral objective.
2. Consider the amount of time required for students to study and interpret any stimulus material that might accompany the items.
3. Consider the amount of time required for students to respond to each item.
4. Multiply the total amount of time required to answer each item by the number of items prescribed for each objective.
5. Sum the times estimated for each objective to project the total amount of time required for students to answer the items.
6. Add to this item-based estimate the administration time required to introduce the test, distribute the test, and collect materials when students have finished.

When the estimated time for the examination fits your ball-park figure of time allocated for the test, the table of test specifications is complete. Should any of the time estimates represent impossible allocations for the time available or the attention span of the students, you may either reduce the number of items specified or administer the prescribed test in more than one test session. Reducing the number of items may not be the wisest approach to solving the problem since the skills, objectives, and items were prescribed to maximize score reliability and decision validity.

An Example

The instructional goal on writing paragraphs is used to illustrate a table of test specifications for a unit of instruction. A sample table of test specifications for the pretest, unit posttest, and practice tests is included in Table 4.2. The readiness test is omitted from the table since it is based on objectives from a prior instructional unit on constructing sentences. Notice in Table 4.2 that the goal analysis matrix for paragraphs is used as the foundation for the table of test specifications. The levels of learning are listed across the top of the table and the main content areas are listed down the left side. Using the instructional goal matrix as the basis for your tables will help you balance the levels of learning and content for each test prescribed. The far right column in the table contains the total number and percentage of both objectives and items prescribed for each content area and the total test. This column will help you determine whether you have the content areas balanced. The totals row at the bottom of the matrix for each type of test will help you see how the different

TABLE 4.2
Table of Test Specifications for the Intellectual Skill "Write a Paragraph"

CONCEPTS/ CONTENT	A State/Recall Physical Characteristics	B State/Recall Functional Characteristics	C State/Recall Quality Characteristics	D Discriminate Examples & Nonexamples	E Evaluate Given Examples	F Produce Examples	TOTALS Objectives Items # %	
PRETEST								
I. Paragraph	I.A.3 (1)*	I.B.3 (1)		I.D.1 (1) I.D.2 (1)			4 (4)	18 11
II. Topic Sentence	II.A.3 (1)	II.B.3 (1)	II.C.3 (1)	II.D.1 (2)	II.E.1 (3)	II.F.1 (3)	6 (11)	27 30
III. Supporting Sentences	III.A.3 (1)	III.B.3 (1)	III.C.3 (1)	III.D.1 (2)	III.E.1 (3)	III.F.1 (3)	6 (11)	27 30
IV. Concluding Sentences	IV.A.3 (1)	IV.B.3 (1)	IV.C.3 (1)	IV.D.1 (2)	IV.E.1 (3)	IV.F.1 (3)	6 (11)	27 30
TOTALS Objectives Items Est. Time	4 4 2	4 4 2	3 3 3	5 8 14	3 9 27	3 9 27	22 (37) 75 min.	100 100
UNIT POSTTEST								
I. Paragraph	I.A.4 (1)	1.B.4 (1)		I.D.2 (1)		I.F.1 (1) I.F.2 (1) I.F.3 (1) I.F.4 (1)	7 (7)	23 16
II. Topic Sentence	II.A.4 (1)	II.B.4 (1)	II.C.4 (1)	II.D.1 (2)	II.E.1 (2) II.E.4 (2)	II.F.1 (2)	7 (11)	23 25
III. Supporting Sentences	III.A.4 (1)	III.B.4 (1)	III.C.4 (1)	III.D.1 (2)	III.E.1 (2) III.E.3 (2) III.E.5 (2)	III.F.1 (2)	8 (13)	27 30
IV. Concluding Sentences	IV.A.4 (1)	IV.B.4 (1)	IV.C.4 (1)	IV.D.1 (2)	IV.E.1 (2) IV.E.3 (2) IV.E.4 (2)	IV.F.1 (2)	8 (13)	27 30
TOTALS Objectives Items Est. Time	4 4 2	4 4 2	3 3 3	4 7 10	8 16 32	7 10 110	30 (44) 159 min.	100 100

*Numbers in parentheses represent the number of test items prescribed for each objective.

CONCEPTS/ CONTENT	A State/Recall Physical Characteristics	B State/Recall Functional Characteristics	C State/Recall Quality Characteristics	D Discriminate Examples & Nonexamples	E Evaluate Given Examples	F Produce Examples	TOTALS Objectives (Items) Est. Time
PRACTICE TESTS							
I. Paragraph	I.A.2 (1)	I.B.2 (1)		I.D.1 (2) I.D.2 (2)			4 (6) 10 min.
II. Topic Sentence **1.**	II.A.2 (1)	II.B.2 (1)	II.C.1 (1)	II.D.1 (1)	II.E.2 (2) II.E.3 (2) II.E.5 (3)	II.F.1 (3)	8 (14) 40 min.
2.	II.A.1 (1)	II.B.1 (1)	II.C.1 (1)	II.D.1 (1)	II.E.5 (3)	II.F.1 (3)	6 (10) 30 min.
3.					II.E.1 (3) II.E.2 (2) II.E.3 (2) II.E.4 (2) II.E.5 (3)	II.F.1 (3)	6 (15) 40 min.
III. Supporting Sentences **1. (Relevance)**	III.A.2 (1)	III.B.2 (1)	III.C.2 (1)	III.D.1 (1)	III.E.1 (2) III.E.2 (2)	III.F.1 (2)	7 (10) 25 min.
2. (Sequence)	III.A.4 (1)	III.B.4 (1)	III.C.4 (1)	III.D.1 (1)	III.E.1 (2) III.E.3 (2) III.E.4 (2) III.E.6 (2)	III.F.1 (2)	9 (14) 35 min.
3. (Transition)				III.D.1 (1)	III.E.5 (3) III.E.6 (3)	III.F.1 (2)	4 (9) 30 min.
IV. Concluding Sentences **1.**	IV.A.2 (1)	IV.B.2 (1)	IV.C.1 (1)	IV.D.1 (1)	IV.E.2 (2) IV.E.3 (2) IV.E.5 (3)	IV.F.1 (3)	8 (14) 30 min.
2.	IV.A.1 (1)	IV.B.1 (1)	IV.C.1 (1)	IV.D.1 (1)	IV.E.5 (3)	IV.F.1 (3)	6 (10) 25 min.
3.					IV.E.1 (3) IV.E.2 (2) IV.E.3 (2) IV.E.4 (2) IV.E.5 (3)	IV.F.1 (3)	6 (15) 40 min.
I. Paragraph **1.**						I.F.1 (2)	1 (2) 40 min.
2.						I.F.2 (2)	1 (2) 40 min.
3.						I.F.3 (2)	1 (2) 40 min.
4.						I.F.4 (2)	1 (2) 40 min.

levels of learning are balanced for each test. The following paragraphs describe the design considerations for each of the tests prescribed.

Pretest   All skills except for writing paragraphs are included on the pretest. All objectives selected require objective-style items. This was done to ensure good representation of the skills tested and to minimize testing and scoring time. Thirty percent of the test measures recall-level skills, and 70 percent measures performance-level skills for discrimination, evaluation, and writing. Relative to content balance, topic, supporting, and concluding sentences, each receives 30 percent of the items, and the remaining items are used for overall paragraphs. Objective-based data from such a test should enable the teacher to group students based on their current skill levels and develop appropriate instruction for each group.

Unit Posttest   Similar to the pretest, the posttest covers all skill areas in the domain; however, more items on the posttest are prescribed for evaluation and writing skills. Additionally, students will be required to write four types of paragraphs. Twenty-five percent of the items will cover recall-level skills, and all items prescribed for this level are selected response (see Table 3.6). For the performance-level skills, 52 percent are selected response and 23 percent are written response. This posttest specification should provide the teacher with a test that measures all levels of learning and is balanced across all four content areas.

Practice Tests   The final set of test prescriptions in Table 4.2 is for 14 separate practice tests. There is one initial test for paragraph characteristics, three tests for each type of sentence, and four paragraph writing exercises. Taken together, these practice tests are representative of the entire goal framework. They are separate, however, to support lesson-level learning and practice. Monitoring students' progress on these practice tests should help the teacher pace instruction and provide additional lessons and exercises for students who need them.

DESIGNING COMPREHENSIVE
TERM OR SEMESTER EXAMS

Teachers frequently want to measure students' progress on several instructional units. Such comprehensive tests should be balanced by content areas and learning levels. Because several different frameworks of skills will be tested, prescribing test items that represent all of the enabling skills is not feasible. A table of specifications can help you manage the process of test development and design a test that best represents all the units covered.

Although skipping the development of a table of specifications for a comprehensive exam may save time, it is not recommended. Using items from previous unit tests will not ensure that the comprehensive posttest is balanced according to content, learning levels, and representative behavioral objectives. A posttest developed without appropriate prescriptions may produce scores of limited use and interpretation, thus compromising the entire project.

As you develop a table of specifications for a comprehensive posttest, you should consider the following six elements: (1) balance among the goals selected for the exam, (2) balance among the levels of learning, (3) the test format, (4) the total number of items, (5) the number of test items for each goal and level of learning, and (6) the enabling skills to be selected from each goal framework. A table of specifications incorporating these factors will help ensure a comprehensive posttest that represents each unit and is balanced by goals and levels of learning.

In constructing the table, you should first consider the balance among the goals to be represented on the exam. Study the goals and their respective frameworks and determine the relative complexity of the goals. The more complex a goal, the more emphasis it may need. For example, if 10 goals of approximately equal complexity are represented, the items for each goal may account for 10 percent of the total test. If 5 goals are more complex than the others, test items for these goals may take up a larger proportion of the test, with the 5 less complex goals represented by a smaller percentage of items. Regardless of the rationale you use to determine percentages, you should record the proportion of items for each goal in your table of specifications.

Once the appropriate balance among goals is established, turn to the second important element—balance among the levels of learning within each goal. When allocating the proportion assigned for a goal among the levels of learning, remember that recall-level skills are often subsumed within performance-level skills. Additionally, recall-level skills are less complex than performance skills and thus can be measured using fewer items. Therefore, you will usually want to assign a greater portion of the items allocated for each goal to performance-level skills. A caution is in order, however. If only performance-level skills are included on a test, and students fail to answer these items correctly, you may have difficulty interpreting their scores. You will not be able to detect whether they missed the items because they did not know the rule or definition or because they knew it but had trouble generalizing it.

Table 4.3 contains three tables of test specifications that balance 10 goals differently by goal and by level of learning. The specifications for Test A indicate equal emphasis among the 10 goals; however, 80 percent of the items require performance-level skills. The prescription for Test B emphasizes 5 of the 10 goals and indicates that 75 percent of the items test performance-level skills. The chart for Test C specifies uneven percentages for the 10 goals and requires that 100 percent of the items test performance-level skills. The different balances in goals and levels of learning in Tests A, B, and C will potentially result in different student scores for the three tests and different inferences about students' performance. The most appropriate balance among goals and levels of learning can best be determined by studying the relative complexity of the goals to be measured and assigning a portion of the test to each goal

TABLE 4.3
Partial Test Specifications for Three Comprehensive Posttests, Weighted by Goal
and Learning Level

Goal	Percentage of Items	Percentage Recall[a]	Percentage Performance[b]
Test A			
1	10	2	8
2	10	2	8
3	10	2	8
4	10	2	8
5	10	2	8
6	10	2	8
7	10	2	8
8	10	2	8
9	10	2	8
10	10	2	8
Total	100%	20%	80%
Test B			
1	14	3	11
2	6	2	4
3	14	3	11
4	6	2	4
5	14	3	11
6	6	2	4
7	14	3	11
8	6	2	4
9	14	3	11
10	6	2	4
Total	100%	25%	75%
Test C			
1	14		14
2	6		6
3	10		10
4	8		8
5	12		12
6	8		8
7	16		16
8	6		6
9	14		14
10	6		6
Total	100%	0%	100%

[a] The Recall category prescribes remembering and comprehension items.
[b] The Performance category prescribes classification, evaluation, problem-solving, explanation,
and prediction items.

accordingly. Then, with each goal assigned a portion of the test, you can select
the proportion for each level of learning within the goal.

Once you have weighted all the goals and learning levels to be covered,
you need to select a test format. Depending on the instructional goals to be

measured, you may decide on an objective test, an essay exam, a product development project, an active performance measure, or some combination of these formats. In making your decision, review the behaviors specified in the instructional goals to be measured and the item formats prescribed in the tables of test specifications for each unit.

You are now ready to prescribe the total number of items to be included on the exam and the number of items allocated for each goal. In selecting the total number of test items, consider two factors: the time available for testing and the required level of performance.

The time available for testing depends on the length of the class period and on students' attention spans. Students should be able to complete the test within the class period and before they become fatigued.

The required level of performance will also help determine the total number of questions on the exam. Recall-level items require less time than performance-level items, whatever the test format. Items that ask students to solve problems, analyze or synthesize information, or evaluate examples all require more time than do items that require students to remember a term, fact, definition, rule, or principle. Essay questions require more time than either selected-response or short-answer items.

Suppose, for example, that your class period is 50 minutes long. Of this time, approximately 10 minutes will be needed to distribute the tests, give instructions, and collect the tests; 40 minutes remain. If you estimate that students can answer an average of one short-answer question per minute, then your test can include a maximum of 40 short-answer items. If you plan to administer an essay test, and predict that each question will require approximately 12 minutes to answer, then you can include only three essay items. A test that contains a combination of short-answer and essay questions should allow enough time for each type of question.

After you have determined the total number of test items, then determine the number of items for each goal. For example, if each of 10 goals is to represent 10 percent of the test, and you have a total of 40 questions on the test, then the total number of items can be multiplied by the allocated proportion to determine the appropriate number of items (.10 × 40 = 4). Each goal would be represented on the test by four items.

The number of items allocated for each goal can then be divided between recall and performance-level items. If you choose to measure only performance-level skills for one goal, then all four of the assigned items would be designated for performance-level skills. If you choose to emphasize performance-level items, but also want to include some recall items for another one of the goals, then you probably would assign three of the available items to performance-level skills and one to recall.

Table 4.4 illustrates a partially completed table of test specifications that prescribes the total number of test items, the percentage and number of items for each of 10 goals, and the distribution of items according to learning level. For this comprehensive exam, 25 percent of the items measure recall-level skills and 75 percent measure performance-level skills.

TABLE 4.4
Partial Table of Test Specifications Prescribing Percentage and Number of Items for Each Goal and Level of Learning

| | Levels of Learning | | | |
| | Recall[a] No. of Items (Columns A–C) | Performance[b] No. of Items (Columns D–F) | Total No. | Percentage of Total Items |
Goals				
1	1	3	4	10
2	1	3	4	10
3	1	3	4	10
4	1	3	4	10
5	1	3	4	10
6	1	3	4	10
7	1	3	4	10
8	1	3	4	10
9	1	3	4	10
10	1	3	4	
Total	10	30	40	
Percentage of total items	25%	75%		100%

[a] The Recall category prescribes remembering and comprehension items.
[b] The Performance category prescribes classification, evaluation, problem-solving, explanation, and prediction items.

The final step in developing a table of specifications is the selection of enabling skills from each goal framework. Because the number of items for each goal must be limited, you should select the enabling skills and behavioral objectives that best represent each goal. For example, the test specifications in Table 4.4 limit the number of recall-level objectives for each goal to one. Only three items for each goal can be included at the performance level. In selecting performance-level objectives, you have three options: develop three items for one objective, write one item for one objective and two items for another, or write one item for each of three objectives. Try to choose the option that will result in the best measurement of student performance on the goal.

An Example

Suppose you developed a table of test specifications for comprehensive term and semester examinations in language arts, and you decide the following:

	Total Items	Percentage for Paragraph	Total Items for Paragraph
Term Exam	40	20	8
Semester Exam	50	10	5

Table 4.5 contains the table of test specifications for the paragraph portions of these tests, and the following section explains the paragraph prescriptions for each test.

Comprehensive Term Exam   The term exam will cover several instructional goals besides the one for writing paragraphs. Due to the limited number of items available for this unit, the teacher specified only evaluation- and writing-level objectives. Even with this limitation, the time required to administer this portion of the term exam is estimated at 64 minutes; thus, the teacher may need to administer the term exam in sections. One strategy might be to include the objective-style items (II.E through IV.F) with objective items from the other units and administer the paragraph writing items (I.F.1 and I.F.2) on a separate day (see Table 3.6 for specific objectives selected).

Comprehensive Semester Exam   The semester exam will cover units taught during one-half of the school year, and there will be only five items devoted to the paragraph unit. With this limitation in mind, the teacher prescribed only writing-level skills. Three short-answer items are prescribed (II.F.1 through IV.F.1), and students will be required to write two paragraphs. With total testing time estimated at 51 minutes for just the paragraph items, the teacher may need to separate the objective items and paragraph writing items to ensure that students do not become fatigued during the exam.

Once you have completed tables of test specifications, you are ready to begin writing test items and assembling tests. Guidelines for writing objective test items are covered in Chapter 5. Guidelines for developing and using alternative methods of assessment are provided in Chapters 9 through 13.

COMPUTER TECHNOLOGY

The table of test specifications you create for your instructional goal will serve as your guide for writing test items and as the blueprint you will need to create the pretest, practice test, and posttest that you have prescribed. The chronological sequence of activities that you would follow is:

1. Prepare a table of test specifications.
2. Write test items.
3. Assemble tests.

TABLE 4.5
A Sample Table of Test Specifications for Term and Semester Exams for the Instructional Goal "Write a Paragraph"

CONCEPTS/ CONTENT	A State/Recall Physical Characteristics	B State/Recall Functional Characteristics	C State/Recall Quality Characteristics	D Discriminate Examples & Nonexamples	E Evaluate Given Examples	F Produce Examples	TOTALS Objectives Items Est. Time
COMPREHENSIVE TERM EXAM							
I. Paragraph						I.F.1 (1) I.F.2 (1)	2 (2) 40 min.
II. Topic Sentence					II.E.1 (1)	II.F.1 (1)	2 (2) 8 min.
III. Supporting Sentences					III.E.1 (1)	III.F.1 (1)	2 (2) 8 min.
IV. Concluding Sentences					IV.E.1 (1)	IV.F.1 (1)	2 (2) 8 min.
TOTALS Objectives Items Est. Time					3 3 6	5 5 58	8 (8) 64 min.
COMPREHENSIVE SEMESTER EXAM							
I. Paragraph						I.F.3 (1) I.F.4 (1)	2 (2) 40 min.
II. Topic Sentence						II.F.1 (1)	1 (1) 3 min.
III. Supporting Sentences						III.F.1 (1)	1 (1) 5 min.
IV. Concluding Sentences						IV.F.1 (1)	1 (1) 3 min.
TOTALS Objectives Items Est. Time							5 (5) 51 min.

*Numbers in parentheses represent the number of test items prescribed for each objective.

You learned how to prepare a table of test specifications in this chapter, and you will learn how to write objective test items in Chapter 5. The Computer Technology section of Chapter 5 includes information about the types of objective-style items teachers can store in their computer-based test item bank. The first time you teach a subject, you will probably write just enough test items to comprise each of the tests you need to use, so the final step of assembling each test will be almost automatic. As you teach the subject again or begin working in developmental teams with your colleagues, however, you will begin to add many new items to your bank, edit the existing items, and discard items that prove to be unclear or ineffective with your students. This is the point at which you will really start developing a bank of test items that provides you with many item choices for each of your behavioral objectives. This is also the point at which the computer plays a valuable role, because it provides an automated method for retrieving and selecting items and then formatting, assembling, and printing tests.

It is important to emphasize here that this automated method of assembling a test is based directly on the table of test specifications covered in this chapter, thus it is included in this Computer Technology section. Chronologically, however, it is clear that you cannot assemble a test until you have gone through the process of writing items (Chapter 5), so keep that in mind as you read the rest of this section. You may want to come back and reread this section after you have finished Chapter 5.

Create a Test File

The items you select for a particular test are called a test file. Suppose that you already have multiple test items written and stored in your test item bank for each of the behavioral objectives you wrote for a unit of instruction. To assemble a test from your item bank, you will need to create a test file and name it. The ParTEST (Economics Research, Inc., 1991) program allows you to use eight characters to name your test file. You should choose your test file names carefully since these names are the keys you will use to access the test in the future. In addition, these names become the test column titles in your student roster. When the test file names reflect the nature of the test, the tests will be easier to locate in the program and the student records will be easier for you to interpret.

If you want to create the paragraph tests specified in Table 4.2, you might name the pretest file PREPARAG. The letters PRC might be used to indicate practice tests, and the practice test files might be named PRCPARAG, PRCTOP1, PRCTOP2, PRCTOP3, PRCSUP1, PRCSUP2, PRCSUP3, PRCCON1, PRCCON2, PRCCON3, PRCPARA1, PRCPARA2, PRCPARA3, and PRCPARA4. The posttest file might be named PSTPARAG.

Select Test Items

Once the test file is created for a test you wish to produce from your item bank, you are ready to search for the items you wish to include. The ParTEST program enables you to search your item bank using the six descriptor categories you identified when you created the item bank. Recall that one category was OBJECTIVE. Although you can use any of the six descriptors (SUB-JECT, TOPIC, OBJECTIVE, CHAPTER, SOURCE, COGNITIVE TYPE) or any combination of the six to locate items in the bank, the descriptor category OBJECTIVE will enable you to locate and select items that fit each of the tests prescribed in your table of test specifications.

Suppose you want to create the paragraph pretest specified in the table of test specifications in Table 4.2. First, load the test file PREPARAG. Next, using the "search for items to select" option in the program, type the objective code I.A.3 beside the search criteria OBJECTIVE to indicate that you want to review all items in the bank related to the first objective, I.A.3. The computer will display on the screen all the items stored in the bank for this particular objective. Since there is only one item prescribed in the table of test specifications for this objective, you should select the one item you want for the pretest from those available. Next, "search" for all test items available in the item bank for the second prescribed objective, I.B.3. Choosing this objective code for the search criteria will cause the screen to display all items in the bank available for this particular objective. From those available, locate the one you want and choose it for the pretest. The objective codes for the remaining objectives prescribed for the pretest can be used to locate and select items that fit the test specifications.

You can create any of the tests you have prescribed in your tables of test specifications by creating and naming a test file and then using the objective code you entered when you created the items to search for and retrieve the items. This procedure for creating tests will enable you to produce many different tests according to your test specifications without retyping the items once they are entered into your item bank and classified using your user-descriptor categories.

Edit Items in a Test File

Once you have assembled all the prescribed test items for your tests in a test file, you may edit the items in the file. You may change the wording of items, change the order they will appear on the test, or delete items from the test. Once you have created the test that you want, then print the test, the keys for scoring the test, and the feedback reports for students. You can experiment with test files using the ParTEST demonstration program and the directions provided in your *Student Manual*.

Create Term and Semester Exams

It is as easy to create term and semester exams using your item banks as it is to create unit tests. First, you need to name your comprehensive test file (e.g., TERM1). Next, using your table of test specifications for the comprehensive exam, locate the particular test banks you need for each of the instructional goals covered during the term. Then, using your table of test specifications, search each item bank using the objective codes and select the number of items required for each objective. The test file can assemble test items from a variety of item banks, which makes creating comprehensive exams as easy as creating unit tests.

The next chapter on writing objective items describes the kinds of test items that you may enter into your test bank.

SUMMARY

Carefully designed classroom tests can help you make correct decisions about the quality of your instruction and student progress. Test results can be used to tailor instruction and review for a particular group of students, evaluate the quality of instruction, and identify portions of your lessons that need improvement. Test results are also used to determine whether a group or individuals within a group have the prerequisite skills to begin a unit of instruction; provide students with practice during instruction; evaluate student progress; and determine students' mastery of instructional objectives.

During the design of classroom tests, you need to be concerned with the validity of your decisions based on test scores and the reliability of test scores. *Validity* refers to the appropriateness of inferences made from test scores. *Reliability* refers to the consistency or stability of scores obtained from a test. If the scores are unreliable, decisions or inferences based on them are dubious. Tests must be designed carefully to yield reliable scores and valid decisions about learner performance.

Factors related to ensuring the content validity of a test include how scores will be used; how well the behavioral objectives selected represent the goal framework; the test item formats that would best measure students' achievement of each objective; and the number of items required to measure achievement of each objective.

To help ensure reliable test scores, you should take five steps during the design stage: (1) select a representative sample of objectives from the goal framework; (2) select enough items to represent adequately the skills required in the objective; (3) select item formats that reduce the likelihood of guessing; (4) prescribe only the number of items students can complete in the time available; and (5) determine ways to maintain positive student attitudes toward testing.

The subordinate skills in an instructional goal framework should be divided into prerequisite skills (skills students should have mastered before entering a unit of instruction) and enabling skills (skills that comprise the main focus of instruction for a unit).

Teachers typically design four types of tests to help them with planning and evaluation activities. Entry behaviors tests help determine whether students possess the prerequisite skills needed for a unit of instruction. Pretests provide data useful in developing lesson plans. Entry behaviors tests and pretests are often combined and administered before instruction is planned. Practice tests are usually informal instruments administered during instruction. The data from practice tests permit you to evaluate students' progress, assess the quality of instruction, and provide corrective feedback to students. Posttests are administered after instruction, and the data are used to evaluate student progress, assign grades, and refine the instruction.

Careful planning and the development of tables of specifications substantially increase the likelihood of valid decisions and reliable test scores. The steps in developing test specifications for one unit of instruction are as follow:

1. Prescribe the types of tests needed to support your decisions.
2. Select the most representative set of subordinate skills from the goal framework for the types of tests prescribed.
3. Select one or more behavioral objectives for each subordinate skill.
4. Specify the number of items for each objective.
5. Estimate the time required for students to answer the total number of items for each objective and for the test.

Teachers who want to test students on their mastery of goals from several units of instruction should design test specifications for a comprehensive posttest. The seven steps in this procedure are:

1. Construct a matrix that lists all instructional goals to be measured.
2. Review the goal framework, behavioral objectives, and tables of specifications for each goal listed and insert the appropriate levels of learning across the top of the matrix.
3. Determine the overall portion of the test to be devoted to each goal and to each level of learning and record this information in the matrix.
4. Review the table of test specifications for each goal, note the item formats prescribed in each table, and select the best test format(s).
5. Use the selected test format, the time available for administering the test, and the skills of the students to determine the total number of test items.
6. Determine the number of items for each goal and for each level of learning and record this decision in the table.
7. Select the behavioral objectives to be measured and insert their identifying numbers in the table beside the number of items to be written for each.

When working with computer-based test item banks, you can use tables of test specifications to determine the number of items you need to develop for the bank. They are also used as a guide to help you create test files and tests for any purpose.

PRACTICE EXERCISES

I. **Designing Tests**
    A. Test scores that accurately reflect students' mastery of instructional goals and lead to appropriate inferences about students' achievement are called _valid_ test scores.
    B. Test scores that are consistent and that provide a stable indication of students' performance are called _reliable_ test scores.
    C. List four factors that affect the validity of test scores and that should be considered during test design activities.
    D. List five steps a teacher can take during test planning to help ensure reliable test scores.
    E. The subordinate skills in the goal framework that students should have mastered prior to beginning a unit are called _____ skills.
    F. The subordinate skills in the goal framework that will be the main focus of instruction during a unit are called _____ skills.
    G. List five ways teachers use test results to help plan instruction.
    H. List four ways teachers use test results to help monitor student progress.
    I. Table 4.6 includes a column for each of the four types of tests described in the chapter. The left-hand column contains statements that describe one or more tests. Match the descriptions with the appropriate type of test by checking the correct test columns. Check your responses in the completed version of Table 4.6F in the Feedback section.
    J. Design Test Specifications. Suppose you need to design the tests to support an instructional unit on writing compound sentences. This is a fundamental goal of schooling that is taught across elementary, secondary, and university levels. The instructional goal framework and accompanying behavioral objectives are located in the Feedback section of Chapter 3 in Tables 3.7 and 3.9, respectively.
        1. Prescribe the types of tests that should be developed for the unit.
        2. Divide the subordinate skills in Table 3.7 into prerequisite and enabling skills.
        3. Design a pretest, four practice tests, and a posttest for the unit using tables of test specifications.
        You may compare your test designs with those illustrated in Table 4.7.
    K. Assume you wanted to design a comprehensive posttest that could include only 45 items. Also assume that only 20 percent of the test would be devoted to the compound sentence unit.
        1. How many items on the test would relate to compound sentences?
        2. Given that you are limited to this number of items, select the major skill areas and objectives you would include, the item format you would use, and the number of items you would include for each objective.
    L. Enrichment. For the goal analysis framework and behavioral objectives you have developed in your own content area, construct a table of test specifications for:
        1. An entry behaviors test.
        2. A pretest.
        3. A practice test.
        4. A unit posttest.

TABLE 4.6
Types of Tests and Their Descriptions

Descriptions	Entry Behaviors Test	Pretest	Practice Test	Posttest
A. Main purpose for test				
1. Plan instruction				
2. Evaluate instruction				
3. Revise instruction				
4. Monitor student progress				
5. Grade student performance				
B. When test is administered				
1. Before planning lessons				
2. During instruction				
3. After instruction is completed				
C. Objectives included on a test				
1. Only objectives for prerequisite skills				
2. A representative sample of objectives for enabling skills from the goal framework				

FEEDBACK

I. Designing Tests
- **A.** Valid
- **B.** Reliable
- **C.** Factors related to validity include:
  - **1.** The purpose for the test and how the results will be used.
  - **2.** How well the behavioral objectives selected represent the goal framework.
  - **3.** The match between the behavior described in the objective and the test item format.
  - **4.** The adequacy of the number of items used to measure performance on each objective.
- **D.** The five steps for reliability are to:
  - **1.** Select a representative sample of subordinate skills from the goal framework.
  - **2.** Select items that adequately represent the skills required in each objective.
  - **3.** Select item formats that reduce the likelihood of guessing.
  - **4.** Include only the number of items that students can comfortably complete.
  - **5.** Determine ways to maintain positive student attitudes toward testing.

TABLE 4.7
Table of Test Specifications for the Intellectual Skill, Write a Compound Sentence

CONCEPTS/ CONTENT	**A** State/Recall Physical Characteristics	**B** State/Recall Functional Characteristics	**C** State/Recall Quality Characteristics	**D** Discriminate Between Examples & Nonexamples	**E** Evaluate Given Examples	**F** Produce Examples	**TOTALS** Objectives Items Minutes	
PRETEST							f	%
III. Coordinating Conjunction	III.A.2 (1)*	III.B.3 (1)	III.C.3 (1)	III.D.1 (4)	III.E.1 (4)	III.F.1 (4)	6 (15)	50 39
IV. Compound Sentences	IV.A.3 (1)	IV.B.2 (1)	IV.C.2 (1)	IV.D.1 (8)	IV.E.1 (8)	IV.F.1 (4)	6 (23)	50 61
TOTALS Objectives Items Est. Time	2 2 1 min.	2 2 1 min.	2 2 1 min.	2 12 10 min.	2 12 10 min.	2 8 16 min.	12 (38)	100 100 39 min.
UNIT POSTTEST							f	%
III. Coordinating Conjunction	III.A.2 (1)	III.B.4 (1)	III.C.4 (1)	III.D.2 (4)	III.E.1 (2) III.E.2 (2)	III.F.1 (4)	7 (15)	47 36
IV. Compound Sentences	IV.A.4 (1)	IV.B.2 (1)	IV.C.2 (1)	IV.D.1 (8)	IV.E.1 (4) IV.E.2 (4)	IV.F.1 (4) IV.F.2 (4)	8 (27)	53 64
TOTALS Objectives Items Est. Time	2 2 1 min.	2 2 1 min.	2 2 1 min.	2 12 10 min.	4 12 24 min.	3 12 24 min.	15 (42)	100 100 61 min.
PRACTICE TESTS								
I. Simple Sentence & Coordinating Conjunction	II.D.1 (4) III.A.1 (1)	III.B.1 (1)	III.C.1 (1)	III.D.2 (8)			5 (15) 12 min.	
II. Coordinating Conjunction				III.D.1 (8)	III.E.1 (8)	III.F.1 (8)	3 (24) 20 min.	
III. Compound Sentences	IV.A.1 (1)	IV.B.1 (1)	IV.C.1 (1)	IV.D.1 (15)			4 (18) 14 min.	
IV. Compound Sentences				IV.D.1 (10)	IV.E.1 (10)	IV.F.1 (10)	3 (30) 30 min.	
COMPREHENSIVE TERM EXAM								
Coordinating Conjunction & Compound Sentences				IV.D.1 (2)	III.E.2 (2) IV.E.1 (2) IV.E.2 (3)		4 (9) 5 min.	

*Numbers in parentheses reflect the number of items prescribed for each objective selected.
Note: Objective codes correspond to the behavioral objectives in Table 3.9.

E. Prerequisite skills
F. Enabling skills
G. Teachers use test results to help them:
  1. Determine whether prescribed instructional goals are at the appropriate level for students.
  2. Separate the enabling skills that have been previously mastered from those that must be learned.
  3. Plan remedial, enrichment, and review activities.
  4. Evaluate the quality of the instruction.
  5. Revise instruction.
H. In monitoring students' progress, teachers use test scores to help them:
  1. Determine who is ready to begin a unit of instruction and who should receive remedial instruction prior to beginning a unit.
  2. Identify subgroups of students to receive remedial or enrichment activities.
  3. Identify students who have mastered the enabling skills for a unit.
  4. Assign grades.
I. The completed version of Table 4.6 follows.

TABLE 4.6(F)
Test Types and Purposes

Descriptions	Entry Behaviors Test	Pretest	Practice Test	Posttest
A. Main purpose for test				
1. Plan instruction	X	X		
2. Evaluate instruction			X	X
3. Revise instruction			X	X
4. Monitor student progress			X	X
5. Grade student performance				X
B. When test is administered				
1. Before planning lessons	X	X		
2. During instruction			X	
3. After instruction is completed				X
C. Objectives included on a test				
1. Only objectives for prerequisite skills	X			
2. A representative sample of objectives for enabling skills from the goal framework		X	X	X

J. Design Test Specifications
  1. Tests should include a readiness test, a pretest, several practice tests, and at least one posttest.

2. Referring to Table 3.7, the prerequisite skills should include Row I, skills I.A through I.F, and Row II, skills II.A through II.F, all pertaining to the content areas of commas and simple sentences. The enabling skills should include all the remaining cells, III.A through IV.F, pertaining to coordinating conjunctions and compound sentences.
3. Review the test specifications for a pretest, four practice tests, and a posttest in Table 4.7.
K. Your comprehensive posttest would include:
1. Nine items related to compound sentences.
2. See the bottom row of Table 4.7. All the objectives prescribed are at the discrimination and evaluation levels. These objectives require selected response item formats due to administration and scoring time constraints that are always present at the end of a term or semester.

REFERENCE

Economics Research, Inc. (1991). *ParTEST user's manual.* Costa Mesa, CA: Author.

SUGGESTED READINGS

Ebel, R. L., & Frisbee, D. A. (1991). *Essentials of educational measurement* (5th ed.) (pp. 77–132). Englewood Cliffs, NJ: Prentice Hall.

Gronlund, N. E. & Linn, R. L. (1990). *Measurement and evaluation in teaching* (6th ed.) (pp. 48–140). New York: Macmillan.

Hopkins, C. D. & Antes, R. L. (1990). *Classroom measurement and evaluation* (3rd ed.) (pp. 129–173). Itasca, IL: F. E. Peacock.

Hopkins, K. D., Stanley, J. C., & Hopkins, B. R. (1990). *Educational and psychological measurement and evaluation* (3rd ed.) (pp. 165–192). Englewood Cliffs, NJ: Prentice Hall.

Kubiszyn, T., & Borich, G. (1990). *Educational testing and measurement* (3rd ed.) (pp. 60–67). Glenview, IL: Scott, Foresman/Little, Brown.

Mehrens, W. A., & Lehmann, I. J. (1991). *Measurement and evaluation in education and psychology* (4th ed.) (pp. 55–65). New York: CBS College Publishing.

Messick, S. (1989). Validity. In R. L. Linn (Ed.), *Educational measurement* (3rd ed.) (pp. 63–76). New York: American Council on Education/Macmillan.

Oosterhof, A. (1990). *Classroom applications of educational measurement* (pp. 21–30). Columbus, OH: Merrill.

Popham, J. W. (1990). *Modern educational measurement* (2nd ed.) (pp. 203–234). Englewood Cliffs, NJ: Prentice Hall.

Sax, G. (1989). *Principles of educational and psychological measurement and evaluation* (3rd ed.) (pp. 79–89). Belmont, CA: Wadsworth.

Wiersma, W., & Jurs, S. G. (1990). *Educational measurement and testing* (2nd ed.) (pp. 34–40). Boston: Allyn and Bacon.

CHAPTER 5

Writing Objective Test Items

OBJECTIVES

- Name and describe the five primary criteria for writing any type of test item.
- Describe the formatting criteria for the following objective test items: completion, short answer, alternate response, clustered alternate response, matching, keyed, and multiple choice.
- Use the five primary criteria and the formatting criteria to evaluate objective test items.
- Write objective test items following primary and formatting criteria.
- Assemble an objective test and write directions for responding to the items.

With the behavioral objectives written for each enabling skill in the instructional goal framework, you are ready to begin writing test items that can be used to judge students' mastery of the objectives and instructional goal. This chapter includes the five main quality criteria for creating any type of test item, the formatting criteria for each type of written and selected-response objective test item, and procedures for formatively evaluating objective items.

Objective test items require students to write or select a correct or best answer. These items are called *objective* because they can be *scored* more objectively than any other type of item used to measure students' performance. Written-response items include sentence completion and short-answer questions. Selected-response items include alternative-response, matching, keyed, and multiple-choice items.

Objective test items are popular with classroom teachers for several reasons. First, a teacher can use them to measure many types of learning, from verbal information to the use of rules and principles, and many levels of learning, from knowledge through evaluation. Second, a wide range of content can be measured because the items can be answered relatively quickly. Third, objective tests are easier to administer, score, and analyze than are other types of tests. Fourth, they can often be adapted for use with computers and can be scored and analyzed by machine. Finally, fewer scoring errors are likely to be made, yielding scores generally more reliable than those from other types of tests.

Despite their positive features, objective tests cannot be used to measure many of the skills found in curriculum guides. For example, objective test items cannot measure students' ability to write a report, deliver a speech, construct a mobile, operate equipment, paint a picture, or play the piano. Although objective items can measure certain aspects of these skills (e.g., related terminology, rules, or procedures), actual performance tests provide a more valid measure of these skills.

USING FIVE PRIMARY CRITERIA TO WRITE TEST ITEMS

The concepts of validity and reliability were introduced in the previous chapter, and the objective of all classroom test creators is to produce tests that yield valid and reliable test scores. You will recall that *validity* refers to whether a test measures what it is supposed to measure (e.g., the behavioral objective and instructional goal) and whether teachers can make valid judgments about a student's skill level based on the test score, and that *reliability* refers to whether scores obtained from a test are consistent. A test covering the same objectives that yields three very different test scores without additional instruction in a short period of time would not be considered reliable. In addition to the general guidelines in Chapter 4, there are five primary criteria that should be used to guide item writing, regardless of the particular item format, to help ensure that the tests teachers create result in reliable scores and valid decisions about a student's achievement level. The five criteria are:

1. Congruence of items with the conditions, behavior, and content specified in the behavioral objective
2. Congruence of items with the characteristics of students to be tested
3. Freedom from bias
4. Clarity of items
5. Accuracy of measures

Writing test items that meet these five criteria will help guarantee that the scores students earn on your tests are reliable and valid representations of their skills. The following sections describe the five criteria and ways you can use these standards in writing quality test items.

Congruence of Items with Objectives

Congruence between items and objectives helps ensure that test scores are valid. When writing items, you should pay careful attention to the behavior, content, and conditions prescribed in the objectives.

Behavior The response format selected for test items should match the behavior prescribed in the objective. It is important to note whether the student needs to define, list, select, solve, construct, perform, or evaluate. As you write each item, consider alternative ways the student might respond to demonstrate the behavior, and then write the items to solicit the prescribed behavior.

Content The content subsumed in each objective may be simple or quite complex. Instances of content selected for test items should clearly reflect all facets of the content students are likely to encounter. For example, if you were selecting instances of proper nouns, you would need to select some related to persons, places, and things. Writing items related to only one or two areas of content would be insufficient.

In writing test items, be careful not to confound the rules or principles measured. Items that measure two or more skills at once will be difficult to interpret because the student may select the correct answer for the wrong reason. For example, when measuring students' ability to capitalize a proper noun, the word used to measure this skill should not be placed first in a sentence. Students may respond correctly using the rule for capitalizing sentences rather than the one for capitalizing proper nouns.

Finally, you need to ensure that the instances of content you select for items are precise and relate only to the content measured. Using nouns again as an illustration, words that have multimeanings, such as *park*, *season*, and *field*, can be either nouns or verbs. Students will respond to multimeaning words depending on how they define them. If multimeaning words are used, they should always be placed in a context in which their meaning is precise.

Conditions Many intellectual and motor skills can be measured only in a situation that allows students to demonstrate their skill. In order to perform, operate, analyze, synthesize, or evaluate, students must be given appropriate resources. Test items that require supplementary resources are called *context-dependent* or *interpretive* items.

For most teacher-made tests, the conditions specified in the objective can be matched closely or realistically simulated. The conditions of behavioral objectives, which describe what students are to be given, can specify a variety of resource materials. They may require that students be provided with such materials as short stories, pictures, charts, diagrams, data tables, models, slides, specimens, or particular products. They may also specify such equipment as computers, saws, dissecting tools, sewing machines, weighing instruments, or automobiles. In addition, conditions sometimes include facilities, such as the school library or a learning resource center. The resource materials provided to students during testing must be congruent with the conditions specified in the objective. These materials are just as critical to valid measurement as is the nature of the items.

Of the five primary criteria for designing test items, the congruence between the elements of the behavioral objective and the elements of the test item is the most critical. When objectives and test items are not congruent, then something besides the intended objective is most likely measured by the item.

Congruence of Items with Target Students' Characteristics

In order to create tests that result in valid and reliable scores, the items must be congruent with the characteristics of target students. Factors that can influence the validity of a test are students' reading levels, vocabulary, and experience. Students of any age who are poor readers will have difficulty responding to items that require a lot of reading, and their answers may reflect their reading skills more than their achievement of the objective. Therefore, vocabulary used in either written or oral items should be familiar to students to ensure that their response reflects their achievement of the objective and not their vocabulary. For example, if you are selecting words to use in measuring students' ability to classify nouns, each word used to measure the skill should be one that all students in the group can define. Students' experience and age should also be used to create the context for an item. The word *context* refers to the situation posed to test the objective. For example, if you want students to punctuate sentences or analyze a short story, the sentences and story used should be about topics and situations familiar to them.

Freedom from Bias

Test items and resources should be free of stereotyping and of cultural, racial, and gender biases. People described in the items and resources should positively reflect the cultural, racial, and sexual characteristics of students in the group. The contexts and problem situations used should also be appropriate for males and females and for the cultural groups represented in the class. Students who are offended by items or unfamiliar with cultural-dependent contexts used may be less able to answer correctly, thus reducing the accuracy of the scores. Carefully designing items with potential bias in mind should help eliminate unconscious stereotyping and biases.

You should also avoid using contextual material that may unnecessarily arouse students' sensitivities. Contextual references to such topics as religion or church, political affiliations, or sexual behaviors are not appropriate in items unless the *content* of the instructional goal specifies religion, politics, or sexual behavior. Consider the following item intended to measure verb choice:

1. Fritz _____ to church last Sunday.
   a. go
   b. gone
   c. went

The religious context used in this item is inappropriate and may arouse the sensitivities of students who do not attend church or who do so on different days.

Clarity of Items

The clarity of items also affects the validity and reliability of a test. To ensure valid measures, items should be carefully constructed to avoid ambiguity and unintended complexity. Clearly written items allow students to focus their attention on the actual skill being measured. The language should be clear and precise; grammar, sentence structure, and punctuation should be correct. Each item should pose only one question. Questions that contain multiple ideas or that address several issues will confuse students of any age. Irrelevant or extraneous materials should be avoided. Instructions for responding should be clear, explaining how students are to respond as well as how resource materials are to be used.

To help ensure reliability, items should have only one correct or clearly best answer. Including more than one correct answer confuses students and can result in inconsistent answers, scoring, analysis, and interpretation.

Accuracy of Measures

Some items may measure students' skills more accurately than others. Factors related to the accuracy of measures are the novelty of items, susceptibility to guessing, susceptibility to cheating, and familiarity with item and test format.

The novelty of items and resources used on a test can influence test validity. Test items should not simply duplicate those previously used in classroom instruction or on earlier tests. Whenever feasible, novel items should be used each time an objective is measured. Otherwise, students may answer the questions correctly by remembering the correct answer from a previous unit test, practice test, or pretest. To ensure that students can perform the skill and are not simply recalling a previous instance, novel items should be used. The duplication of test items can lead to incorrect inferences about students' achievement levels.

Novelty of resource material and equipment is a different matter. Resources, such as charts, stories, pictures, and data tables, should contain novel information, but the organization and kinds of information as well as the degree of complexity and detail included should remain the same as that used during instruction. Such resources as computers, saws, sewing machines, and dissecting tools should not be changed for tests. Students should be tested using the same equipment they used to practice, particularly if changing equipment might increase the complexity of the task.

Guessing behavior tends to affect the reliability of test scores. While writing items, you should consider the probability of students' answering the question by guessing correctly. Test items that require students to select an answer are most susceptible to this problem. For example, students who do not know the answer to a two-choice item still have a 50 percent chance of answering correctly. Items containing three, four, or five choices reduce the probability of guessing correctly, but guessing remains a factor nevertheless. Items that require students to write rather than select answers also reduce the likelihood of guessing correctly.

Inadvertent clues in the item directions, or resources, also increase the probability that students will correctly guess an answer. For example, it is relatively easy for students to classify proper nouns in a list of words where all proper nouns are capitalized and all common nouns are not. Some students may use the capital letter rather than the meaning of the word to select correct examples of proper nouns. To avoid clues in this instance, capitalize all words in the list, capitalize no words in the list, or capitalize only some proper nouns and some common nouns. Removing potential clues from items will increase the reliability of students' scores.

Another factor that affects score reliability is the ease with which students can cheat on a test. When students are seated close together and their responses are brief, they can easily copy answers from other students' tests. When writing items that are susceptible to cheating, you should use strategies to reduce the likelihood of its occurrence. One such strategy is to create multiple forms of the test that contain the same questions but use a different item sequence on each form. With answers reordered, students' ability to locate corresponding answers at a glance will be eliminated.

Finally, students' familiarity with the item format and test medium can influence their scores. Their first experience with an essay, multiple-choice, matching, oral, or public performance exam should not be on a posttest. Likewise, testing procedures that require students to respond using such resources as a machine-scored answer sheet or a computer should not be introduced on a posttest. Students should practice using unfamiliar item formats and responding resources in a nongraded situation, such as a pretest or practice test, to avoid creating unnecessary confusion and anxiety during a posttest.

With these five primary criteria in mind, you are ready to consider the formatting criteria for written and selected-response objective items.

DEVELOPING WRITTEN-RESPONSE TEST ITEMS

Written-response test items require students to recall information from memory or to apply a skill before they write the answer. These items have several positive features. Because no alternatives are provided from which students can select an answer, students are less likely to guess correctly. By analyzing students' original responses, you can identify misconceptions and problems students have. The ability to identify misconceptions will help you tailor review materials to real problems and write plausible distractors for subsequent selected-response test items. Written-response items are very versatile because they can be constructed in a variety of formats and used to measure both verbal information and intellectual skills. The following list of possible uses is not exhaustive, but it illustrates the versatility of these items:

1. Students may be given a definition and asked to write the name of the concept defined.
2. Students may be given the name of a concept and asked to write a brief definition for it.
3. Students may be given the name of a concept and asked to list its unique characteristics.
4. Students may be asked to supply a missing word or words in a given definition, rule, or principle.
5. Students may be given a resource paragraph and asked to recall specific details from the paragraph, supply correct punctuation, reorder information, or edit it.
6. Students may be given a written passage to analyze and then asked to list the main ideas and the relationship among them.
7. Students may be given an incomplete paragraph and asked to write an introductory or concluding sentence for it.
8. Students may be given a product and asked to list its qualities and inadequacies.
9. Students may be asked to view materials, such as slides or specimens set up at different test stations, and then to write short answers for questions posed about each exhibit.

Despite their versatility, written-response items have their limitations. First, the item must be clearly written to produce the anticipated answer. More than one logical answer to an item will cause scoring problems and may reduce reliability. You must decide whether to accept logical, yet unanticipated, answers, whether to reduce credit for misspelled answers, and how much credit to allow for incomplete answers. Second, written answers cannot be machine scored. Scoring items, synthesizing answers by objectives, and analyzing individual and group responses all take time. Even though written-response items are time consuming and more difficult to score reliably, they should be the item format of choice when the behavior in the objective requires a written response.

Completion Items

The distinguishing characteristic of completion (sometimes called *fill-in-the-blank*) items is that the items are complete sentences that have key terms replaced with a blank. An example completion item is: "Tests administered prior to instruction that measure students' performance on enabling skills are called _____ ." The following are suggestions for writing clear, effective items in this format.

1. *Remove only key words from the statement.* A statement containing too many blanks does not adequately communicate the desired answer. For example, the item, "_____ _____ are words that refer to particular _____ , _____ , or _____ ," would be quite confusing to students. This ambiguity can be corrected in either of the following ways:

   a. Proper nouns are words that refer to particular _____ ,
      _____ , or _____ .
   b. Words that refer to particular persons, places, or things are called
      _____ .

2. *Place blanks for key words near or at the end of the statement.* Students should be able to anticipate the correct missing word before they encounter the blank. Placing the blank near or at the end of a statement does not change the meaning of the sentence, but students may find the item easier to read and answer.

The following suggestions will help you structure a completion item. First, write the complete statement. Second, select the key word or words you wish to eliminate. Third, if the key word is not located toward the end of the statement, rewrite the statement so the key word comes toward the end and replace it with a blank. Finally, read the statement with the words removed to ensure that enough information remains to guide students to the desired answer. The following series of statements illustrates these steps:

   a. Write statement: Nouns are words that refer to persons, places, things, or ideas.
   b. Select key word: *Nouns* are words that refer to persons, places, things, or ideas.
   c. Rewrite statement: Words that refer to persons, places, things, or ideas are called _____ .

3. *Eliminate the possibility of several plausible answers.* Often, incomplete sentences can logically be completed using several different words. For example, the item, "Proper nouns are words that refer to _____ persons, places, or things," would likely produce a variety of responses. Students might insert the words *particular, specific, given, proper,* or *some.* When there are several plausible answers to an item, replace the word that was taken out and remove another instead. A much superior item would be, "Words that refer to particular persons, places, or things are called _____ ."

4. *Eliminate clues to the correct answer.* Students will find clues to answers in blanks that are the length of desired words, in a blank preceded by *a* or *an,* and in the use of singular or plural verbs. You can eliminate these clues by making all the blanks the same length; by using *a(an)* instead of either *a* or

an; and by avoiding singular or plural verbs that may suggest a correct response.

5. *Paraphrase statements taken from instructional materials.* Test items that consist of verbatim statements taken from text promote rote memorization and tend to reduce students' need to read for comprehension. A much better test item would paraphrase key ideas in the text.

6. *Reduce scoring time by using answer sheets or other devices that simplify scoring.* Scoring completion items is time consuming, but there are several ways to make the task easier. Many teachers have students use a separate answer sheet with blanks numbered to correspond with those on the test. Another method is to make a column of blanks in either side margin of the test itself. Both techniques shorten the time required to score students' responses.

Short-Answer Items

Short-answer items are very versatile, and there are several ways in which they can be formatted. One type of short-answer item is a complete statement or question that requires students to insert a word, a phrase, or a sentence. Examples include:

1. Briefly define the term *proper noun.* _____
2. What are words that refer to *particular* persons, places, or things called? _____
3. John had $5.00. He bought a model kit for $2.56 and glue for $1.29. He paid 5% sales tax on his purchase. How much money did he have left? $_____
4. In the story *Habits,* describe why Clarissa may have acted as she did.
   _____

   _____

A second type of short-answer item frequently appears on mathematics tests. A group of items is presented with one set of directions. See Table 5.1 for an example.

A third type of short-answer format is association items that require students to associate a given stimulus with a response. Students are asked to

TABLE 5.1
Short-Answer Items with One Set of Directions

Directions: Use the sign in each problem to find the answer.

(1) 56	(2) 78	(3) 56	(4) 80	(5) 24	(6) 52
+ 43	+ 25	− 43	− 45	× 12	× 46

TABLE 5.2
Short-Answer Association Items: Stimulus and Response

Directions: Write a matching capital letter for each letter given.

a _____   m _____

e _____   q _____

i _____   u _____

---

associate a word, a symbol, or a picture with something else. The directions explain what the association should be. The examples in Tables 5.2 through 5.5 illustrate this format.

The following three suggestions will help you prepare good short-answer items.

1. *Provide a blank for each item that suggests whether the response should be one word or several (i.e., a phrase or sentence).* If you expect a one-word answer, the blank should be the length of one word. To avoid providing clues, make all word-sized blanks the same length. If the answer is a phrase or sentence, the blank or space should not permit students to write more than that. Some students will feel compelled to fill whatever space is allowed and will write an essay when a short answer is asked for.

2. *Specify the units required in the answer.* If the answer is to be in inches, dollars, or some other unit, specify the unit both in the question and beside the blank. Otherwise, some students may use alternative or inappropriate units in their answers. Clearly indicated units help ensure that an incorrect answer was not the result of misreading or misunderstanding the question.

3. *Ensure that the directions for a cluster of items are appropriate for all items in the set.* If one set of directions is used for a set of items, ensure that all items included are compatible with the directions. When a set of associations is to be made, state the basis for the association and the type of response sought. Include only homogeneous stimuli in the set.

TABLE 5.3
Short-Answer Association Items: Stimulus and Response

Directions: The names of several traffic signs appear below. <u>Draw the traffic sign</u> that matches each sign name in the blank provided.

1. Stop _____

2. Yield _____

3. Do not enter _____

4. Railroad crossing _____

5. School zone _____

TABLE 5.4

Short-Answer Association Items: Stimulus and Response

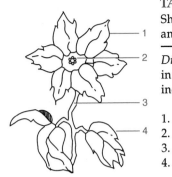

Directions: Name parts of flowers. For each arrow in the diagram (1–4), write the <u>name</u> of the part indicated by the arrow.

1.
2.
3.
4.

TABLE 5.5

Short-Answer Association Items: Stimulus and Response

Directions: Write the <u>time</u> each clock indicates: minutes after the hour; minutes before the hour.

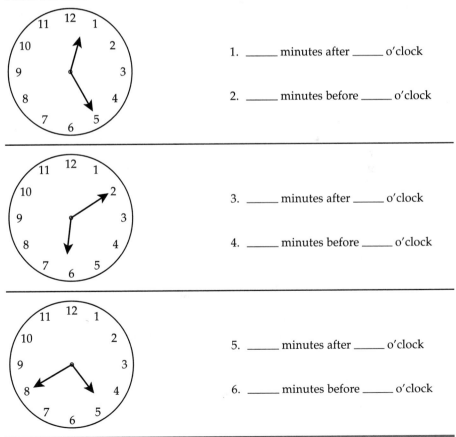

1. _____ minutes after _____ o'clock

2. _____ minutes before _____ o'clock

3. _____ minutes after _____ o'clock

4. _____ minutes before _____ o'clock

5. _____ minutes after _____ o'clock

6. _____ minutes before _____ o'clock

DEVELOPING SELECTED-RESPONSE TEST ITEMS

Selected-response items require students to choose an answer from a given set of plausible, alternative choices. Because each item must include one or more incorrect alternatives, selected-response items can be difficult to construct. Incorrect alternatives, sometimes called *distractors* or *foils,* should not be tricky or obscure and should not contain material unfamiliar to the students. Instead, they should represent plausible misconceptions that students may have developed. Because the correct answer appears in each item, students have a better chance of guessing correctly than they would with written-response items, and their potential for guessing correctly is increased when distractors do not appear reasonable.

Despite these drawbacks, using selected-response items has several advantages. First, each item requires students to choose among alternative responses that they may not have considered otherwise. These items can require students to make fine distinctions among several plausible answers. Therefore, teachers can use them to test aspects of students' skills that cannot be tested with other item formats. Second, students can answer more selected-response items than written-response items in the same period of time. Thus, a selected-response test can measure a wider range of skills than can a written-response test, when the two testing times are equal. Third, selected-response tests can be adapted for computer administration, or scoring can be done by machine. The following sections describe different types of selected-response items and present suggestions for item development.

Alternative-Response Items

Alternative-response items give students a choice of two responses. Each item presents a statement that students are to judge. The directions may ask students to make such decisions as whether the statement is true or false, correct or incorrect, or fact or opinion. The alternative-response format is desirable because it can be used to measure several types and levels of learning. For example, it can be used to:

1. Test students' ability to recall information. For example, students can be asked to determine whether a definition, a rule, or a principle is stated correctly.
2. Determine whether students can use a definition to classify examples and nonexamples of a concept.
3. Determine whether students can judge the correctness of given analyses or syntheses material.
4. Assess students' ability to evaluate material. For example, after reviewing selected materials, students can be asked whether they agree or disagree with given evaluations of the materials.

5. Apply principles in order to judge the accuracy of statements of causality or correlation.

In spite of its versatility, students have a 50 percent chance of guessing the correct answer to an alternative-response item. To reduce the potential for guessing correctly, some teachers modify the format by asking students to change an underlined word or words in an item if they believe the item is incorrect as stated. The students are directed to write the correct information either above the underlined word or in a blank provided beside the item. The following example illustrates a traditional and a modified true-false item.

Traditional
T F   1. A served tennis ball that strikes the net before landing in the appropriate area is called a net ball.

Modified
T F <u>let</u> 1. A served tennis ball that strikes the net before landing in the appropriate area is called a <u>net</u> ball.

Because it reduces the probability of guessing, the modified alternative-response item results in more valid and reliable test scores than does the traditional item. Students may recognize that the statement in a traditional item is incorrect, but they still may not know the correct answer or the reasons they thought the statement was wrong. With the modified format, students must first recognize that the statement is false and then supply the correct information. Although this modification reduces the probability of guessing correctly, it also increases scoring time. It can no longer be totally machine scored unless the test is administered by computer. The desirability of this modification will depend on the time and resources available for scoring.

The following suggestions for developing alternative-response items deal primarily with the directions for items and with the statements students are asked to judge.

1. *Explain judgments to be made in the directions.* Alternative-response items can be used to have students make a variety of judgments, such as true-false, yes-no, correct-incorrect, and fact-opinion. The nature of the required judgment should be clearly described.

2. *Ensure that answer choices logically match the necessary judgments.* For example, if students are to determine whether statements are *true* or *false,* the best answer choices are *true* and *false.* If a statement logically requires a *yes* or *no* answer, the item should offer students these two choices. If students are to determine whether a statement reflects fact or opinion, the two answer choices should be *fact* and *opinion.*

3. *Explain in the directions how students are to record their answers.* Without explicit instructions, students are likely to respond in a variety of ways. Directions should indicate whether students are to circle letters or words, fill in circles or spaces on a machine-scored answer sheet, or write words in blanks beside the items.

4. *Include only one idea to be judged in each statement.* Statements that include several ideas or that are only partially true will confuse students and affect their answer choices. A simple sentence with clear, precise wording at an appropriate vocabulary level is most appropriate. One exception to this rule is an item intended to check students' ability to detect causality or correlation.

5. *Word statements in a positive manner.* Negatively stated items are more complex and difficult to interpret than are positive statements. Negative words, such as *no* and *not*, add confusion that can reduce both the validity and reliability of students' responses. In effect, such items may be measuring the students' ability to read carefully rather than their objective-based skills. For example, students attempting to respond to the statement, "The word *boy* is not a noun," would have to recall the definition for nouns and then determine whether the word *boy* fit the definition. If they decided that the word was a noun, they would then need to note the word *not* and select false as the correct response. Some students may know that the word *boy* is a noun, miss the word *not* in the statement, and incorrectly mark the statement as true. If there is a legitimate reason for including negative words in a statement, they should be underlined or written in all capital letters to attract students' attention.

6. *Avoid designing questions to trick students.* Teachers who intentionally create items meant to trick students may also be tricking themselves. Such items not only confuse students but may also make the students' scores uninterpretable. A teacher using trick items would not be able to determine whether the instruction was effective or whether students were ready to begin the next lesson.

7. *Avoid providing clues to the correct answer.* Unintended clues help students guess the correct answer to test items. Any type of pattern, either in the directions, items, or responses, will guide students toward the right responses. An obvious example is the use of statements that are either all true or all false. Some students will quickly detect and accept this pattern, whereas other students will distrust the pattern of their answers and change some of them to the alternative. Less obvious, but still detectable, patterns can affect test results. Such patterns include the consistent use of true and false statements of different lengths, the obvious preference for one answer type, and the alternate placement of true and false items. For example, students will quickly recognize a pattern in which true statements are always longer than false ones. To avoid providing these types of clues, you should make statements of both types approximately the same length, review the list of statements to ensure that one type is not dominant, and review the sequence of responses to ensure that no pattern exists.

A final type of clue is the use of determiners or qualifiers, such as *always,* *never,* and *absolutely.* A statement that includes these and similar words strongly suggests an answer of false or no. This type of clue is one of the easiest to avoid.

Table 5.6 contains poor and improved examples of test items for the objective, "Given the definition of a noun, identify it as such." The behavioral objective appears at the top of the table. The suggestions discussed in this section are listed on the left. The second column provides examples of items that do not incorporate these suggestions, and the third column shows revisions of the same items.

Clustered Alternative-Response Items

A useful modification in the alternative-response item is called the *clustered* *alternative-response format.* The purposes for this format are to eliminate redundancy in items and to reduce reading time. These items include a common set of directions and short items of only one or a few words. For example, the following set of repetitive items could easily be clustered.

T F 1. The word *house* is a noun.
T F 2. The word *happy* is a noun.
T F 3. The word *bird* is a noun.
T F 4. The word *ran* is a noun.

To reduce the redundancy, redesign the items to appear as follows:

Directions: Identify nouns. For each of the following words, circle <u>YES</u> if the word <u>is</u> a noun and <u>NO</u> if the word <u>is not</u> a noun.

Yes No 1. house
Yes No 2. happy
Yes No 3. bird
Yes No 4. ran

The following suggestions will help you write good clustered alternative-response items:

1. Ensure that every item in the cluster is congruent with the response directions.
2. Ensure that only one of the two response options can be correct for each item.
3. Ensure that the instances included adequately sample the content in the objective.
4. Ensure that no clues are provided through patterns of answers or the number of items included in each category.

TABLE 5.6
Alternative-Response Test Items for the Behavioral Objective "Given the Definition of a Noun, Identify It as Such"

Suggestion	Item	Improved Item
Ensure that answer choices logically match the judgments to be made.	**1 2** 1. Nouns are words that refer to people, places, things, and ideas.	**T F** 1. Nouns are words that refer to people, places, things, and ideas.
Include only one idea in each statement.	**T F** 1. Nouns are words that refer to people, actions, places, conjunctions, things, and modifiers.	**T F** 1. Nouns are words that refer to people, places, things, and ideas. **T F** 2. Nouns are words that refer to actions, conjunctions, and modifiers.
Use clear, precise wording.	**T F** 1. Words used in the English language to reference persons we are speaking or writing about are called *nouns*.	**T F** 1. Words that refer to people are called *nouns*.
Statements should clearly relate to one of the alternatives.	**T F** 1. Words that refer to any physical object are sometimes called *nouns*.	**T F** 1. Words that refer to physical objects are nouns.
Make the wording of statements positive.	**T F** 1. Nouns are not words that refer to action.	**T F** 1. Nouns are words that refer to action.
Make both correct and incorrect statements about the same length.	**T F** 1. Nouns are words that refer to persons, places, things, and ideas. **T F** 2. Nouns are words that refer to actions. **T F** 3. Nouns are words that refer to conjunctions.	**T F** 1. Nouns are words that refer to persons, places, things, and ideas. **T F** 2. Nouns are words that refer to actions, conjunctions, and adjectives.
Avoid specific determiners, such as *always* and *never*.	**T F** 1. Nouns are words that always refer to people.	**T F** 1. Nouns are words that refer to people.

Table 5.7 contains 12 clustered alternative-response items for the objective "Given a list of words containing nouns and other parts of speech, select words that are nouns." Using the suggestions as a guide, review the directions and cluster of items in Table 5.7 to see whether you can locate potential problems.

Initially, it appears that all the items in the set are congruent with the directions (suggestion 1). However, each word in the list cannot be answered correctly with only one of the options (suggestion 2). Of the words chosen for the list, both *farm* and *park* fail to meet this criterion because they can be either nouns or verbs. Some students may visualize *park* as a place, whereas others may interpret it as an action. Some may visualize *farm* as a place, whereas others may define it as what a farmer does to obtain crops. This means that both responses could be correct for these terms, thus creating scoring problems.

According to the third suggestion, the words in the cluster should adequately sample the content of the objective. Two items, *man* and *aunt*, refer to persons. *Farm, library,* and *park* refer to places, and *mouse* and *book* refer to things. There are no examples included to represent the idea category of nouns. Therefore, the list does not adequately cover the content.

Finally, you should look for potential clues in the cluster. Clues might be found in the order of items in the list, in the number of instances included in

TABLE 5.7
Clustered Alternative-Response Test Items for the Behavioral Objective "Given a List of Words Containing Nouns and Other Parts of Speech, Select Words That Are Nouns"

Directions: Identify nouns. Each of the following words is either a noun or some other part of speech. If the word is a noun, circle <u>yes</u>. If the word is not a noun, circle <u>no</u>.

Words	*Noun*	*Not a Noun*
1. farm	yes	no
2. mouse	yes	no
3. library	yes	no
4. happy	yes	no
5. swiftly	yes	no
6. man	yes	no
7. tall	yes	no
8. aunt	yes	no
9. park	yes	no
10. book	yes	no
11. took	yes	no
12. where	yes	no

each content category, and in the number of nonexamples. In Table 5.7, nouns related to persons, places, and things are dispersed throughout the list, and nonexamples are interspersed as well, so no clue is provided there. The number of instances for each category is varied—two words relate to persons, three to places, two to things, and five to nonexamples. Therefore, no clues related to the number of items in each category are provided.

Several adaptations could be made to the directions for responding to the clustered items in Table 5.7 to simplify responding and scoring. One would be to instruct students simply to place a check (√) in the blanks before words that are nouns and to make no mark in the blanks before words that are not nouns. Another set of directions could be used to adapt these items for machine scoring. Students could be instructed to darken response 1 on the answer sheet for items that are nouns and to darken response 2 for items that are not nouns. If answer sheets are to be used, it is a good idea to modify the cluster of items as well to help students remember which space on the answer sheet corresponds to the response they wish to make. The list of words could be modified for machine scoring, as illustrated in Table 5.8.

Matching Items

Matching items are another popular selected-response format. These items require students to match information in two columns. Items in the left-hand column are called premises, and those in the right-hand column are called responses. Students are required to locate the correct response for each premise.

Although this format cannot be used to measure all levels and types of learning, matching exercises permit a teacher to measure many related facts, associations, and relationships quickly. It is an excellent way to measure students' ability to associate terms with their definitions, associate symbols

TABLE 5.8
Word List Modified for Machine Scoring

Directions: Identify nouns. Each of the following words is either a noun or some other part of speech. If the word is a noun, darken ① on your answer sheet beside the item number. If the word is not a noun, darken ② on your answer sheet beside the item number.

Word	Noun	Not a Noun
1. farm	①	②
2. mouse	①	②
3. library	①	②

with their names, name parts of an illustration, relate dates with names or events, match individuals with their accomplishments, and classify examples of concepts. Additionally, this item format is easily adapted for machine scoring. The one difficulty teachers have with the matching format is identifying multiple, plausible responses for each premise in the set. The following suggestions for writing matching items address the directions, the premises, and the responses.

1. *Provide clear, informative directions.* The directions should describe the types of items in each column and the basis for matching them. The directions should also indicate how and where responses are to be made and whether a response can be used more than once.

2. *Ensure that a set of premises is homogeneous and includes the more difficult reading material.* A set of premises should contain items that present the same kind of information (e.g., either authors, inventors, explorers, or politicians). Information on a variety of topics should not be included. If long phrases or sentences are to be used, they should be placed in the premise rather than the response column. For example, if definitions and symbols are to be matched, the premise should be the definition and the shorter symbol the response. The set should be limited to four to six items to help avoid irrelevant complexity.

3. *Ensure that responses are homogeneous, brief, and logically ordered.* Like the set of premises, the set of responses should be homogeneous; unrelated information is not likely to function well as distractors. The set of responses should contain more than one plausible response for each premise to avoid students guessing the correct answer through the process of elimination. Because students will reread the responses several times while matching items in the set, the responses should be as brief as possible. The responses should be arranged in chronological, alphabetical, or numerical order to help students locate their chosen answers and to help avoid pattern clues.

4. *Avoid one-to-one correspondence between premises and responses.* A different number of premises and responses should be included in a set. For example, if there are only four of each included, when three of the four items are matched, the answer to the fourth becomes automatic. This problem can be avoided in one of two ways. First, the set can be designed so that one response is correct for two or more of the premises. Second, more responses than premises can be included in the set. Either solution helps avoid the problem. The directions should always indicate whether a response can be used more than once.

Table 5.9 contains a set of matching items for the instructional goal "Name common traffic signs." The set, which measures students' ability to associate traffic sign names with their shapes, applies the suggestions just outlined. The directions describe the enabling skill, the types of information in the columns, the basis for matching items, and how to mark responses.

TABLE 5.9
Matching Items for the Instructional Goal "Name Common Traffic Signs"

Directions: Match traffic signs with their names. Column A contains the names of common traffic signs. Column B contains the shapes of traffic signs. For each sign named in Column A, select the matching shape in Column B. Place the letter of the matching shape in the blank before the name of each sign. A response may be used more than once or not at all.

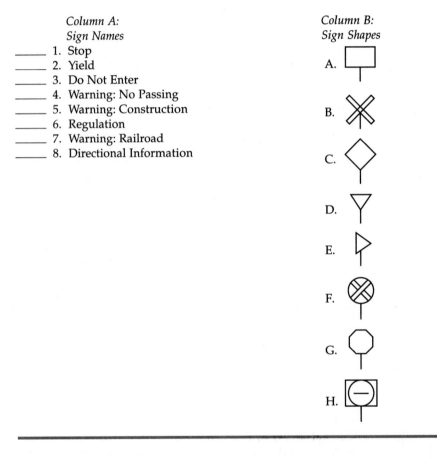

Column A:
Sign Names

_____ 1. Stop
_____ 2. Yield
_____ 3. Do Not Enter
_____ 4. Warning: No Passing
_____ 5. Warning: Construction
_____ 6. Regulation
_____ 7. Warning: Railroad
_____ 8. Directional Information

Column B:
Sign Shapes

A.

B.

C.

D.

E.

F.

G.

H.

Both the premise and response columns contain homogeneous material. Notice that sign colors have not been included in the response list. Mixing colors and shapes would break the homogeneity of the list and substantially and unnecessarily increase the complexity of the item. Although there are eight premises and eight responses, multiple premises match the same response in order to avoid providing clues. The matching format is an efficient way to measure the verbal information skills in this goal.

Keyed Items

Keyed items are similar in format to matching items. Like matching items, they include a set of responses for several different questions. Unlike matching items, the sets of premises and responses are placed one above the other, rather than side by side, to facilitate spacing on the page. The suggestions for writing matching items also apply to keyed items. Table 5.10 provides an example of this format. The homogeneous set of responses appears above the item statements. Each item asks for the name of a learning level, and to avoid clues, there are more responses than items. Notice that the responses are placed in the defined order of complexity from knowledge to evaluation to help students locate the answer they choose. The definitions, presented as items, are mixed in their order of complexity.

WRITING MULTIPLE-CHOICE ITEMS

Multiple choice is one of the selected-response test item formats, but it is given its own section in this chapter because it is the most popular and most frequently used of the selected-response formats. It commonly appears on classroom tests in all grade levels and subjects and is used almost exclusively on standardized tests. Although multiple-choice items can be formatted in

TABLE 5.10
Keyed Items That Measure Knowledge of Bloom's Levels of Learning

---

Directions: Define Bloom's levels of learning. The following items contain descriptions of Bloom's levels of learning. The responses name the levels of learning. Place the letter for the correct learning level in the blank before each description.

Responses
a. Knowledge
b. Comprehension
c. Application
d. Analysis
e. Synthesis
f. Evaluation

_____ 1. Divide a communication into its component parts and describe the relationship among the parts.
_____ 2. Use prescribed criteria to judge the quality of a product.
_____ 3. Recall the exact definition of a term.
_____ 4. Use rules and principles to solve a problem.
_____ 5. Paraphrase a given idea.

several ways, these items have certain common characteristics: an initial stem that introduces a problem or asks a question and a list of three or more alternative responses following the stem. The list of responses includes a correct answer and several incorrect answers.

The versatility of multiple-choice items has caused teachers to select this item format more than any other. A test made of such items can be an excellent diagnostic tool with the following advantages:

1. Multiple-choice items can measure both verbal information and intellectual skills. Within the intellectual skill category, they can measure all levels, from knowledge through evaluation.
2. These items can be used to focus students' attention on particular aspects of a problem.
3. By providing multiple responses, these items can force students to choose among alternatives that they may not have otherwise considered.
4. By instructing students to select the best answer, these items can measure students' ability to make fine discriminations.
5. Multiple-choice items permit the use of more than one correct alternative in a set of responses (e.g., Both A and B are correct).
6. They enable measurement of a wide range of content in a relatively short time period.
7. They can be reliably scored.
8. They are easily adapted for machine scoring and for computer administration and scoring.
9. Multiple-choice items are easily compiled into item banks.

At the same time, multiple-choice items have their limitations. First, like other objective items, they cannot directly measure attitudes or motor skills that require demonstration and active performance. However, they can measure the intellectual skills and verbal information that support attitudes and motor skills. Second, students who do not know the correct answer to a multiple-choice question can often guess correctly. Third, teachers usually have difficulty in thinking of plausible incorrect answers that reflect students' actual misconceptions and problems. Incorrect alternatives that are illogical to students diminish the diagnostic value of these items as well as the validity of the test results. The following suggestions for writing multiple-choice items relate to the stem, the responses, and the placement of items.

The Stem

The stem of a multiple-choice item poses a problem or asks a question; it can be formatted in several ways. The most common format is a complete sentence or question. Using this format, the stem resembles the short-answer item except that students select rather than write their answers. A second

popular format is the incomplete statement that students complete by selecting one of the responses. This stem format closely resembles the completion
item. A third widely used format embeds the stem in the directions. The stem
in this case poses a single problem for a series of items that contain only
responses. This format avoids repeating the same problem numerous times.
Table 5.11 contains an example of each of these stem formats.

Many teachers prefer stems that are complete questions or statements,
such as those in examples I and III, to the incomplete statement format
illustrated in example II. Complete questions and statements provide all the
information students need to answer the question before they consider the
response choices. Students may need to read an incomplete statement several
times before they understand what is being asked. The complete question or
statement is usually less confusing to them and, therefore, more efficient.
When the incomplete statement format is used, all information required to
formulate the responses from memory should precede the colon. In other
words, students should not need to read the responses in order to determine
the nature of the question.

Regardless of the format used for stems, the suggestions for writing them
are the same as those for writing other objective items. The wording should

TABLE 5.11
Common Formats for the Stem of a Multiple-Choice Item

I. *Complete Question*	What level of learning requires breaking a message into its parts and showing the relationships among the parts? a. Knowledge b. Comprehension c. Application d. Analysis e. Synthesis
II. *Incomplete Statement*	The level of learning that requires breaking a message into its parts and showing the relationships among the parts is called: a. Knowledge b. Comprehension c. Application d. Analysis e. Synthesis

III. *Common Stem Embedded in Directions*	Locate the nouns in the following sentences. Place the letter of the words that are nouns in the blank before the sentence.
	 _____ 1. The plump squirrels ran up and down.
	              a b c d
	 _____ 2. The band was energetic and noisy, if not melodious.
	              a b c d

be clear and precise, and the punctuation should be accurate. If negative words are necessary, they should be underlined or highlighted to ensure that they will not be overlooked. When embedding the stem in directions, the stem or problem should precede the directions for marking responses.

Responses

The responses for a multiple-choice answer consist of a correct answer and two or more incorrect answers, which are called *distractors* or *foils.* The responses can be designed using a variety of formats. They may be symbols, words, phrases, or sentences that are listed vertically beneath the stem (the traditional format). However, responses can also be embedded in contextual material, such as sentences, paragraphs, or articles. They can be the labeled parts of pictures, illustrations, or data tables. When testing young children or nonreaders, responses may be a series of pictures or illustrations. They may also consist of a set of real objects, such as rocks, tools, equipment, slides of specimens, or beakers of liquid. In addition, an object can have its parts labeled as responses. Examples of these response formats appear in Table 5.12.

Correct Responses   Good correct responses should be brief, clear, grammatically consistent with the stem, and clearly labeled with a number or letter. Information taken from the textbook should be paraphrased. Key words from the stem should not be repeated in the correct answer as this will provide a clue. When it is necessary to repeat a key word in the correct response, then the same word should be included in at least one of the distractors. An item should contain only one best answer, even when two or more of the options are correct. A single-answer choice can be used to combine multiple correct options into a best answer—for example, "Both A and B are correct" or "All of the above are correct." Although multiple correct answers add to the versatility of the multiple-choice item, do not use them simply because you cannot think of good distractors for the item.

Distractors   Ideally, an item should enable you to differentiate between students who know the correct answer and those who do not. Quality distractors that reflect common misconceptions and problems are more likely to help you make this differentiation. If unskilled students can immediately eliminate incorrect responses, the item is not functioning as it should.

Quality distractors are much more difficult to write than is the correct response. One problem is the difficulty of identifying misconceptions and problems students are likely to have. Plausible distractors can be found in the content of other enabling skills in the same or related lessons, in questions students ask in class about your presentations or their homework, and in students' written responses on pretests and practice exercises. If you analyze the nature of their questions and errors, you will be able to construct quality distractors that help detect persistent problems.

TABLE 5.12
Response Formats for Multiple-Choice Items

Type of Response	Test Items
1. Vertical list of symbols, words, phrases, or sentences following a stem	What is the name of a word that refers to a person, a place, or a thing? a. A noun b. A pronoun c. An adjective d. An adverb
2. Set of pictures or illustrations	Teacher says, "Color the square."

3. Labeled parts of an illustration or picture	*Directions:* Locate direction in a map. The map in Figure 1 has its edges labeled A, B, C, and D. Choose the edge that answers questions (1) through (4).

_____ (1) Which edge is north?
_____ (2) Which edge is west?
_____ (3) Which edge is south?
_____ (4) Which edges bound the northeast?

Figure 1

4. Labeled objects	At station 1 you will find a set of four leaves. Each leaf is labeled either A, B, C, or D. Which leaf was taken from a *deciduous* tree? (Assume four different leaves are labeled and placed at station 1.)

5. Embedded in sentences

Directions: Find the *verbs* in the following sentences. Write the letter under the verb in the space before the item number.

_____ 1. Beth <u>ran</u> <u>swiftly</u> <u>down</u> the <u>path</u>.
            A   B   C   D   E

_____ 2. <u>John</u> <u>felt</u> <u>superb</u> <u>after</u> the <u>award</u>.
            A   B   C   D   E

6. Embedded in paragraphs, stories, or articles

Directions: Read the following paragraph and decide whether you think all the sentences in it relate to the topic. If you find a sentence that does *not* fit the topic, underline it.

    I can see so many things on a hike in my neighbor- hood. The trees, bushes, and flowers in my neighbors' yards are always interesting because they change with the seasons. Sometimes I can even see people in their yards mowing the grass, pruning the bushes, or weeding the flower beds. I enjoy planting flowers. Once I saw workmen sawing down a large oak tree and loading it into a big truck. I decided to sit down and watch them work. It was interesting to see how the appearance of the yard and house changed as more and more of the tree was removed. I see something different every time I take a walk.

Even though you may have identified actual misconceptions to use as distractors, several factors can reduce their attractiveness to unskilled students. The use of unfamiliar words or ideas unrelated to the lessons, the lack of homogeneity in the list of responses, and grammatical incompatibility between the distractor and stem can cause students to avoid otherwise attractive distractors. One strategy for increasing the attractiveness of a distractor to students who are guessing is to repeat a key word from the stem in a distractor. Students who are using key words as clues to the correct answer will be drawn to this option.

Machine-Scored Responses   When machine-scored answer sheets are used, students can become confused and mark the wrong space. Marking errors affect both the validity and reliability of the scores. Labeling the test responses so that they correspond to the response letters and numbers on the answer sheet will reduce the probability of marking errors. For example, answer sheets are designed so that either letters or numbers can be used to identify responses. One type of response will appear at the top of the column, and the other type will appear within the circles, parentheses, or brackets beside the item number. The following example illustrates such an arrangement.

	Responses				
Item	*A*	*B*	*C*	*D*	*E*
1.	①	②	③	④	⑤
2.	①	②	③	④	⑤
3.	①	②	③	④	⑤

As students continue down the answer sheet, they will have more and more difficulty using the response codes across the top of the column (in this example, A, B, C, D, and E). Thus, using the response codes beside the items on the answer sheet when constructing your items is a better method. One caution should be made. If the options beside the item number are numbers (as illustrated), and the answer to the question is also a number between one and five, then students are likely to confuse the answer number with the response code number. The following example illustrates this problem:

Question: 1. $2 + 0 =$ _____   *Correctly coded:* 1. 1 2 ③ 4 5
　　　　　　 1. 0   *Misplaced:* 1. 1 ② 3 4 5
　　　　　　 2. 1
　　　　　　 3. 2
　　　　　　 4. 3
　　　　　　 5. 4

When numbers are used to code the responses, students will often darken the numbered space that matches the numeric answer rather than the correct answer code. For such items you should use the letter codes across the top of the column or match the answer code and response numbers if possible. Other types of items on the same test can require students to use the more convenient numbered responses.

Editing Items

Once the stem, correct response, and distractors are written, you should evaluate the entire item. Words repeated in each response should be removed and placed in the stem to avoid unnecessary redundancies. The set of responses should be sequenced logically using an alphabetical, chronological, numerical, or procedural order whenever possible. Additionally, you should check to see whether clues to the correct answer have been provided. The following mistakes are common in writing multiple-choice items that provide clues:

1. Only the correct response repeats a key word from the stem.
2. Distractors are consistently longer or shorter than the correct answer.
3. The correct answer is more technical and detailed than the distractors.
4. Answer options that indicate multiple responses, such as "Both B and D are correct," appear only when these options are the correct answers. If other test items do not include these options as distractors, students will quickly identify the pattern.
5. The correct response frequently appears in the same position in the set. Some teachers consider the first and last positions too obvious, and they tend to place the correct answer in the middle. Using a logical sequencing strategy for the responses, such as alphabetical or numerical, will help you avoid such detectable patterns.

Item Format and Placement

Practice in writing multiple-choice items will help you gain the skill necessary to write good diagnostic items. The following suggestions for item format and placement can help you develop multiple-choice tests that are easy for students to use.

1. List single-sentence, phrase, or word responses vertically beneath the stem and begin each response on a separate line.
2. Underline and code responses embedded in a sentence or paragraph.
3. Place the stem and all responses on the same page.
4. Place resource materials that cannot be included on the same page on a separate, unattached page for easy reference.
5. Label resource materials with titles, such as Figure 1 or Table 1, so they can be clearly identified in the directions.
6. Place directions for locating and using resource materials before the resource materials.

7. Place resource materials included on the same page before the related items.
8. For items requiring the use of real objects, set up work stations with numbers that correspond to related items on the test.
   a. Sequence work stations to match the order of items on the test.
   b. Label each object or part of an object to match a response code on the test paper.

WRITING OBJECTIVE TEST ITEMS

With the five primary criteria for writing test items and the formatting criteria for each type of objective test item in mind, you are ready to begin writing items. These test items should be linked to the behavioral objectives you have written for the enabling skills in your instructional goal. Selected behavioral objectives from the paragraph instructional goal contained in Table 3.6 are used to illustrate the link between objective test items and behavioral objectives. Table 5.13 contains sample test items for the selected objectives. The first column in the table includes the objective code and objective. The second column contains the types of items that can be created to assess students' acquisition of the skill, and the third column includes sample test items. When you have the behavioral objectives before you as a reference while you write items, you are more likely to create items that are congruent with them.

In addition to linking items to behavioral objectives, you should construct items at the appropriate language and complexity level for your students. Notice the three multiple-choice items at the end of Table 5.13. All three items can test the objective, "Locate the topic sentence in a paragraph." They differ, however, in the complexity of the subjects addressed, vocabulary level, sentence complexity, and the responding behavior. Elementary-age pupils would have difficulty responding to the first two items, and most senior high level students would be bored with the paragraph on baking cupcakes. Senior high students with lower reading abilities, however, may have more success with the second paragraph than the first.

You should also take care during item construction not to stereotype characters included in your scenarios. Notice in the second multiple-choice item that a boy, not a girl, is baking the cupcakes. Without conscious effort, many teachers illustrate girls helping around the house or providing an audience for others, while boys are depicted adventuring, earning cash, or being admired for some accomplishment.

ASSEMBLING AN OBJECTIVE TEST

With the test items written and each objective test designed to serve a particular purpose, you are ready to assemble your tests. The order in which items are placed on the test is important, and there are three criteria to consider before determining item order. These criteria include the following:

1. Ensure that the item order does not contribute to inadvertent test complexity for students taking the test.
2. Ensure that the item order does not provide students with unintended clues to the correct answers.
3. Ensure that the item order does not make scoring the test or analyzing students' performance more difficult than necessary.

TABLE 5.13
Objective Test Items Linked to Behavioral Objectives for the Instructional Goal "Write a Paragraph"

Objective Code	Item Format	Item
II.B.1 Given the term *topic sentence*, recall its functional characteristics.	Short Answer	• What purpose does the **topic sentence** serve in a paragraph? _____ • Why are **topic sentences** included in a paragraph? _____
II.F.1 Given an incomplete paragraph that is missing a topic sentence (time series, feelings, procedure, or description), write a topic sentence to introduce the paragraph.	Short Answer	**Write Topic Sentences.** For the following incomplete paragraphs, write topic sentences to introduce them. Please write your sentences in the blank provided on your answer sheet. 1. _____ One product that always surfaces on TV at Christmas is the "Clapper" that can turn off and on lights and appliances with a clap of the hands. Another relatively late comer, yet persistent cyclical product, is the "Chia Pet" that grows plants into an animal shape when seeds and water are added to the planter. A third holiday cycle product is the Remington "micro-shave" that "shaves as close as a blade or your money back." If the number of people who receive these products as gifts is proportional to the number of commercials aired for them around the holidays, a lot of clean-shaven men with bushy pottery pets who are clapping on and off their razors will ring in the new year.
II.B.2 Given the functional characteristics of a topic sentence, recall its name.	Completion	• The sentence that **introduces the subject** of a paragraph is called the _____ sentence. • The sentence that tells what a paragraph is about is called the _____ sentence. • The introductory sentence of a paragraph is called a _____ sentence.
	Alternate Response	• **T F** Topic sentences conclude the information presented in a paragraph. • **T F** Topic sentences introduce the subject of a paragraph.

(continued)

TABLE 5.13 Continued

Objective Code	Item Format	Item
II.A, II.B, III.A, III.B	Matching	**Characteristics of Paragraphs.** Column A contains descriptions of the types of sentences found in a paragraph, and Column B contains sentence names. Match each description with the type of sentence described. Place the letter of the sentence name in the space before each description. **You may use each name more than once or not at all.**

Column A

____ The middle sentences in a paragraph

____ Introduces the subject

____ Typically comes last in a paragraph

____ Elaborates the subject

____ Summarizes the ideas in a paragraph

____ Typically comes first in a paragraph

Column B

a. Compound Sentence

b. Concluding Sentence

c. Supporting Sentence

d. Topic Sentence

e. Complex Sentence

| | Keyed | **Recognizing Characteristics of Paragraphs.** Darken the letter indicating the type of sentence in the space beside the item number on your answer sheet. |

Types of Sentences

a. Complex Sentence

b. Concluding Sentence

c. Simple Sentence

d. Supporting Sentence

e. Topic Sentence

1. What sentence is used to elaborate the topic of a paragraph?
2. What sentence is most typically located first in a paragraph?
3. What sentence is used to summarize the ideas in a paragraph?
4. What sentence is typically located last in a paragraph?
5. What sentence is used to introduce the ideas in a paragraph?
6. What sentence is usually located in the middle of a paragraph?

| II.B.3 Given the term *topic sentence* and a list of possible functional characteristics related to the concept, choose those for a topic sentence. | Multiple Choice | 1. What is the function of a topic sentence in a paragraph?
    a. Elaborate the topic
    b. Conclude the topic
    c. Introduce the subject
    d. Provide transition within the paragraph

2. The purpose of the topic sentence within a paragraph is to provide:
    a. Indention
    b. Relevance
    c. An introduction
    d. An ending |

Objective Code	Item Format	Item

		3. What is the role of the topic sentence in a paragraph?
		  a. Present ideas on one topic
		  b. Introduce the subject
		  c. Sequence information
		  d. Express feelings

II.D.1 Given a complete paragraph, correctly indented, locate the topic sentence.	Multiple Choice (Modified)	**Locate Topic Sentence.** For each of the following paragraphs, locate the topic sentence and darken the letter preceding the topic sentence for that item on your answer sheet.
		
		1. Which of the following sentences is the topic sentence of the paragraph?
		
		  (A) The president's priority is to revive the nation's economy and citizens' incomes, and many economists believe he should start by changing some federal regulations. (B) Their research shows that agricultural subsidies cost consumers and taxpayers almost 6 billion dollars a year more than they benefit farmers. (C) Regulated minimum prices for milk cost consumers 500 million dollars a year, and sugar growers reap more than 1 billion tax dollars through price supports. (D) More startling, the federal paperwork to monitor our regulations costs Americans an estimated 100 billion dollars a year, and state and local governments add another 22 billion dollars. (F) The total cost of federal regulations is estimated at 392 billion annually, or $4,000 for each household. (G) It seems the president might benefit by examining federal regulations as one important step in economic recovery.
		
		Underline the **topic sentence** in the following paragraph.
		
		  To save our tax dollars, the president should change some laws. For example, the law that protects farmers' incomes costs us 6 billion dollars. The law that protects dairy farmers costs us 500 million dollars a year. The law that protects sugar farmers costs us more than 1 billion dollars every year. The paperwork we must complete to see that such laws are kept costs us about 100 billion dollars a year. The total cost of these laws is about 392 billion dollars each year, or $4,000 for each household. If the president really wants to save our tax dollars, he should look at these laws.
		
		Underline the **topic sentence** in the following paragraph.
		
		  Jerry is very good at baking cupcakes. He puts the mix from the box into a bowl. Then he adds an egg and some milk. He stirs it all with care. He pours his mix into cupcake papers that he has placed into a cupcake pan. While they are baking, he mixes the icing. As soon as they cool, he adds the icing. When he makes cupcakes, his father calls him "the chef."

To the degree possible, cluster together items that measure the same enabling skills and instructional goals. This strategy is beneficial for both examinees and teachers since it helps provide students with a context for items on the test, and it aids teachers in analyzing students' mastery of objectives and goals. When items for one goal are scattered throughout the test, they must be rearranged for mastery analysis.

Occasionally, however, items for one goal will need to be scattered throughout the test to avoid providing clues to the correct answer. One example where scattering items would be necessary is a comprehensive capitalization test that measures capitalizing the first word of a sentence, the pronoun *I*, proper nouns, and so forth. If you place these goal-based items together on a test, students could quickly detect the error patterns in the items.

Writing Directions for Objective Test Items

Directions help clarify for students what they are to do and how to indicate their chosen response. Two criteria are important for ensuring that directions aid rather than confuse students. The first relates to the order of information provided in directions and the second has to do with highlighting or separating directions from items on the test.

Order of Information.   The best order for presenting directions is the following:

1. State the skill measured.
2. Describe any resource materials required to answer the item (e.g., maps, charts, paragraphs).
3. Describe how students are to respond.
4. Describe any special conditions.

The following example directions illustrate this order:

> Capitalize proper nouns. The following paragraph contains both common and proper nouns. Locate the common and proper nouns that have capitalization errors and <u>underline</u> each noun that is wrong. Some sentences may have more than one mistake, and other sentences may have no errors.

Highlight Directions.   Directions should be highlighted to enable students to locate them easily before they begin to answer a set of questions and to review them while they are answering the questions. There are many ways to highlight directions, including placing a box around them, using all capital letters, using bold print, or changing the page margins. The following example illustrates the procedure.

> Create compound sentences. The following test items each contain two simple sentences. In the space provided just below each pair of sentences, write one compound sentence for each set of simple sentences. In writing your compound sentences, you may want to: (1) change some proper nouns to pronouns or (2) omit some of the words in the simple sentences for clarity. Take care that the coordinating conjunctions you choose clarify the relationships between the simple sentences.

FORMATIVE EVALUATION OF ITEMS

Even though objective items are written carefully, the first draft of a test may contain many errors. Before administering any posttest, a draft copy should be evaluated to locate and remove potential problems. Some errors in item construction are more critical than others. The primary consideration in evaluating an item is its congruence with the objective it measures. Without this congruence, the appropriateness of the item for target students, the clarity of item wording, and the accuracy of measures are irrelevant. The second most important consideration is the congruence of the item with the characteristics of target students. Once you are sure items meet these two criteria, next consider whether subtle biases exist and, if so, eliminate them. After bias, you should consider the clarity of each item. Finally, check to see whether the items are likely to result in accurate measures.

In addition to the criteria and their order of importance, consider who would be the best judge of each criterion. Table 5.14 lists each criterion and the individuals who can judge it. Like the criteria, the evaluators are listed in their order of importance because some may be better judges than others for each factor.

Congruence Between Items and Objectives

The primary consideration in evaluating a test item is its congruence with its behavioral objective. Colleagues are recommended as the primary evaluators of this criterion; authors are recommended as secondary reviewers because they will tend to see both what they intended to include in the item and what they actually included. This tendency may cause them to overlook important problems, whereas colleagues, unaware of authors' intentions, can judge only what is present. Whether the item is being evaluated by colleagues or by the author, the following procedure is recommended for judging the congruence between items and objectives.

TABLE 5.14
Criteria and Evaluations for Test Items

Criteria in Order of Importance	Evaluators in Order of Importance
1. Congruence between the item and the objective	1. Colleagues 2. Author
2. Congruence between items and target students' characteristics	1. Target students 2. Author 3. Colleagues
3. Freedom from bias	1. Colleagues 2. Group representatives
4. Clarity of items	1. Colleagues 2. Author 3. Target students
5. Accuracy of measures	1. Author 2. Target students 3. Colleagues

1. Place the objective and item side by side.
2. Break down both the objective and the item into their separate elements.
3. Relate comparable elements in the objective and item.
4. Judge whether comparable elements are congruent.

Table 5.15 illustrates the first two steps in the procedure. The objective contains three elements: conditions, behavior, and content. The item also contains three elements: response directions, content, and stimulus material.

The third step is to relate comparable elements in the behavioral objective and the item. The conditions in the objective should be compared with the stimulus material in the item; the behavior in the objective should be compared with the response direction; and the content in the objective should be compared with the content specified in the directions and in the stimulus material.

The fourth step is to judge whether comparable elements are congruent. Stimulus material in the item should match the material prescribed in the conditions. For example, if the conditions prescribe that students be given a paragraph with the topic, supporting, and concluding sentences out of order, then the stimulus material in the item should be an unorganized paragraph. The behavior in the response directions should be compatible with the behavior in the objective. For instance, if the objective behavior prescribed sequencing the sentences in a paragraph, then the response directions should include comparable behaviors, such as reorder, reorganize, rearrange, or even sequence. The content in the objective should match the content in both the directions and the stimulus material. If the content in the objective specified

TABLE 5.15
Objective and Items Separated into Elements

Objective	Item
Given a list of words containing nouns and other parts of speech, select words that are nouns.	*Directions:* Locate the nouns in the following list, and place a check beside each one. ___ 1. sun ___ 5. library ___ 2. run ___ 6. religion ___ 3. boy ___ 7. flower ___ 4. happy ___ 8. smooth
Objective Elements	*Item Elements*

Conditions: Give a list of words containing nouns and other parts of speech,
Behavior: select
Content: words that are nouns.
	Response directions:
	  Locate
	  place a check beside
	Content: nouns
	Stimulus materials:
	  ___ 1. sun ___ 5. library
	  ___ 2. run ___ 6. religion
	  ___ 3. boy ___ 7. flower
	  ___ 4. happy ___ 8. smooth

a chronological sequence, then the directions should specify chronological order and the sentences included in the paragraph should have a clear chronological relationship.

The elements for the objective and items on discriminating between nouns and other words are compared in Table 5.16. The objective elements are included in the first column, the item elements are included in the second column, and the judgments about congruence are included in the last column. Based on these comparisons, these items and their objective would be judged congruent.

Now consider the objective and sample items in Table 5.17. The first column contains the objective with its elements separated, the second column contains items that are not congruent with the objective, and the last column contains items that are congruent. Consider first the incongruent items. Notice that the conditions specified in the objective do not match the stimulus material. The conditions specify that the sets of simple sentences be complete with proper capitalization and punctuation. However, the items in the stimulus material are already combined into compound sentences. The stimulus material in the items in the third column are congruent: two separate simple sentences are presented.

Consider next the behavior specified in the objective and that included in the directions. The objective specifies that students rewrite the sentences, whereas the item directions in column two tell students to punctuate only.

TABLE 5.16
Comparison of Elements in Behavioral Objectives and Test Items

Objective Elements	Item Elements	Congruent?
Conditions Given a list of words containing nouns and other parts of speech,	*Stimulus Materials* 1. sun 2. run 3. boy 4. happy 5. library 6. religion 7. flower 8. smooth	*Yes* 1. A list of words is provided. 2. The list contains five words that are clearly nouns. 3. The list contains three words that clearly are not nouns.
Behavior select	*Directions for Responding* Locate Place a check beside	*Yes* 1. Students must discriminate between nouns and other words. 2. They can demonstrate their selections by checking the nouns.
Content words that are nouns.	*Directions* Nouns *Stimulus Materials* 1. board 2. run 3. boy 4. happy 5. library 6. religion 7. flower 8. smooth	*Yes* 1. The content in the objective and item directions is the same. *Yes* 1. Nouns included in the list refer to persons, places, things, and ideas; thus, they are representative of the content. 2. Other words presented represent verbs and adjectives.

Rewriting would require students to punctuate; select a coordinating conjunction, if needed; omit the ending punctuation in the first sentence; and omit the beginning capital letter in the second sentence. Obviously, rewriting the sentences is more complex than punctuating given compound sentences that already have these modifications. Thus, the behaviors in the objective and items are not congruent. The rewrite response specified in the third column is congruent with the objective.

Last, compare the content in the objective with that included in the items. The objective names compound sentences, the directions for the items in the second column specify compound sentences, and the stimulus material in the

TABLE 5.17
An Example Behavioral Objective with Incongruent and Congruent Test Items

Objective	Incongruent Item	Congruent Item
1. Given sets of two simple sentences, complete with their first words capitalized and their ending punctuation, <u>rewrite</u> them as <u>compound sentences</u>.	*Directions:* <u>Punctuate</u> the following <u>compound sentences</u>. 1. John is taller than Paul but Bill is taller than John. 2. Jill really enjoys the animals at the zoo but she likes the elephants best.	*Directions:* <u>Rewrite</u> the following sets of simple sentences to form <u>compound sentences</u>. a. John is taller than Paul. b. Bill is taller than John. 1. _____ _____ a. Jill really enjoys the animals at the zoo. b. She likes the elephants best. 2. _____ _____

second column contains compound sentences. Thus, these items and the objective are congruent in content even though they are not congruent in conditions and behavior. The items in the third column also contain content congruent with that in the objective.

Congruence Between Items and Students' Characteristics

After ensuring that items and objectives are congruent, you should next evaluate the appropriateness of items for given students. For this review you will need from one to three students typical of the target population. If you have a homogeneous group, the judgments of one student should suffice. However, if you have a heterogeneous group, you might want one student who is above average, one who is average, and one who is below average in achievement to review the items.

Ask the student reviewers to read the directions, to underline all words they do not understand, and to inquire about any instructions that are unclear. They should then read and respond to each item. Again, they should underline any words that are unfamiliar and inquire about questions that confuse them. Based on their inquiries and on their responses to items, you can locate unfamiliar, ambiguous, or awkward material and rephrase it as needed. Although it is not important for these students to know the correct answers to items, it is important for them to understand what they are to do (directions) and the meaning of the questions. If these students can respond as you intend, then you can assume that the items are appropriate for similar students in your classes. You might also ask these student reviewers to show you answer clues that they find in either the directions or the items because students can often find clues that escape teachers.

If you have no student reviewers available, review the items for their appropriateness yourself since you are the one most familiar with the characteristics of students in your classes. In addition, colleagues who teach similar students can be asked to evaluate the appropriateness of the language and examples for their students.

Freedom from Bias

The best persons to judge whether test items are free from bias are your colleagues and perhaps members of particular groups such as women, men, different racial or ethnic representatives, or different religious or political groups. It is important when asking colleagues and group representatives to evaluate test items for bias that you specifically tell them the purpose for the review. Bias can be so subtle that you are unaware that it is creeping into your items, and reviewers are unaware that it is in the items without consciously looking for it.

Clarity of Items

The fourth criterion is the clarity of items. The most appropriate evaluators are your colleagues. The items may appear clear and grammatically correct to you, but colleagues can independently judge what you actually wrote instead of what you intended to write. These evaluations are especially tricky because many reviewers do not simply indicate errors in items; instead, they often rephrase the items to suit themselves. This problem usually can be avoided by providing reviewers with the following instructions: First, mark *errors* in grammar and punctuation; second, eliminate unnecessary words or phrases; and third, only rephrase items that remain unclear after the first and second steps are complete.

The best colleagues to use for this review are those who judged the congruence between your items and objectives. This preliminary exercise helps clarify your intentions and helps critics avoid rewriting items so they are no longer congruent with the objective.

If colleagues are not available to assist with this review, evaluate the items for clarity yourself. This is best done after enough time has passed for you to forget what you intended to express.

Accuracy of Measures

You are the best person to judge the potential of your items for producing accurate measures. You are the only one who knows whether an item is novel or repeated; you know as well as anyone whether particular item formats are amenable to guessing behaviors; and you know the seating arrangements in your class and whether students can readily obtain answers from other students.

Item Formatting Criteria

Besides these five general criteria, remember that several recommendations were presented for formatting each type of objective item, and these suggestions also provide criteria for formatively evaluating your items in each format. The only individuals who can judge whether your items are correctly formatted are people familiar with the suggestions for writing each type of item. People unfamiliar with item formatting rules will tend to focus on the general clarity of your items rather than on their structure.

COMPUTER TECHNOLOGY

Formatting Items

There is a wide variety of objective-style item formats that you can use in your test item bank. The ParTEST (Economics Research, Inc., 1991) program enables you to enter the following types of items:

Written-response items: Completion items (called "fill-in" in the program) and short-answer items. The short-answer items are entered into the bank using the essay/problem item format.

Selected-response items: Alternative-response, multiple choice, and matching items.

Entering Test Items

You can create your test items working at the computer terminal. Following the program prompt, "Add Items to an Item Bank," you are asked to indicate the item bank you want to expand. Once you are in the correct item bank, you will be prompted to choose the item format you want. Using your list of behavioral objectives as a guide, select the test item format that is most congruent with the behavior specified in the objective. Once you select the format, the program prompts you to enter the type of information needed, when to enter it, and how to enter it. The program enables you to underline text and use boldface letters to call students' attention to particular aspects of a question or problem. Superscription and subscription are also available for those who choose to use it. Additionally, you can edit test items at any time after you have entered them.

Besides the items themselves, you can enter exhibits such as written passages, tables, charts, and figures that can be linked to a particular item or set of items in the bank. You can also specify a particular number of lines to be left blank either preceding or following a test item. Such blank areas provide even greater flexibility for attaching a picture or other reference material that is required to answer an item.

After entering each item, do not forget to complete the six user-descriptor categories for each one. You should be especially careful to enter the enabling skill codes since, as you saw in the previous chapter, these codes are extremely important for searching your item bank to locate items and assemble tests according to your tables of test specifications. You can experiment with writing and editing objective test items using the ParTEST demonstration program and the directions provided in your *Student Manual*.

Working as a Team

Your test bank should contain multiple items for each behavioral objective you specify for a unit of instruction. Having multiple items for each objective increases the flexibility and utility of your item bank. With the availability of item banking programs, teachers at a given grade level or who teach a particular subject area are beginning to work together as teams to create outstanding item banks. The teams perform the instructional goal analysis together and share the task of writing appropriate behavioral objectives for the instructional goal framework. They also agree to the name of the item bank and the descriptor categories they will use to classify items. Then, each member of the team creates an item bank that includes a few original test items for each of the behavioral objectives. When each member of the team finishes her or his bank, the team merges their test banks to create a large item bank that is almost always bigger and usually better than a bank that any single member of the team could create. (The user's manual describes how to merge item banks.) Finally, they copy the combined item bank to give each member of the team a personal copy.

Assembling a Test

Procedures for selecting particular test items for a test were described in the Computer Technology section of the preceding chapter. In addition to selecting items according to your table of test specifications, you have several options available for creating your test. You can: (1) specify a title for each test, (2) write directions for the overall test, and (3) write directions for particular sets of items on the test. As noted previously, the assembly program prints a copy of the test for you, prints an answer key for scoring the test, and prints a feedback report for students. With this complete set of test documents, you are ready to copy, administer, and score your test. You may also experiment with these tasks using the ParTEST demonstration program and your *Student Manual*.

SUMMARY

In writing objective items, your primary concerns should be the validity and reliability of the resulting scores. Important factors in achieving these qualities are the congruence between the item and the behavioral objectives and characteristics of target students, freedom from bias, the clarity of language used, and the accuracy of the measure. In addition to these primary considerations, there are several suggestions for writing items using each format.

Objective tests typically consist of written-response and selected-response items. Written-response formats include completion and short-answer items; selected-response formats include alternative-response, matching, keyed, and multiple-choice items. Several features of these items make them desirable for classroom tests. First, they can be used to measure several types and levels of learning. Second, a wide range of content can be tested in a relatively short period. Third, each format has several variations for flexibility. Finally, objective tests can be scored more reliably and quickly than can other types of tests.

Written-response items can be used to measure a variety of types and levels of learning, minimize the probability of students guessing correctly, and help teachers analyze misconceptions and problems that students have. These items can either be single statements and questions that require an answer or clusters of items with one set of common directions. Clustered items usually have words, phrases, pictures, or symbols that act as stimuli. Two drawbacks of written-response items are lengthy scoring time and the difficulty of scoring items objectively.

Selected-response items require students to select an answer from a given set of alternatives. They are versatile and can be used to measure several types and levels of learning. One unique feature is that a well-constructed selected-response item can measure students' abilities to see different facets of a problem and to make fine discriminations. These items can be administered quickly, and a wide range of material can be tested. In addition, they can be hand scored quickly, adapted for computer administration, or adapted for machine scoring. Formats include the alternative-response item that requires students to select one correct answer from two alternatives; the matching item in which students match a set of premises and responses; the keyed item that requires students to use the same set of responses for a group of items; and the multiple-choice item that requires students to choose responses from among three or more alternatives.

Table 5.18 contains a checklist that you can use for formatively evaluating objective test items. The first section of the checklist names criteria for evaluating test items regardless of their particular format, and the remaining sections name criteria for evaluating each type of objective test item.

Computer-based test item banks enable you to use all the objective-style items described in this chapter. In fact, they are quite easy to enter into an item bank and edit once they are entered. In addition to your items, you can link exhibits, such as passages, tables, or graphs, to the items. Many teachers work independently to create their item banks, but working in teams to create large, flexible item banks for a grade level or subject is becoming more popular.

TABLE 5.18
Checklist for Evaluating Objective Test Items

I. Internal Criteria for All Item Formats

<u>Yes</u> <u>No</u>   A. Congruence with Behavioral Objective: Are the items congruent with:
___ ___   1. The objective behavior?
___ ___   2. The objective content?
___ ___   3. The objective conditions?

<u>Yes</u> <u>No</u>   B. Congruence with Target Group: Are the items appropriate for learners related to the:
___ ___   1. Language and vocabulary level?
___ ___   2. Contexts and examples used?
___ ___   3. Problem complexity level?

<u>Yes</u> <u>No</u>   C. Freedom from Bias: Are the items free from biasing material related to:
___ ___   1. Cultural/ethnic groups?
___ ___   2. Gender issues?
___ ___   3. Religious issues?
___ ___   4. Political issues?

<u>Yes</u> <u>No</u>   D. Language Clarity: Do the items have:
___ ___   1. Correct grammar and spelling?
___ ___   2. Precise terms for the intended meaning?
___ ___   3. Correct punctuation?
___ ___   4. Directions that present, first, the skill measured; second, a description of any materials required to answer the item; and last, instructions for how to respond to the item (if applicable)?

<u>Yes</u> <u>No</u>   E. Accuracy of Measures: Are the items:
___ ___   1. Novel or different than those used during instruction or on previous tests?
___ ___   2. Free from clues that enable students to guess the correct answer?
___ ___   3. Formatted in a manner that is familiar to students?

II. Formatting Criteria for Written-Response Test Items

<u>Yes</u> <u>No</u>   A. Completion Test Items
___ ___   1. Are only key words removed from a statement?
___ ___   2. Is all information required to answer a question presented *before* any blanks are provided for answering the question?
___ ___   3. Has the possibility of several reasonable answers been eliminated?
___ ___   4. Have all clues to the correct answer been eliminated?
___ ___   5. Have key statements taken from instructional materials been paraphrased?

<u>Yes</u> <u>No</u>   B. Short-Answer Test Items
___ ___   1. Do blanks for each response suggest the length of anticipated answers?
___ ___   2. Are the units required for an answer specified (e.g., lbs., yds.)?
___ ___   3. Are directions for a cluster of items appropriate for all items in the set?
___ ___   4. Does a statement of the skill measured (e.g., "Identify nouns") precede explanations of materials provided *and* directions for answering the question(s)?

III. Formatting Criteria for Selected-Response Test Items

Yes No A. Alternative-Response Items
___ ___   1. Are judgments to be made explained in the directions?
___ ___   2. Do answer choices logically match the judgments?
___ ___   3. Does each statement include only one item to be judged?
___ ___   4. Are statements worded positively?
___ ___   5. Are questions avoided that purposefully may trick or mislead students?
___ ___   6. Are clues to the correct answer avoided?

Yes No B. Clustered Alternative-Response Items
___ ___   1. Is every item in the set congruent with the response directions?
___ ___   2. Is only one of the two options clearly correct?
___ ___   3. Do instances contained in the set adequately represent all aspects of the content in the objective?
___ ___   4. Are clues through patterns of answers, number of items, length of items, and so on avoided?

Yes No C. Matching Items
___ ___   1. Do directions indicate the skill measured?
___ ___   2. Do directions indicate the basis for matching elements in the columns?
___ ___   3. Does the column on the left side (premise) contain homogeneous content (from one general area)?
___ ___   4. Does the column on the left side (premise) contain the more difficult or lengthy reading material?
___ ___   5. Are the responses located in the right-hand column?
___ ___   6. Are the responses homogeneous?
___ ___   7. Are the responses as brief as possible, and more brief than the elements in the left column?
___ ___   8. Are the responses logically ordered in the list (e.g., alphabetically, chronologically, procedurally)?

IV. Formatting Criteria for Multiple-Choice Test Items

Yes No A. The Stem
___ ___   1. Does the stem contain all the information required for the learner to formulate a correct answer from memory?
___ ___   2. Are any negative words in the stem underlined for emphasis?
___ ___   3. Do common stems that are embedded in directions contain, first, the skill measured; second, a description of the item if needed; and third, instructions for how to mark answers?

Yes No B. The Correct Response: Does the correct response:
___ ___   1. Grammatically fit the stem?
___ ___   2. Contain paraphrased rather than textbook language?
___ ___   3. Have only one correct or best answer?
___ ___   4. Contain the options "All of the above are correct" or "None of the above are correct" only when logical?
___ ___   5. Contain "All of the above are correct" and "None of the above are correct" for *both* correct responses and for distractors?
___ ___   6. Avoid key terms from the stem whenever possible?

(continued)

TABLE 5.18 Continued

Yes	No		7. Appear similar to the distractors in:
—	—		a. Technical detail?
—	—		b. Specificity?
—	—		c. Length?
—	—		8. Vary in position within the set of responses across a group of items?

NA	Yes	No	C. The Distractors: Do the distractors:
—	—	—	1. Reflect common misconceptions and problems?
—	—	—	2. Logically answer the problem posed in the stem?
—	—	—	3. Grammatically fit the stem?
—	—	—	4. Repeat key words from the stem to attract students who are guessing?
—	—	—	5. Avoid repeating common words or phrases?

NA	Yes	No	D. The Set of Responses: Does the set of responses:
—	—	—	1. Contain homogeneous material/ideas?
—	—	—	2. Reflect logical ordering (e.g., alphabetical, chronological, procedural)?
—	—	—	3. Avoid the confusion between the numeric responses 1 through 5 and the response codes one through five?
—	—	—	4. Use the response codes directly adjacent to question numbers on answer sheets?

PRACTICE EXERCISES

I. **Criteria for Writing Objective Test Items**
   A. Name two quality characteristics of all test items.
   B. List the five primary criteria for producing test items to ensure these quality characteristics.
   C. Five criteria can be used while writing test items to help ensure that the items result in valid and reliable measures of students' achievement. In the following exercise, match each recommendation to its criterion.

   Criteria
   a. Congruence between items and behavioral objectives
   b. Congruence between items and characteristics of target students
   c. Freedom from bias
   d. Clarity of items
   e. Accuracy of measures

Recommendations
_____ **1.** Include only one question in each item.
_____ **2.** Use a response format for items that is appropriate for the prescribed behavior.
_____ **3.** Exclude extraneous material from the item.
_____ **4.** Construct items to minimize guessing correctly.
_____ **5.** Use a familiar context.
_____ **6.** Select or develop resources that accurately reflect the conditions.
_____ **7.** Select instances of content that are clearly examples and nonexamples.
_____ **8.** Use vocabulary that is readily understood.
_____ **9.** Include instances that cover the scope of content that students are likely to encounter.
_____ **10.** Select an item format that is familiar.
_____ **11.** Use correct grammar and punctuation.
_____ **12.** Construct items to reduce the probability of guessing the correct answer.
_____ **13.** Use contexts that are free from cultural, racial, and sexual stereotypes.

D. Match the physical descriptions of test items in Column A with the names of objective test items in Column B. Place the letter preceding the name of the item in the space preceding the description. You may use any answer more than once or not at all.

Column A	*Column B*
_____ **1.** A test item that contains a stem and three to five alternative responses.	a. Alternative response
	b. Completion
_____ **2.** A set of test items preceded by a single list of three or more response options that are used to answer all items in the set.	c. Keyed
	d. Multiple choice
	e. Short answer
_____ **3.** A complete statement with one or two key terms omitted and replaced with a blank.	f. Modified alternative response
_____ **4.** A complete statement that students are to judge as true/false, correct/incorrect, fact/fiction, etc.	
_____ **5.** Two columns of elements that students are to equate.	
_____ **6.** An item for which students must supply a term, phrase, number, sentence, or other brief response.	

E. The following items are statements about formatting criteria for objective test items. For each statement, identify the type of item described. You may use each answer more than once or not at all, or you may have more than one answer for an item.

Responses
a. Alternative-response items
b. Clustered alternative-response items
c. Completion items
d. Keyed items
e. Matching items
f. Multiple-choice items
g. Short-answer items

Statements
_____ **1.** Remove only key words from a statement.
_____ **2.** Avoid specific determiners.
_____ **3.** Ensure that the directions for a cluster of items are appropriate for all items in the set.
_____ **4.** Avoid designing questions to trick students.
_____ **5.** Eliminate the possibility of several reasonable answers.
_____ **6.** Include only one idea to be judged in each statement.
_____ **7.** Specify the units (e.g., lbs, inches, miles) required in an answer.
_____ **8.** Avoid double negatives.
_____ **9.** Ensure that the premises are homogeneous and contain the more difficult reading material.
_____ **10.** Ensure that responses are homogeneous, brief, and logically ordered.

F. The following items relate to formatting criteria for multiple-choice items. Place the letter corresponding to the best answer in the blank beside the question number.

_____ **1.** Which of the following characteristics is *unique* to multiple-choice items?
  a. A complete statement that asks a question or poses a problem
  b. A complete statement that is correct in grammar and punctuation
  c. A set of three or more responses from which a student must select the answer
  d. An item that matches the conditions, behavior, and content specified in the objective
  e. Both c and d are correct

_____ **2.** What part of a multiple-choice item contains the problem statement?
  a. Distractor
  b. Foil
  c. Responses
  d. Stem

_____ **3.** Which of the following terms is used for incorrect responses?
  a. Distractor
  b. Foil
  c. Response set
  d. Stem
  e. Both a and b are correct

_____ **4.** Which of the following statements reflects a *positive* feature of multiple-choice items? They can be used to measure
   a. Various types of learning including attitudes.
   b. Students' ability to make fine discriminations.
   c. A student's unique or novel solutions to a problem.
   d. Both a and b are correct.

_____ **5.** Which of the following statements reflects *limitations* of multiple-choice items? They *cannot* be written to
   a. Measure complex intellectual skills.
   b. Measure several levels of learning.
   c. Diagnose misconceptions and problems students have.
   d. Avoid the probability of students guessing the correct answer.
   e. Measure the intellectual skills that are subordinate to a motor skill.

Directions: The following items may have more than one correct answer. Indicate the responses that apply.

_____ **6.** Which of the following characteristics does a good stem have?
   a. It is congruent with the behavioral objective.
   b. The vocabulary, the context, and the complexity are appropriate for the students being tested.
   c. It clearly poses the question or problem.
   d. The grammar and punctuation are correct.

_____ **7.** Which of the following suggestions would help you develop correct responses for multiple-choice questions?
   a. Repeat key words from the stem in the answer.
   b. Use statements as they appear in the textbook.
   c. Do *not* use such options as "Both A and B are correct" as the answer.
   d. Ensure that the answer is grammatically consistent with the stem.

_____ **8.** Which of the following suggestions would help you write good distractors?
   a. Construct responses that are plausible to students.
   b. Ensure that distractors are grammatically consistent with the stem.
   c. Include common misconceptions and problems students may have with the skill measured.
   d. Construct them to be either longer or shorter than the correct answer.

_____ **9.** Which of the following characteristics does a good set of responses have?
   a. They are homogeneous.
   b. They all contain the same key words from the stem.
   c. When the responses are numerals, the answer code should also be a numeral for consistency.
   d. They are placed in a logical order.

_____ **10.** Which of the following statements describes clues commonly found in multiple-choice items?
   a. Distractors are consistently longer or shorter than the correct answer.
   b. Using such responses as "Both A and C are correct" only when this is the correct response.
   c. Key words in the stem appear in one or more of the distractors.
   d. The correct answer frequently appears in the same position in the set.

_____ **11.** Which of the following suggestions would help you arrange multiple-choice items on a test?

    a. List responses horizontally on a line.

    b. Place resource materials between the directions and the questions when they are on the same page.

    c. Place resources that require a lot of space, or that are needed for questions on several pages, on a separate, unattached page.

    d. For economy, place some or all of the responses on the page following the one containing the stem.

II. Evaluate Objective Test Items

  A. The left column contains behavioral objectives taken from Table 3.6; the center column contains target grade level(s) for students, and the right column contains sample objective test items. Using the primary criteria, judge the quality of the item presented. In judging the item, make the following responses:

    a. Flawed by objective congruence

    b. Flawed by target student congruence

    c. Flawed by bias

    d. Flawed by clarity

    e. The item has no apparent flaws

Objective	*Grade Level*	*Item*
IV.A.1 Given the term *concluding sentence,* recall its physical characteristics.	Primary (K–2)	**1.** Where is the concluding sentence typically located in a paragraph? _____
IV.A.2 Given the physical characteristics of a concluding sentence, recall its name.	Intermediate (3–6)	**2.** The sentence that comes last in a paragraph is called the _____ sentence. **3.** **T F** The last sentence in a paragraph is called a topic sentence.

IV.B.1 Given the term *concluding sentence,* recall its function characteristics.	Middle School (6–8)	**4.** The purpose of the concluding sentence in a paragraph is to:
		  a. Introduce the subject
		  b. Elaborate the subject
		  c. Entertain the reader
		  d. Summarize the ideas

IV.D.1 Given a complete paragraph, correctly indented, locate the concluding sentence.	High School (Basic)	**5.** Mark the letter before the **concluding sentence** in the following paragraph on your answer sheet.

    (a) Each time we elect a president, we turn into a nation of advice oracles. (b) From every rooftop and laptop, someone's shouting out another set of instructions for the president-elect. Words of council, caution, and exhortation fill every newspaper and talk show. (c) At heart, we are a know-it-all society.

    6. The purpose of the concluding sentence in a paragraph is to:

      a. Introduce the subject

      b. Elaborate the subject

c. Entertain the reader

d. Summarize the ideas

7. Mark the letter before the **concluding sentence** in the following paragraph on your answer sheet.

(a) Mr. Garcia, the janitor, works very hard at school. (b) He arrives at 5:30 A.M., before anyone else, to start his day. (c) By mid-morning he often walks two miles completing his chores. (d) It is hard for him to com- plete his schedule of tasks each day because students and teachers always call him to solve their problems around the school. (e) By the end of the day, he is not finished and is always exhausted, but he is also proud of the positive contributions he makes for so many people.

B. For the next four examples, evaluate the congruence between the objectives and test items. Use the responses below to indicate your judgments. You may use more than one response for each item.

a. The objective and item(s) *are* congruent.

b. The objective *conditions* and item *stimulus material* are *not* congruent.

c. The objective *behavior* and item *response directions* are *not* congruent.

d. The objective *content* and item *directions* and/or *stimulus material* are *not* congruent.

Objective	*Item*
1. Given a list of words containing common and proper nouns with all words capitalized, identify the proper nouns.	*Directions:* Place a check (√) in the space before the <u>proper nouns</u> in the following list. _____ 1. french fries _____ 2. Burger King _____ 3. Whopper _____ 4. Big Mac _____ 5. hamburger _____ 6. McDonalds

2. Given a specified liquid capacity amount,

state an <u>equivalent amount of liquid</u> in the specified unit.

Directions: For each of the liquid measures named in column A, identify an equivalent amount for the unit of measure specified in column B.

	A		B
1.	16 tablespoons	= _____	cup(s)
2.	3 cups	= _____	quart(s)
3.	2 quarts	= _____	gallon(s)
4.	8 quarts	= _____	gallon(s)

3. Given a lower case letter,

write the <u>corresponding upper case letter</u> from memory.

Say, "For each of the letters I write on the board, circle the capital letter that matches it on your paper."

Letters on Board	*Responses on Answer Sheet*				
f	B	G	E	F	C
a	B	C	P	T	A
l	I	L	J	T	M

4. Given simple sentences containing proper nouns without the proper nouns capitalized,

locate the proper nouns.

Directions: Underline the words in the following sentences that should be capitalized.

1. he arrived early at school with his father.
2. they all enjoyed the picnic.
3. Barney went to the game with Mary and Fred.
4. seattle is located in the northwest.

C. Evaluate the formatting of the following completion, alternative-response, matching, and keyed items. Write any problems you identify on a separate sheet.

1. Completion Items

   Directions: Reading a map. Complete each statement by writing the missing word or words in the blank provided.

   a. The top of the map is traditionally _____ .

   b. The _____ contains the names of symbols used on a map.

   c. The _____ is used to locate towns on a map.

   d. The _____ of town names is included in an _____ .

2. Short-Answer Items

   Directions: Reading a map. Use the map in Figure A to answer the following questions. Write your answer in the blank before each question. (Assume that the map is appropriate for target students.)

   _____ miles a. Use the mileage scale and your ruler to estimate the number of miles between Carter and Doyle.

   _____ miles b. How far is it from Hyatt to Bryne?

   _____ c. What is the name of the city to the north of Jackson?

3. Alternative-Response Items

   Directions: Reading a map. Circle T if the statement is true and F if it is false.

   T F a. A map legend identifies symbols used in a map and can be used to locate particular cities.

   T F b. The direction arrow on a map does not usually point north.

   T F c. The map legend always contains the direction indicator and the mileage scale.

4. Matching Items

   Directions: Reading a map. Place the letter from Column B in the space before the matching item in Column A.

Column A	*Column B*
_____ 1. Legend	a. A sphere that contains a map of the earth
_____ 2. Grid	b. An alphabetical list of places contained on a map
_____ 3. Index	c. A key or legend used to identify symbols on a map
_____ 4. Globe	d. An organization that provides maps
_____ 5. AAA Automobile Club	e. A matrix of lines running through the map top to bottom and side to side

   5. Keyed Items
   Directions: Reading a map. The items in Column A describe aids that can be used to interpret maps. Identify the aid in Column B that each item describes. You may use each of the responses in Column B more than once or not at all.

	Column A	*Column B*
_____	**1.** An alphabetical list of cities and towns	a. Legend
_____	**2.** Lines that divide the face of the map into blocks	b. Grid
		c. Index
_____	**3.** A key that contains map symbols and their names	d. Mileage scale
_____	**4.** A table that contains the names of major cities and the distances between them	e. Mileage table
_____	**5.** A line marked off in miles	
_____	**6.** An aid used to locate specified towns	
_____	**7.** An aid used to estimate distance between small towns	
_____	**8.** An aid used to locate types of highways	

III. Write Objective Items

Using your own paper, write two objective test items for each of the following behavioral objectives taken from the compound sentence examples in Table 3.9. Select any objective item format that you believe will appropriately assess the behavior stipulated in the objective. Before beginning to write the items, imagine a particular group of students. Then write the items so they are appropriate in vocabulary, content, and complexity for the group. You may want to use the item writing criteria in Table 5.18 to guide your item development. Compare your items with the sample ones included in the Feedback section; they were created for students in the upper elementary grades.

Code	Behavioral Objective
III.B.1	Given the term *coordinating conjunction,* state its role or function.
III.B.2	Given a description of the function of the coordinating conjunction, name the word described.
III.D.1	Given a compound sentence, locate the coordinating conjunction.
III.D.2	Given a compound sentence with various elements of the sentence underlined and numbered (e.g., subject, verb, comma, and coordinating conjunction), locate the coordinating conjunction.
III.E.1	Given two simple sentences and a coordinating conjunction, judge whether the conjunction is logical.
III.E.2	Given (a) two simple sentences joined by a comma and a blank space and (b) a list of alternative coordinating conjunctions, choose the most logical conjunction.
III.F.1	Given two simple sentences separated by a comma and a blank space, write an appropriate coordinating conjunction in the space.

IV. **Enrichment**

Using behavioral objectives you have developed from your own content area, complete the following activities:

A. Write appropriate objective test items. Use the ParTEST demonstration program to create your objective items. See the *Student Manual* for directions.

B. Evaluate your test items for:
1. Congruence with the behavioral objectives
2. Congruence with the characteristics of your target students
3. Bias of any kind
4. Clarity (grammar, punctuation, precision)
5. Accuracy of measure (novelty, clues)
6. Formatting suggestions

C. Ask a colleague to evaluate your items and directions and suggest revisions. Have the evaluator compare the items with your objectives.

D. Have any available target students read the items and mark any directions and items that they do not understand. Additionally, have them circle any words that they cannot define.

E. Use your colleague's suggestions and students' remarks to revise the directions and items.

FEEDBACK

I. **Criteria for Writing Objective Test Items**

A. Two quality characteristics of all test items are *validity* of decisions made based on test scores and *reliability* of test scores.

B. The five primary criteria are congruence with behavioral objective, congruence with target students' characteristics, free from all bias, clarity, and accuracy.

C. Designing Test Items

1. d	**5.** b	**9.** a	**13.** c
2. a	**6.** a	**10.** b	
3. d	**7.** a	**11.** d	
4. e	**8.** b	**12.** e	

D. Descriptions and Names of Test Items

1. e	**4.** a
2. c	**5.** d
3. b	**6.** f

E. Formatting Objective Items

1. c	**6.** a
2. a	**7.** g
3. all formats	**8.** a
4. all formats	**9.** e
5. c	**10.** d, e, f

F. Formatting Multiple-Choice Items

1. c	**7.** d
2. d	**8.** a, b, c
3. e	**9.** a, d

4. b   **10.** a, b, d
5. d   **11.** b, c
6. a, b, c, d

II. **Evaluating Objective Test Items**
   A. Behavioral Objectives and Objective Test Items
      1. b   **5.** b
      2. e   **6.** a
      3. e   **7.** c
      4. a

      Note: The Hispanic gentleman in the scenario is stereotyped as a janitor. Notice that changing the word *janitor* to *principal* works very well in the paragraph.
   B. Objectives and Test Items
      1. b
      2. a
      3. c
      4. b, d
   C. Evaluate Objective Items. The sample items reflect the following problems:
      1. Completion Items
         a. The item is vague and many answers are possible.
         b. The blank is at the beginning of the item.
         c. The blank is at the beginning of the item, and there are two correct answers (index, grid).
         d. The first blank is placed toward the beginning of the item and does not require a key term. Additionally, the word *an* preceding the second blank suggests that the response begins with a vowel.
      2. Short-Answer Items
         a. This item contains no major problems.
         b. This item does not indicate how students are to determine the mileage. Instructions about whether they should use a mileage table, mileage scale, or miles printed along the highway should be added.
         c. This item should be clarified as several towns are likely to be north of the one specified. Adding such information as "the first town north of Jackson" would help clarify the item.
      3. Alternative-Response Items
         a. The statement includes more than one idea.
         b. The item contains an unnecessary negative word.
         c. The item contains the determiner *always* and two ideas.
      4. Matching Items. These items contain many problems.
         a. The directions:
            (1) do not explain the contents of the premise or response list.
            (2) do not describe the basis for matching the items.
            (3) refer to columns that are not titled.
            (4) do not specify if a response can be used more than once.
         b. The premises:
            (1) are shorter than the responses.
            (2) do not all have more than one plausible answer for each premise.
            (3) are not homogeneous. Although both premises and responses are all related to maps, the sets are not homogeneous.

5. Keyed Items. The examples have these weaknesses:
   a. The questions and the answers are placed in the same order.
   b. Item four contains the word *table*, which matches the word *table* in the answer, thus providing a clue to the answer.

III. Write Objective Items

Code	Behavioral Objectives	Items

III.B.1 Given the term *coordinating conjunction*, state its role or function.

1. What **purpose** does the coordinating conjunction serve? _____
2. What is the role of the coordinating conjunction in a compound sentence? _____

III.B.2 Given a description of the function of the coordinating conjunction, name the word described.

3. The word that links two simple sentences to form a compound sentence is called a/an _____ .
4. The term that bridges two simple sentences and shows the relationship between them is called a/an _____ .

III.D.1 Given a compound sentence, locate the coordinating conjunction.

Directions: Underline the **coordinating conjunction** in the following sentence(s).

5. The boat rolled and twisted in the storm, and the passengers feared for their lives.
6. The cat passed by the butcher shop for breakfast each morning, but today there was no one there.

III.D.2 Given a compound sentence with various elements of the sentence underlined and numbered (e.g., subject, verb, comma, and coordinating conjunction), locate the coordinating conjunction.

Directions: **Locate Coordinating Conjunctions** in the following sentences. Mark the letter beneath the coordinating conjunction on your answer sheet beside the item number.

7. Jill had to finish painting the deck before she was
   A   B   C
   allowed to talk with her friends, so she painted
                                     D
   faster than she ever painted before.
          E

8. The pep rally was fun on Friday, because all the girls
       A   B
   and boys who play on any team were honored by
              C   D
   the student body.
                E

III.E.1 Given two simple sentences and a coordinating conjunction, judge whether the conjunction is logical.

Directions: Evaluate the coordinating conjunctions in the following sentences. If the conjunction **logically connects** the two simple sentences, mark **(1)** on your answer sheet beside the item number. If the conjunction forms an **illogical link,** mark **(2)** on your answer sheet.

9. Everyone was gathered on the lawn outside the science museum, but there was a lunar eclipse tonight.
10. The earth's shadow moved slowly across the moon's surface, and soon the entire moon was dark.

III.E.2 Given (a) two simple sentences joined by a comma and a blank space and (b) a list of alternative coordinating conjunctions, choose the most logical conjunction.

Directions: **Evaluate Coordinating Conjunctions.** For each of the following sentences, choose the **best** coordinating conjunction from the list beneath the sentence. Mark the letter of your choice beside the item number on your answer sheet.

11. Benjamin Franklin is known for discovering electricity, _____ he also was renowned for editing Poor Richard's Almanac.
   a. and
   b. because
   c. however
   d. thus

12. Deep sea fishing can be a lot of fun, _____ you must be careful not to get too much sun.
   a. and
   b. because
   c. but
   d. moreover

III.F.1 Given two simple sentences separated by a comma and a blank space, write an appropriate coordinating conjunction in the space.

Directions: **Supply Coordinating Conjunctions.** Read each of the following compound sentences carefully and identify the relationship between the two sentences. Based on this relationship, write the best coordinating conjunction in the blank to link the two sentences.

13. We are going to plant a rose garden this spring, _____ the price of roses is too high.

14. Sara was a wonderful pitcher, _____ she occasionally hit a home run.

REFERENCE

Economics Research, Inc. (1991). *ParTEST user's manual.* (pp. 40–61). Costa Mesa, CA: Author.

SUGGESTED READINGS

Ebel, R. L., & Frisbee, D. A. (1991). *Essentials of educational measurement* (5th ed.) (pp. 133–187). Englewood Cliffs, NJ: Prentice Hall.

Gronlund, N. E., & Linn, R. L. (1990). *Measurement and evaluation in teaching* (6th ed.) (pp. 143–210). New York: Macmillan.

Hopkins, C. D., & Antes, R. L. (1990). *Classroom measurement and evaluation* (3rd ed.) (pp. 174–245). Itasca, IL: F. E. Peacock.

Hopkins, K. D., Stanley, J. C., & Hopkins, B. R. (1990). *Educational and psychological measurement and evaluation* (3rd ed.) (pp. 224–266). Englewood Cliffs, NJ: Prentice Hall.

Kubiszyn, T., & Borich, G. (1990). *Educational testing and measurement* (3rd ed.) (pp. 68–96). Glenview, IL: Scott, Foresman/Little, Brown.

Mehrens, W. A., and Lehmann, I. J. (1991). *Measurement and evaluation in education and psychology* (4th ed.)

(pp. 106–149). New York: CBS College Publishing.

Oosterhof, A. (1990). *Classroom applications of educational measurement* (pp. 87–174). Columbus, OH: Merrill.

Popham, J. W. (1990). *Modern educational measurement* (2nd ed.) (pp. 235–264). Englewood Cliffs, NJ: Prentice Hall.

Sax, G. (1989). *Principles of educational and psychological measurement and evaluation* (3rd ed.) (pp. 93–128). Belmont, CA: Wadsworth.

Wiersma, W., & Jurs, S. G. (1990). *Educational measurement and testing* (2nd ed.) (pp. 41–64). Boston: Allyn and Bacon.

CHAPTER 6

Evaluating Group Performance

OBJECTIVES

- Set expectations for the distribution of scores, measures of central tendency, and measures of variability based on:
  a. The complexity of the tasks measured
  b. The achievement characteristics of the group
  c. The perceived quality of the instruction and the test
- Describe the group's performance by:
  a. Creating a frequency distribution
  b. Calculating measures of central tendency
  c. Calculating measures of variability
- Evaluate the group's performance by comparing the anticipated to the calculated measures.

After you have administered and scored your test, you are ready to evaluate a group's performance. To evaluate performance, you need to calculate several measures of the group's performances and then compare these measures with criteria and standards you establish. You need to answer one basic question: <u>Are these measures reasonable given the circumstances?</u> There are <u>four main factors to consider</u> when establishing criteria for judging the reasonableness of the measures, including:

1. The complexity of the tasks measured
2. The achievement characteristics of the group
3. The quality of the instruction
4. The quality of the test

The first two factors are relatively fixed, that is, your instruction is not likely to change the nature of the task or the characteristics of the group. However, the quality of your instruction and test can make a difference in how students perform.

When estimating levels of performance, teachers generally assume that their instruction was effective and their test was good. Therefore, expectations for group performance are set using only the complexity of the tasks and the group's characteristics. Should the group's performance not meet the expected levels, then the instruction and test are usually reviewed to locate the cause for the discrepancy.

Three main areas of indicators are used to describe a group's test performance: (1) the location and shape of the raw score distribution; (2) measures of central tendency, including the mean, median, and mode; and (3) measures of variability, including the range and standard deviation. The following sections present procedures for calculating and interpreting these measures to describe a group's performance. In addition, there are procedures for identifying criteria and setting standards for evaluating a group's performance. Practically speaking, calculating these group performance indicators by hand is tedious and unnecessary. However, basic paper-and-pencil methods are illustrated to ensure that you understand the logic behind the indices. Without this understanding, your ability to interpret the data would be affected. Whenever possible, obtain these indices from machine-scoring services and spend your time interpreting rather than calculating. When machine scoring is not feasible, use an inexpensive hand calculator with the capacity to compute measures of central tendency and variability from raw scores.

DESCRIBING THE DISTRIBUTION OF TEST SCORES

To describe the distribution of test scores, you can use either a frequency table or a frequency polygon.

Creating a Frequency Table

Table 6.1 shows a frequency table for hypothetical objective test scores. The first column lists all the possible scores, starting with the highest and ending with the lowest. A second column indicates the number of times each score occurs. The third column indicates frequencies, or the total number of times each score appears. Notice that the term *raw score* and the symbol X are used to represent the number of items each student answered correctly. These widely accepted terms are used to represent students' individual scores throughout the chapter. Summarizing the scores on such a table will permit you to determine the highest and lowest scores quickly and to identify the score distribution pattern.

Creating a Frequency Polygon

A *frequency polygon* is a graph that provides the same information as a frequency table. Plotting a graph of the frequency of scores will help you determine the shape of the distribution, which you can then use to interpret the results. A frequency polygon has a horizontal axis and a vertical axis placed

TABLE 6.1
Frequency Distribution of Objective Test Scores

	Raw Scores X	Tally	Frequency
Highest Possible Score	20	ЖHT	5
	19	III	3
	18	II	2
	17	II	2
	16	II	2
	15	III	3
	14	I	1
	13	I	1
	12	I	1
	•		
	•		
Lowest Possible Score	0		

at right angles to each other. Each point on the horizontal axis represents a possible raw score, and each point on the vertical axis represents the frequency or the number of times each score occurs. To complete the graph, place a dot at the intersection of each raw score and its frequency. Figure 6.1 shows how the frequency of one score is plotted. The dot at the intersection of a raw score of 5 on the horizontal axis and the frequency 4 on the vertical axis indicates that 4 students in the group answered 5 of 20 items correctly.

After you have plotted the frequency of each raw score, connect the dots to complete the polygon, as shown in Figure 6.2. This graph indicates that (1) everyone in the group answered more than eight and fewer than twenty items correctly, (2) one person correctly answered nine items and two correctly answered ten items, and (3) thirteen correct items was the most frequently earned score.

Figure 6.3 contains a frequency polygon for the raw scores summarized in Table 6.1. The slashes at the beginning of the horizontal axis indicate that no students earned raw scores from 0 to 11. The graph begins with a raw score of 12 and ends with 20, the maximum score possible.

Table 6.1 and Figure 6.3 both illustrate the distribution of raw scores for the class. To interpret this distribution, you need to understand the different shapes that distributions can take and what these shapes indicate.

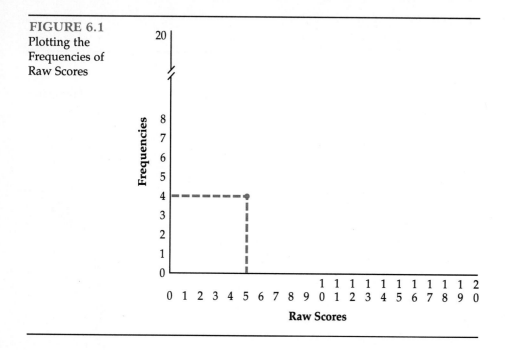

FIGURE 6.1
Plotting the
Frequencies of
Raw Scores

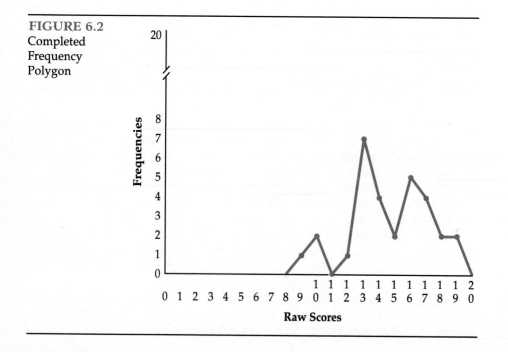

FIGURE 6.2
Completed
Frequency
Polygon

FIGURE 6.3
Frequency
Polygon for
Students' Test
Scores in
Table 6.1

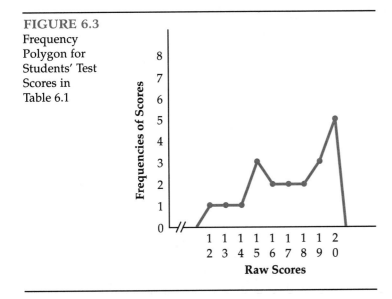

General Shapes of Test Score Distributions

A test score distribution reflects one of several commonly observed shapes. It can be *symmetrical, skewed, unimodal, bimodal,* or *multimodal.* The normal distribution (sometimes called the *bell-shaped curve*), the rectangular distribution, and the U-shaped distribution illustrated in Figure 6.4 are all symmetrical. In a normal distribution, most scores are near the center of the distribution. The low and high ends of the score scale contain very small frequencies of scores. The rectangular distribution, while also symmetrical, indicates that an equal number of students received each score. There is no common area of perform-

FIGURE 6.4
Symmetrically Shaped Test Score Distributions

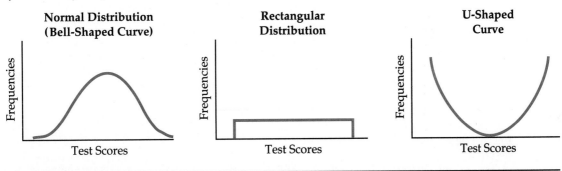

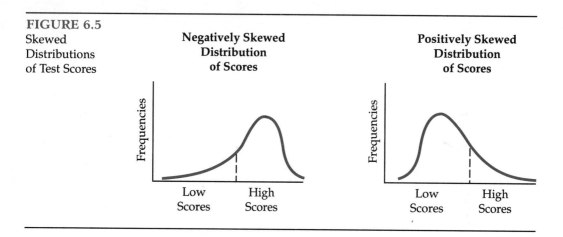

FIGURE 6.5
Skewed
Distributions
of Test Scores

ance. In the U-shaped distribution, a large number of scores occur at the low
and the high ends, but none or few occur in the middle of the distribution.

In a skewed distribution, more scores occur at either the high or low end
of the score scale. When most scores occur at the high end of the scale, the
distribution is *negatively skewed.* Notice that in the negatively skewed distribution in Figure 6.5, the highest frequencies appear to the right of the midpoint on the raw score scale. If the curve were folded in half at the midpoint,
the two sides of the distribution would not be equal. A negatively skewed
distribution indicates that more students received high scores than low scores.
For this reason, it is sometimes called a *mastery curve.*

A distribution in which most scores appear toward the lower end of the
score scale is *positively skewed*. A positively skewed distribution is illustrated
to the right in Figure 6.5. Such a distribution indicates that a test was difficult
for most of the class.

Distributions can also be unimodal, bimodal, or multimodal. The raw
score that occurs most frequently in a distribution is called the *mode*. If only
one score appears most frequently, the distribution is unimodal. The bell-
shaped curve in Figure 6.4 and the skewed distributions in Figure 6.5 are
examples of unimodal distributions. If two scores, some distance from each
other on the scale, have higher frequencies than the scores surrounding them,
the distribution is bimodal. The center distribution in Figure 6.6 represents a
bimodal curve. The right-hand illustration represents a multimodal distribution in which more than two scores have atypically high frequencies compared to the scores around them.

Interpreting a Score Distribution
Using Its Location and Shape

To interpret test results, consider both the location and the shape of the
distribution on the raw score scale. The distribution can spread out across the

FIGURE 6.6
Unimodal, Bimodal, and Multimodal Distributions of Test Scores

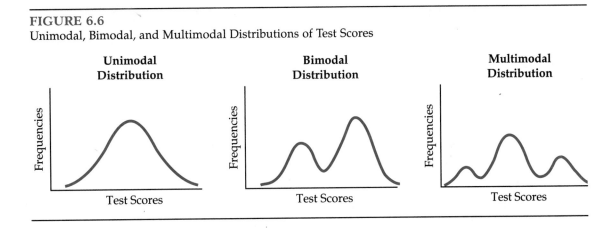

range of possible test scores, or it can cover only a small portion of the scale. Tall, narrow shapes indicate homogeneous group performance; a wide distribution of scores reflects heterogeneous performance. High, narrow distributions located at the upper end of the score scale represent high achievement; those toward the lower end of the scale suggest inadequate achievement. Consider the shapes and locations of the score distributions in Figure 6.7. Although all three distributions are unimodal, bell-shaped curves, each reflects a different level of performance. The distribution in illustration A is short and wide, reflecting heterogeneous group performance. The one in illustration B is high and narrow and located toward the high end of the scale, indicating homogeneous, high test performance. Such a distribution suggests that the group was made up of high-achieving students, or that the skills tested were very easy for the group, or that the instruction was very effective. The distribution in illustration C is also tall and narrow but located toward

FIGURE 6.7
Width and Location of Score Distributions

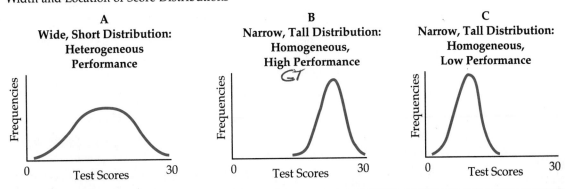

the lower end of the scale. This distribution indicates that the group contained low-achieving students, or that the skills tested were too complex for the group, or that the test, the instruction, or both were inadequate.

Evaluating a Group's Performance Using the Score Distribution

In order to use the observed score distribution to evaluate a group's performance, you need to judge whether the observed distribution is reasonable, given the circumstances. Two factors can be used to establish reasonable levels of performance: the complexity of the tasks measured by the test and the achievement characteristics of the group. Using your perceptions related to these two factors, estimate a reasonable score distribution for the situation. When the distribution you observe does not resemble one you anticipate, investigate the cause.

Consider the class that took the test illustrated in Figure 6.3. Suppose that based on their previous achievement the class was described as heterogeneous, and the skills measured by the test were described as relatively easy. In this case, you would expect to see a relatively wide distribution of scores to reflect the group's heterogeneity. However, since the tasks were considered relatively easy, the shape should be negatively skewed. Now, review the distribution obtained for the test in Figure 6.3. As expected, the distribution is relatively wide. It is also located in the top half of the raw score scale, making it negatively skewed. This means that the instruction was effective and the test good, as anticipated.

A score distribution considered reasonable for one group may not be acceptable for another. For example, if the class taking the test contained only high achievers, the teacher would undoubtedly be disappointed with the score distribution in Figure 6.3. Instead of this shape, the teacher would have expected a narrow, tall distribution located toward the high end of the scale. This mismatch between the anticipated and obtained distributions would cause the teacher to question the instruction and test.

USING MEASURES OF CENTRAL TENDENCY

Measures of central tendency that identify the center of a score distribution include the mean and the median. The *mean* is a group's average raw score, and the *median* is the central point in the distribution of scores.

Calculating the Mean and Median

To calculate the mean for a set of raw scores, add all the scores together and divide the sum by the number of students in the group. For example, if raw scores for a group of five students were 5, 6, 7, 8, and 9, you would calculate the mean as follows:

1. Add   2. Divide
    5      $\dfrac{35}{5} = 7$ 7 is the mean score for the set of scores.
    6
    7
    8
  +9
  ——
  35

The following formula is used to represent this calculation:

$$\overline{X} = \frac{\Sigma X}{N}$$

In the formula, the symbol $\overline{X}$ represents the mean; the symbol Σ means to sum the raw scores, represented by X; and N is the number of scores, or students, in the group.

The median is a point that divides the distribution of scores in half. You can approximate a median by locating the middle score in an ordered set of scores. For example, the median for the scores 5, 6, 7, 8, and 9 is the middle score, or 7. For an uneven number of scores, the median is simply the middle score. The median for an even number of scores is a point halfway between the two middle scores. For example, the median for the scores 5, 6, 7, 8, 9, and 10 is halfway between 7 and 8, which are the two middle scores. Thus, the median for this set of scores is 7.5.

When there are several tied scores in a distribution, calculating the median is a bit more complex. In this situation, each score is considered to extend .5 point below and .5 point above the actual scores. For example, a score of 18 would extend from 17.5 to 18.5. The score 17.5 is called the *lower real limit* for the observed score 18. The median is calculated using the following formula:

$$\text{Median} = L + \frac{\dfrac{N}{2} - \text{Sum of students below the score containing the median}}{\text{Frequency of students at the score containing the median}}$$

where:

L = The lower real limit of the raw score containing the median
N = The number of students in the group

Table 6.2 illustrates the use of this formula to calculate the median for a set of scores.

Now, review the data for the test in Table 6.1 and calculate the mean and median. To find the mean, add all the raw scores together (ΣX). You should have five scores of 20, three scores of 19, two scores of 18, and so on. Next,

TABLE 6.2
Calculating the Median

X	f	
20	I	1. The number in the group is 26 and half this number is 13. Therefore, the median will divide the scores such that 13 scores are below and above it.
19	I	
18	III	2. Count from the bottom of the distribution to locate the raw score that contains the thirteenth and fourteenth scores. In this example, the raw score 16 contains these scores.
17	IIII	
16	JHT	
15	IIII	3. The median is then calculated using the formula:
14	III	
13	II	
12	I	
11	I	
10	I	
N = 26		

$$\text{Median} = 15.5 + \frac{\frac{26}{2} - 12}{5} = 15.5 + \frac{1}{5} = 15.5 + .20 = 15.70$$

divide the sum of the scores by 20, the number of students in the group. Your calculation should look like this:

1. Sum scores.

   20 + 20 + 20 + 20 + 20 + 19 + 19 + 19 + 18 + 18 + 17 + 17 +
   16 + 16 + 15 + 15 + 15 + 14 + 13 + 12 = 343

2. Divide the sum by the number of students.

$$\overline{X} = \frac{343}{20} = 17.15$$

The group's average score on the test is 17.15.

You may have already concluded that multiplying each raw score by its frequency and then adding the products is a faster way to obtain ΣX. Whenever you use a frequency table to calculate a mean, you can save time by doing some simple multiplication, as illustrated in Table 6.3.

Because there is an even number of scores (20), the median will be halfway between the two middle scores. The tenth score from the top of the distribution is 18, and the tenth score from the bottom is 17. Thus, the median is halfway between 18 and 17, or 17.5.

TABLE 6.3
Calculating the Mean and Median Using a Frequency Table

1. Multiply each score by its frequency and sum the products.

Raw Scores X		Frequency f		Product fX
20	×	5	=	100
19	×	3	=	57
18	×	2	=	36
17	×	2	=	34
16	×	2	=	32
15	×	3	=	45
14	×	1	=	14
13	×	1	=	13
12	×	1	=	12
			$\Sigma X =$	343

Median → (at raw score 17)

2. Divide ΣX by the number of students (20).

$$\overline{X} = \frac{343}{20} = 17.15$$

Relating the Mean and Median to the Distribution of Scores

To interpret measures of central tendency, compare (1) the relative positions of the mean and median in the distribution, (2) their distance from the highest earned score, and (3) their distance from the highest possible raw score.
The illustrations in Figure 6.8. show the relative positions of the mean and median in three distributions. In distribution A, which is normal and symmetrical, the mean and median occupy the same central point. In a negatively skewed distribution, like the one in example B, the atypically low scores in the group produce a mean lower than the median. A positively skewed distribution, as the one in example C, has a few extremely high scores that raise the mean above the median. These illustrations show that the mean is influenced by the size of each raw score in the distribution, whereas the median is not. Extreme scores raise or lower the mean, but they have no effect on the median. In the latter case, very high or very low scores are simply scores, regardless of their values. The relative position of the mean and median in a distribution helps you determine whether its shape is symmetrical or skewed, and if skewed, in what direction.

FIGURE 6.8
Relative Positions of the Mean and Median in Score Distributions

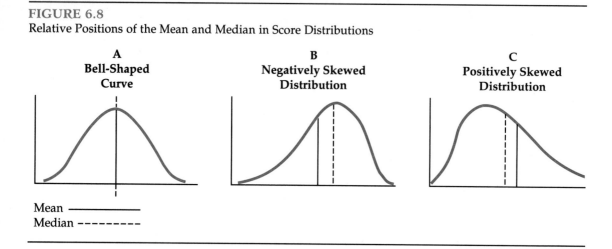

Mean ——————
Median - - - - - - -

To assess the difficulty of a test for a group, compare the mean, the highest earned score, and the highest possible raw score for the test. When the mean is relatively close to the highest earned score, you have evidence that the overall group's performance was rather similar. Additionally, when the highest earned score is the same as, or close to, the highest possible score, you have evidence that the group performed similarly and well on the test. This situation is illustrated in example A of Figure 6.9.

When the mean score is close to the highest earned score (X_H), yet the highest earned score is quite a bit below the highest possible score, then a different interpretation would result. This finding would indicate that the group's performance was rather homogeneous and that the test was rather difficult. This situation is illustrated in example B of Figure 6.9.

Another pattern could emerge in which the highest earned and the highest possible scores were the same, or similar, yet the mean score was quite a bit below them on the scale. This result, illustrated in example C, would tend to reflect heterogeneous group performance on relatively complex tasks.

Evaluating a Group's Performance

To evaluate the group's performance using measures of central tendency, you need to estimate reasonable values for the mean and median and compare the estimated scores with those observed. In deciding what to expect, you should again consider the difficulty of the tasks measured and the achievement characteristics of the group. For example, if you have a homogeneous group of high achievers and relatively complex tasks, then you would expect to find the mean and median relatively close to the highest possible score. When the tasks measured are judged to be relatively easy for such a group, you might

FIGURE 6.9
Describing a
Group's Perfor-
mance Using the
Mean, Highest
Earned Score,
and Highest
Possible Score
on a Test

A Total possible points = 50
   Highest earned score (X_H) = 50
   Mean score ($\overline{X}$) = 43 (86%)

Raw
Scores   0   10   20   30   40   50
                                                              $\overline{X}$ X_H

B Total possible points = 50
   Highest earned score (X_H) = 43 (86%)
   Mean score ($\overline{X}$) = 38 (76%)

Raw
Scores   0   10   20   30   40   50
                                                   $\overline{X}$ X_H

C Total possible points = 50
   Highest earned score (X_H) = 50 (100%)
   Mean score ($\overline{X}$) = 38 (76%)

Raw
Scores   0   10   20   30   40   50
                                               $\overline{X}$ X_H

expect to see these scores located even closer to the highest possible score.
Your expected mean and median would be lower for a homogeneous, average
group and even lower for a homogeneous, below-average group. When setting expectations for the mean and median, you should select an area in which
these scores will fall rather than particular scores because estimating precise
scores would be very difficult. When the mean and median fall outside a
reasonable area, you have reason to question the instruction and test.

Now, use the measures of central tendency to evaluate the group's performance on the test illustrated in Table 6.3. As previously described, the
group is heterogeneous, and most of the tasks are relatively easy. These two
factors would lead you to anticipate that:

1. The mean and median will be relatively close to the highest earned and
   the highest possible scores.
2. The mean will be lower than the median to reflect the anticipated negatively skewed curve.

Comparing the mean (17.15) and the median (17.5) with the highest
earned score (20) and the highest possible score (20), you find that the obtained scores fall within the area anticipated. Comparing the relative positions of the mean and median, you find that the mean is lower than the
median, which reflects the anticipated negatively skewed distribution. Therefore, the measures of central tendency reflect that the group's performance on
the capitalization test is reasonable given the circumstances.

USING MEASURES OF VARIABILITY

The variability of performance among students in the group is indicated by the range and standard deviation. The range is set by the two extreme scores, and the standard deviation is a measure of how widely the scores in a group differ from the average score. Both measures reflect the amount that individual performances differ and thus describe the homogeneity or heterogeneity of a group's performance.

Calculating the Range

Some measurement specialists define the range (R) as the difference between the highest score and the lowest score earned on a test. The formula for this calculation is:

$$\text{Range } (R) = X_H - X_L$$

Other specialists define the range as including all observed scores in the set. Using this definition, the formula for calculating the range is:

$$R = (X_H - X_L) + 1$$

The latter procedure ensures that the range extends to include all scores. For example, if the highest observed raw score on a test is 28 and the lowest is 12, then the range would be:

$$R = 28 - 12 = 16$$
$$R = (28 - 12) + 1 = 17$$

Whether you use the first or second calculation method is a matter of personal choice, although most teachers use the first one. For all practical purposes, the interpretation of the index would be the same.

Interpreting the Range

One caution should be made about using the range to interpret a group's performance. Because the range is based only on the two extreme scores in a set, an atypical high or low score for the group will distort your interpretation. Atypical scores are called *outliers;* they reflect the performance of an atypical student rather than overall group performance. Thus, before calculating and interpreting the range, determine that the high and low scores are not extreme compared to the other scores in the distribution. If you find an outlier score on either end of your distribution, eliminate it and calculate the range using the next closest score to it in the set.

There are some rules of thumb you can use to interpret a range. A range that covers about one-quarter or less of the total raw score scale generally reflects homogeneous performance. Thus, if a test contains 40 items and the range is about 10, then the group's performance can be considered homogeneous. As the width of the range increases, so does the heterogeneity of the performance. A range spanning about one-third of the raw score scale indicates a somewhat heterogeneous group performance; one that spans about one-half of the raw score scale signals a very heterogeneous group performance. Therefore, for a 40-item test, a range of about 13 (or one-third of 40) would reflect somewhat heterogeneous group performance; a range of about 20 would reflect very heterogeneous performance.

As previously noted, the group's achievement characteristics and the complexity of the tasks measured should be considered when using the range to evaluate a group's performance on a given test. Again considering the data from the test in Table 6.2, you would expect to see a range that spans between one-third to one-half the raw score scale because the group is heterogeneous. One-third of the raw score scale is 6.6, or 20 (items) divided by 3. The observed range is 8, or 20 minus 12. Therefore, the observed range comes close to the expected range, indicating that the group's performance is rather heterogeneous. Like the performance indicators previously described, the range reflects that the group's overall test performance was as anticipated.

Calculating the Standard Deviation

Because all scores in the distribution and the mean are used in calculating the standard deviation, the procedure is more complex. It involves the following series of steps:

1. Calculate the mean score $(\overline{X})$.
2. Subtract the mean score from each raw score (X) to find the deviation score (x).
3. Square each deviation score (x^2).
4. Add together all the squared deviation scores (Σx^2).
5. Divide the sum by the number of scores (N).
6. Find the square root of the quotient.

The formula for calculating the standard deviation is:

$$\sigma = \sqrt{\frac{\sum(X - \overline{X})^2}{N}} \quad \text{or} \quad s = \sqrt{\frac{\sum(X - \overline{X})^2}{N-1}}$$

The first formula, using the symbol σ for the standard deviation and N in the denominator of the formula, is used when the group tested is the target population, which typically is the case for classroom teachers. The second formula, using the symbol s for the standard deviation and $N - 1$ in the denominator, is used when the group tested represents only a sample of the target population rather than the population itself. For the purpose of describing the variability of students' performance on a classroom test, it does not matter whether you use the population or the sample formula. The difference between the indices obtained using the two formulas will be negligible and not cause you to reach a different conclusion about the variability of your class on a test.

Although the procedure for calculating the standard deviation appears complicated, you can easily master it with practice. Moreover, most hand calculators can automatically square numbers and calculate square roots.

Working through an example will help you understand the procedure. Given a set of five raw scores (5, 6, 7, 8, and 9), rank and list the scores from highest to lowest. Next, add all the scores and divide by the number of scores to obtain the mean. The sum of the five scores is 35, and the mean is 7, or 35 divided by 5. The next step is to calculate the deviation score (x), and the easiest way to do this is to set up a table of columns as follows:

Raw Scores (X)		Mean $(\overline{X})$		Deviation Score x
9	–	7	=	2
8	–	7	=	1
7	–	7	=	0
6	–	7	=	–1
5	–	7	=	–2

Notice that the mean score, 7, is subtracted from each raw score. The resulting differences are the deviation scores.

The reason for the next step, squaring each deviation score, now becomes obvious. The sum of 2, 1, 0, –1, and –2 is 0. Zero divided by the number of scores is also 0. To eliminate this problem, change all the negative deviation scores to positive numbers by squaring each score. Next, the squared deviations should be summed to obtain Σx^2. Your calculations should appear as follows:

$(X - \overline{X})$	x	x^2
9 – 7	2	4
8 – 7	1	1
7 – 7	0	0
6 – 7	–1	1
5 – 7	–2	4
	$\Sigma x^2 =$	10

Now you can calculate the standard deviation using the formula:

$$\sigma = \sqrt{\frac{\Sigma(X - \overline{X})^2}{N}}$$

You already have the numerator, 10, which is the sum of your x^2 column. Divide 10 by 5, which is the number of scores in the set. Your formula now is:

$$\sigma = \sqrt{\frac{10}{5}} = \sqrt{2} \quad \text{or} \quad s = \sqrt{\frac{10}{4}} = \sqrt{2.5}$$

Use your calculator to find the square root of 2, which is 1.41. This standard deviation of 1.41 for this set of scores is a measure of the distance between the scores and the mean of those scores. Because the computation includes the step where the sum of deviations from the mean is divided by the number of scores, the standard deviation *has the effect of* being the average amount that the scores deviate from the mean.

Table 6.4 presents the calculations needed to figure the standard deviation for the test data illustrated in Tables 6.1 and 6.3. The procedure illustrated is the one typically used when there are several tied scores in a data set. The first column (X) contains each raw score, and the second column (f) indicates the frequency of each raw score. The third column (x) includes the deviation of each raw score from the mean, or $X - \overline{X}$, and the fourth column (x^2) contains the squared deviation scores. The last column (fx^2) includes the squared deviation scores multiplied by the frequency with which each occurs in the data. Summing the fx^2 column, you will obtain the numerator in the formula, or $\Sigma(X - \overline{X})^2$. This sum divided by the number of students in the group yields the value 6.128, and the square root of this value is the standard deviation, or 2.48. If you were to use $N - 1$ as the denominator in the formula, then the standard deviation, s, for the test would be 2.54, a difference of .06 from σ.

Interpreting the Standard Deviation

Two factors influence the size of the standard deviation: the range and the distribution of scores within the range. Because both the range and the standard deviation are measures of a group's variability, larger ranges will produce larger standard deviations. A wide range and standard deviation both reflect heterogeneous performance, and narrow ones reflect performances that are more similar.

TABLE 6.4
Calculating the Standard Deviation for the Test Data in Tables 6.1 and 6.3

X	f	x	x^2	fx^2	
20	5	2.85	8.12	40.61	$\sigma = \sqrt{\dfrac{\Sigma(X - \overline{X})^2}{N}}$
19	3	1.85	3.42	10.27	
18	2	.85	.72	1.45	
17	2	−.15	.02	.05	$= \sqrt{\dfrac{122.56}{20}}$
16	2	−1.15	1.32	2.65	
15	3	−2.15	4.62	13.87	
14	1	−3.15	9.92	9.92	$= \sqrt{6.128}$
13	1	−4.15	17.22	17.22	
12	1	−5.15	26.52	26.52	$= 2.48$
				$\Sigma(X - \overline{X})^2 = 122.56$	

For a given range size, the size of the corresponding standard deviation will vary based on the distribution of scores within the range. For example, the ranges and mean scores are the same in the score distributions illustrated in Figure 6.10, yet the score patterns within these distributions are very different. These different score patterns produce different standard deviations.

Most scores are close to the mean score in the rather bell-shaped curve in example A. In distributions in which there is a short distance between the mean and most other scores in the set, the standard deviation will be small for the range. A relatively small standard deviation for a given range reflects rather similar performance for most students in the group. The scores in the rectangular distribution, illustration B, are farther from the mean. The standard deviation for such a distribution will be larger than one for a distribution in which most of the scores are clustered in one area. A rectangular distribution reflects heterogeneous performance within the range with no area of similar performance. The bimodal, U-shaped distribution in example C produces the largest standard deviation because the distance between the mean and other scores in the set is greater. This distribution reflects two divergent groups within the class.

You can estimate the distribution of scores within the range using a few quick calculations and comparisons. The largest possible standard deviation for any given range is the range divided by two. Such a large standard deviation would reflect a U-shaped distribution (see example C in Figure 6.10). Although so large a standard deviation is unlikely, you can use this figure as a basis of comparison for the obtained standard deviation value. The following rules will help you determine the variability of a group's performance within the range.

1. A standard deviation close to one-half of the range indicates that the group's performance is very diverse within the range.
2. A standard deviation close to one-third of the range reflects scores that are dispersed throughout the range.
3. A standard deviation spanning one-quarter or less of the range indicates that most scores are clustered within an area.

For example, if the range were 20, an observed standard deviation approaching one-half this value, or 10, reflects two diverse groups in the class. An observed standard deviation of around 6.6, or one-third of the range, reflects a more even distribution of scores throughout the range. However, a standard deviation of about 5 or less, one-quarter of the range, reflects a majority of scores clustered within an area.

Evaluating a Group's Performance

To evaluate a group's performance using the standard deviation, you should first decide what value you expect. Using the previously obtained information for the test data in Tables 6.1 and 6.3, you would undoubtedly expect a

FIGURE 6.10
Three Score
Distribution
Shapes Having
the Same Mean
and Range but
Different Stan-
dard Deviations

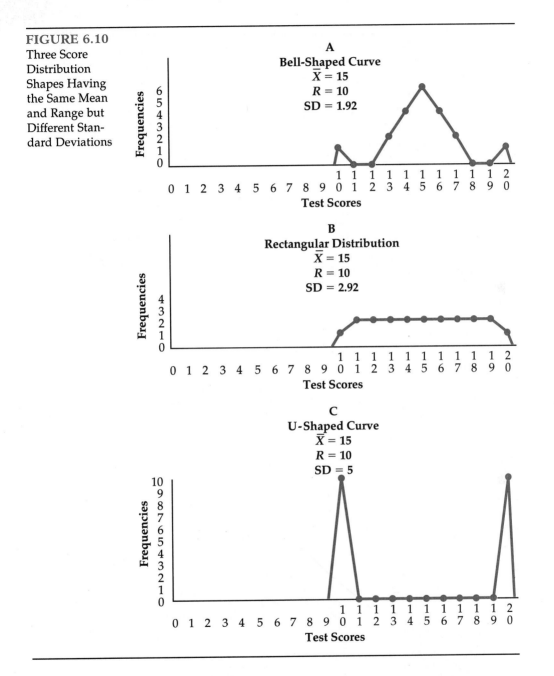

A
Bell-Shaped Curve
$\overline{X} = 15$
$R = 10$
$SD = 1.92$

Frequencies

Test Scores

B
Rectangular Distribution
$\overline{X} = 15$
$R = 10$
$SD = 2.92$

Frequencies

Test Scores

C
U-Shaped Curve
$\overline{X} = 15$
$R = 10$
$SD = 5$

Frequencies

Test Scores

standard deviation somewhere around one-third to one-quarter of the range
because, although the group is heterogeneous, the tasks were relatively easy.
Given the range of 8 for the test, you would expect the standard deviation to
be between 2.66 and 2, rather than between 2.66 and 4. Once you have selected

an area for the standard deviation, you should compare it with the one obtained. The standard deviation calculated for the test is 2.48 (see Table 6.4), and the expected standard deviation is about 2.66. Therefore, the scores are distributed as anticipated and reflect the heterogeneous nature of the group on relatively easy tasks.

The machine-scoring services available for selected-response tests eliminate the tedium of calculating measures of central tendency and variability. These scores are provided on the computer printout of student performance and need only be compared with those you anticipate.

An Example

Figure 6.11 contains raw scores for the paragraph unit posttest prescribed in the table of test specifications in Table 5.2. The objective portion of the posttest contains 43 items covering behavioral objectives I.A.4 through IV.E.4. (Objectives I.F.1 through I.F.4 on writing paragraphs were not scored with the

FIGURE 6.11
Group Performance Measures for a Paragraph Unit Posttest

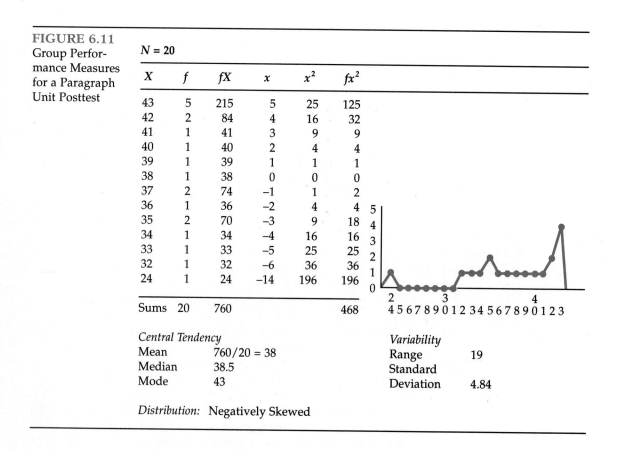

$N = 20$

X	f	fX	x	x^2	fx^2
43	5	215	5	25	125
42	2	84	4	16	32
41	1	41	3	9	9
40	1	40	2	4	4
39	1	39	1	1	1
38	1	38	0	0	0
37	2	74	−1	1	2
36	1	36	−2	4	4
35	2	70	−3	9	18
34	1	34	−4	16	16
33	1	33	−5	25	25
32	1	32	−6	36	36
24	1	24	−14	196	196

| Sums | 20 | 760 | | | 468 |

Central Tendency

Mean	$760/20 = 38$
Median	38.5
Mode	43

Variability

Range	19
Standard Deviation	4.84

Distribution: Negatively Skewed

objective items; these performance objectives will be discussed later in Chapter 9.)

Scenario   Some skills measured by the paragraph posttest are relatively easy (recall and discrimination), whereas others are quite complex (evaluation and production). The class that took the test is somewhat heterogeneous, containing average and above-average students. The class contains one mainstreamed student whose achievement is well below that of other class members. The paragraph posttest was administered following all instruction on paragraphs. The teacher expects the class to perform very well on the exam, with many students earning near perfect scores. A negatively skewed score distribution is anticipated, with the mean score located near the highest score. The mainstreamed student struggled through the instruction and is expected to score much lower than classmates. This student's raw score is expected to affect the mean, range, and standard deviation for the group.

Results   Notice in Figure 6.11 that the class contained 20 students ($N = 20$ or Σf). The raw scores are listed in the far left column, followed by the frequency for each one. Measures of central tendency, the distribution shape, and measures of variability are listed at the bottom of the figure. A frequency polygon of raw scores is also pictured in the figure.

The mean score, 38, represents 88 percent of the items included on the paragraph test ($38 \div 43 = .88$), which indicates that instruction was effective for the majority of the class. The median, 38.5, is higher than the mean, and it reflects a negatively skewed distribution of raw scores. The mode, 43, is a perfect score on the test.

As anticipated, the variability measures were affected by the mainstreamed student whose raw score of 24 could be considered an outlier for the class. The range, 19, is greater than one-third of the items included on the test ($19 \div 43 = .44$) and reflects quite heterogeneous performance. With the lowest score eliminated from calculations, however, the range would be 11. This value is approximately one-quarter of the 43 items, and it more closely reflects the teacher's observations of students' progress during the unit. This difference in ranges was great enough to warrant recalculation of the group's data with the outlier score removed.

Figure 6.12 contains the measures of central tendency and variability recalculated after eliminating the atypical raw score for the mainstreamed student. These modified group performance measures reflect better the overall group's posttest performance. The adjusted mean is 38.74, the median is 39, and the mode remains 43. Even without the mainstreamed student's raw score in the calculations, the distribution remains negatively skewed. The range is now 11, which reflects the anticipated homogeneous performance. The recalculated standard deviation is 3.71 (approximately one-third of the range reflecting the negative skew of raw scores).

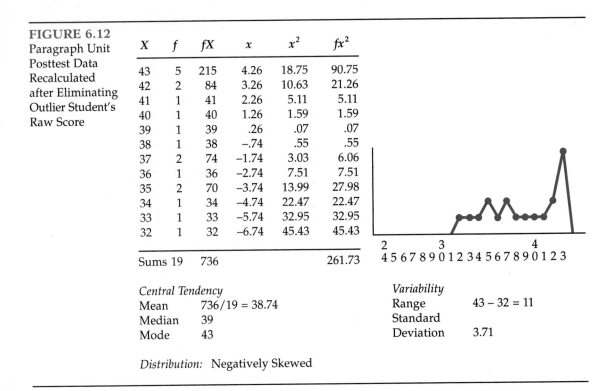

FIGURE 6.12
Paragraph Unit Posttest Data Recalculated after Eliminating Outlier Student's Raw Score

X	f	fX	x	x^2	fx^2
43	5	215	4.26	18.75	90.75
42	2	84	3.26	10.63	21.26
41	1	41	2.26	5.11	5.11
40	1	40	1.26	1.59	1.59
39	1	39	.26	.07	.07
38	1	38	−.74	.55	.55
37	2	74	−1.74	3.03	6.06
36	1	36	−2.74	7.51	7.51
35	2	70	−3.74	13.99	27.98
34	1	34	−4.74	22.47	22.47
33	1	33	−5.74	32.95	32.95
32	1	32	−6.74	45.43	45.43
Sums	19	736			261.73

Central Tendency
Mean   736/19 = 38.74
Median   39
Mode   43

Variability
Range   43 − 32 = 11
Standard
Deviation   3.71

Distribution: Negatively Skewed

COMPUTER TECHNOLOGY

If you have the appropriate automated equipment, computers can save you many hours of scoring time, and they can produce very useful reports for analyzing and evaluating a group's achievement and progress.

Procedures for Scoring a Test

Your tests can be scored by a computer quite easily and quickly if students record their responses to items on *mark sense sheets*, sometimes called *scan sheets*, and your school system provides automated scanning equipment. You create answer keys for scoring students' tests using a blank answer sheet to record the correct answer(s) for each item. Students' answer sheets are read by a scanner, and the answers they select are compared with those on the answer key. When a student's answer matches the answer on the key, the item is counted as correct. When the answer does not match the keyed answer, the distractor chosen is typically printed to facilitate distractor analysis. Through automation, hundreds of answer sheets can be scored and reports produced in a few minutes. Once a test is scored, there are several group performance reports provided for users of ParSCORE and ParGRADE (Economics Research, Inc., 1992). Some of these reports include the distribution of scores and a histogram of scores.

Distribution of Scores

The score distribution report quickly provides teachers with a variety of information about a group's performance. First, the report contains the information about the class that was entered in the roster (Chapter 2). Recall that this information includes the teacher's name, the class, and the time and day the class meets. The report also includes the name of the test. The name of the test is the same as the test file name described in Chapters 4 and 5 (e.g., PREPARAG for paragraph pretest). It also indicates the particular form of the test used. The computer will generate multiple forms of a test with answers to items scrambled and/or question numbers scrambled. Multiple test forms are typically used by teachers who need to minimize copying behavior among their students. The score distribution report summarizes student data for all forms of a single test used. The report also includes the total number of points on the test and the total number of students who took the test.

Relative to measures of central tendency, both the mean and median are reported. For variability, the standard deviation, the highest earned score, and the lowest earned score are reported. From these scores, you can readily determine the range. The report also includes students' raw scores and percentage correct scores, and the number and percentage of students in the group who earn each score. Scanning a score distribution report for any test, you can determine whether the students' performance was about as expected or atypical for the group. A sample score distribution report is included in Figure 6.13.

Histogram

The ParGRADE (Economics Research, Inc., 1992) program also provides a histogram of the group's performance. The top of the graph includes the same identifying information as the score distribution report. The bottom of the graph includes the number of students on the vertical axis and the percentage correct scores on the horizontal axis. This graph provides a visual representation of the location and spread of students' scores within the range. An example ParGRADE histogram is included in Figure 6.14. To read the histogram, locate any percentage score on the horizontal axis (e.g., 80). Follow the dots above the score 80 to the top of the column. From this point, follow across the chart to the left side. From this chart, the teacher can see that 24 of the 326 students earned a score of 80% on the exam.

FIGURE 6.13
A Sample Score Distribution Report

```
Report Date: 3-4-1994        Time: 16:24:46            STATE COLLEGE
--------------------------------------------------------------------
                 S C O R E   D I S T R I B U T I O N

  Instructor: RALPH LEWIS              Total Possible Points:  50
       Class: ECON 100              Students in this Group: 320
    Time/Day: -Combined-                       Mean Score:  32.47
        Date: 03-04-1994                     Median Score:  32.00
        Test: EXAM 2                   Standard Deviation:   8.68
        Form: All forms                     Highest Score:  50
                                             Lowest Score:  10
                             Reliability Coefficient (KR20):   0.77
```

Raw Score	Percent Correct	Number of Students	Percent of Class	Cumulative Percent	Percentile
50	100.00	2	0.6	0.6	99.4
48	96.00	5	1.6	2.2	97.8
46	92.00	14	4.4	6.6	93.4
44	88.00	19	5.9	12.5	87.5
42	84.00	17	5.3	17.8	82.2
40	80.00	23	7.2	25.0	75.0
38	76.00	26	8.1	33.1	66.9
36	72.00	30	9.4	42.5	57.5
34	68.00	22	6.9	49.4	50.6
32	64.00	34	10.6	60.0	40.0
30	60.00	20	6.3	66.2	33.8
28	56.00	21	6.6	72.8	27.2
26	52.00	20	6.3	79.1	20.9
24	48.00	18	5.6	84.7	13.3
22	44.00	10	3.1	87.8	12.2
20	40.00	14	4.4	92.2	7.8
18	36.00	8	2.5	94.7	5.3
16	32.00	10	3.1	97.8	2.2
14	28.00	4	1.3	99.1	0.9
12	24.00	1	0.3	99.4	0.6
10	20.00	2	0.6	100.0	0.0

Source: Economics Research, Inc. (1992). *ParSCORE & ParGRADE User's Manual* (p. 143). Costa Mesa, CA.

Various testing programs will provide printouts (reports) that differ in format, but most will include the standard descriptions of central tendency and variability that you have studied in this chapter. You will appreciate the ease with which the computer manages group performance data for you.

FIGURE 6.14
A Sample Histogram

```
 Report Date:   3-4-1994    Time: 16:24:46           STATE COLLEGE
 ---------------------------------------------------------------------

                        H I S T O G R A M

   Instructor: RALPH LEWIS          Total Possible Points:  50
        Class: ECON 100          Students in this Group: 320
    Time/Day: -Combined-                   Mean Score:  32.47
         Date: 03-04-1994                Median Score:  32.00
         Test: EXAM 2              Standard Deviation:   8.68
         Form: All forms               Highest Score:  50
                                        Lowest Score:  10
                        Reliability Coefficient (KR20):   0.77


       36                            o
                                     o
                                     o
                                     o    o
                                     o    o
                                     o    o
                                     o    o  o
                                     o    o  o
       24                            o    o  o  o
                                     o  o  o  o  o
                                 o   o  o  o  o
   Number                 o  o  o  o  o  o  o  o       o
     of                   o  o  o  o  o  o  o  o       o
  Students               o  o  o  o  o  o  o  o  o  o
                         o  o  o  o  o  o  o  o  o  o
                     o   o  o  o  o  o  o  o  o  o  o  o
                     o   o  o  o  o  o  o  o  o  o  o  o
       12            o   o  o  o  o  o  o  o  o  o  o  o
                  o   o  o  o  o  o  o  o  o  o  o  o  o
                  o   o  o  o  o  o  o  o  o  o  o  o  o
                o  o  o  o  o  o  o  o  o  o  o  o  o  o
                o  o  o  o  o  o  o  o  o  o  o  o  o  o
                o  o  o  o  o  o  o  o  o  o  o  o  o  o  o
             o  o  o  o  o  o  o  o  o  o  o  o  o  o  o
          o   o  o  o  o  o  o  o  o  o  o  o  o  o  o  o  o
          o  o  o  o  o  o  o  o  o  o  o  o  o  o  o  o  o

          0   10   20   30   40   50   60   70   80   90   100
                               Percent
```

Source: Economics Research, Inc. (1992). *ParSCORE & ParGRADE User's Manual* (p. 145). Costa Mesa, CA.

SUMMARY

The following outline summarizes the procedure used to describe and evaluate a group's test performance.

A. Describe and compare test results.
 1. Create a frequency table or frequency polygon of the test scores.
 2. Compare the location of the highest and lowest earned scores with the highest possible score and decide whether they are reasonable, given the complexity of the tasks measured by the test and achievement characteristics of the group.
 3. Calculate and compare measures of central tendency.
   a. Calculate the mean and note its position in the score distribution.
   b. Locate the median and note its position in the score distribution.
   c. Locate any mode (or modes) and note its position in the score distribution.
   d. Compare the mean, median, and mode and describe the distribution as being symmetrical or skewed based on these measures.
 4. Compare the observed measures of central tendency and their location in the score distribution to those you would expect, given the complexity of the tasks and the achievement characteristics of the group.
 5. Calculate and compare the measures of variability.
   a. Calculate the range.
   b. Calculate the standard deviation.
 6. Compare the variability measures with those you would expect, given the complexity of the tasks and the group's characteristics.
B. Note any discrepancies between measures you expected and those you observed.
C. Try to explain any discrepancies you find. Discrepancies are usually caused by misjudging the quality of instruction or the test. They are also potentially related to misinterpreting the complexity of the tasks or the group's achievement characteristics.
D. Judge the group's performance as being better than expected, as expected, or lower than expected.

Table 6.5 summarizes the group's performance on the paragraph test. The performance indicators are listed in the far left column, and the teacher's estimations for the class are listed in the second column. The observed results are listed in the third column, and any discrepancies between the estimated and observed measures are listed in the last column. Comparing the information summarized in the table, you can see that the teacher was very good in synthesizing factors that relate to group performance since there are only two discrepancies between the estimated and observed measures. This teacher would undoubtedly conclude that the group's test performance was better than expected and very good for a heterogeneous class.

Computer-based testing programs can be used to score students' tests, calculate measures of central tendency and variability, and plot histograms that

TABLE 6.5
Summary of the Estimated and Observed Measures of Group Performance on the Paragraph Posttest
(Outlier Removed)

Performance Indicator	Estimation Based on Relatively Easy Tasks and a Heterogeneous Group	Observation	Discrepancy
Location of highest earned score	Highest possible score	Highest possible score	None
Location of lowest earned score	Slightly more than half the number of items correct	32 (or 74%) of the items correct	Better than anticipated
Location of mean score	Close to the high end of the distribution	38.42 (or 84% correct)	None
Location of median score	Higher than the mean score	39	None
Location of mode	Toward the top of the scale	At the top of the scale	None
Range	Between one-third and one-half of the total number of items $\dfrac{43}{3} = 14.3$ $\dfrac{43}{2} = 21.5$	11	More narrow than anticipated
Standard deviation	Somewhere around one-third of the range $\dfrac{11}{3} = 3.66$	3.71	None
Distribution shape	Negatively skewed	Negatively skewed	None

graphically represent a group's test performance. Teachers who can interpret these indices and graphics can obtain the information they need for class management from the student performance reports generated by the computer.

PRACTICE EXERCISES

I. Measures of Central Tendency and Variability
    A. Central Tendency
        1. What is the name of the average score in a set of test scores?
            a. Mode
            b. Standard deviation
            c. Mean
            d. Median

2. Fifty percent of the scores fall below which point in a distribution?
   a. Mean
   b. Median
   c. Mode
   d. A score half way between the highest and lowest raw score

B. Distributions

Column A contains the location of the mean and median in a distribution of test scores. Column B contains the shapes of score distributions. Match the location of the mean and the median with the corresponding distribution shape.

Column A	*Column B*
_____ 1. The mean and median are the same value.	a. Positively skewed
	b. Negatively skewed
_____ 2. The mean is greater than the median.	c. Symmetrical, bell-shaped
	d. Symmetrical, rectangular
_____ 3. The median is greater than the mean.	e. Both c and d

C. Variability

Column A describes distributions of scores within a range. Column B lists possible values of the standard deviation for a range of 9. Match each distribution with the standard deviation value that would reflect it.

Column A	*Column B*
_____ 1. The majority of the scores in the set are located close to the mean.	a. $\dfrac{9}{2} = 4.5$
_____ 2. The scores are spread throughout the range.	b. $\dfrac{9}{3} = 3$
_____ 3. The scores are divided between the upper and lower end of the range reflecting a bimodal, U-shaped distribution.	c. $\dfrac{9}{4} = 2.5$

II. Score Distributions

Examine the following score distributions and name each type.

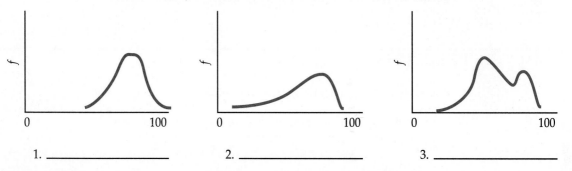

1. _____   2. _____   3. _____

III. **Describe Group Performance**
Using Figure 6.15, calculate group performance measures for the compound sentences posttest prescribed in the table of test specifications in Table 5.7. There is a total of 42 items on the posttest covering 15 behavioral objectives (III.A.2 through IV.F.2). Check your work in the Feedback section in Figure 6.15(F).

IV. **Enrichment**
Use a test you have developed and administered to complete the following exercises:
1. Use information about the complexity of the tasks measured and the achievement characteristics of the group to estimate the group's performance. You should estimate:
   a. The areas in which the highest and lowest raw scores will occur.
   b. The area between the highest and the lowest scores in which the mean will be located.
   c. The area in which the median will occur.
   d. The shape of the distribution.
   e. The range.
   f. The standard deviation based on the estimated range.
2. Determine the shape of the distribution, measures of central tendency, and measures of variability.
3. Use the observed measures to describe the group's performance.
4. Compare the anticipated and observed performances and try to explain any discrepancies.

FIGURE 6.15
Group Performance Measures for a Compound Sentence Unit Posttest

X	f	fX	x	x^2	fx^2
42	2				
41	2				
40	5				
39	2				
38	1				
37	1				
36	1				
35	2				
34	1				
33	1				
31	1				
27	1				

Sums __ ___   ___

```
5 |
4 |
3 |
2 |
1 |
0 |_____
   2   3              4
   7 8 9 0 1 2 3 4 5 6 7 8 9 0 1 2
```

Central Tendency
Mean _____
Median _____
Mode _____

Variability
Range ___ (~__ % of items)
Standard
Deviation ___ (~__ % of range)

Distribution: _____

FEEDBACK

I. **Measures of Central Tendency and Variability**
   A. Control Tendency
      1. c
      2. b
   B. Distributions
      1. e
      2. a
      3. b
   C. Variability
      1. c
      2. b
      3. a

II. **Score Distributions**
    The score distributions are:
    1. Bell-shaped
    2. Negatively skewed
    3. Bimodal

III. **Describe Group Performance**
     See Figure 6.15F.

FIGURE 6.15F
Group Performance Measures for a Compound Sentence Unit Posttest

X	f	fX	x	x^2	fx^2
42	2	84	4.5	20.25	40.50
41	2	82	3.5	12.25	24.50
40	5	200	2.5	6.25	31.25
39	2	78	1.5	2.25	4.50
38	1	38	.5	.25	.25
37	1	37	−.5	.25	.25
36	1	36	−1.5	2.25	2.25
35	2	70	−2.5	6.25	12.50
34	1	34	−3.5	12.25	12.25
33	1	33	−4.5	20.25	20.25
31	1	31	−6.5	42.25	42.25
27	1	27	−10.5	110.25	110.25
Sums	20	750			301.00

Central Tendency
Mean   750/20 = 37.5
Median   38.5 + [(20/2 − 9)/2] = 39
Mode   40

Variability
Range   15 (~36% of items)
Standard
Deviation   3.88 (~26% of range)

Distribution: Negatively Skewed

REFERENCE

Economics Research, Inc. (1992). *Par-SCORE & ParGRADE user's manual.* Costa Mesa, CA: Author.

SUGGESTED READINGS

Ebel, R. L., and Frisbee, D. A. (1992). *Essentials of educational measurement* (5th ed.) (pp. 55–75). Englewood Cliffs, NJ: Prentice Hall.

Hopkins, C. D., & Antes, R. L. (1990). *Classroom measurement and evaluation* (3rd ed.) (pp. 346–402). Itasca, IL: F. E. Peacock.

Hopkins, K. D., Stanley, J. C., & Hopkins, B. R. (1990). *Educational and psychological measurement and evaluation* (3rd ed.) (pp. 19–41, 288–318). Englewood Cliffs, NJ: Prentice Hall.

Kubiszyn, T., & Borich, G. (1990). *Educational testing and measurement* (3rd ed.) (pp. 205–260). Glenview, IL: Scott, Foresman/Little, Brown.

Mehrens, W. A., and Lehmann, I. J. (1991). *Measurement and evaluation in education and psychology* (4th ed.) (pp. 209–223). New York: CBS College Publishing.

Popham, J. W. (1990). *Modern educational measurement* (2nd ed.) (pp. 66–97). Englewood Cliffs, NJ: Prentice Hall.

Sax, G. (1989). *Principles of educational and psychological measurement and evaluation* (3rd ed.) (pp. 184–284). Belmont, CA: Wadsworth.

Wiersma, W., & Jurs, S. G. (1990). *Educational measurement and testing* (2nd ed.) (pp. 91–115). Boston: Allyn and Bacon.

CHAPTER 7

Analyzing Objective Test Items and Tests

OBJECTIVES

- Define, calculate, and interpret indices of item difficulty.
- Define, calculate, and interpret indices of item discrimination.
- Define, calculate, and interpret data for an item distractor analysis.
- Define, calculate, and interpret indices of test internal consistency.
- Evaluate test items and tests.

In developing classroom tests, teachers must synthesize many factors related to the skills to be measured, the instruction delivered, and the characteristics of target students. The tests they develop reflect their perceptions of the best way to measure prescribed skills. Teachers often check their perceptions of the clarity and technical accuracy of items by asking a colleague and a few students to review new items. These reviews help them detect problems and revise the items before administering new tests.

Like classroom teachers, test specialists have content experts and sample students review new items they write. However, they also administer new tests to a large, representative group of students before the tests are finalized. They evaluate a new item using three quality characteristics, including (1) its *difficulty* for the group, (2) its ability to *discriminate* between those students who possess the most knowledge and skill in a domain and those students who possess the least, and (3) its *distractor* plausibility for the group. Using data from these field trials, test specialists usually find problems in the items that were not detected during item reviews. Defective items are then revised or eliminated before a new test is actually used.

Since defective items are commonly found during field trials, it is unfortunate that most teachers do not have the time or resources to conduct such trials before administering new tests in the classroom. Even though defective items cannot always be identified before a test is administered, teachers can use the item analysis procedures used by test specialists to locate defective items after the test is administered. Teachers who simply score, record, and return test papers without performing item analyses are missing opportunities to identify and discount defective items, improve their item-writing skills, and evaluate the quality of their test and instruction.

In spite of the importance of these item analyses for developing quality achievement tests, the technology for enabling classroom teachers to perform item analyses routinely was not available in schools until recently. Most schools today have computer-scoring services for selected-response tests that quickly calculate and summarize the data teachers need to perform item analysis. If computer-scoring services are available in your school, and your class is mature enough to manage a separate answer sheet, use them. When machine scoring is not feasible, item analysis can be performed manually, although it is time consuming and typically not done.

This chapter describes item and test evaluation procedures for selected-response objective tests. The first section explains item difficulty analysis; the second, item discrimination analysis; the third, item distractor analysis; and the fourth, internal consistency measures for the overall test. The derivation of the indices used for each analysis is explained to aid your interpretation of them on test analysis reports generated by a computer. Classroom teachers typically do not have time to generate item and test data by hand, but relatively little time is required to interpret them from the test evaluation reports once their meaning is clear. Typical item analysis reports are included for practice in using them to evaluate items and tests.

One caution is necessary before beginning this chapter. The illustrations of calculating the various indices use very small numbers of items and students in order to simplify and clarify the calculation procedures. In reality, much larger samples of items and students would be required for the indices to reflect meaningful properties of the items or characteristics of a student group. Even when calculating these indices for a realistic classroom test and a typical size group, you should be cautious. The item and test data you obtain will differ from group to group due to factors such as differences in the groups' achievement characteristics and differences in instructional activities. Faulty, unclear items, scoring errors, and ineffective tests can often be detected using the data from only one class; therefore, item analysis procedures are appropriate for classroom teachers to use in the development and evaluation of their tests. It would not, however, be appropriate to use test data from one class to make generalizations about other classes or the students in an entire grade level.

ITEM DIFFICULTY ANALYSIS

The first measure used to evaluate the quality of a test item is its difficulty for the group. The item difficulty index, p, is the proportion or percentage of students in the analysis group who answer the item correctly. Difficulty indices can be arbitrarily divided with those expressed as proportions ranging from .00 to 1.00, and those expressed as percentages ranging from 0 to 100 as follows:

	Very Difficult	*Fairly Difficult*	*Moderately Easy*	*Very Easy*
Proportion	.00–.49	.50–.69	.70–.89	.90–1.00
Percentage	0%–49%	50%–69%	70%–89%	90%–100%

As you can see, the higher the p value, or difficulty index, the easier the item is for the group.

Calculating Item Difficulty Indices

The item difficulty index, p, is easy to calculate. The number of students in the group who answer each item correctly is divided by the total number of students who took the test. The formula for calculating p is:

$$P = \frac{R}{N}$$

R represents the number of students who answer each item right, and N represents the total number of students in the class.

Suppose you administer a five-item test to a class that contains 40 students, and you obtain the item results displayed in Table 7.1. The first column contains each item number; the second column, R, lists the number of students who answered each item right; the third column, N, indicates the number of students who took the test; and the last column, p, illustrates how the difficulty index is calculated for the five items.

Interpreting the difficulty indices for these five items, you would conclude that item 1, $p = 1.00$, was very easy for the group since all members answered it correctly. Each subsequent item is more difficult for the group, and item 5, $p = .375$, was extremely difficult.

TABLE 7.1
Item Difficulty Indices for a Five-Item Test

Item	R	N	p
1	40	40	40/40 = 1.00
2	36	40	36/40 = .90
3	32	40	32/40 = .80
4	20	40	20/40 = .50
5	15	40	15/40 = .375

Evaluating Items Using the Item Difficulty Index

The *difficulty index* is a *measure* of each item's difficulty for the students tested. This measure can be used to describe the difficulty of the item (e.g., this item is very easy, moderately easy, fairly difficult, or very difficult for this group). It can also be used to evaluate or judge the quality of the item using criteria and standards. Evaluation requires that you identify variables that influence the difficulty index and standards for judging the quality of the item. In essence, you are judging the reasonableness of the measure considering the variables that influence it. When an observed difficulty index does not seem reasonable given the circumstances, then you have evidence to question the quality of the item. The following four variables can be used to evaluate the item using the difficulty index:

1. The complexity of the skill measured
2. The achievement characteristics of the group
3. The comparability of difficulty indices for multiple items that measure the same objective
4. The comparability of difficulty indices for items that measure hierarchically related skills

Skill Complexity   To determine whether an observed difficulty index is reasonable, you should first estimate the complexity of the skill measured by the item and set expectations for the percentage of students likely to answer correctly. For example, if a test item requires students to recall simple verbal information, make a relatively obvious discrimination, or perform a simple calculation, you would expect most of the students to answer the item correctly. If, on the other hand, the item measures a complex skill, some students undoubtedly will miss the item. If many students miss an item you believe measures a simple skill, then you have reason to believe that something is wrong either with the item or with the instruction. Likewise, a very high proportion of correct responses for a relatively complex task may signal the presence of a clue in the item. Therefore, the reasonableness of an observed difficulty index depends in part on the complexity of the skill measured.

The Group's Achievement Characteristics   In addition to the complexity of the skill measured, interpreting difficulty indices requires considering the group's achievement characteristics. Given the same skill complexity and item to measure the skill, you would adjust the anticipated difficulty index depending on whether the group was heterogeneous or homogeneous. The expected proportion of students who answer the item correctly in a very heterogeneous group should be lower than that expected for a homogeneous group of high achievers. The expected difficulty index for a homogeneous, high-achieving group should be higher than one for a homogeneous group of average achievers. Likewise, a homogeneous group of average achievers should have a higher expected difficulty index than a homogeneous group of low-achieving students.

Using information about the complexity of the task measured and about the group's achievement characteristics, you can make decisions about the reasonableness of an observed difficulty index. In a group of high achievers, a large proportion of students would probably answer an item correctly, regardless of task complexity, if instruction was adequate and the item was clearly written. In a group of average achievers, items measuring easy skills would probably produce a high proportion of correct responses; items measuring more complex skills would produce a smaller proportion of right answers. You might expect most students in a group of low achievers to answer complex items incorrectly and to produce high difficulty indices only on very easy questions. Similarly, you would not expect all of the students in a heterogeneous group to answer an item correctly, unless the task was very simple or the item contained a clue. Item difficulty indices that seem unrealistically high, given the task's complexity and the group's characteristics, usually signal clues in the items; those that seem unreasonably low signal either defective items or inadequate instruction.

Multiple Items for the Same Objective Comparing the difficulty indices for different items that measure the same objective can usually help you determine whether problems detected are caused by the item or by instruction. Test items that measure the same objective should result in approximately the same difficulty indices. For example, if you include three items on a test to measure the same objective, and all students answer one item correctly but only 60 percent answer the other two items correctly, you should look for a clue in the easy item. On the other hand, if only 55 percent of the students answer one of a set of three items correctly, and more than 90 percent answer the other two items correctly, it might signal a complexity in the difficult item not experienced by students in the easier ones. The following example illustrates this situation. The set of five items requires students to select words that are nouns. Notice that the difficulty index is at about the same level on all but one item.

	Difficulty Index
Word	p
1. barn	.70
2. busy	.65
3. brown	.75
4. barrel	.70
5. barrister	.40

The first four items have difficulty indices between .65 and .75. Item 5, however, is obviously more difficult than the other four. The atypically low proportion of correct responses to this item suggests some sort of problem. From this example, you would probably conclude that most students did not know the meaning of the word *barrister,* which influenced their responses.

Locating an atypical difficulty index in a set of items does not always pinpoint the defective item. You should also use your estimation of a reasonable difficulty index in deciding whether the atypical item is the one posing the problem. Consider, for example, a set of three items that measures a rather complex skill administered to a very heterogeneous group of students. If you estimated that approximately two-thirds of the class had mastered the skill, yet observed difficulty indices of .60, .90, and 1.00 for the three items, you probably would not conclude that the more difficult item contained inadvertent complexity. Instead, you might review the two easier items to see whether they contained clues to the correct answer. Although this type of situation is possible, the atypical difficulty index usually reflects the problem item.

Hierarchically Related Items   In interpreting difficulty indices, it is also important to compare them for items that measure hierarchically related skills. For instance, students may be required to:

1. State the identifying characteristics of nouns.
2. Select nouns from a list of words containing nouns and other parts of speech.
3. Select proper nouns from a list of nouns.
4. Capitalize proper nouns.

Obviously, students who do not know the characteristics of nouns cannot consistently separate nouns from other parts of speech. If they cannot recognize nouns, they will not be able to recognize proper nouns without clues. Also, if they cannot recognize proper nouns, they can only guess which nouns should be capitalized. Consider the reasonable difficulty indices for three test items based on each of the skills in Table 7.2.

TABLE 7.2
Difficulty Indices for Hierarchical Tasks

Difficulty Indices			
Item 1	Item 2	Item 3	**Skills**
.60	.60	.65	Capitalize proper nouns.
.65	.60	.65	Select proper nouns from a list of nouns.
.70	.75	.70	Select nouns from a list of nouns and other parts of speech.
.80			State the identifying characteristics of nouns.

In Table 7.2, 80 percent of the group correctly answered the item that required them to state the characteristics of nouns. Therefore, no more than 80 percent should correctly answer higher-level skills. Notice that 70 percent correctly selected nouns, and fewer, or 60 percent, correctly selected proper nouns. All the students who were able to identify proper nouns could also capitalize them. Considering the hierarchical relationship among these skills, the difficulty indices for the items seem reasonable.

Now, compare these data with a second set of unreasonable difficulty indices in Table 7.3. Here, 90 percent or more of the students could locate proper nouns, yet only 80 percent knew the characteristics of nouns and only 70 percent could correctly select nouns from a list of words containing nouns and other parts of speech. These illogical percentages can be explained in two ways. First, proper noun items may have contained clues—for example, being capitalized when other words in the list were not. The other possibility could be faulty reasoning in establishing the relationship among skills in the hierar-chy. If you encounter difficulty indices that imply that higher-level skills have been mastered by more students than have subordinate skills, you should look for (1) clues in items that measure higher-order skills, (2) errors in logic in identifying skills included in the hierarchy, and (3) errors in sequencing skills in the hierarchy.

In summary, interpreting the reasonableness of item difficulty indices requires comparing observed indices with those anticipated given the com-plexity of the skills measured and the achievement characteristics of the group; comparing difficulty indices for multiple items that measure the same behavioral objective; and comparing difficulty indices for items that measure hierarchically related skills. These comparisons should enable you to pinpoint items that either contain clues or introduce unintended com-plexity.

You can also use difficulty indices to evaluate the quality of your instruc-tion. If many students incorrectly answer some or all of the items related to

TABLE 7.3
Unreasonable Difficulty Indices for Hierarchical Tasks

Difficulty Indices			
Item 1	Item 2	Item 3	**Skills**
.60	.60	.60	Capitalize proper nouns.
.90	.95	.90	Select proper nouns from a list of nouns.
.70	.70	.70	Select nouns from a list of nouns and other parts of speech.
.80	.80	.80	State the identifying characteristics of nouns.

an important skill, you need to reconsider the instruction for these behavioral objectives. Although an analysis of item difficulty will not identify the instructional weaknesses, it will indicate where to look for problems.

Caution is required when interpreting item difficulty indices. In a small group, one wrong answer or a careless mistake will produce a different difficulty index. Therefore, in making your comparisons, you should look for a reasonable range of scores. A difference of as much as 10 to 15 percentage points in a small group will be due to chance errors on the part of students rather than to actual differences in item difficulty. Thus, you should be concerned only with large, obvious differences in your analysis.

Some measurement specialists recommend comparing the difficulty indices of items on pretests and posttests in order to evaluate the quality of items on criterion-referenced tests. To perform such an item analysis, you need to administer a pretest and posttest that contain the same items. Then calculate the difficulty indices for the items on each test and subtract each item's p value on the pretest from its p value on the posttest. The difference between these values is considered one indicator of item quality. This procedure is illustrated in Table 7.4.

Items that exhibit high, positive differences, such as 1, 3, and 4, supposedly reflect good technical characteristics. Items that have small or no differences, or negative differences, such as items 2 and 5, supposedly reflect technical problems with the item, the instruction, or both.

Using a pretest-posttest comparison to evaluate the quality of items on your criterion-referenced tests has several limitations. First, pretest data are not always available for comparison. Pretests are usually administered only when teachers have reason to believe that some students in the class already possess some of the enabling skills in the goal framework. When this is the case, pretests are administered to aid in grouping students for instruction or for differentiating between skills that need to be taught and those that simply need to be reviewed. Second, when pretests are used to aid planning, different or novel items should be used on posttests to measure students' accomplishment of the same enabling skills and objectives. When exactly the same items

TABLE 7.4
Comparing Item Difficulty on Pretests and Posttests

Item	Enabling Skill 1				
	1	2	3	4	5
Posttest p	.60	.40	1.00	.85	.20
Pretest p	.20	.40	.50	.50	.80
Difference (post – pre)	.40	.00	.50	.35	−.60

are included on pretests and posttests, it is impossible to determine whether students have learned the enabling skill or simply remember the example used in the previous measure. Third, when different items are used to measure the same skill on the pretest and posttest, comparing them would not make sense because it is impossible to ensure that different items are precisely equal in difficulty. Although comparing students' pretest and posttest performances is valuable for evaluating the quality of instruction, these comparisons are best made at the objective or enabling skill level rather than at the item level. Procedures for judging students' progress at the objective level are described in Chapter 8. Item analysis for criterion-referenced tests is best accomplished by comparing the reasonableness of observed difficulty indices against your perceptions of the complexity of the skill measured and the achievement characteristics of your class.

Sometimes teachers do not have time to perform all these comparisons between their expectations for item difficulty and their observed item data. When this is the case, and often it is, they set a minimum acceptable p value for all posttest items. A typical minimum acceptable p value is set at .50, reflecting that at least one-half the class answered correctly. This criterion is based on the assumption that items presented following instruction should be tailored to the ability level of the group; thus, if instruction was clear and the item was clear, then at least one-half of the group should be able to identify the correct answer. Using such a rule of thumb, all items on a test failing to meet the minimum difficulty criterion would be flagged for further analysis. Obtaining a difficulty index lower than .50 does not automatically reflect a problem with the item since it may instead reflect inadequate instruction for the enabling skill. Further analysis of the item should help you determine whether the problem is rooted in the item or in the instruction.

ITEM DISCRIMINATION ANALYSIS

Item discrimination analysis is based on the assumption that students who receive high scores on the overall test should score better on an item-by-item basis than students who receive low scores on the overall test. An index of item discrimination permits a teacher to determine whether students' performances on individual items are consistent with their overall performances. Discrimination indices can range from 1.00 to –1.00 as follows:

Maximum Negative Discrimination Between Groups	*No Discrimination Between Groups*	*Maximum Positive Discrimination Between Groups*
–1.00	.00	1.00

A discrimination index of 1.00 for an item indicates maximum positive discrimination between the highest- and lowest-scoring students. To observe such an index, all students in the upper group would have to answer the item correctly, whereas all students in the lower group would have to miss the item. An index of .00 indicates that the item does not discriminate at all between the highest- and lowest-scoring students. When the same number of students in each group answers an item correctly, a discrimination index of .00 results. Maximum negative discrimination is −1.00, which results when all students in the lower-scoring group answer an item correctly and all students in the upper-scoring group miss it. Generally, high negative discrimination indices reflect problems.

The highest-quality tests are those that contain all items that have positive discrimination indices. A positive discrimination index indicates that more higher-scoring than lower-scoring students answered the item correctly. When the reverse is true, and a test contains many negatively discriminating items, the overall test scores fail to differentiate as they should between those who know the most and the least in the domain. Thus, in evaluating the quality of test items and tests, teachers should flag negatively discriminating items for further analysis.

There are several different discrimination indices used to judge the quality of test items. Two are presented because they are the ones most commonly used on computer-generated item analysis reports for classroom tests. One is the discrimination index, d, and the other is the point-biserial correlation index, r_{pbi}. Both discrimination measures reflect whether students' performance on a single item is consistent with their overall test scores; however, there are some differences in the calculation procedures and interpretations.

Calculating d for Item Discrimination

Prior to calculating the discrimination index, d, two subgroups of class members must be identified. One subgroup selected typically contains approximately 27 percent of the class who earn the highest overall test scores, and it is called the *upper subgroup*. The other subgroup contains approximately 27 percent of the class who earn the lowest overall test scores, and it is called the *lower subgroup*. For example, if a class contains 40 students, the upper and lower subgroups would each contain 10 students, or about 27 percent of the total class of 40. Should a class contain 100 students, then the upper and lower subgroups would each contain 27 students. The performance of these two extreme subgroups is then compared on an item-by-item basis following the assumption that if an item differentiates between those who do and do not know the content, it will be most readily detectable by comparing the performance on that item of the extreme upper- and lower-scoring subgroups.

Although computer-generated reports typically include only 27 percent of the students in the subgroups, it is not incorrect to include more, and including 50 percent in each subgroup is acceptable. Discrimination indices calculated on only the highest- and lowest-scoring students tend to be higher than those obtained using all members of a class.

To identify the particular students included in each subgroup, the raw scores (total number of items answered correctly) of all students who took the test are calculated and then students are ranked by raw score from the highest to the lowest performance. From these ranked raw scores, the number of students required to complete the upper subgroup are selected from the high end of the raw score scale, and the number of students required for the lower subgroup are selected from the bottom end of the scale. Each subgroup must contain an equal number of students.

With these two subgroups identified, the discrimination index, d, can be calculated. The procedure is to (1) calculate the proportion of students in the upper subgroup who answer the item correctly (p_u), (2) calculate the proportion of students in the lower subgroup who answer the item correctly (p_l), and (3) subtract the proportion correct in the lower group from the proportion correct in the upper group to obtain the difference. The formula for this calculation is:

$$d = p_u - p_l \quad \text{or} \quad \frac{R_u}{n_u} - \frac{R_l}{n_l}$$

where

p_u = the proportion in the upper subgroup who answers correctly
p_l = the proportion in the lower subgroup who answers correctly
R_u = the number in the upper subgroup who answers correctly
R_l = the number in the lower subgroup who answers correctly
n_u = the number of students in the upper subgroup
n_l = the number of students in the lower subgroup

This difference between subgroup difficulty indices reflects whether the item was easier for the upper- than the lower-scoring subgroup, as one would reasonably expect.

Table 7.5 contains a five-item test administered to 40 students. Columns II and III repeat the total group item difficulty (p) information from Table 7.1. Column IV contains the difficulty index for only the 10 students in the upper subgroup (p_u). This index is calculated by dividing the number of students in the upper subgroup who answered the item correctly (R_u) by the number of students in the upper subgroup (n_u). Column V includes the difficulty index for the lower subgroup (p_l) obtained by dividing the number of students in the lower subgroup who answered the item correctly by the number of students in the lower subgroup (n_l). Column VI contains the discrimination index (d) for each item. It is obtained by subtracting the difficulty index of the lower subgroup (p_l) from the difficulty index of the upper subgroup (p_u).

TABLE 7.5
Item Discrimination Indices for a Five-Item Test

I Item	II R	III p_n	IV $R_u/n_u = p_u$	V $R_l/n_l = p_l$	VI $p_u - p_l = d$
1	40	1.00	10/10 = 1.00	10/10 = 1.00	1.00 – 1.00 = .00
2	36	.90	10/10 = 1.00	8/10 = .80	1.00 – .80 = .20
3	32	.80	6/10 = .60	6/10 = .60	.60 – .60 = .00
4	20	.50	8/10 = .80	2/10 = .20	.80 – .20 = .60
5	15	.375	1/10 = .10	3/10 = .30	.10 – .30 = –.20

Interpreting the Discrimination Index d

Recall that the discrimination index (d) reflects the difference between the difficulty of the item for the upper and lower subgroups. Notice that item 1 was very easy for the entire class ($p = 1.00$), for the upper group ($p_u = 1.00$), and for the lower group ($p_l = 1.00$). The discrimination index of .00 for item 1 reflects that there was no difference at all in the difficulty of the item for the two extreme subgroups; thus, it fails to discriminate between those who know the most (highest overall exam scores) and those who know the least (lowest overall exam scores) in the domain tested.

Item 2 was easy for the overall class ($p_n = .90$), yet it was easier for the upper subgroup ($p_u = 1.00$) than for the lower subgroup ($p_l = .80$), resulting in a discrimination index of .20 for the item. The third item was more difficult for the class ($p_n = .80$), although it was equally difficult for the upper subgroup ($p_u = .60$) and the lower subgroup ($p_l = .60$), resulting in no discrimination between the two extreme groups ($d = .00$). Item 4 was quite difficult since only one-half the class answered correctly ($p_n = .50$). The item, however, was relatively easy for the upper group ($p_u = .80$) and very difficult for the lower group ($p_l = .20$), resulting in good discrimination between those students who knew the most and the least on the overall exam. Quite a different result was observed for item 5. It was very difficult for the entire class ($p_n = .375$), extremely difficult for the upper group ($p_u = .10$), and very difficult for the lower group ($p_l = .30$). Since the lower subgroup performed better on item 5 than the upper subgroup, the discrimination index is a negative value, –.20, which occurs when an item is less difficult for the extreme lower subgroup.

The negative discrimination index of –.20 for the item 5 reflects some type of ambiguity in the item. The item is quite difficult for the class ($p_n = .375$) and even more difficult for the upper subgroup ($p_u = .10$). Such a difficult item with a negative discrimination index might reflect rampant guessing behavior, a distractor that was also correct, a miskeyed item, or any number of other problems. This illogical data for the item indicates that the item should be analyzed carefully prior to using it again. The p value of .375 indicates that there is either a problem with the item or the instruction was inadequate. The low *p* value, coupled with the negative discrimination index, indicates clearly that further analysis of the item is warranted.

The Item Difficulty-Discrimination Relationship

Undoubtedly, you noticed during the preceding discussion that the discrimination index was interpreted relative to the difficulty index. The discrimination index is partially a function of the difficulty index in that for each difficulty index, there is a limited range of discrimination indices possible. Figure 7.1 illustrates the relationship between the difficulty and discrimination indices. Difficulty indices are listed along the bottom of the figure from 0.00 on the left, indicating that no student answered an item correctly, to 1.00 on the right side of the scale, indicating that all students answered correctly. These difficulty indices are calculated based on the performance of the sub-

FIGURE 7.1
The Test Item Difficulty-Discrimination Relationship

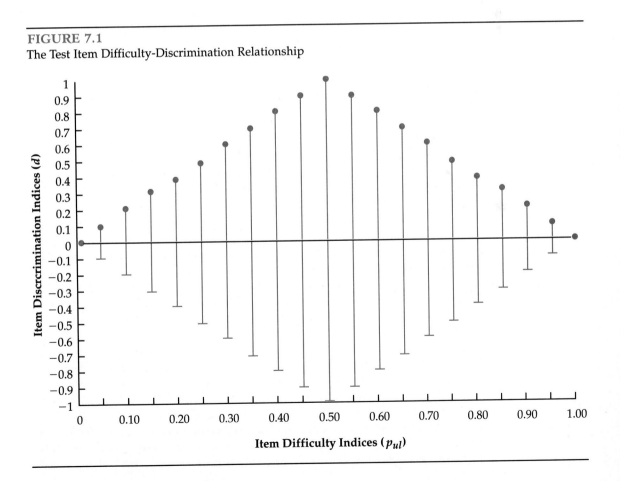

groups (p_{ul}) rather than the overall class (p_n). The numbers along the left side of the figure reflect the possible range of discrimination indices from 1.00 at the top through –1.00 at the bottom. Recall that discrimination values above .00 reflect that an item was easier for the upper group than the lower group, and negative values below 0.00 reflect that an item was easier for the lower subgroup than for the upper.

Directly above each difficulty index is a vertical line. The dot at the top of each line indicates the highest possible positive discrimination value for the given difficulty index, and the bar at the bottom of the line indicates the lowest possible negative discrimination index for the item difficulty level. Notice, for example, that for a difficulty value of .10, the highest positive discrimination value is .20 and the lowest negative value is –.20. The maximum discrimination values for a difficulty level of .20 are .40 and –.40. The vertical line connecting the two extreme discrimination values indicates that discrimination values may fall at points between the two extremes for any difficulty index, depending on the difference in item difficulty between the two extreme comparison groups. The horizontal line across the figure at $d = 0.00$ indicates the point at which there is no discrimination between the two groups, and $d = 0.00$ can occur across the range of difficulty indices.

Notice the symmetrical nature of discrimination values in Figure 7.1. For each difficulty value, the discrimination value range extends an equal distance above and below the $d = 0.00$, or no discrimination line. Notice also that the extreme possible values of discrimination increase steadily from a p_{ul} value of 0.00 to a p_{ul} value of 0.50 and then steadily decrease from $p_{ul} = 0.50$ to $p_{ul} = 1.00$. This symmetry is explained easily when you understand the relationship between the p_{ul} and d values.

Consider first the symmetry of the range of positive and negative discrimination indices for each p_{ul} value. Suppose your total class contains 40 students and that the upper and lower subgroups each contain 10 students. Based on these numbers, the possible range of discrimination indices for items with p_{ul} values of 0.30 and 0.70 will be examined. Notice in Figure 7.1 that the extreme values and the range of possible discrimination values are the same for these two difficulty indices.

Table 7.6 contains all the possible item discrimination data for the selected p_{ul} values. The left data set illustrates all the possible combinations of right responses to the item if 14, or 70 percent, of the upper and lower subgroups answer correctly ($20 \times .70 = 14$). The highest positive discrimination index will be observed when all 10 members of the upper subgroup answer correctly, while only 4 members of the lower subgroup answer correctly ($d = 1.00 - .40$, or .60). There are, however, six other combinations of upper- and lower-subgroup correct responses when the number of students answering correctly totals 14, and they are also illustrated in the table. Each time 1 less student from the upper subgroup responds correctly, 1 more in the lower subgroup must answer correctly since for a p value of .70, the total number of correct responses is fixed at 14. Each combination of R_u and R_l

TABLE 7.6

The Possible Discrimination Indices for Difficulty Indices of .70 and .30 and an Analysis Group Containing 20 Students

P_{ul} = .70					P_{ul} = .30				
R_u	R_l	P_u	P_l	d	R_u	R_l	P_u	P_l	d
10	4	1.00	.40	.60	6	0	.60	.00	.60
9	5	.90	.50	.40	5	1	.50	.10	.40
8	6	.80	.60	.20	4	2	.40	.20	.20
7	7	.70	.70	.00	3	3	.30	.30	.00
6	8	.60	.80	−.20	2	4	.20	.40	−.20
5	9	.50	.90	−.40	1	5	.10	.50	−.40
4	10	.40	1.00	−.60	0	6	.00	.60	−.60

Note: The total number of students in the upper and lower subgroups for each p value is calcualted as: p = .70, 20(.70) = 14; p = .30, 20(.30) = 6.

results in a different discrimination index. When each subgroup has 7 members responding correctly, then a d value of .00, or no discrimination between the upper and lower subgroups, results. The maximum negative discrimination index occurs when all members of the lower subgroup and only 4 members of the upper subgroup answer the item correctly.

You can see that the same phenomenon occurs in the right side of the table for items with difficulty indices (p_{ul}) of .30. In this instance, however, only 6 of the 20 students have answered the item correctly (.30 × 20 = 6). Again, only seven different combinations of R_u and R_l are possible, and they are illustrated. The maximum positive discrimination index possible is .60 and the maximum negative is −.60. The remaining five discrimination values fall between these two extremes.

Table 7.7 illustrates the various levels of discrimination possible for difficulty indices of .60 and .40. Notice in Figure 7.1 that the vertical discrimination line above p_{ul} values of .60 and .40 are longer than the ones for items with p_{ul} values of .30 and .70. The longer length of the lines reflects that there are more combinations of R_u and R_l possible at p values of .60 and .40. When the analysis group contains 20 students and the p_{ul} value is .60, then 12 students have answered the item correctly (.60 × 20 = 12). There are nine combinations of R_u and R_l possible in this case, and the discrimination index that would result from each combination is illustrated. Why is there no R_u – R_l combination of 12 and 0 or 11 and 1 listed in the table? These combinations are not possible since the upper and lower subgroups contain only 10 students; thus, the highest possible R value is 10 for either group. Notice the symmetrical

TABLE 7.7

The Possible Discrimination Indices for Difficulty Indices of .60 and .40 and an
Analysis Group Containing 20 Students

$P_{ul} = .60$					$P_{ul} = .40$				
R_u	R_l	P_u	P_l	d	R_u	R_l	P_u	P_l	d
10	2	1.00	.20	.80	8	0	.80	.00	.80
9	3	.90	.30	.60	7	1	.70	.10	.60
8	4	.80	.40	.40	6	2	.60	.20	.40
7	5	.70	.50	.20	5	3	.50	.30	.20
6	6	.60	.60	.00	4	4	.40	.40	.00
5	7	.50	.70	−.20	3	5	.30	.50	−.20
4	8	.40	.80	−.40	2	6	.20	.60	−.40
3	9	.30	.90	−.60	1	7	.10	.70	−.60
2	10	.20	1.00	−.80	0	8	.00	.80	−.80

Note: The total number of students in the upper and lower subgroups for each p value is
calcualted as: $p = .60$, $20(.60) = 12$; $p = .40$, $20(.40) = 8$.

nature of d values for a difficulty index of .40. Eight students have answered
the item correctly with nine possible d values.

The fact that the highest possible discrimination index varies with the
level of the difficulty index makes the discrimination index somewhat abstract to interpret. For example, you cannot set one value of discrimination to
reflect good item discrimination. Suppose you established $d = .50$ as a value
below which item discrimination is judged questionable. Notice in Figure 7.1
that it is impossible to obtain such a high value unless the item difficulty level
is between .25 and .75. This criterion of $d \geq .50$ presents a problem since many
quality items on classroom tests yield p_{ul} values of .80 or higher. To solve this
dilemma, many measurement specialists suggest judging any positive discrimination value as acceptable.

Calculating the Point-Biserial Correlation Index
for Item Discrimination

A third discrimination measure provided in item analysis reports generated
by the computer is the point-biserial correlation index (r_{pbi}). This index indicates how well you can predict the total test scores of students from an
individual item on the test. An item is judged consistent with students' overall
test scores when students who earn the highest overall test scores answer the

item correctly and students who earn the lowest overall scores answer incorrectly. When more higher- than lower-scoring students answer an item correctly, a positive r_{pbi} index results; when the students who answer correctly are equally represented among the higher- and lower-scoring groups, a value near .00 results; and when more lower- than higher-scoring students answer correctly, a negative r_{pbi} index is obtained.

The possible scale for the point-biserial correlation index extends from −1.00 to 1.00, although obtaining values this high in either a positive or negative direction on classroom tests is unlikely. More typically, they are observed to range between −.30 and .70.

Unlike the previously described discrimination index, d, the point-biserial correlation index does not compare the performance of only the upper and lower extreme subgroups; instead, it uses the item and total test scores for all students who complete the exam. The formula used to calculate the point-biserial correlation index is:

$$r_{pbi} = \frac{\overline{X}_p - \overline{X}}{\sigma} \sqrt{\frac{p}{q}}$$

where:

$\overline{X}_p$ = the mean or average overall test score for only the subgroup of students who answers the item correctly.

$\overline{X}$ = the mean or average overall test score for the total class.

σ = the standard deviation for the total test.

p = the proportion of the total class who answers the item correctly.

q = the proportion of the total class who answers the item incorrectly $(1 - p)$.

A quick look at the terms in this formula makes it clear that teachers do not calculate the r_{pbi} index by hand for items on their tests. Since the item analysis reports generated in your school are likely to include the point-biserial correlation index instead of the discrimination index, d, it is important for you to be able to interpret the r_{pbi} values provided. The following discussion is for those readers who want to understand the indices they are expected to interpret. The calculation of each element in the formula and the combination process are described in Table 7.8. Students are listed in column A, and their responses to each of five test items are included in section B. For each item, correct answers are indicated with a 1, and incorrect answers are assigned a 0. Column C contains each student's raw score and the total group's mean score. The standard deviation for the test is calculated in column D.

Column E illustrates the calculation of the mean test scores for only the students who answered each of the five items correctly ($\overline{X}_p$). Column F illustrates the calculation of the difficulty index (p) for the five items, and column

TABLE 7.8
Calculation of the Point-Biserial Correlation Index

I.

A	B Test Item					C	D Standard Deviation		
Student	1	2	3	4	5	Raw Score	$(X - \bar{X})$	x^2	σ
1	1	1	1	1	1	5	$5 - 3 = 2$	4	$\sigma = \sqrt{10/5}$
2	1	1	1	1	0	4	$4 - 3 = 1$	1	
3	1	1	1	0	0	3	$3 - 3 = 0$	0	$= 1.41$
4	1	1	0	0	0	2	$2 - 3 = -1$	1	
5	1	0	0	0	0	1	$1 - 3 = -2$	4	
p_n	1.00	.80	.60	.40	.20	$\Sigma = 15$	$\Sigma x^2 = 10$		
r_{pbi}	.00	.70	.87	.86	.71	$\bar{X} = 15/5 = 3$			

II.

Item	E $\bar{X}_p$	F p	G q	H $r_{pbi} = \dfrac{\bar{X}_p - \bar{X}}{\sigma} \sqrt{\dfrac{p}{q}}$
1	$15/5 = 3$	$5/5 = 1$	$1 - 1\ = .00$	$[(3 - 3)/1.41]\ \sqrt{1.00/.00}\ =\ .00(1.00) = .00$
2	$14/4 = 3.5$	$4/5 = .80$	$1 - .80 = .20$	$[(3.5 - 3)/1.41]\ \sqrt{.80/.20} =\ .35(2)\ \ \ = .70$
3	$12/3 = 4$	$3/5 = .60$	$1 - .60 = .40$	$[(4 - 3)/1.41]\ \sqrt{.60/.40}\ \ =\ .71(1.22) = .87$
4	$9/2 = 4.5$	$2/5 = .40$	$1 - .40 = .60$	$[(4.5 - 3)/1.41]\ \sqrt{.40/.60} = 1.06(.816) = .86$
5	$5/1 = 5$	$1/5 = .20$	$1 - .20 = .80$	$[(5 - 3)/1.41]\ \sqrt{.20/.80}\ \ = 1.42(.5)\ \ \ = .71$

G shows the calculation of q, or $1 - p$, for each item. Column H illustrates the calculation of the point-biserial correlation index for each item.

The difficulty and point-biserial correlation indices are repeated in the bottom rows of the top portion of the table in section B. Notice that all students answered item 1 correctly; thus, the difference between the two means is .00, which can only result in a r_{pbi} discrimination index of .00. The remaining r_{pbi} indices are all high and positive. These results could have been predicted from the pattern of incorrect responses since all errors committed for any items were made by the lower-scoring students. Except for item 1, you could conclude that the items on this test discriminated well between those who earned the highest and lowest scores on the exam.

Table 7.9 contains another set of test scores with less than ideal discrimination for some items. The test scores range from 10 to 2, the overall mean is 5.6, and the standard deviation is 2.37. The highest difficulty index is .80, and

TABLE 7.9
The Point-Biserial Correlation Index Calculated for a Ten-Item Test

Student	Test Item 1	2	3	4	5	6	7	8	9	10	Raw Score X	$(X - \overline{X})$	x^2
1	1	1	1	1	1	1	1	1	1	1	10	4.4	19.36
2	1	1	1	1	0	1	0	1	1	1	8	2.4	5.76
3	1	1	1	1	0	1	0	1	1	0	7	1.4	1.96
4	1	1	1	0	1	1	0	1	1	0	7	1.4	1.96
5	1	1	1	0	0	1	0	1	0	1	6	.4	.16
6	1	1	0	0	1	0	1	1	0	0	5	-.6	.36
7	1	1	0	0	1	0	1	0	0	1	5	-.6	.36
8	1	0	0	1	0	0	1	0	0	0	3	-2.6	6.76
9	0	0	0	1	0	0	1	0	0	1	3	-2.6	6.76
10	0	0	0	1	0	0	1	0	0	0	2	-3.6	12.96
p_n	.80	.70	.50	.60	.40	.50	.60	.60	.40	.50	$\overline{X} = 56/10$	$\sigma = \sqrt{56.4/10}$	
r_{pbi}	.66	.81	.84	-.05	.40	.84	-.48	.81	.83	.34	$= 5.6$	$= 2.37$	

Item	$\overline{X}_p$	$\overline{X}_p - \overline{X}$	$\dfrac{\overline{X}_p - \overline{X}}{\sigma}$	$\sqrt{\dfrac{p_n}{q}}$	r_{pbi}
1	6.38	.78	.329	2.00	.66
2	6.86	1.26	.532	1.53	.81
3	7.60	2.00	.844	1.00	.84
4	5.50	-.10	-.042	1.22	-.05
5	6.75	1.15	.485	.82	.40
6	7.60	2.00	.844	1.00	.84
7	4.67	-.93	-.392	1.22	-.48
8	7.17	1.57	.662	1.22	.81
9	8.00	2.40	1.013	.82	.83
10	6.40	.80	.338	1.00	.34

the lowest is .40. The point-biserial correlation indices are calculated in the bottom portion of the table. Notice that two of the items, 4 and 7, have negative r_{pbi} indices. These negative values resulted from the fact that the average test score for students who passed these items is lower than the mean score for the class. For item 4, the means were very close, so the r_{pbi} index is slightly lower than 0 at -.05. For item 7, the difference between the two means is -.93, so the r_{pbi} index is much lower.

Consider the three items with p_n values of .50. Both items 3 and 6 yield a very high r_{pbi} index of .84, indicating that the items discriminate extremely well between the two groups. Item 10, on the other hand, has students at the upper and lower end of the raw score scale who answered the item correctly, so a much lower r_{pbi} index of .34 resulted. It remains a positive value because one more higher- than lower-scoring student answered correctly, which yielded a positive difference between the two mean scores.

Comparing the Discrimination Indices d and r_{pbi} for Test Items

Two different indices of item discrimination have been described. Although they are calculated quite differently, they indicate the same characteristics: an item's ability to discriminate between those who performed the best and the least well on the exam. Comparing the information provided by each index for the same items and tests, you typically would reach the same conclusion about the items' discrimination quality. To illustrate this, review the item data from Table 7.9 that are presented in Table 7.10. All the item difficulty and discrimination indices described thus far are included. The first four rows contain various difficulty values for each item calculated from the total group and the upper and lower subgroups. The last two rows contain the discrimination indices.

Would your overall conclusions about the items' ability to discriminate be different if you used one or the other of the indices? No. All items besides 4 and 7 yield credible discrimination. Both indices for item 4 indicate that the item yielded no or negligible discrimination, and both indices for item 7 indicate a high level of negative discrimination.

The d value and the r_{pbi} value for an item can sometimes provide conflicting evidence about an item's discrimination quality. When this occurs, the d value will reflect stronger discrimination for an item, whereas the r_{pbi} index

TABLE 7.10
Item Difficulty and Discrimination Indices for the Item Data in Table 7.9

Difficulty/ Discrimination	Test Item									
	1	2	3	4	5	6	7	8	9	10
p	.80	.70	.50	.60	.40	.50	.60	.60	.40	.50
p_u	1.00	1.00	1.00	1.00	.33	1.00	.33	1.00	1.00	.67
p_l	.33	.00	.00	1.00	.00	.00	1.00	.00	.00	.33
p_{ul}	.67	.50	.50	1.00	.17	.50	.67	.50	.50	.50
r_{pbi}	.66	.81	.84	−.05	.40	.84	−.48	.81	.83	.34
d	.67	1.00	1.00	.00	.33	1.00	−.67	1.00	1.00	.34

Note: p_u, p_l, and p_{ul} are calculated on the performance of the upper- and lower-scoring three students, or 33 percent, rather than the typical 27 percent due to the small group size.

will reflect weaker discrimination for the same item. What could cause this difference? It stems from the fact that the d value reflects the test performance of only the highest- and lowest-scoring students, whereas the r_{pbi} index is calculated using the scores of all students who completed the test. Discrimination indices calculated on only the extreme scoring groups will typically reflect higher discrimination for an item than those calculated using all group members.

Evaluating Test Items Using Difficulty and Discrimination Indices

In order to judge an item's quality using the difficulty and discrimination indices, you must establish minimally acceptable criteria for each index. The criteria established depend on multiple factors related to the inherent complexity of the skill measured and the characteristics of the students, including the variability of their performance on the overall test.

In a preceding discussion on item difficulty, a minimum p value of .50 was recommended for posttests under the assumptions that if (1) the instruction was clear, (2) the item was clear and was tailored to students' developmental level, and (3) the students were trying to succeed, then at least 50 percent of them should be able to identify the correct response. Under special circumstances, you may choose to lower or raise this criterion of $p \geq .50$, but it will serve as a good rule of thumb for quickly screening items for potential problems when you have not specifically identified reasons why the p values should be lower or higher for a particular group on a particular test.

In setting a minimally acceptable criterion for judging item discrimination using either of the discrimination indices, you need to consider the variability of the group's overall test performance. A group's performance would be considered homogeneous when there is a narrow range and standard deviation for test scores, and it would be considered heterogeneous when there is a wide range and standard deviation. This suggestion usually causes teachers to ask, How wide is wide, and how narrow is narrow? Obviously, there is no correct answer to such reasonable questions, so a rule of thumb can be cautiously applied to help you determine the homogeneity or heterogeneity of a group's test performance. Test performance can be considered homogeneous when you obtain a range of raw scores that spans approximately 25 percent or less of the total number of items on the test and a standard deviation that spans approximately 25 percent or less of the range. Test performance would be considered heterogeneous when the range spans approximately 33 percent of the total number of items on the test and the standard deviation spans approximately 25 percent or more of the range. Test performance would be considered very heterogeneous when the range is approximately 50 percent or more of the total number of items on the test and the standard deviation is approximately 25 percent or more of the range. When you obtain a relatively wide range and standard deviation for a test, you can reasonably expect the items on the test to yield high positive discrimination indices. Conversely, when you obtain a relatively narrow range and standard deviation, lower item discrimination generally can be expected.

What levels of discrimination should be considered minimally acceptable for typical class-size groups containing fewer than 50 students? When your group's overall test performance is homogeneous, then .00 or any positive value for d or r_{pbi} would be acceptable for all items.

Heterogeneous group performance on a test means that you can expect higher levels of item discrimination. General rules of thumb for judging item discrimination using d and r_{pbi} are listed in Table 7.11. Notice that the d index has various difficulty and discrimination levels recommended. These levels reflect the fact that the maximum discrimination available varies with the difficulty level. It is easier to recommend minimum criteria for the r_{pbi} index since it does not vary with the item difficulty levels. With these criteria in mind for both the difficulty and discrimination indices, you are ready to perform a distractor analysis.

ITEM DISTRACTOR ANALYSIS

The third type of item analysis performed by teachers is the distractor analysis. Unlike the difficulty and discrimination indices that reflect the group's performance relative only to the correct answer, the incorrect answers chosen by group members are the focus of the distractor analysis. The index used is the proportion of students who select each incorrect response. Distractors chosen by a large portion of the group possibly reflect misconceptions, and those chosen by no one potentially reflect choices considered illogical by

TABLE 7.11
Criteria for Judging Item Discrimination on Classroom Tests Given Heterogeneous Test Performance

Discrimination Judgment	d		r_{pbi}	
	p_{ul}	d	p	r_{pbi}
Excellent	.30 – .70	$\geq .40$		$\geq .30$
	.71 – .90	$\geq .20$		
	> .90	$\geq .00$		
Acceptable	.30 – .70	$\geq .20$		$\geq .20$
	.71 – .90	$\geq .10$		
	> .90	$\geq .00$		
Questionable	< .90	.00	< .90	.00

group members. Similar to the difficulty and discrimination analyses, the data required to perform this analysis are generated by the computer as the tests are scored, and they are printed in a summary table for teachers to interpret.

There are two main reasons why teachers perform an item distractor analysis: to facilitate instructional planning and to determine why the items yielded unreasonable difficulty and discrimination indices. Recall from Chapter 5 that distractors should reflect common misconceptions or incomplete learning observed among students during instruction. When item distractors do reflect common misconceptions, it is important to understand which ones students select so that instruction for correcting these errors can be provided in subsequent review sessions. Through performing a distractor analysis, teachers can diagnose the actual problems students are having and prescribe targeted instruction. Some items come to your attention because you judge the difficulty index to be too high or low for the inherent complexity of the skill measured or because they yield a negative discrimination index.

Items that all members of the group answer correctly ($p = 1.00$) are immediately suspect. If the skill measured is not extremely easy or one particularly emphasized during instruction, then you might conclude that the distractors did not reflect plausible alternatives, even for students who did not know the correct answer. Items that unskilled students can answer correctly by default are often called *"gimmes"* by students. Although students tend to like gimmes, tests that contain too many of them will not yield test scores that lead to valid decisions about the students' skill level in the domain. Each distractor for such an item should be analyzed carefully to ensure that it is a plausible alternative. Some potential problems are that distractors contain (1) information not studied in the lessons, (2) unfamiliar terminology, (3) grammatical mismatches between the stem and the distractors, or (4) obviously more or less information than the correct answer. You may also find that clues to the correct answer are in the stem of the question, the directions for a set of questions, or in other items on the test.

Items also attract attention because they are more difficult for students than anticipated based on the inherent complexity of the skill measured. Very difficult items may result from problems with item construction or inadequate instruction, and the distractor analysis will help you determine whether the root of the problem is the item. Potential problems include (1) unfamiliar vocabulary in the stem or distractors, (2) two correct answers, (3) a distractor rather than the correct answer keyed as correct, or (4) a confusing, unclear question.

Negatively discriminating items with p values lower than .90 also signal that an item may be flawed, and an analysis of the response choices selected by the upper and lower subgroups may provide clues to the problem. Typical problems resulting in negative discrimination include (1) miskeyed items, (2) unfamiliar terminology, (3) a distractor that appears correct to the upper subgroup, or (4) a confusing, unclear question. If instruction was misleading, students in the upper subgroup could have actually learned an incorrect response. Inadequate instruction in the skill measured can also lead to negatively discriminating items. If the upper subgroup of students does not know the answer to the question, then they, like members of the lower subgroup, try to guess the correct answer, and the discrimination index is as likely to be negative as positive.

Interpreting Item Distractor Data

Table 7.12 illustrates different item data formats commonly provided by computers for distractor analysis. The item numbers are listed in the second column, and students' responses for five-option test items are illustrated in the columns to the right. The far right column, NR, indicates no response, or the number of students who did not answer the question. Data sets I and II report the proportion of the total group that selected each option. In set I, the correct answer is printed in the second column beside the item number, and in set II, the correct answer is indicated by an asterisk beside the proportion

TABLE 7.12
Item Data Useful for Performing a Distractor Analysis

	Item	Key	Total Group Performance Responses						
			1	2	3	4	5	NR	
I.	1	2	.20	.40	.10	.10	.20	.00	
	2	4	.00	.00	.00	1.00	.00	.00	
II.	1		.00	.20	.80*	.10	.00	.00	
	2		.70*	.10	.00	.10	.10	.00	
III.	1	f	0	16*	24	4	4	.00	
		%	.00	.40*	.60	.00	.00	.00	
	2	f	0	0	32*	8	0	0	
		%	.00	.00	.80*	.20	.00	.00	

	Item	Key	Upper-Lower Group Performance						p
IV.	1	u	.50*	.00	.50	.00	.00	.00	.60
		l	.50*	.00	.20	.20	.10	.00	
	2	u	.00	.80*	.00	.00	.20	.00	.60
		l	.20	.20*	.20	.30	.10	.00	
	3	u	.60	.00	.40*	.00	.00	.00	.75
		l	.20	.00	.80*	.00	.00	.00	

Note: Decimal numbers reflect the proportion of students selecting each response.

of students choosing it. The same format is used in set III, with the only difference being that both the frequency (f) and the proportion (%) of the students who selected each option are indicated.

Examining these item data in the first three sets will help you see what you can infer about the items. In set I, the difficulty index (p) for the first item is .40, indicating a relatively difficult item. The proportion of students choosing the keyed answer is the difficulty index. All distractors were chosen by some member of the group, which illustrates that the teacher had included distractors that were all plausible. You might also conclude from the data that the item was not miskeyed since the keyed answer was selected by the largest proportion of the class. For item 2 in set I, 100 percent of the class selected the keyed answer 4, reflecting either an easy item, a clue, or unreasonable distractors.

Now consider the data for the two items in set II. Both items appear to be functioning well since they were easy for the majority of the class (p = .80 and .70). In addition, both items contained distractors considered plausible by the group, which provides information for planning the review session. In set III, the majority of the class chose distractor 3 (p = .60) for the first item, providing a hint that this item may either be miskeyed or contain two correct answers. The item should be reviewed for both possibilities. The second item was relatively easy for the group (p = .80), and only one distractor was functioning.

Much information about the items can be obtained from analysis programs that provide whole group data, but the information provided in set IV is much more helpful. For each of the three items, three difficulty indices—p_u, p_l, and total group p—are provided. This analysis program reports separately the options chosen by the upper and lower 27 percent of the class. Notice that for item 1, one-half of both the upper and lower subgroups selected the correct answer. Based on this information, can you calculate the discrimination index d? It is .00. The distractor most attractive to the remaining upper subgroup students was 3, whereas members of the lower subgroup selected options 3, 4, and 5. This information should cause you to investigate the following:

1. Why was distractor 3 so attractive? Is it also a correct answer? Was adequate instruction provided to enable the students to correctly distinguish between responses 1 and 3?
2. What is wrong with distractor 2? Does it really reflect a misconception or problem students have?

Consider the pattern of responses for item 2 in set IV. The item was moderately difficult for the class (p = .60), and it discriminated well between the upper and lower subgroups (d = .80 − .20 = .60). Distractor 5 should certainly be explained to students during the test review, and overall instruction on the skill should be provided for the lower group since these students appear to have all the misconceptions identified by the item distractors. For item 3, you should first check to see whether it is miskeyed since the difficulty and discrimination data for distractor 1 seem more plausible than for the keyed response (1: $p_{ul} = .40$, $d = 40$; 3: $p_{ul} = .60$, $d = -.40$).

EVALUATING ITEMS USING STUDENT PERFORMANCE DATA

As you can see, it is relatively easy to generate hypotheses about the problems students experience with your test items using only the item analysis reports. To check your hunches, however, you will need to transfer the item data to a copy of your test and examine the actual items using the data. This transfer can be accomplished easily by hand when it is not done for you by the computer. Table 7.13 contains three sample multiple-choice items with the item analysis data inserted beside the item and responses. Beside each item number, you

TABLE 7.13
Item Analysis Data for Distractor Analysis

p_n/d		1. What is the sentence called that introduces the subject in a paragraph?	
.60/.10			
p_u	p_l		
.50	.30	A. First sentence	(physical criterion)
	.20	B. Introduction sentence	(repeat stem term)
	.00	C. Relevant sentence	(quality criterion)
	.10	D. Subject sentence	(repeat stem term)
.50	.40	*E. Topic sentence	

p_n/d		2. What are the sentences in a paragraph called that elaborate the topic?	
.80/.50			
p_u	p_l		
	.10	A. Elaboration sentences	(repeat stem term)
	.20	B. Relevant sentences	(quality criterion)
	.10	C. Sequenced sentences	(quality criterion)
1.00	.50	*D. Supporting sentences	
	.10	E. Topic sentences	(repeat stem term)

p_n/d		3. What is the largest standard deviation possible for a test that contains 20 items, has a mean of 10, and has a range of 8?	
.20/.00			
p_u	p_l		
	.10	A. 2	(divisor: $R/2$)
.90	.50	B. 4	
.10	.10	*C. 5	($\overline{X}/2$)
	.20	D. 10	(# of items/2)
	.10	E. None of these	

can see the difficulty (p) and discrimination (d) indices. To the left of each item response, you will find the proportion of the upper and lower subgroups who selected it. To the right of each distractor in parentheses, you will find the logic used to create the distractor.

Items 1 and 2 are both easy; verbal information recall items related to the paragraph instructional goal previously described. The teacher undoubtedly judged that both items would be very easy for the class on the posttest; however, item 1 was much more complex than anticipated, and it did not discriminate well. Reviewing the data, you can see that an equal number of students in the upper group selected the responses "First sentence" and "Topic sentence," possibly indicating that the students did not read the question carefully enough. The teacher would either emphasize this difference in subsequent instruction or replace the distractor "First sentence" with information more readily distinguished by the group for subsequent tests. The other two distractors chosen by members of the lower group were key terms repeated from the stem, which possibly reflects that students were reaching for an answer using clues. The distractor not chosen by anyone in the group was "Relevant sentence," a quality criterion for topic sentences.

The teacher would probably judge that the second item was quite good based on the p and d values of .80 and .50, respectively. Additionally, the distractors used were all considered plausible by some group members.

The third item relates to the standard deviation described previously. If these item p and d values (.20, .00) were obtained, they would surely reflect a mistake; however, just from these indices, you could not determine whether the error was in teaching the concept or in developing the item. The distractor analysis data indicate that both these hunches are wrong. Reviewing the data for the upper group, it becomes obvious that the item is miskeyed. The correct answer is 4 since the range, 8, divided by 2, is 4 rather than 5. Can you calculate the actual item indices for p_{ul} and d from the data for response B? They are .70 and .40, values considerably more reasonable.

Using a distractor analysis report, you will be able to improve the quality of your feedback to students following the exam, and you will be able to improve the quality of items you use to judge students' performance—both worthwhile pursuits.

Interpreting a Typical Item Analysis Report Generated by a Computer

Prior to reviewing item analysis data, it might be helpful to list the steps a teacher would take in analyzing the data. The following procedure is recommended:

1. Determine whether the group's overall test performance is homogeneous or heterogeneous using the range and standard deviation.
2. Based on your perceptions of the group's achievement and motivation characteristics, the complexity of the skills measured, and the quality of the

instruction delivered, set minimally acceptable criteria for difficulty and discrimination levels.

3. Scan the item analysis report to locate questionable items based on difficulty and discrimination. Mark any items that are more difficult than anticipated. Locate the discrimination index column on the report, and mark any items that do not yield the established minimum criterion. For items that do not yield acceptable discrimination, locate the corresponding p value. If the p value is greater than .90, review the item to determine whether such high performance is reasonable for the skill measured. The negative and negligible discrimination indices can be ignored when the high difficulty indices are logical for the skill measured. If the p value is lower than .90, review each response to see whether you can identify problem distractors.

4. Check the distractors selected by upper and lower subgroup members to help locate potential problems within items.

Each of these steps is illustrated in the following example.

Determine Group Homogeneity   The first step is to determine whether the group's performance should be classified as heterogeneous or homogeneous. The following information from a report for an actual classroom test should be useful:

> *Number of test items:* 20
> *Range:* 20 – 12 = 8, or 38 percent of 20 items
> *Standard deviation:* 1.76, or 22 percent of the range
> *Number of students:* 34
> *Number of students in upper-lower subgroups:* 9

The range is greater than one-third of the total items on the test, and the standard deviation is approximately one-quarter of the range. Based on these data, the group's overall test performance will be classified as heterogeneous, although the standard deviation is borderline. The small number (nine) of students in the subgroups means that you should be cautious in interpreting the d index. If even one more or less student answers an item correctly, then the p_u and p_l values will change by 11 percent.

Set Criteria for Item Difficulty and Discrimination   The next steps are to set minimum criteria for the difficulty and discrimination indices. The minimum criterion for the difficulty index is set at $p \geq .50$ since the exam was a unit posttest, the instruction was considered good, and the group contained high-achieving students. Based on the group's heterogeneous overall test performance, minimum standards for the discrimination index are set at the acceptable level in Table 7.11, or $d \geq .20$ or .10 based on the p value and $r_{pbi} \geq .20$. For items with $p \geq .90$, any positive or negative discrimination index will be considered acceptable if the high p value is reasonable for the skill measured.

Table 7.14 contains the item analysis data for a 20-item objective test that will be used for locating potential problem items. The item number is listed in the first column, and the keyed correct answer is listed in the second column. The next 10 columns contain the percentage of students in the upper and lower subgroups who selected each of the four response options. The columns corresponding to the keyed response for each item contain the p_u and p_l values. The two columns marked NR reflect the percentage of students who made no response or failed to answer the question. The five columns on the

TABLE 7.14
Computer-Generated Item Analysis Data for an Objective Test

Item	Key	Upper Group 1	2	3	4	NR	Lower Group 1	2	3	4	NR	Difficulty/Discrimination p_n	d	r_{pbi}
1	4			.11	.89			.22	.33	.33	.11	.68	.56	.481
2	3			1.00					1.00			1.00	.00	.000
3	4			.22	.78				.33	.67		.65	.11	.081
4	1	.67	.22	.11			.89		.11			.76	−.22	−.057
5	2		.78		.22			1.00				.82	−.22	−.270
6	4				1.00		.44	.11	.11	.33		.68	.67	.454
7	4				1.00		.11	.11	.33	.44		.76	.56	.652
8	1	1.00					1.00					.97	.00	.010
9	4				1.00		.22	.22		.56		.79	.44	.168
10	1	1.00					.89		.11			.94	.11	.334
11	2		1.00				.11	.22	.67			.68	.78	.696
12	3			1.00					1.00			.97	.00	−.064
13	4			.11	.89				.33	.67		.74	.22	.247
14	2	.22	.78				.22	.78				.65	.00	.029
15	2	.11	.89				.22	.67	.11			.76	.22	.342
16	3			1.00					1.00			.85	.00	−.047
17	4				1.00				.33	.67		.88	.33	.468
18	1	.78	.11	.11			.22	.33	.22	.22		.59	.56	.455
19	3			1.00			.11	.11	.78			.79	.22	.060
20	3	.11	.22	.67			.33	.44	.11	.11		.35	.56	2.86

far right of the table contain the difficulty index for the entire group of 34 students (p); the d item discrimination value based on performance of the 18 students in the upper and lower subgroups; and the r_{pbi} discrimination index based on the performance of all 34 students.

Locate Questionable Items Based on Difficulty and Discrimination

The next step is to locate the subset of items that have potential problems. Begin by locating the item difficulty column (p_n) in Table 7.14. Scan the difficulty indices in the column and mark all items in the table that were extremely difficult ($p < .50$) and extremely easy ($p > .95$) for the group. You should mark item 20 as very difficult and items 2, 8, 10, and 12 as extremely easy.

Next, locate the two item discrimination index columns on the right side of the table (d and r_{pbi}) and mark all items that do not yield acceptable discrimination. If one of the two indices indicate adequate discrimination, you may wish to accept this as evidence that the item discriminates adequately and not mark these items. You may also want to exclude items with difficulty indices greater than .90 since these very easy items may not discriminate well. Items with p values less than .90 that clearly produce inadequate discrimination include numbers 3, 4, 5, 14, and 16. Of the 20 items, 5 should be reviewed based on their difficulty levels for the group and 5 should be examined due to inadequate discrimination.

Examine Distractor Data for Questionable Items

Once you have pinpointed potentially flawed items, you should examine the proportion of upper- and lower-group students who selected each distractor for the items. This analysis may help you locate particular parts of the items that appear to cause the problem. Examine the distractor data for the 10 items you have checked in Table 7.14, and develop hunches about which distractor or distractors appear to warrant further examination. See whether the conclusions you reach about the distractors match those in Table 7.15.

Comparing Item Data for Multiple Class Groups

In order to illustrate the tentative nature of item data from one class group, the same test of 20 items was administered to another class studying the same unit, and the following test data were obtained:

	$\overline{X}$	Range	σ	σ/R	N	Subgroup #
Group 1	17.00	20 − 12 = 8	1.76	.22	34	9
Group 2	17.32	20 − 13 = 7	2.31	.33	28	8

The mean scores were very similar for the two groups, which indicates that you can expect the item difficulty indices (p) to be relatively similar for the two groups since $\Sigma p = \overline{X}$. The range is smaller for group 2, yet their standard deviation is larger, at 33 percent of their range. The larger standard deviation indicates a wider dispersion of test scores within the range for the second

TABLE 7.15
Analysis of Potentially Faulty Items Based on Student Performance Data

Item	Conclusions about Items Flagged for Difficulty	Analysis Procedure
20	Too difficult for group All distractors chosen Keyed response most selected Good discrimination	1. Check item vocabulary, context 2. Provide more emphasis on skills during instruction
2 8 10 12	Extremely easy for group No (or 1) distractors chosen by upper or lower subgroups	1. Check stem, distractors for clues 2. Check distractors for plausibility 3. Check distractors to determine whether they reflect common misconceptions

	Conclusions about Items Flagged for Discrimination		
Item	Nonfunctioning Distractors	Distractor Most Attractive for Upper Group	Analysis Procedure
3	1, 2	3	1. Examine nonfunctioning distractors to determine whether they reflect common misconceptions/problems and revise as needed.
4	4	2	2. Check distractor most attractive for upper group to determine whether it also reflects a correct answer and revise as needed.
5	1, 3	4	
14	3, 4	1	
16	1, 2, 4		

group; thus, you might expect better item discrimination for the second group than you observed for the first group.

Table 7.16 contains the item data for both groups. First, compare the groups' performance for item 20 that was judged too difficult for the first group. Notice that group 2 earned an acceptable difficulty index of .61, and their discrimination indices for the item would be judged excellent. The additional data from group 2 reflect that item 20 is a good test item and that the discrepant p values most likely stem from different instructional emphases in the two classes.

Now compare the item discrimination data for the two class groups. Items 3, 4, 5, 14, and 16 were observed to yield inadequate discrimination when the test was administered to group 1. Reviewing the discrimination indices from group 2, note that items 3, 14, and 16 again failed to yield acceptable discrimination, providing further evidence that these three items contain some type of flaw. A different item discrimination pattern emerges for the other two items. Items 4 and 5 yielded adequate discrimination indices for group 2.

TABLE 7.16
Item Discrimination Data for Two Groups of Students

Item	Group	P_n	d	r_{pbi}
3	1	.65	.11	.081
	2	.82	.00	.007
4	1	.76	−.22	−.057
	2	.82	.25	.278
5	1	.82	−.22	−.270
	2	.71	.50	.285
14	1	.65	.00	.029
	2	.71	.13	−.012
16	1	.85	.00	−.047
	2	.89	.13	−.026
20	1	.35	.56	.286
	2	.61	.62	.684

Based on all item discrimination data from the two groups, you might conclude that only items 3, 14, and 16 appear inadequate. Examining the distractors chosen by members of the upper and lower subgroups from both classes may help determine where to look for problems in these items, and Table 7.17 includes the complete data for items 3, 14, and 16. One potential problem with these items is that they have only one distractor considered plausible by students in either group. The two nonfunctioning distractors might be revised to see whether the items' discrimination quality can be improved with subsequent class groups.

Adjusting for Flawed Items

Finding faulty items on a test you have administered to your class means that you must decide what to do about the items. Of course, you will want to revise flawed items prior to using them again, but what about the class that was subjected to the problematic items? The scores students earn on your tests are used to describe their achievement in the course. When these test scores are based on some flawed items, they reflect your errors as well as the students' errors. There is no rule for solving these problems but ignoring them does not seem prudent. Many teachers give all students in the class credit for items that were too difficult. Others eliminate the items and rescore the exam.

When the items you use on a test are new, you should not be surprised to find that approximately 10 percent of them do not yield the anticipated

TABLE 7.17
Distractor Analysis Data for Three Items with Consistently Inadequate
Discrimination Indices

			Upper Group					Lower Group					Difficulty/ Discrimination		
Item	Key	Group	1	2	3	4	NR	1	2	3	4	NR	p_n	d	r_{pbi}
3	4	1			.22	.78				.33	.67		.65	.11	.081
		2			.25	.75				.25	.75		.82	.00	.007
14	2	1	.22	.78				.22	.78				.65	.00	.029
		2	.13	.88				.25	.75				.71	.13	−.012
16	3	1			1.00					1.00			.85	.00	−.047
		2			1.00					.87	.13		.89	.13	−.026

difficulty indices. Even very experienced test developers find this to be the case. Take care in setting unreasonable standards for yourself as a test developer, and avoid holding your students responsible for your inadvertent errors.

An Example

Table 7.18 contains the item analysis data for the topic sentence portion of the unit posttest on writing paragraphs. Objective codes are included in the top row, and items that measure each objective are listed beneath the codes. The correct answers are located in the third row. Students' names are listed in the far left column, and an asterisk in the student-by-item cell indicates a correct answer. A number in the intersecting cell indicates the number of the distractor selected by the student. The teacher used an x in the intersecting cell to indicate unacceptable original topic sentences.

Item data are included in the bottom rows of the table. The names of indices are listed in the far left column, and the value calculated for each item appears in the intersecting index-by-item cell. These indices can be used to locate potentially flawed items on the test. First, examine the difficulty indices for all items to locate any items that are too difficult for the class. The total group difficulty indices illustrate that this portion of the test was quite easy for most class members; no items had difficulty indices lower than .50. Second, look for items that contain possible clues. All students in the class answered 4 of the 15 items correctly (3, 4, 6, 7). The text of these items should be examined to determine whether clues are present or the items are simply easy for class members. Items 3 and 4 reflect physical and functional characteristics, and items 6 and 7 are discrimination items requiring students to locate topic sentences in a paragraph. These should be easy enabling skills for

TABLE 7.18

Item Analysis for the Topic Sentence Portion of the Paragraph Posttest (Objectives II.A.4 to II.F.1 in Tables 3.6 and 4.2)

TOPIC SENTENCE OBJECTIVES													
Objective Codes	II.A.4		II.B.4		II.C.4		II.D.1		II.E.1		II.E.4		II.F.1	
Items	3		4		5		6	7	8	9	10	11	12	13
Correct Answers	4		4		4		1	1	2	4	1	4	Hand Scored	
Augustine	*		*		*		*	*	*	*	*	*	*	*
Prince	*		*		*		*	*	*	*	*	*	*	*
Deddens	*		*		*		*	*	*	*	*	*	*	*
Talbot	*		*		*		*	*	*	*	*	*	*	*
McComas	*		*		*		*	*	*	*	*	*	*	*
Rust	*		*		*		*	*	*	*	*	*	*	*
Carey	*		*		*		*	*	*	*	*	*	*	*
Cromer	*		*		*		*	*	*	*	*	*	*	*
Hager	*		*		*		*	*	*	*	*	*	*	*
McLaughlin	*		*		*		*	*	*	*	*	*	*	*
White	*		*		*		*	*	*	*	*	*	*	*
Otto	*		*		*		*	*	*	*	*	*	*	*
Lovejoy	*		*		*		*	*	*	*	*	*	*	*
Hill	*		*		*		*	*	*	*	*	*	*	*
Scragg	*		*		2		*	*	*	*	*	*	*	*
Gormley	*		*		3		*	*	*	3	*	*	*	*
Bailey	*		*		2		*	*	1	*	*	*	*	*
Deiters	*		*		2		*	*	*	3	*	*	*	x
Stewart	*		*		3		*	*	*	*	2	*	*	x
Smith	*		*		2		*	*	*	3	2	2	x	x
Total *p*	1.0		1.0		.70		1.0	1.0	.95	.85	.90	.95	.95	.85
p_{ul}	1.0		1.0		.50		1.0	1.0	.90	.70	.80	.90	.90	.70
d	.00		.00		1.00		.00	.00	.20	.60	.40	.20	.20	.60
r_{pbi}	.00		.00		.79		.00	.00	.19	.63	.69	.67	.67	.72

students following instruction, and it seems reasonable that all students answered them correctly.

After examining items for potential problems related to item difficulty, you should examine the discrimination indices for potentially confusing items. All discrimination indices for all items with p values lower than 1.00 appear quite reasonable. One possible exception is item 8, with a point-biserial correlation index of .19. In contrast, the d index based on upper-lower group comparisons reflects adequate discrimination between the two extreme scoring groups for this item. Based on these item data, it appears that all topic sentence items are functioning well for this group of students. With the item data analyzed, you are ready to consider the internal consistency of the total test.

TEST INTERNAL CONSISTENCY ANALYSIS

The preceding sections described procedures for evaluating the quality of individual items on a test. To check the discrimination quality of a particular item, the consistency was judged between students' performance on that item and their performance on the overall test. This question of the consistency of students' performance can be expanded to apply to an entire test. A test is said to have good internal consistency if the students who answer each question correctly are the same students who tend to answer the other questions correctly. Stated in a different way, a test has good internal consistency when the pattern of student performance on the overall test matches the pattern of student performance on most items on the test, where the students who have the highest overall scores on the test comprise the group that has the highest rate of correct responses on most items on the test. In other words, a test will have good internal consistency if most of the items on the test show good, positive discrimination.

The measure of a test's internal consistency described is the Kuder-Richardson formula 20, referred to as K-R$_{20}$. This particular index is used with objective-style tests when answers are scored as either correct or incorrect.

Calculating the Kuder-Richardson Internal Consistency Reliability Index

The K-R$_{20}$ index is the internal consistency reliability measure most often reported on computer-generated test analysis reports. The following formula is used for computing it:

$$\text{K-R}_{20} = \frac{n}{n-1}\left(1 - \frac{\Sigma p_i q_i}{\sigma^2}\right)$$

where

n =   the total number of test items.

p_i =   the proportion of students who answer each item correctly.

q_i =   the proportion of students who answer each item incorrectly, or $1 - p$.

$p_i q_i$ =   the proportion answering correctly times the proportion answering incorrectly. This value is called the *item variance*, and it is sometimes symbolized as s_i^2.

Σ =   sum the values for all test items.

σ^2 =   the total test variance. This value is the square of the standard deviation. The variance is calculated as $\Sigma(X - \overline{X})^2/N$. When the group tested represents a sample rather than the population, this value will be written as s^2 and calculated using $N - 1$ in the denominator.

The subscript $_i$ refers to item data.

Table 7.19 illustrates the calculation of the K-R$_{20}$ internal consistency reliability index. Two tests are included in the table. Each test includes data for six items and six students. The bottom rows for each test list item difficulty and discrimination data. The far right side of each test's data includes the calculation of the mean, test variance, and internal consistency reliability index.

Test I has a perfectly U-shaped distribution of raw scores, maximum item variance for each item (pq), and perfect item discrimination for all items at 1.00 for the point biserial correlation index. Such a configuration of item characteristics yields the maximum sum of item variances ($\Sigma p_i q_i$). It also yields maximum test variance given the range of scores since $[(6 - 0)/2]^2 = 3^2 = 9$. Notice that the maximum sum of item variances divided by the maximum test variance results in a K-R$_{20}$ index of .999. Such a high K-R$_{20}$ index reflects that the test is completely internally consistent.

Now review the item and test data in Table 7.19 for Test II. The items vary in difficulty and thus in item variances. This variability will reduce the internal consistency reliability index. These items probably do not measure the exact same skill since all students answered item 1 correctly and only one student answered item 6 correctly. Such item data usually reflect heterogeneous test content. In spite of test content differences, all items but the first one discriminate very well, which results in a wide range of scores and large test variance for a content-heterogeneous test containing only six items. The observed K-R$_{20}$ index of .80 reflects good internal consistency for a test measuring heterogeneous content.

Now consider the item and test data for the two tests illustrated in Table 7.20. These tests both have lower K-R$_{20}$ indices than the tests in Table 7.19. Notice that Test III has the same mean, range, and variance as Test II in Table

TABLE 7.19
Two Tests with Good Internal Consistency Reliability

			Test I					Data for Test Variance			Test Data
			Item				*Raw Score*	x^*	x^2		
Student	*1*	*2*	*3*	*4*	*5*	*6*					
1	1	1	1	1	1	1	6	3	9		$\overline{X}$ = 18/6 = 3
2	1	1	1	1	1	1	6	3	9		σ^2 = 54/6 = 9
3	1	1	1	1	1	1	6	3	9		K-R$_{20}$ = 6/5 [1 − (1.5/9)]
4	0	0	0	0	0	0	0	−3	9		= 1.2 (.833)
5	0	0	0	0	0	0	0	−3	9		= .99
6	0	0	0	0	0	0	0	−3	9		
p	.50	.50	.50	.50	.50	.50					
pq	.25	.25	.25	.25	.25	.25					
r_{pbi}	1.00	1.00	1.00	1.00	1.00	1.00					

			Test II					Data for Test Variance			Test Data
			Item				*Raw Score*	x^*	x^2		
Student	*1*	*2*	*3*	*4*	*5*	*6*					
1	1	1	1	1	1	1	6	2.5	6.25		$\overline{X}$ = 21/6 = 3.5
2	1	1	1	1	1	0	5	1.5	2.25		σ^2 = 17.5/6 = 2.92
3	1	1	1	1	0	0	4	.5	.25		K-R$_{20}$ = 6/5 [1 − (.97/2.92)]
4	1	1	1	0	0	0	3	−.5	.25		= 1.2 (.668)
5	1	1	0	0	0	0	2	−1.5	2.25		= .80
6	1	0	0	0	0	0	1	−2.5	6.25		
p	1.00	.83	.67	.50	.33	.17					
pq	.00	.14	.22	.25	.22	.14					
r_{pbi}	.00	.65	.83	.88	.82	.66					

*Note: $x = X - \overline{X}$.

7.19, yet the internal consistency index is smaller. The smaller K-R$_{20}$ index results from the item characteristics. Item 2 discriminates negatively, and all items are relatively difficult, yielding higher item variances than those in Test II.

Test IV in Table 7.20 has an internal consistency reliability index of −.456, indicating internal inconsistency for the test. Students' responses were ran-

TABLE 7.20
Two Tests Yielding Lower Internal Consistency

			Test III								Test Data	

Test III

			Item				Data for Test Variance			Test Data
Student	1	2	3	4	5	6	Raw Score	x^*	x^2	
1	1	1	1	1	1	1	6	2.5	6.25	$\overline{X}$ = 21/6 = 3.5
2	1	0	1	1	1	1	5	1.5	2.25	σ^2 = 17.5/6 = 2.92
3	1	0	0	1	1	1	4	.5	.25	K-R$_{20}$ = 6/5 [1 − (1.41/2.92)]
4	1	1	1	0	0	0	3	−.5	.25	= 1.2 (.52)
5	0	1	1	0	0	0	2	−1.5	2.25	= .62
6	0	1	0	0	0	0	1	−2.5	6.25	
p	.67	.67	.67	.50	.50	.50				
pq	.22	.22	.22	.25	.25	.25				
r_{pbi}	.83	−.42	.42	.88	.88	.88				

Test IV

			Item				Data for Test Variance			Test Data
Student	1	2	3	4	5	6	Raw Score	x^*	x^2	
1	1	0	1	0	1	0	3	0	0	$\overline{X}$ = 18/6 = 3
2	0	1	0	1	0	1	3	0	0	σ^2 = 0/6 = 0
3	0	1	0	1	0	1	3	0	0	K-R$_{20}$ = 6/5 [1 − (1.38/.00)]
4	1	0	0	1	0	1	3	0	0	= 1.2 (−.38)
5	1	0	1	0	1	0	3	0	0	= −.456
6	0	1	0	1	0	1	3	0	0	
p	.50	.50	.33	.67	.33	.67				
pq	.25	.25	.22	.22	.22	.22				
r_{pbi}	.00	.00	.00	.00	.00	.00				

*Note: $x = X − \overline{X}$.

dom, the items were difficult, and all six students obtained the same raw score of 3. In this case:

1. The mean score is 3.
2. The test variance and standard deviation are .00 since no score varies from the mean.

3. The item point-biserial correlation indices (r_{pbi}) are all .00 since there is no difference between means for item passers and the total group, and the test's standard deviation is .00.

Notice the impact of these data on the K-R$_{20}$ index for Test IV. The first element in the formula remains 1.2 since there are six items. The item variances for the six items are relatively high since the items are difficult, yet the test variance is .00. Only the sum of the item variances is subtracted from 1, yielding −.38, which, multiplied by the correction factor 1.2, is −.456. This K-R$_{20}$ index reflects great internal inconsistency for the test. The difficult items are not accompanied by good item discrimination and reasonable test variance. Test inconsistency can be expected when students do not possess the skills measured by a test and are randomly guessing answers.

Interpreting the K-R$_{20}$ Internal Consistency Reliability Index

The K-R$_{20}$ index typically ranges between .00 and 1.00, although negative values are possible. A K-R$_{20}$ index of .00 reflects no internal consistency for a test, and obtaining a value this low following instruction is highly unlikely. Indices greater than .90 reflect excellent internal consistency reliability. Obtaining a value this high or higher on a classroom test administered following instruction would be rare. Values this high are frequently observed for large standardized tests designed to discriminate among students. Indices near .80 are frequently obtained for classroom tests that measure complex skills and that are administered to heterogeneous groups of students. Values as low as .50 are also common for classroom tests administered following instruction to homogeneous groups of students. Values lower than .50 would be considered questionable unless one knows that the students tested were very similar in their skill levels.

As the previous calculation examples illustrated, four main factors influence the size of the K-R$_{20}$ internal consistency reliability index. They include:

1. Group homogeneity
2. Content homogeneity
3. Test length
4. Item difficulty

Group Homogeneity The achievement characteristics of the group examined will affect internal consistency reliability. The same test will yield a lower K-R$_{20}$ index when it is administered to a homogeneous group than when it is administered to a heterogeneous one. Students who are very similar in skill level will achieve similar raw scores on an examination, resulting in lower item discrimination, a more narrow range of scores, and a smaller test variance. Thus, you should not be surprised when the same posttest yields different $K-R_{20}$ indices when administered to different student groups.

Group homogeneity is influenced by instruction, and the same test administered to a group as a pretest and again as a posttest will yield different $K-R_{20}$ indices. Suppose you administered a pretest covering unencountered skills to a heterogeneous group. Students typically guess on pretests, the raw scores are usually low, and test variance is usually low. On the pretest, students' performance would be homogeneous, and a low internal consistency index would undoubtedly result. Administering the test again following quality instruction, you would most likely observe a much higher $K-R_{20}$ index for the same group due to differential learning rates in heterogeneous groups.

Content Homogeneity A second factor that influences measures of internal consistency is the homogeneity of skills measured on a test. A purely homogeneous test is one that measures only one skill or objective. For example, a test measuring students' skill in capitalizing proper nouns would be considered homogeneous. Students who possess this single skill would be expected to answer all items correctly, and students who did not understand proper nouns or capitalization would be expected to miss all items. Such a skill-specific exam administered to a heterogeneous class would yield a relatively large test variance and corresponding large internal consistency reliability index. It probably would not yield a perfect index of 1.00 due to the presence of inadvertent errors and guessing behavior.

The more skills measured by a test, the less homogeneous the test content. Tests that include a variety of skills typically yield a lower internal consistency reliability index than those that cover only one. For example, a term examination that measures 10 different capitalization objectives would be considered heterogeneous in content. Some students may know most capitalization rules very well but not all 10, and they may be proficient in different rules. The resulting uneven pattern of responses across the items on the test will tend to yield a lower $K-R_{20}$ index than a test containing the same number of items that covers only 1 capitalization rule. Heterogeneity of test content is an important factor for classroom teachers to consider in judging their tests since most unit, term, and semester examinations contain a variety of instructional objectives and goals.

Test Length The number of test items included on a test will influence the internal consistency reliability index. Basically, the longer the test, the better the internal consistency reliability indices. For example, a test on capitalizing proper nouns that contains 40 items will be much more reliable than one that contains only 10 items. With 40 items, you can adequately measure all four types of nouns with multiple examples and nonexamples for each type. Presenting only 10 items would limit the representativeness of items for the domain, thus potentially reducing the reliability. The correction factor in the formula ($n/n - 1$) will also differentially affect the K-R$_{20}$ index based on the number of items on the test.

Item Difficulty   The difficulty of the items and the overall test will affect the internal consistency reliability index. Tests that are extremely easy or difficult for a group yield little item and test variance, and lower K-R$_{20}$ indices will result. Very easy items are less problematic than very difficult ones since easy items tend to increase everyone's score by a constant. Extremely difficult items, on the other hand, tend to reduce reliability when guessing is rampant within the group.

COMPUTER TECHNOLOGY

The item and test analysis information described in this chapter is readily available from the ParSCORE (Economics Research, Inc., 1992) program. Figure 7.2 illustrates one type of report you can produce for a test. If multiple forms of a test are administered (e.g., item order scrambled and/or response order scrambled), the program can integrate item data from the different forms and produce reports as though only one form was administered.

Test Item Indices

The item numbers are located in the first column of Figure 7.2. Item difficulty indices (p values) for the total class are located in the second column, those for the upper group (27 percent) are located in the third column, and those for the lower group (27 percent) are provided in the fourth column.

For indices of item discrimination, you can obtain the discrimination index (d) by subtracting the lower group's p value in column 4 from the upper group's p value in column 3. The point-biserial correlation index is listed in column 5. You can use the next six columns, labeled Response Frequencies, to perform a distractor analysis. Notice that correct answers are indicated by an asterisk and that the last column lists distractors that were not chosen by any member of the class.

Test Internal Consistency

The Kuder-Richardson Internal Consistency Reliability Index (K-R$_{20}$) is located on the report following the group performance indices in the top right side of the page. In this example, the K-R$_{20}$ is 0.88.

A good testing program is invaluable for generating and summarizing item and test analysis data. Although a classroom teacher rarely has the time to devote to lengthy calculations, interpreting data from a computer-generated report requires relatively little time. Using data from these reports to improve both classroom tests and instruction helps teachers improve their work on an ongoing basis.

FIGURE 7.2
Sample Test Response and Item Analysis Report Form

```
Report Date:    7-7-1994    Time: 9:55:5        ParSCORE STATE COLLEGE
-----------------------------------------------------------------------------
                      TEST RESPONSE AND ITEM ANALYSIS

Instructor: RALPH LEWIS                      Total Possible Points: 100
      Class: ECON 100                        Students in this Group:  39
   Time/Day: 9 MWF                                      Mean Score:  49.85
       Date: 5-21-1994                                Median Score:  48.00
       Test: EXAM 3                       Standard Deviation:  16.87
       Form: A                                       Highest Score:  86
                                                       Lowest Score:  22
                              Reliability Coefficient (K-R_{20}):  0.88
```

| | Correct Responses as a Percentage of | | | Discrimination (Point Biserial) | Response Frequencies | | | | | | Nondistractors |
Item No.	The Total Group	Upper 27% of Group	Lower 27% of Group		A	B	C	D	E	O	
1	77	82	55	0.23	4	1	3	30*	1	0	
2	62	91	18	0.64	24*	3	2	2	8	0	
3	67	82	36	0.42	8	26*	5	0	0	0	DE
4	79	91	45	0.41	1	31*	4	2	1	0	
5	38	73	9	0.60	15*	13	6	3	2	0	
6	56	100	18	0.70	2	3	11	22*	1	0	
7	33	45	9	0.28	13*	15	9	2	0	0	E
8	13	27	9	0.29	18	5*	8	4	4	0	
9	26	0	27	-0.25	3	10*	16	3	7	0	
10	46	64	27	0.27	4	2	18*	2	13	0	
11	59	82	36	0.43	23*	6	4	2	4	0	
12	56	82	27	0.38	1	22*	1	7	8	0	
13	64	82	55	0.17	25*	3	4	3	4	0	
14	62	82	36	0.46	5	2	24*	7	1	0	
15	10	18	9	0.12	22	4*	4	8	1	0	
16	28	73	9	0.53	11*	15	1	4	8	0	
17	10	9	9	0.08	10	6	11	8	4*	0	
18	72	91	64	0.24	5	1	28*	4	1	0	
19	69	100	45	0.58	3	1	4	27*	4	0	
20	44	82	18	0.50	6	12	2	2	17*	0	
21	62	82	45	0.37	7	3	24*	2	3	0	
22	67	82	64	0.19	2	26*	4	7	0	0	E
23	36	73	18	0.43	6	12	14*	4	3	0	
24	54	64	45	0.29	5	21*	6	4	3	0	
25	41	100	9	0.66	16*	1	10	9	3	0	
26	51	100	27	0.48	3	2	3	11	20*	0	
27	36	45	18	0.18	3	8	12	14*	2	0	
28	64	91	36	0.46	3	3	5	25*	3	0	
29	59	91	36	0.47	2	2	2	23*	10	0	
30	31	45	9	0.44	3	7	15	2	12*	0	

Source: Economics Research, Inc. (1992). *ParSCORE and ParTEST User's Manual* (p. 139). Costa Mesa, CA.

SUMMARY

Due to limited time and resources, teachers usually cannot field test and revise items before a test is administered to a class. However, analyzing test items after students have taken the test can help teachers locate faulty or ineffective items and identify areas where instruction might be improved.

The three types of item analysis are item difficulty analysis, item discrimination analysis, and distractor analysis. The difficulty index is a measure of the difficulty of an item for a given group of students; it is the proportion of students who answer the item correctly; and it can range from 0 to 1.00. To describe the difficulty of an item using this measure, the indices can be classified into four categories: very easy ($p = .90$–1.00), moderately easy ($p = .70$–.89), fairly difficult ($p = .50$–.69), and very difficult ($p = .00$–.49). The overall difficulty of a test depends on the number of items falling into each category. The difficulty index can be used to evaluate an item by comparing (1) an item's difficulty with the difficulty anticipated, given the skill's complexity and the group's achievement characteristics; (2) the difficulty indices for items measuring the same objective; and (3) the difficulty indices for hierarchically related items. Difficulty measures that are very different from those anticipated signal a problem with the item, the instruction, or your perception of the circumstances.

Item discrimination analysis compares the performances of students who earn higher overall test scores with those of students earning lower total scores. Discrimination indices can range from 1.00 to –1.00. Positive numbers indicate that students with higher overall scores performed better on an item than did students with lower test scores. A discrimination index of .00 indicates that the upper and lower groups performed the same on an item; a negative index indicates that the lower scoring group performed better.

Evaluating an item using the discrimination index depends on two factors: the difficulty level of the item and the group's achievement characteristics. For homogeneous groups, relatively little discrimination is anticipated for an item, regardless of its difficulty level. For heterogeneous groups, little or no discrimination is anticipated for items that are extremely easy or extremely difficult. However, moderate-to-high, positive values should be anticipated for midrange difficulty indices.

Distractor analysis is performed for selected-response items. It provides information about the plausibility of distractors, helps teachers identify common misconceptions, and pinpoints parts of an item that are causing problems. In performing a distractor analysis, the number or percentage of students in the upper and lower groups who select each response are identified and analyzed. If teachers have ample time, they analyze the distractors for all items. However, when time is limited, they analyze only items that were (1) less difficult or more difficult than anticipated, (2) negative discriminators, and (3) designed to measure relatively complex skills.

Item analysis data do not indicate what is wrong with an item. Instead, they suggest that an item and perhaps the related instruction need to be reconsidered. Before calculating students' grades, you should eliminate items found to be defective, as they tend to distort the results and affect the validity of your interpretations.

One measure, the K-R$_{20}$ index, can be used to evaluate the internal consistency of an objective test. The K-R$_{20}$ index compares the sum of the item variances with the total test variance. This index is affected by group homogeneity, content homogeneity, test length, and item difficulty. The maximum K-R$_{20}$ value is 1.00, though obtaining values this high for classroom tests is unlikely. Typically, K-R$_{20}$ indices around .80 reflect good internal consistency for classroom tests, given students' inadvertent errors, guessing behavior, and common instruction; K-R$_{20}$ values near .50 are common; but ones much below this level should be questioned.

Table 7.21 contains a summary of the indices used to evaluate test items and tests. It includes the purpose for each measure, its formula, and the criterion values for judging the item and test quality. These criterion values are appropriate for classroom posttests.

TABLE 7.21
A Summary of Indices Used to Conduct an Item and Test Analysis

Analysis	Purpose	Measure	Formula	Criterion Values for Classroom Tests
Item Difficulty	Locate items more or less difficult than anticipated.	p	$p = \dfrac{R}{N}$ range = .00 to 1.00	Scanning Criterion: $p \geq .50$ $p \geq 90$: Very Easy $p = .70-.89$: Moderately Easy $p = .50-.69$: Fairly Difficult $p \leq .49$: Very Difficult
Item Discrimination	Determine consistency of students' item and total test performance.	d	$d = p_u - p_l$ range = −1.00 to 1.00	Scanning Criterion: $d \geq .00$ $\overline{p_{ul}}$ $\overline{d}$ $.30-.70$ $\geq .40$ $.71-.90$ $\geq .20$ $\geq .91$ any ± value
		r_{pbi}	$\dfrac{\overline{X}_p - \overline{X}}{\sigma}\sqrt{\dfrac{p}{q}}$ range = −1.00 to 1.00	Scanning Criterion: $r_{pbi} \geq .20$
Item Distractor	Locate students' misconceptions for subsequent instruction. Locate faulty items for revision.	Proportion of students selecting each response		
Test Internal Consistency Reliability	Compare item variance with total test variance.	K-R$_{20}$	$\dfrac{n}{n-1}\left(1 - \dfrac{\Sigma pq}{\sigma^2}\right)$	K-R$_{20}$ > .80 Excellent K-R$_{20}$ < .50 Questionable

Calculating by hand the item and test indices described in this chapter is not feasible, but computer generated programs such as ParSCORE (Economics Research, Inc., 1992) will calculate them for you. When you understand the indices included on computer-generated test reports, it is relatively easy to locate both the areas of strengths and problems in your tests, which is the first step in improving the quality of tests you use in your classroom.

PRACTICE EXERCISES

I. **Types of Item Analysis**

In the following exercise, Column A contains descriptions of item analysis activities and Column B names the three types of item analyses. Match each activity with its corresponding type of analysis.

Column A

_____ 1. Calculate the proportion of students who answer each item correctly.

_____ 2. Summarize the number or proportion of students in the upper and lower groups who select each response option.

_____ 3. Compare the proportion of the upper and lower groups who answer each item correctly.

_____ 4. Compare the perceived item complexity with the proportion of students who answer correctly.

_____ 5. Locate responses that were not plausible as well as common misconceptions.

_____ 6. Compare the proportion of students who correctly answer items related to the same objective.

Column B

a. Difficulty analysis
b. Discrimination analysis
c. Distractor analysis

II. **Calculating Difficulty and Discrimination Indices**

Table 7.22 contains objective and item data for the coordinating conjunction portion of the unit posttest prescribed in Table 5.7. The behavioral objectives for this section of the exam are described in Table 3.9. All item data are provided for items 1 through 11. For items 12, 13, 14, and 15, use your own paper to calculate the following indices and then insert them in the table in the appropriate cells.

A. Total group difficulty indices (p)
B. Discrimination indices (d)
C. Point-biserial correlation indices (r_{pbi})

TABLE 7.22

Item and Behavioral Objective Data for Only the Coordinating Conjunction Portion of the Compound Sentences Posttest (Objectives III.A.2 to III.F.1 in Tables 3.9 and 5.7)

Mean = 37.5   Standard Deviation = 3.88

Objective Codes	III.A.2	III.B.4	III.C.4	III.D.2				III.E.1		III.E.2		III.F.1				Overall Test Raw Score
Items	1	2	3	4	5	6	7	8	9	10	11	12	13	14	15	42
Correct Answers	*2*	*3*	*1*	*3*	*2*	*4*	*1*	*4*	*2*	*1*	*4*	*Hand Scored*				
McComas	*	*	*	*	*	*	*	*	*	*	*	*	*	*	*	42
Talbot	*	*	*	*	*	*	*	*	*	*	*	*	*	*	*	42
Deddens	*	*	*	*	*	*	*	*	*	*	*	*	*	*	*	41
Prince	*	*	*	*	*	*	*	*	*	*	*	*	*	*	*	41
Augustine	*	*	*	*	*	*	*	*	*	*	*	*	*	*	*	40
Rust	*	*	*	*	*	*	*	*	*	*	*	*	*	*	*	40
Carey	*	*	*	*	*	2	*	*	*	*	*	*	*	*	*	40
White	*	*	*	*	*	*	*	*	*	*	*	*	x	*	*	40
Hager	*	*	*	*	*	*	*	*	*	*	*	*	*	*	*	40
McLaughlin	*	*	*	*	*	2	*	*	*	*	*	*	*	x	*	39
Cromer	*	*	*	*	*	2	*	*	*	*	*	*	*	x	*	39
Otto	*	*	*	*	*	2	*	*	*	*	*	*	*	x	*	38
Scragg	*	*	*	*	*	2	*	*	*	*	3	*	*	x	*	37
Hill	*	*	*	*	*	2	*	*	*	*	3	*	*	*	x	36
Lovejoy	*	*	*	*	*	*	*	*	*	4	3	*	*	x	*	35
Bailey	*	*	3	*	*	2	*	*	*	2	3	*	*	x	*	35
Gormley	*	*	*	*	*	2	*	*	3	*	3	*	*	x	x	34
Deiters	*	*	*	*	*	1	*	*	3	2	1	x	*	x	*	33
Stewart	*	*	2	*	*	1	*	3	3	*	2	x	*	x	x	31
Smith	*	1	*	*	*	1	*	1	1	*	1	x	x	x	x	27
Total *p*	1.0	.95	.90	1.0	1.0	.45	1.0	.90	.80	.85	.60					
d	.00	.20	.40	.00	.00	1.0	.00	.40	.80	.40	1.0					
r_{pbi}	.00	.62	.39	.00	.00	.61	.00	.73	.81	.34	.84					

III. **Using Item Data to Locate Potentially Flawed Objective Items and Distractors**
In the preceding chapter on group performance analysis, the group's overall perform-ance on the compound sentences posttest was described as somewhat heterogeneous (range $42 - 27 = 15$ or 36 percent of the total number of items on the test and standard deviation of 3.88 encompasses 26 percent of the range). Use the item data in Table 7.22 to locate potentially flawed items based on their difficulty and discrimination indices, and record your answers in Table 7.23. Check your analysis in Table 7.23F.

IV. **Determining the Internal Consistency of the Overall Test**
Using the item data and standard deviation reported for the coordinating conjunction items in Table 7.22, calculate the K-R$_{20}$ index. (*Note:* This index is typically only calculated for the total test. There were 42 items on the total test, and that seems a few too many calculations for practice!)

V. **Interpreting Item Analysis Reports**
Interpreting a computer-generated item analysis report using difficulty, discrimina-tion, and distractor data. Table 7.24 contains 16 items selected from an item analysis report for a 56-item unit test. The following data were obtained for the test:

$\overline{X}$	R	σ	N students	N subgroups
$47, 86\%$	$56 - 37 = 19$	5.6	28	8

The small number of students means that the data should be considered tentative.
A. Classify the group performance as heterogeneous or homogeneous, and set mini-mum values for the r_{pbi} and d indices.
B. Using Table 7.24, locate any items with total group difficulty indices (p) lower than .50.
C. Locate any items that all students answered correctly.
D. Locate all items with r_{pbi} and d indices lower than the established minimum criteria. Can any of these items be ignored based on the p value?

TABLE 7.23
Chart for Summarizing Potentially Flawed Objective Test Items in Table 7.22

Item Evaluation Criteria	Potentially Flawed Coordinating Conjunction Items	Potentially Problematic Distractors for Identified Items
1. Too difficult ($p < .50$)		
2. All students answering correctly (potential clues)		
3. Much more or less difficult than other items measuring the same objective		
4. Inadequate discrimination for a somewhat heterogeneous group		

TABLE 7.24
Difficulty and Discrimination Data for Selected Items from a Unit Test

Item	Key	Upper 27% Responses					Lower 27% Responses					Difficulty/Discrimination		
		1	2	3	4	NR	1	2	3	4	NR	p	d	r_{pbi}
1	3			1.00			.13	.26	.50	.13		.79	.50	.787
2	3		.13	.88			.25	.13	.63			.57	.25	.277
3	3		.13	.88			.25	.25	.25	.25		.64	.63	.460
4	1	.75		.13	.13		.50	.13	.13	.25		.57	.25	.162
5	3	.13		.88			.38		.63			.64	.25	.141
6	2		1.00					.50	.38	.13		.82	.50	.512
7	3	.13		.88			.25		.75			.82	.13	.130
8	3	.13		.88				.13	.75	.13		.86	.13	.016
9	2		.13	.88				.25	.63	.13		.25	−.12	−.260
10	3			1.00				.25	.75			.75	.25	.452
11	1	1.00					.88			.13		.86	.12	.052
12	3			1.00					.38	.63		.79	.63	.059
13	3	.13		.88			.25		.75			.75	.13	.114
14	4			.13	.88				.25	.75		.79	.13	.012
15	2		1.00				.13	.88				.93	.13	.393
16	2		1.00					.88		.13		.96	.13	.102

Note: A blank space indicates that no student selected the response, and the number beneath each response option indicates the proportion of the upper or lower subgroup that selected the response.

E. The same 56-item test was administered to a second class containing 32 students. Compare these overall test data to determine whether the two groups' performances were similar.

Overall Test Data for Two Groups

Group	$\overline{X}$	%	Range	Range as % of Total Items	σ	σ as % of Range
I	47	84	19	34%	5.6	29%
II	45.4	81	25	45%	5.6	22%

F. Using the selected data in Table 7.25, determine whether any items yielded consistently low r_{pbi} indices across class groups.

G. Consider the distractors chosen by subgroup students for item 4. Based on this information, what might you conclude about the item?

H. Consider the distractors chosen by subgroup students for item 9. What might you conclude about this item?

I. Items 13 and 14 yielded inconsistent item discrimination data for the two groups. What might have caused these inconsistencies?

TABLE 7.25
Selected Data from Two Groups for Items That Yield Inadequate Point-Biserial Correlation Indices

Item	Key	Group	Upper 27% Responses				Lower 27% Responses				p	r_{pbi}
			1	2	3	4	1	2	3	4		
4	1	I	.75		.13	.13	.50	.13	.13	.25	.57	.162
		II	.89			.11	.78		.11	.11	.78	.082
7	3	I	.13		.88		.25		.75		.82	.130
		II		1.00					1.00		.91	−.013
8	3	I		.13	.88			.13	.75	.13	.86	.016
		II		.11	.78	.11		.11	.67	.22	.84	.172
9	2	I		.13	.88			.25	.63	.13	.25	−.260
		II	.11		.89			.33	.44	.22	.30	−.162
13	3	I	.13		.88		.25		.75		.75	.114
		II	.11		.89		.44		.56		.72	.422
14	4	I			.13	.88			.25	.75	.79	.012
		II				1.00			.33	.67	.78	.379

VI. Enrichment

Obtain a computer-generated item analysis report for a test that either you or someone else has administered. If the test was administered to two different class groups, obtain both data sets to enable comparison of the data for two occasions. Obtain a copy of the examination.

A. Locate the mean, range, and standard deviation. (You may need to calculate the range since it frequently is not provided.)

B. Classify the group's performance as heterogeneous or homogeneous.

C. Set your minimum standards for difficulty and discrimination.

D. Locate the difficulty indices (p) for each item, and circle those items more difficult than your set criterion. Transfer the difficulty and discrimination data for these items to a copy of the test. Analyze the text of the test item and generate hunches about why the item was more difficult than anticipated.

E. Locate all items on the test that measure the same behavioral objectives or enabling skills. Compare the p values for item sets, and locate any items that are very much more or less difficult than others in the set. Copy difficulty, discrimination, and distractor data for items identified as potentially flawed onto the test copy, and examine the items carefully for inadvertent item construction errors.

F. Locate the discrimination index. Your report will typically include only one of the two indices described. If your report contains difficulty indices for upper and lower subgroups, you can use p_u and p_l to obtain d when it is not provided. Discrimination is usually considered acceptable when either of the discrimination indices reflects an adequate level. Circle all items that did not yield adequate discrimination. Copy difficulty, discrimination, and distractor data for these items onto the test form, and analyze the item context and content.

    G. In analyzing the content of items judged potentially flawed based on difficulty and discrimination indices:
       1. Locate and review distractors not chosen by any class members.
       2. Locate and review distractors selected by many of the students in the group.
       3. Locate and review distractors chosen by more students in the upper subgroup.
    H. Revise items you consider faulty.

FEEDBACK

  I. **Types of Item Analysis**
     1. a   4. a
     2. c   5. c
     3. b   6. a

  II. **Calculating Difficulty and Discrimination Indices**

	Item			
	12	13	14	15
A. Total p	.85	.90	.50	.80
B. d	.60	.20	1.00	.60
C. r_{pbi}	.78	.34	.70	.71

  III. **Using Item Data to Locate Potentially Flawed Objective Items and Distractors**
     See Table 7.23F.

  IV. **Determining the Internal Consistency of the Overall Test**
     The K-R$_{20}$ index is .95, and this value represents very good internal consistency for the coordinating conjunction portion of the unit posttest.

  V. **Interpreting Item Analysis Reports**
     A. The range spans approximately 33 percent of the items, and the standard deviation spans 29 percent of the range. Based on these data, the group's performance would be classified as somewhat heterogeneous. The minimum value for r_{pbi} should be set at 20. Minimum values for d should be .20 for p values between .30 and .70 and .10 for values outside this range. Any d value is acceptable when p values are .90 or greater.
     B. Item 9 has a p value of .25; thus, it does not meet the minimum difficulty criterion.
     C. There are no items that all students answered correctly; however, 96 percent answered item 16 correctly, and 93 percent answered item 15 correctly.
     D. Items with inadequate r_{pbi} indices include 4, 5, 7, 8, 9, 11, 12, 13, 14, and 16. Item 16 can be ignored based on its extremely high difficulty index (.96). Only one item, 9, yielded an inadequate d index.
     E. The two groups' average test performances were similar. Based on their ranges and standard deviations, both groups' performances would be classified as somewhat heterogeneous.

TABLE 7.23F
Chart for Summarizing Potentially Flawed Objective Test Items in Table 7.22

Item Evaluation Criteria	Potentially Flawed Coordinating Conjunction Items	Potentially Problematic Distractors for Identified Items
1. Too difficult ($p < .50$)	Item 6	Distractor 2 chosen by 8 students
2. All students answering correcting (potential clues)	Items 1, 4, 5, 7. These items are recalling verbal information and locating the coordinating conjunction within a sentence. It is reasonable for all members of the class to answer them correctly.	
3. Much more or less difficult than other items measuring the same objective	Item 6, more difficult

Item 11, more difficult

Item 14, more difficult | • Distractor 2 chosen by 8 students
• All distractors functioning, 3 is the most chosen misconception
• (No distractors—student supplied conjunction for given sentences) |
| 4. Inadequate discrimination for a somewhat heterogeneous group | None except those items answered correctly by all students | |

F. Items that yielded consistently low discrimination indices across class groups are 4, 7, 8, and 9.

G. For item 4, all distractors were chosen by at least one group member, indicating that they were plausible for students. The item does not appear to be miskeyed since the majority of both subgroups selected the keyed answer. Distractors 3 and 4 should be analyzed carefully to determine why they might be attractive to upper subgroup members.

H. For item 9, all distractors were chosen by at least one member of the groups. The item is possibly miskeyed since distractor 3 had p_{ul} values of .76 (calculated as $[.88 + .63] \div 2$) and .67 and d values of .25 (calculated as $p_u - p_l$) and .45 for the two groups. If option 3 is not the correct answer, it should be analyzed carefully to determine why it was so attractive to students in both classes.

I. The small number of students in each class and the even smaller number of students in the upper and lower subgroups undoubtedly resulted in item data that were not generalizable across groups. Notice in Table 7.24 that the d values for group I on these two items were acceptable at .13; thus, the higher discrimination values for group II were not completely unexpected.

REFERENCE

Economics Research, Inc. (1992). *Par-SCORE user's manual* (p. 139). Costa Mesa, CA: Economics Research, Inc.

SUGGESTED READINGS

Ebel, R. L., & Frisbee, D. A. (1991). *Essentials of educational measurement* (5th ed.) (pp. 220–240). Englewood Cliffs, NJ: Prentice Hall.

Hopkins, C. D., & Antes, R. L. (1990). *Classroom measurement and evaluation* (3rd ed.) (pp. 267–292). Itasca, IL: F. E. Peacock.

Mehrens, W. A., & Lehmann, I. J. (1991). *Measurement and evaluation in education and psychology* (4th ed.) (pp. 160–170; 248–264). New York: CBS College Publishing.

Oosterhof, A. (1990). *Classroom applications of educational measurement* (pp. 253–269). Columbus, OH: Merrill.

Popham, J. W. (1990). *Modern educational measurement* (2nd ed.) (pp. 286–308). Englewood Cliffs, NJ: Prentice Hall.

Sax, G. (1989). *Principles of educational and psychological measurement and evaluation* (3rd ed.) (pp. 227–256). Belmont, CA: Wadsworth.

Wiersma, W., & Jurs, S. G. (1990). *Educational measurement and testing* (2nd ed.) (pp. 239–253). Boston: Allyn and Bacon.

CHAPTER 8

Evaluating Individual Performance and Instruction

OBJECTIVES

- Perform a norm-referenced analysis and an evaluation of an individual's test performances.
- Perform a criterion-referenced analysis and an evaluation of an individual's test performances.
- Evaluate the quality of instruction for each goal.

Once you have analyzed a group's performance and the test, you need to interpret each individual's performance. A test score by itself has little meaning. To interpret a student's score, you can compare it with scores of other students or relate it to the number of skills measured by the test. Comparing a student's performance with that of other students is called *norm-referenced analysis.* Teachers use this type of analysis to determine whether a student's test performance is above average, average, or below average compared to classmates. Norm-referenced analysis can be used to interpret students' scores from any test, regardless of the logic used in the test design. *Criterion-referenced analysis* refers only to the interpretation of test scores obtained from criterion-referenced tests. Remember that the design of a criterion-referenced test is based on the carefully specified set of enabling skills that make up an instructional goal framework. Thus, a high score on a criterion-referenced test reflects that the student has mastered the criterion or set of skills embedded in the goal. Likewise, a low score reflects that a student has made little, if any, progress on the criterion. Since the classroom tests described in this chapter are criterion referenced, both criterion-referenced and norm-referenced analyses can be performed.

Each of these analyses provides a different type of information. For example, if a criterion-referenced analysis indicated that a student had mastered only half of the skills measured, you might consider the student's performance inadequate. If you then performed a norm-referenced analysis and discovered that the same student's performance was well above average in the class, your interpretation of the score would probably change. In addition to evaluating individual performances, you should evaluate the group's performance on each goal, enabling skill, or objective. Information from this analysis will help you evaluate the quality of the instruction and identify lessons or portions of lessons that were not effective.

CONDUCTING A NORM-REFERENCED ANALYSIS

To compare an individual's performance to the group's, you need to determine whether (1) the student's performance is above average, average, or below average and (2) the student's performance is consistent with her or his past performance.

Comparing Individual Performance to the Group

An easy way to compare a student's performance to the group is to divide the raw scores into categories of above average, average, and below average, and then compare the student's score with these categories. You can use the mean and the standard deviation to categorize the raw scores. Raw scores equal to and higher than one standard deviation above the mean are classified as above average. Raw scores equal to and lower than one standard deviation below the mean are classified as below average. Scores between these two anchors are categorized as average-level performance on the test. Raw scores equal to and greater than two standard deviations above the mean are classified as being well above average. Likewise, scores equal to and lower than two standard deviations below the mean are considered to be well below average compared to the class.

Consider, for example, the following achievement categories for a 25-item test. Remember the following symbols: X_H = the highest earned score, X_L = the lowest earned score, $\overline{X}$ = the mean, and σ = the standard deviation. The standard deviation in the example is 4.73. This value is added to and subtracted from the mean score, 19.1, to locate the categories of above average, average, and below average. According to this chart, no scores would be classified as very high performance compared to the class, and scores of 24 and 25 would be considered above average in the group. Raw scores ranging from 15 to 23 would be classified as average-level performance compared to the class. Scores ranging from 11 to 14 would be classified as below average, and scores from 8 to 10 would be categorized as well below average for this group.

Score Category	Very Low Performance		Below-Average Performance	Average Performance	Above-Average Performance		Very High Performance
Scores	8	9.64	14.37	19.91	23.83	25	
	X_L	-2σ	-1σ	$\overline{X}$	$+1\sigma$	X_H	$+2\sigma$

Comparing a student's performance with the group's performance is sometimes accomplished through the use of standard scores and percentile scores. Standard scores and percentile scores are often reported on computer-generated reports.

Calculating and Using Standard Scores

Often, standard scores are used to compare an individual's test performance with that of the group. The most commonly reported standard scores on computer-generated test analysis reports are the z and T scores. Standard scores are derived from an individual's raw score, the group's average score, and the group's variability as measured by the standard deviation. Thus, students' raw scores are modified to reflect their group standing.

These norm-referenced z and T scores are called standard scores because they convert all posttest scores to a standard scale that has a constant mean and a constant standard deviation. Holding the mean and standard deviation constant enables interpreting students' relative performance on a single test and across tests using only the standard score. The z score has a constant mean of 0 and a constant standard deviation of 1, and the T score has a constant mean of 50 and a standard deviation of 10.

The standard score scale for z and T scores is illustrated in the following chart:

z Scores		−3	−2	−1	0	+1	+2	+3
T Scores		20	30	40	50	60	70	80
Standard Deviations		-3σ	-2σ	-1σ	$\overline{X}$	$+1\sigma$	$+2\sigma$	$+3\sigma$

A z score of 0 and a T score of 50 both reflect that the student earned the mean score on the test. A z score of 1 and a T score of 60 both are one standard deviation above the mean; therefore, they reflect the lower boundary of above average performance. Likewise, a z score of −1 and a T score of 40 both are one standard deviation below the mean and reflect the upper boundary of below average performance. Scores farther from the mean in either direction reflect performance farther removed from average. Thus, regardless of the original raw scores, original mean score, or original standard deviation on a test, the standard scores can be used to locate a student's comparative performance level.

The formulas for calculating the z and T scores are:

$$z = \frac{X - \overline{X}}{\sigma} \qquad T = 10z + 50$$

The z score is calculated by subtracting the mean score on the test from each student's raw score. This difference, or the amount the individual's score deviates from the mean, is divided by the standard deviation to determine how much larger or smaller the individual's deviation is than the group's standard deviation. In other words, a z score of .5 or −.5 indicates that a student's deviation from the mean score is half as large as the group's standard deviation. Negative numbers reflect deviation below the mean. A z score of 1 or −1 indicates that the student's deviation from the mean score is the same as the group's standard deviation. Scores of 1.5 and −1.5 indicate that a student's deviation from the mean is one and one-half times larger than the group's standard deviation.

The *T* score is calculated from the z score. The z score is multiplied by 10 to change the size of the standard deviation from 1 to 10. This product is added to 50 to change the size of the mean from 0 to 50. These *T* scores have the same meaning as the z scores. Scores of 45 or 55 indicate that a student's deviation from the mean is only half as large as the group's standard deviation. *T* scores rather than z scores are frequently used to report a student's relative performance to avoid using the negative and decimal numbers on the z score scale. Regardless of whether the z or *T* score is reported on your analysis reports, its indication of a student's group standing remains the same.

Table 8.1 illustrates the calculation of z and *T* scores for the hypothetical set of test data previously described. The raw scores are listed in the first column and the frequency with which each score occurs in the set is shown in the second column. The z scores are provided in the third column and the corresponding *T* scores are listed in the last column. Recall that the mean for this set of scores is 19.1 and the standard deviation is 4.73. Notice that the raw

TABLE 8.1
Standard Scores for Hypothetical Objective Test Data

Mean = 19.1	Standard Deviation = 4.73			
X	f	z	T	
25	2	1.25	62	Above Average Compared to Classmates
24	1	1.04	60	
23	2	.82	58	
22	2	.61	56	
21	4	.40	54	Average Achievement Compared to Classmates
19	2	−.02	50	
18	1	−.23	48	
17	2	−.44	46	
14	1	−1.08	39	
12	1	−1.50	35	Below Average Compared to Classmates
10	1	−1.92	31	
8	1	−2.35	26	Well Below Average Compared to Classmates

Note: The z score for a raw score of 25 is calculated as follows: $(25 − 19.1)/4.73 = 1.25$. The *T* score for a raw score of 25 is calculated as follows: $(10 \times 1.25) + 50 = 62$.

score 24 is closest to one standard deviation above the mean, 23.83, and that this score has a z score of 1.04 and a T score of 60. The raw score 19 is closest to the mean score 19.01 and it has a corresponding z score of –.02 and T score of 50. The raw score nearest one standard deviation below the mean is 14 and its z and T scores are –1.08 and 39, respectively. The raw score 8 is lower than two standard deviations below the mean and it has z and T scores of –2.35 and 26, respectively. When standard scores are provided with computerized test analysis forms, you can simply use these scores to classify students' test performance as above average, average, or below average.

Calculating and Using Percentile Scores

Percentile scores range from 1 to 99, and they reflect the percentage of students surpassed at each raw score in a distribution of test scores. Typically, scores at the 75th percentile and above are considered to be above average (upper quartile), and scores at the 25th percentile and below are considered to be below average (lower quartile). Midrange percentiles between these two anchors are interpreted as average-level performance compared to the class group.

Calculating Percentile Scores   Table 8.2 contains hypothetical raw scores for 20 students. The first column contains the raw scores, and the highest possible score is 25. The second column contains the percentage of items correct for each raw score. The third column contains the frequency with which each raw score occurred in the class. The fourth column contains the *cumulative frequency of students* below each raw score, or the total number of students scoring *below* each raw score. The fifth includes one-half of the students who earn each raw score. The sixth column contains the *cumulative frequency at midpoint*, and it is the sum of the values in columns 4 and 5. The cumulative frequency at midpoint value includes the total number of students scoring below each raw score and one-half the number of students who earn that raw score. The seventh column contains the proportion of students represented in the cumulative frequency at midpoint. This proportion is obtained by dividing the cumulative frequency at midpoint by the total number of students in the group. The eighth column contains the percentile score, and it is obtained by multiplying the proportion of students in column 7 by 100.

Interpreting Percentile Scores   Each percentile score represents the percentage of students in the class surpassed at each raw score point on the test. For example, a student who earns a percentile score of 13 is said to have scored better than 13 percent of the students in the class, and a student who earns a percentile score of 80 has surpassed 80 percent of the group.

Teachers need to be cautious and not confuse percentile scores with the percentage of items answered on a test. Notice in Table 8.2 that for a raw score

TABLE 8.2
Calculating Percentile Scores for Objective Test Data

N = 20							
1	2	3	4	5	6	7	8
Raw Scores X	Percentage Correct	f	cf Below	1/2 f within	cf at Midpoint	Proportion Surpassed	Percentile
25	100	2	18	1.0	19.0	.95	95
24	96	1	17	.5	17.5	.88	88
23	92	2	15	1.0	16.0	.80	80
22	88	2	13	1.0	14.0	.70	70
21	84	4	9	2.0	11.0	.55	55
20	80						
19	76	2	7	1.0	8.0	.40	40
18	72	1	6	.5	6.5	.31	31
17	68	2	4	1.0	5.0	.25	25
16							
15							
14	56	1	3	.5	3.5	.18	18
13							
12	48	1	2	.5	2.5	.13	13
11							
10	40	1	1	.5	1.5	.08	8
9							
8	32	1	0	.5	.5	.03	3

of 21, the percentage of items answered correctly is 84, whereas the corresponding percentile score is 55. The percentage correct score reflects the proportion of *test items* answered correctly, and the percentile score represents the proportion of *students* surpassed on the exam.

One final comment should be made. Teachers cannot determine the percentage of items answered correctly using only norm-referenced scores. For example, a student may earn a *T* score of 70 and a percentile score of 99, yet only answer correctly 60 percent of the items included on a test. Norm-referenced scores indicate how well a student performed compared to classmates, but not how much of a domain a student has mastered. Percentile scores will be discussed again in Chapter 15.

Comparing Current with Past Performances

Comparing a student's performance with the group's performance provides a general indication of how the student is performing. To interpret properly a student's performance that is classified as above average, average, or below average, you need to compare it with his or her usual or typical performance level. For example, an average test performance can be considered as not good, typical, or excellent, depending on the student's previous record. An average-level performance would undoubtedly be considered good for a student who typically earns below-average scores. Likewise, an average performance would be viewed negatively for a student who typically earns one of the highest scores in the group.

The achievement characteristics of the group will also influence your interpretation of high, average, and low performance. An average performance in a high-achieving, homogeneous group is different from an average performance in a heterogeneous group. Because norm-referenced interpretations are relative, you should also evaluate students on the number of skills they have mastered.

An Example

Students' raw scores from the objective portion of the paragraph posttest are used to demonstrate norm-referenced analysis. Table 8.3 includes the test scores of all class members in the left portion of the table, and the right portion contains norm-referenced data with the mainstreamed student's outlier score removed. The first column contains students' raw scores, followed by the percentage of items correct for each raw score. The third column contains the frequency with which each raw score occurred for the exam. The remaining columns include the z, T, and percentile scores for each raw score.

Examine first the data in the left side of the table that includes all members of the class. Only students who earned perfect scores on the exam would be classified as above average in this class (z and T scores of 1.03 and 60, respectively). Raw scores of 34 and 42 set the boundaries for average-level performance on the test ($z = -.83$ to .83 and $T = 42$ to 58). Raw scores 32 and 33 are classified as below average with z and T scores lower than one standard deviation below the mean score. The mainstreamed student earned a raw score of 24, a z score of -2.89, and a T score of 21. This achievement level would be classified as well below average in this class since it is lower than two standard deviations below the mean.

The percentile scores are located in the last column for the total class. Notice that the highest percentile score is 88 and the lowest is 2. Even though students earned perfect scores on the exam (43 and 100% correct), they did not obtain a percentile score of 100 because they cannot surpass themselves. Why did these five students not receive percentile scores of 99? The percentile score of 88 was the highest on this test because there were five students who tied for a perfect raw score. All students earning scores lower than 43, plus one-half the students tied at 43, results in a cumulative frequency at midpoint of 17.5. This value divided by the number of students in the class yields a percentile score of 88.

TABLE 8.3
Norm-Referenced Analysis of Students' Achievement on the Objective Portion of the Paragraph Unit Posttest

$N = 20$ Mean = 38	Standard Deviation = 4.84					$N = 19$ Mean = 38.74	Standard Deviation = 3.71	
		Total	Class	Group		Recalculated	without	Outlier
X	Percentage Correct	f	z	T	Percentile	z	T	Percentile
43	100	5	1.03	60	88	1.15	61	87
42	98	2	.83	58	70	.88	59	68
41	95	1	.62	56	63	.61	56	61
40	93	1	.41	54	58	.34	53	55
39	91	1	.21	52	53	.07	51	50
38	88	1	.00	50	48	.20	48	45
37	86	2	−.21	48	40	−.47	45	37
36	84	1	−.41	46	33	−.74	43	29
35	81	2	−.62	44	25	−1.00	40	21
34	79	1	−.83	42	18	−1.28	37	13
33	77	1	−1.03	40	13	−1.55	35	8
32	74	1	−1.24	38	8	−1.82	32	3
24	56	1	−2.89	21	2			

Note: Using the total class group: A z score for the raw score 43 is calculated as follows: $(43 − 38)/4.84 = 1.03$. A T score for the raw score 43 is calculated as follows: $(1.03 \times 10) + 50 = 60$. A percentile score for the raw score 43 is calculated as follows: $(15 + 2.5)/20 \times 100 = 88$.

Comparing the percentage of items correct and the percentile for each score should illustrate why it is important not to confuse these two scores when interpreting students' test performance. For a percentage correct score of 100, the corresponding percentile score is 88, and for a percentage correct score of 86, the percentile score is 40.

The right side of Table 8.3 includes the recalculated z, T, and percentile scores with the outlier score removed. Similar to the previous data, only a raw score of 43 is classified as above average in this class. Removal of the outlier score, however, resulted in decreasing the size of the average group and increasing the number of students classified as below average in the class. Average raw scores now range from 36 to 42 ($T = 43$ to 59) and below-average scores range from 32 to 35 ($T = 32$ to 40). This decreases the number of students classified as average from 12 to 9 and increases the number classified as below average from 2 to 5 (excluding the mainstreamed student). These recalculated data illustrate how the nature of the comparison group can influence the norm-referenced scores and the classification of students as above average, average, and below average.

CONDUCTING A CRITERION-REFERENCED ANALYSIS

All the performance analysis procedures presented thus far use students' raw scores. Raw scores alone do not provide the type of information you need to evaluate a student's progress on prescribed skills. Consider, for example, the test performances of J. Allen and T. Baker shown in Table 8.4. The top row of the table identifies the six objectives measured by the examination. The second row identifies the item numbers from 1 to 24. Notice that numbers 10 through 24 are written vertically. The third row identifies the keyed correct answer for each item. Notice that there are four items measuring each of the six objectives. The rows for Allen and Baker contain the responses made by each student. A dot (.) indicates that the student's response matched the keyed correct response, and a number in a student-by-item cell indicates the particular incorrect response selected by the student. From the raw score column, you can see that both students answered 18 of 24 test items correctly. If the mean score on the test is also 18, you might conclude that their performances are the same and that they are average for the group. After looking at the students' prior performance records, you might also conclude that their test performances are typical for them. Now, compare the two students' responses by objective and item.

Although both students answered 18 items correctly, their performances on the objectives were quite different. Allen correctly answered 3 of 4 items for each objective. Baker, however, correctly answered all of the items for four of the objectives, failed objective 4 completely, and answered half the items correctly for objective 6. This information sheds new light on the divergence of the students' performances and suggests very different instructional needs.

Reviewing your students' response patterns can help you determine their mastery of the objectives, enabling skills, or goals you are measuring. By using such a mastery analysis, you can better judge the quality of each student's performance and prescribe appropriate follow-up activities.

TABLE 8.4
Student Performance by Objective and Item

OBJECTIVE	1	2	3	4	5	6	TOTAL	
Item **Answer**	1 2 3 4 3 2 1 4	5 6 7 8 4 3 1 4	1 1 1 9 0 1 2 2 3 5 1	1 1 1 1 3 4 5 6 2 2 1 3	1 1 1 2 7 8 9 0 5 1 4 3	2 2 2 2 1 2 3 4 2 1 1 5	Raw Score	%
Allen, J.	. . 2 .	. 1 . .	. . 4 .	1 . . .	. 2 . .	. . 3 .	18	75
Baker, T.	. . . .	. . . .	. . . .	1 3 2 2	. . . .	3 . 3 .	18	75

To perform a mastery analysis you need to do the following:

1. Compare items by objective, enabling skill, or goal.
2. Determine the number of correct answers that will indicate minimal mastery of each skill.
3. Determine whether each student mastered each objective.
4. Prescribe follow-up activities.
5. Develop a student progress chart.
6. Evaluate students' performances.

Comparing Items by Objective, Enabling Skill, or Goal

For the comparison, you can use the student response matrix you obtain when you use machine scoring. To separate items by objectives, enabling skills, or goals, simply draw vertical lines in the matrix between items measuring different skills. Tables 8.4 and 8.6 both illustrate the way a test report can be subdivided by objective or enabling skill. Teachers also create their own formats for organizing classroom test information by objective or enabling skill to make it easier to determine whether students are mastering the content.

Establishing Mastery Criteria

After you have separated the test items by skill, decide the level of performance on each skill that you consider mastery. If a skill is represented by multiple test items, minimal mastery is generally defined as correctly answering a majority of the items. If a skill is measured by only one or two items, the student would need to answer one or both items correctly. For example, the test described in Table 8.4 measured six different objectives with four items each. Students would have had to answer three of the four items correctly to master each objective. If a skill is extremely important or includes a variety of subskills, you might want to set the criterion at a level higher than a simple majority of correct items.

Determining Individual Mastery of Skills

To determine an individual student's mastery of the skills, you need to (1) count the items that the student answered correctly for each skill and (2) count the number of skills that the student mastered. Referring to the example test in Table 8.4, if a student missed two or more items per objective, you should circle these items on your chart. Next, count the number of objectives mastered and record them in the right-hand column of your chart. Your mastery chart should look like Table 8.5 for the two students.

TABLE 8.5
Describing Students' Mastery

OBJECTIVE	1	2	3	4	5	6	TOTAL		
Item	1 2 3 4	5 6 7 8	1 1 1 9 0 1 2	1 1 1 1 3 4 5 6	1 1 1 2 7 8 9 0	2 2 2 2 1 2 3 4	Raw Score	%	OBJ.
Answer	3 2 1 4	4 3 1 4	2 3 5 1	2 2 1 3	5 1 4 3	2 1 1 5	24		6
Allen, J.	. . 2 .	. 1 . .	. . 4 .	1 . . .	. 2 . .	. . 3 .	18	75	6
Baker, T.	. . . .	. . . .	. . . .	(1 3 2 2)	. . . .	(3 . 3 .)	18	75	4

According to the chart, Allen correctly answered a majority of the items for each objective, achieving at least minimal mastery on all six objectives. For Baker, objectives 4 and 6 are circled. The number in the right-hand column indicates that this student mastered only four of the six objectives.

Prescribing Follow-Up Activities

To prescribe appropriate follow-up activities, you need to consider the importance of the skills that students failed and the students' previous achievement. For example, if subsequent lessons build on a particular skill, a student who failed to master the skill will undoubtedly have difficulty. The simplest way to avoid such problems is to divide the group into two categories: students who have mastered the goals and students who need more instruction and practice. You can then prescribe enrichment activities for the first group and developmental activities for the second, or you could organize peer-tutoring or cooperative learning activities to involve the entire group in bringing all students up to an acceptable level of mastery.

In establishing follow-up activities, also consider each student's previous achievement. If a student's test performance is inconsistent in terms of the number of goals or objectives typically mastered, you may wish to interview the student to determine what factors contributed to the sudden decline or improvement in achievement.

Developing a Student Progress Chart

Some teachers like to keep a student progress chart that indicates the skills that remain to be mastered by each student. This type of chart usually lists all student names in the left-hand column and indicates the objectives, enabling skills, or goals to be mastered across the top. The teacher can either post the chart on a bulletin board for student use or refer to the chart during private consultations with students or their parents.

Evaluating Students' Performances

Students' performances can be evaluated by comparing the raw scores and the number of skills mastered. Reviewing either of these scores independently does not provide the same insight. Earning a high test score and mastering all skills would obviously be considered a good test performance. Likewise, earning a low score and failing several skills would be judged an inadequate performance. However, it is not uncommon to find rather average test scores for students who have mastered all the skills, at least at a minimum level. When such a pattern is found, a student's overall performance can be judged as good because mastering all the skills reflects good work. However, the student may have a reading problem, may not be motivated to be very careful in answering questions, or may work too quickly. Such a pattern warrants a student conference to investigate and hopefully resolve the problem.

An Example

Table 8.6 contains students' scores by item and objective for the topic sentence strand of the unit posttest on writing a paragraph. The behavioral objectives are described in Table 3.6 and the table of test specifications for the unit posttest are described in Table 4.2. The top three rows of the table contain the behavioral objective codes, the test item numbers, and the correct answers. Notice that objective II.F.1 indicates that these test items were hand scored. This objective required students to write topic sentences for incomplete paragraphs. Students' names are listed in the far left column. Asterisks placed in the item columns reflect correct answers. The numbers listed in test item columns reflect incorrect responses, and the particular number indicates the distractor selected by the student.

Using the rule that minimal mastery requires answering a simple majority of the items correctly for each objective, you can see that students needed to answer all items correctly for objectives II.A.4 through II.F.1. Objectives not mastered are highlighted in the table using a dark box. All students in the class mastered the recall objectives related to the physical and functional characteristics of topic sentences (objectives II.A.4 and II.B.4). Six students did not demonstrate mastery of the objective related to the quality characteristics of topic sentences (II.C.4). All students mastered the objective related to discriminating between topic sentences and other sentences included in a paragraph (II.D.1). Considering the two objectives for evaluating topic sentences, four students failed objective II.E.1 and two students failed objective II.E.4. Three students also did not master the objective for writing topic sentences for given incomplete paragraphs.

Table 8.7 includes the original goal analysis matrix, and it is often used to summarize the names of students who require additional instruction on particular enabling skills in the unit. Although only the mastery data for the topic sentence portion of the test is included in the table, the names of students who failed to master other enabling skills on the posttest can be inserted into the

TABLE 8.6

Mastery Analysis of Students' Performance for Only the Topic Sentence Portion of the Paragraph Posttest (Objectives II.A.4 to II.F.1 in Tables 3.6 and 4.2)

	TOPIC SENTENCE OBJECTIVES							
Objective Codes	**II.A.4**	**II.B.4**	**II.C.4**	**II.D.1**	**II.E.1**	**II.E.4**	**II.F.1**	**Total Objectives Mastered**
Items:	3	4	5	6 7	8 9	10 11	12 13	7
Correct Answers:	4	4	4	1 1	2 4	1 4	*Hand Scored*	
Augustine	*	*	*	* *	* *	* *	* *	7
Prince	*	*	*	* *	* *	* *	* *	7
Deddens	*	*	*	* *	* *	* *	* *	7
Talbot	*	*	*	* *	* *	* *	* *	7
McComas	*	*	*	* *	* *	* *	* *	7
Rust	*	*	*	* *	* *	* *	* *	7
Carey	*	*	*	* *	* *	* *	* *	7
Cromer	*	*	*	* *	* *	* *	* *	7
Hager	*	*	*	* *	* *	* *	* *	7
McLaughlin	*	*	*	* *	* *	* *	* *	7
White	*	*	*	* *	* *	* *	* *	7
Otto	*	*	*	* *	* *	* *	* *	7
Lovejoy	*	*	*	* *	* *	* *	* *	7
Hill	*	*	*	* *	* *	* *	* *	7
Scragg	*	*	2	* *	* *	* *	* *	6
Gormley	*	3	*	* *	* 3	* *	* *	5
Bailey	*	*	2	* *	1 *	* *	* *	5
Deiters	*	*	2	* *	* 3	* *	* x	4
Stewart	*	*	3	* *	* *	2 *	* x	4
Smith	*	*	2	* *	* 3	2 1	x x	3
Number of Students Who Mastered	20	20	14	20	16	18	17	
Percentage of Students Who Mastered	100%	100%	70%	100%	80%	90%	85%	

TABLE 8.7
Prescribed Instructional Activities Based on Mastery Analysis

CONCEPTS/ CONTENT	A State/Recall Physical Characteristics of:	B State/Recall Functional Characteristics of:	C State/Recall Quality Characteristics of:	D Discriminate Between Examples & Nonexamples	E Evaluate Given Examples	F Produce Examples of:
I. Topic Sentence			Bailey Deiters Gormley Scragg Smith Stewart		Bailey Deiters Gormley Smith Stewart	Deiters Smith Stewart
III. Supporting Sentences						
IV. Concluding Sentence						

appropriate cells. The completed chart will provide the teacher with a good class summary for prescribing follow-up activities. As students master the skills following subsequent instruction, their names can be removed from the table.

Table 8.8 includes a partial student progress chart for the instructional goal, "Write a paragraph." The summary chart does not list particular behavioral objectives for the unit; instead, the original enabling skills from the goal analysis matrix are used to indicate learner progress. The far left column of the table lists students' names, and the enabling skills for the paragraph unit are listed across the top of the chart. The teacher has placed an x in the intersecting student-by-enabling skill cells to indicate the students who have mastered each skill. In addition, an **M** for mastery is inserted in the total topic sentence column (**II**) for those students who mastered all topic sentence enabling skills. A **PM** is used to identify the students who mastered the majority of the enabling skills. The blank cells indicate nonmastery of a concept area, and they are used to identify the students who did not master the majority of enabling skills. In the example class group, Bailey and Gormley partially mastered the topic sentences area, whereas Deiters, Smith, and Stewart failed to master topic sentences. The other 15 students mastered all enabling skills for topic sentences.

EVALUATING THE QUALITY OF INSTRUCTION

Analyzing individual performances provides useful information about each student's progress. To evaluate the quality of instruction, however, you need

TABLE 8.8
A Partial Student Progress Chart for the Instructional Goal,
"Write a Paragraph"

	PARAGRAPH			TOPIC SENTENCES							
ENABLING SKILLS	I A	I B	I D	II A	II B	II C	II D	II E	II F	**II**	Etc.
Augustine	x	x	x	x	x	x	x	x	x	**M**	
Bailey	x	x	x	x	x		x		x	**PM**	
Carey	x	x	x	x	x	x	x	x	x	**M**	
Cromer	x	x	x	x	x	x	x	x	x	**M**	
Deddens	x	x	x	x	x	x	x	x	x	**M**	
Deiters	x	x	x	x	x		x				
Gormley	x	x	x	x	x		x		x	**PM**	
Hager	x	x	x	x	x	x	x	x	x	**M**	
Hill		x	x	x	x	x	x	x	x	**M**	
Lovejoy	x	x	x	x	x	x	x	x	x	**M**	
McComas	x	x	x	x	x	x	x	x	x	**M**	
McLaughlin	x	x	x	x	x	x	x	x	x	**M**	
Otto	x	x	x	x	x	x	x	x	x	**M**	
Prince	x	x	x	x	x	x	x	x	x	**M**	
Rust	x	x	x	x	x	x	x	x	x	**M**	
Scragg	x	x	x	x	x		x	x	x	**M**	
Smith	x	x	x	x	x		x				
Stewart	x	x	x	x	x		x				
Talbot	x	x	x	x	x	x	x	x	x	**M**	
White	x	x	x	x	x	x	x	x	x	**M**	

Note: x = at least minimal mastery of enabling skill; **PM** = Partial Mastery of concept strand
(e.g., topic sentences, supporting sentences, and concluding sentences); **M** = Mastery of
concept strand.

to analyze the entire group's mastery of each goal. To conduct a group mastery analysis, you need to do the following:

1. Establish a minimum standard for group mastery of each skill.
2. Describe the proportion of the group that mastered each skill.
3. Compare the group's performance to the minimum standards.
4. Evaluate the quality of the instruction for each skill.

Setting Minimum Standards for Group Performance

To set minimum standards for the group, again consider the achievement characteristics of the students and the complexity of the skills measured. In addition, consider each skill's importance as a prerequisite for subsequent goals. For example, if a class contains average and above-average students, and if the skills measured are relatively easy, you might reasonably expect 80 percent or more of the students to master each skill. However, if the skills are important prerequisites for subsequent lessons, you might raise your criterion to 100 percent. If you have a very low-achieving group of students who are learning rather complex skills, you might lower your criterion to 75, 70, or 60 percent of the group passing. The mastery criteria you set are relative and should reflect all the factors just described. You can set one mastery criterion for all skills measured or establish a different minimum standard for each.

Describing Group Performance on Each Skill

You can easily calculate a group's performance on each skill using a mastery analysis like the one in Table 8.6. Simply count the number of students who mastered each skill and write the total in a row created at the bottom of the table. To find the percentage who mastered each objective, divide the number who passed the skill by the total number of students and then multiply the proportion by 100. The percentage of students in the class who mastered each objective can be inserted in the last row of the table. Notice the group performance figures in the last two rows of Table 8.6. The physical and functional characteristics objectives (II.A.4 and II.B.4) and the examples discrimination objective (II.D.1) were mastered by 100 percent of the class. Only 70 percent of the group, however, mastered the quality characteristics objective (II.C.4), and 80 and 90 percent of the group mastered the two evaluation objectives (II.E.1 and II.E.5, respectively). More emphasis on identifying quality characteristics and discriminating them in the paragraph context will undoubtedly improve students' achievement in these two areas. Finally, 85 percent of the class wrote acceptable topic sentences for the incomplete paragraphs presented on the objective unit posttest.

Comparing a Group's Performance to Minimum Standards

If 80 percent of the group passing each goal was set as the minimum acceptable standard for each skill, then you can see that group performance on only one objective, quality characteristics, (II.C.4), did not meet the standard. The percentage of students passing the other six objectives was at or above the minimum standard.

Evaluating the Quality of Instruction

As the previous example shows, a group's performance reflects the quality of instruction much more than does individual achievement. When group performance on a skill exceeds your minimum criterion, you can conclude that instruction was very effective. If group performance barely meets the minimum standard, the instruction can be judged as acceptable. If a group fails to meet the established minimum, however, you should review and revise instruction that produced such a poor posttest performance. In the example, instruction related to the quality characteristics of topic sentences should be revised. By revising ineffective lessons throughout the year, you improve the quality of your instruction and, hopefully, raise the level of subsequent group performances.

COMPUTER TECHNOLOGY

Individual performance information is available from computer-based scoring and reporting programs. Among other data, the following norm-referenced and criterion-referenced information is available through the Par-SCORE and ParGRADE programs (Economics Research, Inc., 1992).

Norm-Referenced Data

For any test you administer and score, you can print reports that list each student's *T* score, percentile score, or stanine score. Stanine scores are on a 9-point scale, ranging from a low score of 1 to a high score of 9. (Stanine scores are described in more detail in Chapter 15.)

Criterion-Referenced Data

You can generate an individual student report, such as the one illustrated in Figure 8.1. Such a report is interesting for both students and parents. Information necessary to identify the student, course, and test are printed at the top of the form. The first row of data, labeled Test Key, indicates the

FIGURE 8.1
Individual Student Report

```
Id #: 820048002              Class: ECON 200        Course #: 3333
Name: ABOUNTERI, ALBERT      Time: 2 MWF
Date: 2-15-94

                                                     BA
                                                     ++      A
           Test Key:  CCDAABBBDC ABDAACBBBB CEDDBBABAB CCBCEACBAC AADB*CDDCC
          Items 1-50: 1234567890 1234567890 1234567890 1234567890 1234567890
    Student's Answers: ******C*** **B*CD**** *D*B*AB*** C***DC**** *BC*** A*E
                                                        E      E


              EXAM 3 Form A                        CUMULATIVE
         ----------------------              ----------------------
          Possible Points: 100              Possible Points: 400
               Raw Score:  68                  Raw Score: 308
          Objective Score:  46               Percent Correct:  77%
             Essay Score:  22             In-progress Grade:  B
          Percent Correct: 68%

              Comments: COMPLETED CLASS REPORT   Code: M2
```

Source: Economics Research, Inc. (1992). *ParSCORE and ParGRADE User's Manual* (p. 167). Costa Mesa, CA.

correct answers for each item, and the second row indicates the item number. Items with a plus (+) symbol and an additional letter above them (e.g., items 34 and 35) indicate that both indicated responses are required for the student to receive credit. Items with two responses present without the plus sign (e.g., item 40) indicate that either of the named responses is considered correct. The third row lists the student's responses to the items. An asterisk (*) is used to indicate a correct response, and a letter printed in the student's record indicates the incorrect distractor selected. Using these data, you could circle objectives or enabling skills the student did not master on the test.

Besides the item information, test summary data is provided in the bottom left corner of the report. The total number of points earned, the points earned on the objective-style items, the points earned on essay or other alternative style items, and the overall percentage correct score are listed. The bottom right portion of the figure illustrates the points the student has earned to date during a grading term. Information included is the cumulative number of points, raw score, percentage correct score, and in-progress grade. (More about grades will be discussed later in Chapter 14.)

A second method that is easier for teachers to use for identifying and tracking students' mastery is to generate test reports that include both total scores and subtest scores for each student. The ability to score a total test (all items included on a test) and any number of subtests you wish means that it is quite easy for you to obtain objective- or goal-based mastery data for each student in the class. Subtests for an instructional unit posttest could include the set of items measuring each enabling skill or related clusters of skills (e.g., all items on topic sentences). Subtests for comprehensive term and semester exams could be the set of items that measure each of the instructional goals included on the examination. Scoring tests in this manner will enable you automatically to generate reports of students' mastery levels on each subtest. Additionally, if you report students' subtest scores as percentage correct scores, you can simply read their scores to determine whether they have mastered, partially mastered, or failed to master a given subtest. For example, if there are three items included for an objective, a subtest percentage score of 67 percent (two of three items answered correctly or a simple majority of the items presented for the objective) would indicate minimal mastery on the subtest, and if there were four items included for an objective, a subtest percentage score of 75 percent (three of four items correct) would indicate minimal mastery.

Figure 8.2 illustrates a subtest report from the ParSCORE program (Economics Research, Inc., p. 187, 1992). The top portion of the report identifies the course, instructor, term, and particular exam (Exam 3). The teacher has three subtests on the exam. For each subtest, the total number of items included and the number of items the student must answer correctly for minimal mastery are provided. Teachers set passing levels themselves at any criterion they wish, and they can change their criteria at any time. In this case, the teacher has set answering 50 percent of the items correctly for each subtest as minimal mastery—a very lenient criterion. Notice that the first subtest contains 10 items, and the students must answer 5 of the items correctly to pass. The overall test contains three subtests, and students must pass two of them to pass the overall exam.

The bottom portion of the subtest report contains summary information about each student's achievement. From this summary, you can see that Susan Abbott failed to master subtest 1 and passed subtests 2 and 3. This performance earned her a passing mark on the overall test. In contrast, Donald Borman and Cindy Cummings both failed all three subtests and the overall exam. Such achievement reports would help teachers form subgroups of students for review, additional instruction, or enrichment. They also would be helpful for completing mastery-style report cards that include mastery levels on instructional goals rather than course-level letter grades.

Creating subtest reports is quite easy since they can be generated in a matter of seconds when an exam is scored. They can be made more interpretable by assigning names to overall tests and subtests that reflect the skills covered on the test. The program limits test names to four characters. For the paragraph test, you might name the overall test PRGH and have subtests

FIGURE 8.2
Total Test and Subtest Scores

```
Report Date:      7-8-1994  2:10:49      ParSCORE STATE COLLEGE       Page 1
-----------------------------------------------------------------------------
   Course #: 2222                        Instructor: RALPH LEWIS
     Course: ECON 100                    Description: INTRO TO ECONOMICS
   Day/Time: 9 MWF                       Term/Year: SPRING 1994
```

S U B T E S T   R E P O R T
EXAM 3

* = Failed

	SUBTEST			
	1	2	3	Overall
--Possible Points--	10	27	13	3
--Minimum to Pass--	5	14	7	2
--Required----------		Y		
---ID #-------Name--				
1. 801447147 ABBOTT, SUSAN A	4*	17	8	2 P
	40%	63%	62%	67%
2. 832075207 BALL, ADAM J	6	17	6*	2 P
	60%	63%	46%	67%
3. 820637061 BALL, ANA R	5	16	4*	2 P
	50%	59%	31%	67%
4. 800684066 BANNER, DAN E	6	15	6*	2 P
	60%	56%	46%	67%
5. 782271221 BONN, TOM L	5	18	4*	2 P
	50%	67%	31%	67%
6. 821658165 BORMAN, DONALD M	4*	10*	5*	0 F
	40%	37%	38%	0%
7. 800025003 BRANDON, VIRGINIA M	6	18	7	3 P
	60%	67%	54%	100%
8. 820030007 BRENNER, JERRY T	5	14	3*	2 P
	50%	52%	23%	67%
9. 831529159 CARLETON, SAM R	8	13*	7	2 F
	80%	48%	54%	67%
10. 840841081 CONREY, LYNN T	9	25	7	3 P
	90%	93%	54%	100%
11. 840933099 COPPER, LINDA B	3*	14	8	2 P
	30%	52%	62%	67%
12. 840015008 CUMMINGS, CINDY L	2*	7*	3*	0 F
	20%	26%	23%	0%
13. 841170116 DAILY, DANNY M	5	18	5*	2 P
	50%	67%	38%	67%

Source: Economics Research, Inc. (1992). *ParSCORE and ParGRADE User's Manual* (p. 187). Costa Mesa, CA.

FIGURE 8.3
Individual Student Progress Report

```
                    P R O G R E S S    R E P O R T

Name........: ABOUNTERI, ALBERT        Date........:5/16/1994
I.D. Number.: 8200482                  Course #....:3333
Course......: ECON 200                 Instructor..:RALPH
Day/Time....: 2 MWF                    Code........:LEWIS


                     A S S I G N M E N T S
----------------------------------------------------------------------
Date          Type       Description            Possible   Score
----------------------------------------------------------------------
3/1/94        MIDTERM 1  Chapters 1-10             100      85
4/15/94       MIDTERM 2  Chapters 11-20            100      80
5/15/94       MIDTERM 3  Chapters 21-30            100      68
3/15/94       QUIZ 1     Lecture & Outside Readings  50     41
4/1/94        QUIZ 2     Lecture & Outside Readings  50     34
----------------------------------------------------------------------
Comments:     COMPLETED CLASS REPORT         Total Points     308
                 Please have your parent review Possible Points 400
              this report and sign. This report % of Possible  77.0%
              is due back by June 1, 1994.      Grade            C


Student                            Parent
Signature _____ Signature _____
```

Source: Economics Research, Inc. (1992). *ParSCORE and ParGRADE User's Manual* (p. 171). Costa Mesa, CA.

named PGH, TOPC, SUPP, and CONC. A test in this class covering group performance analysis might be named GRUP, and subtests could be named CNTR and VARI for central tendency and variability.

A third type of individual student report that is quite useful for communicating interim progress to both students and parents is the student progress report. A sample report is included in Figure 8.3. This report includes data for all tests administered up to any given point during a term. The top of the report identifies the student, the instructor, and the class. The body of the report includes the assignments completed, including the date, the type of test, a verbal description of the test, the total number of points included on the test, and the student's raw score on each assignment. The bottom right side of the report contains cumulative information about the student's progress thus far during the grading term.

Using your imagination to have the computer tailor such reports to your particular situation, you might choose to provide parents with their child's pretest scores, practice test scores, and posttest scores for each unit of instruction. This set of tests will illustrate better to parents the progress, or lack there of, that their child is making for each instructional goal covered. You might also choose to include total test posttest scores as well as subtest scores to provide parents with more detailed information about goal areas where their child is progressing nicely or falling behind. These quickly produced progress reports are invaluable for teachers who are required by school or district policy to inform parents of pupils' progress during a grading term. Individual reports for an entire class or group of classes can be generated rapidly from information stored in the computer program when each of the tests was scored or when alternative assessment information was entered into each student's record.

Using such reports helps ensure that parents are informed about their child's work. Notice at the bottom of the progress report that there is space for both the student and parent to sign the form and return it to the teacher. You might also include the times and days that you are available for parent conferences and a telephone number parents can use to make an appointment.

SUMMARY

Test data can be used to analyze and evaluate an individual's performance, a group's performance, and the quality of instruction.

An individual's scores can be evaluated using both norm-referenced and criterion-referenced analysis. To make norm-referenced comparisons, you need to create performance categories of above average, average, and below average. You can then compare each student's score with these categories and with the levels earned by the student on previous tests. The most basic way to make norm-referenced comparisons among students is to use the mean and standard deviation to classify raw scores as above average, average, or below average.

A second method is to calculate standard scores and use them to locate students' normative performance levels. The most commonly used standard scores are the z and T scores. Scores equal to and greater than 1.0 on the z score scale and 60 on the T score scale are classified as above average. Scores equal to and less than -1.0 on the z score scale and 40 on the T score scale are considered to be below average. Scores between these two anchors are classified as average-level performance.

The third norm-referenced procedure is to rank raw scores and convert them to percentile scores. The upper quartile and lower quartile on the percentile scale are classified as above and below average. Scores between these two anchors are classified as average level performance.

Using criterion-referenced analysis, you can evaluate individual students' progress on prescribed instructional goals, enabling skills, or objectives. To conduct such an analysis, you need to organize items within objectives, enabling skills, or goals; establish minimum criteria for mastering each; and determine whether each student mastered each skill. This information can be used to prepare follow-up activities and to judge the quality and consistency of each student's performance. Progress charts will help you keep track of skills that individual students still need to learn.

Evaluating the quality of instruction requires a third type of analysis. First, prescribe the minimum percentage of students who must master each skill for instruction to be considered adequate. Next, calculate the percentage of students who pass each skill and compare these figures with the established minimums. If the percentage of students who pass a skill exceeds the minimum standard, then instruction is considered good; if the minimum is met, instruction is considered adequate. However, if the proportion passing does not meet the minimum standard, the instruction is considered inadequate, and you should analyze and revise related lessons.

Although these analysis procedures may seem complex and time consuming, they are easily mastered with practice. Today, machine-scoring services can provide most of the required data summaries that you need. Once you recognize the value of these analyses for aiding your evaluation and planning, you will want to use them whenever possible.

PRACTICE EXERCISES

I. **Norm-Referenced Analysis of a Student's Performance**
   Table 8.9 contains the raw scores from the objective portion of the compound sentences unit posttest. Using the raw scores, the mean score, and the standard deviation, calculate the following indices (check your calculations in Table 8.9F in the Feedback section):
   A. The raw scores comparable to one standard deviation above the mean, the mean, one standard deviation below the mean, and two standard deviations below the mean. Plot these scores on the scale provided at the bottom of the table.
   B. The z score for each raw score in the first column.
   C. The T scores for each raw score.
   D. The percentiles for each raw score. Columns are provided in Table 8.9 for the cumulative frequency below, one-half frequency within, cumulative frequency at midpoint, proportions, and percentiles.
   E. Using the mean and standard deviation scale at the bottom of Table 8.9, how would you interpret the performance of a student who earned a raw score of 42 on the test?
   F. Using the z scores, how would you interpret the performance of a student who earned a z score of $-.39$ on the test?
   G. Using the T scores, how would you interpret the performance of a student who earned a 56 on the test?
   H. Using the percentile scores, how would you interpret the performance of a student who earned a score of 68 on the test?

TABLE 8.9
Norm-Referenced Analysis of Students' Posttest Scores for the Compound
Sentences Unit

$N = 20$ Mean = 37.5   Standard Deviation = 3.88

X	f	z	T	fb	1/2 fw	cfmp	Proportion	Percentile
42	2							
41	2							
40	5							
39	2							
38	1							
37	1							
36	1							
35	2							
34	1							
33	1							
31	1							
27	1							

Score						
Anchors	X_L	−2	−1	X	+1	X_H
Raw						
Scores						

II. Criterion-Referenced Analysis of a Student's Performance

Table 8.10 contains the behavioral objectives from the coordinating conjunction portion of the compound sentences posttest. The objectives for this unit are described in
Table 3.9 and the table of test specifications for the unit posttest is included in Table
4.7. Using the item-by-objective data included in Table 8.10, perform the following
tasks (check your work in Table 8.10F in the Feedback section):

A. Determine the number of items that need to be answered correctly to master each
behavioral objective.

B. Examine the item data in the table and highlight (circle or square) the objectives
not mastered by particular students in the class.

C. Count the number of objectives mastered by each student, and insert the sum in
the last column on the right marked Total Objectives Mastered.

D. Count the number of students in the class that mastered each objective, and insert
the sum in the Number of Students Who Mastered row at the bottom of the table.

TABLE 8.10
Mastery Analysis of Students' Performance for Only the Conjunction Portion of the Compound Sentences Posttest (Objectives III.A.2 to III.F.1 in Tables 3.6 and 5.7)

Objective Codes	III.A.2	III.B.4	III.C.4	III.D.2				III.E.1		III.E.2		III.F.1				Total Objectives Mastered
Items:	1	2	3	4	5	6	7	8	9	10	11	12	13	14	15	7
Correct Answers:	2	3	1	3	2	4	1	4	2	1	4	*Hand Scored*				
McComas	*	*	*	*	*	*	*	*	*	*	*	*	*	*	*	
Talbot	*	*	*	*	*	*	*	*	*	*	*	*	*	*	*	
Deddens	*	*	*	*	*	*	*	*	*	*	*	*	*	*	*	
Prince	*	*	*	*	*	*	*	*	*	*	*	*	*	*	*	
Augustine	*	*	*	*	*	*	*	*	*	*	*	*	*	*	*	
Rust	*	*	*	*	*	*	*	*	*	*	*	*	*	*	*	
Carey	*	*	*	*	*	2	*	*	*	*	*	*	*	*	*	
White	*	*	*	*	*	*	*	*	*	*	*	*	x	*	*	
Hager	*	*	*	*	*	*	*	*	*	*	*	*	*	*	*	
McLaughlin	*	*	*	*	*	2	*	*	*	*	*	*	*	x	*	
Cromer	*	*	*	*	*	2	*	*	*	*	*	*	*	x	*	
Otto	*	*	*	*	*	2	*	*	*	*	*	*	*	x	*	
Scragg	*	*	*	*	*	2	*	*	*	*	3	*	*	x	*	
Hill	*	*	*	*	*	2	*	*	*	*	3	*	*	*	x	
Lovejoy	*	*	*	*	*	*	*	*	*	4	3	*	*	x	*	
Bailey	*	*	3	*	*	2	*	*	*	2	3	*	*	x	*	
Gormley	*	*	*	*	*	2	*	*	3	*	3	*	*	x	x	
Deiters	*	*	*	*	*	1	*	*	3	2	1	x	*	x	*	
Stewart	*	*	2	*	*	1	*	3	3	*	2	x	*	x	x	
Smith	*	1	*	*	*	1	*	1	1	*	1	x	x	x	x	
Number of Students Who Mastered																
Percentage of Students Who Mastered																

E. Calculate the percentage of students who mastered each objective and insert these percentages in the bottom row of the table. Suppose you set a criterion of 80 percent of the class mastering each objective. Are there any objectives for which instruction should be reconsidered?

F. Examine Smith's response pattern and compare it with the correct answers in the fourth row of the table. Based on the pattern, do you suspect that Smith really missed items 3, 7, and 10? What evidence makes you suspect this?

III. Prescribing Instructional Activities Based on Mastery Analysis

Table 8.11 is a goal analysis framework for the instructional goal, "Write a compound sentence." Based on the mastery data in Table 8.10, list the names of students who need more instruction in each of the coordinating conjunction enabling skills cells. Check your work in Table 8.11F in the Feedback section.

IV. Monitoring Student Progress

Table 8.12 contains a sample student progress chart for the instructional goal, "Write a compound sentence." Using the mastery information summarized in Tables 8.10 and 8.11, complete the mastery chart for students in the class. Check your decisions in Table 8.12F in the Feedback section.

V. Enrichment

A. For a test you have developed and administered, complete the following:

1. Establish above-average, average, and below-average categories of scores using the mean and the standard deviation.

2. Compare each student's score to the established categories and determine whether the performance is above average, average, or below average within the group.

3. Calculate z, T, and percentile scores for each raw score. Using these scores, judge each student's performance level.

TABLE 8.11
Prescribed Instructional Activities Based on Mastery Analysis

CONCEPTS/ CONTENT	A State/Recall Physical Characteristics of:	B State/Recall Functional Characteristics of:	C State/Recall Quality Characteristics of:	D Discriminate Between Examples & Nonexamples	E Evaluate Given Examples	F Produce Examples of:
I. Comma						
III. Simple Sentence						
IV. Coordinating Conjunction						
IV. Compound Sentence						

TABLE 8.12

A Sample Student Progress Chart for the Instructional Goal,
"Write Compound Sentences"

COORDINATING CONJUNCTION ENABLING SKILLS								
Enabling Skills	III A	III B	III C	III D	III E	II C	III F	III	Etc.
Augustine									
Bailey									
Carey									
Cromer									
Deddens									
Deiters									
Gormley									
Hager									
Hill									
Lovejoy									
McComas									
McLaughlin									
Otto									
Prince									
Rust									
Scragg									
Smith									
Stewart									
Talbot									
White									

Note: x = at least minimal mastery of enabling skill; **PM** = Partial Mastery of concept strand (e.g., simple sentences, commas, coordinating conjunctions, compound sentences); **M** = Mastery of concept strand.

4. Establish criteria for minimal mastery of each skill measured and:
    a. Determine the number of skills each student mastered.
    b. Prescribe follow-up activities for each student. Identify students who should receive enrichment activities and those who need additional instruction and practice on each skill.

5. Evaluate instruction:
   a. Establish a criterion for the minimal percentage of students who should master each skill.
   b. Calculate the percentage of students who master each skill.
   c. Compare the percentage who passed each skill to the criterion established and judge instruction as good, adequate, or inadequate.
   d. Revise lesson plans for ineffective instruction.

FEEDBACK

I. **Norm-Referenced Analysis of a Student's Performance**
   A. See Table 8.9F.
   B. See Table 8.9F.
   C. See Table 8.9F.
   D. See Table 8.9F.

TABLE 8.9F
Norm-Referenced Analysis of Students' Posttest Scores for the Compound Sentences Unit

$N = 20$ **Mean = 37.5**   **Standard Deviation = 3.88**

X	f	z	T	fb	1/2 fw	cfmp	Proportion	Percentile
42	2	1.16	62	18	1.0	19.0	.95	95
41	2	.90	59	16	1.0	17.0	.85	85
40	5	.64	56	11	2.5	13.5	.68	68
39	2	.39	54	9	1.0	10.0	.50	50
38	1	.13	51	8	.5	8.5	.43	43
37	1	−.13	49	7	.5	7.5	.38	38
36	1	−.39	46	6	.5	6.5	.33	33
35	2	−.64	44	4	1.0	5.0	.25	25
34	1	−.90	41	3	.5	3.5	.18	18
33	1	−1.16	38	2	.5	2.5	.13	13
31	1	−1.68	33	1	.5	1.5	.08	08
27	1	−2.71	23	0	.5	.5	.03	03

Score Anchors	X_L	−2	−1	X	+1	X_H
Raw Scores	27	29.74	33.62	37.5	41.38	42

TABLE 8.10F

Mastery Analysis of Students' Performance for the Conjunction Portion of the Compound Sentences Posttest (Objectives III.A.2 to III.F.1 in Tables 3.6 and 5.7)

Objective Codes	III.A.2	III.B.4	III.C.4	III.D.2				III.E.1		III.E.2		III.F.1				Total Objectives Mastered
CONJUNCTION OBJECTIVES																
Items:	1	2	3	4	5	6	7	8	9	10	11	12	13	14	15	7
Correct Answers:	2	3	1	3	2	4	1	4	2	1	4	*Hand Scored*				
McComas	*	*	*	*	*	*	*	*	*	*	*	*	*	*	*	7
Talbot	*	*	*	*	*	*	*	*	*	*	*	*	*	*	*	7
Deddens	*	*	*	*	*	*	*	*	*	*	*	*	*	*	*	7
Prince	*	*	*	*	*	*	*	*	*	*	*	*	*	*	*	7
Augustine	*	*	*	*	*	*	*	*	*	*	*	*	*	*	*	7
Rust	*	*	*	*	*	*	*	*	*	*	*	*	*	*	*	7
Carey	*	*	*	*	*	2	*	*	*	*	*	*	*	*	*	7
White	*	*	*	*	*	*	*	*	*	*	*	*	x	*	*	7
Hager	*	*	*	*	*	*	*	*	*	*	*	*	*	*	*	7
McLaughlin	*	*	*	*	*	2	*	*	*	*	*	*	*	x	*	7
Cromer	*	*	*	*	*	2	*	*	*	*	*	*	*	x	*	7
Otto	*	*	*	*	*	2	*	*	*	*	*	*	*	x	*	7
Scragg	*	*	*	*	*	2	*	*	*	*	3	*	*	x	*	6
Hill	*	*	*	*	*	2	*	*	*	*	3	*	*	*	x	6
Lovejoy	*	*	*	*	*	*	*	*	*	4	3	*	*	x	*	6
Bailey	*	*	3	*	*	2	*	*	*	2	3	*	*	x	*	5
Gormley	*	*	*	*	*	2	*	*	3	*	3	*	*	x	x	4
Deiters	*	*	*	*	*	1	*	*	3	2	1	x	*	x	*	4
Stewart	*	*	2	*	*	1	*	3	3	*	2	x	*	x	x	3
Smith	*	1	*	*	*	1	*	1	1	*	1	x	x	x	x	3
Number of Students Who Mastered	20	20	18	20				16		12		16				
Percentage of Students Who Mastered	100%	100%	90%	100%				80%		60%		80%				

    E. The two students who earned scores of 42 performed above average compared to their classmates.

    F. A z score of –.39 reflects average level performance in the class.

    G. A T score of 56 reflects average level performance in the class.

    H. Students who earned a percentile score of 68 performed better than 68 percent of the students in the class.

II. Criterion-Referenced Analysis of a Student's Performance

    A. See Table 8.10F.

    B. See Table 8.10F.

    C. See Table 8.10F.

    D. See Table 8.10F.

    E. See Table 8.10F.

    F. Instruction should be reconsidered for objective III.E.2.

    G. It appears that Smith selected response option 1 for all items on the last half of the objective part of the test. Since the correct answer for items 3, 7, and 10 is 1, Smith may have inadvertently answered them correctly. It seems wise to follow up with some oral questions for Smith.

III. Prescribing Instructional Activities Based on Mastery Analysis

See Table 8.11F. Note that Smith was added to the list for enabling skill III.C.

IV. Monitoring Student Progress

See Table 8.12F. In order to be judged "master," students had to master all enabling skills for the strand. Partial mastery was assigned for students who had mastered a majority of the enabling skills for the coordinating conjunction strand. Nonmastery (blank cells) was assigned for students who mastered half or less of the enabling skills in the strand.

TABLE 8.11F

Prescribed Instructional Activities Based on Mastery Analysis

CONCEPTS/ CONTENT	A State/Recall Physical Characteristics of:	B State/Recall Functional Characteristics of:	C State/Recall Quality Characteristics of:	D Discriminate Between Examples & Nonexamples	E Evaluate Given Examples	F Produce Examples of:
I. Comma						
III. Simple Sentence						
IV. Coordinating Conjunction		Smith	Bailey Stewart Smith?	Smith?	Bailey Deiters Gormley Hill Lovejoy Scragg Smith Stewart	Deiters Gormley Smith Stewart
IV. Compound Sentence						

TABLE 8.12F
A Sample Student Progress Chart for the Conjunction Portion of the Instructional
Goal, "Write Compound Sentences"

COORDINATING CONJUNCTION ENABLING SKILLS								
Enabling Skills	**III A**	**III B**	**III C**	**III D**	**III E**	**III F**	**III**	**Etc.**
Augustine	x	x	x	x	x	x	**M**	
Bailey	x	x		x		x	**PM**	
Carey	x	x	x	x	x	x	**M**	
Cromer	x	x	x	x	x	x	**M**	
Deddens	x	x	x	x	x	x	**M**	
Deiters	x	x	x	x			**PM**	
Gormley	x	x	x	x			**PM**	
Hager	x	x	x	x	x	x	**M**	
Hill	x	x	x	x		x	**PM**	
Lovejoy	x	x	x	x		x	**PM**	
McComas	x	x	x	x	x	x	**M**	
McLaughlin	x	x	x	x	x	x	**M**	
Otto	x	x	x	x	x	x	**M**	
Prince	x	x	x	x	x	x	**M**	
Rust	x	x	x	x	x	x	**M**	
Scragg	x	x	x	x		x	**PM**	
Smith	x		x	x				
Stewart	x	x		x				
Talbot	x	x	x	x	x	x	**M**	
White	x	x	x	x	x	x	**M**	

Note: x = at least minimal mastery of enabling skill; **PM** = Partial Mastery of concept strand
(e.g., coordinating conjunctions); **M** = Mastery of concept strand. For partial mastery, students
mastered four of the six enabling skills.

REFERENCE

Economics Research, Inc. (1992). *ParSCORE and ParGRADE user's manual* (pp. 167, 171, 187). Costa Mesa, CA: Economics Research, Inc.

SUGGESTED READINGS

Dick, W., & Carey, L. M. (1990). *The systematic design of instruction* (3rd ed.). Glendale, IL: Scott, Foresman.

Dick, W., & Carey, L. M. (1991). Formative evaluation. In L. J. Briggs, K. L. Gustafson, & M. H. Tillman (Eds.), *Instructional design principles and applications* (2nd ed.) (pp. 227–269). Englewood Cliffs, NJ: Educational Technology.

Hopkins, C. D., & Antes, R. L. (1990). *Classroom measurement and evaluation* (3rd ed.) (p. 289). Itasca, IL: F. E. Peacock.

Popham, J. W. (1990). *Modern educational measurement* (2nd ed.) (pp. 412–422). Englewood Cliffs, NJ: Prentice Hall.

Sax, G. (1989). *Principles of educational and psychological measurement and evaluation* (3rd ed.) (pp. 551–556). Belmont, CA: Wadsworth.

CHAPTER 9

Constructing and Using Essay and Product Development Tests

OBJECTIVES

- Define *essay* and *product development tests*.
- Describe the types of skills typically measured using essay and product development tests.
- Discuss the positive and negative features of essay and product development tests.
- Write essay questions and product development instructions.
- Select and include relevant information in directions.
- Define *global scoring* and describe its uses.
- Define *analytical scoring* and describe its uses.
- Develop a checklist for analytical scoring.
- Develop a rating scale for analytical scoring.
- Use a rating scale to score given products.
- Describe typical errors associated with constructing and scoring essay and product development tests.
- Describe benefits of students using checklists and rating scales to evaluate their own work.

Curriculum guides often contain complex instructional goals that require students to demonstrate their ability to create a unique response. In constructing unique responses, students need to determine how they will approach a given problem, plan and organize their responses, and present their ideas. Objective tests do not require students to produce original pieces of work that demonstrate these capabilities.

Often these complex goals can be measured with essay questions, which typically require students to discuss, analyze, compare for similarities and differences, synthesize, or evaluate. For example, students may be asked to discuss a product, a procedure, an event, a political action, a natural phenomenon, historical characters, a scientific experiment, a piece of literature, or a philosophical viewpoint. They may be expected to analyze and describe the components of a concrete or defined concept, rule, or principle, or to analyze and describe the steps in a procedure or the components in a system. Essay questions also can be used to measure their ability to compare or contrast concepts, theories, systems, procedures, events, people, and numerous other subjects. They can measure students' abilities to synthesize pieces of literature, articles, events, or other phenomena. In addition, students may be asked to evaluate the quality of a product or event, the execution of some procedure or motor skill, or an instance of behavior.

Some instructional goals, such as higher-level intellectual skills and cognitive strategies, cannot be adequately measured by either objective or essay questions. To demonstrate their skill, students need to develop some type of product either with pencil and paper or by some other method. Such products include letters, themes, poems, abstracts, term papers, flowcharts, computer programs, original songs, photographs, videotapes, maps, bookcases, blueprints, and drawings. Each student's product will be unique and will vary in complexity, originality, and accuracy. Even when students are following detailed instructions, their responses will vary.

Both essay and product development tests require students to synthesize many enabling skills in their responses. For example, students writing a summary of a book must form sentences and paragraphs, write legibly, select ideas and information, and organize their presentation. One advantage of these tests is the teacher's ability to separate and comment on particular elements of students' responses, such as their approach, organization, logic, and accuracy.

Unfortunately, this type of testing has several major drawbacks. First, a teacher must spend considerable time selecting the task, writing the instructions, scoring the products, analyzing students' work, and evaluating both individual and group performance. Second, more class time is usually required for essay and product exams than for objective-style exams, which often limits the breadth of the material tested. Third, because responses vary, only experts can make the fine distinctions that determine whether an answer is acceptable. Responses cannot be machine scored or given to an aide or student assistant for scoring. Finally, scoring is less reliable on these exams than on objective exams for several reasons. Teachers' standards may shift during scoring, and fatigue can cause lapses in concentration. Scoring bias is another serious problem. Some teachers tend to be lenient, whereas others consistently give all the students average or below-average marks. Teachers' perceptions of individual students also can bias the scores they assign. In addition, students with excellent verbal and organizational skills can bluff an answer and often receive better scores than less verbally skilled students whose answers contain superior content. In spite of these limitations, essay and product development tests provide the best means of determining whether students can actually perform complex skills such as writing paragraphs and themes, conducting and reporting scientific experiments, or critiquing literature and plays.

ANALYZING INSTRUCTIONAL GOALS THAT REQUIRE ESSAY OR PRODUCT DEVELOPMENT RESPONSES

The same procedures described in Chapter 3 for analyzing instructional goals that are intellectual skills and verbal information are used to analyze instructional goals that require product development. Recall that intellectual skills goals are typically analyzed using a goal matrix diagram, tree diagram, or flowchart to identify key enabling skills. Objective tests are used to assess students' mastery of enabling skills in the goal framework, whereas essay and product development exams are usually used to determine whether students can synthesize all the enabling skills to perform the goal.

The instructional goal is typically located in the far right column (Produce) of the goal matrix, at the far left of a tree diagram, and at the top of a flowchart, and one or more behavioral objectives should have been written for the goal during the analysis process. These objectives specify the conditions appropriate for performing the goal, and they sometimes include the criteria for an acceptable product. More often, however, there are multiple criteria required to judge the quality of a product, and there are usually too many criteria to include them all in the behavioral objectives.

The criteria for judging students' essays and products are located in the goal analysis framework. In a matrix analysis, they are located in the first three columns of the matrix, and they include the physical, functional, and qualitative characteristics of a product that are specified for a particular group. In the tree diagram and flowchart, they are typically located toward the basic ends, and they include the characteristic descriptions of a product. You may wish to review the goal analysis frameworks in Chapter 3 to examine the enabling skills that describe the physical, functional, and qualitative characteristics of paragraphs. The matrix diagram is located in Figure 3.6, the tree diagram is in Figure 3.7, and the flowchart is in Figure 3.8. When scoring a student's product, such as a paragraph, drawing, or bookcase, you need to question whether the product (1) has the prescribed physical characteristics, (2) functions as intended, and (3) includes the quality characteristics specified to an acceptable degree for the developmental level of the target students.

Essay tests are really just one specific type of product development test, so the foundation for essay questions is also the instructional goal matrix. Essay questions typically require students to describe, explain, contrast, compare, analyze, and so forth. Recall also from Chapter 3 that essay questions are usually created by combining cells in the goal framework. For example, students can describe something by combining the cells within an enabling skill concept strand, and they can compare for similarities and differences the physical, functional, and qualitative characteristics of concepts within these columns of the matrix. Related to the geography goal matrix in Table 3.3, students might be asked to describe a particular country in North America (Row I), and you would score their answer by the particular number of identifying facts the students could recall (e.g., the capital city [I.B], location on map [I.D], area size [I.C], population size [I.E], climate [I.F], etc.). On the other hand, you may want students to compare the similarities and differences among North, Central, and South American countries using characteristics such as area size, population size, gross national product, or form of government. Once you have located the skills you want to measure on the goal analysis framework, you are ready to write questions and instructions and to develop scoring procedures.

WRITING QUESTIONS AND INSTRUCTIONS

Many of the suggestions for writing objective test items also apply to essay questions and instructions for product development. Questions and instructions should match the behavior, content, and conditions specified in the behavioral objective; the vocabulary, complexity, and context should be appropriate for target students; and questions and instructions should be clearly written using correct grammar and punctuation.

An essay question or set of instructions should describe the type of response that you expect. For example, if students are to compare two things, the instructions should begin with the word *compare*. If they are to critique something, the instructions should begin with the word *critique*. Students should know the meaning of these words and how to demonstrate these skills. If all or some students do not understand what these terms are, their responses may reflect their misunderstanding of what they are told to do.

Providing Guidance

The amount of guidance in the question or instructions depends on the skill being measured and the sophistication of the students. Related to the skill, instructions may require students to discuss or compare things using components they select themselves, or the instructions may specify which components they are to use. Students may have to select and use evaluation criteria, or they may be given the criteria to apply. Related to students' characteristics, older students and high achievers tend to work well with minimum guidance. However, younger students and average or below-average achievers need more structure in the directions.

Students' responses will depend on the amount of guidance in the instructions. Consider the amount of guidance provided in the three essay questions included in Table 9.1. The questions in the left-hand column have the content removed to illustrate the item format. Any content could be

TABLE 9.1
Degrees of Guidance in Essay Questions

1. Compare X and Y.	1. Compare *pretests* and *posttests*.

2. Compare X and Y for the following:
   a.
   b.
   c.
	2. Compare *pretests* and *posttests* for the following:
	   a. the test's relationship to the goal framework
	   b. the time the test is administered
	   c. uses for test scores

3. Compare the similarities of and differences between X and Y for the following:
   a.
   b.
   c.
	3. Compare the similarities of and the differences between *pretests* and *posttests* for the following:
	   a. the test's relationship to the goal framework
	   b. the time the test is administered
	   c. uses for test scores

substituted for the letters X and Y and the letters a, b, and c. The questions in the right-hand column use the same format, but content is included in each.

Notice that the three sets of instructions vary considerably in the amount of guidance provided. The first question requires students to decide which aspects of the pretest and posttest they will compare and how they will compare them. This is the most complex question because students must determine all the elements in their response. The lack of guidance will produce greater variety in students' answers.

The second question provides more guidance. Students are told which aspects of pretests and posttests they are to compare. The third set directs students' responses even more by specifying that students compare similarities and differences. Each question is of value. The amount of guidance to include in an essay question depends on whether you want students to recall the facets to be compared or whether you want to provide them. In determining the appropriate amount of guidance, you should always consider what skills you want to measure and the skill level of students being tested.

The amount of guidance to include is also a consideration when writing instructions that require development of a product. For example, the instructions for producing a paragraph can vary considerably in the amount of guidance provided. Consider the following three sets of instructions:

1. Write a paragraph about a fire drill.
2. Write a paragraph about a fire drill. Your paragraph should include:
    a. A topic sentence
    b. At least four supporting sentences
    c. A concluding sentence

3. Write a paragraph that describes fire drill procedures. Your paragraph should include:
   a. A topic sentence
   b. At least four supporting sentences
   c. A concluding sentence

Each set of directions will undoubtedly produce very different paragraphs. The second set is more specific than the first and the third more specific than the second. The third set limits the topic to fire drill procedures and specifies the number and types of sentences to be included. To determine which set of instructions would be best, you would first need to decide how much guidance should be provided for a particular group of students and what skills you want to measure. Specific instructions like those in the third set would not be appropriate if you wanted to measure whether students remembered to include topic and concluding sentences in their paragraphs. However, they would be appropriate for measuring students' skill in ordering events in a prescribed procedure (such as a fire drill). Regardless of the test's purpose, the directions must include enough information to provide clear and unambiguous guidance for the task.

Providing Organizational Information

Besides specifying the nature of the task to be performed, instructions can include additional information to help students determine the relative importance of different questions or sections of the test. Information that can help students organize their work includes (1) the length and scope of the response sought, (2) the number of points each question is worth, and (3) the time available for completing the test or the recommended time students should spend on each question. This type of information is incorporated in the paragraph test in the following example:

1. Write a paragraph that describes fire drill procedures. Your paragraph should include 6 to 10 sentences. Be sure to include:
   a. A topic sentence (5 points)
   b. At least four supporting sentences (8 points)
   c. A concluding sentence (4 points)
   You will have 20 minutes to write and revise your paragraph.

The paragraph is a relatively small product, but other intellectual skills products are quite complex, span a long period of time, and require quite detailed instructions. Table 9.2 contains sample directions and organizational information for the term project in a classroom measurement and evaluation course. The directions are quite detailed, yet many students request additional information prior to beginning work and intermittently throughout

TABLE 9.2
Sample Instructions for One Product in a Classroom Measurement and
Evaluation Course

Directions for Developing Your Item Bank and Producing Tests

1. Form a discipline/major-based team (no more than four members per team) with classmates.

2. Using a local school district curriculum guide (or State Curriculum Standards), choose an instructional goal for a small unit of instruction (about same in scope as writing a paragraph).

3. Create page 1.0 of your project:
   a. Name team members and your major areas of study.
   b. Describe the instructional goal selected by your team and its source.
   c. Describe the achievement characteristics of students for which your instruction/tests are intended.

4. Create page 2.0 of your project:
   a. Use an analytical procedure (matrix diagram, tree diagram, flowchart, etc.) to create a goal framework for the instructional goal you have chosen. Name your goal framework (e.g., **Table 1 Goal Framework for the Instructional Goal** _____). See page 2 of the example projects and Figures 3.6, 3.7, and 3.8 in the text.

5. Create page 3.0+ of your project:
   a. Develop a Table of Test Specifications for an Instructional Goal that includes:
      (1) The enabling skill codes from your instructional goal framework
      (2) The behavioral objectives for the enabling skills in the goal framework
      (3) The number of items that should be used to determine a learner's mastery level for each objective
   b. Name your test specifications (e.g., **Table 2 Table of Test Specifications for the Instructional Goal** _____). See page 3 of the sample projects and Table 3.6 in the text.

6. Create page 4.0+ of your project:
   a. Develop prescriptions for individual tests within your unit, including readiness tests, pretests, practice tests, and posttests. Name these prescriptions (e.g., **Table 3 Test Prescriptions for Individual Tests for the Instructional Goal** _____). See page 4 of the samples and Table 4.5 in the text.

7. Create an item bank for your instructional goal:
   a. Go to the computer lab, register as a member of this class, sign up for creating an item bank, and purchase one floppy disk for each team member and one to submit as part of the term project. (Purchase the type recommended by the lab assistant for use with the item banking program.)
   b. Enter the item bank program, and name an item bank for your instructional goal.
   c. As a team, develop a set of descriptor codes for the items in your bank. Your descriptors might include the following categories: objective code, learning level of the objective, concept or topic, grade level, test use (e.g., pretest, practice test, unit exam, term exam), reference chapter, etc. Create item descriptors that seem most reasonable to you as a team.
   d. Enter your item descriptor categories into your item bank.
   e. Each team member should create (enter into the item bank) the number of test items specified in 5.a.(3) above for each behavioral objective in the goal framework. Use the

(continued)

TABLE 9.2 Continued

       item format most appropriate for each behavioral objective in your set. Link appro-
       priate graphics, tables, charts, textual material, rating scales, and checklists to the items
       in your bank. Remember to maintain a backup copy of your bank.

    f. When you have completed your portion of the bank, print a reference copy of your
       entire bank.

8. Have a team meeting to *evaluate* the items in your item bank. Date: _____

    a. The items for all objectives should be written by this team meeting. During the meeting,
       members should exchange items so that all items are evaluated by all members of the
       team. The checklist for quality items (Tables 5.18 and 9.13 in the text) should be used to
       evaluate items. Descriptors for items should also be reviewed to ensure the
       compatibility of descriptors and items across authors. Evaluators should write their
       suggestions for item improvements directly on the author's item printout.

9. Revise items based on colleagues' critiques. Item authors should reenter their item banks,
    locate, and edit their items based on evaluators' comments.

10. Assemble tests for the unit. All tests prescribed in Table 3 of your project should be
    assembled, printed, and submitted as a portion of the term project.

    a. Each team member should use his or her own integrated item bank to assemble the
       pretest, the practice tests, or a unit posttest. As a team, all prescribed tests should be
       assembled, printed, and submitted as part of the project.

11. The pretest for your team should become **Table 4,** and it should be named appropriately.
    The practice tests should become **Tables 5** and **6** and named appropriately. The unit
    posttest should be the last table in your project. You should submit a copy of your item
    bank disk as part of the project.

12. Team projects are due on _____ .

their projects. The directions provide the basic understandings for how students are expected to proceed, what they are expected to produce, and when
their products are due.

DEVELOPING SCORING PROCEDURES

Teachers typically use two types of scoring procedures to evaluate the quality
of students' responses to essay questions and products. With *global* scoring
(also called *holistic* scoring), the teacher uses general impressions to judge the
quality of an answer or product. A teacher using *analytical* scoring divides a
response into its relevant components and evaluates each part separately.

Global Scoring of Essay and Product Tests

Global scoring is appropriate whenever a test is *not* used to provide corrective
feedback to students or to evaluate instruction. Its purpose is to sort students'

responses into categories that indicate quality. For example, global scoring would be sufficient for a writing test used to place students in an English class. When a teacher has many papers to score, and it is not important to communicate the nature of the errors, global scoring is adequate.

The procedure for global scoring consists of the following seven steps.

1. *Establish the scoring categories you will use.* For example, you may have responses that fall into such categories as pass or fail; good, adequate, and poor; or excellent, good, adequate, poor, and unacceptable. The number of categories selected depends on the purpose for the evaluation and on your ability to place similar responses consistently into the same category. If you create too many categories or do not carefully define each category, you will find scoring difficult.

2. *Characterize a response that fits each category.* If, for example, you were to use the three categories of excellent, adequate, and poor, you should describe the particular characteristics that a response should have to be classified into one of the categories. What characteristics should be present for a response to be considered excellent? What would be absent or present in an adequate response? What would be absent in a poor response? Listing these characteristics helps you classify responses more consistently.

3. *Read each response rapidly and form an overall impression.* During the reading, look for the characteristics you used to describe each rating category.

4. *Sort the responses into the designated categories.*

5. *Reread the papers that have been placed within a category.* After all papers have been classified, you should consider only those within a set for their comparability.

6. *Move any clearly superior or inferior responses to other categories.*

7. *Assign the same numerical score to all responses within a category.* For example, papers in the excellent category can be assigned a score of 5, those in the adequate category can be assigned a score of 3, and so forth.

Although global scoring is relatively fast and reliable, two limitations make it less appropriate for classroom tests. First, it does not provide students with adequate feedback about their work. Most students will want to know why they received the assigned score and will not be satisfied with a global rating. Second, global evaluations do not permit the teacher to analyze the responses and identify specific instructional problems. Thus, students do not have the information they need to correct their mistakes, and teachers cannot classify errors and relate them to problems in their lessons.

Analytical Scoring of Product Tests

Analytical scoring is more time consuming than global scoring, but it is a superior method for instructional purposes. This procedure helps a teacher focus on relevant aspects of students' responses and provides a systematic way to assign partial credit. Just as important, it allows students to see where they lost points. Using this method, teachers can summarize the group's performance on main components, analyze errors, and use error analysis to evaluate and revise instruction.

At the same time, analytical scoring also has some disadvantages. First, constructing a scoring instrument and marking responses take considerable time. If the teacher has not identified and sequenced all the components desired in an answer in the order they are likely to appear in students' responses, searching for these components in students' work will take even longer. Second, developing a flexible scoring procedure that accommodates unanticipated responses can also be difficult. Teachers using analytical scoring may struggle with the problem of scoring correct, unusual answers that do not fit the structure and that cannot be compared to other students' responses.

Analytical scoring can be simplified by using a form that indicates the desired elements of a response and the number of points to be awarded for each. To construct such a form, first identify and order the desired components and subcomponents of each response. The major components you select should always be based on an instructional goal and its framework of subordinate skills. In addition to these skills, you may want to use other elements, such as the students' approach, organization, and originality, to judge their work. Some teachers believe that grammar, neatness, punctuation, and spelling should always count whereas others choose not to emphasize these elements in every task. If you choose to include elements not contained in the goal framework and not included in instruction for the unit, you should inform students of this intention in the test directions.

Table 9.3 includes a hypothetical goal analysis matrix with two main concept areas and six levels of learning. Main components for the product include I. First Concept and II. Second Concept. The characteristics listed in columns A, B, and C make up the subcomponents that are included within

TABLE 9.3
Hypothetical Instructional Goal Analysis Framework

CONCEPTS/ CONTENT	A State/Recall Physical Characteristics of:	B State/Recall Functional Characteristics of:	C State/Recall Quality Characteristics of:	D Discriminate Between Examples & Nonexamples	E Evaluate Given Examples	F Produce Examples of:
I. First Concept	1. _____ 2. _____	1.	1. _____ 2. _____ 3. _____			
II. Second Concept	1. _____	1. _____ 2. _____	1. _____ 2. _____ 3. _____			

each main component. The skeleton of the hypothetical analytical scoring form with the main concepts and their characteristics included is outlined in Table 9.4. Notice that the top of the form has a title, a space for the student's name, a space to record the date, and a space to record the student's score. The far left column, labeled Criteria, contains the enabling skills codes (e.g., I.A.1), the main concepts (main components), and the key characteristics of the concepts (subcomponents) that are to be judged.

Pay careful attention to how you word or phrase the criteria in your rating form. All criteria should be either positively or neutrally worded. The wording of some elements should not reflect positive features of a product while others reflect negative feature or errors. Consistency in the direction of the criteria is critical for maintaining congruence between the criteria and your ratings of students' products. For example, one criterion should not be "good sequence" while another is "poor transition." A rating of yes for each of these criteria would result in a nonsensical score for students. With the analytical scoring form completed to this point, you are ready to decide how

TABLE 9.4
Main Components and Subcomponents in an Analytical Scoring Form

TITLE OF THE TEST	
Name _____	**Date** _____ **Score** _____
Criteria	
I. First Concept	
A.1 Physical Characteristic 1	
A.2 Physical Characteristic 2	
B.1 Functional Characteristic 1	
C.1 Quality Characteristic 1	
C.2 Quality Characteristic 2	
C.3 Quality Characteristic 3	
II. Second Concept	
A.1 Physical Characteristic 1	
B.1 Functional Characteristic 1	
B.2 Functional Characteristic 2	
C.1 Quality Characteristic 1	
C.2 Quality Characteristic 2	
C.3 Quality Characteristic 3	

to score each of the subcomponents identified. There are two basic rating choices in analytical scoring: checklists and rating scales.

Checklists   A checklist permits you only two categories to judge the quality of each component or subcomponent of a student's product. These two categories might be the presence or absence of a given characteristic, or they might be the acceptability or unacceptability of a characteristic present in the work.

When using a checklist to score a student's product, simply check each subcomponent that is present or that is acceptable in the product. The check marks can be summed to obtain a total score for the student, and this sum of checks is comparable to a student's raw score on an objective test. Raw scores can be converted to percentage correct scores by dividing the number of acceptable components by the total number of criteria used to evaluate the product and then multiplying by 100. Table 9.5 contains the hypothetical

TABLE 9.5
A Skeleton Checklist for Analytically Scoring Students' Products and Essays

TITLE OF THE TEST			
Name _____		Date _____ Score ___8___/(12) ___67___%	
Yes	No	Criteria	Comments
		I. First Concept	
√		A.1 Physical Characteristic 1	
√		A.2 Physical Characteristic 2	
	√	B.1 Functional Characteristic 1	
√		C.1 Quality Characteristic 1	
	√	C.2 Quality Characteristic 2	
√		C.3 Quality Characteristic 3	
		II. Second Concept	
√		A.1 Physical Characteristic 1	
	√	B.1 Functional Characteristic 1	
√		B.2 Functional Characteristic 2	
√		C.1 Quality Characteristic 1	
√		C.2 Quality Characteristic 2	
	√	C.3 Quality Characteristic 3	

evaluation criteria from Table 9.4 configured into a checklist. In the example, the teacher has left space for comments on the far right. Sample check marks are inserted to illustrate how raw scores and percentage correct scores are obtained.

One note to keep in mind about checklists is that when planning to use scores for grading purposes, you must remember that the points assigned to each component of the checklist should be proportional to the importance of the component. The scoring in the example checklist in Table 9.5 would indicate that all components are considered to be of equal importance, because each check mark is worth one point. If, however, you judged several components of the product being evaluated to be two or three times as important as the other components, then a check mark by those components would be worth two or three points instead of one point. This way of scoring a checklist will automatically assign the most weight to the components that you judge to be most important.

Checklists can be used to evaluate written products such as term papers, and they can be used to evaluate other types of student products, such as a bookcase or a picture frame constructed in an industrial arts class, a dress or meal produced in a home economics class, or a mobile constructed in either a math or art class. For example, students being tested on the goal "Construct a mobile" would need to construct mobiles to demonstrate their skill even though the principles involved could be measured at the knowledge and comprehension levels using an objective test. The instructional goal framework should be used as the basis for both objective tests and the product evaluation form. A goal framework that a math teacher might develop is illustrated in Figure 9.1. Table 9.6 is a corresponding checklist for evaluating students' mobiles. Notice that the criteria included on the checklist are observable and reflect the teacher's judgment of major components that should be included. An instructional goal framework and checklist created by an art teacher would undoubtedly be different from these examples because art teachers would need to include additional enabling skills related to the artistic quality of the mobile.

Notice in the example in Table 9.6 that assigning one point for each check mark will automatically give Part IV of the checklist twice as much weight as Part I, II, or III, because Part IV has six components instead of three. For judging this product, however, the natural weighting built into the checklist is probably appropriate, because the double-wire mobile is more complex than any of the single-wire mobiles.

Rating Scales   The rating scale, an extension of the checklist, lets you judge not only the presence or acceptability of a characteristic but also its degree of quality. A rating scale contains all the main components and key subcomponents identified from the instructional goal framework. Similar to the checklist, these components should be stated in a consistently positive or neutral manner so that a low or high rating has the same meaning across all criteria.

FIGURE 9.1
Instructional Goal Framework for Constructing a Mobile

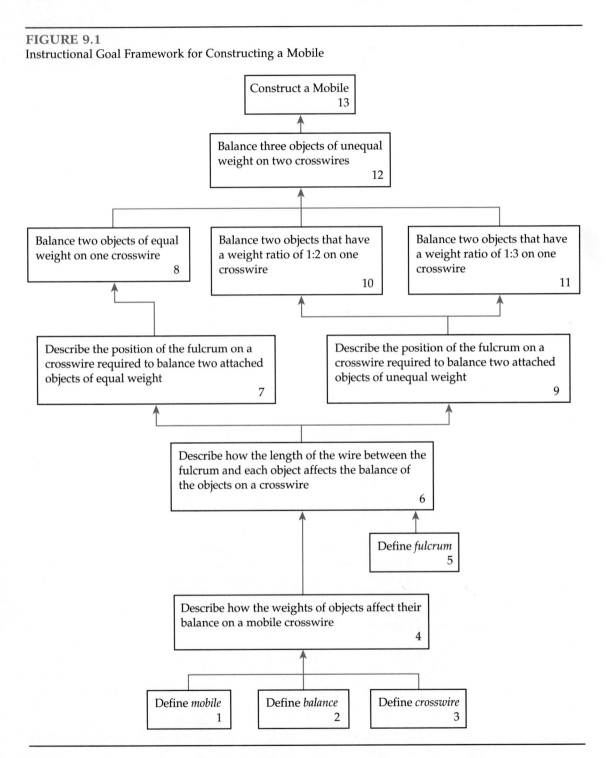

TABLE 9.6
Checklist for Evaluating Mobiles

Name _____ Date _____ Score _____
Total (15)

   I. Mobile with 1:1 weight ratio between two objects
      _____ 1. Objects correctly selected by weight
      _____ 2. Objects correctly positioned on crosswire
      _____ 3. Fulcrum found on crosswire

  II. Mobile with 1:2 weight ratio between two objects
      _____ 1. Objects correctly selected by weight
      _____ 2. Objects correctly positioned on crosswire
      _____ 3. Fulcrum found on crosswire

 III. Mobile with 1:3 weight ratio between two objects
      _____ 1. Objects correctly selected by weight
      _____ 2. Objects correctly positioned on crosswire
      _____ 3. Fulcrum found on crosswire

 IV. Mobile having three objects of unequal weight and two crosswires
      _____ 1. Objects correctly selected by weight
      _____ 2. Wires correctly selected by length
      _____ 3. Objects attached to correct crosswires
      _____ 4. Objects positioned correctly on crosswires
      _____ 5. Fulcrum found on lower crosswire
      _____ 6. Fulcrum found on upper crosswire

In addition, the rating scale has a sequence of numbers that represent degrees of quality for each product characteristic. The lowest end of a rating scale may have either the number 0 or 1. A rating of 0 is used *only* when a component or characteristic can be totally absent from a student's product. It should never be used to represent an unacceptable level of a characteristic that is present in a student's work. Remember that the purposes for the ratings are evaluation and communication—not demoralization!

There is no clear limit for setting the high end of the rating scale, but there is a good rule of thumb for determining one. You should never include more quality categories than you can clearly differentiate and consistently (reliably) rate. Teachers are probably most consistent with checklists where they are judging the acceptability or unacceptability of a particular characteristic. They can remain relatively reliable in their judgments when they add one more category, so there are three levels of quality to judge for a single characteristic. Three levels typically are used to reflect unacceptable (1), acceptable (2), and good (3) levels of a characteristic in a product. Four quality levels usually reflect unacceptable (1), acceptable (2), good (3), and excellent (4). Above this level, you should be very cautious. Only very complex characteristics can be judged consistently using four or more quality characteristics.

The number of quality levels you prescribe for each characteristic depends on the nature and complexity of the particular concept and characteristic to be rated. For example, judging whether a paragraph is indented does not require three or four levels of quality differentiation. Indentation is basically a checklist, yes/no, type of characteristic. Likewise, rating whether a student has the topic sentence properly located within a paragraph is also very straightforward, and a three- or four-point rating scale would be very difficult to use consistently to judge this characteristic. On the other hand, rating characteristics such as the sequence of information presented in a message or the quality of transitional words and phrases used in the message is more complex and can warrant differentiated levels of quality.

This paragraph example provides an opportunity for illustrating yet another quality characteristic you should consider in the construction of product and essay rating scales. The components and subcomponents in the rating scale do not need, nor should they necessarily have, the same number of quality points. The symmetrical four- or five-point rating scales included on attitude surveys and questionnaires, although attractive, are most often inappropriate for scoring products since the criteria differ by concept and characteristics.

Finally, once you have settled on the appropriate number of quality categories for each characteristic, it is a good idea to identify verbal descriptions for each of the numerical points on the scale. These verbal or qualitative descriptions will help you be more consistent in using the quantitative levels in your scales. For example, a rating of 0 could have the descriptor "Not Present." This particular label would help ensure that you only assign a score of 0 for missing ideas or components and not for inadequate examples. The better the descriptors fit the positive and negative features of individual components in your rating scale, the more consistent your ratings will be and the better they will communicate strengths and weaknesses to students.

In summary, the best rating scales for instructional purposes are those that include a thorough list of main components and subcomponents, but include a limited and appropriate number of quality levels to be differentiated for each component. Such a rating scale not only focuses the rater on the important elements of a product and aids consistent judgment but it also communicates expectations and judgments better to students.

Table 9.7 contains a hypothetical rating scale developed from the checklist in Table 9.5. Notice that the components and subcomponents are the same

TABLE 9.7
A Skeleton Rating Scale for Analytically Scoring Students' Products and Essays

TITLE OF THE TEST				
Name _____ Date _____ Score __25__ / (30) = _83_ %				
Criteria	Not Present 0	Present 1	Adequately Developed 2	Well Developed 3
I. First Concept (15)				
A.1 Physical Characteristic 1	0	①		
A.2 Physical Characteristic 2	0	1	②	
B.1 Functional Characteristic 1	0	1	2	3
C.1 Quality Characteristic 1	0	1	2	3
C.2 Quality Characteristic 2	0	1	②	3
C.3 Quality Characteristic 3	0	1	2	3
II. Second Concept (15)				
A.1 Physical Characteristic 1	0	①		
B.1 Functional Characteristic 1	0	1	②	
B.2 Functional Characteristic 2	0	1	2	3
C.1 Quality Characteristic 1	0	1	②	3
C.2 Quality Characteristic 2	0	1	2	3
C.3 Quality Characteristic 3	⓪	1	2	3

as for the checklist. The checklist has been expanded from two rating categories to three for the majority of the subcomponents. Note also that quality descriptors are provided above the quality levels at the top of the rating scales.

To use such a rating scale, you would locate each component in the product and then locate each subcomponent prescribed within the main category. For example, if you were rating topic sentences in a paragraph (a main component), you would first locate the topic sentence. With it in view, you would then rate its physical characteristics, how well it functions within the paragraph, and whether it meets the qualitative characteristics prescribed for a particular student group. You indicate your rating of each subcomponent by circling the quality-level number that best reflects the level of work.

These ratings for each subcomponent can be summed to obtain the student's raw score on the product. In the example, the student earned 14 of the

15 points available for the first concept and 11 of the 15 points available for the second one. The student's raw score is 25. The percentage correct score is obtained by dividing the student's assigned points (25) by the total possible number of points on the rating scale (30) and then multiplying by 100. The student's percentage correct score is 83. For grading purposes, it is important to understand that the score of 83 percent does not necessarily mean that the student has mastered the skill at an 83 percent level. It means only that the student was credited with 83 percent of the points available on the rating scale. *If* the points available for each of the components (e.g., 1, 2, or 3) reflect the relative importance of the components, *then* you can feel more comfortable using the 83 percent score for grading purposes.

Analytical Scoring of Essay Tests

The preceding examples illustrate the development of checklists and rating scales for scoring students' products. An extension of these same procedures is used to develop analytical scoring forms for essay tests. Scoring forms for essay tests differ somewhat because these tests usually contain several questions that represent broader content areas. The basic procedure for developing the scoring form for each essay question is the same as that previously described—that is, (1) identify and sequence the main components and subcomponents for each essay question, (2) determine whether a checklist or rating scale would be most useful, and (3) develop the scoring form according to a plan.

The rating form for an essay test might contain a rating scale for each question, a checklist for each question, or a combination of the two formats. In fact, the rating plan for one question might contain some components to be checked as present and others to be rated on a quality scale. Consider the hypothetical rating form in Table 9.8 for a four-question essay test. A checklist containing five components is used to score the first question; the second and third questions are scored using rating scales that contain 16 points each; and a checklist worth 6 points is used to score the fourth question. Using such a form, the topic of each question can be inserted beside the question number, and the components can be inserted beside the capital letters. The number of points a student earns can be inserted in the space beside each question and then multiplied by a desired weight, if additional weighting is needed to balance the questions. In the example, weights were chosen to increase the value of questions 1 and 4 to approximate the value of questions 2 and 3.

Using such a rating form to score the questions on an essay test will help you be more objective during scoring, show students where they earned and lost points, and aid your analysis of the group's responses, which is necessary for evaluating instruction and planning review sessions. It will also reduce the time you spend scoring students' tests, since you can illustrate where and why they lost points without rewriting their answers for them.

TABLE 9.8
Hypothetical Rating Form for an Essay Test Containing Four Questions

Name _____ Date _____ Score __53.5 of 62 = 83%__

Question 1 (Checklist, 5 Points)		*Points*	×	*Weight*	=	*Score*
Present Component						
✓ A. _____		4	×	3	=	12
✓ B. _____						
✓ C. _____						
___ D. _____						
✓ E. _____						

Question 2 (Rating Scale, 16 Points)

Components		Ratings							
	(1)	(2)	(3)	(4)					
A. _____	___	✓	___		15	×	1	=	15
B. _____	___	___	✓						
C. _____	___	___	___	✓					
D. _____	___	___	✓						
E. _____	___	___	✓						

Question 3 (Rating Scale, 16 Points)

Components		Ratings							
	(1)	(2)	(3)	(4)					
A. _____	___	___	✓		14	×	1	=	14
B. _____	___	✓	___						
C. _____	___	___	___	✓					
D. _____	___	✓	___						
E. _____	___	___	✓						

Question 4 (Checklist, 6 Points)						
Present Component						
✓ A. _____		5	×	2.5	=	12.5
___ B. _____						
✓ C. _____						
✓ D. _____						
✓ E. _____						
✓ F. _____						

Evaluating Checklists and Rating Scales

Before you use a checklist or rating scale to score students' work, you should evaluate the form and revise it if necessary. First, select two or three students' responses or products and rate their work using the form. Determine whether the components on the form are observable and whether they are listed on the form in the sequence they most frequently occur in the products. Delete components that are not observable, change the sequence of components if necessary, and add components observable in the products that you may have inadvertently overlooked. When adding components, be sure they are appropriate for the instructional goal measured and not an artifact of the particular subset of responses you have chosen. Adjust students' scores on the few products rated to reflect any changes made in the rating form. Second, score each paper again. It is good to allow some time to lapse between the two ratings so that you forget the scores assigned the first time. Compare the two ratings you assigned each paper and locate any inconsistencies. Where inconsistent scores occur, either revise the form to include fewer categories of quality that need to be differentiated or write more descriptive titles for each of the categories.

You might also ask a colleague to rate the same papers using the form. Compare your ratings with those of your colleague, discuss any inconsistencies, locate ways in which the form can be changed to improve consistency, and revise the form as needed. Once you begin to score students' work, do not alter the form. Any changes at this point may produce inconsistent ratings.

AVOIDING COMMON ERRORS IN TEST DEVELOPMENT, SCORING, AND GRADING

Development Errors

In producing essay and product development tests, teachers tend to commit two kinds of errors. First, some teachers teach skills at the lower levels of learning and test them at the higher levels. You should not teach lessons at the knowledge and comprehension levels and then expect students to perform at an application level on the test. Likewise, you should not teach at the comprehension level and then write tests to measure skills at the analysis, synthesis, or evaluation levels. If students are required to develop a product or analyze a piece of literature, they should have been instructed at these levels and given ample opportunity to practice these skills before the posttest. To avoid this problem, make sure that novel items used on the posttest mirror those used on practice tests.

Teachers also err in constructing essay and product development tests when the items or directions do not provide adequate guidance. One way to ensure that items and directions are clear and the task posed is feasible is to construct the evaluation form before you administer the test. Constructing the evaluation form will help ensure that you have a clear notion of what you are asking students to do. After the evaluation form is complete, recheck your questions and directions to see whether they provide adequate guidance for the responses you anticipate.

Essay tests can include several questions that require relatively brief answers, or they may contain only one or two questions that require lengthy responses. Whatever the number of questions, the entire class should be directed to answer all the questions included on the test. One relatively common practice in developing essay tests, which is *not* recommended by test specialists, is to provide several questions on an essay test and allow students to select a subset of questions to answer. This practice would be similar to letting students answer 20 of 30 objective items. Both essay and objective test items represent only a few of those a teacher could construct, and the same sample should be used to evaluate all students. When students' responses are not comparable, your ability to evaluate your instruction and students' performance is compromised.

Scoring Errors

Two common scoring errors are inconsistency and bias. Even when teachers use checklists and rating scales, they can score students' responses inconsistently. They may become stricter or more lenient as they work through a set of papers, and their attitudes can change when they become tired, hurried, or bored. You can avoid such inconsistencies in several ways. First, instead of marking all the essay questions on one student's paper, score all the students' responses to one question before going on to the next question. Complete the scoring of one question during one marking period rather than in several. After you have completed all the papers on each question, check your consistency by again scoring the first few papers. If a student's first and second scores are the same, your scoring was probably consistent for all students. Noticeable inconsistencies in marking might indicate that your attitude, rather than the quality of students' work, determined test scores. If the scores are different, you should rescore the tests.

Besides attitude, the inclusion of too many quality categories for each component can lead to inconsistent scoring. For example, the paragraph rating scale in Table 9.9 lists only main components with no physical, functional, or quality characteristics. The rating scales for each main component have eight quality levels for each component with only two descriptor categories. Although it would take little time to develop such a scale, the probability of the teacher's marking paragraphs inconsistently is high. It would be more difficult to identify distinct quality descriptors for all eight category numbers. It would also be difficult to differentiate consistently between adjacent categories (e.g., determining when a student should receive a 3 instead of a 4 or a 6 instead of a 7). When inconsistencies are present, you might want to revise your rating scale and use strategies to minimize potential attitude shifts before rescoring tests.

Scoring bias is another common problem. Some teachers give all the students high test scores regardless of quality. Others give all average or all very low marks. In your own marking, you should compare the range of

TABLE 9.9
Rating Scale with Inappropriate Quality Categories

Component	Rating	
	Inadequate	Excellent
I. Topic Sentence	1 2 3 4 5 6 7 8	
II. Supporting Sentences	1 2 3 4 5 6 7 8	
III. Concluding Sentence	1 2 3 4 5 6 7 8	

scores you assign with the heterogeneity or homogeneity of the group. If you have a homogeneous group of students, a small range of high, average, or low scores may accurately reflect the quality of students' work. If you are assigning similar scores to a heterogeneous group, however, your marking may be biased.

Teachers' opinions of individual students can also bias their scoring. Teachers are often inclined to score particular students' papers more leniently than they score others, and disruptive or uncooperative students sometimes receive scores lower than they deserve. Students who are struggling can evoke a great deal of sympathy, and teachers who want to encourage their efforts may score these students' papers quite leniently. However you choose to justify unearned scores, keep in mind that they are, indeed, unearned.

Because teachers are often unaware of their bias, they may find it difficult to avoid. Test specialists recommend that teachers maintain objectivity by dissociating students' names from their responses. For example, you could instruct your students to put their names on the backs of their papers or you could cover their names with removable labels until you finished scoring the papers. Students could also write their names and an identifying number on a separate sheet of paper and indicate only the identifying number on their work. If you have difficulty scoring papers that do not identify the student, your impressions of students are probably influencing the way you score. If this is the case, you should keep in mind that you are scoring responses and not individuals.

Another common error sometimes observed in scoring essay tests is to use *subtractive* rather than *additive* scoring. Subtractive scoring occurs when a teacher decides subjectively that a test will be worth a given number of total points, divides these points equally among the questions on the test, and then scores students' answers by subtracting a subjective number of points from each answer for errors and omissions present in the answers. Students' raw scores are obtained by subtracting the negative points from the total number of points allocated. To illustrate subtractive scoring, a teacher may administer a four-question essay test and decide that the total exam will be worth 100 points, with 25 points allocated to each of the four questions. Before grading begins, all students have a score of 100 in the exam. As the teacher reads each answer, points are subtracted from the total for omissions and errors. For one omission, a student's score may be reduced by 2 points, for an error it may be reduced by 5 points, and 1 point might be subtracted for each spelling error. The sum of the negative points the student earns is then subtracted from the total points allocated to determine the student's score on the question. If the student made one omission, one content error, and misspelled five words, the score for the question would $25 - 12 = 13$. This method of subtractive grading is very subjective, does not clearly communicate to students the strengths in their answers, and tends to result in inconsistent scoring across items on one student's test and across students in the class on one test item.

Additive scoring, on the other hand, enables teachers to allocate a specified number of points for each component of an answer, locate that component in the answer, and assign an appropriate number of the allocated points. Students' raw scores are then obtained by adding the points earned for each component. Additive, analytical scoring helps teachers be more objective, and it better communicates the strengths and weaknesses in a student's answer.

A Grading Error

One common grading error is to count practice tests as posttests and include them in the term grade. This tends to happen more on essay and product development practice tests than on objective-style practice tests because of the time and effort required for essay and product tests by both the teacher and students. But the required effort is not what differentiates between practice exercises and posttests. The purposes of practice tests, regardless of the format, are to provide students with the opportunity to rehearse skills and to provide them with corrective feedback. Despite the degree of effort required, students' scores on essay and product development practice tests should not be considered when calculating term achievement grades.

USING PRODUCT RATING FORMS AS AN INSTRUCTIONAL TOOL

Used as self-assessment tools, rating scales and checklists can help students identify and use appropriate criteria for developing their responses. During practice exercises, they can use an evaluation form to rate the quality of their work and to compare their ratings with yours. You can then discuss differences in ratings with students who have difficulty finding problems in their work. Students can also use the rating forms to evaluate example answers and products that you provide. They can discuss similarities and differences among their evaluations and between theirs and yours. Using the criteria when developing their responses for practice exercises and when reviewing work samples will help students focus on the important aspects of a skill. Such involvement should help them not only produce better work but also feel a greater sense of responsibility for the quality of their work and the scores they receive.

The use of product rating forms can also serve to keep cooperative learning activities and group projects on track. Notice in the instructions for developing a test item bank (Table 9.2) that students are directed to use the test item checklists included in Tables 5.18 and 9.13. Using the checklists as a guide, students evaluate the items they have written as well as those written by their teammates. This evaluation activity during the production of term projects serves as instruction for students, and it results in superior item banks.

AN EXAMPLE

The instructional goal framework and behavioral objectives on writing a paragraph are used to illustrate the development of evaluation forms for rating the original paragraphs written by students. The product-level behavioral objectives written for the instructional goal are the following:

I.F.1 Given a topic requiring a description of something, write a four- to six-sentence paragraph.

I.F.2 Given a topic that requires time series, write a four- to six-sentence paragraph.

I.F.3 Given a topic that is a procedure for doing something, write a four- to six-sentence paragraph.

I.F.4 Given a topic that is an expression of feelings or attitude, write a four- to six-sentence paragraph.

The following sections contain examples of instructions, a checklist, and a rating scale.

Writing Instructions

The following instructions are for behavioral objective I.F.3, "Write a paragraph that describes a procedure." Very few directions about the paragraph itself are given because the teacher wants to evaluate whether students remember to include all three types of sentences, order their sentences according to the procedure they describe, and use transitional words to illustrate sequence.

Write a four- to six-sentence paragraph that **describes how** to wash a dog. Use a clean sheet of paper, and write your name in the top, left corner of the page. Put today's date in the top, right corner of the page. You will have 20 minutes to write and revise your paragraph. You may want to outline your dog-washing ideas before you begin to write.

Developing Scoring Procedures

The instructional goal framework for writing a paragraph is repeated in Table 9.10. There are four main concepts in the framework: paragraphs, topic sentences, supporting sentences, and concluding sentences. These main components will comprise the major sections of the evaluation form. Recall that the criteria for evaluating these main components should be located in the physical, functional, and qualitative characteristics columns of the matrix. The goal framework will be used to create a checklist and a rating scale for evaluating students' paragraphs.

A Checklist for Scoring Paragraphs   The main components in rows I, II, III, and IV and their subcomponents in columns A, B, and C are configured into the checklist in Table 9.11. The title of the checklist reflects the instructional goal and the particular assignment within the goal. Space is also included at the top of the form for inserting students' names, the date, their raw

TABLE 9.10

Matrix Diagram Analysis for the Instructional Goal, "Write a Paragraph"

CONCEPTS/ CONTENT	A State/Recall Physical Characteristics	B State/Recall Functional Characteristics	C State/Recall Quality Characteristics	D Discriminate Examples & Nonexamples	E Evaluate Given Examples	F Produce Examples
I. Paragraph	Series of sentences Indented	Express ideas on one topic		Correct vs.: Not indented Many topics		Time Series Feelings Procedure Description
II. Topic Sentence	Typically first Indented	Introduce topic	Relevance Scope Interest	Topic vs.: Supporting Concluding	Correct vs. flawed by: Relevance Scope Interest	Time Series Feelings Procedure Description
III. Supporting Sentences	Middle sentences	Elaborate topic	Relevance Sequence Transition	Supporting vs.: Topic Concluding	Correct vs. flawed by: Relevance Sequence Transition	Time Series Feelings Procedure Description
IV. Concluding Sentence	Typically last	Concludes/ summarizes topic	Transition Relevance Sums up Scope	Concluding vs.: Topic Supporting	Correct vs. flawed by: Transition Relevance Conclusion Scope	Time Series Feelings Procedure Description

TABLE 9.11
A Sample Checklist for Rating Students' Original Paragraphs

WRITING PROCEDURAL PARAGRAPHS (WALKING A DOG)			
Name _____		**Date** _____ **Score** _____ (19) ____%	
Yes	**No**	**Criteria**	**Comments**
		I. Paragraph	
____	____	A.1 Four to six sentences	
____	____	A.2 Indented	
____	____	B.1 Only one idea	
____	____	B.2 Describes procedure	
		II. Topic Sentence	
____	____	A.1 Location (first)	
____	____	B.2 Introduces topic	
____	____	C.1 Relevant to paragraph	
____	____	C.2 Appropriate scope	
____	____	C.3 Interest for reader	
		III. Supporting Sentences	
____	____	A.1 Location (middle)	
____	____	B.2 Elaborates topic	
____	____	C.1 Relevant to topic	
____	____	C.2 Sequence of ideas	
____	____	C.3 Transition	
		IV. Concluding Sentence	
____	____	A.1 Location (last)	
____	____	B.2 Summarizes	
____	____	C.1 Transition	
____	____	C.2 Relevance	
____	____	C.3 Scope	

scores, and the percentage of total points earned. This information is important later for monitoring students' writing progress and for sequencing writing samples in a portfolio of their work.

The left side of the checklist includes spaces for indicating the presence or acceptability of each facet of students' paragraphs. The second column contains the four main components and their subcomponents extracted from the instructional goal framework. The last column includes space for commenting on students' paragraphs. This comment area can be used to praise particularly good characteristics and to point out areas the student needs to reconsider. Using a comments section with your checklists will help you avoid marking over or rewriting students' paragraphs.

Students' raw scores are obtained by checking the acceptable characteristics in the left column and then summing the check marks. The percentage of total points earned is obtained by dividing the student's raw score by the number of possible points (19) and then multiplying the quotient by 100.

A Rating Scale for Scoring Paragraphs   Table 9.12 contains the paragraph checklist reformatted into a rating scale. The project title and other identifying information remains the same. Notice that the main components and subcomponents also remain the same but they are moved to the first column of the form. The second column contains the descriptive categories and numbers to indicate quality levels. The comments column is again included to allow highlighting particularly good components as well as ones that need to be improved.

COMPUTER TECHNOLOGY

Although some teachers believe that computer-based item banks are inappropriate for essay and product tests, this is not the case. Using the ParTEST programs (Economics Research, Inc., 1991), there are several options you can use to enter a checklist or rating scale into an item bank. Probably the easiest method is to enter the performance directions using the essay item format and then enter the accompanying evaluation form in the student feedback section for the item. Any time the item (directions) is printed, the rating scale or checklist will also be printed as the student feedback report. Another method is to enter the evaluation form itself, using either the essay or problem format, and then classify it as a rating scale or checklist with the user descriptors (e.g., subject, topic, test type) for easy retrieval. A third option would be to enter it as a figure that accompanies the item directions. Recall from Chapter 5 that you can link graphs, charts, and tables to designated items using the figure feature. Each time the directions are printed, the accompanying figure is also printed.

Although you must hand-score students' essay questions and products, you can enter their raw scores into their computer-based records using either scan sheets or the key board. For combination essay and objective tests, there is space on each student's answer sheet to insert his or her raw score on the essay part of the exam. The computer will sum the scores from the two portions of the test or it will keep them as separate test scores if you wish.

Once essay or product tests are entered into the program, you can obtain the same types of group performance and individual student performance

TABLE 9.12

A Sample Rating Scale for Evaluating Students' Original Paragraphs

WRITING PROCEDURAL PARAGRAPHS (WASHING A DOG)					
Name _____		Date _____	Score _____	(44) _____%	
Criteria	No 0	Vaguely 1	Mostly 2	Well 3	**Comments**
I. Paragraph (7)					
A.1 Four to six sentences	0	1 (Yes)			
A.2 Indented	0	1 (Yes)			
B.1 Only one topic		1	2		
C.1 Describes procedure		1	2	3	
II. Topic Sentence (10)	0	1 (Included)			
A.1 Location (first)	0	1 (Yes)			
B.2 Introduces topic		1	2		
C.1 Relevant to paragraph		1	2		
C.2 Appropriate scope		1	2		
C.3 Interest for reader		1	2		
III. Supporting Sentences (14)	0	1 (Included)			
A.1 Location (middle)	0	1 (Yes)			
B.2 Elaborates topic		1	2	3	
C.1 Relevant to topic		1	2	3	
C.2 Sequence of ideas		1	2	3	
C.3 Transition		1	2	3	
IV. Concluding Sentence (13)	0	1 (Included)			
A.1 Location (last)	0	1 (Yes)			
B.1 Summarizes		1	2	3	
C.1 Transition		1	2	3	
C.2 Relevance		1	2	3	
C.3 Scope		1	2		
Totals		( ) + ( ) + ( )			= _____

information that is available for objective-style tests. In addition, results from essay and product tests can be included on interim reports to parents.

SUMMARY

Essay tests and product development tests measure students' skills in producing original responses. Essay questions can ask students to discuss, explain, analyze, summarize, or evaluate something. Product development tests can be used to measure students' skill in producing a variety of verbal products, such as paragraphs, book reports, and themes. Product tests can also be used to measure students' skill in creating such objects as mobiles, photographs, and maps.

Essay and product tests allow students to select their approach to a given problem, the information they will include, and the methods of organization and presentation they will use. (Such skills cannot be measured using objective tests.) These tests enable a teacher to determine both what and how students think. Test drawbacks include the time required to develop, analyze, and score them; difficulties in scoring responses consistently and without bias; and the advantage essay tests give to students with well-developed verbal skills.

The procedure for developing and using essay and product development tests consists of three phases: (1) writing questions and directions, (2) developing scoring procedures, and (3) scoring students' responses.

The criteria for developing valid and reliable test items also apply to essay questions and directions for products. The behavior, content, and conditions included should match those in the objectives; the complexity, context, and vocabulary should be appropriate for students; and grammar, punctuation, and sentence structure should be correct. Good questions and directions also provide adequate guidance for responding. Questions and directions that provide little guidance require students to exercise considerable judgment in responding. A lot of guidance guarantees that students will address specific issues, but it also limits the approaches they can take. Considering the main purpose for your test and the skill level of students will help you select an appropriate amount of guidance.

Besides describing the task to be performed, you should provide information that can help students determine the scope of the anticipated responses. You might want to include such information as how long their response should be, the amount of time they should spend, and the number of points each question or section is worth. Developing an evaluation form before administering the test will help you evaluate the clarity and feasibility of your questions or directions.

Essay and product development tests can be scored using either global or analytical scoring methods. Global scoring provides information on the overall quality of students' responses. Analytical scoring provides information on the quality of specific components and subcomponents of a response. Although analytical scoring is more time consuming than is global scoring, it provides students with better feedback and teachers with specific information they can use to analyze and evaluate the quality of instruction.

Analytical scoring requires the use of either a checklist or rating scale. Both should list the components and, if needed, the subcomponents of a skill to direct your attention to particular aspects of a response. The components and subcomponents should be taken directly from the enabling and prerequisite skills in the instructional goal framework. A checklist allows you to mark the presence or absence of a component, whereas a rating scale enables you to differentiate various quality categories for each component using a scale. The number of quality categories included on the scale should not exceed the number you can consistently judge. Verbal descriptors should be written for each quality category. Once the checklist or rating scale is designed, review the number of points allocated to each component. If the value assigned does not contribute an appropriate amount to the total score, use weighting schemes to adjust the relative value of components.

When the evaluation form is complete, review the questions and directions to ensure that they provide students with the guidance necessary to produce the responses you anticipate. At this point, revisions can be made in the questions, directions, or evaluation form as needed. After the test is administered, the rating form should again be evaluated using a few tests. Determine whether the components listed are observable in students' responses, whether they are sequenced in the most efficient order on the form, and whether you can score responses consistently. You should make necessary revisions before beginning to score students' work.

Teachers experience two problems when rating students' responses: inconsistent scoring and bias. Inconsistent scoring can be caused by shifts in attitude that may lead to stricter or more lenient scoring. It can also result when you include more categories of quality for each component than you can consistently judge or use vague descriptors for each category. Bias results from marking all students as good, average, or poor regardless of the quality of their work. Bias also results when you consider not only the nature of the response but also the characteristics of the student who made the response. After scoring all papers, rescore the first two or three to see whether you were consistent. Also check to see whether the range of scores assigned is reasonable given the heterogeneity or homogeneity of the group. If inconsistency or bias is detectable, you should rescore the papers. Table 9.13 includes a checklist you can use for evaluating forms designed to rate students' products and essay questions.

Similar to objective-style items, essay questions and product development directions can be entered into a computer-based test item bank. Keeping test questions or directions and scoring forms in an item bank enables easy retrieval of the materials and convenient editing when changes are necessary. Additionally, scores from product tests are easy to enter into students' records for inclusion on interim and term progress reports.

TABLE 9.13
Checklist for Evaluating Product and Essay Tests

CRITERIA FOR EVALUATING PRODUCT/ESSAY TESTS AND RATING FORMS		
Yes	**No**	**I. Internal Criteria for All Test Formats:** Are instructions, directions, and rating forms:
____	____	A. Congruent with the behavorial objective?
____	____	B. Congruent with the developmental level and experiences of students?
____	____	C. Free from biasing material related to cultural/ethnic groups, gender, and religious and political ideas?
____	____	D. Clearly written with correct grammar, spelling, and punctuation?
		II. Directions: Do the directions and instructions:
____	____	A. Provide appropriate guidance for students' skill level?
____	____	B. Provide appropriate guidance for the skill measured?
____	____	C. Provide adequate organizational information (e.g., time allowed, point values for questions, length and scope of response sought)?
		III. Global Scoring: Are there:
____	____	A. Established scoring categories that will be used?
____	____	B. Only the number of scoring categories that can be consistently differentiated?
____	____	C. Clearly described characteristics of a response that fits each of the categories?
		IV. Analytical Scoring—Criteria (Stems): Are the evaluation criteria:
____	____	A. Congruent with the main concepts (components) in the instructional goal framework?
____	____	B. Congruent with the physical, functional, and qualitative characteristics included in the instructional goal framework (product development)?
____	____	C. Congruent with the main categories of information to be described (rows) or contrasted (columns) in the instructional goal framework (essay)?
____	____	D. Paraphrased clearly in the rating form?
____	____	E. Ordered/sequenced logically/conveniently for observation?
____	____	F. Stated either positively or neutrally so that both criteria and ratings are consistent in meaning?
		V. Analytical Scoring—Checklists: Are the:
____	____	A. Descriptors for categories (yes/no, acceptable/unacceptable) listed at the top of the rating column?
____	____	B. Blanks for checking clearly marked and conveniently located?
		VI. Analytical Scoring—Rating Scales: Are there:
____	____	A. Only the number of quality levels that can consistently be differentiated for each characteristic?
____	____	B. Verbal descriptors for each quality level?

PRACTICE EXERCISES

   I. **Develop and Score Product Tests**
   A. Which of the following skills could be measured only with essay or product development tests?
      1. Recall verbal information.
      2. Design a solution to a problem.
      3. Discriminate among examples and nonexamples of a concept.
      4. Use a rule to solve a problem.
      5. Decide how two or more things should be compared and make the comparisons.
      6. Evaluate a rule, a principle, an object, or a product.
      7. Synthesize facts and information.
      8. Organize facts and information.
      9. Follow rules to produce an original piece of work.
     10. Recall, select, organize, and present information.

TABLE 9.14

Goal Framework for the Instructional Goal, "Outline a Passage"

Components	Define Levels	Paraphrase Entries	Sequence Entries within Level	Label Entries	Align Entries in Outline
Main topics	Define main topics as key main ideas in total passage.	Use sentence or topic outline. Do not mix sentences and phrases in one outline.	Place entries in order defined by passage.	Use roman numerals to label main ideas.	Place all main topics flush with left margin.
Secondary topics	Define secondary topics as key ideas within each main topic. There should be at least two entries.	Make all entries within a main topic parallel in structure. Structure may differ from that of main topics and from that of secondary topics for other main ideas.	Place secondary topics in order defined by passage.	Use capital letters to label secondary topics.	Indent secondary entries 5 spaces from left margin and align.
Level-three topics	Define level-three topics as key ideas *within* each secondary level topic. There should be at least two entries.	Make all entries within a secondary level topic parallel.	Place level-three topics in order defined by passage.	Label level-three topics with arabic numerals.	Indent all level-three topics 10 spaces from left margin and align.
Level-four topics	Define level-four topics as key ideas *within* each level-three topic. There should be at least two entries.	Make all entires within a level-three topic parallel.	Place level-four topics in order defined by passage.	Label level-four topics with lower-case letters.	Indent all level-four topics 15 spaces from left margin and align.

   B. Table 9.14 includes an instructional goal framework for outlining a passage. Use the framework to:
1. Write instructions for a test that measures students' skills in outlining given passages. Assume that the given passages each have three main topics, three secondary ideas, and no level-three or level-four ideas.
2. Write instructions for a practice test in outlining in which students will use a rating form to guide their practice.
3. Develop an evaluation form for scoring students' outlines. (See Table 9.14F in the Feedback section.)

   C. Score the three paragraphs entitled "Washing a Dog" in Figure 9.2 using the paragraph rating form in Table 9.15. Assume the paragraphs were written by sixth-grade students. Record your scores for each paragraph in the last three columns of the form. When you have finished:
1. Compare the scores you assigned with those of classmates.
2. Discuss inconsistencies and try to determine why the scores were different.
3. If you attribute differences to inadequacies in the rating scale, suggest ways to improve the form.
4. Compare your scores to those in Table 9.15F (in the Feedback section) that reflect the judgment of another rater.

II. Enrichment

Select a skill from your own field that can only be measured with an essay or product development test and do the following:
1. Analyze the skill to identify its subordinate skills and create a goal framework that illustrates the relationship among the skills.
2. Write a behavioral objective for the skill; be sure to include relevant conditions.
3. Write an essay question or questions or the instructions for product development. Include adequate guidance for the skill being measured and for the sophistication of target students.
4. Develop a scoring checklist or rating scale.
5. If you have students' work available, score their work using your form.
6. Revise the rating form if necessary.

FEEDBACK

I. Develop and Score Product Tests

   A. The following skills could be measured only with essay and product development tests: 2, 5, 9, and 10.

   B. Instructions for a test of outlining skills.
1. Read the article titled _____ . Make a <u>topic</u> outline of the information in the article. You have 20 minutes to complete the task.
2. Instructions for a practice test of outlining skills.
Make a <u>sentence</u> outline of the information in the article entitled _____ . You have 30 minutes to complete the following:
   a. Read the article.
   b. Review the rating form attached to the article that will be used to score your outline.

FIGURE 9.2
Three Paragraphs Entitled "Washing a Dog"

Paragraph 1

> One of my chors on Saturday is to wash my dog Rover. I use warm water to get him wet all over. Then I rub him with a special soap that doesn't hurt his eyes and keeps his coat glossie. When he is clean, I rinse him twice to make sure all the soap is gone. After he shakes off most of the water, I rub him with a clean old towel. He thinks I do a good job.

Paragraph 2

> Put a wash tub in the yard. Fill it with water and sope. Put the dog in the tub. Scrub the dog. Rinse the dog with a hose. Stand back when the dog gets out of the tub.

Paragraph 3

> My dog hates to get a bath. When anyone gets out the tub she runs and hides. It is easy to find her because she always hides in the same place. You have to hold her the whole time or she will run away again. She shivers and barks the whole time. My cousin's dog likes to get a bath.

    c. Select and organize the information you think should be included.
    d. Write your outline.
    e. Use the rating form to:
        (1) review your outline and <u>correct</u> any problems you find.
        (2) <u>score</u> your outline.
    f. Turn in both your outline and your completed rating form when you have finished.
   3. See Table 9.14F.
  C. Compare your scores with those of classmates and students included in Table 9.15F.

TABLE 9.15
A Rating Scale for Evaluating Students' Paragraphs in Table 9.15

WRITING PROCEDURAL PARAGRAPHS (WASHING A DOG)							
Name _____		Date _____ Score _____ (44) _____%					
Criteria	No 0	Vaguely 1	Mostly 2	Well 3	#1	#2	#3
I. Paragraph (7)							
A.1 Four to six sentences	0	1 (Yes)					
A.2 Indented	0	1 (Yes)					
B.1 Only one topic		1	2				
C.1 Describes procedure		1	2	3			
II. Topic Sentence (10)	0	1 (Included)					
A.1 Location (first)	0	1 (Yes)					
B.2 Introduces topic		1	2				
C.1 Relevant to paragraph		1	2				
C.2 Appropriate scope		1	2				
C.3 Interest for reader		1	2				
III. Supporting Sentences (14)	0	1 (Included)					
A.1 Location (middle)	0	1 (Yes)					
B.2 Elaborates topic		1	2	3			
C.1 Relevant to topic		1	2	3			
C.2 Sequence of ideas		1	2	3			
C.3 Transition		1	2	3			
IV. Concluding Sentence (13)	0	1 (Included)					
A.1 Location (last)	0	1 (Yes)					
B.1 Summarizes		1	2	3			
C.1 Transition		1	2	3			
C.2 Relevance		1	2	3			
C.3 Scope		1	2				
Totals		( ) + ( ) + ( )					

TABLE 9.14F
Rating Scale for Evaluating Outlines

Name _____ Date _____ Score _____
Total　　(35)

I. Main Ideas	1	2	3
A. Main ideas identified	Secondary ideas included — 1	Some ideas missing — 2	All main ideas included — 3
B. Clearly paraphrased	Some meaning changed — 1	Too brief/wordy — 2	Clearly paraphrased — 3
C. Parallel structure	Mixed sentence/phrase — 1	All sentences or phrases — 2	Consistent word format — 3
D. Consistent order	Out of order — 1	Most in order — 2	All in order — 3
E. Consistent labels	Inconsistent — 1	Consistent — 2	
F. Alignment	Flush with left margin — 1	Aligned — 2	

II. Secondary ideas	1	2	3
A. Secondary ideas identified	Main ideas included — 1	Some ideas missing — 2	All secondary ideas included — 3
B. Related to main idea	Scrambled placement — 1	Most within right topic — 2	All within right topic — 3
C. Clearly paraphrased	Some meaning changed — 1	Too brief/wordy — 2	Clearly paraphrased — 3
D. Parallel structure	Mixed sentence/phrase/word — 1	All sentences, phrases, or words — 2	Consistent word format — 3
E. Consistent order	Out of order — 1	Most in order — 2	All in order — 3
F. Consistent labels	Inconsistent — 1	Consistent — 2	
G. Alignment	Indented five spaces — 1	Aligned — 2	

TABLE 9.15F
Ratings for Students' Original Paragraphs on Washing a Dog

WRITING PROCEDURAL PARAGRAPHS (WASHING A DOG)						
Name _____ Date _____ Score _____ (44) _____%						
Criteria	No 0	Vaguely 1	Mostly 2	Well 3	#1	#2	#3
I. Paragraph (7)							
A.1 Four to six sentences	0	1 (Yes)			1	1	1
A.2 Indented	0	1 (Yes)			1	0	0
B.1 Only one topic		1	2		2	2	1
C.1 Describes procedure		1	2	3	3	3	1
II. Topic Sentence (10)	0	1 (Included)			1	0	1
A.1 Location (first)	0	1 (Yes)			1		1
B.2 Introduces topic		1	2		2		2
C.1 Relevant to paragraph		1	2		2		2
C.2 Appropriate scope		1	2		2		2
C.3 Interest for reader		1	2		2		2
III. Supporting Sentences (14)	0	1 (Included)			1	1	1
A.1 Location (middle)	0	1 (Yes)			1	0	1
B.2 Elaborates topic		1	2	3	3	3	3
C.1 Relevant to topic		1	2	3	3	3	3
C.2 Sequence of ideas		1	2	3	3	3	3
C.3 Transition		1	2	3	3	1	1
IV. Concluding Sentence (13)	0	1 (Included)			1	0	1
A.1 Location (last)	0	1 (Yes)			1		1
B.1 Summarizes		1	2	3	3		1
C.1 Transition		1	2	3	1		1
C.2 Relevance		1	2	3	3		1
C.3 Scope		1	2		2		1
Totals	( ) + ( ) + ( )				42	17	31

REFERENCE

Economics Research, Inc. (1991). *ParTEST user's manual*. Costa Mesa, CA: Economics Research, Inc.

SUGGESTED READINGS

Ebel, R. L., & Frisbee, D. A. (1991). *Essentials of educational measurement* (5th ed.) (pp. 188–193). Englewood Cliffs, NJ: Prentice Hall.

Gronlund, N. E., & Linn, R. L. (1990). *Measurement and evaluation in teaching* (6th ed.) (pp. 211–227). New York: Macmillan.

Hopkins, C. D., & Antes, R. L. (1990). *Classroom measurement and evaluation* (3rd ed.) (pp. 100–128). Itasca, IL: F. E. Peacock.

Hopkins, K. D., Stanley, J. C., & Hopkins, B. R. (1990). *Educational and psychological measurement and evaluation* (3rd ed.) (pp. 193–223). Englewood Cliffs, NJ: Prentice Hall.

Kubiszyn, T., & Borich, G. (1990). *Educational testing and measurement* (3rd ed.) (pp. 97–114; 181–191). Glenview, IL: Scott, Foresman/Little, Brown.

Mehrens, W. A., and Lehmann, I. J. (1991). *Measurement and evaluation in education and psychology* (4th ed.) (pp. 81–105). New York: CBS College Publishing.

Oosterhof, A. (1990). *Classroom applications of educational measurement* (pp. 69–85). Columbus, OH: Merrill.

Popham, J. W. (1990). *Modern educational measurement* (2nd ed.) (pp. 266–284). Englewood Cliffs, NJ: Prentice Hall.

Sax, G. (1989). *Principles of educational and psychological measurement and evaluation* (3rd ed.) (pp. 128–144). Belmont, CA: Wadsworth.

Wiersma, W., & Jurs, S. G. (1990). *Educational measurement and testing* (2nd ed.) (pp. 65–90). Boston: Allyn and Bacon.

CHAPTER 10

Constructing and Using Tests That Require Active Performance

Many skills students learn in school involve some type of performance, such as delivering an oral report, driving a car, changing a tire, operating audiovisual equipment, and performing athletic skills. Teachers can rate and assign grades to these performances, just as they do for the skills measured by objective, essay, and product development tests. Performance tests enable teachers to analyze students' performances and to comment on such aspects as timing, speed, precision, sequence, and appearance. Like other types of tests, they provide a basis for evaluating the quality of instruction for separate aspects of the skill. For outgoing students, they are also motivational. Some students enjoy the opportunity to demonstrate their skill for the teacher and their classmates.

At the same time, performance tests have their disadvantages. First, because individuals must be evaluated separately, they are time consuming. Second, teachers have to observe closely because important aspects of the performance may be rapid and difficult to see. Asking students to repeat a performance because something was missed may affect their performance negatively. Third, some students become extremely self-conscious and uncomfortable when they are asked to perform in front of the teacher or the group. If a teacher is not sensitive to the needs and feelings of these students, performance tests might actually inhibit learning and reduce the quality of performance. Finally, a teacher must have excellent classroom management skills in order to (1) maintain a positive atmosphere for the performing student, (2) keep other students engaged in some activity, and (3) focus attention on the performing student. In spite of these limitations, performance tests are the most appropriate method for measuring skills that require action.

The procedure teachers use to evaluate students' performance is similar to that for developing and scoring essay exams and products. Teachers should (1) define and analyze the expected performance, (2) select the components to be evaluated, (3) develop an evaluation form with procedures and instructions, (4) formatively evaluate the form and procedures, and (5) observe and rate students' performances.

The following sections describe general procedures for measuring students' performance. The particular steps you take as a teacher will depend on the content of your instruction, your classroom environment, and the characteristics of your students.

ANALYZING INSTRUCTIONAL GOALS THAT REQUIRE ACTIVE PERFORMANCE

The instructional goals that require active performances are both intellectual skills and motor skills. The analysis procedures for intellectual skills were described in Chapter 3, and motor skills were introduced at that point. The analysis of motor skills is explained in this chapter since evaluation of student's performances requires complete, accurate observation and rating forms for helping ensure the objectivity of teachers' judgments.

Gagné (1985) describes *motor skills* as those skills requiring the coordination of muscular movement, such as walking, running, jumping, and lifting. We acquire some of these skills by watching other people perform them, trying them ourselves, and refining them through trial and error. Complex motor skills, such as driving a race car, forming a clay pot on a potter's wheel, and blowing glass into predesigned forms, require instruction and considerable practice. In school, students use motor skills to form printed and cursive letters, draw pictures, operate scientific equipment, perform in athletic events, use tools and machines, play musical instruments, and sing in a chorus.

Many motor skills can be separated into action steps, which may take place sequentially or simultaneously. These steps, often called *part skills*, make up the complete performance or total skill. Students may learn and practice part skills separately, but they must eventually integrate them into practice of the total skill (Gagné, 1985).

A flowchart is used most often to analyze an instructional goal for a motor skill. During the analysis, you need to identify the total skill, the main part skills, and the proper sequence of the parts. Once the part skills are identified, each skill is further separated into required subskills.

A common method used for beginning the analysis of a motor skill is to videotape a performance of the skill by someone you would consider to be proficient. Then view the performance with the person and talk through the sequence of physical actions and mental activities that accompany the physical actions. At that point, you can begin to put your observations and notes into a flowchart of the part skills and subskills.

Figure 10.1 contains a partial analysis of the goal, "Execute a golf swing." The statement for the total skill appears at the top. Five part skills are listed next: grip the club, address the ball, execute the backswing, execute the downswing, and execute the follow through. In this partial analysis, only the overlap

FIGURE 10.1
Partial Analysis of a Motor Skill Goal: Execute a Golf Swing

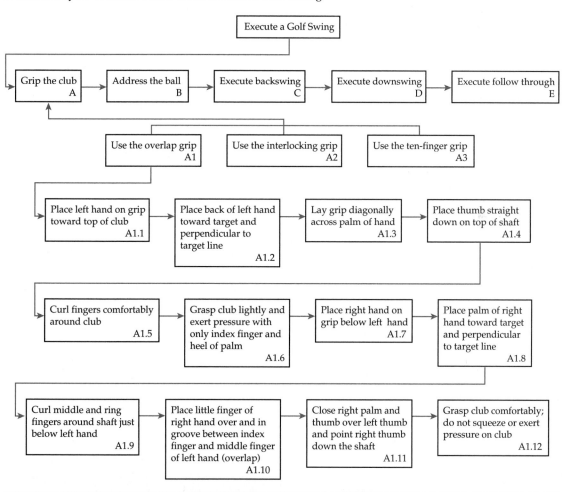

grip is broken down into subskills, which appear in their proper sequence. In a complete analysis, each of the five part skills in the top row would be broken down into subskills. Although some of the part skills might be taught separately, a person learning how to execute a golf swing eventually would have to integrate and practice all of the skills in one smooth, continuous motion.

Some instructional goals do not fall neatly into a single category of learning; instead, they seem to integrate or combine levels. The instructional goal, "Make an oral presentation," is such a goal, and it includes both motor and intellectual skills. Table 10.1 includes a matrix analysis for this combination goal. There are three main performance areas: physical expression, vocal expres-

TABLE 10.1
Instructional Goal Framework for the Goal, "Make an Oral Presentation"

	A Identify/Recall Physical Characteristics	**B** Identify/Recall Functional Characteristics	**C** Identify/Recall Quality Characteristics	**D** Evaluate Instances	**E** Demonstrate
I. Physical Expression	• Posture • Movement • Gestures • Facial expression • Eye contact I.A	• Gain attention • Communicate comfort/ interest I.B	• Posture: alert/ comfortable • Movements: fluid • Facial expression: pleasant • Eyes: encompass audience I.C	Effective vs. Ineffective: • Posture • Movements • Gestures • Facial expressions • Eye contact II.D	• Effective physical expression while speaking before a group II.E
II. Vocal Expression	• Voice • Intonation • Volume • Speed • Enunciation II.A	• Gain and maintain audience attention/ interest II.B	• Voice: steady/calm • Intonation: varied • Volume: varied • Speed: enables clarity II.C	Effective vs. Ineffective: • Steadiness • Calmness • Intonation • Volume • Speed II.D	• Effective vocal expression while speaking before a group II.E
III. Verbal Expression	Message III.A	• Gain attention • Inform • Entertain III.B	• Words: fluid/precise • Avoids repetition • Ideas: complete/ sequenced III.C	Effective vs. Ineffective: • Fluidity • Precision • Repetition • Completeness • Organization III.D	• Effective verbal expression while speaking before a group III.E

sion, and verbal expression. There are five learning levels with three columns for descriptive characteristics (physical, functional, and qualitative), one for evaluation, and one for active demonstration. The discrimination of examples and nonexamples column was classified by the teacher as prerequisite skills for this unit and omitted. For example, all students learning to make oral presentations should be able to locate facial expressions, eyes, and so forth.

Another instructional goal that may appear to be only a motor skill is, "Serve a tennis ball." Certainly someone learning to serve a tennis ball must develop and combine several complex motor skills. At the same time, however, the person will need to know tennis serving rules and strategies. The person should also be able to identify parts of the playing court related to the serve. Finally, the person will need to acquire positive attitudes about cooperation, fair play, consideration of other players, and practice. Because the goal includes motor skills, intellectual skills, verbal skills, and attitudes, it is considered a combination goal. This type of goal requires a combination of analysis procedures.

Figure 10.2 contains a partial analysis for the goal, "Serve a tennis ball." Section I contains a partial analysis of serving procedures. Only step B, "Toss ball," is broken down into subskills. Section II, Intellectual Skills, lists serving rules a player would need to know. The list also includes serving strategies. Section III, Verbal Information, includes the names of parts of the court used during the serve, and Section IV identifies desired attitudes.

In analyzing instructional goals for active performances, you should use the analysis procedure or combination of analysis procedures that works best for a particular goal. Goals that are procedural will probably be most easily analyzed using a flowchart, whereas others that do not have sequential steps, such as oral presentations, may be more easily analyzed using a matrix or tree diagram. If you have difficulty analyzing a particular goal using one of the analysis procedures, switch to one of the others or try a combination.

DEVELOPING PERFORMANCE TESTS

Selecting and Organizing the Components to Observe

Many of the same procedures for developing essay- or product-rating forms can also be used to develop performance-rating forms. With performance tests, however, you must be especially careful in selecting the components.

There are important differences in the procedures for evaluating products and performances. One is the timing of the observations and ratings. To evaluate performance, a teacher must observe and score students while they perform. Because students are usually tested individually, considerable class time must be reserved for performance and observation. Another difference is that the teacher always knows the identity of each student evaluated; thus,

FIGURE 10.2
A Partial
Analysis of a
Combination
Goal: Serve a
Tennis Ball

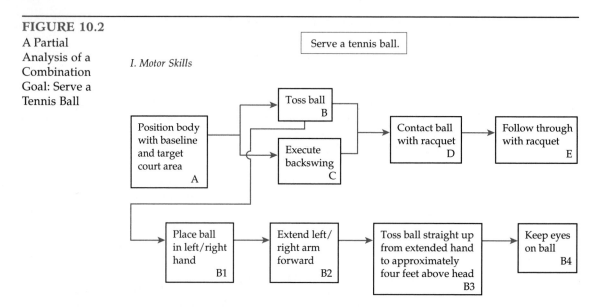

I. Motor Skills

II. Intellectual Skills

Demonstrate the following rules related to designated tasks:

Task
A   When serving into the left-hand court, the player must stand between the center mark and the right sideline.

A   When serving into the right-hand court, the player must stand between the center mark and the left sideline.

A   The player must keep both feet behind the baseline during each serve.

D   After the player contacts the ball with the racquet, the player's feet may touch the baseline.

Goal   When serving into either court, the ball must clear the net without touching it and land within the designated court area or on its boundary line.

Demonstrate the following strategies of serving:

1. Vary speed of ball.
2. Vary direction of ball.
3. Serve to opponent's demonstrated weak hand.

III. Verbal Information

1. Label court lines.
2. Label playing areas.
3. Label net.

IV. Attitudes

Affective Component
The player has positive attitudes toward skill development, fair play, and cooperation.

Behavioral Component
The player:
1. Practices serves when given the opportunity.
2. Accepts the umpire's and opponents' calls.
3. Does not verbally or physically abuse self, equipment, or other people.

avoiding rater bias is more difficult. Another critical difference is that no tangible product remains for reconsideration and feedback unless the performance is videotaped. This means that judgments must be quick and that there is usually nothing except the rating form to show students. Finally, the speed with which some skills are performed restricts the time for observation and detailed analysis of components and subcomponents. This means that evaluation forms must be concise, components must be carefully ordered and easy to find, and score marking must be easy.

The following seven steps are recommended for selecting, sequencing, and paraphrasing the components.

1. Develop an instructional goal framework of the enabling skills and their sequence.
2. Select from the framework the skills you believe will be observable.
3. List these observable skills in the order you believe they will occur.
4. Watch several students who are proficient in the skills and compare the skills on your list with those you are able to observe.
5. Eliminate skills you do not see and add any others you identify during the performance that are not contained on your list.
6. While the students are performing, check your sequence of components and reorder them if necessary.
7. After you have identified and sequenced the components, paraphrase your verbal descriptions of each component into one or two key words.

Developing a Rating Form and Evaluation Procedures

Although you may choose to use either global or analytical scoring methods, analytical scoring is preferable. It is especially helpful for performance tests because global scoring does not usually provide a tangible product to mark and return to students. Analytical scoring enables you to focus on separate aspects of the performances and gather information needed to evaluate the instruction and help students understand their scores. You can use a checklist, a rating scale, or a form that combines the two. The form you develop depends on the type of performance you are observing.

To begin, identify a feasible number of quality categories for each component. If an action cannot be broken down into levels of quality, use a checklist that indicates only its presence or absence. On the other hand, if it is possible to distinguish levels of quality for some or all of the components in the time available, the use of a rating scale will provide better information. The quality categories should represent low to high levels of proficiency. For each category, write a descriptor of the characteristics used to classify an action. The more carefully you select and describe the categories, the more reliable your ratings will be. Assign a score to each category, with low numbers representing low quality and high numbers representing high performance levels.

One caution is in order. Only positive descriptors should be used with a checklist because mixing positive and negative descriptors will result in an uninterpretable score. Consider the meaning of a score of 2 in the following example:

	(0) *No*	(1) *Yes*
A. Good posture	_____	_√_
B. Awkward movements	_____	_√_
Total		2

Checking yes for the presence of each action results in a score that reflects good posture as well as awkward movements. Because a high score is meant to reflect only positive performance, each action should be stated positively. If the second criterion were restated as Fluid movements, a yes rating would reflect a positive performance for that criterion as well. If you need to rate distracting behaviors, such as lengthy pauses and hesitations or the overuse of certain words, the word *avoids* can be added to these components to make a yes rating a positive score.

Finally, as in working with checklists and rating scales in the previous chapter, the points assigned to each component should be proportional to the importance of the component if the score is going to be used for grading. If the importance of some components is not adequately represented, then a weighting scheme will need to be used.

Writing Instructions for Performance Tests

Before students are tested, they should understand exactly what they are to do and how they are to do it. Written directions ensure that each student receives the same information, which should include any special conditions of the performance. The suggestions for writing objective, essay, and product development tests are also appropriate for performance tests. The task described should match the behavior, content, and conditions in the objective. Language should be clear and precise, and the vocabulary should be appropriate for target students. It is especially important on performance tests to ensure that (1) the skill is not too complex for target students and (2) the conditions of performance are the same for all students.

After students have read the instructions, they should be allowed to discuss them and ask questions. During discussion, the teacher can clarify the task and correct misunderstandings for the entire group. The teacher can also explain what the students are to do and how they are to behave while individuals are being tested.

The requirement that a skill be tested in a novel or unfamiliar context does not apply to all performance tests. Many performance tests require students to demonstrate the skills in the same sequence and with the same equipment they used during instruction and rehearsal. Obviously, a student who has learned to drive a car with an automatic transmission should not be evaluated on the ability to drive a car with a standard transmission. For students' performance to be a valid indication of their skill, the testing situation should require the same equipment, content, sequence, and conditions as in the instruction.

FORMATIVELY EVALUATING THE PERFORMANCE TEST FORM AND PROCEDURES

Taking the time for a formative evaluation of your form and procedures is critical to the success of performance testing. Remember that formative evaluation of a test means trying it out with target students under conditions that are similar to those you will find in the actual performance test. The purpose of the formative evaluation is to find potential problems and make appropriate revisions in the directions, content, forms, or procedures for the test.

You should not modify the instructions or the evaluation form for a performance test after the test begins. Certainly, you would not want to ask students to repeat a performance because the instructions were unclear or the evaluation form was cumbersome. To avoid an awkward situation, always evaluate and, if necessary, revise both the instructions and evaluation form you plan to use. One evaluation method is to observe students informally as they practice their skills. The information you gather during their rehearsals will help you modify both the assignment and the rating form.

A good place to begin the formative evaluation is with the task itself. Do the students' actions during rehearsal reflect an understanding of what they are to do? Are they able to demonstrate the desired actions in the time set aside for their evaluation? Can you observe and rate all the actions you have delineated? Are you able to differentiate all the quality categories you have included? Are the components in the best order? Answers to these questions will help you revise the form and estimate the amount of time needed to administer the test to all students.

RATING STUDENTS' PERFORMANCES

Students who know they are being scored on a performance are bound to be influenced by the teacher's behaviors. Nonverbal expressions of anger, disappointment, displeasure, surprise, boredom, or fatigue will produce some type of reaction in students. Often, they will adjust their performance according to the behavioral clues they receive from you. Thus, as you evaluate students' performances, you should always appear positive, noncommittal, and interested in the task. Although you want students to perform well, you should also avoid verbal and nonverbal coaching during a performance. Such assistance, although appropriate during rehearsal, is not appropriate during a posttest.

Rating bias is especially problematic on performance tests. The limited time available for scoring each student's performance can contribute to rating patterns that are consistently generous, neutral, or critical on all components, even though the student was better in some areas than others. If you find that each student was rated consistently in all areas, it could reflect the presence of response bias. Being aware of this potential danger will help you differentiate the quality of different aspects of the performance.

Rating students' performances and behaviors requires both professional judgment and self-awareness. Unlike evaluating essay and product development tests, you usually cannot check previous ratings of the same performance to determine whether you are consistently judging behaviors. Review the range and location of scores you have assigned a class and determine whether they are realistic given the group's characteristics. When the range of scores appears restricted and inappropriately high, average, or low for a given group, your judgments may have been biased.

Eliminating personal bias from scoring is also difficult because students' identities are not separated from their performance. Thus, a teacher's perception of individual students can influence ratings. Obviously, the more a teacher's biases affect students' scores, the more the validity of the test is threatened. You can help avoid this tricky problem by not forming expectations for each student's performance. Although easier said than done, you can try to find positive indicators in a typically weak student's performance and problems in a typically strong student's performance. If you look only for the type of performance you expect, your ratings may not accurately reflect the performance.

A final problem in performance tests is the tendency of students to demonstrate their skills inconsistently. In athletic skills, they may be inconsistent in their ability to serve a tennis ball, shoot baskets, pitch a softball, or execute a particular dive. When such skills are being measured, students can be given several opportunities during the test to perform the skill, and the final score can be determined not only by judging their form and execution each time but also by judging the number of times they succeed in placing a serve or scoring a basket. Some teachers prefer to sum the total scores students receive on each trial and then determine an average score by dividing the sum by the number of trials. Inconsistencies also occur in other types of performances. For example, students delivering oral reports may initially demonstrate nervousness through trembling hands, looking only at their notes, and halting speech. However, as they continue their presentations, some may gain their composure, which will reduce or eliminate these types of behaviors. Others may begin in a composed manner and grow more nervous as they proceed. Inconsistent performance can be communicated to students using a rating category, such as Sometimes Effective or Inconsistent.

AN EXAMPLE

The instructional goal framework for the goal, "Make an oral presentation," in Table 10.1 is used to demonstrate the development of a checklist and rating scales to evaluate students' active performance.

Paraphrasing Components and Subcomponents

The list of behaviors in Table 10.2 shows how one teacher identified, sequenced, and paraphrased the components to be judged. Notice that the teacher selected only observable skills from the framework. Because the skills had no inherent order, the teacher decided on a sequence that would permit efficient observation.

Paraphrasing is an important aspect of writing component descriptors. Notice in Table 10.2 that each component is paraphrased using only one or two words. This minimizes the amount of reading required during the students' performance.

Developing a Checklist

Table 10.3 is a sample checklist for evaluating an oral presentation. It contains only two rating categories, Needs Improvement and Yes. A teacher using this

Example

TABLE 10.2

Behaviors to Evaluate during Oral Presentation

I. Physical Expression
  A. Posture
  B. Movements and gestures
  C. Facial expression
  D. Eye contact
II. Vocal Expression
  A. Calmness
  B. Intonation
  C. Volume
  D. Speed
  E. Enunciation
III. Verbal Expression
  A. Word flow
  B. Word choice
  C. Repetition
  D. Complete thoughts and ideas
  E. Organization

TABLE 10.3
Checklist for Evaluating Oral Presentations

Name _____ Date _____ Score _____		
	Total	**(14)**

Criteria	Needs Improvement	Yes
I. Physical Expression		
A. Good posture	_____	_____
B. Fluid, natural movements	_____	_____
C. Effective facial expression	_____	_____
D. Good eye contact		
II. Vocal Expression		
A. Calm voice	_____	_____
B. Good intonation	_____	_____
C. Good volume	_____	_____
D. Appropriate speed	_____	_____
E. Clearly enunciates		
III. Verbal Expression		
A. Avoids hesitation	_____	_____
B. Effective word choice	_____	_____
C. Avoids repetition	_____	_____
D. Completes thoughts and ideas	_____	_____
E. Good organization of ideas	_____	_____
Total Score		_____

(Handwritten annotations in margin: "Actual Checklist")

format would judge only whether the defined action was acceptable. Notice that an indicator of performance quality is added to each component statement; thus, checking the Yes column reflects a positive score. A student demonstrating all fourteen behaviors on the checklist would receive a total score of 14 on the test.

Developing Rating Scales

Table 10.4 illustrates a rating scale for an oral presentation. The components are listed in the left column and all quality categories are included in the right columns. Four general quality levels are used to rate all 14 components. The lowest rating is Distracting, which would indicate negative actions for the component. The second category, Sometimes Effective, would be used to score an action that was sometimes distracting and sometimes acceptable. The third category, Generally Effective, indicates that no distracting actions were ob-

TABLE 10.4
Rating Scale for Oral Presentations

Name _____ Date _____ Score _____
                                               Total   (56)

Component	Distracting	Sometimes Effective	Generally Effective	Very Effective
I. Physical Expression				
A. Posture	1	2	3	4
B. Movements/gestures	1	2	3	4
C. Facial expression	1	2	3	4
D. Eye contact	1	2	3	4
II. Vocal Expression				
A. Calmness	1	2	3	4
B. Intonation	1	2	3	4
C. Volume	1	2	3	4
D. Speed	1	2	3	4
E. Enunciation	1	2	3	4
III. Verbal Expression				
A. Word flow	1	2	3	4
B. Word choice	1	2	3	4
C. Repetition	1	2	3	4
D. Thoughts/ideas complete	1	2	3	4
E. Ideas organized	1	2	3	4

served and that the student was consistent in demonstrating the behavior. The fourth category, Very Effective, would be used for students who consistently demonstrated the skill in an effective, polished manner. As students are observed, the assigned rating can be circled. The student's total score could then be obtained by summing the circled numbers. A student who received a perfect rating in all 14 components would earn a total score of 56 points.

If the general categories of quality included in the rating scale in Table 10.4 were not adequate to express the reasons for rating a particular component as distracting or effective, the rating scale could be expanded to allow for additional quality descriptors. For example, the facial expression component could be expanded to differentiate among different types of facial expressions. Such expressions as boredom, lack of expression, frowning, and nervousness could be distracting. In actuality, a student may exhibit one of these negative expressions but not others.

The expanded rating scale in Table 10.5 enables you to differentiate among different types of facial expressions and better explain why students

TABLE 10.5

Expanded Rating Scale for Oral Presentations

Name _____ Date _____ Score _____

Total   (60)

Component	Negative Quality	Rating			Positive Quality
		Distracting	Sometimes Effective	Very Effective	
I. Physical Expression					
A. Posture	1. Slouched	1	2	3	Straight
	2. Awkward	1	2	3	Relaxed
B. Movements/ Gestures	1. Hands trembling	1	2	3	Hands steady
	2. Awkward gestures	1	2	3	Fluid gestures
C. Facial Expression	1. Bored	1	2	3	Interested
	2. Unexpressive	1	2	3	Animated
	3. Frowning	1	2	3	Pleasant
	4. Nervous	1	2	3	Relaxed
D. Eye Contact	1. With few people	1	2	3	With many people
	2. Reading notes	1	2	3	Looks at audience
II. Vocal Expression	A. Wavering/cracking	1	2	3	Steady/calm
	B. Monotonous	1	2	3	Varied
	C. Too loud/quiet	1	2	3	Natural
	D. Too rapid/slow	1	2	3	Natural
	E. Poorly enunciated	1	2	3	Enunciated well
III. Verbal Expression	A. Long pauses	1	2	3	Fluid
	B. Slang expressions	1	2	3	Precise vocabulary
	C. Needless repetition	1	2	3	Effective/varied
	D. Incomplete thoughts	1	2	3	Complete thoughts
	E. Poorly organized	1	2	3	Well organized

received a low rating in this area. The components are listed in the far left column. Negative and positive descriptions of expression border each end of the rating scale. Negative descriptors are listed down the left side beside low ratings, and positive ones are listed in the far right column beside high ratings. The ratings of Distracting, Sometimes Effective, and Very Effective are positioned in the middle columns. Such a scale would help you be more precise in marking your ratings and in communicating the meaning of each rating to students. Be careful, however, not to create a scale with so much detail that it is cumbersome to use while observing a student's performance. To use the rating scale, simply circle the rating desired and sum the circled numbers to obtain the total score for each student. A student who received the highest possible rating in each category would earn a total test score of 60 points.

COMPUTER TECHNOLOGY

Similar to essay and product tests, it is appropriate and convenient to put your instructions for active performance tests directly into your test item bank. Using the ParTEST programs (Economics Research, Inc., 1991), you can use the essay- or problem-style item format to enter instructions for the required performance. Likewise, you can insert your checklist or rating scale for scoring students' performances as a separate item, as a student feedback category for the instructions, or as a figure attached to the instructions. Also similar to objective, essay, and product items, your active performance instructions can be classified using your user descriptors (e.g., subject, topic, objective code, etc.). Your active performance instructions, as well as your rating scales and checklists, can be edited at any time.

Although you must hand-score students' performances, you can enter their raw scores into their computer-based records using either scan sheets or the keyboard. Once the performance scores are entered into the program, you can obtain the same types of group performance and individual student performance information that is available for objective-style tests. In addition, active performances can be included on interim reports to parents.

SUMMARY

The procedure for evaluating students' performances and behaviors consists of four major steps: (1) analyze instructional goals and select the skills to include on the performance test; (2) prepare testing procedures, forms, and instructions; (3) try out the performance test and revise as needed; and (4) use the test to evaluate students' performances. Each of these four steps has several substeps:

1. To analyze goals and select skills:
   a. Use a matrix, tree diagram, or flowchart to analyze the performance goal. A combination of these procedures may be required since performance goals can contain procedures composed of motor skills, intellectual skills, verbal information, and even attitudes.
   b. Review the goal framework and select only those skills you believe can be observed during a performance.
   c. Observe someone performing the task and verify that the chosen skills are observable and that none has been omitted.

    d. Sequence the skills in the order they can be observed most efficiently.

2. To prepare testing procedures, forms, and instructions:
   a. Paraphrase each skill using only one or two key words. Either make all statements neutral or all statements positive.
   b. List the paraphrased actions or behaviors in the left column.
   c. Select the number of quality categories that you can consistently distinguish for each.
   d. Write a descriptor for each category and assign each a number, with low numbers representing inadequate performance or negative behaviors.
   e. Determine the relative value of each component rated and devise a weighting plan, if needed, so that the points available are proportional to the importance of each component.
   f. Plan testing procedures and write specific instructions to help ensure uniform performance conditions for all students.

3. To do a formative evaluation of the performance test forms and procedures:
   a. Ask a few students to read the instructions, and revise as needed if there are problems of accuracy or clarity.
   b. Try using the checklist or rating form during the students' practice sessions to review the skill components and rating categories. Revise as needed if there are problems observing skills or distinguishing different quality levels in the rating categories.
   c. While trying the checklist or rating scale during practice sessions, review your own ability to use the form in a smooth, timely manner. Revise as needed if it is confusing, tedious, or cumbersome.

4. To use the test forms and procedures to evaluate students' performances:
   a. Set up performance testing sessions that afford all students equal time and opportunity to demonstrate their skills.
   b. When judging students' behaviors that reflect an attitude, select a time when you are *not* fatigued, disappointed, or unhappy. Your own attitude will influence your interpretation of students' behaviors.
   c. Be aware of how your perceptions of individual students can influence the scores you assign. Take care to look for good qualities in the performance of students who usually score lower than others and look for problems in the performance of students who usually score high. This will help you avoid seeing what you expect to see when it is not there.
   d. When judging a performance test, be especially careful not to exhibit nonverbal gestures that will influence a student's performance.
   e. Be careful not to coach students during a performance posttest because coaching will tend to alter their performance.
   f. Use multiple trials of the performance when needed to improve the validity and reliability of the test.
   g. After summarizing the scores for a group, check to see whether the range and pattern of scores is realistic for that group.

h. Use the checklists or rating scales and videotape (if appropriate) to provide corrective feedback and instructional guidance to students after the test.

By following these steps, you can evaluate students as objectively as possible; provide students with specific, corrective feedback; and have the information you need to evaluate the quality of your instruction.

PRACTICE EXERCISES

I. **Analyzing Motor Skill Instructional Goals**
Identify and sequence the steps students would need to achieve the goal, "Bounce a ball while standing still." Compare your answer with Figure 10.3 in the Feedback section.

II. **Rating Students' Performances**
A. Use Figure 10.1 to develop either a checklist or a rating scale for evaluating students' overlap grip. Compare your evaluation form with the example checklist provided in Table 10.6 in the Feedback section.
B. Use Figure 10.2 to develop a rating scale for evaluating component B of that figure, Toss ball. Compare your rating scale with the example provided in Table 10.7 in the Feedback section.

III. **Enrichment**
A. Rating Student Performance
1. Select an active performance skill that is relevant for the subject and grade level you teach or plan to teach.
2. Analyze the skill to identify the main components and subcomponents within each main step.
3. Develop either a rating scale or checklist for the skill.
4. Use your evaluation form to rate students or other individuals as they perform the skill.
5. Evaluate the form's feasibility and convenience and revise it if necessary.
6. Use the rating form to develop an appropriate performance summary form.

FEEDBACK

I. **Analyzing Motor Skill Instructional Goals**
See Figure 10.3.

II. **Rating Students' Performances**
A. See Table 10.6.
B. A blank copy of the checklist in Table 10.7 can be used as a summary form.

FIGURE 10.3
Subordinate
Skills for the
Instructional
Goal: Bounce a
Ball while
Standing Still

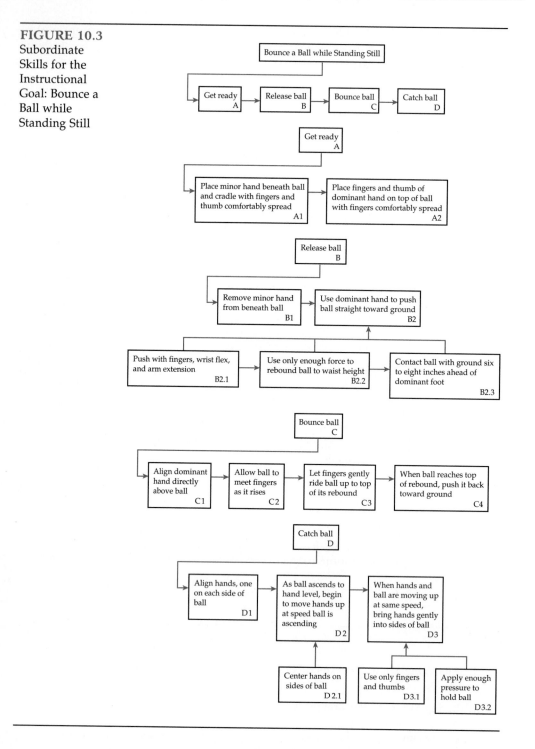

TABLE 10.6
Checklist for Rating an Overlap Grip

Name _Joseph Augustine_   **Period** _2_   **Date** _10/15_   **Score** _12_
                                                                Total   **(15)**

Observed		
No	**Yes**	**A. PLACEMENT OF LEFT HAND**
	X	1. Hand toward top of club
	X	2. Back of hand toward target
	X	3. Back of hand perpendicular to target line
	X	4. Grip diagonally across palm
	X	5. Thumb down topside of shaft
	X	6. Fingers curled comfortably
X		7. Club grasped lightly
		B. PLACEMENT OF RIGHT HAND
	X	1. Hand just below left hand
	X	2. Palm facing target
	X	3. Palm perpendicular to target line
	X	4. Middle and ring finger curled around shaft
X		5. Little finger overlapping left hand
	X	6. Right palm and thumb over left thumb
	X	7. Right thumb pointed down topside of shaft
X		8. Club grasped lightly
Total	12	

Note: This checklist is for a right-handed person. For a left-handed person, the right and left hands would be reversed.

REFERENCES

Economics Research, Inc. (1991). *ParTEST user's manual.* Costa Mesa, CA: Economics Research, Inc.

Gagné, R. M. (1985). *The conditions of learning and theory of instruction.* New York: Holt, Rinehart and Winston.

TABLE 10.7
Partial Rating Scale for the Toss Ball (B) Portion of Serving a Tennis Ball (from the
Instructional Goal Analysis in Figure 10.2)

SERVING A TENNIS BALL				
Name _____	Date _____			Score _____
	Inadequate	Adequate	Good	
	1	2	3	**Comments**
A. Position Body				
B. Toss Ball				
B.1 Ball in hand	1	2		
B.2 Arm extension	1	2	3	
B.3.1 Ball trajectory	1	2	3	
B.3.2 Ball height	1	2	3	
B.4 Eyes on ball	1	2	3	
C. Backswing				
D. Contact Ball				
E. Follow Through				
Totals	( ) +	( ) +	( )	= _____

SUGGESTED READINGS

Ebel, R. L., & Frisbee, D. A. (1991). *Essentials of educational measurement* (5th ed.) (pp. 241–262). Englewood Cliffs, NJ: Prentice Hall.

Gronlund, N. E., & Linn, R. L. (1990). *Measurement and evaluation in teaching* (6th ed.) (pp. 375–398). New York: Macmillan.

Hopkins, C. D., & Antes, R. L. (1990). *Classroom measurement and evaluation* (3rd ed.) (pp. 69–98). Itasca, IL: F. E. Peacock.

Kubiszyn, T., & Borich, G. (1990). *Educational testing and measurement* (3rd ed.) (pp. 155–179). Glenview, IL: Scott, Foresman/Little, Brown.

Mehrens, W. A., & Lehmann, I. J. (1991). *Measurement and evaluation in education and psychology* (4th ed.) (pp. 173–206). New York: CBS College Publishing.

Oosterhof, A. (1990). *Classroom applications of educational measurement* (pp. 176–197). Columbus, OH: Merrill.

Popham, J. W. (1990). *Modern educational measurement* (2nd ed.) (pp. 309–327). Englewood Cliffs, NJ: Prentice Hall.

Sax, G. (1989). *Principles of educational and psychological measurement and evaluation* (3rd ed.) (pp. 147–165). Belmont, CA: Wadsworth.

CHAPTER 11

Constructing and Using
Measures of Students' Attitudes
and Classroom Behavior

- Analyze instructional goals that are attitudes.
- Develop a rating form and evaluation procedures.
- Describe procedures for rating students' behavior.
- Develop questionnaires to gather students' self-reported attitudes.

In addition to measuring students' achievement of verbal information, intellectual skills, cognitive strategies, and motor skills, teachers are often expected to assess students' attitudes and classroom behavior. Rating attitudes and behaviors can be much more difficult than judging achievement. Attitudes and behaviors, such as the attitudes toward learning and classroom conduct, are abstract and difficult to define. In judging a skill, a teacher has to make very few syntheses and inferences. When judging attitudes and behavior, however, a teacher must classify individual instances of behavior over time and synthesize them into a general impression of the underlying attitude. These actions often require inferences about intentions and motives, which are very difficult. The same action or statement can be interpreted many different ways, depending on the context, tone of voice, facial expression, or physical mannerism accompanying the behavior. Because human social behavior is interactive, a teacher must be aware of the effects that the actions and reactions of other group members can have on individual students. Teachers should also have some sense of how their own attitudes and behaviors influence those of students.

343

Gagné (1985) defines *attitudes* as internal states that influence an individual's choice of personal action. According to Gagné, an attitude consists of three elements:

1. An *affective* component includes the positive and negative feelings a person has.
2. A *behavioral* component is made up of behaviors or acts that result from a person's feelings and knowledge.
3. A *cognitive* component consists of a person's knowledge about how to do something and the rewards or consequences for doing it.

Our feelings about people, things, events, and concepts affect our behavior. Learning theorists propose that human beings acquire many of their attitudes by watching and mimicking people they respect or want to emulate. In our society, teachers are expected to play an important role in developing their students' attitudes. For example, most teachers would encourage their students to demonstrate the following attitudes:

1. A negative attitude toward cheating
2. A positive attitude toward learning and toward participation
3. A positive attitude toward classroom and community rules for acceptable behavior
4. A negative attitude toward drug use, smoking, and other activities that are considered dangerous or harmful
5. A positive attitude toward thorough, careful work
6. A positive attitude toward responsible behavior

This chapter describes procedures for (1) locating attitudes and behaviors teachers are expected to monitor and assess, (2) analyzing attitudes to identify their affective and behavioral components, (3) developing forms to assess students' classroom behaviors, (4) rating students' behavior and actions in the classroom, and (5) developing questionnaires that students can use to assess their own attitudes and behavior.

IDENTIFYING ATTITUDES TO BE EVALUATED

Most curriculum guides focus on the achievement of verbal information, intellectual skills, and motor skills, and they do not always identify the student attitudes and behaviors that teachers may be asked to report. This information usually appears on the school district's report card. Occasionally, related information will be included in a student or teacher handbook. Report cards typically indicate categories of attitudes to be rated, and the handbooks explain school policy and rules of student conduct. Some teachers add rules to those specified by the district to suit their subject area, classroom environment, and particular students.

Students to be rated on certain attitudes and behaviors need to understand the meaning of each category of behavior on a report card. Teachers required to judge attitudes and behaviors should define them for students and explain how the ratings will be done.

To define a district's affective goals to students and parents, a teacher must first understand the categories and have evaluation procedures already developed. The most appropriate place to begin is with the information on the report cards. Although report cards often vary from school to school, and typically from district to district, most list attitudes or behaviors on which students are to be rated. Consider the secondary-level report card shown in Table 11.1. In addition to grading achievement, teachers in this district are required to evaluate a student's citizenship, attitude toward learning, and study habits for each grading period. Teachers using such report

TABLE 11.1
Secondary School Report Card for One Semester

			Grading Period I					Grading Period II					Semester I	
Course	Per	Teacher	GRD	CIT	ATL	SH	ABS	GRD	CIT	ATL	SH	ABS	EX	SAG
	1													
	2													
	3													
	4													
	5													
	6													
	7													

STUDENT PROGRESS REPORT

(Name) (School District) (Year)

(School) (Home Room)

Abbreviations

PER = Class period during day
GRD = Achievement grade
CIT = Citizenship
ATL = Attitude toward learning
SH = Study habits
ABS = Absences (frequency)
EX = Semester exam score
SAG = Semester average grade

Grade Codes

A = Excellent (93–100%)   I = Incomplete work
B = Good (85%–92%)   P = Pass
C = Fair (77–84%)   S = Satisfactory
D = Poor (69%–76%)   N = Needs improvement
F = Failure (68% and below) U = Unsatisfactory

cards must decide what attitudes and behaviors a mark in each category would reflect.

Table 11.2 illustrates the behaviors that elementary-level teachers in two different school districts are expected to rate. Besides achievement grades in the subjects studied, teachers using report card A must comment on students' conduct, citizenship, and work habits. Rather than including just these general categories, Citizenship is divided into five specific behaviors that must be rated and Work Habits includes four separate categories. Teachers report students' progress in each area using the ratings of satisfactory, needs improvement, and unsatisfactory. Elementary report card B includes nine categories of behavior that are not organized according to areas. Similar to report card A, teachers use satisfactory, needs improvement, and unsatisfactory to rate each of the nine areas. A comparison of the nonachievement categories included on the secondary and two elementary examples shows that these three school districts are interested in reporting similar types of behaviors to students and parents.

To identify attitudes that you will need to consider during a grading period, go first to report cards and state, district, and school handbooks. Then add any particular attitudes and behavior that are required in your subject area, such as safety habits in an industrial arts class or chemistry laboratory.

TABLE 11.2
Attitudes and Behaviors Rated on Two Elementary-Level Report Cards

Report Card A		**Report Card B**	
Attitude/Behavior	Rating	Attitude/Behavior	Rating
I. Conduct		1. Practices self-discipline	
II. Citizenship		2. Works independently	
A. Respects authority		3. Works well in group activities	
B. Uses self-control		4. Makes good use of time	
C. Respects property		5. Respects persons and property	
D. Respects others' rights		6. Is thoughtful and considerate	
E. Obeys school rules		7. Completes classroom assignments	
III. Work Habits		8. Completes homework assignments	
A. Listens attentively		9. Respects authority	
B. Works quietly			
C. Follows directions			
D. Completes assignments			

Scale:
S = Satisfactory
N = Needs improvement
U = Unsatisfactory

Scale:
S = Satisfactory
N = Needs improvement
U = Unsatisfactory

ANALYZING INSTRUCTIONAL GOALS THAT ARE ATTITUDES

Once you have located attitudes you are expected to teach or monitor and assess, you are ready to analyze them. Recall that they are comprised of an affective component that includes positive and negative feelings, a behavioral component that includes actions that reflect the feelings, and a cognitive component that includes verbal information and intellectual skills required to act in the desired manner. To analyze attitudinal goals, you should identify the relevant components for each of the three elements. This chapter addresses only the affective and behavioral components of an attitude since analysis of intellectual skills and verbal information was described in preceding chapters. The following steps can aid your analysis:

1. Generally define the attitudes to be taught and assessed.
2. Further define or operationalize each attitude by listing the positive feelings or beliefs your students should possess or acquire.
3. For each of the feelings you identify, list actions or behaviors that will demonstrate a student's status on the feeling. This collection of behaviors represents how you have operationalized the general attitude.

The following paragraphs describe and illustrate each of these steps.

Generally Define the Attitudes

The first step is to define the attitudes you are expected to assess. The purpose of this step is to differentiate among the various attitudes included in the curriculum guide and report card. For example, the secondary report card in Table 11.1 has one attitude category called Attitude Toward Learning and another called Study Habits. In what ways do students' attitudes toward learning differ from their study habits? Elementary report card A in Table 11.2 includes both Conduct and Citizenship. If you were using this report card, how would you distinguish between the two? As a teacher in this district, you would need to determine what these terms mean and how they relate to each other, to the subject taught, to the classroom environment, and to your students. Your interpretations will undoubtedly differ from those of other teachers due not only to the abstractness of the terms but also to differences in students' ages, classroom environments, and subjects.

Consider, for example, one teacher's definitions of the following categories:

1. *Citizenship* is the social interactions students have with their peers and with their teacher. It includes their individual contributions to the classroom society.
2. *Conduct* relates to observing established school and classroom rules of behavior (e.g., safety, property, and permissible actions).

3. *Attitude toward learning* relates to the student's approach to learning new ideas and skills.
4. *Study habits* relates to the procedures a student uses to accomplish assigned work.

Definitions such as these serve only as a beginning for the analysis process. With these general definitions in mind, you are ready to define further each attitude by identifying the positive feelings you believe are associated with each attitude.

List Associated Positive and Negative Feelings

No one or two feelings would be adequate to define an attitude. Attitudes are abstractions, sometimes called *constructs,* that must be defined using a set or combination of associated feelings. A person possessing one or two of the feelings in a set may or may not possess the attitude, but someone who possesses the entire set can reasonably be said to hold the attitude.

A good way to identify the best set of feelings for an attitude is to brainstorm and list all the possible associated feelings that you can imagine. With this so-called laundry list of feelings in hand, you can evaluate the list and eliminate those you consider redundant, irrelevant, more related to other attitudes, or inappropriate for a given group of students in a particular environment.

In considering feelings that are related to a student's approach to learning, one teacher settled on these six positive feelings: interest, curiosity, self-confidence, independence, perseverance, and a desire to improve one's skills and abilities. With the list selected, the next step is to identify behaviors that reflect a student's status on each feeling.

List Behaviors That Demonstrate Each Feeling

The six feelings described in the previous section partially explain the teacher's perceptions of students' attitudes toward learning. Generating a list of the behaviors students would exhibit in the classroom relative to each feeling would further operationalize the attitude. The best way to generate the list is to imagine the actions of a person who possesses and does not possess each positive feeling identified. As you consider the actions, brainstorm, and write down all the behaviors you can generate. Once you have exhausted your ideas, evaluate the list and remove actions you consider irrelevant, redundant, unobservable, or inappropriate for your age group and classroom environment. The behaviors that remain after your evaluation provide the basis for developing checklists and rating scales to evaluate students' behavior.

Table 11.3 contains the classroom behaviors the teacher considered relevant for the six feelings linked to students' attitudes toward learning. The left side of the table includes positive actions, and the right side contains associ-

TABLE 11.3
Teacher-Constructed List of Behaviors That Reflect a Student's Attitude
toward Learning

Positive Behaviors	Negative Behaviors
1. Appears interested in the topics being studied	1. Appears disinterested in or bored by topics being studied
2. Shows curiosity by asking questions or seeking more information	2. Rejects ideas presented and does not seek additional information
3. Demonstrates confidence in ability to learn new information and skills; is eager to try	3. Lacks confidence in ability to perform new tasks; resists trying
4. Works independently	4. Quits working on tasks when not monitored
5. Demonstrates perseverance in accomplishing tasks	5. Becomes frustrated and quits before completing tasks
6. Seeks and accepts corrective feedback; adjusts performance accordingly	6. Rejects corrective feedback and resists adjusting performance

ated negative behaviors for each of the feelings. This list of classroom behaviors represents the teacher's operationalization of the construct, attitude toward learning. With the attitude operationalized, the teacher has the necessary foundation for developing checklists or rating scales to observe and rate students' related behaviors in the classroom. From these behaviors, the teacher can infer the students' attitudes toward learning.

The process just described for analyzing attitudes might seem rather subjective to you. It is subjective, but not nearly as subjective as simply marking and communicating students' attitudes toward learning without carefully considering what you are judging. Defining attitudes as carefully as possible will enable you to reflect on your definitions and refine them, communicate better with students and parents about attitudes and classroom behavior, and identify attitudinal areas where instructional interventions appear warranted.

DEVELOPING FORMS TO ASSESS CLASSROOM BEHAVIOR

The type of rating form you develop depends on the behaviors you are observing and the number of times you plan to evaluate students. The behaviors on your list probably range from very abstract to very concrete, and each type of behavior requires a different evaluation method. For example, you may wish to record the number of times a student fails to turn in a homework assignment or fails to bring required materials to class. If you assign homework 15 times during a grading period, your form should permit you to record the number of times a student either submits incomplete assignments or fails to turn in an assignment. The totals for each student can then be converted to descriptors, such as Always, Usually, and Rarely.

Abstract behaviors, such as Displays Interest in Topic, are much more difficult to evaluate. A rating form might include two or three rating categories for such a behavior. For example, the categories Disinterested/Bored, Easily Distracted, and Interested/Engaged might be used to rate students on their interest. If you include too many categories for an abstract behavior, you undoubtedly will have difficulty scoring students consistently.

The following sections illustrate a sample checklist and rating scale the teacher could use to rate students' behaviors that reflect their attitudes toward learning.

Checklist

Table 11.4 contains an observation checklist based on the behaviors listed in Table 11.3. There are three behaviors included for each of the six feelings. All the behaviors are positively stated such that a check mark in the Typically column reflects a positive action, and the sum of the check marks will reflect the level of a student's demonstrated attitude toward learning.

Notice the teacher has included space for rating the student's behaviors on three separate dates. Including space for three dates on one page has its benefits and its drawbacks. From a beneficial perspective, it cuts down on the amount of paper the teacher needs to manage and keeps information together. The drawback is that seeing your previous ratings of the student may influence your judgments on subsequent occasions. To avoid this inadvertent influence problem, you may want to cover your prior ratings so you cannot see them until after you finish rating the student. Comparing your ratings across occasions after you have finished is sometimes quite informative.

Rating Scale

Rating scales can also be created from the list of positive and negative behaviors you generate for each attitude. Table 11.5 illustrates one rating scale that could be developed for the list of behaviors in Table 11.3. The six feelings are listed in the left column as anchors, and each feeling has three levels of behavior listed on the right side. Notice that each level or number includes a behavioral descriptor to aid rating students' actions consistently.

You could also configure the behavioral rating scale to accommodate several evaluation dates by adding three or four columns to the right or left of the items and recording your rating in the column rather than circling your response. It is important to keep your descriptions of each value, however, to help ensure the consistency of your judgments.

TABLE 11.4
A Sample Checklist Based on the Affective Feelings in Table 11.3

CLASSROOM BEHAVIORS REFLECTING STUDENTS' ATTITUDES TOWARD LEARNING			
Date _____ Score _____	Date _____ Score _____	Date _____ Score _____	Name _____
Typically	Typically	Typically	

_____ _____ _____	_____ _____ _____	_____ _____ _____	1. Student demonstrates *interest* and engagement in:
			  a. Explanations and demonstrations
			  b. Assignments
			  c. Classwork

_____ _____ _____	_____ _____ _____	_____ _____ _____	2. Student demonstrates learning *curiosity* through:
			  a. Asking questions
			  b. Seeking additional resources in the classroom
			  c. Locating additional materials in the library

_____ _____ _____	_____ _____ _____	_____ _____ _____	3. Student demonstrates *confidence* by:
			  a. Volunteering to answer questions in class
			  b. Offering to help others understand ideas
			  c. Proposing alternative ideas/solutions

_____ _____ _____	_____ _____ _____	_____ _____ _____	4. Student demonstrates *independence* by:
			  a. Beginning assignments without being asked
			  b. Working along without being monitored
			  c. Completing assignments before they are due

_____ _____ _____	_____ _____ _____	_____ _____ _____	5. Student demonstrates *perseverance* by:
			  a. Working through complex problems
			  b. Returning to complex problems independently
			  c. Not complaining about complex assignments

_____ _____ _____	_____ _____ _____	_____ _____ _____	6. Student demonstrates *desire to improve* by:
			  a. Seeking corrective feedback from teacher
			  b. Accepting corrective feedback
			  c. Correcting errors and problems in work

RATING STUDENTS' ATTITUDES AND BEHAVIOR

Rating students' behavior in the classroom can be quite complex; each teacher's observation forms, students, and classroom environment are different. This complexity is increased because each teacher has rather different notions about what constitutes good, acceptable, and unacceptable behavior in the classroom. Additionally, teachers' interactions with their students and

TABLE 11.5
Rating Scale for Attitude toward Learning

Name _____ Date _____ Score _____			
			Total (18)
Behavior	**Rating**		
	Disinterested/ Bored	Easily distracted	Interested/ Engaged
1. Interest	1	2	3
	Does not seek additional information	Occasionally questions topic	Seeks resources, enrichment
2. Curiosity	1	2	3
	Resists trying	Apologizes for questions/work	Eager to try
3. Confidence	1	2	3
	Needs encouragement to begin	Quits working when unmonitored	Begins promptly, works independently
4. Independence	1	2	3
	Easily frustrated, usually quits	Occasionally frustrated and quits	Works steadily, completing tasks
5. Perseverance	1	2	3
	Ignores comments, does not correct work	Occasionally argues, sometimes corrects work	Seeks correction, adjusts work
6. Accepts corrective feedback	1	2	3

students' interactions with each other are within a culture that is unique to the classroom and that has its own spoken and unspoken rules of conduct. Within the context of the classroom culture, some behaviors are acceptable under some circumstances and inappropriate in others, making the teacher's task even more complex. If you are unsure about a student's behavior or motives for a certain behavior, it is a good idea to withhold judgment until you have more information.

In determining what constitutes good behavior in your classroom, avoid Never or Always categories. Distinguishing consistently between good behavior and behavior that needs improvement for a given student can be difficult because most students fluctuate somewhere between these two categories. What you are attempting to communicate is whether a student's behavior is mostly good or whether it mostly needs improvement. This situation is reflected in behavioral checklists and rating scales that contain descriptors such as Typically, Mostly, and Usually. If you really feel the need for a category that includes the notion of Always, you might want to preface it with the term *almost.*

The inclusion of several areas of attitudes, conduct, and behaviors to be rated on report cards can be problematic for middle and high school teachers who see well over 100 students each day. These teachers encounter so many students daily that they sometimes do not have a clear picture of the behavior patterns and motivations of students unless they are particularly well behaved or ill mannered. If you find yourself in the situation of needing to rate and communicate students' conduct, yet are unclear about how to rate them, solve the problem by rating these students' actions and attitudes as satisfactory until you have specific reasons to do otherwise. To avoid this problem, establish a schedule and make notations of behavior and attitudes several times during a grading period.

The number of times during a term that students' behavior is formally rated must be determined. Although students are informally observed on a daily basis, formal observations need not be as frequent. The number of evaluations will depend on the nature of the behavior observed. Concrete behaviors, such as submitting or completing assignments and bringing required materials to class, should be recorded at the appropriate time. Behaviors that are used to infer attitudes, such as attitude toward learning and citizenship, are not usually measured as frequently. Certainly, you want to rate the behaviors you have chosen to reflect these attitudes more than once during a grading term. Multiple ratings help ensure that students' term marks reflect their attitude throughout the term, not just the week preceding report card distribution. Some teachers choose to rate students weekly, some biweekly, and others less frequently. The number of times you choose to rate students' behavior formally depends in part on the subject and on the students you teach. A good rule of thumb is to have at least three measures of behaviors that reflect attitudes. This helps ensure that the ratings students receive on report cards are not peculiar to a special set of circumstances.

Select times when you are fresh, unhurried, and in a positive mood to do your ratings. Because of the degree of inference required, teachers' ratings can reflect their own attitudes more than those of students. As with performance tests, rating bias can affect the validity of students' attitude scores. While rating students' behavior, you should be aware of the potential bias from rating patterns and from general impressions of students and try to be as objective as possible.

DEVELOPING ATTITUDE QUESTIONNAIRES

Some teachers convert their behavior observation forms into questionnaires to gather attitudinal information directly from students. In interpreting students' self-reported attitudes, however, you should keep in mind that students, like the rest of us, often mark responses they consider socially acceptable. Their responses may or may not reflect their actual feelings or beliefs. Because of this natural tendency, you cannot describe students' actual attitudes from questionnaires they complete themselves. What you can describe from these forms is how they are willing to tell you they feel. Comparing students' reported attitudes with those obtained through teacher observation can be very interesting and informative.

Converting observation forms to self-report questionnaires is quite straightforward since most of the analysis work was done during the creation of the teachers' observation forms. The following conversions remain to be done:

1. Instructions to the respondent need to be added.
2. The language used to describe the behaviors and rating categories should be phrased appropriately for the students' reading levels.
3. Wording to indicate that the students are judging themselves should be added.

Table 11.6 contains a questionnaire based on the six key feelings included in Table 11.3. This questionnaire is a checklist that students use to indicate their most typical feelings. The example is developed for use with a mark-sensitive answer sheet that can be scanned and scored using a computer.

The instructions direct students to respond by shading either a 1 or a 2 on the answer sheet for each item. Students' scores can be obtained by summing the numbers they indicate for each item. For example, there are 18 items on the questionnaire, each worth a possible two points. A student who marked a 2 for each item would receive a score of 36, a student who marked all 1s would receive a score of 18, and a student who marked half 2s and half 1s would receive a score of 27.

Table 11.7 contains a rating scale for students to use in describing their attitudes toward learning. It contains the same six key feelings described in Table 11.3 and three optional statements that relate to varying strengths or degrees of feeling in each of these key areas. Students' scores on this rating scale can be obtained by summing the numbers circled by students. For example, if a student chose all statements preceded by the number 2, the score would be 12. You could also format such a rating scale for computer scanning and scoring if your class group is proficient using such forms. This modification would only require changing the instructions for how students are to respond.

TABLE 11.6

A Sample Checklist Based on the Affective Feelings in Table 11.3

MY FEELINGS ABOUT LEARNING IN THIS CLASS

Instructions: This form contains statements that describe how students may feel about their work in school. Read each statement and decide whether it describes **your** feelings in this class **most often** or **not usually**. *Please use the answer sheet provided and a pencil to indicate your feelings. Insert your name and student number before you begin to answer.* If a statement does **not** describe how you usually feel, darken a (1) on your answer sheet. If it describes how you **most often** feel, darken a (2) on your answer sheet.

Not Usually	Most Often	
		A. I am very interested in:
1	2	1. The teacher's explanations and demonstrations
1	2	2. The homework assignments I am asked to complete
1	2	3. The projects and problems we work on in school
		B. I locate more information about the topics we study by:
1	2	4. Asking questions
1	2	5. Looking through resources in the classroom
1	2	6. Finding additional materials in the library
		C. In this class, I like to:
1	2	7. Volunteer answers to questions the teacher asks
1	2	8. Help others understand ideas
1	2	9. Suggest different ideas or solutions for problems we study
		D. When assigned work to do, I:
1	2	10. Begin my work without being asked
1	2	11. Continue working even when no one is watching me
1	2	12. Like to complete my work on time
		E. When asked to do tough assignments, I:
1	2	13. Work through them without being frustrated
1	2	14. Keep trying until I get them done
1	2	15. Keep working on them even after they are due
		F. I really want to do a good job, and I:
1	2	16. Ask the teacher how I can do better
1	2	17. Am pleased when the teacher shows me areas I can do better
1	2	18. Fix problems and mistakes I make in my work

TABLE 11.7
A Sample Attitude Questionnaire Based on the Teacher Observation Form in Table 11.5

ATTITUDES ABOUT LEARNING AND STUDYING

Name _____ Period _____ Date _____

Instructions: Please describe your feelings about learning and studying in this class. In column A below, there are terms that describe feelings about learning. In column B, there are statements about how students sometimes feel. For each of the six feelings, circle the one statement that **best describes** your feelings **most of the time.**

A   **B**

A. Interest in Learning
1. I am usually very bored in class.
2. The things we study in this class are sort of interesting, but my mind keeps thinking about other things.
3. The things we study in class are pretty interesting, and I am rarely bored in class.

B. Curiosity
1. I do not want to know any more about the things we have to learn in this class.
2. I usually want to know more about the things we learn.
3. I almost always want to know more about the ideas we learn in this class.

When I think about my work in this class, I think:
C. Confidence
1. I am not good at doing the assignments.
2. I am sometimes good at doing the assignments.
3. I almost always do a good job.

When an assignment is made in this class, I usually:
D. Independence
1. Don't even start it until the very last minute.
2. Start working but quit when there is no one to help me.
3. Work along and finish the task on time.

When I try to do school work by myself and get stuck, I:
E. Perseverance
1. Usually get flustered and quit before I finish.
2. Sometimes get flustered and quit before I finish.
3. Usually keep working on the problem until I finish.

When the teacher criticizes my work, I:
F. Desire to Improve
1. Usually ignore the comments and do not correct the work.
2. Occasionally argue, and sometimes correct the work.
3. Ask for more information on how to fix it, and I almost always fix my mistakes.

Once you have developed and administered your checklists or rating scales, you will need to summarize students' scores for evaluating their behavior and attitudes. Chapter 13 describes procedures for summarizing responses to locate strengths and find problem areas requiring attention.

COMPUTER TECHNOLOGY

Most teachers do not consider putting their behavior observation checklists or rating scales in their item banks, but it is not difficult to do so using ParTEST (Economics Research, Inc., 1991). You could create an item bank just for the attitudes and behaviors you are expected to observe, rate, and report for a grading term. Remember—you are allowed eight characters to name an item bank, so you might call this bank ATTITUDE. You can store your behavior observation and self-report instruments in the ATTITUDE item bank using the following strategy:

1. Use the essay- or problem-item format to enter the name and definition of the attitude to be rated (e.g., citizenship, attitude toward learning).
2. Enter the checklist or rating scale in the accompanying student feedback section.
3. Classify each attitude with user descriptors you create for your attitude item bank.

You may use the same strategy to create and store attitude rating scales that you design to gather students' responses about their attitudes. With your behavior checklists and rating scales stored in your item bank, you will only need to create them once. You can produce an original copy each time you need to use one, and you can edit or update your instruments at any time.

SUMMARY

Teachers are often expected to judge students' attitudes and to report these judgments to students as well as parents. It is sometimes difficult to locate these attitudes in the curriculum guide for a school district, but they can typically be found on report cards and in the school's handbook for teachers and students.

Gagné (1985) defines *attitudes* as internal states that influence an individual's choice of personal action. He suggests that attitudes have three parts, including an affective component, a behavioral component, and a cognitive component.

Analyzing attitudes from curriculum guides and report cards is quite different from analyzing intellectual or motor skills. The procedure used, sometimes referred to as *operationalizing* an attitude, has the following suggested steps:

1. Generally define each of the attitudes you must evaluate.
2. Compare the general definitions generated to ensure that you have differentiated adequately among the attitudes.
3. Further define each attitude by naming particular positive and/or negative feelings that are associated with the general attitude definition.

4. For each of these feelings, list behaviors that are demonstrable in the classroom that would best reflect the feeling.
5. Create a checklist or rating scale of these behaviors.

Checklists and rating scales should not include absolute rating categories such as Always and Never. Instead, they should contain categories that enable you to rate the general frequency of occurrences or the tendencies in students' behavioral patterns.

Students' attitudes and behaviors should be rated more than once during a term to ensure the ratings students are assigned reflect their behavior patterns and not behavior related to specific instances that occurred near the time of the ratings. You should always rate students' behavior when you are fresh, unhurried, and in a positive mood. This strategy will help ensure that students' ratings reflect more their attitudes than yours.

Checklists and rating scales used by teachers to observe students' behavior can be converted to questionnaires that students use to report their own feelings and attitudes. Teachers must be cautious in interpreting students' self-reported attitudes and feelings, since students tend to select socially acceptable responses that may or may not reflect their true feelings.

Both observation and self-report forms for assessing students' attitudes can be formatted for computer scanning and scoring. Using this equipment reduces the amount of clerical work required to score students' ratings. These forms can also be placed in a test item bank for easy editing and retrieval.

PRACTICE EXERCISES

I. **Rating Attitudes and Behaviors**
   A. Many school districts require teachers to report students' progress in citizenship. Develop a rating scale you could use to judge behaviors you believe reflect citizenship. In developing your rating scale, follow these steps:
   1. Write a definition for the term *citizenship* that can be used to guide your work.
   2. List all the positive feelings you believe are associated with the attitude as you have defined it.
   3. List the positive behaviors you believe reflect each feeling and the negative behaviors that demonstrate a student's lack of citizenship. Your list should be appropriate for the students and subject you teach or plan to teach.
   4. Evaluate the list and remove behaviors that are redundant, unobservable in the classroom, irrelevant, or inappropriate for your situation.
   5. Paraphrase and list selected behaviors on the left side of a sheet of paper. Check to ensure that all are either neutrally or positively worded.
   6. Select rating categories for each behavior and write a verbal description for each.
   7. Assign a number for each category with low numbers reflecting negative or inappropriate categories.

8. Design the form so you can rate students' behavior three times during a term. Compare your definition and rating scale with those included in Table 11.8 in the Feedback section. Because definitions, subjects, grade levels, classroom environments, and target students vary, your form will undoubtedly differ from the example provided.

B. Using the steps outlined in I.A, develop a behavior rating scale for study habits. Compare the definition and rating scale you develop with the one in Table 11.9 in the Feedback section.

C. For the attitude goal "Choose to be punctual" analyze the following (see Figure 11.1 for feedback):
1. The positive feelings (affective component) a student is expected to possess
2. The overt behaviors that will indicate whether a student chooses to be punctual
3. The verbal information (cognitive component) a student should possess (the information should include cultural expectations, rewards, and consequences)
4. A procedure for punctuality a student could follow

II. Enrichment
A. Rating Attitudes and Behaviors
1. Locate the attitudes and behaviors to be communicated on a report card for your subject and grade level.
2. Locate the rating categories for the attitudes and behaviors on the report card.
3. Define each attitude and behavior category.
4. Develop rating forms for evaluating the attitudes and behaviors.
5. If you are teaching a class, use the forms to evaluate the behavior of students in the class. Revise the form as needed for feasibility and convenience.

FEEDBACK

I. Rating Attitudes and Behaviors
A. See Table 11.8.
B. See Table 11.9.
C. See Figure 11.1.

REFERENCES

Economics Research, Inc. (1991). *ParTEST user's manual.* Costa Mesa, CA: Economics Research, Inc.

Gagné, R. M. (1985). *The conditions of learning and theory of instruction.* New York: Holt, Rinehart and Winston.

SUGGESTED READINGS

Ebel, R. L., & Frisbee, D. A. (1991). *Essentials of educational measurement* (5th ed.) (pp. 241–262). Englewood Cliffs, NJ: Prentice Hall.

Gronlund, N. E., & Linn, R. L. (1990). *Measurement and evaluation in teaching* (6th ed.) (pp. 410–412). New York: Macmillan.

Hopkins, C. D., & Antes, R. L. (1990). *Classroom measurement and evaluation* (3rd ed.) (pp. 69–98). Itasca, IL: F. E. Peacock.

Kubiszyn, T., & Borich, G. (1990). *Educational testing and measurement* (3rd ed.) (pp. 193–196). Glenview, IL: Scott, Foresman/Little, Brown.

Mehrens, W. A., & Lehmann, I. J. (1991). *Measurement and evaluation in education and psychology* (4th ed.) (pp. 173–206). New York: CBS College Publishing.

Oosterhof, A. (1990). *Classroom applications of educational measurement* (pp. 176–197). Columbus, OH: Merrill.

Popham, J. W. (1990). *Modern educational measurement* (2nd ed.) (pp. 328–350). Englewood Cliffs, NJ: Prentice Hall.

Sax, G. (1989). *Principles of educational and psychological measurement and evaluation* (3rd ed.) (pp. 147–165). Belmont, CA: Wadsworth.

TABLE 11.8
Definition and Behavior Rating Scale for Citizenship

Definition: Citizenship is the social interactions that students have with their peers and with their teacher. It includes their contributions to the classroom society.				

Name _____ **Term** _____ **Score** _____

                                                   Total   (153)

Observation Dates: _____ _____ _____ **Total**

I. Citizenship
  A. Self-discipline
    1. Minds own affairs
    2. Controls emotions
    3. Is honest
    4. Is truthful
  B. Interactions with peers
    1. Shows interest in classmates
    2. Listens to classmates
    3. Helps and encourages classmates
    4. Shares resources and materials
    5. Contributes to group activities
  C. Interactions with teacher
    1. Listens when teacher is talking
    2. Follows directions
    3. Seeks guidance and help
    4. Accepts suggestions and comments about classroom interactions
  D. Support of a positive classroom environment
    1. Helps define and analyze class problems
    2. Suggests solutions for class problems
    3. Accepts responsibility for personal contributions to class problems
    4. Helps maintain class property
                                        Totals: _____ _____ _____ _____

Scale: 1 = Rarely; 2 = Inconsistently; 3 = Almost always
Note: Write quality ratings in blanks opposite each behavior.

TABLE 11.9
Definition and Rating Scale for Study Habits

Definition: Study habits are the procedures students use to accomplish assigned work.

Name _____ **Term** _____ **Score** _____

Behavior	**Observation Dates:** ____	____	____	**Total**
I. Class Preparation				
A. Reads assignments before class	____	____	____	____
B. Brings required materials to class	____	____	____	____
II. During presentations/demonstrations				
A. Listens	____	____	____	____
B. Takes notes	____	____	____	____
C. Follows instructions	____	____	____	____
III. During class work				
A. Organizes material	____	____	____	____
B. Works carefully and accurately	____	____	____	____
C. Uses time productively	____	____	____	____
Totals	____	____	____	____

Number of homework assignments during term: ____

IV. Homework
  A. Number submitted on time _____
  B. Number submitted complete _____
  C. Number accurate _____

Scale: 1 = Rarely; 2 = Inconsistently; 3 = Almost always
Note: Write quality ratings in blanks opposite each behavior.

FIGURE 11.1

Analysis of Instructional Goal: Choose to Be Punctual

Affective Component	*Behavioral Component*
The individual has a:	The individual chooses to:
1. Positive attitude toward planning and self-discipline	1. Keep a calendar of appointments
2. Positive attitude toward being punctual	2. Plan activities to enable punctuality
3. Negative attitude toward inconveniencing others	3. Arrive shortly before the scheduled beginning time
	4. Begin scheduled activity on time
	5. End activity on or before scheduled ending time

Cognitive Component (Verbal information)

Cultural Expectations	Rewards	Consequences of Habitual Lateness
1. We live in a time-oriented culture.	The individual gains increased respect from others because he or she has demonstrated:	The individual loses the respect of other people for being discourteous and undisciplined.
2. Punctuality is considered to be an indicator of a person's ability to plan and exercise self-control.	1. Good planning skills	The individual causes other people to worry.
3. Other people expect a person to be punctual.	2. Good self-control	
4. Other people dislike waiting for people who are not on time.	3. Respect for other people's time	The individual causes other people to become annoyed and angry.
5. Being late is considered discourteous because it causes worry for your safety and demonstrates lack of regard for the feelings of other people.	4. Respect for other people's opinions	
	5. The ability to be dependable	

Cognitive Component (Procedure)

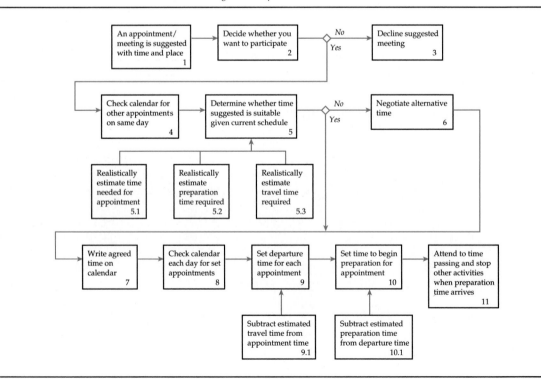

CHAPTER 12

Developing and Administering Tests for Nonreaders

Many students in the early elementary grades and some special education students throughout the grades are nonreaders. Although the preceding suggestions for designing and developing tests might seem irrelevant for teachers of nonreaders, this is not the case. These teachers do encounter some distinct technical problems; however, the suggestions for designing tests for readers also apply to designing tests for nonreaders. For example, teachers of nonreaders need to analyze instructional goals to create a framework of subordinate skills, write behavioral objectives, and create tables of specifications and sample objectives to design readiness tests, pretests, practice tests, and posttests. At the point of test development, these teachers must make some significant departures. Rather than writing directions and questions for students to read, they need to write direction and item scripts that they read to students. Instead of writing responses for students to read, they must create other ways for students to demonstrate that they can recall a fact or perform a skill. They must also use different methods for administering their tests and for recording students' responses. The following sections contain recommendations for testing nonreaders in groups and individually.

TESTING GROUPS OF NONREADERS

Testing an entire class at once requires less time than administering the same test individually to each student in a class. Testing nonreaders simultaneously, however, requires care because following oral instructions is difficult for students. Without clear directions, the group becomes baffled and frustrated, their responses become meaningless, and you become convinced that group testing is not feasible for your class. Most classes can successfully take group tests when the tests are carefully developed and administered. Developing such tests requires writing a script for yourself, creating a response form for students, and using special techniques during test administration.

Writing the Introduction Script

Good tests for readers contain introductory remarks and instructions for completing the test; nonreaders need the same information. Because they cannot read the instructions themselves, you need to provide instructions orally. Your introductory remarks should include what the test is about and an explanation and accompanying demonstration of what students are to do. To help ensure that you have their attention, this information should be provided before response forms are distributed. Table 12.1 provides an example introductory script for a test. Notice that the objective measured is written at the top and that the script includes (1) a general statement of the skill to be performed, (2) a demonstration of the skill that shows what students will find on their response forms and how they are to respond, and (3) a call for questions from the group.

Before using such instructions with an entire class, you should field test them with one or two students. Pay careful attention to the clarifying questions they ask and revise your instructions as needed. This trial will reduce the number of questions asked during the test, which will decrease the amount of time required for the test and help avoid frustrating the students.

Writing the Questions Script

You need to write a script for each question on the test. Students cannot reread a question they do not initially understand. Therefore, carefully ordering the directions, pausing to allow students time to perform a step, and repeating key information will help students perform the tasks with a minimum amount of confusion. Directions should be ordered in the following manner:

1. Tell students how to locate their place (e.g., "Find the star on your paper.").
2. Tell them what kinds of objects they will find in that location (e.g., "See the boxes beside the star?").

TABLE 12.1
Teacher's Script and Student's Response Form for a Nonreader Group Test

---

Introduction and Directions

Objective B.2: Given multiple sets of objects that contain up to 10 objects, select the set that contains a specified number of objects.

Introduction: "Today I want you to show me that you can count the number of marbles in a box. On the paper I will give you, you will see a picture of something that will help you find the right boxes. (Draw a typical locator symbol on the chalkboard.) Beside the cat you will find three boxes of marbles." (Draw three boxes of marbles on the chalkboard beside the object.)

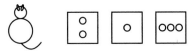

"See, one box contains two marbles (point to correct box), one box contains one marble (point to correct box), and one box contains three marbles (point to box). Only one of the boxes beside the cat will contain the number of marbles that I say. If I asked you to find the box with one marble in it, you would find this box (point to box) because it is the only one *beside the cat* that has one marble in it. I want you to put an *x* on this box (put large *X* on box) to show me that you can find the box with one marble in it. Do you have any questions?"

Distribute response forms.

"Do you have any questions about your paper? Let's begin. I will read the questions, and you will mark your answers with an *X*."

Teacher's Question Script (Obj. B.2)	Student's Response Form (Obj. B.2)
	Name _____ Date _____ Score _____
1. "Find the star on your paper. Do you see the star? (pause) See the boxes behind the star? (pause) Find the box that has four marbles in it. Find the box that has four marbles in it. (pause) Place an *X* on the box that has four marbles in it." (pause)	
2. "Find the sailboat on your paper. Do you see the sailboat? (pause) See the boxes beside the sailboat? (pause) Find the box that has five marbles in it. Find the box that has five marbles in it. (pause) Put an *X* on the box that has five marbles in it." (pause)	
3. "Find the apple on your paper. Do you see the apple? (pause) See the boxes beside the apple? (pause) Find the box that has seven marbles in it. Find the box that has seven marbles in it. (pause) Put an *X* on the box that has seven marbles in it." (pause)	

3. Describe the skill measured (e.g., "Find the box beside the star with four marbles in it.").
4. Tell them how to show that they can perform the skill (e.g., "Put an X on the box that has four marbles in it.").

This question script, with the recommended pauses and repetition inserted, appears in Table 12.1.

Initially, you might think that creating such scripts constitutes busywork. However, writing a script has four benefits. First, it helps you avoid omitting important information needed for smooth test administration. Second, the script can be evaluated and refined to avoid the same problems in future test administrations. Third, it enables you to use teacher's aides to help with testing. Using your script, they can administer the test (1) to the class, freeing you to circulate among students and provide additional assistance when needed; (2) to individual students who were absent during the group test; and (3) to small groups or individuals who need to retake the test following additional instruction. Fourth, the script will be available when you need to measure the same skill for a new class.

Developing the Response Form

As you write the question scripts, you should develop the corresponding paper-and-pencil response form. Space for the student's name, the date, and the score should be included at the top. The illustrations on the form must match the information in the introduction and question scripts. The symbols used to help students locate their place should be familiar to the class. If they are familiar with numerals or letters, use them. If not, use such symbols as a star, ball, dog, cat, moon, bike, or sailboat. The responses in each set should be clearly separated and easy for children to distinguish. Similar to other selected-response tests, they should contain one clearly correct answer and one to three distractors that represent plausible misconceptions or errors. A sample response form is included in Table 12.1.

Administering the Test

Once the scripts and response form are developed, you are ready to administer the test. If you have a teacher's aide or parent volunteer available, he or she can provide valuable assistance with this challenging task. The person who reads the script should watch the group closely for clues about pacing and needed repetition. Having a second person who can circulate among students and provide additional attention (e.g., pointing to the correct location) will make the procedure progress more smoothly. If you have no help, seat those students you predict will need assistance close by you. The pauses built into the question scripts enable you to scan the entire group for potential problems.

TESTING INDIVIDUAL NONREADERS

It is not always feasible to test a group; thus, individual tests need to be given. This situation is common for special education teachers who provide individualized instruction and have each student in the class studying a different lesson. Developing individually administered tests for nonreaders requires a question script, sometimes objects that students manipulate, and a student response record. Keeping the required materials together in a test packet or kit will save time because you will need the same materials each time the test is administered. These kits can be labeled to identify the objectives measured and the material enclosed. They can be filed in sequence with other test kits that measure subordinate skills related to the same instructional goal.

Developing the Script and Response Form

Unlike group-administered tests, the script for individually administered tests is usually included on the same form as the student response record. They can be included on the same form because the teacher both reads the script and records the student's responses. The form should contain space for recording the student's name, the date the test is administered, the objective measured, the script used to introduce the test, the directions/questions script, and space for recording the student's responses. Consider the example test form in Table 12.2. The objective measured and introduction script are included at the top; the directions/questions script is included on the left side; and spaces to record the student's responses are in the right-hand columns. Notice the space to record each response the student makes and spaces for repeating the test if necessary.

Manner of Responding

Because these tests are administered individually, a student can respond orally to your questions or can manipulate given objects to demonstrate skill. For example, a student can choose a specified picture from a set; sequence a set of pictures, numbers, or letters; count a specified number of objects; choose a particular shape, letter, number, or color from a set; or classify similar objects in a set. Objects needed for a test should be kept in the test kit along with the script and response record.

Administering the Test

To begin the test, introduce the skill to be measured and answer any questions the student might have about what you want her or him to do. When there are objects to be manipulated, you will find that demonstrating the skill using a simple example is helpful. As with group tests, such a demonstration will help ensure that the student's errors relate to skill rather than to under-

TABLE 12.2
Teacher's Script and Student's Response Record for an Individualized
Nonreader Test

Name _____

Objective A.4: Given a set of 10 objects, count out two sets of objects containing a
specified number and sum and total number of objects removed.

Introduction: "See the pile of <u>beans</u> I have given you? Today I want you to count
the number of beans I say and take them from the pile. (Demonstrate with one bean
and two beans.) Then I want you to tell me how many beans you have taken from
the pile altogether." (Demonstrate 1 + 2 = 3). "Are you ready?"

	Student's Responses	
Directions/Questions Script	Dates Tested	
	9-12	9-30
1. "Take three beans from the pile and place them here."	3	3
2. "Take two beans from the pile and place them there."	2	2
3. "How many beans have you taken from the pile altogether?"	5	5
"Put the beans back in the big pile."		
4. "Take four beans from the pile and place them here."	4	4
5. "Take four beans from the pile and place them there."	4	4
6. "How many beans have you taken from the pile altogether?"	8	8
"Put the beans back in the big pile."		
7. "Take five beans from the pile and place them here."	̶4̶	5
8. "Take four beans from the pile and place them there."	4	4
9. "How many beans have you taken from the pile altogether?"	̶8̶	9
Total Correct Responses	7	9

standing your directions. Watch the student carefully and pace your test
according to his or her ability to follow your directions.

As the student responds to each question, you should record *all* the
responses. Recording only incorrect or correct responses will affect a student's
attitude and may influence performance on subsequent items. For the same
reason, incorrect answers should be marked or identified only after the test is
completed.

In addition to how you record responses, the way you behave during the
test is important; the student will watch you closely to detect your reactions
to responses. You should remain pleasant and patient regardless of whether
the student makes an incorrect response or asks to have information repeated
a third or fourth time. Coaching, rewarding (e.g., "Great, Johnny"), or criticizing behaviors will influence the validity of the measure.

Providing Corrective Feedback

Provide feedback to the student immediately following an individual test, if time permits. You can review errors the student made, explain or show why the response was incorrect, and demonstrate how the task is performed correctly. After this additional instruction, you might give the student an opportunity to perform the skill correctly and include the amount of verbal guidance or coaching the student appears to need. However, a correct response after coaching should not be counted as a correct answer on the test. The student's ability to perform the skill should be checked on another day to see whether the skill was remembered over time.

SUMMARIZING AND ANALYZING STUDENTS' RESPONSES

The suggestions for organizing, summarizing, and analyzing students' responses presented in Chapter 13 are appropriate for both individual and group tests. You summarize and analyze the data you recorded on students' records during individual tests or the data students created using their own response forms on group tests. From these group summaries, you can evaluate the quality of both your tests and your instruction.

COMPUTER TECHNOLOGY

The creation of tests for nonreaders using a computerized item bank and test assembly program is quite easy when compared to the process of creating them by hand. The scripts (items) you create for nonreaders can be entered into ParTEST (Economics Research, Inc., 1991) using the essay question or problem format. Your item scripts can then be classified and systematically stored through the program's user descriptors (e.g., subject, topic, behavioral objective code, etc.). Students' response forms can be linked to your item scripts using the student feedback section.

Computerized script (item) storage and test assembly capabilities are especially useful for primary grade teachers of nonreaders. These capabilities provide primary-level teachers with the flexibility necessary either to assemble many different versions of a test or to create many very small tests that contain only a few items. In order to meet the needs of their students, primary teachers tend to include fewer items on their tests. When considering readiness tests, pretests, practice tests, and posttests, however, primary teachers typically need a greater number of tests than other teachers. The item bank can help primary teachers assemble a variety of tests for the same instructional goal that will help meet the needs of their total class, different achievement-level groups within their class, or individuals who require specialized materials.

Special education teachers will also find computerized item banks invaluable. Their needs are different from those of typical classroom teachers since they tend to have fewer students, with each student at a different grade level or studying unique materials. Computerized item banks and assembly programs will enable these teachers to create any number of tests, each designed to meet the special needs of individual students. One adjustment special education teachers can make to maximize the utility of the item bank for themselves is to change one of the user descriptors to a grade-level category. When using search criteria to locate items in the bank for a student at a particular grade level, they can add this search criterion to find the most appropriate items relative to context and vocabulary.

SUMMARY

Nonreaders can be tested in groups or individually. Group tests require you to write scripts for directions and questions, develop a student response form, and administer the test carefully. Suggestions for developing and administering these tests include:

Directions Script
1. Describe the skill to be measured.
2. Write a script for demonstrating the skill.
3. Ask for clarifying questions.

Questions Script
1. Sequence instructions in the following order:
   a. Tell students how to find the correct location on the response form.
   b. Describe what they will find in that location.
   c. Describe the skill to be performed.
   d. Tell students how to mark their response.
2. Include pauses between instructions that enable students to perform the specified task.
3. Repeat key information (e.g., the skill to be performed).

Response Form
1. Include familiar symbols that students can use to locate the correct response set.
2. Clearly separate the responses within and across sets.

Administration
1. Seat students you predict will need extra help close by you.
2. Read the directions script.
3. Demonstrate the skill to be performed.
4. Ask for clarifying questions.
5. Distribute the response form.
6. Call for questions.
7. Read the questions script.

8. Observe the group during pauses to identify potential problems.
9. Repeat any instructions as needed.

Individual tests for nonreaders require a form that includes a script for directions and questions, space to mark a student's responses, objects to manipulate (sometimes), and special administration techniques. The procedures for developing the script are the same as those described for group tests. Procedures for creating the response form and administering the test are:

Response Form
1. Include space to record the student's response to each task.
2. Include space for administering the test several times.

Administration
1. Read the directions script.
2. Demonstrate the skill to be performed.
3. Ask for clarifying questions.
4. Read the questions script, pausing and repeating information as needed.
5. Record all responses.
6. Remain pleasant and patient throughout the test.
7. Avoid using coaching, rewarding, or criticizing behaviors.
8. Mark incorrect responses only after the test is completed.
9. Provide students with corrective feedback immediately following the test, if time permits.

PRACTICE EXERCISES

I. **Group Testing Intellectual Skills for Nonreaders**
   For nonreaders, perform the following tasks:
   A. Analyze the instructional goal "Write upper-case and lower-case letters from memory." (See Table 12.3 in the Feedback section.)
   B. Develop behavioral objectives for all enabling skills included in your analysis. (See Table 12.4 in the Feedback section.)
   C. Develop a script and response form for testing students' mastery of objective II.F.2 in Table 12.4. This objective is: Given each lower-case letter in writing, write the corresponding upper-case letter. (See Table 12.5 in the Feedback section.)

II. **Individually Testing Motor Skills for Nonreaders**
   Many teachers in the early primary grades are concerned with students' eye-hand coordination and their motor development. One very good task for assessing a student's status and progress is this developmental area is bouncing a playground ball while standing still, while walking, and while running. Using the goal analysis in Figure 12.1 for bouncing a ball while standing still, develop a checklist that can be used on four separate occasions during a term to assess your student's status on this skill. (See Table 12.6 in the Feedback section.)

FIGURE 12.1
Subordinate
Skills for the
Instructional
Goal: Bounce a
Ball while
Standing Still

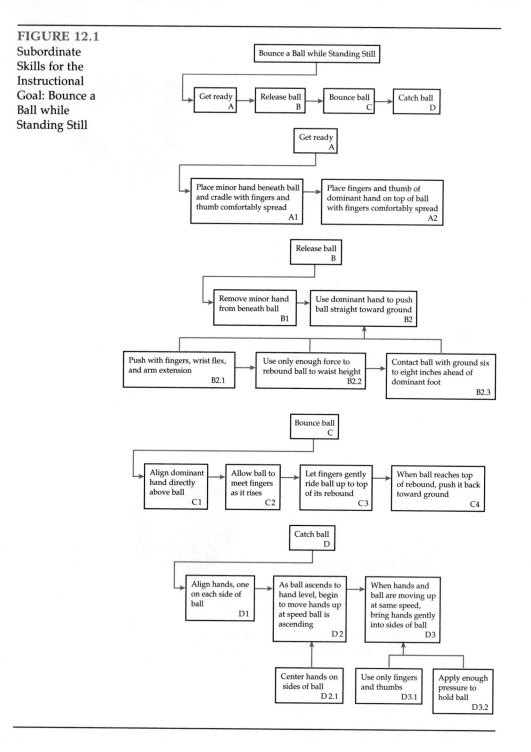

III. Enrichment
    A. Locate a curriculum guide for preschool, kindergarten, or first grade and perform the following:
        1. Choose an instructional goal from the guide that is either an intellectual skill, a motor skill, or a social development skill.
        2. Use either a matrix diagram, tree diagram, or flowchart to analyze the goal.
        3. Write behavioral objectives for each enabling skill identified.

FEEDBACK

I. Group Testing Intellectual Skills for Nonreaders
    A. See Table 12.3.
    B. See Table 12.4.
    C. See Table 12.5.

II. Individually Testing Motor Skills for Nonreaders
See Table 12.6.

TABLE 12.3
Matrix Diagram for the Intellectual Skill, "Write Lower-Case and Upper-Case Letters"

CONCEPTS/ CONTENT	A State/ Recall Physical Characterstics of:	B State/ Recall Functional Characteristics of:	C State/Recall Quality Characteristics of:	D Discriminate Between Examples & Nonexamples	E Evaluate Given Examples	F Produce Examples of:
I. Lower-case letters				a through z		a through z
II. Upper-case letters				A through Z		A through Z

TABLE 12.4
Behavioral Objectives for Enabling Skills in Table 12.3

  I.D Given a response sheet that contains lower-case letters in sets of 10, circle the letter in each set that is named by the teacher. To the degree possible, the letters included in each set should be similar in appearance.

  I.F When each of the lower-case letters is named by the teacher, draw the letter named.

  II.D Given a response sheet that contains upper-case letters in sets of 10, circle the letters named by the teacher. To the degree possible, the letters included in each set should be similar in appearance.

  II.F.1 When each of the upper-case letters is named by the teacher, draw the letter named.

  II.F.2 Given the illustration of each lower-case letter, write the corresponding upper-case letter.

TABLE 12.5
Teacher's Script and Students' Response Form for a Test on Writing Upper-Case Letters

---

TEACHER'S SCRIPT

1. "Today I want you to write capital letters on a special paper that I give you. While I pass out the papers, please get out a pencil that has a good point for writing your letters. Do not write on the paper I give you until I tell you how I want you to write." (Distribute response sheets.)
2. "Does everybody have a paper and a pencil?" (Pause while readiness determined.)
3. "Let's begin. See the line at the top of your paper beside the word *Name?*" (Point out line on sample response sheet on overhead projector so students can see example on projector screen.)
4. "Print your name on this line." (Print sample name in space for overhead display.)
5. "See the line beside your name where it says *Date?* On this line write the numbers *2-6* just like this." (Demonstrate on overhead.)
6. "Do you see all the lower-case letters on your paper?" (Point out letters on overhead.)
7. "I want you to write the capital letter for each lower-case letter."
8. "Write each capital letter on the line beside each lower-case letter." (Point to line beside letter on overhead.)
9. "Let's do one together. See the first letter? It is a lower-case *a*." (Point to *a* on overhead.)
10. "See the line beside the letter *a?* Let's write a capital *A* on the line to show that it belongs to the lower-case *a*." (Write a capital *A* on overhead.)
9. "Do you have any questions about what you are supposed to do?"
10. "Let's begin. Write the capital letter for each lower-case letter on your paper."

STUDENTS' RESPONSE FORM

II.F.2 Writing Capital Letters for Given Lower-Case Letters

Name _____   Date_____

a _____   b _____   c _____   d _____   e _____

f _____   g _____   h _____   i _____   j _____

k _____   l _____   m _____   n _____   o _____

p _____   q _____   r _____   s _____   t _____

u _____   v _____   w _____   x _____   y _____

z _____

TABLE 12.6
A Sample Checklist for Assessing Students' Ability to Bounce a Ball
While Standing Still

BOUNCING PLAYGROUND BALL WHILE STANDING STILL								
Name _____	Date ___		Date ___		Date ___		Date ___	
	Yes	No	Yes	No	Yes	No	Yes	No
A. Getting ready								
1. Minor hand supporting underneath	—	—	—	—	—	—	—	—
2. Dominant hand over	—	—	—	—	—	—	—	—
3. Dominant hand relaxed, fingers curved	—	—	—	—	—	—	—	—
B. Release								
1. Remove minor hand	—	—	—	—	—	—	—	—
2. Push with "fingers" of dominant hand	—	—	—	—	—	—	—	—
3. Force adequate to rebound ball to waist	—	—	—	—	—	—	—	—
4. Ball bounces about 6 inches ahead of dominant foot	—	—	—	—	—	—	—	—
C. Bounce								
1. Dominant hand aligned above ball	—	—	—	—	—	—	—	—
2. Rising ball meets flexed fingers	—	—	—	—	—	—	—	—
3. Fingers "ride" ball to top of rebound	—	—	—	—	—	—	—	—
4. Push ball back to ground with flexed fingers	—	—	—	—	—	—	—	—
D. Catch Ball								
1. Align hands, palms in	—	—	—	—	—	—	—	—
2. Hands move toward and ascend with ball	—	—	—	—	—	—	—	—
3. Hands move gently into ball	—	—	—	—	—	—	—	—
4. Use only fingers and thumb to contact ball	—	—	—	—	—	—	—	—

REFERENCE

Economics Research, Inc. (1991). *ParTEST user's guide*. Costa Mesa, CA: Economics Research, Inc.

SUGGESTED READINGS

Gearheart, C., & Gearheart, B. (1990). *Introduction to special education assessment: Principles and practices* (pp. 95–114). Denver, CO: Love Publishing.

Payne, D. A. (1992). *Measuring and evaluating educational outcomes* (pp. 328–330). New York: Macmillan.

Standardized test publishing companies' Examiners' Manuals: Review the teachers' scripts and the student response forms for kindergarten, first-, and second-grade tests. These materials are typically available from the guidance counselor of most elementary schools.

CHAPTER 13

Developing and Using Portfolios and Mastery Charts

OBJECTIVES

- Develop portfolios of individual students' work to demonstrate initial status and progress on instructional goals.
- Describe guidelines for choosing portfolio exhibits that are not related to instructional goals and objectives.
- Summarize a group's objective-based scores from product, performance, or attitude rating forms in order to evaluate instruction.
- Summarize a group's progress on one instructional goal across time to evaluate the quality of instruction.

One of the most important tasks that teachers perform is to communicate clearly and accurately their students' progress in school. Teachers can have difficulty clearly communicating achievement to students and parents when using abstract numbers and grades, and many choose to supplement test scores and grades with portfolios that contain samples of a student's work throughout the term. Although teachers have used portfolios for decades to collect work samples and describe pupils' progress, there is increased interest among educators in encouraging their use to improve communication. Whether you personally decide to develop and maintain student portfolios or you are required to do so by school administrators, carefully planning will help ensure that your portfolios are useful.

As you studied the previous chapters on alternative means of assessment, it may have become obvious to you that the most logical approach to reporting many of these assessments would be through organizing a collection of students' work for criterion-referenced analyses. It is possible to use norm-referenced analysis procedures with checklists and rating scales and to calculate group performance measures for central tendency and variability, but it makes more sense to use criterion-referenced reviews of students' progress on instructional goals and objectives. Teachers who choose to calculate norm-referenced indices for their checklist and rating scale data can do so by using students' raw scores and by following the procedures described in the norm-referenced section of Chapter 8.

Most of the conceptual work for producing quality portfolios was addressed in preceding chapters since portfolios do require ideas and materials that you studied on goal analysis, test development, test analysis, and alternative assessment. Portfolios are unique, however, in that they enable you to pull everything together into a coherent picture of a student's development in your class. The design of portfolios should enable a balanced view of your students that includes (1) a picture of students' status at the outset of instruction on academic goals and objectives and documentation of their progress through instruction and posttests, (2) a broader picture of growth that is not tied to specific instructional goals and objectives, and (3) when viewed as a class set, a composite picture of strengths and weaknesses in the instructional program.

DEVELOPING PORTFOLIOS TO MONITOR GROWTH ON INSTRUCTIONAL GOALS AND OBJECTIVES

Effective portfolios are not simply chronological collections of students' work from a particular time. Rather, their design should enable illustration of students' status at the outset of instruction and provide documentation of their progress through instruction and posttest. The following paragraphs describe planning and design activities for quality portfolios. An example portfolio assessment form for the instructional goal "Write a paragraph" is used to illustrate the process. In developing a portfolio, you might take the following steps:

1. Examine the instructional goals in the curriculum guide and identify the types of information that can illustrate students' status and growth on the goals.
2. Plan a testing strategy that will enable demonstration of progress.
3. Develop a portfolio assessment form.
4. Select a container for your portfolios.
5. Enter information and work samples into the portfolio.
6. Compare students' initial status with posttest performance and assess development.
7. Write a descriptive summary of students' status and growth.

The following paragraphs describe each of these steps.

Examining Instructional Goals

Developing and maintaining portfolios can be quite time consuming, so you should ensure that the instructional goals you select for portfolio assessment are the most critical ones for analyzing and communicating your students' progress. Skills you might judge as most critical are ones that are foundational not only for your subject but also for the students' development in other subject areas. For example, a language arts teacher might choose to document oral and silent reading goals in a portfolio because reading is foundational for all school subjects; a math teacher might choose to document calculations as well as particular kinds of quantitative reasoning; and a physical education teacher might choose to demonstrate physical fitness and strength development goals. Basic life skills such as these warrant the additional time required for portfolio assessment. When you have selected the goals you believe should receive the most attention from you, your students, and their parents, you need to consider your strategy for examining students' skills on the goals.

Planning a Testing Strategy That Will Enable Illustration of Student Progress

Well-designed portfolios should illustrate students' progress during a term, semester, or year. It is unlikely that any portfolio system will enable you to store all the work samples your students produce, so samples chosen should be relevant for your instructional goals and they should illustrate students' progress on the goals.

To demonstrate students' progress during your course, you will need to have a measure of their status at the outset of instruction and then subsequent measures of their skill at various points across the term, semester, or year. Initial status assessments could include pretests (and perhaps readiness tests), observations, interviews, samples of work, and other formal and informal assessments, since students' achievement levels on these materials provide baseline data for reviewing progress. Students' achievement on practice tests can provide illustrations of interim progress, and posttest data, when compared with pretest information, will illuminate the skills changes that occur. Recall that the design of all these types of tests was described in Chapter 4. For the critical goals you select, planning methods to assess students' status before or during the beginning of instruction is the only way to guarantee that you have the information required to develop a good portfolio. Remember that such testing could include objective tests and any of the other alternative tests that you have studied.

Along with the work samples you choose for your students' portfolios, you might want to encourage your students to evaluate their own work and to volunteer samples for inclusion in their portfolios. Engaging in exercises to evaluate their own work and selecting samples they consider their best work can be very good learning experiences. Additionally, comparing initial products with those they develop after instruction and seeing their progress in the class can also be illuminating for students.

Developing a Portfolio Assessment Form

Designing an effective portfolio assessment form requires consideration of how to format the information you need. Since the purpose of portfolios is to communicate both status and growth, the manner in which you organize work samples and describe them is very important. Portfolios should *not* be only a chronological collection of students' papers and projects; instead, they should contain work samples organized to enable direct comparisons of initial work with work samples produced following instruction and practice. Early planning for organizing and describing materials in the portfolio can ensure that you identify the best way to display and describe students' progress.

Table 13.1 contains a sample portfolio assessment form for the instructional goal "Write a paragraph." The first row of the table identifies the purpose for the form; the second indicates the particular instructional goal from the curriculum guide; the third row names the student, grade level, and teacher; and the fourth row is used to identify the products the teacher plans to include in the portfolio. Notice that the objective-style pretest and posttest for paragraphs are listed as well as the four types of paragraphs students wrote during the unit. It is quite appropriate to include objective tests as work samples in portfolios.

The fifth row, labeled Exhibits, contains numbers that are used to identify and sequence students' products in the portfolio. The sixth row, labeled Purpose, identifies whether each work sample is a baseline measure or a measure obtained following instruction. In this example, only pretest and posttest samples are included; however, teachers can include interim work as well. The seventh row of the summary form identifies the date the student produced the work. Notice that work samples are sequenced in pretest/posttest pairs rather than chronologically. This ordering strategy will enable teachers, parents, and students to examine progress better since contiguous products are the same assignments collected early and late during the unit. The information described in these top rows is similar to a textbook's table of contents in that it informs readers of what they will find in the portfolio and where they will find it. Moreover, the information helps teachers classify and file information in the portfolio as it is completed by students and evaluated.

The criteria for judging students' paragraphs are listed in the far left column. Notice that only main paragraph components (I. through IV.) are included on the form. This is done because the purpose for this form is to provide a summary of the students' work. Listing each criterion within the components could create information overload for the reader. Notice also that this teacher has opted to include criteria other than paragraph structure on the summary form. Criteria related to the students' choice of content and ideas, as well as their sentence structure, grammar, punctuation, and spelling, are being monitored in the work samples. These criteria will not be considered in evaluating students' ability to structure paragraphs, but they are being

TABLE 13.1
A Sample Portfolio Assessment Form for the Instructional Goal, Write a Paragraph

PORTFOLIO ASSESSMENT										

Instructional Goal: Write a paragraph

Name _____ Grade _____ Teacher _____

Objectives	Paragraph Objective Tests		Rating Scale Totals	I.F.1 Descriptive Paragraph		I.F.2 Time Series Paragraph		I.F.3 Procedure Paragraph		I.F.4 Feelings Paragraph	
Exhibits:	#1	#2		#3	#4	#5	#6	#7	#8	#9	#10
Purpose:	Pre	Post		Pre	Post	Pre	Post	Pre	Post	Pre	Post
Criteria *Date*	___	___		___	___	___	___	___	___	___	___
I. Paragraph	___	___	7	___	___	___	___	___	___	___	___
II. Topic Sentence	___	___	10	___	___	___	___	___	___	___	___
III. Supporting Sentences	___	___	14	___	___	___	___	___	___	___	___
IV. Concluding Sentence	___	___	13	___	___	___	___	___	___	___	___
Raw Score **Percentage Correct**	___ ___	___ ___	44	___ ___	___ ___	___ ___	___ ___	___ ___	___ ___	___ ___	___ ___
V. Content	___	___		___	___	___	___	___	___	___	___
VI. Sentence Structure	___	___		___	___	___	___	___	___	___	___
VII. Grammar	___	___		___	___	___	___	___	___	___	___
VIII. Punctuation	___	___		___	___	___	___	___	___	___	___
IX. Spelling	___	___		___	___	___	___	___	___	___	___
Comments:											
General Progress:											

monitored in the paragraph writing samples to enable communication of progress in these important skills.

The last two rows in the summary form are reserved for the teacher's descriptive comments. The first of these rows is for comparison of each pair of products, and the last row is reserved for the teacher's general impressions of the students' development during the unit. These descriptive summaries serve to focus parents' and students' attention on facets of students' work that the teacher considers important.

Completing the design of your portfolio assessment summary form for a unit of instruction is, in essence, completing the design of that section of the portfolio. The assessment form can be attached in some manner to the front of the portfolio where it will be convenient to use. It is a good idea to keep it inside the cover, however, as students undoubtedly will consider the information it contains to be confidential. All that remains at this point is to collect students' work, score it, enter the scores on the summary form, assign each sample an exhibit number, and place it—along with a copy of the checklist or rating scale used to judge the work—into the portfolio.

Selecting a Container for Your Portfolios

Several criteria should be considered for selecting portfolio containers that best suit your needs. Some include the available storage space and facilities, the number of students you teach, and the type and size of appropriate work samples. If appropriate work samples are limited to paper-and-pencil products, you teach over 150 students a day, and you have very limited storage facilities, then the file folder will undoubtedly be the container of choice. On the other hand, if you teach a subject where products other than paper-and-pencil ones are common (e.g., computer discs, videotapes, notebooks, woodcuttings), then you will need to balance product size and storage capabilities in determining the best portfolio containers. It is important to remember that the type of container chosen will influence the nature of the work samples that can be stored.

Entering Information on the Summary Form and Placing Products into the Portfolio

Table 13.2 contains the portfolio assessment form with all the pretest information inserted for one student. Ruby's objective pretest was administered on October 2. The number of questions she answered correctly for each main paragraph component is inserted in the form, along with the total number of items the pretest contained for each component. For example, she answered all 4 general paragraph questions correctly and 7 of 11 topic sentence questions correctly.

The writing sample pretests were administered on October 3, 4, 5, and 6. The points Ruby was awarded for each main component are inserted for each of these pretests. With her data from these different samples collected together, the teacher can analyze patterns in her initial work. For example, Ruby had already mastered the general idea of paragraphs since she earned all possible points in this category. She appears to need work, however, on topic

TABLE 13.2
A Sample Paragraph Portfolio Assessment Form for One Student

	PORTFOLIO ASSESSMENT					
Instructional Goal: Write a paragraph						
Name _Ruby Hager_ Grade _8_ Teacher _Ms. Jones_						
Objectives	**Paragraph Objective Tests**	**Rating Scale Totals**	**I.F.1 Descriptive Paragraph**	**I.F.2 Time Series Paragraph**	**I.F.3 Procedure Paragraph**	**I.F.4 Feelings Paragraph**
Exhibits:	#1 #2		#3 #4	#5 #6	#7 #8	#9 #10
Purpose:	Pre Post		Pre Post	Pre Post	Pre Post	Pre Post
Criteria Date	10/2 ____		10/3 ____	10/4 ____	10/5 ____	10/6 ____
I. Paragraph	4/4 ____	7	7 ____	7 ____	7 ____	7 ____
II. Topic Sentence	7/11 ____	10	6 ____	6 ____	7 ____	6 ____
III. Supporting Sentences	8/11 ____	14	7 ____	6 ____	7 ____	8 ____
IV. Concluding Sentence	7/11 ____	13	10 ____	9 ____	9 ____	10 ____
Raw Score	26 ____		30 ____	28 ____	30 ____	31 ____
Percentage Correct	70 ____	44	68 ____	64 ____	68 ____	70 ____
V. Content	____ ____		____ ____	____ ____	____ ____	____ ____
VI. Sentence Structure	____ ____		____ ____	____ ____	____ ____	____ ____
VII. Grammar	____ ____		____ ____	____ ____	____ ____	____ ____
VIII. Punctuation	____ ____		____ ____	____ ____	____ ____	____ ____
IX. Spelling	____ ____		____ ____	____ ____	____ ____	____ ____
Comments:						
General Progress:						

sentences, supporting sentences, and concluding sentences. Her writing samples, with their rating scales attached, document her initial status on writing paragraphs. They should be numbered for reference and filed in the appropriate place in the portfolio. Notice that there are no general comments inserted on the assessment form since data from the posttests are unavailable at this point for comparison. As posttest measures are obtained, they can be scored and compared with these baseline data.

Comparing Pretest/Posttest Performance and Assessing Progress

Table 13.3 includes Ruby's posttest scores for the paragraph unit. Dates the exams were administered are inserted at the top of the posttest columns, and her scores are listed beside the pretest scores. Notice that her performance on the objective posttest demonstrates good progress across all main components of a paragraph. Her total score changed from 70 percent of the items answered correctly on the pretest (26/37) to 91 percent on the posttest (40/44), which reflects marked improvement.

Ruby's performance on each of the four writing samples improved as well. She moved from earning 68 to 89 percent of the points on the descriptive paragraph, 64 to 91 percent on the time series paragraph, 68 to 91 percent on the procedures paragraph, and 70 to 100 percent on the feelings paragraph. From these data comparisons, the teacher can see that Ruby's overall development was at a consistent level across all writing samples. Examining her progress for each paragraph component, you can see that she was already proficient in general paragraph skills at the outset, and she made good progress during the unit in writing both topic and concluding sentences. She still has room for improvement in the supporting sentences area. The descriptive information included at the bottom of the form can provide insights into particular areas of supporting sentences that require additional instruction and practice.

Writing a Descriptive Summary of Students' Status and Progress

As you analyze a student's work and make descriptive comments about its features, it is important to point out uniqueness within and across work samples. Otherwise, these features may be missed by you, parents, and students when the portfolio is reviewed during conferences. Additionally, it is important to describe both strengths and areas that need to be improved in a student's work. Stressing strengths is important because it is discouraging to a student and parent to review a summary of work that stresses only faults and weaknesses. Calling attention to good points, and pointing them out *first*, often ensures that students and parents have a receptive mindset for accepting information about areas that need to be improved.

In writing your summaries, keep in mind that the nature and tone of words you use in your descriptions are important for the students and parents. Avoid using terms on these assessment forms such as *failed, inadequate,* or *unacceptable.* These terms are not only discouraging to students but they

TABLE 13.3
Paragraph Portfolio Assessment Form for One Student Completed for a Unit of Instruction

PORTFOLIO ASSESSMENT									

Instructional Goal: Write a paragraph

Name _Ruby Hager_____ Grade __8__ Teacher __Ms. Jones_____

Objectives	Paragraph Objective Tests		Rating Scale Totals	I.F.1 Descriptive Paragraph		I.F.2 Time Series Paragraph		I.F.3 Procedure Paragraph		I.F.4 Feelings Paragraph	
Exhibits:	#1	#2		#3	#4	#5	#6	#7	#8	#9	#10
Purpose:	Pre	Post		Pre	Post	Pre	Post	Pre	Post	Pre	Post
Criteria Date	10/2	11/22		10/3	11/23	10/4	11/24	10/5	11/25	10/6	11/26
I. Paragraph	4/4	7/7	7	7	7	7	7	7	7	7	7
II. Topic Sentence	7/11	11/11	10	6	10	6	10	7	10	6	10
III. Supporting Sentences	8/11	10/13	14	7	10	6	10	7	12	8	14
IV. Concluding Sentence	7/11	12/13	13	10	12	9	13	9	11	10	13
Raw Score	26	40		30	39	28	40	30	40	31	44
Percentage Correct	70	91	44	68	89	64	91	68	91	70	100
V. Content				✓	+	✓	+	✓	+	✓	+
VI. Sentence Structure				+	+	+	+	+	+	+	+
VII. Grammar				+	+	✓	+	+	+	+	+
VIII. Punctuation				+	+	+	+	+	+	+	+
IX. Spelling				NI	NI	NI	NI	NI	NI	NI	NI
Comments:	Good effort and improvement			Good desc. Needs to work on sequence		Topic sentence good improv.		Over generalized conclusions		Very good at expressing personal feelings	

General Progress: Ruby has a good concept of paragraph structure and purpose. She is imaginative and detailed in her descriptions. Her writing developed nicely over the term. She needs to work on transition and sequence. Her spelling needs attention—a personel dictionary may help.

also connote a misleading sense of finality to skill development. Language that implies future development and growth is far more appropriate. Problematic areas in students' work samples might be positively described as skills that need improvement, future focus, or strengthening.

CHOOSING GOAL-FREE EXHIBITS FOR PORTFOLIOS

When you consider the purpose for a portfolio, you can see why teachers often choose to include materials that are not directly related to a student's progress on a specific goal or objective. These extras can help provide a richer picture of a student's intellectual and social growth. A problem arises when the portfolio becomes a cluttered catchall for *everything* that is cute, colorful, humorous, inventive, or unique in even the smallest way. Then the portfolio begins to resemble a bulletin board or the refrigerator door in households, and the value of the portfolio is diminished as a method of communication among teachers, students, and parents. There are three guidelines that will help ensure that extra material inserted into portfolios is useful for your periodic reviews of a student: focus, chronology, and documentation.

Providing a Focus

Sometimes it is fun to include a few things in a portfolio just because you want to, but usually what is included should focus on aspects of a student that you think deserve additional notice. Such aspects could include attitudes and behavior not listed on report cards, academic abilities or deficiencies not related to your subject area, artistic tendencies, social accomplishments, career goals, or a myriad of other areas that would help you communicate with students and their parents. If material does not focus on something that needs to be said about a student, then do not include it in the portfolio.

Portraying a Chronology

The most useful exhibits in a portfolio are those that sustain their focus across time, whether it be a grading period or an entire school year. Exhibits will occasionally be entered into a portfolio as isolated comments on a student, but those exhibits that have a sequence and demonstrate a pattern will have more value in your periodic reviews of students.

Providing Documentation

A good rule of thumb is that if it is not worth taking a moment to document a potential exhibit for a portfolio, then do not include it. Documenting what you include will help tie together the contents of a portfolio and emphasize the focus of the exhibits. Table 13.4 is a generic form to use for documenting exhibits included in a portfolio. You could adapt the format to meet your needs in a particular classroom setting.

Assume that you have decided to include something in a student's portfolio; these are the steps you could take to document the exhibit:

TABLE 13.4
Generic Form for Documenting Portfolio Exhibits

	Description of Exhibits		
	No. _____ Date _____ Description _____	No. _____ Date _____ Description _____	
Focus of Exhibits			Etc.
1.			
2.			
Etc.			

1. In the heading for the first column on the top of the form, enter:
   a. An identifying number for the exhibit
   b. The date
   c. A description of the exhibit that could include:
      (1) Notes from an interview or informal observation
      (2) A rating scale or checklist from some product or process
      (3) An objective test or quiz
      (4) An actual product
      (5) Anecdotal comments written on a slip of paper
      (6) A lab report or technical drawing
      (7) A sample of writing
      (8) Any other document or product that would support a focus on an aspect of a student
2. In the space in the left side of the first row on the form, enter a description of the focus of the exhibit. Remember that the focus is student centered. It is the particular aspect of the student that you have chosen to highlight by inserting this exhibit into the portfolio. The focus could be on:
   a. Career goals
   b. Social adjustment
   c. Athletic ability
   d. Academic skills
   e. Classroom behavior
   f. Any other aspect of the student that you have chosen

3. In the cell where the focus row intersects the description column, enter any notes that will add more meaning to this summary document or help you remember details of the exhibit. Such notes might include:
   a. Anecdotal impressions
   b. Test scores, grades, percentage correct, objectives mastered, and so on
   c. Comments on progress
   d. Other information that will help jog your memory so that you will not need to refer to the original exhibit each time you review the portfolio

When you decide to insert another exhibit into the student's portfolio, just move over one column to the right and down one row and repeat the three steps. On the other hand, if the new exhibit is focused on the same aspect of the student as exhibit number 1, then you would use the same row and just move over one column to the right for your new entry. By documenting your exhibits in this manner, you automatically create the focus and the sense of chronology that are so valuable in making a portfolio an effective tool for communicating with students and parents.

SUMMARIZING GROUP PERFORMANCE TO EVALUATE INSTRUCTION

Emphasis thus far in this chapter has been on student portfolios and how they are used to communicate a students' progress. The rest of the chapter focuses on summarizing the information from alternative forms of assessment that are often included in portfolios, and using the summary information for tracking group progress and identifying strengths and weaknesses in the instructional program. When you use checklists to evaluate students' work, the procedures to use for evaluating instruction are similar to those described in Chapter 8. Since each student who does satisfactory work for each subcomponent gets one point on a checklist, you simply determine the level of performance that you expect for group mastery of each component, calculate the percentage of the group that mastered each subcomponent, and then locate those subcomponents where fewer than the anticipated number of students received a satisfactory mark.

Data obtained from rating scales, however, are a little different since students can earn differing numbers of quality points for the subcomponents. Recall that a rating scale may include some criteria that are judged using a checklist, while others are judged using a three- or four-point scale. Table 13.5 contains group summary data for the general paragraph (I.) and topic sentence (II.) portions of the paragraph rating scale. Students' names are listed down the left column and the main components and subcomponents are listed in the rows across the top. The actual scores students were assigned for each criterion are inserted in each student-by-criterion cell.

TABLE 13.5
Group Summary Data from a Portion of the Paragraph Rating Scale Included in Table 9.12

| | WRITE DESCRIPTIVE PARAGRAPHS (I.F.1) | | | | | | | |
| | Paragraph | | | Topic Sentence | | | | |
Date: 11-23	Indent I.A	One Topic I.B	Description* I.C	Location II.A	Introduces II.B	Relevant II.C.1	Scope II.C.2	Interest II.C.3
Total Points:	1	2	3	1	2	2	2	2
Students								
Augustine	1	2	3	2	2	2	2	2
Bailey	1	1	2	2	1	1	1	2
Carey	1	2	3	2	2	2	2	2
Cromer	1	2	2	2	2	2	2	2
Deddens	1	2	3	2	2	2	2	2
Deiters	1	1	1	2	1	1	1	1
Gormley	1	1	1	2	1	1	1	1
Hager	1	2	3	2	2	2	2	2
Hill	1	2	3	2	2	2	1	1
Lovejoy	1	2	1	2	2	2	1	1
McComas	1	2	3	2	2	2	2	2
McLaughlin	1	2	3	2	2	2	2	2
Otto	1	2	2	2	2	2	2	2
Prince	1	2	3	2	2	2	2	2
Rust	1	2	3	2	2	2	2	2
Scragg	1	1	1	2	2	2	1	1
Smith	1	1	1	2	1	1	1	1
Stewart	0	1	2	2	1	2	1	1
Talbot	1	2	3	2	2	2	2	2
White	1	2	3	2	2	2	1	1
Sum:	19	34	46	40	35	36	31	32
Total Possible:	20	40	60	40	40	40	40	40
Percentage:	95	85	77	100	88	90	78	80
			**				**	

Note: This quality characteristic is used to judge whether students' paragraphs actually contained descriptions of something.

The first step in determining the quality of instruction for each subcomponent is to determine the percentage of points you feel your students should earn following instruction. Similar to checklists and objective tests, this decision is a matter of professional judgment based on the complexity of the subcomponent and the characteristics of the group examined.

The second step is to sum the points earned by the class for each subcomponent. This is accomplished by summing the points awarded within a column. For example, the sum of points earned by the group for the indention objective is obtained by adding the points in column I.A. The sum for the group is 19. This sum is inserted in the row marked Sum at the bottom of the table.

The third step is to determine the total possible number of points available for the subcomponent. The total points possible is obtained for each subcomponent by multiplying the quality points assigned for the subcomponent by the total number of students in the class. For example, there are three quality points students can earn for the subcomponent "Paragraph meets descriptive assignment" in column I.C. This value (3) times the number of students in the class (20) is the total number of points possible for that subcomponent. This number is inserted in the row marked Total Possible at the bottom of the table.

The fourth step is to determine the percentage of total points earned by the class for each subcomponent. The percentage is obtained by dividing the sum of points the group earned by the total possible number of points. This index is inserted in the last row of the table marked Percentage. For example, students earned 95 percent of the points available for indenting their paragraphs and 85 percent of the points available for including only one topic in their paragraphs.

The final step is to locate subcomponents where the designed percentage of points were not earned. Suppose you decided that students in the group should earn 80 percent of the available points for instruction to be considered adequate. Using this standard, instruction for two subcomponents in Table 13.5 should be reconsidered. Only 77 percent of the total possible points were earned for writing an acceptable description of something in their paragraphs (column I.C), and 78 percent of the points were earned for the scope of their topic sentences.

EVALUATING GROUP PROGRESS

Often, the types of skills measured using alternative assessment procedures are evaluated multiple times during a term or semester using the same rating scale or checklist. Procedures similar to those just described for assessing students' performance on one occasion can be repeated to examine the quality of instruction indicated by students' achievement each time the instructional goal is assessed. To illustrate how you might proceed, the general paragraph and topic sentence subcomponents of the paragraph goal are used to demonstrate the summary and analysis procedure. Other main components and subcomponents of the assignment would be evaluated in the same manner.

Table 13.6 contains a summary form useful for evaluating group progress across time. The top of the table again identifies the behavioral objective (I.F.1) for writing descriptive paragraphs, and the column headings name the subcomponents. Rather than listing individual students' names in the far left column, the dates on which the writing samples were taken are included. For each subcomponent, the percentage of possible points earned by the class is listed.

A summary table such as this will enable you to determine whether your students are progressing as a group on the main components and subcomponents of the instructional goal. For example, the teacher appears to have corrected the problem occurring with students not actually writing a description of something (I.C) in their paragraphs. Each time the writing sample was taken, students did a better job with descriptions. Likewise, problems with the scope of students' topic sentences (II.C.2) appears to be resolved for most students in the class. With data summarized in this manner, you can also monitor progress for skills not actually considered problematic. Notice that the group is making good progress in the area of writing to suit the interest of their intended audience (II.C.3).

Group performance summaries across time will also help you locate areas where the students' achievement was initially considered adequate, but no progress or improvement is being made. Consider the introductory quality of students' topic sentences (II.B). The class has made no progress on this subcomponent, and the teacher may want to rethink the instructional strategy relative to this important characteristic.

TABLE 13.6
Group Progress Data from a Portion of the Paragraph Rating Scale Included in Table 9.12

WRITE DESCRIPTIVE PARAGRAPHS (I.F.1)								
	Paragraph			**Topic Sentence**				
	Indent I.A	One Topic I.B	Descrip-tion I.C	Loca-tion II.A	Intro-duces II.B	Rele-vant II.C.1	Scope II.C.2	Interest II.C.3
Date: 11/23 Percentage:	95	85	77	100	88	90	78	80
Date: 12/18 Percentage:	100	85	80	100	85	86	80	95
Date: 1/21 Percentage:	100	86	86	100	86	88	84	90
Date: 2/28 Percentage:	100	88	90	100	88	89	86	92

Note: The number in the cell reflects the percentage of total possible points the group earned for each subcomponent.

COMPUTER TECHNOLOGY

Teachers might not consider computer technology very helpful for portfolio assessment or mastery analysis based on alternative assessments, but it can be quite helpful. It is true that product, active performance, and behavior observation checklists and rating scales must be hand-scored; however, students' subtest (e.g., main component) and total test scores from such assessments can be entered into the student roster using the computer keyboard. Including alternative assessment scores in students' term records enables teachers to monitor students' developmental progress from pretests, practice tests, objective posttests, and alternative assessments. Such a comprehensive record provides teachers and parents with multifaceted information about a student's development. Imagine, for example, the instructional goal on writing a paragraph. A student roster that includes a student's readiness test, pretest, practice test, and objective posttest scores, as well as the scores on the four types of paragraphs written, would provide a better view of the student's development than would either the objective test scores or the paragraph product scores alone. Thus, although many teachers do not initially consider computers as particularly helpful for alternative assessments, it is important to remember that programs such as ParSCORE and ParGRADE (Economics Research, Inc., 1992) have utility for record keeping, information synthesis, and performance analysis.

Computer technology currently under development by National Computer Systems (NCS) will undoubtedly revolutionize the manner in which students' work samples are catalogued, stored, and retrieved for analysis and communication. NCS has developed the capability to store efficiently written materials, photographs, audiotapes, and videotapes of students' performances on a single disk. When this technology is available to teachers for routine class work, meaningful portfolios that document students' status and growth in a myriad of achievement areas can be easily created and managed.

SUMMARY

Procedures for evaluating students' progress using alternative assessments are described in this chapter. The three methods discussed include portfolio assessment, group summary charts, and group progress charts.

Portfolios are collections of students' work that are used to document progress on instructional goals, and their main purpose is to improve communication with students and parents. Portfolios do not contain simply a chronological collection of random work samples; instead, they include carefully selected sets of materials that demonstrate students' initial status on key instructional goals and the progress they make on these goals during a course. The following procedures are recommended for designing and developing effective portfolios to demonstrate students' progress:

1. Examine the instructional goals in the curriculum guide and identify the types of information that can illustrate students' status and growth on the goals.
2. Plan a testing strategy that will enable demonstration of students' progress.
3. Develop a portfolio assessment form.
4. Select a container for your portfolios.
5. Enter information and work samples into the portfolio.
6. Compare students' pretest and posttest performance and assess development.
7. Write a descriptive summary of students' status and growth.

Many teachers use the portfolio as an instructional tool by encouraging students to assist with selecting materials for inclusion. Moreover, many encourage students to evaluate their own progress during a course using the work samples collected.

Teachers sometimes choose to include in portfolios exhibits that do not relate directly to instructional goals or objectives. Guidelines for incorporation of such exhibits include: (1) having a clear focus for the materials selected, (2) portraying a chronology or focus across time, and (3) providing documentation of what is included and why.

Work samples included in a portfolio provide an illustration of one individual's progress. To evaluate instruction, however, you will need to summarize the group's achievement data that were gathered using alternative assessment methods. Group performance data gathered using a checklist is analyzed in the same manner as described in Chapter 8. The following steps are used to summarize a group's achievement on product, performance, and behavior rating scales:

1. Create a summary table that includes the points earned by all students for each component on your checklist or rating scale.
2. Use your professional judgment to set a standard for the minimum percentage of points that should be earned by your class on each subcomponent.
3. Calculate the percentage of points earned by the group for each subcomponent.
4. Locate any subcomponents where the percentage of points earned is less than the established standard.
5. Evaluate your instruction and instructional schedule for subcomponents where students' achievement does not meet the established standard.

Besides summarizing a group's achievement on one test, you should evaluate their progress across several work samples. The procedures for summarizing data to evaluate group progress are the same as those for evaluating group performance on one measure with one exception. To examine progress, you will need to summarize the percentage of points the total group earned for each subcomponent across the times the skills were assessed. Using these data, you can detect areas where the group is improving, maintaining status, or regressing. These progress assessments provide information about whether instructional interventions are effective.

PRACTICE EXERCISES

I. **Portfolio Assessment**
   A. What is the *main purpose* for creating and maintaining portfolios of students' work?
   B. What kinds of information are summarized in portfolio assessment forms?
   C. What type of products can you use to document a student's initial skill status on instructional goals?
   D. What type of products can you use to document students' progress and growth?
   E. What is a good strategy for describing the strengths and weaknesses in a student's skills that become apparent in a portfolio?
   F. Design a portfolio assessment form for the chapter outline rating scale included in Table 13.7. Compare your assessment form with the one included in Table 13.7F in the Feedback section.

II. **Evaluating Instruction Using a Group Summary Form**
   Using the group summary form for chapter outlines included in Table 13.8, perform the following steps (assume a group score of earning 80 percent of the points available for each subcomponent as your minimum standard for evaluating instruction):
   A. Sum the total number of points earned by the group for each subcomponent and insert this value in the Sum row at the bottom of the table.
   B. Determine the total number of points possible for the group to earn for each subcomponent, and insert this number in the Total Possible row at the bottom of the table.
   C. Calculate the percentage of possible points earned by the class for each subcomponent, and insert this percentage in the row marked Percentage Earned.
   D. Locate subcomponents for which additional instruction and practice appear warranted. See Table 13.8F in the Feedback section for calculations.

III. **Evaluating Instruction Using a Group Progress Chart**
   Table 13.9 contains a partially completed group progress chart for the instructional unit on outlining chapters in a textbook. Using this chart, perform the following steps:
   A. Complete the table by inserting into the first data row the group's percentage of points earned from the bottom of Table 13.8.
   B. Examine trends in students' performance over the term, and identify subcomponents where students' learning appears to be:
      1. Progressing (improving)
      2. Staying about the same
      3. Regressing (getting worse)
   C. Using a minimum standard of 80 percent of the total points earned and lack of progress on subcomponents, identify subcomponents where additional group instruction appears necessary.

TABLE 13.7
Rating Scale for Evaluating Outlines

Name _____ Date _____ Score _____
                                                  Total   (35)

I. Main Ideas	1	2	3
A. Main ideas identified	Secondary ideas included — 1	Some ideas missing — 2	All main ideas included — 3
B. Clearly paraphrased	Some meaning changed — 1	Too brief/wordy — 2	Clearly paraphrased — 3
C. Parallel structure	Mixed sentence/phrase — 1	All sentences or phrases — 2	Consistent word format — 3
D. Consistent order	Out of order — 1	Most in order — 2	All in order — 3
E. Consistent labels	Inconsistent — 1	Consistent — 2	3
F. Alignment	Flush with left margin — 1	Aligned — 2	

II. Secondary ideas	1	2	3
A. Secondary ideas identified	Main ideas included — 1	Some ideas missing — 2	All secondary ideas included — 3
B. Related to main idea	Scrambled placement — 1	Most within right topic — 2	All within right topic — 3
C. Clearly paraphrased	Some meaning changed — 1	Too brief/wordy — 2	Clearly paraphrased — 3
D. Parallel structure	Mixed sentence/phrase/word — 1	All sentences, phrases, or words — 2	Consistent word format — 3
E. Consistent order	Out of order — 1	Most in order — 2	All in order — 3
F. Consistent labels	Inconsistent — 1	Consistent — 2	3
G. Alignment	Indented five spaces — 1	Aligned — 2	

TABLE 13.8
Evaluating Instruction Using Group Performance Data

OUTLINE TEXTBOOK CHAPTERS							
II. Secondary Ideas							
Subcomponent	A	B	C	D	E	F	G
	Identify	Relate	Paraphrase	Parallel	Order	Label	Align
Students *Points:*	3	3	3	3	3	2	2
Augustine	3	3	3	3	3	2	2
Bailey	1	1	2	2	1	1	2
Carey	2	2	3	3	2	2	2
Cromer	2	2	2	3	2	2	2
Deddens	3	3	3	3	2	2	2
Deiters	1	1	1	2	1	1	2
Gormley	1	1	1	1	1	1	2
Hager	3	3	3	3	3	2	2
Hill	1	2	1	2	2	2	2
Lovejoy	1	2	1	2	2	2	2
McComas	3	3	3	3	3	2	2
McLaughlin	2	2	3	2	3	2	2
Otto	1	2	2	2	2	2	2
Prince	3	3	3	3	3	2	2
Rust	3	3	3	3	3	2	2
Scragg	1	1	1	2	2	2	2
Smith	1	1	1	1	1	1	1
Stewart	1	1	2	2	1	2	1
Talbot	3	3	3	3	3	2	2
White	2	2	3	2	2	2	2
Sum:							
Total Possible:							
Percentage:							
Review Inst.:							

TABLE 13.9
Evaluating Instruction Using Group Performance Data

		A	B	C	D	E	F	G
OUTLINE TEXTBOOK CHAPTERS								
II. Secondary Ideas								
Subcomponent		A	B	C	D	E	F	G
		Identify	Relate	Paraphrase	Parallel	Order	Label	Align
Date	*Totals:*	3	3	3	3	3	2	2
1/12	Percentage							
1/19	Percentage	66	68	72	80	78	92	95
1/28	Percentage	72	67	78	81	80	90	94
2/10	Percentage	78	69	84	79	86	91	96

Note: Numbers in cells represent the percentage of points earned by the total class on each subcomponent.

IV. **Enrichment**
Select an instructional goal from a curriculum guide for the subject and grade level that you teach or plan to teach. For this goal:
A. Name possible work samples that could be used to provide baseline data for students' skills at the outset of instruction.
B. Name possible work samples that could be included to illustrate students' interim progress.
C. Name possible work samples that could provide outcome measures of students' achievement during the class.
D. Plan ways to organize the portfolio.
E. Develop a portfolio assessment form for recording performance data, contrasting work samples, describing students' strengths, and describing areas where they need additional instruction and practice.
F. Locate a teacher who has a good portfolio system developed and request permission to examine the following:
   1. The materials it contains that are anchored to instructional goals
   2. The materials that are unique to a particular student
   3. The assessment form(s) used to locate, contrast, and describe both goal-based and student-based materials included in the portfolio

FEEDBACK

I. **Portfolio Assessment**
   A. The main purpose for creating and maintaining portfolios of students' work is to provide better communication to students and parents about students' learning and their progress in school. The letter grades and skills checklists typically provided to summarize students' progress cannot illustrate as clearly the instructional goals that students have mastered, partially mastered, or not mastered

during a term. They also cannot communicate noncurricular aspects, talents, and characteristics of a student that should be recognized and communicated.

B. The kinds of information typically included in portfolios are samples of students' work that demonstrate their status on instructional goals at the outset of instruction and their growth on these goals during and following instruction. Many teachers also choose to include materials students produce that are not anchored

TABLE 13.7F

A Sample Portfolio Assessment Form for the Instructional Goal, Outline Chapters in the Text

PORTFOLIO ASSESSMENT							
Instructional Goal: Outline text chapters including main ideas and secondary ideas in the outline							
Name _____ Grade _____ Teacher _____							
Objectives		Initial Chapter 4	Chapter 5	Chapter 6	Chapter 7	Etc.	
Exhibits:		#1	#2	#3	#4		
Criteria Date	*Total Points*						
I. Main ideas							
A. Identified	3						
B. Paraphrased	3						
C. Parallel	3						
D. Consistent order	3						
E. Consistent labels	2						
F. Alignment	2						
II. Secondary Ideas							
A. Identified	3						
B. Related to main	3						
C. Paraphrased	3						
D. Parallel	3						
E. Consistent order	3						
F. Consistent labels	2						
G. Alignment	2						
Total	35						
Percentage of Total	100						
General Progress:							

to any particular instructional goal but that do illustrate students' status and growth on both cognitive and social skills. Moreover, many teachers frequently include samples of work that students choose to include in their portfolios, regardless of whether these student selected samples are anchored to the curriculum or are particularly good at illustrating the student's progress.

C. Students' initial skill status can be documented using any work sample produced at the outset of instruction. The samples can be formally or informally produced materials or they can be formally administered pretests for the instructional unit. Teachers sometimes use formal or informal readiness tests as a part of the initial documentation. These work samples can be objective-style exams, products students develop, active performances, and attitude rating scales or questionnaires.

D. Students' progress and growth can be documented using practice exercises (interim) and posttests designed to measure their goal-based knowledge and skill. These tests can be objective-style exams, product development tests, active performance tests, and attitude rating scales or questionnaires. The posttests can include unit exams, term exams, or semester exams. These formal assessment materials can be supplemented with other work samples the teacher considers unique and important for describing a student's progress.

E. The best strategy for communicating students' strengths and weaknesses is to address the strengths first. After discussing all the strong points in a student's work, especially areas where the student is making strides and improving, the student will be more receptive to critical comments concerning how they can improve. Critiques should be phrased positively, connoting growth, progress, and future development.

F. Compare your portfolio assessment form with the example in Table 13.7F. The students' baseline skills will be recorded in the column labeled Chapter 4. Space is included for data from their outlines for subsequent chapters. Notice that space is provided for recording the total points available for each subcomponent.

II. **Evaluating Instruction Using a Group Summary Form**
For items A through D, compare your calculations with the ones included in Table 13.8F. More instruction and rehearsal are needed for subcomponents II.A, II.B, II.C, II.D, and II.E.

TABLE 13.8F
Evaluating Instruction Using Group Performance Data

OUTLINE TEXTBOOK CHAPTERS							
II. Secondary Ideas							
Subcomponent	A	B	C	D	E	F	G
	Identify	Relate	Paraphrase	Parallel	Order	Label	Align
Students *Points:*	3	3	3	3	3	2	2
Sum:	38	41	44	47	42	36	38
Total Possible:	60	60	60	60	60	40	40
Percentage:	63	68	73	78	70	90	95
Review Inst.:	***	***	***	***	***		

TABLE 13.9F

Evaluating Instruction Using Group Performance Data

	OUTLINE TEXTBOOK CHAPTERS						
	II. Secondary Ideas						
Subcomponent	A	B	C	D	E	F	G
	Identify	Relate	Paraphrase	Parallel	Order	Label	Align
Date *Totals:*	3	3	3	3	3	2	2
1/12 Percentage	63	68	73	78	70	90	95
1/19 Percentage	66	68	72	80	78	92	95
1/28 Percentage	72	67	78	81	80	90	94
2/10 Percentage	78	69	84	79	86	91	96

Note: Numbers in cells represent the percentage of points earned by the total class on each subcomponent.

  III. **Evaluating Instruction Using a Group Progress Chart**
     A. See Table 13.9F.
     B. Subcomponents include the following:
        1. Progressing: II.A, II.C, and II.E
        2. Staying about the same: II.B, II.D, II.F, and II.G
        3. Regressing: none
     C. Additional instruction appears warranted for the following subcomponents: II.A, II.B, and II.D.

REFERENCE

Economics Research, Inc. (1992). *ParSCORE and ParGRADE user's manual.* Costa Mesa, CA: Economics Research, Inc.

SUGGESTED READINGS

Arter, J. A., & Paulson, P. (1991). *Composite portfolio work group summaries.* Portland, OR: Northwest Regional Educational Laboratory.

Arter, J. A., & Spandel, V. (1991). *Using portfolios of student work in instruction and assessment.* Portland, OR: Northwest Regional Educational Laboratory.

Hewitt, G. (1989). *Vermont portfolio assessment project.* Montpelier, VT: Vermont State Department of Education.

Vavrus, L. (1990). Put portfolios to the test. *Instructor, 100*(1), 48–53.

Worthen, B. R., Borg, W. R., & White, K. R. (1993). *Measurement and evaluation in the schools* (pp. 436–444). White Plains, NY: Longman.

Grading and Reporting Student Progress

- Design a gradebook based on your teaching assignment.
- Create a daily record to record and summarize instances of behavior and manage classroom business.
- Create a posttest record to document and summarize students' progress on instructional goals during the term.
  - a. Combine individual posttest scores into a composite score.
  - b. Convert composite scores to term grades.
- Create a conduct record to document and summarize students' scores on conduct rating scales.
- Identify factors that confound achievement grades and result in invalid interpretations.
- Create a performance summary form to use as a reference during parent-teacher conferences.

Teachers are usually expected to monitor and report three types of student behavior: achievement, attendance, and conduct. School districts use report cards to communicate this information to students, parents, school personnel, and other interested parties. Students use their achievement grades and other marks to verify the quality of their work and the acceptability of their conduct. Parents use report cards to help determine the amount of study time their children need and to make educational plans. School personnel also use grades, along with other information, for a number of purposes, such as the following:

1. To review the scope and sequence of the curriculum
2. To plan supplementary programs
3. To help students plan their education
4. To determine students' eligibility for special programs
5. To compare with standardized achievement test scores
6. To manage students' promotion

Employers and admission officers for colleges and universities use grades to determine whether an individual will be hired or admitted. Because grades can significantly influence decisions about a student's future, teachers should ensure that students' achievement grades and marks for conduct accurately reflect their behavior.

DESIGNING A GRADEBOOK

Teachers use gradebooks to document students' progress throughout a year. Although teaching assignments and information requirements vary, most teachers need a daily record of students' attendance and other information related to daily classroom management, a record of posttest scores, and a record of conduct scores obtained from behavior rating scales. Like most efficient accounting systems, the gradebook should separate the different types of information to reduce the probability of recording and analysis errors.

Your gradebook's design should reflect the nature of your teaching assignment. For example, an elementary teacher who teaches five different subjects to the same group needs to create one daily record, one conduct record, and a different posttest record for each subject. On the other hand, a teacher who is assigned five different groups needs a gradebook that contains a daily record, a posttest record, and a conduct record for each class.

Although commercially produced gradebooks are available, many are scanty and contain inadequate space for good documentation. You may be more satisfied with a gradebook you construct yourself using a loose-leaf notebook; large block, two-sided graph paper; and divider pages with tabs. After students' names are recorded on the first page, subsequent pages can be trimmed so the names remain visible as new pages are added. Such a gradebook has several advantages. You can add new pages as needed, remove and store information from previous terms, and insert records you might generate using the various computer programs available for gradebooks. If you are skilled in using a personal computer and spreadsheet programs that enable you to design a record for summarizing and manipulating data, you will want to use these resources to create and manage your gradebook. Commercial gradebook computer programs are now available, and they save teachers hours of clerical work and tedious calculations. Keep in mind the availability of these resources as you study the procedures recommended in this chapter.

CREATING THE DAILY RECORD

The daily record is used to document information related to daily classroom management. It contains information about attendance, homework and classroom assignments, particular instances of conduct you want to record, and other school matters. This record helps you complete behavior rating scales throughout the term, complete the attendance section of the report card, and conduct conferences with parents, students, and others. Your notations can help you explain the term marks for study habits and conduct and can also help identify factors, such as attendance or lack of participation, that contributed to students' posttest scores.

Selecting Symbols

In creating this section of the gradebook, you need to select symbols to record information. For example, you can use symbols like those in Figure 14.1 to record instances of behavior related to attendance, study habits, participation, and conduct.

Symbols should be selected for their efficiency and convenience. Consider the symbols in the attendance column of Figure 14.1. When you first record attendance, you can use the symbol / to note a student is absent. Should the student appear during the class session with an acceptable excuse for the lateness, the symbol can be converted to an X to indicate an excused tardiness. If the student does not have an adequate excuse, a circle can be placed around the X to signal an unexcused tardiness. However, if the student does not appear, the symbol / will indicate that the student was absent that day. If the student brings an acceptable excuse for the absence, no other mark is necessary. However, if the student does not present a legitimate excuse for the absence, a circle can be placed around the / to signify an unexcused absence.

Create a legend in the daily record that explains each symbol. Otherwise, you might use different symbols for the same behavior or forget what a particular symbol means. You can create new symbols as needed and add them to the legend.

Labeling Columns and Recording Information

In creating the daily record, you should reserve at least two rows at the top of the page to label columns. The date of each class session can be recorded in

FIGURE 14.1 Legend of Symbols for Recording Behaviors	Attendance	Study Habits	Participation	Conduct

	/ = Absent
	⊘ = Unexcused
	  absence
	X = Tardy
	Ⓧ = Unexcused
	  tardy
		H = Homework
		Ⓗ = Homework
		  accurate
		XH = No homework
		IH = Inaccurate
		  homework
		CH = Homework not
		  complete
		LH = Late homework
			M = Materials not
			  present
			C = Clothing
			  inadequate
			P = Did not
			  participate
			T = Time wasted
				A = Agressive
				D = Disruptive
				CT = Cheating on
				  test

the top row. The second row can be used to label specific types of information—for example, homework due, parent permission slips due, laboratory fees paid, or materials borrowed from a class resource center. Since more than one column may be needed for some dates, it is best to complete this record on a day-to-day basis. An example of a daily record is shown in Figure 14.2.

Summarizing Information

At the end of the grading period, you need to summarize the information. The two rows at the top of this record can be used to organize the data. The first row can identify the behavior category, and the second row can label the particular type of behavior within each category. The total number of times a student exhibits each behavior can be recorded in the remaining rows. Figure 14.3 is a sample summary section of a daily record.

CREATING THE POSTTEST RECORD

The posttest section is used to record information about students' progress on instructional goals and objectives studied during the term. Keeping adequate posttest records saves you time at the end of a grading term by providing the information needed to analyze tests, combine scores, and assign term grades. Adequate records also help you conduct conferences with students, parents, and other school personnel. To ensure that you have all the information needed, you should include the following items for each posttest:

1. The title and format of the test and the date it was administered
2. The total number of items or points
3. The group's mean score and standard deviation
4. The specific goals and the number of goals measured
5. Each student's raw score, percentage of items correct or points earned, number of goals or objectives mastered, and assigned grade.

If you plan to use a norm-referenced grading system, you will also want to record students' *T* scores for each test.

FIGURE 14.2
Sample Daily Record

Dates	9-1	2	3	4	5		8		9	10	11		12
Students								H				Trip	
Allen, B.					⃝/		X	IH	X	P		ok	
Baker, J.								H	/			ok	

FIGURE 14.3
Sample Term
Summary Section
of Daily Record

Students	Attendance				Study Habits					Participation				Conduct		
	/	(/)	X	(X)	(H)	XH	IH	CH	LH	M	C	P	T	A	D	CT
Allen, B.	0	1	1	0	12	2	1	0	0	1	0	0	0	0	0	1
Baker, J.	3	0	1	0	2	4	6	1	2	7	0	2	0	0	1	0

At first, this amount of information may seem unreasonable. At the end of the term, however, you will need this information in order to analyze the relationship among tests, devise a plan for combining scores, and calculate term grades. You may also need to explain the nature and meaning of particular test scores to other people. Referring to the information in your gradebook will be much easier than reconstructing it by sorting through your files.

Formatting the Information

You can reduce recording time by designing a systematic way to record test information. Reserve at least four rows at the top of the page to label columns and record general information about the test. The remaining rows can be used to record individual's performances. Consider the sample record for one student shown in Figure 14.4.

The top row is used to identify the particular test and the date it was administered. The second row identifies the mean score ($\overline{X}$), the total number of items on the test (Items), and the instructional goals tested (GL). The third row contains the standard deviation and space for recording the amount of weight the test will contribute to the term grade. The fourth row contains the symbols for the percentage correct score (%), the weighted percentage correct score (Wt.%), the T score (T), the weighted T score (Wt.T), and the grade (Gr.). The weighted percentage correct scores and the weighted T scores are not calculated until the end of a grading period, but you should reserve space for them as you record the data for each test. These weighted scores are described later in this chapter.

Although this may seem to be a lot of information about a test, having adequate information recorded in the gradebook will help you prepare quickly for parent conferences, and it will facilitate your discussions of students' achievement during conferences with students, parents, or counselors. From just the information contained in this sample gradebook, we can see that the first unit test was administered on September 10th, had a mean score of 16 and a standard deviation of 4, contained 20 items, and covered instructional goals 1 through 3 in the curriculum guide. B. Allen's raw score of 14 was below the group's mean score (16), and his T score was 45. His test performance was average in his class since his raw score was not lower than one standard deviation below the mean. He answered 70 percent of the items

FIGURE 14.4
Sample Posttest
Record

Unit Test 1: Sept. 10								Unit Test 2: Sept. 17							
	$\overline{X} =$	16	Items =	20		GL		$\overline{X} =$	21	Items =	25		GL	
	SD =	4	Wt. =			1–3		SD =	3	Wt. =			4–6	
Students		%	Wt.%	T	Wt.T		Gr.		%	Wt.%	T	Wt.T		Gr.
Allen, B.	14	70		45		2	C	19	76		43		2	C

correctly, mastered two of the three instructional goals tested, and was assigned a grade of C on the exam.

Combining Posttest Scores into a Composite Score

At the end of each term, you need to combine posttest scores into a *composite score* that reflects each student's achievement throughout the term. A composite score is created by combining two or more test scores. The steps in creating a composite score include (1) analyzing the relationship among posttests administered during the term to determine the weight each posttest should contribute to the composite score, (2) identifying weighting factors, (3) calculating weighted scores so each test contributes the desired amount, and (4) combining weighted scores into the composite score.

Analyzing the Relationship among Posttests When combining scores from multiple tests in a composite score, you need to decide how much weight each test will contribute. Analyzing the relationship among the tests will help you determine an appropriate weight for each one. There are at least two factors to consider in analyzing tests: their interdependence and their complexity.

The first comparison is whether tests measure different or overlapping sets of instructional goals. For example, if only unit tests are administered, each will most likely measure a different set of goals and objectives. However, posttests are frequently interdependent because they overlap in the goals measured. Suppose you administer quizzes, unit tests, midterm exams, and a final exam. Unit tests will measure many of the goals previously measured by quizzes; midterm exams will overlap unit tests; and comprehensive finals will overlap all previous tests. When posttests are interdependent, you should compare them across these categories as well as within each category.

A second comparison is the relative complexity of the tests. Factors that influence a test's complexity are its scope and the difficulty level of goals it measures. The scope of tests can be compared using the number of goals measured and the length of time between instruction and testing. Difficulty can be compared using the relative complexity of the goals measured by each test.

Comparing tests on the basis of scope, quizzes administered immediately following instruction that measure the objectives for only one goal are undoubtedly the least complex. A unit test that measures more goals and spans more time is more complex. Similarly, a comprehensive final exam that measures all the goals studied during the term and spans many weeks of study is more complex than any other test during the term. Based on these differences in complexity, you might decide that (1) a comprehensive final should contribute more to the composite score than any midterm exam, (2) a midterm exam should contribute more than any unit test, and (3) a unit test should contribute more than any quiz.

In addition to scope, the relative difficulty of goals measured is used to compare tests. Most likely, the goals measured by different tests are unequal in difficulty. For example, one test may measure students' skills in capitalizing the pronoun *I* and the first word of a sentence, whereas another measures their skill in capitalizing proper nouns and the titles of artistic works. Obviously, the goals measured by the second test are more difficult. The format of a test can sometimes provide a clue to the difficulty of the skills measured. For instance, essay tests, product development tests, and performance tests that require recall, analysis, organization, synthesis, and presentation skills might be judged more difficult than some objective tests. Based on differences in skill difficulty, you might decide to assign more weight to tests that measure more difficult goals.

Although tests may differ in the number and difficulty of goals measured, their overall complexity might be considered equal. For example, one test that measures several less difficult goals might be considered comparable in overall complexity to another that measures fewer more difficult ones. Thus, based on overall complexity, you might decide to assign them equal weight in the composite score.

You need to summarize information about posttests in order to compare them. Table 14.1 contains two summary charts for nine tests administered during a term. The information required to create such a summary should be available in the gradebook. In the top chart, the left-hand column identifies the test, and the second column identifies its format. The next set of columns identifies the instructional goals studied during the term, and the particular goals measured by each test are identified using an X. The right-hand column lists the total number of goals measured by each test.

Using the information in the top chart, tests can be compared for interdependence. From the table, the following relationships are evident:

1. Tests 1, 2, 3, 5, 6, and 7 are independent in the goals they measure. They appear to be unit tests because each measures either 2 or 3 goals. Collectively, they measure all 16 goals.
2. Test 4 measures goals previously measured by unit tests 1, 2, and 3.

TABLE 14.1
Summary of Posttests Administered during One Term

Test	Format	Goals Measured 1	2	3	4	5	6	7	8	9	10	11	12	13	14	15	16	Total Goals
1	Objective	X	X	X														3
2	Objective				X	X	X											3
3	Objective							X	X	X								3
4	Objective	X	X	X	X	X	X	X	X	X								9
5	Objective										X	X	X					3
6	Objective													X	X			2
7	Objective															X	X	2
8	Objective										X	X	X	X	X	X	X	7
9	Objective	X	X	X	X	X	X	X	X	X	X	X	X	X	X	X	X	16

Test Categories

	Unit Tests						Midterm Exams		Comprehensive Final
Test	1	2	3	5	6	7	4	8	9
Number of Goals	3	3	3	3	2	2	9	7	16
Format	0	0	0	0	0	0	0	0	0
Difficulty of Goals					X	X	X		X

Note: An X reflects more complex goals.

3. Test 8 measures the same goals as unit tests 5, 6, and 7.
4. Together, tests 4 and 8 measure all 16 goals.
5. Test 9 measures all 16 goals studied during the term.

This example includes three categories of interdependent tests: (1) six unit tests, numbers 1, 2, 3, 5, 6, and 7; (2) two midterm exams, tests 4 and 8; and (3) one comprehensive final exam, test 9. Based on the fact that the tests are interdependent, you could first compare categories to determine how much weight each category should contribute to the term composite score. Once the weight for each category is selected, you can compare tests within each category to determine how much weight to assign each one.

To compare categories, consider the number and complexity of goals measured by tests across categories. In this example, all three categories measure the same 16 goals. Therefore, one category probably would not be considered more complex than another, and they would be weighted equally in the composite score. To weight the categories equally, the unit tests collectively would contribute one-third, or 33.3 percent, to the composite score; the two midterm exams together would contribute one-third; and the final exam would contribute one-third, as illustrated in Figure 14.5.

FIGURE 14.5
Percentage
Contributed to
the Composite
Score by Each
Test Category

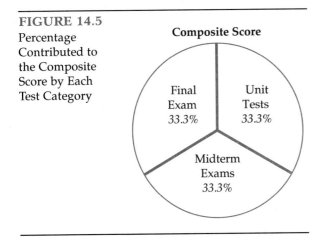

When you have determined the percentage each category is to contribute to the composite score, the next step in the analysis is to compare the tests within a category. The purpose for this comparison is to determine how much weight each test should contribute to the total percentage allotted for the category. The lower portion of Table 14.1 contains information about the nine tests' scope and difficulty arranged by category.

Comparing unit tests by scope, tests 1, 2, 3, and 5 all measure three goals, whereas tests 6 and 7 measure only two. Comparing them by the relative difficulty of goals measured, tests 6 and 7 are considered more difficult than the other four tests. If you decide that scope is balanced by skill difficulty and that the overall complexity of the six tests is approximately equal, then each test should contribute an equal percentage to the composite score.

Identifying Weighting Factors for Each Test   The percentage that each unit test will contribute to the composite score can now be determined. The total percentage allocated for unit tests (33.3 percent) is divided by the number of tests (6) to identify the percentage for each. Therefore, each unit test will contribute 5.55 percent to the term composite score.

The midterm exam category contains two tests to be compared. Test 4 measures nine skills, whereas test 8 measures only seven; however, the goals measured by test 8 are considered more complex. Thus, balancing scope and skill difficulty, you might decide to weight the two midterm exams equally.

To determine the percentage each midterm exam will contribute to the composite score, divide the percentage allocated for midterm exams (33.3 percent) by the number of exams (2). In this case, each midterm exam will contribute 16.65 percent to the composite score.

FIGURE 14.6
Percentage
Contributed to
the Term
Composite Score
by Each Test
Category and
Individual Test

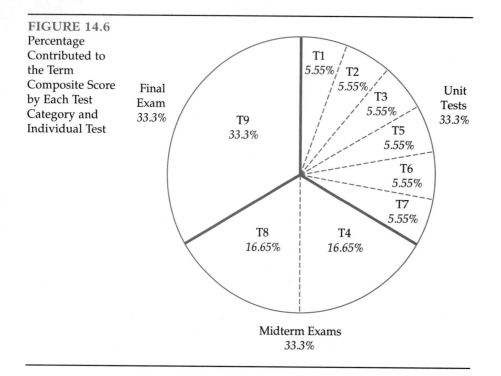

The percentage of weight assigned to categories and to individual tests is illustrated in Figure 14.6. Note that each of the three categories contributes an equal amount to the composite score (the six unit tests combined and the two midterm exams combined contribute equal amounts). Notice also that the final exam contributes more weight than either midterm exam and that each midterm exam contributes more weight than any unit test.

Usually, the manner in which you weight your tests is a matter of professional judgment. Some school districts, however, have grading policies that prescribe the weight final exams are to contribute to the composite score. Should your district prescribe the percentage allotted to final exams, you would assign weights to individual tests using a procedure similar to the one described in the previous example.

Suppose your district's grading policies state that final exams must contribute 25 percent to the composite score. With this given, you need to determine how the remaining 75 percent will be divided among the other tests. Using the nine tests in the preceding example and the same decisions about their relative weights, you could assign percentages to categories and to individual tests as follows:

1. Assign 25 percent to the final exam.
2. Divide the remaining 75 percent by the number of categories (2) and assign 37.5 percent to the unit test and the midterm exam categories.

3. Divide the percentage allocated for unit tests (37.5 percent) by the number of tests (6), and assign 6.25 percent to each unit test.
4. Divide the 37.5 percent allocated for midterm exams by 2, and assign 18.75 percent to each midterm.

Figure 14.7 illustrates the percentages assigned to each category and test. The unit test category and the midterm exam category each contribute more weight to the composite score than the final exam. However, the final exam contributes more than either midterm exam, and each midterm exam contributes more than any unit test. Thus, the assigned weights should reflect the relative complexity of the tests.

Calculating Weighted Scores   After selecting the weight each test will contribute to the term composite score, the next task is to calculate the weighted score for each test. This is accomplished using these two steps:

1. Convert the percentage assigned for each test to a proportion by dividing the percentage by 100. For example, 5.55 percent becomes .056, 16.65 percent becomes .167, and 33.3 percent becomes .333. These weights are inserted in the sample gradebook in Table 14.2.
2. Multiply each test score (percentage correct and/or T score) by its designated proportion to obtain its weighted score.

FIGURE 14.7
Weight Assigned to Nine Tests Using School District Policy

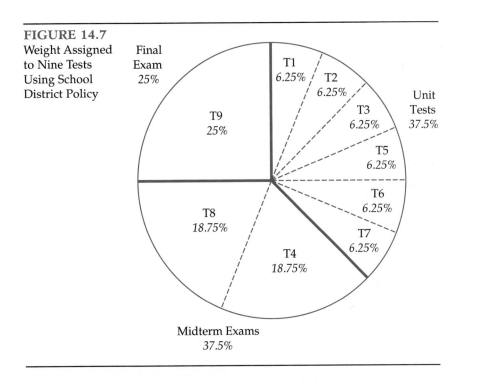

TABLE 14.2
Weighted Scores for the Nine Posttests

Unit Test 1: Sept. 10

	X̄ = 16	Items = 20		GL	
	SD = 4	Wt. = .056		1–3	Gr.
Students	%	Wt.%	T	Wt.T	
Allen, B.	14	70	3.92	45	2.52	2	C
Baker, J.	18	90	5.04	55	3.08	3	A

Unit Test 2: Sept. 17

	X̄ = 21	Items = 25		GL	
	SD = 3	Wt. = .056		4–6	Gr.
	%	Wt.%	T	Wt.T	
Allen, B.	19	76	4.26	43	2.42	2	C
Baker, J.	25	100	5.6	63	3.54	3	A

Unit Test 3: Sept. 24

	X̄ = 24	Items = 30		GL	
	SD = 3	Wt. = .056		7–9	Gr.
Students	%	Wt.%	T	Wt.T	
Allen, B.	22	73	4.09	45	2.42	2	C
Baker, J.	28	93	5.21	63	3.54	3	A

Midterm Exam Test 4: Oct. 1

	X̄ = 43	Items = 50		GL	
	SD = 4	Wt. = .167		1–9	Gr.
	%	Wt.%	T	Wt.T	
Allen, B.	43	86	14.36	50	8.35	7	B
Baker, J.	47	94	15.7	60	10.02	9	A

Unit Test 5: Oct. 8

	X̄ = 16	Items = 20		GL	
	SD = 2	Wt. = .056		10–12	Gr.
Students	%	Wt.%	T	Wt.T	
Allen, B.	15	75	4.20	45	2.52	2	C
Baker, J.	20	100	5.60	70	3.92	3	A

Unit Test 6: Oct. 15

	X̄ = 16	Items = 20		GL	
	SD = 3	Wt. = .056		13–14	Gr.
	%	Wt.%	T	Wt.T	
Allen, B.	15	75	4.2	47	2.62	2	C
Baker, J.	19	95	5.32	60	3.36	2	A

Unit Test 7: Oct. 22

	X̄ = 26	Items = 30		GL	
	SD = 3	Wt. = .056		15–16	Gr.
Students	%	Wt.%	T	Wt.T	
Allen, B.	25	83	4.65	47	2.62	2	B
Baker, J.	27	90	5.04	53	2.98	2	A

Midterm Exam Test 8: Nov. 3

	X̄ = 38	Items = 45		GL	
	SD = 4	Wt. = .167		10–16	Gr.
	%	Wt.%	T	Wt.T	
Allen, B.	39	87	14.53	52.5	8.77	5	B
Baker, J.	42	93	15.53	60	10.02	7	A

Final Exam: Nov. 5

	X̄ = 42	Items = 50		GL	
	SD = 5	Wt. = .333		1–16	Gr.
Students	%	Wt.%	T	Wt.T	
Allen, B.	45	90	29.97	55	18.65	14	A
Baker, J.	50	100	33.3	66	21.98	16	A

Term 1 Summary
Composite Scores

	%	T	GL	Gr.
			16	
Allen, B.	84	51	14	
Baker, J.	96	62	16	

The weighted percentage correct and weighted T scores for each of the nine tests are calculated in the sample gradebook in Table 14.2 for two students. The first column identifies the students. The first column within each test section contains their raw scores, and the next two columns contain the students' percentage correct scores (%) and weighted percentage correct scores (Wt.%). For B. Allen, the weighted percentage correct score for unit test 1 was obtained by multiplying his percentage correct score (70) by the assigned weight (.056) to obtain the weighted percentage correct score of 3.92. The next two columns within each test section contain the students' T scores (T) and weighted T scores (Wt.T). B. Allen's T score of 45 was multiplied by the assigned weight .056 to obtain his weighted T score of 2.52. Notice in the example that all unit tests have a weighting factor of .056, the midterms have weighting factors of .167, and the final exam has a weighting factor of .333.

Combining Weighted Scores into Term Composite Scores You should reserve columns in the gradebook to record term summary data. You will need one column for the students' composite percentage correct scores, one column for their composite T scores if you choose, one column for the total number of goals mastered, and one column for the assigned grade. An example of the term summary section of the gradebook is illustrated in the bottom right-hand section of Table 14.2.

With the weighted scores calculated for each test and summary columns designated in the gradebook, you are ready to calculate and record the term composite scores. The term composite percentage correct scores are obtained by summing the weighted percentage correct scores for all tests administered during the term. In the example, B. Allen's term composite percentage correct score is 3.92 + 4.26 + 4.09 + 14.36 . . . + 29.97, for a term composite percentage correct score of 84. The sum of J. Baker's weighted percentage correct scores is 96. These criterion-referenced composite scores generally reflect the proportion of test items that students answered correctly during the term, and they are used as the basis for students' grades when a school district's grading standards are defined using a 100-point scale.

Term composite scores can also be based on the weighted T scores, and these scores reflect the student's norm-referenced standing in the class. B. Allen's term composite T score is obtained by summing his weighted T scores for the term, and his composite T score is 2.52 + 2.42 + . . . 18.65, for a total of 51. His term composite T score of 51 is very close to the mean score of the class ($T = 50$), and it reflects that his achievement during the term was average compared to class members. J. Baker's composite T score of 62 is greater than one standard deviation above the mean ($T = 60$), and it reflects that his achievement during the term was above average compared to his classmates.

Converting Composite Scores into Term Grades

After calculating the composite scores, you need to convert them to grades. This conversion requires selecting a range of composite scores for each grade.

These score ranges are called *grading standards*. Some school districts have policies that set common grading standards throughout the district. When this is the case, each grade and the range of composite scores required to earn it are described on the report card or in the teacher's manual. The three sets of grading standards shown in Table 14.3 are common.

These standards differ in the range of composite scores assigned for each grade. The first set assigns the highest eleven scores a grade of *A*, and the *B*, *C*, and *D* grade categories each contain 10 scores. It is the most lenient of the three standards. The grades in the second set have equal score ranges, but they include only 8 points instead of 10. The third set differs from the first two in that it has unequal score ranges for the grades. The range of scores for an *A* is only 6 points, the range for a *B* is 7 points, and the range for both *C* and *D* grades is 9 points. Therefore, this set is more rigorous at the high than at the low end of the scale.

Converting your students' composite scores to grades is easy when your district prescribes grade standards. You simply locate and assign the grade that corresponds to the earned composite scores. For example, if your district prescribed the first set of grade standards, B. Allen, who earned a composite score of 84, would receive a *B*. However, this student would be assigned a *C* if the second or third set of standards were applied. J. Baker, who earned a composite score of 96, would be assigned an *A* using any of the three grade standards.

When the district does not prescribe composite score ranges for grades, you need to set your own. There are two options to use in setting grade standards. One is to set standards based solely on students' achievement of the goals, called *criterion-referenced grading*. The other is to set standards based on students' relative performances, called *norm-referenced grading*. Criterion-referenced grading is preferable because it more clearly communicates the amount of information and skills each student has achieved.

TABLE 14.3
Three Sets of Grading Standards

| Grade | Standards and Ranges of Corresponding Composite Scores | | |
	Standard 1	Standard 2	Standard 3
A	90–100	93–100	95–100
B	80–89	85–92	88–94
C	70–79	77–84	79–87
D	60–69	69–76	70–78
F	59 and below	68 and below	69 and below

Using Criterion-Referenced Standards Setting standards for criterion-referenced grading is a matter of professional judgment. You need to select the composite score ranges that reflect outstanding, good, questionable, and inadequate achievement. You also need to select a score below which students will be assigned a failing grade. An outstanding, or *A*, grade should communicate to other people that a student has mastered all the skills covered and has done so at a high level. A grade of *B* should communicate that a student has mastered all or most skills, at least at a minimum level. A grade of *C* should reflect that the student has mastered the majority of the skills but is struggling. A grade of *D* should reflect that the student is having difficulty with many of the skills, and an *F* should reflect that the student has made little, if any, progress on the goals studied during the term.

To set your own grading standards, you need to select the lowest composite score that reflects each of the five grade levels. The minimum score for each grade can be set by (1) predicting a score range within which you believe the minimum score should fall, (2) reviewing the number of goals mastered by students who earn composite scores within the chosen range, and (3) selecting a cut-off score that best reflects that grade. For example, you might predict that the cut-off score for an *A* should be somewhere between 90 and 95. The total goals mastered column in the gradebook should be reviewed for students who earn composite scores in this range to determine whether they have mastered all the goals. If students who earn scores of 90 have mastered all the goals, then 90 could be set as the minimum score. However, if students who earn this score fail to master some of the goals, then you might want to set a higher cut-off score for an *A*. The same procedure can be followed to select the minimum score for each grade.

An alternative method for setting cut-off scores that is quicker, but not as thorough, is to (1) establish the lower limit for *A* and *D* grades, using the previously described method; (2) find the score range between the minimum *A* and *D* grades; and (3) divide this range by 3 to set the score ranges for the *D, C,* and *B* grades. For example, if you set 90 as the cut-off score for an *A* and 65 as the cut-off score for a *D*, the difference between these two scores is 25 points (90 minus 65). Dividing 25 by 3, you obtain 8.3 points. Therefore, the *D, C,* and *B* ranges will each contain about 8 points.

Next, you need to locate the minimum score for each grade. You can do so using the following steps:

1. Select the exact number of points for each grade. Assume you decide to make the *D* and *B* ranges equal 8 points and the *C* range equal 9 points.
2. Subtract the assigned number of points for a *B* (8) from the lowest *A* score (90) to identify the minimum score for a *B* (90 − 8 = 82).

3. Subtract the assigned number of points for a *C* (9) from the lowest *B* score to identify the minimum score for a *C* (82 – 9 = 73).
4. Subtract the assigned number of points for a *D* (8) from the lowest *C* score to identify the minimum score for a *D* (73 – 8 = 65). This score should match the one initially selected as the minimum *D* score, 65, which it does.

Thus, your grading standards would be the following:

Grade	Composite Score Range
A	90–100 (11 points)
B	82–89 (8 points)
C	73–81 (9 points)
D	65–72 (8 points)
F	64 and below

After establishing a range of scores for each grade, you can convert each student's term composite score to the matching letter grade. Using these standards, B. Allen, who earned a term composite score of 84 in the preceding example, would be assigned a grade of *B*; J. Baker, who earned a composite score of 96, would be assigned an *A*.

Using Norm-Referenced Standards   Although it is not recommended, some teachers choose to assign grades based on the relative performance of students in the class. If you want to use a purely norm-referenced grading system, you will need to base the grades you assign on term composite *T* scores. Recall that a *T* score is comprised of the student's raw score, the class's mean score, and the class's standard deviation. In essence, the *T* score reflects the student's relative performance on the test compared to the class. It is the ratio of the deviation of the student's raw score from the group's mean score compared to the group's standard deviation. The term composite *T* score reflects a student's achievement compared to the class on all tests administered during the term.

Rather than how much curriculum content the student has mastered, norm-referenced grades reflect a student's achievement level within a group. A norm-referenced grade of A should communicate to other people that a student's achievement is outstanding *compared to other students in the class*. A grade of B should indicate above-average achievement, and a grade of C should communicate average-level achievement in the group. A grade of D should reflect below-average achievement, and an F grade should communicate progress well below that of classmates.

Similar to criterion-referenced grading, setting standards for norm-referenced grades is a matter of professional judgment since there are no exact rules for establishing the range of *T* scores that should be equivalent to each letter grade assigned. Perhaps the best way to proceed in equating composite *T* scores with term grades would be the following:

1. Create a frequency distribution of term composite *T* scores.
2. Locate benchmark scores reflecting the mean and standard deviations below and above the mean (e.g., 20, 30, 40, 50, 60, 70).
3. Examine the shape of the distribution relative to the benchmarks (e.g., wide, tall, symmetrical, skewed).
4. Consider the achievement characteristics of the class (e.g., heterogeneous or homogeneous; high, average, or low).
5. Equate composite *T* score ranges with the letter grades that appear most reasonable based on the group's achievement characteristics and the distribution of *T* scores.

This list of steps implies that two factors—score distribution and group achievement characteristics—can influence the matching of composite *T* scores and letter grades. Consider first how the score distribution might influence your decisions. You might assign different grades to different scores for a distribution that is a symmetrical, narrow, bell-shaped curve than for a distribution that has an extreme negative skew. The two different distributions in Figure 14.8 illustrate this situation. In the top, bell-shaped distribution, T scores range from 30 to 70, whereas in the bottom, negatively skewed distribution, *T* scores range from 20 to 59. Obviously, the assignment of letter grades to *T* scores would differ for the two distributions.

The second factor to consider is the achievement characteristics of the class. Suppose you teach a homogeneous group of high-achieving students. Regardless of the shape of the distribution of *T* scores, does this mean that

FIGURE 14.8
Possible
Composite
T Score
Distributions

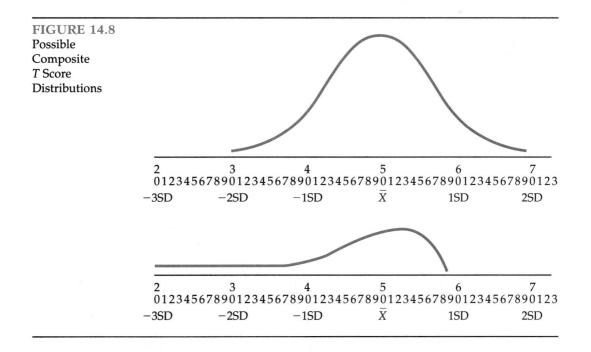

some students should be assigned grades of F simply because their scores are at the bottom in a high-achieving class? Should a student who earned a *T* score of 50 be assigned a C grade to reflect average performance in the class even though the *T* score of 50 equates to a composite percentage correct score of 85 or above? The answer to these questions is obviously no, and these examples illustrate the difficulties teachers encounter when trying to use purely norm-referenced standards for assigning term grades. They also illustrate why school districts typically specify percentage correct scores in their grading policies.

At this point you are probably wondering why teachers would want to calculate *T* scores for each test and for a term composite score when they are not particularly useful for assigning term grades. *T* scores help teachers communicate information about a student's performance that cannot readily be illustrated using percentage correct scores. For example, *T* scores are used to analyze a student's performance across time and tests since they have a common mean (50) and standard deviation (10). They help teachers determine and communicate whether students are holding their own, gaining ground, or losing ground compared to other students in the class. A downward trend in a student's *T* scores over the term could signal a problem that should be communicated to parents, whereas an upward trend would undoubtedly please the parents of a student who earned a low grade for the term.

Comparing Composite Score Outcomes Using Different Grading Systems and Weighting Plans

If you calculate both term composite percentage correct scores and term composite *T* scores, you should not be surprised to find that a student's rank in the class differs for the two types of composite scores. Differentially weighting tests administered during a term can also affect students' class ranks using either type of composite score. Table 14.4 illustrates how using one or the other composite score and different weighting plans can affect the term rank of three students on two tests. The top portion of the table illustrates the outcome of composite percentage correct and *T* scores when the two tests are weighted equally, with each test contributing 50 percent to the composite score. For each student, the raw scores, percentage correct scores, weighted percentage correct scores (Wt.%), *T* scores, and weighted *T* scores (Wt.*T*) are listed for the two tests. The far right columns contain the students' composite scores. Notice that when using the percentage correct composite scores, all three students earn composite scores of 90, illustrating the same overall achievement level for the three students. In contrast, the composite *T* scores differ for the three students. Jones earned a *T* score of 52, Miller a score of 50, and Thomas a score of 49. Were grades to be assigned based on the composite *T* scores, the students could possibly be assigned different grades depending on where the established cut-off score was placed.

TABLE 14.4
A Comparison of the Rank of Composite Scores Using Percentage Correct Scores, *T* Scores, and Different Weights of Tests

Test One Weighted 50% and Test Two Weighted 50%

	Test One					Test Two					Term Composites	
	X̄/SD	%	Wt.%	T	Wt.T	X̄/SD	%	Wt.%	T	Wt.T	%	T
	18/3	20	.5		.5	18/5	20	.5		.5		
Jones	20	100	50	57	29	16	80	40	46	23	90	52
Miller	18	90	45	50	25	18	90	45	50	25	90	50
Thomas	16	80	40	43	22	20	100	50	54	27	90	49

Test One Weighted 80% and Test Two Weighted 20%

	Test One					Test Two					Term Composites	
	X̄/SD	%	Wt.%	T	Wt.T	X̄/SD	%	Wt.%	T	Wt.T	%	T
	18/3	20	.8		.8	18/5	20	.2		.2		
Jones	20	100	80	57	46	16	80	16	46	9	96	55
Miller	18	90	72	50	40	18	90	18	50	10	90	50
Thomas	16	80	64	43	34	20	100	20	54	11	84	45

Test One Weighted 20% and Test Two Weighted 80%

	Test One					Test Two					Term Composites	
	X̄/SD	%	Wt.%	T	Wt.T	X̄/SD	%	Wt.%	T	Wt.T	%	T
	18/3	20	.2		.2	18/5	20	.8		.8		
Jones	20	100	20	57	11	16	80	64	46	37	84	48
Miller	18	90	18	50	10	18	90	72	50	40	90	50
Thomas	16	80	16	43	9	20	100	80	54	43	96	52

The middle set of scores contains the same raw score for the three students on the two tests with the same means and standard deviations. The second set of scores differs only in that Test One will contribute 80 percent and Test Two will contribute 20 percent to the composite scores. Using this weighting plan for the two tests, the students' composite percentage correct scores no longer equal 90; instead, they range from 96 to 84. Such large differences in term composite percentage correct scores would undoubtedly result in different term grades for the three students. Notice also the greater differences in the students' composite *T* scores. The resulting range (55 – 45 = 10) is as wide as the standard deviation for *T* scores.

The third set of scores in Table 14.4 contains the same raw scores, means, and standard deviations as the first two sets. In this set, however, the first test contributes 20 percent and the second test contributes 80 percent to the composite score. Using this weighting plan, the students' composite percentage correct scores are not equal at 90, as in the first set, and they are in the reverse order of the scores in the second set. Weighting the second test by .80 results in reversing the rank of Jones and Thomas for both the composite percentage and *T* scores.

One final observation about the test data in Table 14.4 should be noted. It is not possible to use the norm-referenced *T* score to determine students' criterion-referenced skill levels in a domain. Notice in the first set of equally weighted scores that Miller earned a composite *T* score of 50. Such a score reflects that Miller's performance was quite average in the class. Now match this average-level *T* score with Miller's percentage correct composite score of 90. Obviously, Miller's average group performance reflects very good achievement of the skills taught during the term.

In summary, teachers need to be thoughtful about whether to use a criterion-referenced or a norm-referenced grading system. They also should take care in deciding whether and how to weight test scores differentially that are obtained during a term. Regardless of students' raw scores, different types of composite scores and different weighting plans can influence the final term grades assigned to students.

Calculating Semester and Annual Grades

At the conclusion of two or more terms, you need to combine term grades into a semester grade; at the end of the year, you may need to combine semester grades into an annual grade. Suppose you teach in a school district that has two terms in a semester and a comprehensive semester exam that, by district policy, contributes 25 percent to the semester grade. In your gradebook, you need to create semester summary columns for the composite score for each term, the semester exam raw score and percentage or *T* score, the weighted scores for each measure, the semester composite score, and the semester grade.

The first step is to identify the percentage each measure is to contribute to the semester composite score. Since the semester exam contributes 25 percent to the semester grade, the term composite scores will contribute the remaining 75 percent. Undoubtedly, you will want to weight the terms equally, so each term composite score will contribute one-half the 75 percent, or 37.5 percent.

The second step is to convert the percentages assigned to weighting factors. The 25 percent assigned for the semester exam is converted to a weighting factor of .25, and the 37.5 percent for each term composite score is converted to a weighting factor of .375 to ensure that each measure contributes the desired amount to the semester composite scores. Next, you should

TABLE 14.5
Semester I Summary

	Term I: .375			.375	Term II: .375			.375	Sem. Exam: .25				.25	Sem. Summary		
	% Comp	Wt. %	T Comp	Wt. T	% Comp	Wt. %	T Comp	Wt. T	$\overline{X}$/SD 40/4	% 50	Wt. %	T	Wt. T	%	T	Grade
Students									$\overline{X}$							
Allen, B.	84	32	51	19	88	33	55	21	42	84	21	55	14	86	54	B
Baker, J.	96	36	62	23	93	35	60	23	45	90	23	63	16	94	62	A

TABLE 14.6
Annual Summary

Students	Semester 1 Composite %	T	Semester 2 Composite %	T	Total %	T	Annual Composite %	T	Grade
Allen, B.	86	54	80	55	165	109	83	55	B
Baker, J.	94	62	95	60	189	122	95	61	A

(1) calculate the weighted scores and (2) sum the weighted scores to obtain the semester composite scores. These calculations for two students are illustrated in Table 14.5. The last task is to convert these semester composite scores to semester grades using the scale established for term grades.

A slightly different process is used to calculate annual grades. Usually, the two semesters are weighted equally when combined into a composite score for the year, and there is no comprehensive annual exam to be combined with the semester composite scores. Table 14.6 illustrates how semester composite scores are combined to obtain the annual grade. The students' composite scores for the two semesters are added together and this sum is divided by 2 to obtain the annual composite score. These scores are then converted to the annual grade using the established grading scale.

CREATING THE CONDUCT RECORD

In addition to reporting achievement, teachers are often expected to measure and report students' conduct in such areas as study habits, attitude toward learning, and citizenship. The procedures for developing behavior rating scales to judge conduct are described in Chapter 11. During the grading period, you would follow an observation schedule and use the rating scales to score students' behavior. Similar to achievement test scores, these conduct scores should be recorded in the gradebook, combined into composite scores, and converted to the marks prescribed on the report card.

Recording Scores

Since different behaviors are reported separately, you can create an area for each in the conduct section of the gradebook. For example, if you are expected to report attitude toward learning, study habits, and citizenship, you would need three separate areas in the record. The number of columns required for each behavior depends on the number of times it was rated during the term. If you rated each behavior three times, you would need three columns to record students' scores. To accommodate your work at the end of the term, you should reserve three additional columns: one for the total score, one for the composite score, and one for the assigned mark. The gradebook section for attitude toward learning might appear as follows:

Conduct:			Attitude toward Learning			
Date	9-21	10-10	10-30	Total	Composite	Grade
Possible score:	18	18	18	54		
Allen, B.	12	13	14	____	____	____
Baker, J.	18	16	18	____	____	____

The conduct is identified in the top row, and the dates when students were rated and column titles appear in the second row. The third row is reserved for the total number of points included on the attitude-toward-learning instrument on page 352, and students' scores are listed in the remaining rows.

Combining Scores into a Composite Score

There are two factors to consider before combining conduct scores into a composite score: converting all scores to a common scale and determining the amount of weight each measure should contribute. Relative to a common scale, the same rating scale is usually used each time a behavior is scored, and no conversion should be necessary. Also, you will probably want each measure to contribute an equal amount of weight to the term composite score. Therefore, you will not assign any weights. If you want to weight the measures differently, you should identify weighting factors as you did for posttest scores, reserve space in the gradebook for weighted scores, and convert raw scores to weighted scores before summing them.

Composite scores for conduct are calculated the same way as composite scores for achievement. For equally weighted measures, the steps are (1) Sum the individual scores to obtain the total and (2) Divide the total by the number of scores to obtain the average or composite score. The following example shows the calculation of composite scores for B. Allen and J. Baker.

Conduct:				Attitude toward Learning		
Date	9-21	10-10	10-30	Total	Composite	Grade
Possible score:	18	18	18	54		
Allen, B.	12	13	14	39	13	
Baker, J.	18	16	18	52	17	

Converting Composite Scores to Marks

The final step in the procedure is to convert term composite scores into marks. The marks used to communicate conduct are generally described on the report card. Some school districts use a three-category scale, whereas others use four- or five-category scales. The three-category scale is often *S* for satisfactory, *N* for needs improvement; and *U* for unsatisfactory. The four-category scale might use *E* for excellent, *G* for good, *N* for needs improvement, and *U* for unsatisfactory. The five-category scale might use *A* through *F*, or *1* through *5*, to communicate different levels of behavior.

One way to convert composite scores to report card marks is to (1) identify the possible range of composite scores, (2) divide this range by the number of grade categories prescribed by the district, and (3) assign a relatively equal number of scores to each category. Suppose the highest possible composite score for attitude toward learning is 18 and the lowest possible score is 6. You have a potential range of 13 points, including the lowest and highest scores. This range of 13 points might be divided in the following ways for scales that include three, four, and five categories.

Three-Category Scale		Four-Category Scale		Five-Category Scale	
Mark	*Score Range*	*Mark*	*Score Range*	*Mark*	*Score Range*
S	15, 16, 17, 18	E	16, 17, 18	A	16, 17, 18
N	11, 12, 13, 14	G	13, 14, 15	B	13, 14, 15
U	6, 7, 8, 9, 10	N	9, 10, 11, 12	C	10, 11, 12
		U	6, 7, 8	D	8, 9
				F	6, 7

Based on a three-category scale, B. Allen's composite score, 13, would be converted to an *N*; J. Baker's composite score, 17, would be *S*. On the four-category scale, Allen would receive a *G* and Baker an *E*. On the five-category scale, Allen and Baker would receive a *B* and an *A*, respectively. The standards you select should be recorded in the gradebook for reference.

CONFOUNDING THE ACHIEVEMENT GRADE

In their efforts to create a comprehensive index of students' progress, some teachers mix conduct and achievement. Although they may believe that mixing these variables improves the accuracy of students' grades, exactly the opposite occurs. The term used to describe mixing variables is *confounding*. When conduct is confounded with achievement, the meaning of the achievement grade is compromised, and valid interpretation becomes difficult, if not impossible. Four common ways that teachers confound achievement grades are (1) treating practice tests as posttests, (2) administering unannounced posttests, (3) reducing posttest scores for misbehavior, and (4) using extra-credit assignments to alter grades.

It is not uncommon to find teachers who treat practice tests and routine homework assignments as posttests. This is typically done to encourage students to complete their assignments and to do so carefully. When practice tests are used as posttests, students' initial attempts to perform skills are confounded with their progress following instruction, practice, and feedback. Since the purpose for practice tests is rehearsal, they are premature measures of achievement; and students' scores on practice tests tend to be lower than their scores on legitimate posttests. Thus, practice test scores negatively influence the composite score. Teachers who confound practice and achievement usually attempt to minimize this negative influence by reducing the percentage that practice tests contribute to the composite score, eliminating the lowest practice test score, providing opportunities for extra-credit work, or a combination of these three strategies.

A second confounding practice is administering unannounced posttests, sometimes called *pop quizzes*. The usual explanation teachers give for using such tests is to keep students studying on a regular basis rather than cramming just before a scheduled test. This practice, however, confounds study habits and actual achievement. Low scores could be attributed to the fact that either students did not study or they were experiencing difficulty learning the skills. The consequence of administering unannounced posttests is that these scores tend to be lower than scores on scheduled tests. Thus, they also have a negative influence on composite scores and grades. Like teachers who use practice tests as posttests, those who use unannounced tests generally need to develop strategies to counter their negative influence.

A third practice that confounds conduct and achievement is reducing earned posttest scores for unacceptable behavior. These unacceptable behaviors can include habitually submitting product development tests late, talking or being otherwise disruptive during a test, or cheating on a test. The reason usually given for altering the earned scores is to teach students that such misbehaviors will not be tolerated. However, this practice confounds achievement with lack of judgment and immaturity. Students caught cheating on a test should be required to take another form of the test so that a legitimate measure of their progress is obtained. Alternative strategies, besides reducing earned scores, should be sought for encouraging promptness, consideration, and honesty.

A fourth practice that confounds achievement and conduct is using extra-credit assignments to alter grades. Extra-credit assignments are those not required of all students in the regular conduct of the class. The reason typi-cally given for altering grades using extra credit is to give students who are not satisfied with their earned scores an opportunity to improve their grades. However, this practice confounds students' achievement of the prescribed goals and their effort. For example, some students may want a higher grade than their test performance warrants. When given an extra-credit option, these students will complete the additional work to improve their grades. Suppose that students who demonstrated mastery at good (B) and question-able (C) levels are permitted to raise these grades one letter by completing an extra report, paper, or project. Does completing the assignment mean that they have now mastered the skills studied during the term at a higher level? Probably not. Instead, it means they have mastered the skills at the measured level but are willing to expend additional effort to obtain a higher grade. Thus, the higher grade masks their mastery level.

Any one of these confounding practices confuses the meaning of the grade. However, when two or more of them are used, the grade's meaning becomes increasingly distorted. The grade no longer reflects students' mas-tery level, but this level plus rehearsal, study habits, misbehavior, and effort. Parents and school administrators will undoubtedly misinterpret such grades. It is also unlikely that confounded grades will correlate very well with students' scores on districtwide or standardized tests that measure the same skills. The best practice is to assign achievement grades solely for achieve-ment. You can communicate students' inadequate study habits, misbehavior, and outstanding effort using the space for such conduct on the report card.

PREPARING FOR CONFERENCES

Many school districts schedule parent-teacher conferences following the dis-tribution of report cards. These conferences permit teachers to explain stu-dents' grades and answer questions parents may have about their child's achievement, conduct, and attendance.

To prepare for these individual conferences, you need to review each student's record, select the information to present, and decide how you will present your observations. Preparing for conferences will be easier if you develop a generic term summary form that can be completed from data in the gradebook as conferences are scheduled. You might include the following information on the form:

1. The goals covered during the term
2. The goals mastered by the student
3. The student's percentage score on each posttest administered during the term
4. The student's composite score
5. The group's average composite score, standard deviation, and range

TABLE 14.7
Generic Performance Summary Form for Parent Conferences

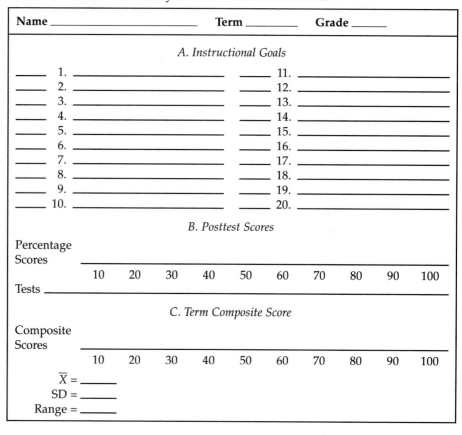

A sample generic form is illustrated in Table 14.7. The top row contains space for the student's name, the term, and the grade earned. Section A contains space for listing the goals covered during the term. The block preceding each goal can be used to indicate whether the student mastered it. Section B contains a percentage scale for recording the student's posttest scores on each test. The area beneath this scale can be used to list quizzes, unit tests, midterm exams, and the final exam. Section C includes another scale that can be used to illustrate the student's composite score, as well as the class mean, standard deviation, and range.

At the conclusion of each term, a master form for the term can be completed by inserting the particular goals studied in section A; listing the posttests administered in section B; and inserting the class mean, standard deviation, and range for the class composite scores in section C. Multiple copies of the master form can be made and then completed for each student as conferences are scheduled.

Table 14.8 contains a sample form completed for Brian Allen for the first term. To complete the form, his name and term grade are inserted in the top row; the goals he mastered are checked in section A; the location of his percentage score on each posttest is inserted in section B; and the location of his composite percentage correct score is added to section C.

During the conference, the form can be used as a reference for presenting and discussing his progress. For example, section A can be used to describe the skills studied during the term and Brian's mastery or failure of each.

TABLE 14.8
Performance Summary Form

Name *Allen, Brian*	Term ___I___	Grade ___B___

A. Instructional Goals (X's indicate at least minimal mastery)

X	1. Group common words or objects	X	11. Select adjectives to modify nouns
X	2. Name synonyms		12. Select adverbs to modify verbs, adjectives, & adverbs
X	3. Name antonyms	X	13. Write plural forms of singular words & vice versa
X	4. Add prefixes to root words	X	14. Match singular subjects and verbs
	5. Add suffixes to root words	X	15. Match plural subjects and verbs
X	6. Form contractions	X	16. Select the correct verb tense
X	7. Use coordinating conjunctions		17.
X	8. Use correlative conjunctions		18.
X	9. Use subordinating conjunctions		19.
X	10. Substitute pronouns for nouns		20.

B. Posttest Scores

Percentage Scores

```
                                        6
                                        5                8
                                       132             749
        _____
        10    20    30    40    50    60    70    80    90    100
```

Tests   *Unit tests: 1, 2, 3, 5, 6, 7; Midterm exams: 4, 8; Final: 9*

C. Term Composite Score ___84___

Composite Scores

```
                                  |—————————————————•————|
        _____
        10    20    30    40    50    60    70    80    90    100
```

$\overline{X}$ = 81
SD = 11
Range = 44 to 96

Section B can be used to explain the level and consistency of his performance throughout the term. Trends in his progress, such as his improved test performance toward the end of the term, will be obvious from the location and sequence of the scores. Section C can be used not only to describe his achievement level but also to compare his progress to that of the class. Although completing such a form will take only a couple of minutes, it will help ensure that you are prepared for conferences and can present factual data for discussion.

If you have developed portfolios of students' work and portfolio assessment forms that demonstrate students' status and progress on key instructional goals studied during a grading period, you should use them during parent conferences. Recall that the main purpose for portfolios is to enhance communication about students' progress. Materials in the portfolio can illustrate strengths in a student's work as well as areas where the student needs to improve. These concrete illustrations of status and progress will communicate achievement to parents in a manner that will enable them to become involved in supplemental learning at home. Real work samples and portfolio assessment forms will communicate development in a way not possible using abstract grades and numbers. You should remember, however, that the grades assigned and the materials included in the portfolio should be congruent with the level of achievement they communicate to parents. If a student is assigned a grade of C or D and the portfolio contains only the student's best samples of work, or it does not illustrate initial status and growth, then parents can become confused about your grading system. Recall that a complete discussion of developing and using student portfolios is included in Chapter 13.

DEVELOPING CRITERION-REFERENCED REPORT CARDS

Many school districts today use performance summary forms similar to the one illustrated in Table 14.8 as the actual report card sent to parents; these are especially popular in the primary grades. Performance summaries that provide information about a student's mastery status on each instructional goal studied during a term aids parents in understanding their child's progress.

There are many formats for criterion-referenced report cards. Some are very similar to the form in Table 14.8, and they include a term summary letter grade, the student's performance level on each goal studied during the term, and a summary of the student's test scores earned during the term. Some report cards include the student's mastery status and test scores but do not contain either a composite score or letter grade. Other forms include only a student's mastery status on key instructional goals studied during a term. When this is the case, mastery levels are often reported as mastery, partial mastery, and nonmastery. Completing these report cards is quite easy when you use mastery summary forms such as the one illustrated in Table 8.8 as the basis for completing the report card.

COMPUTER TECHNOLOGY

One of the real advantages of computerized programs such as ParSCORE and ParGRADE (Economics Research, Inc., 1992) is the flexible grading and reporting options they provide. As you name and score each of your tests during a term, students' raw scores are fed into the student roster under the designated test name. The raw scores in the roster are then converted to common scale scores such as percentage correct or T scores, weighted as you designate, and combined by the program to create cumulative points (composite scores). Using these cumulative points, grades are automatically assigned to students based on the weighting plan and grading criteria you specify. Computer-based gradebook programs have not radically changed teachers' grading tasks, but they have radically changed the time required to perform them. The following paragraphs briefly describe the ParSCORE and ParGRADE gradebook, called the student roster, and some options for weighting tests and assigning grades.

The Student Roster

Recall from Chapter 2 that the initial roster created for a new class contains students' identification numbers, names, telephone numbers, their grading code, and the teacher's comments. That initial roster forms the basis for the sample test roster that is included in Figure 14.9. Information identifying the course and instructor is printed at the top of the page. The first column contains the entry number, and the second column contains the students' assigned numbers. The third column contains the students' names, and the fourth column contains the grading codes assigned for each student. The next seven columns are reserved for students' scores. In this sample, raw scores for three exams and two quizzes are illustrated, and space remains for one more quiz and one report. You can include any number of tests and any category of tests in a student roster that you create. The last column of scores, labeled Cum Pts (cumulative points), contains the sum of raw score points the student has earned during the term. The final column contains the grade assigned by the computer according to the teacher's instructions.

The type of information included in Figure 14.9 is created from the initial class roster and from tests you administer as they are named and scored during a term. With the roster in this raw form, you are ready to weight tests, which will automatically adjust students' cumulative points to reflect the weights you enter.

Weighting Tests

There are several options for weighting test scores contained in the roster. One option includes converting all raw scores in the roster to the same scale (percentage correct and T scores are two options), and then multiplying the

FIGURE 14.9
The Student Roster Illustrating Student's Raw Scores

Course #: 3333
 Course: ECON 200
 Day/Time: 2 MWF

Instructor: RALPH LEWIS
Description: MICROECONOMICS
Term/Year: Spring 92

		Code	Exam			Quiz			Rept	Cum	Final
			1	2	3	1	2	3	1	Pts	Grade
	--Possible points--		100	100	100	50	50			400	
----ID #	Name										
1. 820048002	ABOUNTERI, ALBERT		85	80	68	41	34			308	B
2. 811170116	ALBRIGHT, ALLEN E		75	76	78	35	39			303	B
3. 821841184	ALDERSON, WILLIAM A		59	66	82	35	41			283	C
4. 811111118	ANOLLA, ANTHONY R		45	55	86	38	43			267	C
5. 830745070	BANKER, ROBERT F		78	70	92	40	46			326	B
6. 812014201	BARKLEY, RON R	W	56		70	46				172	W
7. 700932093	BLANCHT, BRADLEY E		85	75	90	40	45			335	B
8. 820656062	BLAND, EDITH A	CR	85	75	64	30	32			286	CR
9. 830274029	BRANDLEY, JOHN A		58	62	74	40	36			270	C
10. 811802182	BRENTT, DENISE W		79	58	84	25	42			288	C
11. 821607161	CRENMAN, ELIZABETH A		65	90	84	45	42			326	B
12. 810976094	DAKER, ALBERT P	CR		74	66	45	33			218	NC
13. 820864088	DENNY, CHARLES J		91	92	80	45	40			348	A
14. 820013004	FREEDMAN, LAWRANCE A		95	66	86	45	43			335	B
15. 792239229	GREEN, TINA B		64	66	86	38	43			297	C
16. 770525055	HAROLD, EDWARDO A		84	84	86	46	43			343	A
17. 822264222	HOLTEIN, ANNA E		67	71	64	34	32			268	C
18. 820416041	HOWARD, JERRY L		58	50	68	45	34			255	D
19. 770841087	HYLAND, NATE W		78	70	94	46	47			335	B
20. 830005001	JONNATON, ROGER Q		46	50	84	26	42			248	D
21. 802663266	JUNE, RICHARD U		85	95	82	25	41			328	B
22. 830632061	KENDSLY, ROBERT F		92	95	86	47	43			363	A
23. 812414241	KNEW, BRUCE L		84	80	84	46	42			336	B
24. 820598053	LAWARNCE, ALBERT R		75	65	76	36	38			290	C
25. 820048000	LEWIS, ROBERT R		71	90	66	38	33			298	C
26. 810050005	MANSON, ENSIGN I		85	55	92	40	46			318	B
27. 820447048	MATHEWS, JOHN W		86	80	86	42	43			337	B
28. 830207024	MCMOORE, LOUISE L		54	66	78	30	39			267	C
29. 811220120	MONTCLIFF, JON A		54	56	86	29	43			268	C
30. 790970096	MOORE, JOHN H		83	80	78	50	39			330	B
31. 811265126	MORANS, ELIZABETH A		74	70	80	40	42			306	B
32. 811225126	MORGAN, TINA V		76	80	88	40	44			328	B
33. 820254024	MOVENTON, WILLIAM B		65	69	80	29	40			283	C
34. 820010000	NIELSON, ABBY R		68	71	74	47	37			297	C
35. 800191014	PAULSON, GARY R		62	66	94	41	47			310	B
36. 782067207	PINFOR, JOHN P		65	85	86	39	43			318	B
37. 820024000	PULLMAN, ANNE A		47	50	76	30	38			241	D
38. 791115117	RALPH, DONALD C		69	69	74	35	37			284	C
39. 812021200	REDSON, GEORGE A		65	56	68	30	34			253	D
40. 831113112	RICE, JOHN S		58	85	86	42	43			314	B
41. 831837185	RICE, WILLIAM W		75	46	88	40	44			293	C
42. 820184019	RUMPSON, TOM N		74	75	56	40	28			273	C
43. 790111017	SAMPSON, THOMPSON A		66		66	40	33			205	F

Source: ParSCORE and ParGRADE user's manual (p. 155). Costa Mesa, CA: Economics Research, Inc., 1992.

converted scores for a given test by a constant (weighting factor). When you use this option, you simply indicate the test column and weighting factor you wish to change. The computer automatically adjusts each student's score on the exam by the assigned weighting factor, adjusts the total possible number of points for the test, adjusts the students' cumulative points for the term, and adjusts the students' assigned term grade.

A second option is to specify the amount of weight that entire categories of tests will contribute to the term grade. For example, you might decide to weight:

1. All quizzes as 15 percent of the term grade
2. All unit tests together as 35 percent
3. The midterm as 15 percent
4. The final as 15 percent
5. Project 1 as 10 percent
6. Project 2 as 20 percent

With only these global specifications for how categories of tests are to be weighted, the computer can automatically adjust the relative weights of each type of test. This will ensure that all tests in a single category contribute only the prescribed units of weight to the cumulative points. When you use this option, the students' raw scores are not changed on the roster. Only the cumulative points and grade assigned (last two columns) are changed to reflect your weighting scheme.

Grading Scales

There are four different default codes for assigning grades to students using ParSCORE and ParGRADE (Economics Research, Inc., 1992). Students can be assigned letter grades (e.g., *A, B, C, D, F*); they can be graded as pass/fail marks (e.g., credit or no credit for their work); they can be assigned a mark of *W* when they withdraw from your class; or they can be assigned an *I* mark for work that is incomplete at the end of the term. If you choose to use these generic categories, you can enter for each mark the percentage correct score required. You may also choose to use other categories and name them yourself, or you could tailor them to those specified in the grading policies of your school or school district. One such alternative might be mastery, partial mastery, and nonmastery.

The top portion of Figure 14.10 contains a sample table of the default criteria for assigning grades in ParSCORE and ParTEST and a sample grade distribution report you can get from the programs. The left side of the figure illustrates the percentage of cumulative points required to obtain each letter grade and the percentage of points required to receive credit for the course. You can change these criteria to suit your needs. The right side of the figure illustrates a sample distribution of grades that might result from the defined

FIGURE 14.10

Sample Grading Criteria and Grade Distribution

GRADING CRITERIA					GRADE DISTRIBUTION		
Description	Code	Minimum Percent	Minimum Points	Grade	Grade	Number of Students	Percent of Class
1. EXCELLENT ------------>		90.00	360	A	A	1	2.0
GOOD ------------------>		80.00	320	B	B	16	32.7
AVERAGE -------------->		70.00	280	C	C	14	28.6
POOR ------------------>		60.00	240	D	D	11	22.4
FAILURE -------------->		0.00	0	F	F	4	8.2
		0.00	0		CR	2	4.1
2. CREDIT/-------------->	CR	70.00	280	CR	NC	0	0.0
NO CREDIT ------------>	CR	0.00	0	NC	W	1	2.0
		0.00	0		I	0	0.0
3. WITHDRAWAL --------->	W	0.00	0	W		0	0.0
INCOMPLETE ---------->	I	0.00	0	I			
		0.00	0				
4. CRITERIA FOR	A- ??	89.00	356	A			
SPECIAL CODED	B- ??	79.00	316	B			
STUDENTS	C- ??	69.00	276	C			
	D- ??	59.00	236	D			

[F1] Edit [F2] RowEdit [F3] ColumnEdit [F9] Print [F10] Quit

GRADING CRITERIA					GRADE DISTRIBUTION		
Description	Code	Minimum Percent	Minimum Points	Grade	Grade	Number of Students	Percent of Class
WITHDRAWAL..............	W	0.00	0	W	W	2	4.0
INCOMPLETE..............	I	0.00	0	I	I	0	0.0
----------------------	--	0.00	0		CR	1	2.0
CREDIT..................	CR	65.00	260	CR	NC	1	2.0
NO CREDIT...............	CR	0.00	0	NC	A	3	6.0
----------------------	--	0.00	0		B	19	38.0
EXCELLENT...............	??	85.00	340	A	C	15	30.0
GOOD....................	??	75.00	300	B	D	6	12.0
AVERAGE.................	??	65.00	260	C	F	3	6.0
POOR....................	??	55.00	220	D		0	0.0
FAILURE	??	0.00	0	F			
----------------------	--	0.00	0				
EOPS STUDENTS..........	E	0.00	0				
		90.00	0				
* DEFAULT *		0.00	0				
GRADING CRITERIA		0.00	0				

[F1] Edit [F2] RowEdit [F3] ColumnEdit [F9] Print [F10] Quit

Source: ParSCORE and ParGRADE user's manual (pp. 124, 132). Costa Mesa, CA: Economics Research, Inc., 1992.

grade scale. When you establish your exam weighting scheme and your grading criteria, the program displays the grading distribution you will obtain for the class using the strategy you have chosen. Should you not like the resulting grade distribution, you can readily change either your weighting scheme or your grading scale. The program will quickly recalculate cumulative points and grades and display the new grade distribution from your alternative strategy. The bottom portion of Figure 14.10 illustrates an alternative set of grading criteria and grade distribution. Regardless of the grading scheme you use, a computer-based gradebook will be a valuable time saver for record keeping and grading.

SUMMARY

Each grading term, teachers are expected to evaluate and report students' progress in achievement and conduct as well as to report their attendance. To document and summarize student data, you need to design a gradebook that matches your teaching assignment.

The gradebook should include a daily record in which you document events that occur during each class session. To prepare this section, select the information you will document, choose symbols that represent each type of information, create a legend for the symbols, list class dates, and record the selected behaviors. You will also need a summary section in which to record the frequencies of selected behaviors. Information in the daily record will help you summarize attendance, complete behavior rating scales, and perhaps explain the grades and other marks students earn.

The gradebook should also contain a posttest record. This section is used to record and summarize students' posttest performance. In documenting achievement, you should record general information about each test, such as (1) the format, title, and date; (2) the group's average score and standard deviation; (3) the number of items or points included on the test; and (4) the particular goals and number of goals measured. This information is used to compare tests at the end of the term and to interpret students' scores on each test. To document students' performance, record their raw scores, percentage and/or T scores, the number of goals they mastered, and the grade earned. You should also reserve a column for weighted scores.

At the end of the term, you need to synthesize individual test scores into a term composite score. The steps in this procedure include (1) analyzing the relationship among posttests to determine the weight each test should contribute to the composite score, (2) identifying weighting factors, (3) calculating weighted scores, and (4) calculating composite scores.

The next task is to convert composite scores to term grades using standards. Grade standards are often prescribed by district policy; when they are not, you need to set your own. Standards can be set using either criterion-referenced or norm-referenced methods, although criterion-referenced methods are preferred. Criterion-referenced standards are based on the level of students' performance on the goals studied during the term, and norm-referenced standards are based on relative group performance.

Most school districts also require you to assign marks for conduct in such areas as attitude toward learning, study habits, and citizenship. A third section of the gradebook should be reserved for recording students' scores from behavior rating scales. Similar to posttest scores, conduct scores should be combined into a composite score at the end of the term. These scores are converted to district-prescribed marks using standards you set yourself.

Some teachers confound achievement grades by combining conduct and achievement. This happens when posttest achievement is confounded with rehearsal, study habits, misbehavior, or effort. Such practices should be avoided because they make valid interpretation of the achievement grade impossible.

Teacher-parent conferences are usually scheduled after report cards are sent home. In preparing for these conferences, you need to select the information you want to communicate and decide how to present it. To save time, prepare a generic summary form that includes the selected information. The form can be completed for each student and used as a basis for discussion during scheduled conferences. Making portfolios of students' work can also facilitate communicating progress during the term to students, parents, and school personnel.

Many school districts today use criterion-referenced report cards. Such reports name the key instructional goals studied during a term and the student's mastery status on each one. Some also include the traditional composite score and letter grade. Regardless of the grading policies in your district, computer-based gradebook programs will aid your work in producing both interim and final achievement reports.

PRACTICE EXERCISES

I. **The Gradebook**
   Identify the section of the gradebook (in Column B) in which each of the following types of information (in Column A) should be recorded.

   Column A

   _____ **1.** Scores from behavior rating scales

   _____ **2.** The particular goals and number of goals measured

   _____ **3.** Materials checked out from the resource center

   _____ **4.** Dates of class sessions

   Column B

   a. The Daily Record
   b. The Posttest Record
   c. The Conduct Record

_____ 5. The format, title, and dates of
        tests given
_____ 6. Particular instances of conduct
_____ 7. The number of items or points
        on a test
_____ 8. Attendance
_____ 9. Parent permission granted for
        a field trip
_____ 10. Raw scores
_____ 11. Group performance measures
         including the mean and
         standard deviation
_____ 12. The percentage of items correct

II. Recording Posttest Information

Information about one posttest is given here. On a piece of graph paper, label columns
and insert the test information as you would in the gradebook. Remember to reserve
several columns on the left side to record students' names and a column to record
weighted scores at the end of the term. For the exercise, assume you will use criterion-
referenced grading.

Posttest Information
1. The test was objective and covered goals 1, 2, 3, and 4 in the punctuation unit.
2. It was administered on December 5.
3. The test included 30 items, and the average score and standard deviation were
   25 and 3, respectively.
4. John Anker's raw score was 28, he mastered all four goals, and he earned an *A*.
5. Alice Brown's raw score was 20, she mastered two of the goals (1 and 3), and
   she earned a *D*.

III. Identifying the Percentage Each Test Will Contribute to the Composite Score

Suppose that during one term you administered five quizzes, three unit tests, and a
comprehensive final exam. Based on an analysis of the tests, you decide that:
1. The five quizzes together should contribute 25 percent to the composite score.
2. The three unit tests together should contribute 50 percent.
3. The final exam should contribute 25 percent.
4. The five quizzes should be weighted equally.
5. The three unit tests should be weighted equally.
   A. What percentage will each quiz contribute to the final score?
   B. What percentage will each unit test contribute to the composite score?

IV. Identifying Weighting Factors for Each Test

Using the percentage allocated for each test, identify in Table 14.9 the weighting factor
for each quiz, each unit test, and the final exam in III.

V. Calculating Weighted Scores

A. The posttest record for the nine tests in III is included in Table 14.10. Insert the
   selected weighting factors in the appropriate cell for each test.
B. Calculate weighted percentage correct and *T* scores for each test for the two
   students illustrated.

TABLE 14.9
Weighting Factors for Posttests

Test	Percentage	Weighting Factor
Quizzes		
Unit Tests		
Final Exam		

VI. Calculating Composite Scores
   A. A section, Posttest Summary, is located at the bottom of Table 14.10. Label columns in this section to record term summary information.
   B. Calculate the term composite scores for the two students and record them in this section.
   C. Sum the number of goals mastered by each student.

VII. Setting Standards for Assigning Grades
   A. Grade standards that are based on the number of goals mastered and points earned during a term are called _____ .
   B. Grade standards that are based on the relative position of students' composite scores are called _____ .
   C. In Table 14.11, describe the meaning of each letter grade for both criterion-referenced and norm-referenced grading systems. Check your definitions in Table 14.11F.
   D. Use the following information to determine the score ranges for grades *B, C,* and *D*.

   Grade   *Score Range*
   A = _93_ to _100_
   B = ___ to ___
   C = ___ to ___
   D = _60_ to ___
   F = _59_ and below

   E. Using these grading standards, convert the students' composite scores in Table 14.10 to grades.

VIII. Enrichment
   A. Obtain your school district's policies on grading and look for information that describes:
      1. The type and number of measures that are to be used to measure the students' progress
      2. The percentage a final exam is to contribute to the composite score
      3. The standards for converting composite scores to grades
      4. Whether grade standards are to be criterion-referenced or norm-referenced.
   B. Review your school district's report card for your grade level and identify the categories of behavior that are to be reported.
   C. Design a gradebook that will enable you to document the required information.

TABLE 14.10
Posttest Record for One Term

Quiz 1: January 15th

Students	$\overline{X} =$ 17	Items = 20		GL		
	SD = 2	Wt. =		1		
Students	%	Wt.%	T	Wt.T	(1)	Gr.
Allen, B.	17	85			1	B
Baker, J.	20	100			1	A

Quiz 2 (partially obscured)

Students	$\overline{X} =$					
	SD = 2					
Students	%	W.			(2)	Gr.
Allen, B.	12	80			2,3	C
Baker, J.	13	87			2,3	B

Unit Test 1: January 30th

Students	$\overline{X} =$ 30	Items = 35		GL		
	SD = 3	Wt. =		1–3		
Students	%	Wt.%	T	Wt.T	(3)	Gr.
Allen, B.	31	89			1–3	B
Baker, J.	34	97			1–3	A

Quiz 3: February 6th

Students	$\overline{X} =$ 16	Items = 20		GL		
	SD = 4	Wt. =		4,5		
Students	%	Wt.%	T	Wt.T	(2)	Gr.
Allen, B.	17	85			4,5	B
Baker, J.	19	95			4,5	A

Quiz 4: February 15th

Students	$\overline{X} =$ 21	Items = 25		GL		
	SD = 2	Wt. =		6		
Students	%	Wt.%	T	Wt.T	(1)	Gr.
Allen, B.	20	80			6	C
Baker, J.	23	92			6	A

Unit Test 2: February 20th

Students	$\overline{X} =$ 32	Items = 40		GL		
	SD = 4	Wt. = 0		4–6		
Students	%	Wt.%	T	Wt.T	(3)	Gr.
Allen, B.	32	80			4,5	C
Baker, J.	38	95			4–6	A

Quiz 5: February 28th

Students	$\overline{X} =$ 16	Items = 20		GL		
	SD = 3	Wt. =		7–9		
Students	%	Wt.%	T	Wt.T	(3)	Gr.
Allen, B.	17	85			7–9	B
Baker, J.	20	100			7–9	A

Unit Test 3: March 5th

Students	$\overline{X} =$ 33	Items = 4		GL		
	SD = 4	Wt. = 0		7–9		
Students	%	Wt.%	T	Wt.T	(3)	Gr.
Allen, B.	35	88			7–9	B
Baker, J.	39	98			7–9	A

Term Final Examination: March 15th

Students	$\overline{X} =$ 40	Items = 50		GL		
	SD = 5	Wt. =		1–9		
Students	%	Wt.%	T	Wt.T	(9)	Gr.
Allen, B.	42	84			1–5	B
					7–9	
Baker, J.	46	92			1–9	A

Posttest Summary Composites

TABLE 14.11
Grading Standards

Grade	Criterion-Referenced Standards	Norm-Referenced Standards
A		
B		
C		
D		
F		

D. Select the behaviors you want to record in a daily record and identify symbols you can use to document each one.

E. Based on your subject and grade level, select the information you need for each posttest. Design a format that can be used to systematically record the information.

FEEDBACK

I. The Gradebook

1. c	**7.** b
2. b	**8.** a
3. a	**9.** a
4. a	**10.** b
5. b	**11.** b
6. a	**12.** b

II. Recording Posttest Information

Your information should look like the following:

	Obj. Punctuation 12-5						
	$\overline{X}$ =	25	Items =	30		GL	
	SD =	3	Wt =			1–4	
Students	$\overline{X}$	%	Wt.%	T	Wt.T	(4)	Gr.
Anker, John	28	93		60		1–4	A
Brown, Alice	20	67		33.4		1, 3	D

Did you remember to reserve columns for percentage correct and T scores? Percentage scores are obtained by:

1. Dividing each student's raw score by the total number of items, or points, on the test to obtain the proportion correct.

2. Multiplying the proportion correct by 100 to obtain the percentage.

John: $\dfrac{28}{30} = .93; .93 \times 100 = 93\%$

Alice: $\dfrac{20}{30} = .666; .67 \times 100 = 67\%$

Did you remember to calculate T scores? T scores are calculated by:
1. Subtracting the test mean from each student's raw score
2. Dividing this difference by the test's standard deviation
3. Multiplying this quotient by 10
4. Adding 50 to this product

John: $\dfrac{28 - 25}{3} \times 10 + 50 = 60$ Alice: $\dfrac{20 - 28}{3} \times 10 + 50 = 33.4$

Did you remember to reserve columns for weighted scores that will need to be calculated at the end of the term?

III. Identifying the Percentage Each Test Will Contribute to the Composite Score
   A. Each quiz will contribute 5 percent.

$\dfrac{\text{Total percentage allocated for quizzes}}{\text{Number of quizzes}} = \dfrac{25}{5} = 5 \text{ percent}$

   B. Each unit test will contribute 16.7 percent.

$\dfrac{\text{Total percentage allocated for unit tests}}{\text{Number of unit tests}} = \dfrac{50}{3} = 16.66; 16.7 \text{ percent}$

IV. Identifying Weighting Factors for Each Test
   See Table 14.9F.

V. Calculating Weighted Scores
   A. See Table 14.10F. The weighting factors for each test are inserted in the cell beside the Wt. = cell.

TABLE 14.9F

Test	Percentage	Weighting Factor
Quizzes	5	.05
Unit Test	16.7	.167
Final Exam	25	.25

TABLE 14.10F
Posttest Record for One Term

Quiz 1: January 15th

	$\overline{X}=$	17	Items =	20		GL	
	SD =	2	Wt. =	.05		1	
Students		%	Wt.%	T	Wt.T	(1)	Gr.
Allen, B.	17	85	4.25	50	2.5	1	B
Baker, J.	20	100	5.00	65	3.25	1	A

Quiz 2: January 24th

	$\overline{X}=$	12	Items =	15		GL	
	SD =	2	Wt. =	.05		2,3	
		%	Wt.%	T	Wt.T	(2)	Gr.
Allen, B.	12	80	4	50	2.5	2,3	C
Baker, J.	13	87	4.35	55	2.75	2,3	B

Unit Test 1: January 30th

	$\overline{X}=$	30	Items =	35		GL	
	SD =	3	Wt. =	.167		1–3	
Students		%	Wt.%	T	Wt.T	(3)	Gr.
Allen, B.	31	89	14.86	53.33	8.91	1–3	B
Baker, J.	34	97	16.20	63.33	10.58	1–3	A

Quiz 3: February 6th

	$\overline{X}=$	16	Items =	20		GL	
	SD =	4	Wt. =	.05		4,5	
		%	Wt.%	T	Wt.T	(2)	Gr.
Allen, B.	17	85	4.25	52.5	2.63	4,5	B
Baker, J.	19	95	4.75	57.5	2.88	4,5	A

Quiz 4: February 15th

	$\overline{X}=$	21	Items =	25		GL	
	SD =	2	Wt. =	.05		6	
Students		%	Wt.%	T	Wt.T	(1)	Gr.
Allen, B.	20	80	4	45	2.25	6	C
Baker, J.	23	92	4.6	60	3	6	A

Unit Test 2: February 20th

	$\overline{X}=$	32	Items =	40		GL	
	SD =	4	Wt. =	.167		4–6	
		%	Wt.%	T	Wt.T	(3)	Gr.
Allen, B.	32	80	13.36	50	8.35	4,5	C
Baker, J.	38	95	15.87	65	10.86	4–6	A

Quiz 5: February 28th

	$\overline{X}=$	16	Items =	20		GL	
	SD =	3	Wt. =	.05		7–9	
Students		%	Wt.%	T	Wt.T	(3)	Gr.
Allen, B.	17	85	4.25	53.33	2.67	7–9	B
Baker, J.	20	100	5	63.33	3.17	7–9	A

Unit Test 3: March 5th

	$\overline{X}=$	33	Items =	40		GL	
	SD =	4	Wt. =	.167		7–9	
		%	Wt.%	T	Wt.T	(3)	Gr.
Allen, B.	35	88	14.70	55	9.19	7–9	B
Baker, J.	39	98	16.37	65	10.86	7–9	A

Term Final Examination: March 15th

	$\overline{X}=$	40	Items =	50		GL	
	SD =	5	Wt. =	.25		1–9	
Students		%	Wt.%	T	Wt.T	(9)	Gr.
Allen, B.	42	84	21	54	13.5	1–5	B
						7–9	
Baker, J.	46	92	23	62	15.5	1–9	A

Posttest Summary Composites

	Percentage	T	Goals 9	Term Grade		
Allen, B.	85	53	8	B		
Baker, J.	95	63	9	A		

440

B. The percentage correct and *T* scores are multiplied by the weighting factors to obtain the weighted scores.

VI. **Calculating Composite Scores**
   A. See Table 14.10F. Columns were created in the summary section to record the composite scores, the total number of goals mastered during the term, and the term grade.
   B. The composite scores were calculated by summing the weighted percentage correct scores for each test and by summing the weighted *T* scores for each test.

VII. **Setting Standards for Assigning Grades**
   A. Criterion-referenced standards
   B. Norm-referenced standards
   C. See Table 14.11F.
   D. *Grade   Score Range*
   　　　A = 93 to 100
   　　　B = 82 to 92
   　　　C = 71 to 81
   　　　D = 60 to 70
   　　　F = 59 and below
   These scores were identified using the following steps:
   　1. Identify the range of scores between the lowest *A* and the lowest *D* (93 − 60 = 33).
   　2. Divide this range by 3 (there are three grade levels—*B*, *C*, and *D*) to obtain the range of scores for each grade (33/3 = 11).
   　3. Subtract 11 from 93 to identify the lower limit for a *B* grade (93 − 11 = 82).
   　4. Subtract 11 from 82 to identify the lower limit for a *C* grade (82 − 11 = 71).
   　5. Subtract 11 from 71 to obtain the lower limit for a *D* grade (71 − 11 = 60).
   E. B. Allen would be assigned a *B*, and J. Baker would be assigned an *A*.

TABLE 14.11F
Grading Standards

Grade	Criterion-Referenced Standards	Norm-Referenced Standards
A	Outstanding number of goals mastered and points earned	Outstanding progress compared to classmates
B	Very good number of goals mastered and points earned	Above-average progress compared to classmates
C	Questionable number of goals mastered and points earned—student is experiencing some difficulty	Average progress compared to classmates
D	Inadequate number of goals mastered and points earned	Below-average progress compared to classmates
F	Unacceptable number of goals mastered and points earned	Very little progress compared to classmates

REFERENCE

Economics Research, Inc. (1992). *ParSCORE and ParGRADE user's guide* (pp. 124, 132, 155). Costa Mesa, CA: Economics Research, Inc.

SUGGESTED READINGS

Ebel, R. L., & Frisbee, D. A. (1991). *Essentials of educational measurement* (5th ed.) (pp. 264–284). Englewood Cliffs, NJ: Prentice Hall.

Gronlund, N. E., & Linn, R. L. (1990). *Measurement and evaluation in teaching* (6th ed.) (pp. 427–452). New York: Macmillan.

Hopkins, C. D., & Antes, R. L. (1990). *Classroom measurement and evaluation* (3rd ed.) (pp. 406–436). Itasca, IL: F. E. Peacock.

Hopkins, K. D., Stanley, J. C., & Hopkins, B. R. (1990). *Educational and psychological measurement and evaluation* (3rd ed.) (pp. 319–338). Englewood Cliffs, NJ: Prentice Hall.

Kubiszyn, T., & Borich, G. (1990). *Educational testing and measurement* (3rd ed.) (pp. 137–153). Glenview, IL: Scott, Foresman/Little, Brown.

Mehrens, W. A., and Lehmann, I. J. (1991). *Measurement and evaluation in education and psychology* (4th ed.) (pp. 479–495). New York: CBS College Publishing.

Oosterhof, A. (1990). *Classroom applications of educational measurement* (pp. 443–445). Columbus, OH: Merrill.

Popham, J. W. (1990). *Modern educational measurement* (2nd ed.) (pp. 400–412). Englewood Cliffs, NJ: Prentice Hall.

Sax, G. (1989). *Principles of educational and psychological measurement and evaluation* (3rd ed.) (pp. 538–550). Belmont, CA: Wadsworth.

Interpreting Standardized Test Results

- Compare criterion-referenced achievement tests, norm-referenced achievement tests, and scholastic aptitude tests using their purposes, design characteristics, and uses.
- Describe the procedures for developing norm-referenced tests.
- Describe the normal curve and anchor points under the normal curve that are used to interpret standard scores.
- Describe scale scores and use them to analyze students' performance on standardized tests.
- Calculate and interpret the following standard scores: percentiles, percentile bands, and stanines.
- Interpret the following standard scores: normalized z and T scores, normal curve equivalent scores, and deviation IQ scores.
- Interpret grade equivalent scores and anticipated achievement scores.
- Describe the performance of individual students and class groups using their test records.

In addition to preparing and using classroom tests, teachers are usually expected to administer and interpret one or more standardized tests each year. These tests are called *standardized* because the same directions are used for administering them in all classrooms and standard procedures are used for scoring and interpreting them. This standardization permits comparing students' performance across classrooms, across schools, and across school districts. The three types of standardized tests used in schools include criterion-referenced achievement tests, norm-referenced achievement tests, and norm-referenced scholastic aptitude tests. These tests differ in purpose and in how they are developed and interpreted.

CRITERION-REFERENCED ACHIEVEMENT TESTS

Criterion-referenced achievement tests are developed by school districts, state departments of education, and commercial testing companies. These tests measure students' progress in such subjects as language arts, mathematics, science, and social studies. The match between these tests and the prescribed curriculum for a particular grade level and subject is of primary importance. Because these tests correspond directly to the curriculum guide, they can be administered at the beginning of the school year to evaluate the appropriateness of the curriculum for the grade level and to plan instruction tailored to students' needs. At the conclusion of a semester or year, they can be used to evaluate students' progress during the course.

The procedures used to develop criterion-referenced achievement tests are similar to those teachers use to develop classroom tests. The goals prescribed in the curriculum guide are analyzed to identify their subordinate skills, which are divided into prerequisite and enabling skills for each grade. The conditions for performing each skill are identified; and item specifications are written to ensure that each item is at an appropriate level of complexity, elicits the appropriate behavior, and includes the intended content. Item specifications prescribe the characteristics of the stem (or question), the correct answer, and each distractor to be included. Multiple-choice items are often used because of their economy, versatility, and objectivity. Tables of specifications are developed to ensure an appropriate balance among goals and their subordinate skills. Using these specifications, a writing team writes many more items than needed for each skill.

The review process used to evaluate these items is more comprehensive than that used by teachers. In addition to the writing team, content experts review the items for congruence with item specifications. Language specialists evaluate the appropriateness of the vocabulary, reading level, and grammar. Representatives from different cultural groups evaluate the items for potential bias in vocabulary and context. Finally, target students are sometimes used to review the items to verify their readability. During the review process, many items are either eliminated or revised.

Items that survive these reviews are assigned to different test forms for a field test. A large, representative sample of students is selected to take each test, which is administered in regular classrooms by the teachers. Like classroom tests, the items are evaluated using their difficulty and discrimination indices. Related to difficulty, items that are more difficult than anticipated, given the complexity of the task, are eliminated. Likewise, those that do not discriminate well for the obtained difficulty levels are eliminated. Items that meet the criteria are stored in an item bank or item pool. Using the table of specifications, items are selected from the bank for tests as needed.

To help ensure the curricular validity of commercial criterion-referenced tests, publishers have begun to provide custom-made or tailor-made tests.

Publishers follow the previously described procedure to create comprehensive item banks for each subject. Working in collaboration with a school district's representatives, they select the goals and objectives to be measured by a test and create a table of specifications tailored to the school's curriculum. Then, using the table of specifications, they select items from their item pool to create tests tailored to the district's curriculum.

Students' performance on criterion-referenced tests is usually reported as nonmastery, partial knowledge, or mastery of each objective. A criterion, or score needed for partial knowledge and mastery, is set using professional judgment. Scores used to report each student's level are either the percentage of items answered correctly for each objective or derived scores created using the number of items correct and other factors, such as the difficulty and discrimination levels of items in a set and the probability of guessing correct answers.

NORM-REFERENCED ACHIEVEMENT TESTS

Norm-referenced achievement tests are used primarily to compare students' achievement to that of a large, representative group of students at the same grade level. This representative group is called a *norm group*. Norm groups can be made up of students from throughout a school district, the state, the region, or the country. The purpose for these tests is to determine whether a student's or a group's achievement level is above average, average, or below average when compared to that of the selected norm group. These tests typically measure students' achievement in basic skills, such as language and mathematics, although other subjects are sometimes included. Norm-referenced tests are extremely time consuming and expensive to develop; therefore, they are usually produced and distributed by commercial test publishers rather than by school districts or state departments of education.

A summary of the process used to develop norm-referenced achievement tests appears in Figure 15.1. There are five main stages in the process: designing, developing, field testing, creating norms, and writing test manuals. During the design of norm-referenced tests, those goals cited most often in curriculum guides throughout the nation are selected to ensure the test's relevance for most school districts. Tasks selected to measure each goal vary in difficulty; for example, some are prerequisite skills, some are enabling skills, and some are too complex for most students at each grade level. Tasks are chosen in this manner to ensure the wide range of scores necessary to discriminate among below-average, average, and above-average achievers.

The item writing and review processes are the same for both criterion-referenced and norm-referenced tests. However, the procedures used to field test and select items for norm-referenced tests are different. During the field test, the different test forms are administered to a large, representative sample of

FIGURE 15.1

Process for Developing Norm-Referenced Achievement Tests

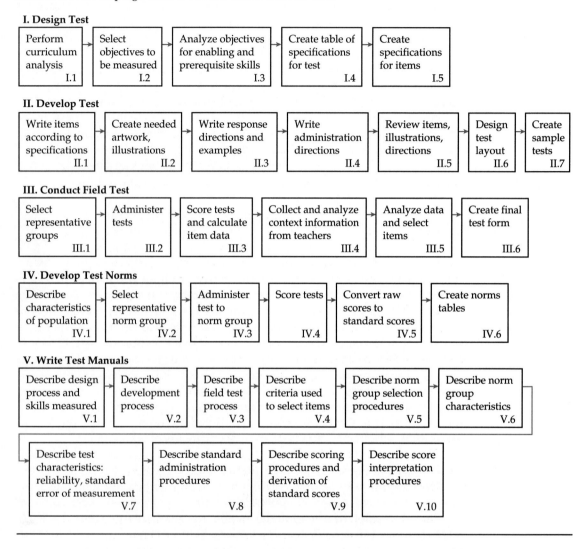

students. Students are selected according to specific characteristics, such as prior achievement or aptitude, age, gender, cultural group, socioeconomic level, school and community type, and geographic region. A sample of students from the grades immediately preceding and following the target grade may also be included. Teachers administer the tests in selected classrooms and follow the prescribed administration procedures, with one exception. Students are allowed ample time to finish the test. Teachers record the time each student requires, note any items or directions that cause confusion, and describe difficulties observed.

Data from the field test are analyzed, and items are selected for the final test version using the following four criteria:

1. Objective balance (inclusion of enough items for all skills)
2. Difficulty range (p values ranging from .90 down to .20, with a median value of about .55)
3. Discrimination indices (the highest positive discrimination index for the accompanying difficulty index)
4. Instructional sensitivity (a larger proportion of students answering items correctly at each higher grade level)

The items that best meet these criteria appear on the final test form, which is professionally formatted and produced.

Scores on norm-referenced tests are based on the performance of students in a reference group, or norm group. To select a representative norm group, the team must first define the population (e.g., all third-graders in the United States) and then select variables that accurately describe the group. If the norm group selected does not adequately represent the population, interpretations of individual students' performances are questionable.

To ensure that a cross-section of students is included, the team establishes categories of students and then determines the proportion of the population that falls into each category. For example, the team must know how the population is distributed according to the following characteristics:

1. Achievement or aptitude
2. Age, gender, race, and cultural group
3. Enrollment in public, private, and parochial schools
4. Enrollment in large, medium, and small schools
5. Residence in the different regions of the country
6. Residence in urban, suburban, and rural communities
7. Residence in high-, medium-, and low-income communities

Once the team has determined the characteristics of the population, a sampling plan is used to select the schools that will be included. The norm group usually includes thousands of students who, all together, are representative of the population.

Teachers then use the standardized procedures to administer the test to students in the norm group. At the same time, the team collects data on the group's characteristics. The tests are scored, and derived scores are calculated and reported in norms tables that appear in the test's technical manual and in the administrator's manual. Although raw scores are used to report students' achievement, they are converted to derived scores to facilitate comparing each student's performance to that of the norm group. Commonly used derived scores include percentiles, percentile bands, stanines, normal curve equivalent scores, grade equivalent scores, scale scores, and anticipated achievement scores. Procedures for interpreting these scores are described later in the chapter.

The team's final task is to develop the test manuals. These manuals usually describe the design and development process, the field test procedures, the item selection process, the sampling plan for the norm group, the characteristics of the norm group, and the group's test performance. They also include a list of the goals and objectives measured, directions for administering and scoring the test, and directions for interpreting the scores.

SCHOLASTIC APTITUDE TESTS

Scholastic aptitude tests are developed by commercial test publishers because they too are time consuming and expensive to develop. Unlike the two types of achievement tests, they do not measure students' achievement in school-related subjects. Instead, their main purpose is to measure students' thinking processes, sometimes called *reasoning skills*. These thinking processes include such skills as recall, concept discrimination, classification, analysis, sequencing, synthesis, inference, and generalization. Students' performances on aptitude tests are used to predict how well they will achieve in given subjects, special training programs, higher education, and careers that require similar reasoning skills.

The procedures used to develop scholastic aptitude tests are similar to those used to develop norm-referenced achievement tests because aptitude tests are norm referenced. The skills measured vary widely in difficulty to enable discrimination among students who are below average, average, and above average in aptitude. The major difference between these tests is that the foundation or framework of skills measured by the aptitude test involves thinking or reasoning skills rather than curriculum-based skills.

Students' performances on aptitude tests are interpreted by comparing them to the performances of the representative norm group. The scores traditionally used to report performance on aptitude tests are deviation IQ scores. However, percentiles are sometimes reported as well.

Table 15.1 summarizes the characteristics of criterion-referenced and norm-referenced achievement tests and scholastic aptitude tests. Because of the differences in these tests, school personnel carefully select the appropriate test for their purpose. For example, if they want to know how many students in each grade have mastered the skills prescribed in the curriculum guide, they should use a criterion-referenced test. However, if they want to know how their students' general achievement in a subject area compares to the achievement of a norm group, they should use a norm-referenced test. Finally, if they want to know which students are most likely to succeed in a particular

TABLE 15.1

Characteristics of Criterion-Referenced and Norm-Referenced Achievement Tests and
Scholastic Aptitude Tests

	Criterion-Referenced Achievement Tests	Norm-Referenced Achievement Tests	Scholastic Aptitude Tests
Typical developers	School districts State departments of education Commercial publishers	Commercial publishers	Commercial publishers
Primary purpose	To measure students' achievement of curriculum-based skills	To measure students' achievement of curriculum-based skills	To measure students' general thinking or reasoning skills
Foundation or item basis	Grade or course-specific curricular goals and their subordinate skills	Curricular goals from multiple grade levels	Generic thinking or reasoning skills
Criteria for including items	Balanced representation of goals and objectives Measured difficulty levels are within bounds for perceived skill complexity Measured discrimination levels are high, positive for given difficulty levels	Balanced representation of goals and objectives Wide range of difficulty levels, from .90 to .20 with a median about .55 Measured discrimination levels are high, positive for given difficulty levels Sensitivity to instruction	Balanced representation of thinking or reasoning skills Wide range of difficulty levels, from .90 to .20 with a median about .55 Measured discrimination levels are high, positive for given difficulty levels
Scores typically reported	Minimum scores for partial and total mastery of main skill areas Number of items correct Percentage of items correct Derived score based on items correct and other factors	Percentile ranks Percentile bands Stanines Normal curve equivalent scores Grade equivalent scores Scale scores Anticipated achievement scores (in conjunction with aptitude scores)	Deviation IQ scores Percentiles
When administered	Before instruction After instruction	After instruction	With achievement tests Before selecting courses of study
Use	Assess the curriculum Plan instruction Evaluate progress Group students for instruction	Classify students' achievement as above average, average, or below average for a given grade Create homogeneous or heterogeneous class groups	Classify students' aptitude as below average, average, or above average for a given age Predict achievement in subjects and courses of study that require similar reasoning skills

subject, they should use an aptitude test that measures the reasoning skills required in the subject.

One type of test cannot serve all three purposes equally well; however, it is not uncommon to find a norm-referenced achievement test used for all three. For example, the publishers of norm-referenced tests have begun to report criterion-referenced or mastery scores in addition to the traditional norm-referenced scores. Using these mastery scores, though, potentially can lead to inaccurate judgments about students' mastery. Remember that items are primarily selected for these tests to create a wide range of scores. Thus, many items are purposefully included that are judged to be too complex for most students at a given grade level. This design feature, which is necessary for norm-referenced achievement tests, will result in lower mastery scores for students than will scores produced from legitimate criterion-referenced tests. Norm-referenced achievement tests are also commonly used instead of aptitude tests to predict achievement. This practice is not as problematic since both previous achievement and aptitude have been found to be good predictors of future achievement. One potential problem with this practice is that the subject-based skills in the new curriculum may require different reasoning skills than those measured by previous achievement tests.

NORM-REFERENCED TEST SCORES

Publishers of norm-referenced tests convert students' raw scores into derived scores that permit each student's performance to be compared to that of the norm group. These derived scores are created using only the raw scores of students in the norm group. Later, when students throughout the country take the test, their raw scores are matched with those of students in the norm group, and the corresponding preset derived scores are assigned to individual students.

Using the Normal Curve to Interpret Standard Scores

Most derived scores are based on the standard normal distribution of scores, frequently called the *normal curve.* This distribution is used to give the scores a common meaning that makes interpreting performance much easier. Obviously, if every standardized test used a different score distribution, interpreting the various scores would be a difficult task.

The area under the normal curve is divided into halves, with the mean score as the center. Notice that in Figure 15.2, the area between the mean score and one standard deviation above the mean score (+1SD) contains approximately 34 percent of the ranked scores in the distribution (.3413). Because a normal distribution is symmetrical, approximately 68 percent of the ranked scores fall between one standard deviation above (+1SD) and one standard deviation below (−1SD) the mean score (.3413 + .3413). Fourteen percent of the

FIGURE 15.2
Areas under the
Normal Curve

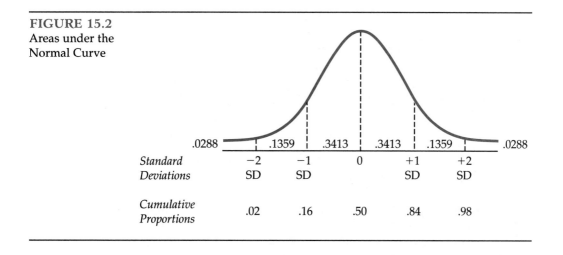

scores fall within the area between one and two standard deviations above the mean, and another 14 percent fall between one and two standard deviations below the mean. The remaining 4 percent of scores are evenly divided between the two remaining plus and minus categories. These percentages total 100 percent of the scores. If you add these percentages cumulatively from left to right, you can locate the proportion of scores that fall below each standard deviation. For example, about 2 percent of the scores fall below two standard deviations below the mean. About 16 percent of the scores fall below one standard deviation below the mean (2 + 14). Likewise, 50 percent fall below the mean (2 + 14 + 34). Eighty-four percent fall below one standard deviation above the mean, and 98 percent fall below two standard deviations above the mean. If you wanted to know the proportion of scores that fall below points between these standard deviation anchors, you could consult a table of areas under the normal curve. These tables are included in most basic statistics books.

It is important to become familiar with the normal curve anchor points illustrated in Figure 15.2 because the interpretation of the majority of derived scores reported for standardized tests depends on these anchor values. Recall how the mean and standard deviation are used in norm-referenced interpretations of students' performance on classroom tests. Scores within one standard deviation of the mean are considered to reflect average-level performance within the class. Scores equal to or greater than one standard deviation above the mean reflect above-average achievement compared to classmates. Scores equal to or lower than one standard deviation below the mean reflect below-average achievement in the group. On standardized, norm-referenced achievement tests, the same interpretation is given to scores located in each of these three areas. The main differences between norm-referenced, standard test scores and norm-referenced, classroom test scores is that standardized scores are interpreted relative to the areas under the normal curve. Scores equal to one standard deviation above the mean reflect above-average performance, and they indicate a score equivalent to the cumulative proportion .84 in Figure 15.2. Students earning scores at this level are comparable in achievement to the upper 16 percent of students in their norm group. Students earning scores within one standard deviation of the mean are comparable to approximately the middle two-thirds of their national norm group. Scores within one standard deviation of the mean are considered to reflect average performance. Students earning scores at one standard deviation below the mean on a standardized test are comparable in achievement to the lowest-scoring 16 percent of the norm group, and performance at this level is considered below average. Students at two standard deviations above the mean are comparable in achievement to the upper 2 percent of students in the norm group. Finally, the scores of students at two standard deviations below the mean are comparable to students in the lowest 2 percent of their national norm group.

In order to make the remainder of this discussion of standardized, norm-referenced tests more concrete, materials from the Comprehensive Tests of Basic Skills (CTBS), published by Macmillan/McGraw-Hill School Publishing Company (1990), will be used as the example. Teachers' materials available from other well-established school test publishers are similar to those contained in the CTBS materials. The CTBS materials also provide a good example because they include a wide variety of the types of test scores reported for norm-referenced tests. The next section describes scale scores and how to use them for analyzing students' performance on standardized tests. Following this discussion are descriptions of various standard scores that are derived from scale scores.

Interpreting Scale Scores

The most basic score, or the first score calculated for a standardized test, is called a *scale score*. Scale scores are derived using either of two scoring methods: pattern scoring based on item response theory (IRT) and number correct scoring. A description of these two scoring methods is beyond the scope of this introductory text; however, readers interested in the process can consult advanced measurement textbooks and the publishers' technical reports that accompany their standardized tests. Generally, publishers use a series of test items that overlap grade levels and a complex, computerized, score-equating system to calculate scale scores for the fall and spring norm groups for each grade level. Factors such as item difficulty, item discrimination, and the likelihood of guessing the correct answer are included in the scoring formulas.

Scale scores generally range from 0 to 999, with students' scores from all grade levels placed within this range. Although different test publishers use a slightly different range of scale scores, students in the lower grades are assigned lower-scale scores, and students in higher grades are assigned higher-scale scores. Scale scores are equal interval scores, which means that the distance or interval between any two numbers is equal at any point on the scale. This equal interval property means that scale scores can be added, subtracted, and averaged.

The best way to become familiar with scale scores is to obtain the norms book for the standardized test that is administered in your school district and to study the range of scale scores used for the grade level(s) and subject(s) you teach. The following paragraphs provide descriptions of how to use scale scores for (1) summarizing students' achievement within a skill area and across the total test battery, (2) analyzing students' achievement within a skill area across grade levels, (3) analyzing a student's achievement across skill areas within a grade level, and (4) evaluating a student's progress from grade to grade.

Summarizing Students' Scale Scores Across Subtests   For the Comprehensive Tests of Basic Skills (CTB/McGraw-Hill, 1990), scale scores are initially calculated for each subtest within a basic skill area. These scores are then averaged to create scale scores for general areas such as reading, language, and mathematics. These average scale scores are again averaged across the three content areas to create the total battery scale scores.

Table 15.2 contains an example of how scale scores from subtests are combined into content area scale scores and how content area scale scores are combined into total battery scale scores. For the reading area, the vocabulary and comprehension subtest scale scores are summed and then divided by two to obtain the average reading scale score ([778 + 774]/2 = 776). The language area scale score is the average of the mechanics and expression subtest scale scores ([786 + 780]/2 = 783), and the total mathematics scale score is the average of the computation and the concepts/applications scale scores ([813 + 797]/2 = 805). The total battery scale score for a student is the average

TABLE 15.2
Summarizing Subtest Scale Scores into Content Area and Total Battery Scale Scores

Reading Subtests	Reading Scale Scores	Language Subtests	Language Scale Scores	Math Subtests	Math Scale Scores	Total Battery	Total Scale Scores
Vocab	778	Mechanics	786	Computation	813	Reading	776
				Concepts/		Language	783
Compre	774	Expression	780	Application	797	Math	805
Total *Reading*	1552/2 = 776	*Total* *Language*	1566/2 = 783	*Total* *Math*	1610/2 = 805	*Total* *Battery*	2364/3 = 788

of the total reading, total language, and total mathematics scale scores ([776 + 783] + 805/3 = 788). Skill areas other than reading, language, and mathematics are typically not included in the total battery scale score. You will need to study the instructor's manual for the standardized tests used in your district to determine how subtest scores are combined to create skill area and total battery scores.

Analyzing Students' Progress Across Grade Levels Within a Subject

The best way to interpret scale scores for any subtest across grade levels is to relate the scale scores to comparable anchor scores from the normal curve. Figure 15.3 contains a selected sample of scale scores from the reading comprehension subtest of the Comprehensive Tests of Basic Skills published by Macmillan/McGraw-Hill. Scale scores appear in the far left column of the figure. The labels beneath the graph represent the grade-level norms. The vertical lines above each grade level indicate the scale scores that correspond to normal curve anchor points for that grade. (See Figure 15.2 for normal

FIGURE 15.3
Scale Scores Corresponding to Normal Curve Anchor Points for the Reading
Comprehension Subtests, Grades 1 Through 12

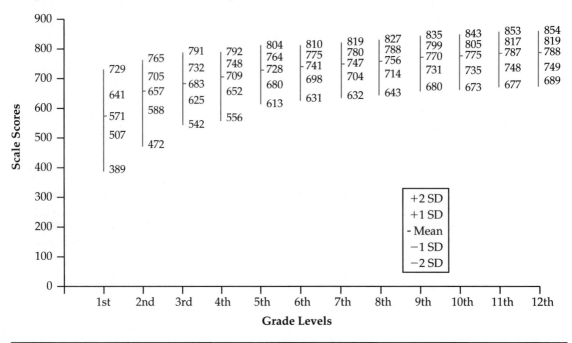

Source: Synthesized from materials in *Comprehensive Tests of Basic Skills, Fourth Edition, Spring Norms Book*, pp. 72–95 (Monterey, CA: Macmillan/McGraw-Hill School Publishing Company, Inc., 1990).

curve anchor point values and their interpretation.) The highest scale score indicated for each grade level reflects the score equivalent to two standard deviations above the mean on the normal curve, and the next score down represents the scale score equivalent to one standard deviation above the mean. The center score reflects the score corresponding to the mean, and the lower two scores reflect those corresponding to one and two standard deviations below the mean, respectively. Notice the first vertical line in Figure 15.3 (first-grade students). The scale score corresponding to two standard deviations above the mean is 729, the mean scale score for first-graders is 571, and the scale score corresponding to two standard deviations below the mean is 389.

What interpretive principles can we glean from the sample scores in Figure 15.3 that will help us interpret students' reading achievement across grade levels? The first principle relates to the consistent increase in scale scores at each normal curve anchor point across grades. For example, the scale score corresponding to two standard deviations below the mean for first-graders is 389, for second-graders it is 472, for third-graders it is 542, and it increases for each grade through grade 12. Notice that the mean scale score for each subsequent grade is higher than the one for the preceding grade. Following the same pattern, the scale score equivalent to two standard deviations above the mean is likewise higher than the one for the previous grade.

The second interpretive principle relates to the overlap in the scale scores across grade levels. Notice in Figure 15.3 that the scale scores overlap from first grade, to second grade, to third grade, and so forth. In other words, students in different grades can be assigned the same scale scores on a standardized test. The meaning attributed to a particular scale score, however, depends on the student's grade level. You can see that a scale score of 650 represents above-average achievement for a first-grade student since it is more than one standard deviation above the mean for this grade. A score of 650 reflects average-level performance for a second-grade student since it is near the mean for second-graders. The same score depicts below-average achievement for a student in the fourth grade or higher since it is more than one standard deviation below the mean for these grades.

The third principle is that variability in achievement among students within a grade is greater in the lower grades than in the upper grades. For example, the range of scale scores in reading comprehension is greater for students in the first grade (729 − 389 = 340) than for students in the twelfth grade (854 − 689 = 165).

The fourth principle is that there are greater achievement gains from grade to grade in the lower grades than in the upper grades. Notice that the difference in mean scale scores for reading comprehension from first to second grade is greater (657 − 571 = 86 points) than the difference in mean scale scores from eleventh to twelfth grade (788 − 787 = 1 point).

The fifth principle is that there is a greater distance in scale scores between the mean and two standard deviations below the mean than between the mean and two standard deviations above the mean. Notice the difference in distance among these three anchor scores across the grade levels in Figure 15.3. The difference between the mean and –2SD for first-graders is 182 scale score points (571 – 389), whereas the distance between the mean and +2SD for the same group is 150 points (729 – 571). This same pattern in scale scores exists across all grade levels.

Analyzing Achievement Across Subjects Within a Grade Level We can also increase our understanding of scale scores by comparing them across various subtests within a particular grade level. Scale scores tend to fall in the same general region of the score distribution for subtests within a grade level. A set of scale score ranges for selected subtests based on sixth-grade norms appear in Table 15.3. Anchor scores for the normal curve are in the far left column, and the subtest names are across the top of the table. The scale score corresponding to each normal curve anchor and subtest is included in the intersecting cell. For example, a scale score of 831 in reading vocabulary is two standard deviations above the mean and represents a score well above average in the sixth-grade norm group. A score of 740 corresponds to the mean and represents average-level achievement for a sixth-grader.

Notice that the scale score ranges across all subtests are in the same general region of the total distribution: Scale scores corresponding to two standard deviations below the mean are located in the low to mid 600s, the mean scale scores are all about 750, and the scores corresponding to two standard deviations above the mean are all in the low 800s region of the distribution. The same pattern is true for subtests within each grade level. Although not illustrated here, the scale scores across subtests for ninth-graders provide an alternative example. The scale scores corresponding to two standard deviations below the mean are in the mid to high 600s across all subtests, the mean scale scores across all subtests are all within the high 700s area, and the scale scores corresponding to two standard deviations above the

TABLE 15.3
Scale Scores Corresponding to Normal Curve Anchors for Selected Subtests
(Sixth-Grade Spring Norms)

Normal Curve Anchors	Reading Vocabulary	Reading Comprehension	Spelling	Language Mechanics	Language Expression	Math Computation	Math Concepts/ Applications	Science	Social Studies
+2 SD	831	810	830	829	816	835	829	827	817
+1 SD	781	775	785	780	777	783	780	784	780
Mean	740	741	743	740	741	750	743	745	745
–1 SD	697	698	697	693	695	700	700	696	699
–2 SD	641	631	641	619	635	637	647	632	627

Source: Material synthesized from the *Comprehensive Tests of Basic Skills, Fourth Edition, Spring Norms Book,* Complete Battery, pp. 82–83 (Monterey, CA: Macmillan/McGraw-Hill School Publishing Company, 1990).

scores are interpreted relative to the areas under the normal curve. Scores equal to one standard deviation above the mean reflect above-average performance, and they indicate a score equivalent to the cumulative proportion .84 in Figure 15.2. Students earning scores at this level are comparable in achievement to the upper 16 percent of students in their norm group. Students earning scores within one standard deviation of the mean are comparable to approximately the middle two-thirds of their national norm group. Scores within one standard deviation of the mean are considered to reflect average performance. Students earning scores at one standard deviation below the mean on a standardized test are comparable in achievement to the lowest-scoring 16 percent of the norm group, and performance at this level is considered below average. Students at two standard deviations above the mean are comparable in achievement to the upper 2 percent of students in the norm group. Finally, the scores of students at two standard deviations below the mean are comparable to students in the lowest 2 percent of their national norm group.

In order to make the remainder of this discussion of standardized, norm-referenced tests more concrete, materials from the Comprehensive Tests of Basic Skills (CTBS), published by Macmillan/McGraw-Hill School Publishing Company (1990), will be used as the example. Teachers' materials available from other well-established school test publishers are similar to those contained in the CTBS materials. The CTBS materials also provide a good example because they include a wide variety of the types of test scores reported for norm-referenced tests. The next section describes scale scores and how to use them for analyzing students' performance on standardized tests. Following this discussion are descriptions of various standard scores that are derived from scale scores.

The most basic score, or the first score calculated for a standardized test, is called a *scale score*. Scale scores are derived using either of two scoring methods: pattern scoring based on item response theory (IRT) and number correct scoring. A description of these two scoring methods is beyond the scope of this introductory text; however, readers interested in the process can consult advanced measurement textbooks and the publishers' technical reports that accompany their standardized tests. Generally, publishers use a series of test items that overlap grade levels and a complex, computerized, score-equating system to calculate scale scores for the fall and spring norm groups for each grade level. Factors such as item difficulty, item discrimination, and the likelihood of guessing the correct answer are included in the scoring formulas.

Scale scores generally range from 0 to 999, with students' scores from all grade levels placed within this range. Although different test publishers use a slightly different range of scale scores, students in the lower grades are assigned lower-scale scores, and students in higher grades are assigned

for students who are above and below the mean scale score. Since we know about these features of scale scores, it would be illogical to use one value as the amount of gain you anticipate for all students in a heterogeneous class or for students in lower and upper elementary grades.

To identify the amount of progress that is typical for norm group students, create a chart of scale scores at each normal curve anchor point for the grade level preceding yours and for your grade level. Using these values, you can calculate the amount of progress anticipated for norm group students by subtracting the preceding year's scale scores from those earned by students at your grade level. For example, if you were a fifth-grade teacher and you wanted to determine how much progress to anticipate in reading by the end of fifth grade, you would subtract the fourth-grade norm group's total reading scale scores from the fifth-grade norm group's total reading scale scores. This difference could then be used as a standard against which to compare the reading progress of students in your fifth-grade class.

The chart in Table 15.4 was constructed from the fourth- and fifth-grade spring norms for the total reading test. Scale scores for both grades were located in the norms tables that corresponded to the normal curve anchor points. Notice that students in the norm group whose scores were two standard deviations below the mean in total reading at the end of the fourth grade (SS = 575) gained 29 scale score points by the end of the fifth grade (SS = 604). Students who were at the mean gained 15 scale score points during the fifth grade, and students who were one standard deviation above the mean at the end of the fourth grade gained 20 scale score points during the fifth grade. These typical scale score gains in reading for norm group fifth-graders will help you determine whether students in your class are generally keeping pace, falling behind, or surpassing students in the norm group.

TABLE 15.4
Scale Scores at Normal Curve Anchor Points for the Total Reading Test for Fourth- and Fifth-Grade Spring Norms

Total Reading Test	Normal Curve Anchors				
	−2 SD	−1 SD	Mean	+1 SD	+2 SD
Fifth-Grade Scale Scores (SS)	604	676	722	759	799
Fourth-Grade Scale Scores (SS)	575	648	707	739	779
Gains Spring 4th to Spring 5th	29	28	15	20	20

Source: Synthesized from materials in the *Comprehensive Tests of Basic Skills, Fourth Edition, Spring Norms Book,* pp. 78–81 (Monterey, CA: Macmillan/McGraw-Hill School Publishing Company, 1990).

You will also need to calculate the scale score gains of students in your class by subtracting their previous year's scale scores from those they earn in your class at the end of the year. Students' spring test scores from the previous year should be available in their permanent school records. (Be sure the scores from the previous year are from the same publisher's test.) You can then compare your students' gains to those of students in the norm group who scored at about the same level. You can make these comparisons from grade to grade for any subtest, area test, or total battery scale scores as long as your students took the same publisher's test the preceding year.

Interpreting Scale Scores Using the Standard Error of Measurement (SEM)

Similar to other forms of human performance, the scores students earn on standardized achievement tests are not perfectly reliable. *Imperfect reliability* means that, upon retesting, students are not likely to earn the same raw score or scale score they obtained the first time they took the test. This phenomenon is best understood when you consider the difficulty we occasionally experience when trying to recall specific facts or procedures on demand. Sometimes we can readily recall details previously learned and other times we have difficulty remembering a familiar name or the steps in a procedure. Furthermore, we commonly forget the names of acquaintances when we introduce them in social situations. The more nervous we are about stating everyone's name correctly, the more likely we are to make errors in recalling names. It is impossible to create perfectly reliable achievements tests for our unreliable minds.

The standard error of measurement (SEM) is the index test publishers use to estimate the degree of score reliability for their standardized tests. Each scale score has its own standard error of measurement; scores toward the center of the distribution for each grade level have smaller standard errors of measurement than those toward the top or bottom of the distribution. The smaller the standard error of measurement, the more reliable the scores from the test. A student's performance level on a standardized test should be interpreted as falling within a range or band of scale scores that is established using the student's earned scale score and the standard error of measurement for that particular score. The standard error of measurement helps teachers avoid overinterpreting the precision of students' scores on standardized tests.

The standard error of measurement works conceptually much like the mean and standard deviation of a set of test scores. The student's earned scale score functions like the mean score since it is located toward the center of the band. The standard error of measurement functions similarly to the standard deviation because it is used to create the intervals around the earned score. A band, sometimes called a *confidence interval,* is placed around the student's earned scale score that is one standard error of measurement above and one standard error of measurement below the earned score. Hypothetically, the student's true score, or true achievement level, on the test is likely to fall within this ±1 SEM band approximately 68 percent of the time. The student's true score is likely to fall within ±2 SEMs approximately 95 percent of the time. (Recall from Figure 12.2 that under the normal curve, approximately 68 percent of the cases fall within ±1 standard deviation from the mean, and approximately 95 percent of the cases fall within ±2 standard deviations from the mean.) The earned scale score should be interpreted as a point within the SEM confidence band where the student's true score is likely to fall.

The standard error of measurement is calculated and reported in the norms tables by test publishers. The size of the standard error of measurement varies from test to test; and within a test, it varies across the range of test scores. The SEM is smallest toward the center of the distribution of scores for each norm group. It is larger toward the highest scores, and it is largest toward the lowest scores on the test. This phenomenon reflects that very high and very low test scores lack the same degree of reliability that scores toward the center of the distribution possess.

To illustrate how the size of the standard error of measurement varies across the range of scale scores within a single test, scores comparable to the normal curve anchor points and their SEM bands are plotted in Figure 15.4. The scale scores in the example are from the CTBS sixth-grade reading comprehension test (Form A, Level 16). The first vertical line on the left side of the figure reflects the SEM confidence band for a scale score equivalent to two standard deviations below the mean. The scale score located at this very low point in the normal distribution is 631, its published SEM is 66 points, and the corresponding confidence band ranges from 565 to 697. Notice that this confidence band is the largest one in the set. At the scale score corresponding to the mean (741), the SEM is only 8 points, and the confidence band ranges from 733 to 749. At two standard deviations above the mean (SS = 810), the published SEM is 15, and the confidence band ranges from 795 to 825. For students earning these particular scale scores, their true scores are expected to fall within these confidence bands 68 percent of the time. Generally, this indicates that you can have most confidence in the reliability of scale scores in the center of the distribution, less confidence in the reliability of scores toward the top of the distribution, and least confidence in the reliability of scores toward the bottom of the distribution. Each scale score for each subtest has its own calculated SEM. The best way to determine the amount of measurement error associated with a particular scale score on a given test is to consult the norms book provided by the test publisher.

Although scale scores are useful to teachers for analyzing a student's standardized test performance, they are difficult to explain to students and parents. In fact, they are difficult for teachers to interpret without the aid of the publisher's norms book. For this reason, scale scores are converted to other derived scores that are more easily interpreted. The most common scores derived from the scale scores are the percentile ranks and percentile bands, stanines, normalized z and T scores, normal curve equivalent scores (NCE), and deviation IQ scores.

Interpreting Percentile Ranks

The first derived score created from scale scores is the percentile rank, and this score is used to anchor scale scores to the normal curve. The range for percentile ranks is 1 to 99. This score indicates the percentage of students in the norm group who earned scale scores below the cumulative frequency at midpoint for each scale score in the distribution. The cumulative frequency at midpoint includes all the students who earned scale scores below a given score plus one-half of the students who earned that scale score. For example, if 38 students earned scale scores lower than 40 and 10 students earned a scale score of 40, the cumulative frequency at midpoint would be 38 plus 5, or 43. A student who earns a percentile rank of 62 is said to have performed better than 62 percent of the students in the norm group. (This percentage includes all students who earned lower scale scores and one-half of the students who earned the same scale score.)

FIGURE 15.4
Width of Standard Error of Measurement (SEM) Bands at Normal Curve Anchor
Points for the Reading Comprehension Test (Form A, Level 16)

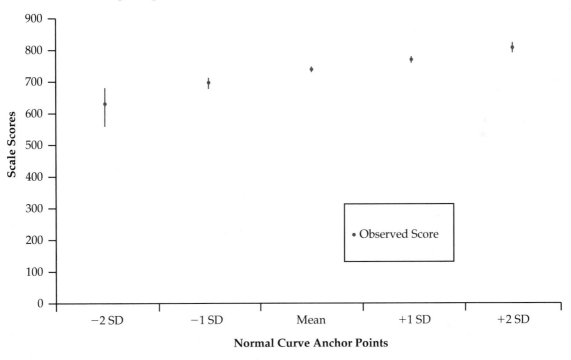

Source: Synthesized from materials in the *Comprehensive Tests of Basic Skills, Fourth Edition, Spring Norms Book*, p. 21 (Monterey CA: Macmillan/McGraw-Hill School Publishing Company, 1990).

Knowing how publishers convert scale scores to percentile ranks is helpful in interpreting them. Although publishers work with a wide range of scale scores and thousands of students, the simplified frequency distribution in Table 15.5 illustrates the process.

First, the scale scores are listed from highest to lowest (column 1), and the number of students who earned each score is tallied (column 2). Although there are several ways to proceed from this point, the most commonly used method is:

1. Sum the frequencies of scores falling below each scale score to obtain the cumulative frequency of scores below each scale score (column 3).
2. Divide the frequency of scores at each scale score in half (column 4).
3. Add the frequency of scores below to half the scores at the scale score to obtain the cumulative frequency at midpoint (column 5).
4. Divide this figure by the number of students in the group to obtain the proportion of students at midpoint (column 6).
5. Multiply this proportion by 100 to obtain the percentile rank for each scale score (column 7).

For example, the percentile rank for a scale score of 445 in Table 15.5 is 50. This conversion was made by:

1. Summing the frequencies of scores falling below 445 ($1 + 2 + 3 + 4 + 5 = 15$).
2. Dividing the frequency of scores at 445 in half ($6/2 = 3$).

TABLE 15.5
Derivation of Percentiles from Scale Scores

$N = 36$

(1) Scale Scores	(2) Frequency of Scores	(3) Cumulative Frequency below		(4) 1/2 Frequency within		(5) Cumulative Frequency at Midpoint	(6) Proportion	(7) Percentile Rank
450	1	35	+	.5	=	35.5	35.5/36 = .99	99
449	2	33	+	1	=	34	34/36 = .94	94
448	3	30	+	1.5	=	31.5	31.5/36 = .88	88
447	4	26	+	2	=	28	28/36 = .77	77
446	5	21	+	2.5	=	23.5	23.5/36 = .65	65
445	6	15	+	3	=	18	18/36 = .50	50
444	5	10	+	2.5	=	12.5	12.5/36 = .35	35
443	4	6	+	2	=	8	8/36 = .22	22
442	3	3	+	1.5	=	4.5	4.5/36 = .13	13
441	2	1	+	1	=	2	2/36 = .05	5
440	1	0	+	.5	=	.5	.5/36 = .01	1

3. Adding the frequency of scores below to half the scores at a scale score of 45 (15 + 3 = 18).
4. Dividing the cumulative frequency at midpoint (18) by the total number of students in the group (36) to obtain the proportion at midpoint (18/36 = .50).
5. Multiplying this proportion by 100 to obtain the percentile rank (.50 x 100 = 50).

There are several factors to consider in interpreting percentiles. One is the distinction between the percentage of correct items and the percentile, since these indices are different. The percentile rank is based on the number of students surpassed, and the percentage correct is based on the number of items correctly answered by an individual student.

Another factor to consider in interpreting percentile ranks is that they are not equal interval scores. An increase of one point on the scale score distribution does not correspond to a similar size increase on the percentile scale. For example, in Table 15.5, a 1-point increase in scale scores (from 445 to 446) results in a 15-point increase on the percentile rank scale (from 50 to 65). An increase in scale scores from 446 to 447 results in a 12-point increase on the percentile scale (from 65 to 77). Similarly, an increase in scale scores from 447 to 448 results in an increase on the percentile rank scale of 11 points. This phenomenon occurs because percentile ranks are based on the frequency of students who earn each scale score, and this number varies across the scale score distribution.

Notice in Table 15.5 that the frequency of students earning each scale score is greater toward the middle of the range than toward the ends of the distribution. This uneven pattern of scores across the range influences the correspondence between scale scores and percentiles ranks. Because there are many tied scores in the center of the distribution, small increases in scale scores result in large increases in percentile scores. As the number of tied scores decreases toward the ends of the scale score distribution, increases in percentile ranks become less dramatic. This uneven correspondence between scale score and percentile increments is not problematic if you know why it occurs and how to explain it to inquiring parents.

Another factor to consider in interpreting percentiles is that the scale scores of the norm group are the basis for the percentiles. Percentiles based on the performance of a nationwide norm group are called *national percentiles*. If other reference groups, such as all the students in a district, are used, then percentiles based on this group would be called *district* or *local percentiles*. Percentiles based on different norm groups are likely to be different even though the underlying scale score is the same for the test. Consider the following data:

Scale Score	*National Percentile*	*District Percentile*
640	60	75

When compared to the national norm group, a scale score of 640 reflects lower achievement than it does when compared to the district norm group. This difference reflects that a scale score of 640 ranked higher in the district group than in the national group. As this comparison shows, any interpretation of percentile ranks depends on the reference group for the scores.

The final factor to consider in interpreting percentile ranks is their relationship to the normal distribution. Because percentile scores reflect the percentage of people in the norm group who earned scores below the midpoint for a scale score, and the areas under the normal curve reflect the percentage of scores falling below a given point on the normal distribution of scores, percentiles can be equated directly to the proportions under the normal curve. The second percentile corresponds to the normal curve cumulative proportion of .02, or two standard deviations below the mean (−2SD). The sixteenth percentile corresponds to the normal curve cumulative proportion of .16, or one standard deviation below the mean (−1SD), and so on. The same correspondence is true for all percentile scores and for all cumulative normal curve proportions. Figure 15.5 illustrates this correspondence. Points between these anchors can be located using a table of areas under the normal curve.

The implication of this correspondence between the percentiles and the normal distribution is that percentiles between plus and minus one standard deviation from the mean are generally interpreted to reflect average test performance. Thus, percentile ranks between 16 and 84 are considered within the average range. Those at one standard deviation above the mean (percentiles of 84) are judged above average. Those at one standard deviation below the mean (percentile scores of 16) are judged below average.

FIGURE 15.5
Relationship of
Percentiles to
the Normal
Curve

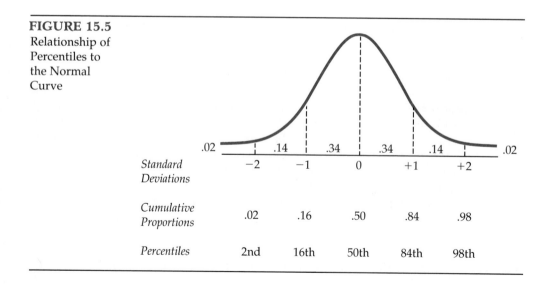

Test publishers use scale scores and the standard error of measurement to create percentile confidence bands. These percentile confidence bands, often simply called *percentile bands,* have the same meaning as the scale score confidence intervals. This means that due to measurement error, a student's true percentile rank can be expected to fall within the percentile confidence band 68 percent of the time. Although these two types of confidence intervals have the same meaning, students' test profiles contain percentile bands because they are easier to explain to parents.

Percentile bands are created directly from scale scores using the standard error of measurement and the percentiles calculated for each scale score. Generally, the procedure is the following:

1. Locate the earned scale score and its corresponding percentile rank in the publisher's norms table. The earned scale score and its percentile rank are the anchor points for calculating both the scale score confidence interval and the percentile confidence band.
2. Add and subtract one standard error of measurement from the earned scale score to create the scale score confidence internal. For example, the mean scale score for reading comprehension is 741 for the sixth-grade norm group. The standard error of measurement published for this scale score is 8, and the confidence interval extends 8 points in either direction from 741. This creates a scale score confidence interval around the mean score from 733 to 749.
3. Equate these boundary scale scores of 733 and 749 to their calculated percentile ranks in the norms book to locate the outer boundaries of the percentile confidence band. For example, the scale score 733 is equivalent to a percentile rank of 42, and the scale score 749 corresponds to a percentile rank of 58.
4. Plot the percentile band for the mean percentile 50 from percentile 42 to 58. You can interpret this percentile confidence band for an earned percentile rank of 50 as the area within which a student's true score is expected to fall 68 percent of the time.

Figure 15.6 contains the percentile bands that correspond to the scale score confidence intervals and normal curve anchor points illustrated in Figure 15.4.

There are two characteristics of percentile bands to consider: (1) the observed percentile score may not fall in the center of the percentile band and (2) the width of percentile bands varies for different percentiles. These characteristics both result from the fact that there are an unequal number of tied scores at each scale score. The obtained percentile does not fall in the center of the percentile band because there are unequal intervals between percentiles. The area of the band between the observed percentile and the center of the scale, the 50th percentile, will be wider than the area between the ob-

FIGURE 15.6

Percentile Confidence Bands Corresponding to the Scale Score Confidence Intervals
and Normal Curve Anchor Points Depicted in Figure 15.4 (Reading Comprehension
Sixth-Grade Norms, Form A, Level 16)

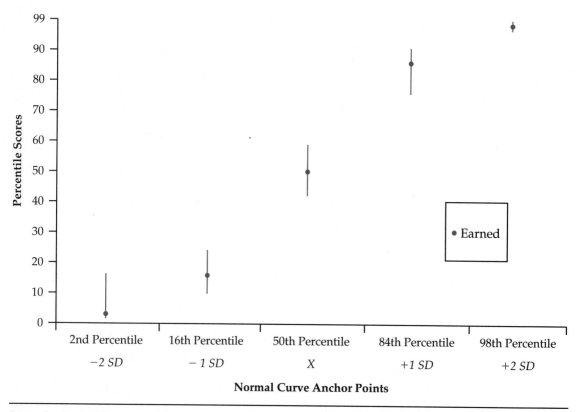

Source: Synthesized from materials in the *Comprehensive Tests of Basic Skills, Fourth Edition,*
Spring Norms Book, pp. 21, 82–83 (Monterey, CA: Macmillan/McGraw-Hill School Publishing
Company, 1990).

served percentile and the outer edges of the scale. This occurs because there
are more tied scale scores toward the center of the distribution. This characteristic can be observed in the five percentile bands in Figure 15.6. Consider
the location of the percentile score 98 within its percentile band. There is a
difference of only one percentile point between the observed score, 98, and the
upper boundary, 99, yet there is a difference of three percentile points between
the observed percentile and the lower boundary. The same characteristic can
be observed for the band surrounding the second percentile. There is a one
percentile point difference between the lower boundary and the second percentile. Toward the mean, there is a 14-point difference between the observed
second percentile and the upper boundary of the band.

The second characteristic is that the width of the percentile band varies for different percentile scores. Generally, percentile bands are wider toward the center of the distribution (the 50th percentile). This occurs because there are more tied scores at each scale score toward the center of the distribution than there are toward the outer edges of the scale score distribution. Remember that many tied scale scores result in dramatic increases on the percentile scale for each increase of one point in the scale scores. This characteristic can also be observed in the five percentile bands in Figure 15.6. The percentile band for a percentile rank of 98 is narrower than the one for a percentile score of 84. Likewise, the percentile band for a percentile score of 89 is narrower than the one for a percentile of 50. Moving from the mean toward the bottom end of the scale, the width of the bands gradually decreases.

Percentiles are used to compare the performances of several students in a class on one test, as well as the performances of one student across several subtests. When percentile bands overlap on the percentile scale, then observed differences between percentiles are considered negligible or due to measurement error. In Figure 15.6, the bands for percentiles 2 and 16 overlap; thus, this difference would be considered negligible. However, if the bands do not overlap, then the percentiles are considered significantly different. For example, the bands in Figure 15.6 for percentiles of 50 and 84 do not overlap. Therefore, the student who earned a percentile of 84 performed significantly better than the student who earned a percentile of 50. This overlap rule provides an important reminder that rather large differences between percentile ranks, or group standing, can be based on small differences between scale scores.

There is a general rule for comparing percentiles when percentile bands are not provided on students' records. The rule is based on the fact that percentile bands are wider toward the center of the percentile scale than toward the ends. Percentile scores in the center of the distribution (between 30 and 70) should be at least 15 percentile points apart before you consider them different. Percentile scores above 70 and below 30 should be at least 10 percentile points apart. Although this procedure permits only general estimates of differences, it is preferable to assuming that small differences in percentile ranks are meaningful.

Interpreting Stanines

Stanine scores are another type of standard score used to report students' performance. This discussion of how publishers create them, their characteristics, and their relationship to the normal curve and percentile scores will help you interpret them.

There are nine scores on a stanine scale; a score of 1 reflects low performance, and a score of 9 reflects high performance. The mean stanine score is 5, and the standard deviation is 2. Each stanine score represents a set proportion of students in the norm group. The proportion of students that corresponds to each score is as follows:

Stanine scores	1	2	3	4	5	6	7	8	9
≈ Proportion of students assigned each score	.04	.07	.12	.17	.20	.17	.12	.07	.04
Cumulative proportions	.04	.10	.22	.40	.59	.77	.89	.95	.99

Publishers create stanine scores directly from a table of proportions under the normal curve. Using cumulative proportions, all students in the norm group who fall at or below the cumulative proportion of .04 are assigned a stanine score of 1. The next 7 percent of the group, from .04 to .10, are assigned a stanine score of 2. The next 12 percent, from .11 to .22, are assigned a stanine score of 3, and so on.

Besides having only a nine-point scale, there are three characteristics of stanine scores you should consider when interpreting them. First, each stanine score represents a band of scale scores and percentile scores; thus, a different stanine score does not exist for each of the other types of scores. Second, stanine scores toward the center of the distribution include a wider band of percentiles than those toward the outer edges of the scale. Finally, stanines 2 through 8 are each one-half a standard deviation wide and have a fixed position on the normal distribution. Thus, they directly correspond to the normal curve and percentile scores.

Figure 15.7 illustrates the relationship among the stanine scores, the normal distribution, and the percentile scores. Stanine 5 extends one-quarter of a standard deviation on each side of the mean, making it one-half a standard deviation wide. Stanines 2 through 4 and 6 through 8 are also one-half a standard deviation wide. Stanines 1 and 9 are wider and extend to the ends of the distribution. Given this position of each stanine on the normal curve, you can equate stanine scores to the normal curve's standard deviation anchors and to percentile scores. For example, a stanine score of 1 is equivalent to standard deviations –3 and –2 and to percentiles 1 through 4. A stanine score of 2 is equivalent to percentile scores 5 through 10. Likewise, a stanine score of 5 is equivalent to the mean and to percentile scores 41 through 59. Because of this relationship, if you know the stanine score, you can locate the percentile scores corresponding to it and vice versa.

Interpreting stanines is rather straightforward. Generally, stanines of 1, 2, and 3 reflect below-average performance compared to the norm group. These scores include the bottom 22 percent of the students in the norm group. Stanines 4, 5, and 6 reflect average performance; these scores include the central 54 percent of the norm group. Stanines 7, 8, and 9 reflect above-average performance; these scores include 21 percent of the students at the top end of the scale. School personnel generally use stanines to classify below-average, average, and above-average performance. Although most publishers use both a percentile and a stanine to report students' performance on each

FIGURE 15.7

Correspondence among Stanines, Percentiles, and the Normal Curve

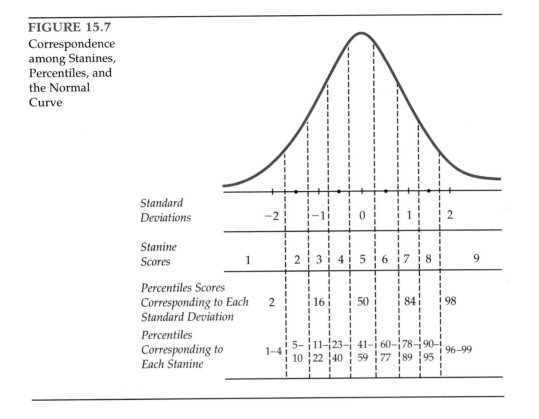

subtest, these scores do not provide different information. Instead, they provide the same information in different forms.

Interpreting Normalized z and T Scores

Two more scores associated with norm-referenced tests are normalized z and normalized T scores. Chapter 8 described linear z and T scores that maintain the shape of their scale score distribution, whether it is symmetrical or skewed. Normalized z and T scores are based on a standard normal distribution, regardless of the shape of the corresponding scale score distribution.

Like its linear counterpart, normalized z scores have a mean of 0 and a standard deviation of 1. In creating normalized z scores, scale scores are converted to percentiles to fix their position under the normal curve. Then, based on the location of the percentiles, the conversion is made to z scores. For example, the scale score corresponding to a percentile of 2, or –2SD, is equated to a normalized z score of –2; the scale score corresponding to a percentile score of 16, or –1SD, is equated to a normalized z score of –1; the scale score corresponding to a percentile of 50 is equated to a normalized z score of 0; and so on.

Normalized *T* scores are equated to scale scores in the same manner. These scores have a mean of 50 and a standard deviation of 10. The scale score corresponding to a percentile score of 2 is equated to a normalized *T* score of 30; the scale score corresponding to a percentile of 16 is equated with a normalized *T* score of 40; and the scale score corresponding to a percentile of 50 is equated to a normalized *T* score of 50. Scores between these points are matched using a table of areas under the normal curve.

Because of their relationship to the normal distribution and percentile scores, normalized *z* and *T* scores are quite easy to interpret. Normalized *z* and *T* scores of 1 and 60 and higher reflect above-average performance because these scores are located at one standard deviation or more above the center of the distribution. Those falling between normalized *z* scores of –1 and +1 and normalized *T* scores of 40 and 60 reflect average performance. Normalized *z* and *T* scores of –1 and 40 or lower are below average compared to the norm group. The anchor points for interpreting normalized *z* and *T* scores are illustrated in the following chart on performance level:

	Very Low	Below Average	Average Performance	Above Average	Outstanding
Normal Curve Standard Deviations	–2	–1	0	+1	+2
z Scores	–2	–1	0	1	2
T Scores	30	40	50	60	70

Interpreting Normal Curve Equivalent Scores (NCE)

You might also encounter a standard score called the *normal curve equivalent score*, or NCE. As its name implies, this score is also based on the normal curve. It has a fixed mean of 50, a fixed standard deviation of 21.06, and a range from 1 to 99. Thus, an NCE score of 29 is equivalent to one standard deviation below the mean (50 – 21.06), and an NCE score of 71 is equivalent to one standard deviation above the mean (50 + 21.06). Additionally, NCE scores are equal interval scores, meaning that the difference between any two adjacent scores on the scale is equal.

Given these properties, NCE scores are easy to interpret. Those scores between 1 and 29 are considered below average; those between 29 and 71 are considered average; and those of 71 and above reflect above-average performance. The proximity of these scores to their mean and the standard deviation anchors can be used to make inferences about the performance level of each score. The NCE scores corresponding to the normal curve standard deviation anchor points are the following:

	Very Low	Below Average	Average Performance	Above Average	Outstanding
Normal Curve Standard Deviations	−2	−1	0	+1	+2
NCE Scores	7.88	28.94	50	71.06	92.12

When using these scores to compare individual students' performances, be cautious not to attribute undue measurement precision to them. Like scale scores and percentiles, these scores should be interpreted as reflecting a probable area of performance rather than a precise point on a scale.

Interpreting Deviation IQ Scores

The deviation IQ score is a standard score used to report students' performance on scholastic aptitude tests. Since it is a standard score, it is interpreted using the properties of the normal distribution. Publishers of aptitude tests use a common mean score of 100; however, some publishers use a standard deviation of 16 points and others use one of 15 points. The technical manual for each publisher's test will report which standard deviation value is used in making score conversions.

When the standard deviation is 16, a deviation IQ score of 84 is located one standard deviation below the mean (100 − 16). Thus, scores of 84 and below are considered to reflect below-average performance compared to the norm group. Scores between 84 and 116 are interpreted as reflecting average-level performance. Scores of 116 and above (100 + 16) are considered above average because they reflect scores that are one standard deviation or more above the mean. Scores of 132 are two standard deviations above the mean and reflect performance at the 98th percentile; these scores reflect outstanding performance compared to the norm group. At the opposite end of the scale, scores of 68 are two standard deviations below the mean and correspond to the 2nd percentile; therefore, they reflect very low performance compared to the norm group. These anchor points for interpreting deviation IQ scores are illustrated in the following diagram on performance level:

	Very Low	Below Average	Average Performance	Above Average	Outstanding
Normal Curve Standard Deviations	−2	−1	0	+1	+2
Deviation IQ Scores	68	84	100	116	132

Interpreting Other Types of Standard Scores

Some publishers use standard scores that are unique to their tests. To interpret any of these scores, you need to consult the test's technical manual to locate the scores that are equivalent to the mean and standard deviation. Interpreting students' performance on these tests is quite easy when these two values are known; otherwise, it can be baffling.

For example, on the Scholastic Aptitude Test (SAT), the College Entrance Examination Board sets the mean at 500 and the standard deviation at 100. Thus, a score of 300 (–2SD) reflects very low performance compared to the norm group; scores between 300 and 400 (–1SD) reflect below-average performance; scores between 400 and 600 reflect average performance; scores between 600 (+1SD) and 700 reflect above-average performance; and those above 700 (+2SD) reflect outstanding performance.

Performance on the Graduate Record Exam (GRE) is reported using a mean score of 1000 and a standard deviation of 200. Thus, scores in the average range extend between 800 to 1200. Scores of 800 and below are considered below average, and those of 1200 and above are considered above average compared to the norm group.

Interpreting Grade Equivalent Scores

Grade equivalent scores enable educators to compare students' variability in each subject within and across grades. Unlike the previously described scores, these scores are not based on the performance of one norm group. Instead, the same test is administered to the norm groups for two or three contiguous grade levels. The mean or median score earned by each group is located and used as the basis for creating all the grade equivalent scores. For example, suppose that the same test is administered to the fourth-, fifth-, and sixth-grade norm groups in September. The grade equivalent scores are matched to scale scores for the test using a chart similar to the one illustrated in Figure 15.8. A hypothetical range of scale scores is used in the example.

Scale scores are ranked vertically from highest to lowest on the left side of the chart. Grade equivalent scores are listed from lowest to highest along the bottom. To begin, three data points are plotted: one at the intersection of the fourth-graders' median score 709 and the grade equivalent score 4.0; a second at the intersection of the fifth-graders' median score 728 and the grade equivalent score 5.0; and the third at the point intersecting the sixth-graders' median score 741 and the grade equivalent score 6.0.

All the remaining grade equivalent scores reported for the test are obtained by interpolation and extrapolation. *Interpolation* is used to match scale scores and grade equivalent scores between the three obtained scores. *Extrapolation* is used to match scale scores and grade equivalent scores outside the measured area (fourth, fifth, and sixth grades).

FIGURE 15.8

Matching Grade
Equivalent
Scores to Raw
Scores Using
Obtained Mean
or Median
Scores and the
Processes of
Interpolation
and
Extrapolation

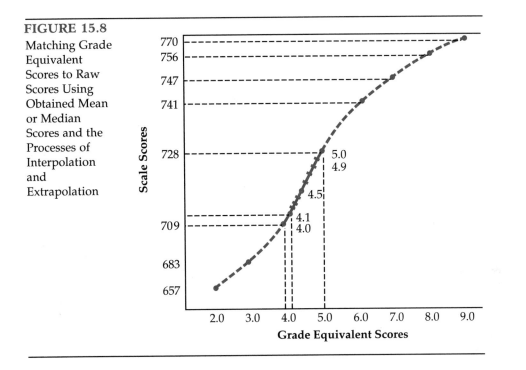

To match grade equivalent scores and scale scores within the grades tested, a line is drawn to connect the three observed data points. The area between each set of points is divided into nine equal segments. Each higher segment is assigned a grade equivalent score. For example, between 4.0 and 5. 0, the first segment is assigned the grade equivalent score 4. 1, the second is assigned the grade equivalent score 4.2, and so on to 4.9. The segments between 5.0 and 6.0 are assigned grade equivalent scores 5.1 through 5.9. Each grade equivalent score is matched to a scale score by assigning the scale score directly across from the intersecting point for each grade equivalent score.

The next step is to use extrapolation to match estimated grade equivalent scores and scale scores for grades outside the three grade levels measured. Points to reflect median scores for grades lower than the fourth and higher than the sixth are estimated because students in these grades did not take the test. In order to match scores outside the measured area, the line connecting the three measured points is extended at both ends. In Figure 15.8, these extensions are illustrated using a broken line. Points on the line that reflect the mean or median score for these outside grades are estimated using the observed distances between the three actual scores. The point on the line that is estimated to locate the median point for each grade is used as the intersecting point on the two scales to equate the grade equivalent scores (2.0, 3.0, 7.0, 8.0, 9.0) to particular scale scores. The interpolation procedure described previously for matching scores between these points is used to complete the matching process.

An important assumption made in creating and interpreting grade equivalent scores is that each grade equivalent score reflects the median score that students in the norm group would earn if they took the test in a given month. For example, a grade equivalent score of 4.0 reflects the median score earned by the norm group in September of the fourth grade. A grade equivalent score of 4.1 reflects the group's expected median score in October; 4.2 reflects the expected median score in November; and so forth to 4.9, which reflects the group's expected median score in June. Research has shown that the amount students progress is not equal from month to month within a year, or from year to year. However, the assumption of even progress will undoubtedly be used until a more realistic, yet systematic, method to describe progress is developed.

There are several important characteristics of grade equivalent scores that you should consider before interpreting them. One is that the observed median score for each grade level in September is set at .0, such as 5.0. This implies that 50 percent of the students in the fifth-grade norm group are assigned a grade equivalent score below this level. A second characteristic is that, because norm-referenced tests are designed to yield a wide range of scores within each grade level, a wide range of grade equivalent scores is assigned to students within each grade. Thus, many students within a given grade will earn grade equivalent scores that are many grade levels lower or higher than their actual grade in school. One way to avoid misinterpreting a low or high grade equivalent score is to equate it to the percentile and stanine assigned to the same scale score. This will help remind you that a grade equivalent score that appears extreme might be within the average performance range for the norm group.

Consider some sample scale scores and their corresponding grade equivalent, percentile, and stanine scores for four subtests of the Comprehensive Tests of Basic Skills (1990). These norms are for the eighth grade and for tests administered in the spring of the year. The first column in Table 15.6 lists the subtests. The second column contains a range of selected scale scores for each subtest. The third, fourth, and fifth columns contain the corresponding grade equivalent, percentile, and stanine scores for each of the scale scores. Since the norm group took the test in the spring, the median grade equivalent score should be 8.8 and correspond to a percentile of 50. Note that the third column contains grade equivalent scores of 8.8 and that the corresponding percentiles are 50. This means that 50 percent of the students in the eighth-grade norm group earned grade equivalent scores below 8.8.

Note the wide range of grade equivalent scores for each subtest. The grade equivalent scores for the reading vocabulary test range from 3.4 to 12.9+. Using the corresponding percentile scores, you can see that a grade equivalent score of 3.4 reflects below-average performance for an eighth-

TABLE 15.6
Selected Scale Scores and Their Corresponding Grade Equivalent Scores,
Percentiles, and Stanines for Eighth Grade, Spring

Subtest	Scale Score	Grade Equivalent Score	National Percentile	National Stanine
Reading	850	12.9+	98	9
Vocabulary	804	12.1	84	7
	763	8.8	50	5
	721	6.0	16	3
	663	3.4	2	1
Reading	827	12.9+	98	9
Comprehension	788	12.9+	84	7
	756	8.8	50	5
	714	5.0	16	3
	643	2.6	2	1
Math	879	12.9+	98	9
Computation	831	12.9+	84	7
	790	8.8	50	5
	739	6.3	16	3
	667	3.8	2	1
Math	846	12.9+	98	9
Concepts	805	12.9+	84	7
	768	8.8	50	5
	726	5.8	16	3
	670	3.5	2	1

Source: Synthesized from materials in *Comprehensive Tests of Basic Skills, Fourth Edition, Spring Norms Book* (Monterey, CA: Macmillan/McGraw-Hill School Publishing Company, 1990).

grader because it corresponds to a percentile of 2 and a stanine of 1. However, a grade equivalent score of 6.0, which might be misinterpreted as very low for an eighth-grader, corresponds to a percentile of 16 and stanine of 3, reflecting below-average performance for eighth-graders. A grade equivalent score of 12.1, which corresponds to a percentile of 84 and a stanine of 7, is just within the above-average range for eighth-grade students. This correspondence is the same between the grade equivalent scores and the percentile and stanine scores for each of the other three tests. Before you interpret a grade equivalent score as reflecting either above- or below-average achievement, check its corresponding percentile and stanine scores to verify your interpretation.

Educators who do not understand these characteristics of grade equivalent scores can make many mistakes in interpreting them. A statement such as, "Our goal is to have all students in Garfield School performing at or above grade level," is usually made by someone who does not understand grade equivalent scores. Reaching this goal is only possible in schools that have no below-average students enrolled. Such a statement as, "Although John is in the eighth grade, he is only working at a third-grade level," also demonstrates a misunderstanding of the grade equivalent score. No third-graders took the eighth-grade form of the test. In addition, very few, if any, of the skills measured by the eighth-grade test would be found in a third-grade curriculum guide or instruction targeted for third-grade students. John's low grade equivalent score simply reflects low performance compared to that of the eighth-grade norm group.

A third characteristic to be aware of is that grade equivalent scores are more variable in some subjects than others. This feature is important to the score's main purpose, which is detecting the norm group's performance patterns in a subject within and across grades. However, these scores should not be used to compare students' performances across subjects. The variability of the norm group's performance across subjects will lead you to conclude that differences exist when they may not.

To illustrate this point, consider the data in Table 15.7. These are scale scores and corresponding grade equivalent and percentile scores from the sixth-grade norms tables accompanying the Comprehensive Tests of Basic Skills (1990). If you used the grade equivalent score to compare a student's performances on the language, reading, and mathematics subtests, you would undoubtedly conclude that the student performed best in language skills (12.9+), less well in reading skills (11.3 and 11.7), and poorest in mathematics

TABLE 15.7

Selected Scale Scores and Their Corresponding Grade Equivalent Scores and Percentiles (Sixth Grade, Spring Norms)

Test	Scale Score	Grade Equivalency	National Percentile
Reading			
Vocabulary	795	11.3	91
Comprehension	786	11.7	91
Language			
Mechanics	793	12.9+	91
Expression	789	12.9+	91
Mathematics			
Computation	796	9.3	91
Concepts and Application	794	11.5	91

Source: Synthesized from materials in *Comprehensive Tests of Basic Skills, Fourth Edition, Spring Norms Book* (Monterey, CA: Macmillan/McGraw-Hill School Publishing Company, 1990).

(9.3 and 11.5). This conclusion would be incorrect, however, because all six of these grade equivalent scores correspond to a percentile of 91.

The differences among these grade equivalent scores simply reflect that the sixth-grade norm group was most variable in language, which resulted in a very wide range of grade equivalent scores. Their performance was less variable in reading, and least variable in mathematics, which resulted in narrower grade equivalent score ranges in these subjects.

Because parents are not familiar with the characteristics of grade equivalent scores and may misinterpret them, school districts and teachers should not use them to communicate students' achievement. If they are included in students' report forms, the easiest way to interpret them to parents is to equate them to their corresponding percentiles and stanines.

Interpreting Anticipated Achievement Scores

Anticipated achievement scores are quite different from those previously described. These scores are calculated separately for each student tested and indicate the student's expected score for each test. These anticipated scores are compared to the obtained scores to determine whether the student's performance was as expected, atypically high, or atypically low.

The publisher establishes anticipated scores for each student by matching the student to a subset of students from the norm group with the same characteristics. Characteristics typically used to match students are age in months, year and month in school, and scores earned on an aptitude test administered at the same time as the achievement test. Sometimes gender is also used as a matching factor.

Once a matched set of students is selected from the norm group, their achievement test scores are ranked from highest to lowest and their mean score is calculated. The anticipated achievement score reported for each student is the mean score earned by the matched set of students from the norm group. Using a measure of the subgroup's variability, a confidence band is placed around the mean score to set boundaries above and below which scores can be considered atypical. The individual's obtained score is then compared to the matched group's score distribution. If the student's score falls within the confidence band, then the obtained score is considered typical. However, if the student's score falls outside the band, then the score is considered atypical or significantly different than anticipated. A plus sign is often used to indicate atypically high scores, and a minus sign is used to indicate atypically low scores.

Derived scores used to report anticipated achievement are the scale score, percentile, grade equivalent score, and normal curve equivalent score. The publisher clearly labels anticipated scores by placing the letters *AA* before the abbreviations for each type of score. *AAGE* is an anticipated grade equivalent score, *AASS* is an anticipated scale score, *AANCE* is an anticipated normal curve equivalent score, and *AANP* is an anticipated national percentile.

TEST RECORDS FOR INDIVIDUAL STUDENTS

Different publishers use different formats to report an individual's test performance. The report forms, sometimes called *profiles*, usually contain the names of the subtests in the battery and a variety of derived scores that match the student's performance to that of the norm group. The derived scores reported often include scale scores (SS), the national percentile (NP), the national stanine (NS), the normal curve equivalent score (NCE), the grade equivalent score (GE), and the anticipated achievement score (e.g., AAGE). The report form includes an anticipated achievement score only if both achievement and aptitude tests were administered at the same time. The form usually includes a chart that illustrates the position of the student's percentile and stanine scores and the percentile bands.

Figure 15.9 contains an individual student's record from the Comprehensive Tests of Basic Skills (CTB/McGraw-Hill, 1992). Biographical information appears at the top and bottom of the left margin. These sections identify the student, teacher, grade, school, city, state, date of testing, particular test form used, and scoring method used to obtain the scale score. In this section, it is important to note that Raina took the test in April of the fifth grade (5.7).

Section A lists the subtests and Raina's derived scores. The names of the scores corresponding to the initials at the top of each score column appear in section D. Consider Raina's scores on the reading vocabulary test. Her scale score is 760. Basically, we are interested in determining whether this scale score represents above-average, average, or below-average achievement compared to students in the fifth-grade norm group. Locate first her national percentile score (NP). Her percentile of 87 reflects above-average achievement for students in the fifth-grade norm group since it is greater than one standard deviation above the mean (84th percentile). It also means that her scale score is better than the scale scores earned by 87 percent of the students in the national norm group. All the other derived scores reported for reading vocabulary simply represent alternative ways of expressing the same level of above-average achievement. Her national stanine score (NS) is 7, which is one standard deviation above the mean for stanine scores. Her normal curve equivalent score (NCE) of 73 is greater than one standard deviation above the mean for NCE scores (50 + 21.06 = 71.06). Although her grade equivalency score (GE) is 8.5, or three grade levels above hers (5.7), information from the

---

FIGURE 15.9 ➤

A Sample Student Interpretive Report from the Comprehensive Tests of Basic Skills, Fourth Edition

Source: Reprinted with permission from a 1992 catalog of materials for the Comprehensive Tests of Basic Skills, Fourth Edition, p. 155 (Monterey: CA: Macmillan/McGraw-Hill School Publishing Company).

◆ CTBS/4 Comprehensive Tests of Basic Skills, Fourth Edition

STUDENT INTERPRETIVE REPORT

STUDENT: STEVENS RAINA   GRADE: 5.7

BIRTH DATE: 8/27/78   CODES: ....

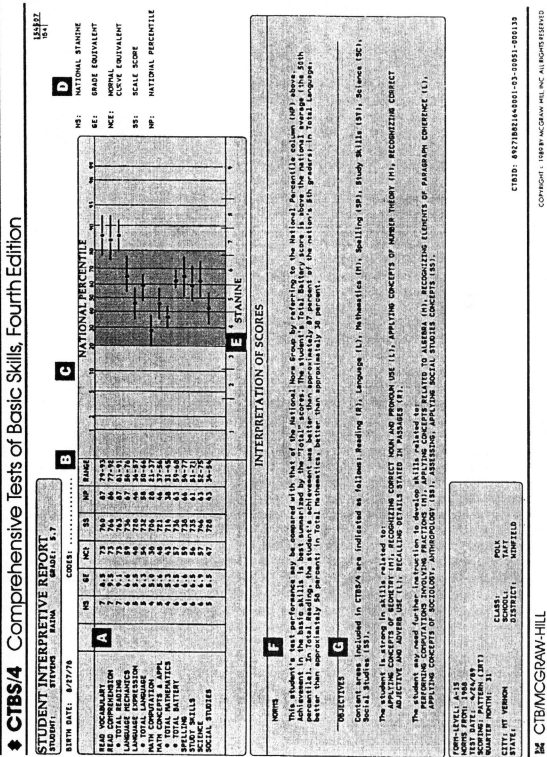

	NS	GE	NCE	SS	NP	RANGE
READ VOCABULARY	7	8.5	73	760	87	79-93
READ COMPREHENSION	7	9.5	73	766	86	77-92
• TOTAL READING	7	9.1	73	763	87	81-91
LANGUAGE MECHANICS	6	6.4	59	736	67	56-70
LANGUAGE EXPRESSION	5	5.5	40	728	44	34-57
• TOTAL LANGUAGE	5	6.3	54	732	58	50-64
MATH COMPUTATION	4	5.0	36	706	38	21-37
MATH CONCEPTS & APPL	4	5.6	48	721	48	37-54
• TOTAL MATHEMATICS	4	5.3	43	715	43	31-45
• TOTAL BATTERY	5	6.6	57	736	63	59-68
SPELLING	6	6.5	56	735	61	54-77
STUDY SKILLS	6	6.9	57	744	61	51-71
SCIENCE	5	5.5	47	728	43	34-54

NATIONAL PERCENTILE

STANINE

D — CODES

- **NS:** NATIONAL STANINE
- **GE:** GRADE EQUIVALENT
- **NCE:** NORMAL CURVE EQUIVALENT
- **SS:** SCALE SCORE
- **NP:** NATIONAL PERCENTILE

INTERPRETATION OF SCORES

F — NORMS

This student's test performance may be compared with that of the National Norm Group by referring to the National Percentile column (NP) above. Achievement in the basic skills is best summarized by the "Total" scores. The student's Total Battery score is above the national average (the 50th percentile). In Total Reading, the student's achievement was better than approximately 87 percent of the nation's 5th graders in Total Language. better than approximately 50 percent in Total Mathematics; better than approximately 38 percent.

G — OBJECTIVES

Content areas included in CTBS/4 are indicated as follows: Reading (R), Language (L), Mathematics (M), Spelling (SP), Study Skills (ST), Science (SC), Social Studies (SS).

The student is strong in skills related to:
APPLYING CONCEPTS OF GEOMETRY (M), RECOGNIZING CORRECT NOUN AND PRONOUN USE (L), APPLYING CONCEPTS OF NUMBER THEORY (M), RECOGNIZING CORRECT ADJECTIVE AND ADVERB USE (L), RECALLING DETAILS STATED IN PASSAGES (R).

The student may need further instruction to develop skills related to:
PERFORMING COMPUTATIONS INVOLVING FRACTIONS (M), APPLYING CONCEPTS RELATED TO ALGEBRA (M), RECOGNIZING ELEMENTS OF PARAGRAPH COHERENCE (L), APPLYING CONCEPTS OF SOCIOLOGY, ANTHROPOLOGY (SS), ASSESSING, APPLYING SOCIAL STUDIES CONCEPTS (SS).

FORM-LEVEL: A-15
NORMS FROM: 1988
TEST DATE: 4/24/89
SCORING: PATTERN (IRT)
QUARTER MONTH: 31

CLASS: POLK
SCHOOL: TAFT
DISTRICT: WINFIELD

CITY: MT VERNON
STATE:

CTBID: 89271B821640001-03-00051-000130

CTB/MCGRAW-HILL

other derived scores means that this GE score is above average compared to students in the fifth-grade norm group.

Notice the far right column in section B, labeled Range. The scores in this column indicate the boundaries of the percentile confidence band for her earned percentile, 87. This means that due to the calculated standard error of measurement for a scale score of 760, Raina's true score can be expected to fall within the percentile range of 79 to 93. Section C includes a graph of the percentile confidence bands. The percentile scores are listed along the top of the chart from 1 to 99. The first band at the top of the graph is the one depicting her reading vocabulary achievement. You can see her observed percentile of 87 represented as a dot toward the center of the band. The lower boundary of the band extends to percentile 79, and the upper boundary reaches percentile 93. The bottom of the graph lists stanine scores. You can look down the chart from her percentile score of 87 (the dot in the center of the confidence band) to see that it falls within stanine 7. This graph of national percentile bands and stanines simply provides a picture of the percentile and stanine scores that appear in the columns of derived scores in section B.

Now consider Raina's performance on the reading comprehension test. Her scale score is 766, which corresponds to a national percentile score of 86. This match means that her reading comprehension is also above average compared to students in the fifth-grade national norm group. Her national stanine score of 7, normal curve equivalency score of 73, and grade equivalency score of 9.5 are alternative ways of expressing her above-average achievement in reading comprehension.

We can compare her achievement in reading vocabulary and comprehension using the percentile bands in section C. Notice that the bands are in the same region and overlap on the scale, indicating that there is no significant difference in her achievement in the two reading areas.

Raina's achievement in language is lower. Her national percentile scores of 67 in mechanics and 46 in expression are both within the average range compared to students in the national norm group. Her total language score represents the average of her scale scores in the two language subtests ([736 + 728]/2 = 732). Her percentile score in total language, 58, is the one that corresponds to her average scale score of 732. Notice that her percentile score in total language is *not* the average of her two percentile scores on the language subtests ([67 + 46]/2 = 57). Since percentile scores are not equal interval scores, it is incorrect to add, subtract, or average them. Her other derived scores in language likewise reflect average-level achievement compared to the fifth-grade national norm group.

We can compare Raina's achievement in reading and language using her percentile bands for total reading and total language in section C. Notice that the bands for these two area scores do not overlap. The fact that the percentile confidence bands do not overlap for these two area scores means that Raina performed significantly better in reading than in language.

Now consider her achievement in mathematics. Her computation scale score is 706, which corresponds to a national percentile score of 28. These scores are located in the lower region of average performance (approximately the middle two-thirds of the students in the norm group). Her stanine score of 4, grade equivalent score of 5.0, and normal curve equivalent score of 38 also reflect low average achievement. Her scale score in math concepts and application of 721 corresponds to a national percentile score of 46, a stanine score of 5, a grade equivalent score of 5.6, and a normal curve equivalent score of 48. These scores all reflect achievement slightly below the mean score compared to students in the national norm group.

We can use her total battery score and her area scores in reading, language, and mathematics to summarize Raina's achievement compared to the fifth-grade national norm group. Her total battery scale score is 736, which corresponds to a national percentile of 63. She performed better on the total battery than 63 percent of the students in the national norm group, and her performance is average since it is slightly above the mean (stanine, 6; grade equivalent score, 6.5; normal curve equivalent, 57; and percentile band, 59 to 68). In comparing her percentile bands for total reading, total language, and total mathematics in section D, we find that her percentile bands do not overlap in the three areas. We can conclude from this comparison that her achievement in reading is superior to her language achievement, and her achievement in language is superior to her achievement in mathematics when compared to the fifth-grade national norm group.

Once you understand derived scores and how they are interpreted, you can interpret the performance of students on standardized achievement tests, regardless of how the scores are formatted on a student's profile sheet. Sometimes publishers provide verbal explanations of a student's performance on the report. Notice sections F and G in Figure 15.9. Section F describes Raina's achievement for parents and school personnel. These descriptions are typically brief, and they cannot substitute for teachers' ability to interpret the derived scores for themselves. Section G indicates the student's particular strengths and weaknesses for particular objectives within each subtest. This information can be helpful to both teachers and parents who want to help students progress.

CLASS RECORDS

The performance of a class is typically summarized for teachers using a class record form. The norm-referenced scores on these forms are the same as those reported on individual students' records. Although norm-referenced achievement tests focus on language and mathematics skills, teachers of all subjects can use the class record to describe the achievement characteristics of their groups. Knowing whether a class is homogeneous or heterogeneous in basic skills can aid both instructional planning and the assessment of any group's progress. Teachers of subjects other than language and mathematics typically use students' scores on the aptitude, total reading, total language, and total math tests to describe a group's achievement characteristics. Teachers of language and mathematics also use students' performances on the subtests to describe the achievement characteristics of their classes.

One good way to describe a group's achievement characteristics is to locate the highest and lowest scores earned by class members and the group's mean score on all tests of interest. If the highest and lowest scores reflect the same general level of performance, then the group can be considered homogeneous. However, if these extreme scores reflect different performance levels, then the class can be described as heterogeneous. The location of the group's average score compared to the two extreme scores provides information about the distribution of the group's scores.

A Sample Class Record Sheet from the Comprehensive Tests of Basic Skills (CTB/McGraw-Hill, 1992) appears in Figure 15.10. The teacher's name (Polk) and grade level (5.7) appear in the top left corner of the report. Information about the test form, test date, and scoring procedures is located in the bottom left corner. The far left column, labeled A, contains an alphabetical list of students in a class, each student's date of birth (DOB), and the test form. Although only three students are illustrated, an actual form would include all members of a class. The second column from the left identifies the types of scores reported. Notice that the class record includes national percentiles, national stanines, grade equivalents, normal curve equivalents, and scale scores for each student. The remaining columns, located in section B, contain the derived scores for all subtests. The bottom portion of the table contains summary data for the class group.

The information provided for each student on the Class Record Sheet is very similar to that provided on the individual student profile form. The main benefit of the class record is to synthesize information across students to enable teachers to describe the class as a whole. The class summary information located at the bottom of the report in section C is additional information not provided on the individual profiles. Using these summary scores, teachers can describe the group's achievement in each of the subtests, area tests, and on the total test battery. On the basis of the total battery scores provided in section C of Figure 15.10, how would you describe the class in the example?

FIGURE 15.10 ➤
A Sample Class Record Sheet from the Comprehensive Tests of Basic Skills, Fourth Edition

Source: Reprinted with permission from a 1992 catalog of materials for the Comprehensive Tests of Basic Skills, Fourth Edition, p. 149 (Monterey: CA: Macmillan/McGraw-Hill School Publishing Company).

◆ CTBS/4 Comprehensive Tests of Basic Skills, Fourth Edition

CLASS RECORD SHEET

CLASS: POLK   **GRADE:** 5.7

A — Reading / Language / Mathematics / Total Battery

STUDENTS	Scores	Reading VOCAB	Reading COMPR	Reading TOTAL	Language MECH	Language EXPR	Language TOTAL	Math COMPU	Math C & A	Math TOTAL	Total Battery	SPELL	STUDY SKILL	SCI	SOC STD
ARNOLD STEPHAN N	NP	46	88	69	77	69	75	54	76	69	73	56	82	70	93
DOB: 7/11/78	NS	5	7	6	6	6	6	5	6	6	6	5	7	6	8
CODES: ·········	GE	5.6	9.7	6.9	8.1	7.5	7.9	5.9	7.7	6.7	7.1	6.1	8.5	7.5	12.+
FORM: A LEVEL: 15	NCE	48	74	60	66	60	65	52	65	60	63	53	70	61	82
	SS	712	769	741	749	750	750	732	755	744	745	728	766	753	791
BRADLEY SHARON	NP	71	60	66	81	75	80	33	51	43	64	56	94	51	59
DOB: 7/25/78	NS	6	6	6	6	6	7	4	5	5	6	6	5	5	5
CODES: ·········	GE	6.7	6.5	6.7	8.5	8.1	8.5	5.2	5.8	5.5	6.5	6.1	12.0	5.9	6.7
FORM: A LEVEL: 15	NCE	62	56	59	68	64	68	40	50	46	58	53	83	50	55
	SS	738	738	738	753	756	755	711	726	719	737	728	793	733	744
BROWN SUSAN F	NP	10	21	16	18	7	12	27	39	33	17	44	23	9	24
DOB: 7/2/78	NS	2	3	3	3	2	3	4	4	4	3	5	3	2	4
CODES: ·········	GE	3.3	4.0	3.6	3.4	2.4	2.7	5.0	5.2	5.1	3.7	5.5	4.4	3.0	4.3
FORM: A LEVEL: 15	NCE	23	33	29	31	18	25	37	44	41	30	47	34	22	35
	SS	659	690	675	675	652	664	704	713	709	682	714	677	662	702

C — CLASS SUMMARY

CLASS SUMMARY	Scores	Reading VOCAB	Reading COMPR	Reading TOTAL	Language MECH	Language EXPR	Language TOTAL	Math COMPU	Math C & A	Math TOTAL	Total Battery	SPELL	STUDY SKILL	SCI	SOC STD
	MDNP	60.0	52.3	59.3	65.0	52.0	61.3	54.0	58.0	51.0	59.0	56.6	66.0	52.0	60.6
	MNS	5.5	5.5	5.5	5.6	5.2	5.5	5.4	5.3	5.4	5.5	5.3	5.8	5.0	5.5
	GME	6.2	6.8	6.5	6.5	6.5	6.6	6.2	6.3	6.2	6.4	6.3	6.8	6.0	7.7
	MNCE	54.5	55.3	55.2	56.8	52.1	55.3	53.3	53.4	53.9	55.0	54.2	53.3	49.9	55.7
	MSS	724.0	735.6	730.0	730.4	731.1	732.0	731.6	731.0	731.5	731.0	727.6	738.8	728.6	744.6
NUMBER OF STUDENTS = 31		31	31	31	31	31	31	31	31	31	31	31	31	31	31

FORM-LEVEL: A-15
NORMS FROM: 1988
TEST DATE: 4/24/89
SCORING: PATTERN (IRT)
QUARTER MONTH: 31

CITY: MT VERNON   SCHOOL: TAFT
STATE: DISTRICT: WINFIELD

Total Battery includes Total Reading, Total Language, and Total Mathematics.

MDNP: MEDIAN NATIONAL PERCENTILE
MNS: MEAN NATIONAL STANINE
GME: GRADE MEAN EQUIVALENT
MNCE: MEAN NORMAL CURVE EQUIVALENT
MSS: MEAN SCALE SCORE

CTB/MCGRAW-HILL

The central tendency scores reported for the class (means and medians) indicate that their average or central achievement is slightly higher than the national norm group's average or central achievement. For example, their median national percentile of 59 is slightly higher than the norm group's center of 50, and their average stanine of 5.5 is also slightly higher than the norm group's average of 5.

Another type of form teachers find useful is the Objectives Performance Report. This form is especially helpful for curriculum planning and evaluation since it describes each student's mastery level for each objective the test measures. Figure 15.11 contains an example of an objectives report. The top and bottom left corners again provide information about the class and the test. The far left column (C) contains a list of the objectives measured by the test, and the percentages of students in both the local school district and the national norm group that mastered each objective are listed beside it. The column just to the right of these group data, labeled DIFF, indicates whether the local group or the national group had a larger percentage of students who mastered the objective. The top row of the table contains an alphabetical list of all the students in the class.

Information about whether a particular student mastered, partially mastered, or failed to master an objective is indicated in the circles placed in the intersection of objective rows and student columns. For example, you can see that Arnold partially mastered the first three objectives listed (word meaning, multimeaning words, and affixes) because the circles in these intersecting cells are partially darkened. We know he failed to master words in context because the circle in his intersecting cell is blank. He mastered the stated information objective since the circle in this cell is completely darkened. You can use such a summary to analyze the objective-by-objective mastery level of each student in your class.

Besides individual student mastery analysis, teachers can use these Objective Performance Reports to analyze the group's mastery of particular objectives. This analysis could be helpful for lesson planning or grouping students for instruction.

The individual and class profile forms illustrated in this chapter represent only a sample of those available from commercial test publishers. Regardless of the publisher or the particular format of the report, the tables and graphs within a report simply indicate whether a student or class group is

FIGURE 15.11 ➤

A Sample Objectives Performance Report from the Comprehensive Tests of Basic Skills, Fourth Edition

Source: Reprinted with permission from a 1992 catalog of materials for the Comprehensive Tests of Basic Skills, Fourth Edition, p. 151 (Monterey: CA: Macmillan/McGraw-Hill School Publishing Company).

◆ CTBS/4 Comprehensive Tests of Basic Skills, Fourth Edition

OBJECTIVES PERFORMANCE REPORT

CLASS: POLK GRADE: 5.7

A

- O : NOT MASTERED (RANGE: .0 - .49)
- ◐ : PARTIALLY MASTERED (RANGE: .50 - .74)
- ● : MASTERED (RANGE: .75 - .99)
- N : NOT ALL ITEMS ATTEMPTED

NUMBER OF STUDENTS: 31

	Students Mastering LOCAL %	NATL %	DIFF %	AVG. OPI
READ VOCABULARY				
18 WORD MEANING	52	45	+ 7	.73
19 MULTIMEANING WORDS	45	47	- 2	.70
20 AFFIXES	39	30	+ 9	.65
22 WORDS IN CONTEXT	26	16	+ 10	.53
READ COMPREHENSION				
25 STATED INFORMATION	58	47	+ 11	.76
27 PASSAGE ANALYSIS	39	39	+ 0	.72
28 CENTRAL THOUGHT	26	32	- 6	
29 WRITTEN FORMS, TECHNIQUE	32	32	+ 0	
30 CRITICAL ASSESSMENT	42	37	+ 5	.72
LANGUAGE MECHANICS				
34 SENTENCE, PHRASE, CLAUSE	65	40	+ 25	.75
35 QUOTATIONS, DIALOGUE	16	19	- 3	.59
36 WRITING CONVENTIONS	84	55	+ 29	.80
37 EDITING SKILLS	29	23	+ 6	.61
LANGUAGE EXPRESSION				
38 NOUNS, PRONOUNS	100	95	+ 5	.97
39 VERBS	77	65	+ 12	.77

NATL % : NATIONAL REFERENCE GROUP 5.8
AVG. OPI : AVERAGE OBJECTIVE PERFORMANCE INDEX

FORM-LEVEL: A-15
NORMS FROM: 1988
TEST DATE: 4/24/89
SCORING: PATTERN (IRT)
QUARTER MONTH: 31

CITY: MT VERNON
STATE:
SCHOOL: TAFT
DISTRICT: WINFIELD

CTB/MCGRAW-HILL

485

above average, average, or below average compared to a representative sample of students at the same grade level. Before administering a standardized test to your students, you should study the examiner's manual carefully to ensure that you are following standard procedures in administering the test. Before interpreting student and class profiles for yourself, your colleagues, or parents, you should review the teacher's and administrator's manuals and the norms book to refresh your memory on the derivation and interpretation of the derived scores used with standardized tests.

SUMMARY

Due to the increasing emphasis on data-based decision making in schools, school personnel must be able to interpret and use information from standardized achievement and scholastic aptitude tests. The achievement tests, which may be either criterion referenced or norm referenced, measure students' knowledge and skills in school subjects. Scholastic aptitude tests measure students' general mental-processing skills.

School districts that intend to use test results for instructional planning, instructional evaluation, or grading students' progress generally select a criterion-referenced test that focuses on the school's curriculum. Districts that want to use test results to compare the performance of individuals or groups to a nationwide sample of students use norm-referenced achievement tests. Those that want to determine which students will probably succeed in a particular program use scholastic aptitude tests to predict students' achievement.

Scoring methods and scores used to report students' performance on the three types of tests differ. Performance on criterion-referenced tests is generally reported as nonmastery, partial knowledge, and mastery. These levels can be based either on the number and percentage of items students answer correctly for each objective or on scores derived using a variety of factors besides the number of correct items. Professional judgment is used to set the cut-off scores for each of the three levels. Performance on norm-referenced tests is reported using derived scores that enable comparisons among students. These scores include scale scores, percentiles, percentile bands, stanines, normal curve equivalent scores, normalized z and T scores, and grade equivalent scores. An anticipated achievement score is also used when both aptitude and achievement tests are administered. Performance on aptitude tests is reported using a deviation IQ score and sometimes a percentile score. Table 15.8 summarizes the characteristics and interpretation of these scores.

Teachers of all subjects use aptitude scores and total scores from the achievement tests to describe the characteristics of their assigned classes. Teachers of language and mathematics use subtest scores and scores on each objective measured by the subtests to aid instructional planning.

TABLE 15.8
Scores Commonly Used to Report Students' Performances on Norm-Referenced Tests

Scores	Characteristics	Interpretation
Scale Scores	These are scores on an arbitrarily set common scale used to measure students' variability in a subject and their progress across grades in a subject. Mean scale scores and standard deviations vary for each subtest and grade level. These measures must be obtained from the test's technical manual for each grade and subject.	Scores 1 standard deviation below the mean and lower reflect below-average performance. Scores within 1 standard deviation from the mean reflect average performance. Scores 1 standard deviation above the mean and higher reflect above-average performance. Students' progress in one subject should be compared using scale scores appropriate to each student's achievement level because students at different levels progress at different rates.
Percentiles	Range from 1 to 99 Midpoint 50 $\overline{X} + 1SD = 84$ $\overline{X} - 1SD = 16$ There are unequal intervals between percentiles.	Percentiles reflect the percentage of students in the norm group surpassed at each raw score in the distribution.
Percentile Bands	These are confidence bands placed around each percentile using the test's standard error of measurement. The width of percentile bands varies across the percentile scale. Those in the center of the distribution are wider than those toward the ends.	A student's score on retesting could fall anywhere within the band. Overlapping bands reflect no significant differences between observed percentile scores.
Stanines	Range from 1 to 9 Midpoint is 5 $\overline{X} + 1SD = 7$ $\overline{X} - 1SD = 3$ Stanines are band scores and encompass several scale scores and percentiles. Stanines in the center of the distribution encompass more percentiles than those toward the ends.	Stanines 1, 2, and 3 reflect below-average performance. Stanines 4, 5, and 6 reflect average performance. Stanines 7, 8, and 9 reflect above-average performance.
Normalized z and T Scores	z: $\overline{X} = 0$ $SD = 1$ $\overline{X} + 1SD = 1$ $\overline{X} - 1SD = -1$	Scores of -1 or lower reflect below-average performance. Scores between $-.99$ and $.99$ reflect average performance. Scores of 1 or above reflect above-average performance.

(continued)

TABLE 15.8 Continued

Scores	Characteristics	Interpretation
	T: $\overline{X} = 50$ $SD = 10$ $\overline{X} + 1SD = 60$ $\overline{X} - 1SD = 40$	Scores of 40 and below reflect below-average performance. Scores of 41 through 59 reflect average performance. Scores of 60 and above reflect above-average performance.
Normal Curve Equivalents	Range from 1 to 99 $\overline{X} = 50$ $SD = 21.06$ $\overline{X} + 1SD = 71.06$ $\overline{X} - 1SD = 28.94$	Scores of 28.94 and lower reflect below-average performance. Scores between 29 and 70 reflect average performance. Scores of 71.06 and higher reflect above-average performance.
Deviation IQ Scores	$\overline{X} = 100$ $SD = 15$ or 16 $\overline{X} + 1SD = 115, 116$ $\overline{X} - 1SD = 85, 84$ These scores are used to report performance on scholastic aptitude tests.	Scores of 85, 84 and lower reflect below-average performance. Scores between 85, 86 and 114, 115 reflect average performance. Scores of 115, 116 and higher reflect above-average performance.
Grade Equivalent Scores	These are scores based on the median score earned by the norm group in two or three consecutive grades. These scores are decimal numbers; the first digit reflects a grade and the second reflects a month within a grade. All scores are derived from the two or three median scores using the processes of interpolation and extrapolation. Grade equivalent scores reflect the estimated median score earned by a group in a given grade and month.	A wide range of grade equivalent scores are assigned to students in each grade level. Match grade equivalent scores to their corresponding percentiles and stanines to determine whether they reflect below-average, average, or above-average performance for students in a particular grade. Do not use these scores to compare one student's performance across subtests. Do not use these scores to describe students' performance to parents and the community.
Anticipated Achievement Scores	These scores are the mean scores earned by a subset of students in the norm group who are matched to each student using aptitude scores and other characteristics. Confidence intervals are placed around these mean scores to differentiate between typical and atypically high or low observed scores.	Although anticipated and observed achievement scores are often different, the differences are considered insignificant unless a plus or minus sign is used to reflect atypically high or low performance.

PRACTICE EXERCISES

I. **Matching Test Types and Purposes**
   Three types of tests are listed in Column B. Indicate the type of test you would use to complete the tasks described in items 1 through of 8 Column A:

   Column A
   _____ 1. Compare the performance of students in your school district to the performance of a nationwide sample of students in basic skills.
   _____ 2. Plan lessons covering the punctuation of declarative, interrogative, exclamatory, and imperative sentences.
   _____ 3. Predict which students are likely to be most successful in an advanced mathematics program.
   _____ 4. Compare a student's performance across reading, language, and mathematics skills.
   _____ 5. Analyze the variability of students' performance in mathematics within and across grades.
   _____ 6. Diagnose problems a student or class has in performing district-prescribed instructional goals.
   _____ 7. Predict the students most likely to succeed in a special mathematics program for gifted students.
   _____ 8. Determine students' mastery of selected language usage skills.

   Column B
   a. Criterion-referenced achievement test
   b. Norm-referenced achievement test
   c. Scholastic aptitude test

II. **Converting Scale Scores to Percentiles**
   Items A through E list the steps you would follow to convert scale scores to percentiles. Use the frequency distribution in Table 15.9 to make these conversions. Check your work using Table 15.9F in the Feedback section.
   A. Beginning at the bottom of the table, calculate the cumulative frequency of scale scores below each scale score and record this number in column 3.
   B. Divide the observed frequency for each scale score by 2 and record this number in column 4.
   C. Sum the frequency below and one-half the frequency within (columns 3 and 4) for each score and record the total in column 5.
   D. Divide the total in column 5 by the total number of students in the group to obtain the proportion of students whose scores fall below the midpoint for each scale score.
   E. Multiply these proportions by 100 to obtain the percentile for each scale score and record this value in column 6.

TABLE 15.9
Worksheet for Converting Scale Scores to Percentiles

(1) Scale Scores	(2) Frequency	(3) Cumulative Frequency below	(4) 1/2 Frequency within	(5) Proportion	(6) Percentile
640	1				
639	1				
638	2				
637	2				
636	3				
635	3				
634	2				
633	2				
632	2				
631	1				
630	1				

III. **Interpreting Percentile Scores**
Judge whether each of the following statements about the characteristics of percentile scores and their interpretation is true.
A. There are equal intervals between percentile scores.
B. Percentiles reflect the percentage of items answered correctly.
C. Percentiles correspond to the standard normal distribution of scores.
D. Percentiles are created using the processes of interpolation and extrapolation.
E. There is an equal number of percentile points between the mean and one standard deviation above the mean and between one and two standard deviations above the mean.
F. There are larger intervals between the percentiles in the center of the distribution than between those toward the ends of the scale.
G. Percentiles range from 0 to 100.
H. Relatively small differences between percentiles toward the center of the scale are not meaningful.
I. Percentiles reflect the percentage of students surpassed at the midpoint for each scale score.
J. One standard deviation above the mean is equivalent to the 60th percentile.
K. Each increase of one scale score point can result in an increase of several percentile points.

IV. **Calculating and Plotting Percentile Bands**
Use the scale score-to-percentile conversions made in Table 15.9 to complete this exercise. Table 15.10 contains three scale scores and their corresponding percentiles from Table 15.9. Follow the directions in items A through C to plot the percentile bands for these three scores. Check your work using Table 15.10F in the Feedback section.
A. Using a standard error of measurement (SEM) of 2, calculate the scale score corresponding to +1 SEM and −1 SEM for each obtained score.
B. Locate the corresponding percentile scores in Table 15.9 for each extended scale score.

TABLE 15.10
Worksheet for Calculating and Plotting Percentile Bands

SEM = 2

	−1 SEM	Obtained Score	+1 SEM	Percentiles 1 5 10 20 30 40 50 60 70 80 90 95 99
Scale Score		639		
Percentile		93		
Scale Score		635		
Percentile		48		
Scale Score		632		
Percentile		15		

C. Using the chart on the right-hand side of Table 15.10, plot the percentile bands for each obtained percentile score. Mark the position of the obtained percentile score within the band.

V. **Interpreting Percentile Bands**
   Judge whether each of the following statements about the characteristics of percentile bands and their interpretation is true.
   A. Percentile bands for percentiles throughout the scale are of equal width.
   B. Percentile bands reflect that norm-referenced tests are imprecise measures of achievement.
   C. The obtained percentile score usually falls in the center of the percentile band.
   D. Percentile bands can be used to compare one student's performance on various subtests.
   E. The performance of several students in the class can be compared on one test using percentile bands.
   F. Scores that have a small standard error of measurement have wider percentile bands than scores that have a large standard error of measurement.
   G. Overlapping bands reflect meaningful differences in obtained percentile scores.
   H. Percentile bands are confidence intervals that reflect the range of scores where a student's score is likely to fall on retesting.

VI. **Interpreting Stanine Scores**
   A. What percentage of the norm group is assigned each stanine score?

Stanine Scores	1	2	3	4	5	6	7	8	9
Percentage									

   B. If there were 1,000 students in the norm group, how many students would be assigned each stanine score?

Stanine Scores	1	2	3	4	5	6	7	8	9
Number of Students									

C. Judge whether each of the following statements about the characteristics of stanine
scores and their interpretation is true.
1. An equal number of students is assigned each stanine.
2. Each stanine encompasses a range of scale scores and percentile scores.
3. An equal range of scale scores corresponds to each stanine.
4. Stanines correspond to the standard normal curve.
5. One standard deviation above the mean corresponds to a stanine score of 7.
6. A stanine of 3 corresponds to one standard deviation below the mean.
7. All nine stanines are one-half a standard deviation wide.
8. A stanine score is more similar to a percentile band than to a percentile.

VII. **Selecting Scores from the Report Form**
Select the score or scores (from Column B) that best answer the questions from
Column A.

	Column A	*Column B*
_____	1. What two scores are used to compare the variability of students' achievement across grade levels?	a. Anticipated achievement scores
		b. Deviation IQ scores
		c. Grade equivalent scores
		d. Normal curve equivalent scores
_____	2. What scores are used to determine whether a student's obtained score is atypical?	e. Normalized z and T scores
		f. Percentile scores
		g. Scale scores
		h. Stanine scores
_____	3. What score is used to report students' aptitude levels?	
_____	4. Of all the scores associated with achievement tests, which one is most likely to be misinterpreted?	
_____	5. Which score is created using the processes of interpolation and extrapolation?	
_____	6. Which achievement scores should not be used to compare a student's achievement on different subtests?	
_____	7. Which score should not be used to report students' performance to parents?	

FIGURE 15.12 ➤

Individual Test Record for the Comprehensive Tests of Basic Skills, Fourth Edition

Source: Reprinted with permission from a 1992 catalog of materials for the Comprehensive
Tests of Basic Skills, Fourth Edition, p. 154 (Monterey: CA: Macmillan/McGraw-Hill School
Publishing Company).

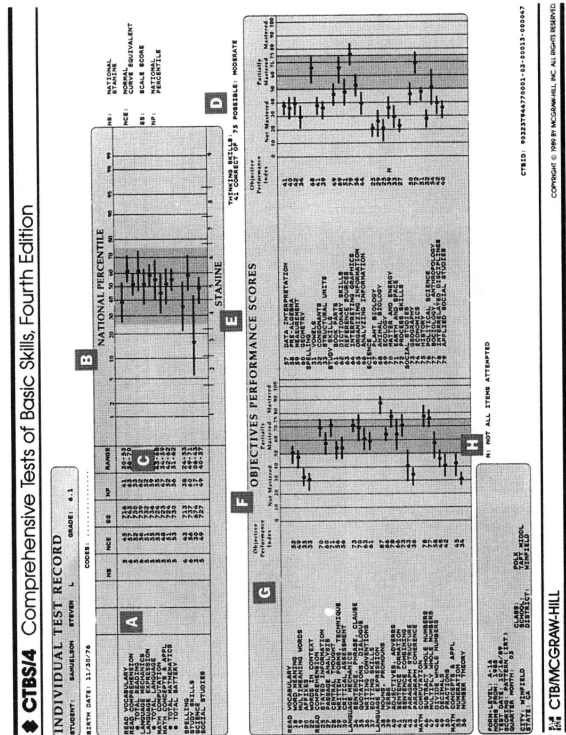

493

VIII. Interpreting Test Records

    A. Use the Comprehensive Tests of Basic Skills Individual Test Record in Figure 15.12 to answer the following questions.

        1. When did Steven take the CTBS (grade, month)?

        2. His scale score (SS) on the language mechanics test is 739. What level of performance does this score reflect?

          a. Above average

          b. Average

          c. Below average

        3. How did you reach this conclusion?

        4. On a retest, his language mechanics percentile score would probably fall within which range?

        5. Which of Steven's scores could you use to compare his performance on the total reading, total language, and total mathematics tests?

        6. On which of these tests did he perform best?

        7. Is his performance in language superior to his performance in reading?

        8. How do you know this?

        9. Steven's national percentile score on the vocabulary test is 41, and his percentile score on the language mechanics test is 62. On which test did he perform better?

       10. His normal curve equivalent score (NCE) in math concepts and application is 48. Is this score lower than one standard deviation below the mean NCE score?

       11. Use Steven's stanine scores to describe his overall performance on the CTBS.

    B. Use the Comprehensive Tests of Basic Skills Class Record Summary Sheet in Figure 15.13 to complete the following exercises.

        1. Use the group's mean national stanine (MNS) to describe the group's standing in total reading.

        2. Use the group's median national percentiles (MDNP) in total reading, language, and mathematics to describe their overall achievement.

IX. Enrichment

    A. Make an appointment with a school guidance counselor to discuss the norm-referenced achievement and aptitude tests used by the district. Ask the following questions:

        1. How are tests selected?

        2. Which tests are used at each grade level?

        3. When are the tests administered?

        4. How do administrators and teachers use the test results?

    B. If district policy permits, review samples of the following test materials:

        1. The administrator's guide for a test used at your grade level. Find a description of the objectives measured, the norm group, administration procedures, and sample report forms.

FIGURE 15.13 ➤

Class Record Summary Sheet for the Comprehensive Tests of Basic Skills, Fourth Edition

Source: Reprinted with permission from a 1992 catalog of materials for the Comprehensive Tests of Basic Skills, Fourth Edition, p. 150 (Monterey: CA: Macmillan/McGraw-Hill School Publishing Company).

◆ CTBS/4 Comprehensive Tests of Basic Skills, Fourth Edition

CLASS RECORD SUMMARY SHEET

CLASS: POLK   GRADE: 5.7

A | **B** Scores

	NUMBER OF STUDENTS	MNS	GHE	MNCE	MSS	MDNP
READ VOCABULARY	31	5.5	6.2	54.5	724.0	60.0
READ COMPREHENSION	31	5.5	6.8	55.3	735.8	52.3
TOTAL READING	31	5.5	6.5	55.2	730.0	59.3
LANGUAGE MECHANICS	31	5.6	6.5	56.8	730.4	65.0
LANGUAGE EXPRESSION	31	5.2	6.5	52.1	733.1	52.0
TOTAL LANGUAGE	31	5.5	6.6	55.3	732.0	61.3
MATH COMPUTATION	31	5.4	6.2	53.3	731.6	54.0
MATH CONCEPTS & APPL	31	5.3	6.3	53.4	731.0	58.0
TOTAL MATHEMATICS	31	5.4	6.2	53.9	731.5	51.0
TOTAL BATTERY	31	5.5	6.4	55.0	731.0	59.0
SPELLING	31	5.3	6.3	54.2	727.6	56.6
STUDY SKILLS	31	5.8	6.8	58.3	738.8	66.0
SCIENCE	31	5.0	6.0	49.9	728.6	52.0
SOCIAL STUDIES	31	5.5	7.7	55.7	744.6	60.6

C MEDIAN NATIONAL PERCENTILE

E MEDIAN NORMAL CURVE EQUIVALENT
■ MEDIAN OBTAINED ACHIEVEMENT

D
MNS: MEAN NATIONAL STANINE
MNCE: MEAN NORMAL CURVE EQUIVALENT
MDNP: MEDIAN NATIONAL PERCENTILE

GME: GRADE MEAN EQUIVALENT
HSS: MEAN SCALE SCORE

F

The Median National Percentiles for this CLASS indicate that the average student's achievement is highest in STUDY SKILLS (66th Percentile) and LANGUAGE MECHANICS (65th Percentile) and lowest in SCIENCE (52nd Percentile) and LANGUAGE EXPRESSION (52nd Percentile). Overall, the TOTAL BATTERY places the CLASS higher than 59 percent of the students in the National Norm Group. This report is a summary only. For a complete description of performance, individual scores should be examined.

FORM-LEVEL: A-15
NORMS FROM: 1988
TEST DATE: 4/24/89
SCORING: PATTERN (IRT)
QUARTER MONTH: 31

SCHOOL: TAFT
DISTRICT: WINFIELD

CITY: MT VERNON
STATE:

CTB/MCGRAW-HILL

2. Sample individual and group report records from the most recent test. The counselor may want to cover or block out students' names before you review these records.

C. If you have kept your own test records or those of your students, analyze these reports and interpret the scores.

FEEDBACK

I. **Matching Test Types and Purposes**

1. b	5. b
2. a	6. a
3. c	7. c
4. b	8. a

II. **Converting Scale Scores to Percentiles**
For items A through E, see Table 15.9F.

III. **Interpreting Percentile Scores.**
The following statements are correct: C, F, H, I, and K.

IV. **Calculating and Plotting Percentile Bands**
For items A through C, see Table 15.10F.

V. **Interpreting Percentile Bands**
The following statements are correct: B, D, E, and H.

TABLE 15.9F
Scale Scores and Their Corresponding Percentiles

(1) Scale Scores	(2) Frequency	(3) Cumulative Frequency below	(4) 1/2 Frequency within	(5) Proportion	(6) Percentiles
640	1	19	.5	19.5/20 = .98	98
639	1	18	.5	18.5/20 = .93	93
638	2	16	1	17/20 = .85	85
637	2	14	1	15/20 = .75	75
636	3	11	1.5	12.5/20 = .63	63
635	3	8	1.5	9.5/20 = .48	48
634	2	6	1	7/20 = .35	35
633	2	4	1	5/20 = .25	25
632	2	2	1	3/20 = .15	15
631	1	1	.5	1.5/20 = .08	8
630	1	0	.5	.5/20 = .03	3

TABLE 15.10F
Percentiles and Their Corresponding Percentile Bands

SEM = 2

	−1 SEM	Obtained Score	+1 SEM	Percentiles 1 5 10 20 30 40 50 60 70 80 90 95 99
Scale Score	637	639	640	
Percentile	75	93	98	————————————— •xxxxxxxxxxxx—
Scale Score	633	635	637	
Percentile	25	48	75	———————— xxxxxxxx•xxxxxxxxx—————
Scale Score	630	632	634	
Percentile	3	15	35	—•xxxxxxxxxxx—————————————

Note: The narrow range of scale scores in the example resulted in abnormally wide percentile bands. Because norm-referenced tests are designed to yield a wide range of scores, the percentile bands are narrower.

VI. **Interpreting Stanine Scores**

Stanine Scores	1	2	3	4	5	6	7	8	9
A. Percentage	4	7	12	17	20	17	12	7	4
B. Number of Students	40	70	120	170	200	170	120	70	40

C. The following statements are correct: 2, 4, 5, 6, and 8.

VII. **Selecting Scores from the Report Form**
1. c and g
2. a and b
3. b
4. c
5. c
6. c and g
7. c

VIII. **Interpreting Test Records**
A. Referring to Figure 15.12 will give you the following answers:
1. 6.1
2. b
3. By determining the performance level indicated by the corresponding percentile or stanine score.
4. It should fall between the 50th and 73rd percentiles. This information was obtained by locating the percentiles that correspond to the outer edges of his percentile band for language mechanics.
5. Percentile bands, stanines, or normal curve equivalent scores.
6. None. The percentile bands overlap for these areas.
7. No.
8. Because the percentile bands for these tests overlap.
9. His performance is equivalent on the two tests since the percentile bands overlap.

    10. No. For the NCE score, the mean is 50 and the standard deviation is 21.06. His score of 48 is not lower than 50 – 21.06, or 28.94.

    11. In comparison with the national norm group, Steven's performances in reading, language skills, and mathematics are average.

B. Referring to Figure 15.13 will give you the following answers:

    1. The group's mean national stanine of 5.5 in total reading indicates average group performance compared to the national norm group.

    2. The group's median percentiles in reading and language are slightly higher than the national norm group's median percentile (50th). Their median percentile in mathematics is close to the center for the national norm group.

REFERENCES

CTB/McGraw-Hill. (1990). *Comprehensive Tests of Basic Skills, fourth edition, Spring norms book.* Monterey, CA: Macmillan/Mc- Graw-Hill School Publishing Company.

CTB/McGraw-Hill. (1992). *1992 Catalog.* Monterey, CA: Macmillan/McGraw-Hill School Publishing Company.

SUGGESTED READINGS

Ebel, R. L., & Frisbee, D. A. (1991). *Essentials of educational measurement* (5th ed.) (pp. 303–341). Englewood Cliffs, NJ: Prentice Hall.

Gronlund, N. E., & Linn, R. L. (1990). *Measurement and evaluation in teaching* (6th ed.) (pp. 265–371). New York: Macmillan.

Hopkins, C. D., & Antes, R. L. (1990). *Classroom measurement and evaluation* (3rd ed.) (pp. 437–475). Itasca, IL: F. E. Peacock.

Kubiszyn, T., & Borich, G. (1990). *Educational testing and measurement* (3rd ed.) (pp. 303–379). Glenview, IL: Scott, Foresman/Little, Brown.

Mehrens, W. A., & Lehmann, I. J. (1991). *Measurement and evaluation in education and psychology* (4th ed.) (pp. 345–394). New York: CBS College Publishing.

Oosterhof, A. (1990). *Classroom applications of educational measurement* (pp. 288–402). Columbus, OH: Merrill.

Popham, W. J. (1990). *Modern educational measurement* (2nd ed.) (pp. 156–180). Englewood Cliffs, NJ: Prentice Hall.

Sax, G. (1989). *Principles of educational and psychological measurement and evaluation* (3rd ed.) (pp. 205–212). Belmont, CA: Wadsworth.

Wiersma, W., & Jurs, S. G. (1990). *Educational measurement and testing* (2nd ed.) (pp. 117–136, 309–331). Boston: Allyn and Bacon.

APPENDIX A

Sample Matrix Diagram

FIGURE 3.6

Sample Matrix Diagram Analysis for the Instructional Goal, "Write a Paragraph"

CONCEPTS/ CONTENT	A State/Recall Physical Characteristics	B State/Recall Functional Characteristics	C State/Recall Quality Charactertistics	D Discriminate Examples & Nonexamples	E Evaluate Given Examples	F Produce Examples
I. Paragraph	Series of sentences Indented	Express ideas on one topic		Correct vs. not indented Many topics		Time Series Feelings Procedure Description
II. Topic Sentence	Typically first Indented	Introduce topic	Relevance Scope Interest	Topic vs. Supporting Concluding	Correct vs. flawed by: Relevance Scope Interest	Time Series Feelings Procedure Description
III. Supporting Sentences	Middle sentences	Elaborate topic	Relevance Sequence Transition	Supporting vs. Topic Concluding	Correct vs. flawed by: Relevance Sequence Transition	Time Series Feelings Procedure Description
IV. Concluding Sentences	Typically last	Conclude/ summarize topic	Transition Relevance Sums up Scope	Concluding vs. Topic Supporting	Correct vs. flawed by: Transition Relevance Conclusion Scope	Time Series Feelings Procedure Description

APPENDIX B

Sample Table of Behavioral Objectives

TABLE 3.6
Table of Behavioral Objectives for the Instructional Goal, "Write a Paragraph"

Enabling Skill	Objective Code	Behavioral Objective
I.A	I.A.1	Given the term *paragraph*, recall its physical characteristics.
	I.A.2	Given the physical characteristics of a paragraph, recall its name.
	I.A.3	Given the term *paragraph* <u>and</u> a list of possible physical characteristics related to the concept, choose those for a paragraph.
	I.A.4	Given a description of the physical characteristics of a paragraph and a list of terms related to paragraphs, select the term *paragraph* as the concept being described.
I.B	I.B.1	Given the term *paragraph*, recall its functional characteristics.
	I.B.2	Given the functional characteristics of a paragraph, recall its name.
	I.B.3	Given the term *paragraph* <u>and</u> a list of possible functional characteristics related to the concept, choose those for a paragraph.
	I.B.4	Given a description of the functional characteristics of a paragraph and a list of terms related to paragraphs, select the term *paragraph* as the concept being described.
I.D	I.D.1	Given a correctly indented and not indented paragraphs, distinguish the correctly formatted paragraph.
	I.D.2	Given paragraphs on one topic and nonparagraphs containing two or more topics, discriminate between them.
II.A	II.A.1	Given the term *topic sentence*, recall its physical characteristics.
	II.A.2	Given the physical characteristics of a topic sentence, recall its name.
	II.A.3	Given the term *topic sentence* <u>and</u> a list of possible physical characteristics related to the concept, choose those for a topic sentence.
	II.A.4	Given a description of the physical characteristics of a topic sentence and a list of terms related to paragraphs, select the term *topic sentence* as the concept being described.
II.B	II.B.1	Given the term *topic sentence*, recall its functional characteristics.
	II.B.2	Given the functional characteristics of a topic sentence, recall its name.
	II.B.3	Given the term *topic sentence* <u>and</u> a list of possible functional characteristics related to the concept, choose those for a topic sentence.
	II.B.4	Given a description of the functional characteristics of a topic sentence and a list of terms related to paragraphs, select the term *topic sentence* as the concept being described.

Enabling Skill	Objective Code	Behavioral Objective
II.C	II.C.1	Given the term *topic sentence*, recall its quality characteristics.
	II.C.2	Given the quality characteristics of a topic sentence, recall its name.
	II.C.3	Given the term *topic sentence* and a list of possible quality characteristics related to the concept, choose those for a topic sentence.
	II.C.4	Given a description of the quality characteristics of a topic sentence and a list of terms related to paragraphs, select the term *topic sentence* as the concept being described.
II.D	II.D.1	Given a complete paragraph, correctly indented, locate the topic sentence.
II.E	II.E.1	Given an incomplete paragraph with the topic sentence omitted and three to four optional topic sentences, choose the best topic sentence.
	II.E.2	Given a complete paragraph with the topic sentence flawed by relevance and a list of possible judgments about the topic sentence that includes "no flaw present," as well as the quality criteria for topic sentences, choose the problem with the topic sentence.
	II.E.3	Given a complete paragraph with the topic sentence flawed by scope and a list of possible judgments about the topic sentence that includes "no flaw present," as well as the criteria for quality topic sentences, choose the problem with the topic sentence.
	II.E.4	Given a complete paragraph with the topic sentence flawed by interest, a list of possible judgments about the topic sentence that includes "no flaw present," as well as the criteria for quality topic sentences, choose the problem with the topic sentence.
	II.E.5	Given complete paragraphs with the topic sentence flawed by either relevance, scope, or interest value, rewrite the given topic sentence to meet quality criteria.
II.F	II.F.1	Given an incomplete paragraph (time series, feelings, procedure, or description), write a topic sentence to introduce the given paragraph.
III.A	III.A.1	Given the term *supporting sentence*, recall its physical characteristics.
	III.A.2	Given the physical characteristics of a supporting sentence, recall its name.
	III.A.3	Given the term *supporting sentence* and a list of possible physical characteristics related to the concept, choose those for a supporting sentence.
	III.A.4	Given a description of the physical characteristics of a supporting sentence and a list of terms related to paragraphs, select the term *supporting sentence* as the concept being described.
III.B	III.B.1	Given the term *supporting sentence*, recall its functional characteristics.
	III.B.2	Given the functional characteristics of a supporting sentence, recall its name.
	III.B.3	Given the term *supporting sentence* and a list of possible functional characteristics related to the concept, choose those for a supporting sentence.
	III.B.4	Given a description of the functional characteristics of a supporting sentence and a list of terms related to paragraphs, select the term *supporting sentence* as the concept being described.
III.C	III.C.1	Given the term *supporting sentence*, recall its quality characteristics.
	III.C.2	Given the quality characteristics of a supporting sentence, recall its name.

(continued)

TABLE 3.6 Continued

Enabling Skill	Objective Code	Behavioral Objective
	III.C.3	Given the term *supporting sentence* <u>and</u> a list of possible quality characteristics related to the concept, choose those for a supporting sentence.
	III.C.4	Given a description of the quality characteristics of a supporting sentence and a list of terms related to paragraphs, select the term *supporting sentence* as the concept being described.
III.D	III.D.1	Given a complete paragraph, correctly indented, locate the supporting sentences.
III.E	III.E.1	Given an incomplete paragraph with the supporting sentences omitted and three to four optional supporting sentences to be used for completing the paragraph, choose the best set of sentences.
	III.E.2	Given a complete paragraph with the supporting sentences flawed by relevance and a list of possible judgments about the supporting sentences that includes "no flaw present," as well as the quality criteria for supporting sentences, choose the problem with the sentences.
	III.E.3	Given a complete paragraph with the supporting sentences flawed by sequence of information and a list of possible judgments about the supporting sentences that includes "no flaw present," as well as the criteria for quality supporting sentences, identify the problem with the sentence.
	III.E.4	Given a complete paragraph with the supporting sentences out of natural chronological/procedural order, reorder the supporting sentences.
	III.E.5	Given a complete paragraph with the supporting sentences flawed by transition, a list of possible judgments about the supporting sentences that includes "no flaw present," as well as the criteria for quality supporting sentences, identify the problem with the sentences.
	III.E.6	Given complete paragraphs with the supporting sentence flawed by either relevance, sequence, or transition, rewrite the highlighted sentence to meet quality criteria.
III.F	III.F.1	Given an incomplete paragraph (time series, feelings, procedure, or description), with one or more supporting sentences missing, write supporting sentences to elaborate the topic introduced.
IV.A	IV.A.1	Given the term *concluding sentence*, recall its physical characteristics.
	IV.A.2	Given the physical characteristics of a concluding sentence, recall its name.
	IV.A.3	Given the term *concluding sentence* <u>and</u> a list of possible physical characteristics related to the concept, choose those for a concluding sentence.
	IV.A.4	Given a description of the physical characteristics of a concluding sentence and a list of terms related to paragraphs, select the term *concluding sentence* as the concept being described.
IV.B	IV.B.1	Given the term *concluding sentence*, recall its functional characteristics.
	IV.B.2	Given the functional characteristics of a concluding sentence, recall its name.
	IV.B.3	Given the term *concluding sentence* <u>and</u> a list of possible functional characteristics related to the concept, choose those for a concluding sentence.

Enabling Skill	Objective Code	Behavioral Objective
	IV.B.4	Given a description of the functional characteristics of a concluding sentence and a list of terms related to paragraphs, select the term *concluding sentence* as the concept being described.
IV.C	IV.C.1	Given the term *concluding sentence,* recall its quality characteristics.
	IV.C.2	Given the quality characteristics of a concluding sentence, recall its name.
	IV.C.3	Given the term *concluding sentence* <u>and</u> a list of possible quality characteristics related to the concept, choose those for a concluding sentence.
	IV.C.4	Given a description of the quality characteristics of a conclud- ing sentence and a list of terms related to paragraphs, select the term *concluding sentence* as the concept being described.
IV.D	IV.D.1	Given a complete paragraph, correctly indented, locate the concluding sentence.
IV.E	IV.E.1	Given an incomplete paragraph with the concluding sentence omitted and three to four optional concluding sentences, choose the best sentence.
	IV.E.2	Given a complete paragraph with the concluding sentence flawed by relevance and a list of possible judgments about the concluding sentence that includes "no flaw present," as well as the quality criteria for concluding sentences, choose the problem with the sentence.
	IV.E.3	Given a complete paragraph with the concluding sentence flawed by redundancy with topic sentence, a list of possible judgments about the concluding sentence that includes "no flaw present," as well as the criteria for quality concluding sentences, identify the problem with the sentence.
	IV.E.4	Given a complete paragraph with the concluding sentence flawed by scope and a list of possible judgments about the concluding sentence that includes "no flaw present," as well as the criteria for quality concluding sentences, identify the problem with the sentence.
	IV.E.5	Given complete paragraphs with the concluding sentence flawed by either relevance, redundancy, or scope, rewrite the given concluding sentence to meet quality criteria.
IV.F	IV.F.1	Given an incomplete paragraph (time series, feelings, procedure, or description), write a concluding sentence to summarize the ideas presented.
I.F	I.F.1	Given a topic requiring a description of something, write a 4- to 6-sentence paragraph.
	I.F.2	Given a topic requiring time series (chronology), write a 4- to 6-sentence paragraph.
	I.F.3	Given a topic that is a procedure for doing something, write a 4- to 6-sentence paragraph.
	I.F.4	Given a topic that is an expression of feelings or attitude, write a 4- to 6-sentence paragraph.

Sample Table of Test Specifications

TABLE 4.2
Table of Test Specifications for the Intellectual Skill "Write a Paragraph"

CONCEPTS/ CONTENT	A State/Recall Physical Characteristics	B State/Recall Functional Characteristics	C State/Recall Quality Characteristics	D Discriminate Examples & Nonexamples	E Evaluate Given Examples	F Produce Examples	TOTALS Objectives Items #	%
PRETEST								
I. Paragraph	I.A.3 (1)*	I.B.3 (1)		I.D.1 (1) I.D.2 (1)			4 (4)	18 11
II. Topic Sentence	II.A.3 (1)	II.B.3 (1)	II.C.3 (1)	II.D.1 (2)	II.E.1 (3)	II.F.1 (3)	6 (11)	27 30
III. Supporting Sentences	III.A.3 (1)	III.B.3 (1)	III.C.3 (1)	III.D.1 (2)	III.E.1 (3)	III.F.1 (3)	6 (11)	27 30
IV. Concluding Sentences	IV.A.3 (1)	IV.B.3 (1)	IV.C.3 (1)	IV.D.1 (2)	IV.E.1 (3)	IV.F.1 (3)	6 (11)	27 30
TOTALS Objectives Items Est. Time	4 4 2	4 4 2	3 3 3	5 8 14	3 9 27	3 9 27	22 (37) 75 min.	100 100
UNIT POSTTEST								
I. Paragraph	I.A.4 (1)	1.B.4 (1)		I.D.2 (1)		I.F.1 (1) I.F.2 (1) I.F.3 (1) I.F.4 (1)	7 (7)	23 16
II. Topic Sentence	II.A.4 (1)	II.B.4 (1)	II.C.4 (1)	II.D.1 (2)	II.E.1 (2) II.E.4 (2)	II.F.1 (2)	7 (11)	23 25
III. Supporting Sentences	III.A.4 (1)	III.B.4 (1)	III.C.4 (1)	III.D.1 (2)	III.E.1 (2) III.E.3 (2) III.E.5 (2)	III.F.1 (2)	8 (13)	27 30
IV. Concluding Sentences	IV.A.4 (1)	IV.B.4 (1)	IV.C.4 (1)	IV.D.1 (2)	IV.E.1 (2) IV.E.3 (2) IV.E.4 (2)	IV.F.1 (2)	8 (13)	27 30
TOTALS Objectives Items Est. Time	4 4 2	4 4 2	3 3 3	4 7 10	8 16 32	7 10 110	30 (44) 159 min.	100 100

*Numbers in parentheses represent the number of test items prescribed for each objective.

CONCEPTS/ CONTENT	A State/Recall Physical Characteristics	B State/Recall Functional Characteristics	C State/Recall Quality Characteristics	D Discriminate Examples & Nonexamples	E Evaluate Given Examples	F Produce Examples	TOTALS Objectives (Items) Est. Time
PRACTICE TESTS							
I. Paragraph	I.A.2 (1)	I.B.2 (1)		I.D.1 (2) I.D.2 (2)			4 (6) 10 min.
II. Topic Sentence 1.	II.A.2 (1)	II.B.2 (1)	II.C.1 (1)	II.D.1 (1)	II.E.2 (2) II.E.3 (2) II.E.5 (3)	II.F.1 (3)	8 (14) 40 min.
2.	II.A.1 (1)	II.B.1 (1)	II.C.1 (1)	II.D.1 (1)	II.E.5 (3)	II.F.1 (3)	6 (10) 30 min.
3.					II.E.1 (3) II.E.2 (2) II.E.3 (2) II.E.4 (2) II.E.5 (3)	II.F.1 (3)	6 (15) 40 min.
III. Support-ing Sentences 1. (Relevance)	III.A.2 (1)	III.B.2 (1)	III.C.2 (1)	III.D.1 (1)	III.E.1 (2) III.E.2 (2)	III.F.1 (2)	7 (10) 25 min.
2. (Sequence)	III.A.4 (1)	III.B.4 (1)	III.C.4 (1)	III.D.1 (1)	III.E.1 (2) III.E.3 (2) III.E.4 (2) III.E.6 (2)	III.F.1 (2)	9 (14) 35 min.
3. (Transition)				III.D.1 (1)	III.E.5 (3) III.E.6 (3)	III.F.1 (2)	4 (9) 30 min.
IV. Conclud-ing Sentences 1.	IV.A.2 (1)	IV.B.2 (1)	IV.C.1 (1)	IV.D.1 (1)	IV.E.2 (2) IV.E.3 (2) IV.E.5 (3)	IV.F.1 (3)	8 (14) 30 min.
2.	IV.A.1 (1)	IV.B.1 (1)	IV.C.1 (1)	IV.D.1 (1)	IV.E.5 (3)	IV.F.1 (3)	6 (10) 25 min.
3.					IV.E.1 (3) IV.E.2 (2) IV.E.3 (2) IV.E.4 (2) IV.E.5 (3)	IV.F.1 (3)	6 (15) 40 min.
I. Paragraph 1.						I.F.1 (2)	1 (2) 40 min.
2.						I.F.2 (2)	1 (2) 40 min.
3.						I.F.3 (2)	1 (2) 40 min.
4.						I.F.4 (2)	1 (2) 40 min.

Entry Behaviors Test for Writing Paragraphs

Name _____ Date _____

Directions: Place a check mark (√) in the space before each **complete** sentence.

_____ 1. Once when I was going to the store.
_____ 2. There are eight kinds of fish in the pond.
_____ 3. John, a friend of mine, likes to camp.
_____ 4. The more people there are in a circus tent.
_____ 5. Both Sarah and Susan enjoy working in the lab.

Directions:

A. Locate the subject or subjects in the following sentences and draw one line under it.
B. Locate the predicate in the following sentences and draw two lines under it.

Example: <u>The big dipper</u> <u>sparkles on clear nights.</u>

6. Bears hibernate in the winter.
7. Ants are very social insects, and they live in colonies.
8. George helped his parents clean the yard.

Directions: Write two complete sentences about any topic you choose.

9. _____
10. _____

Pretest for Writing Paragraphs
(I. Paragraphs and II. Topic Sentences)

Name _____ Date _____

Directions: Use a #2 pencil to grid your name and student number on the answer sheet provided. Mark your answers to the following questions about paragraphs on your answer sheet.

I. PARAGRAPHS

I.A.3   **1.** Which of the following descriptions bests fits a paragraph?
  A. One complete sentence that is either declarative or exclamatory
  B. A set of three or more sentences with the first sentence indented
  C. A compound, complex sentence that is indented
  D. A topic sentence

I.B.3   **2.** Which of the following descriptions best fits a paragraph?
  A. A series of sentences on many topics
  B. A series of sentences on three topics
  C. An indented sentence on one topic
  D. A series of sentences on one topic

I.D.1   **3.** Which of the following paragraphs is correctly indented?

A	B
I don't think it will ever stop raining. It was raining Friday when I came home from school. It rained all day Saturday. It rained so hard Sunday that the picnic was canceled. The sun, if it ever shines again, will certainly be a welcome sight.	I don't think it will ever stop raining. It was raining Friday when I came home from school. It rained all day Saturday. It rained so hard Sunday that the picnic was canceled. The sun, if it ever shines again, will certainly be a welcome sight.

I.D.2   **4.** Which of the following is a paragraph?

A	B
The largest trees grow from very small seeds. Usually the children in my class exchange valentines. If I do my chores without complaining, I get to choose something special I like to do each weekend.	It seems that strawberries are ripe before blackberries. I like raspberries, especially in ice cream. Some people put blueberries in their cereal. Apples ripen after berry season.

C	D
Hot air balloons of all colors soared across the sky last weekend. They reminded me of a hawk sailing along on air currents. I got a pair of stilts last weekend, and I almost broke my neck trying to learn to walk on them.	Sometimes I feel very lonely. I feel lonely when I look across a large, empty pasture. The feeling stirs when I look up and see thousands of stars in the sky or walk at the beach. It is not an unpleasant feeling . . . just a lonely one.

II. TOPIC SENTENCES

II.A.3   **5.** Which of the following descriptions best fits a topic sentence?
      A. Usually the first sentence in a paragraph, indented
      B. Usually the middle sentence in a paragraph
      C. Usually the last sentence in a paragraph

II.B.3   **6.** Which of the following descriptions best fits a topic sentence?
      A. It introduces the subject in a paragraph
      B. It expands the subject or ideas in a paragraph
      C. It summarizes the topic in a paragraph

II.C.3   **7.** Which one of the following qualities is important for topic sentences?
      A. Transition to the topic
      B. Sequence of ideas in the paragraph
      C. Relevant to the ideas presented in the paragraph

II.D.1. *Directions:* Locate the topic sentences in paragraphs 8 and 9. Mark the letter before the topic sentence on your answer sheet for each question number.

Question 8	Question 9
(A) Spring is the Season of beginnings. (B) The spring winds carry the smell of new blossoms through open windows and help birds return to build new homes. (C) Gentle rains nudge buds on trees and lilac bushes. (D) Bright sunshine encourages children to come outside to make new friends and learn new games. (E) These beginnings are so welcome after the long winter.	(A) "This is my first dance, and it seems a little weird. (B) The lights in the gym are dim and romantic, but I can't see who is standing across the room. (C) The music is loud and great, but it's pretty hard to talk without shouting. (D) We all said we were going to dance, but we're just standing here and watching. (E) Would you like to dance? (F) I said, would you like to dance?"

II.E.1 *Directions:* Read the following incomplete paragraphs carefully and then choose the best topic sentence for each one from among the sentences provided.

    10. _____ . An isosceles triangle has two sides that are the same length. An equilateral triangle has three sides that are the same length, while a scalene triangle has three unequal sides. A right triangle has two sides that are perpendicular and form a 90 degree angle.

    Topic Sentences:
    A. There are lots of types of triangles
    B. There are only four kinds of triangles.
    C. Triangles are described by the length of their sides and the angles they form.

11. _____ . They are the queen, the workers, and the drones. The queen bee is the only bee in the colony that can lay eggs, and she can lay enough eggs to form an entirely new colony. The worker bees are female bees, and they gather food, clean the hive, feed the young bees, and tend the queen bee. The drones are the male bees, and their role is to mate with the queen bee.

Topic Sentences:
A. There are three types of bees in a colony, and they differ by gender and role.
B. Entirely new bee colonies are created by the queen bee.
C. Drone bees appear to have an easy life compared to other bees.
D. If it weren't for the workers, members of a bee colony might go hungry.

12. _____ . Inside the state, the governor chooses citizens for important jobs in the state government. He/she develops and proposes a budget for determining how state revenues will be spent each year. Nationally, the governor works with governors from other states to plan and implement cross-state programs. He/she is also the coordinator between federal and state programs. The governor has many jobs as head of the executive branch.

Topic Sentences:
A. The governor and lieutenant governor are a team.
B. The federal and state governments are a team.
C. The governor must work very hard.
D. The governor of a state has many responsibilities.

II.F.1 *Directions:* Write topic sentences for each of the following incomplete paragraphs. Use your own paper to write the topic sentences. Write your name in the upper left corner and today's date in the upper right corner of your paper. Put the question number (e.g., 13, 14, 15) on your paper, and write the topic sentence for each paragraph beside the correct question number.

13. _____ . Hunting tribes moved often, and they lived in "portable" homes that could be built quickly. They moved their homes and villages several times during a year to match the hunting seasons. Farming tribes, on the other hand, stayed in one place to tend their crops. Since the farmers were not mobile, they built sturdy, permanent homes. The type of homes the tribes built depended on their needs.

14. _____ . We can have fluoride treatments for our teeth at the dentist's office. We can brush our teeth carefully using a fluoride toothpaste after each meal. Before bedtime, we can floss our teeth, brush with a fluoride toothpaste, and rinse our mouth with a mild salt-water solution. Good dental hygiene saves smiles, money, and pain.

15. _____ . Valentine's Day isn't about candy and flowers. The Fourth of July isn't about picnics and fireworks. Thanksgiving isn't about turkey and pie. These are the ways in which we celebrate and not the reasons why we celebrate.

HAVE YOU CHECKED YOUR WORK?
DID YOU ANSWER ALL QUESTIONS?
DID YOU ERASE CLEANLY?

IS YOUR NAME ON YOUR ANSWER SHEET AND ON YOUR TOPIC SENTENCES PAPER?

APPENDIX F

First Practice Test for the Topic Sentence Area (II.1)

Name _____ **Date** _____

II.A.2   1. Within a paragraph, the first sentence that is indented is called the _____ sentence.

II.B.2   2. The sentence that introduces the subject of a paragraph is called the _____ sentence.

II.C.1   3. Name three quality characteristics of topic sentences. _____ , _____ , _____ .

II.D.1   4. Underline the topic sentence in the following paragraph.

> Many claim that besides tasting good, garlic has several benefits for people. First, it is believed to help us digest our food after meals. Second, it just might help lower blood pressure and reduce the risk from strokes. Third, some think it is an antiseptic that kills germs. Finally, its use in warding off vampires has been well documented in novels and films.

II.E.2   *Directions:* Judge the quality of the topic sentences in the following paragraphs. After reading
II.E.3   each paragraph, circle the letter before the statement that best describes the topic sentence in the paragraph.

II.E.2   5.   The quality of our school depends on the motivation and skills of many different people in our community. As students, we must want to learn new ideas and skills, and we need to try our best in order to learn. Our teachers must truly want to help us learn and to work with us until we do. Our principals and counselors must work hard to assist teachers in their quest to help us learn. Although not present in the school, the citizens and tax payers of our town must work hard to support our school. When all these different people pull together as a team, an excellent school is the result.

The topic sentence is:
A. Good as it is written
B. **Not relevant** to the information contained in the paragraph
C. **Too narrow in scope** for the paragraph
D. **Too broad in scope** for the paragraph
E. Missing in the paragraph

Note: Answers to verbal information items (1–3) are readily discernible from other items on the test. This cueing problem is difficult to avoid in tests at the lesson (single-concept) level; however, it is not a problem since the test is designed as a practice exercise. Those students who do not yet know the terminology will certainly get a good reminder from the test.

II.E.3   6.   Maps are abstract pictures of the earth. The flat shape of maps makes them very convenient to use. They can be bound into books for study, or they can be folded to take along on a
journey. The round shape of a globe provides a more realistic view of the earth in its natural
form. Globes, however, are not as convenient to use since they cannot be bound into books or
carried along on vacation. Both maps and globes help us view our world.

The topic sentence is:
A. Good as it is written
B. **Not relevant** to the information contained in the paragraph
C. **Too narrow in scope** for the paragraph
D. **Too broad in scope** for the paragraph
E. Missing in the paragraph

II.E.2   7.   It is amazing that birds can find their way home after migrating so far each winter. One
type of feather grows closest to the bird's body, and it is short, soft, and fluffy. The purpose
for these inner feathers is to keep the bird warm. The feathers covering these soft feathers are
longer and stiffer. These cover feathers give the bird its unique color and shape, and they
keep water off the bird's body. A third type of feather can be found on the bird's wings and
tail. These feathers are longer still and stiff, and they are necessary to help birds fly. Each
type of feather is textured, colored, and shaped for its use.

The topic sentence is:
A. Good as it is written
B. **Not relevant** to the information contained in the paragraph
C. **Too narrow in scope** for the paragraph
D. **Too broad in scope** for the paragraph
E. Missing in the paragraph

II.E.3   8.   I do many special things when I visit my grandfather's farm. I take walks in the woods
and identify the different types of plants that grow there. I pet the kittens that live in the
barn and the horses as they graze in the fields. I watch the pigs try to root out a cool spot on
a hot summer day. I follow the cow paths to meet the cows and walk them back to the barn
in the evening. A visit to his farm is like a visit to nature itself.

The topic sentence is:
A. Good as it is written
B. **Not relevant** to the information contained in the paragraph
C. **Too narrow in scope** for the paragraph
D. **Too broad in scope** for the paragraph
E. Missing in the paragraph

II.E.5 *Directions:* Study the following paragraphs and **rewrite** the topic sentences to meet the quality
criteria. Write your sentences in the space provided at the bottom of each paragraph.

9.   Dogs, cats, birds, and fish make very good pets. Dogs serve as companions and friends
for children, adults, and elderly people. They greet you at the door to welcome you home
in the evening. They often accompany you on walks around the neighborhood. Many dogs
play with you by chasing sticks and balls. They can even work for you by barking when stran-
gers come into your yard or near your house. Having a good dog is like having a good friend.

Revised topic sentence:

_____

10.   Roses are very pretty. First, locate a spot in your yard that gets at least five hours of sun daily. Next, dig a hole big enough to hold the rose planter. Line the bottom of the hole with good soil and a small bit of fertilizer. Then, remove the rose from the pot and lower it gently into the hole. Hold the bush upright with one hand while you fill around it with soil. Water around the plant with a hose, and fill any holes that develop in the soil as you water. Water and dust weekly, fertilize monthly, and soon you will have your own roses.

Revised topic sentence:

_____

11.   Houses have windows. Windows are measured in square inches. To find the area of a window, measure the height of the window of inches. Then, measure the width of the window in inches. Multiply the window's height by its width and you have the area of the window. For example, if the window is 30 inches tall and 20 inches wide, its area is 600 square inches.

Revised topic sentence:

_____

APPENDIX G

Paragraph Unit Posttest (Topic Sentence Portion)

Name _____ Date _____

II.A.4 3. In a paragraph, what is the first, indented sentence typically called?
   A. Concluding sentence
   B. Declarative sentence
   C. Supporting sentence
   D. Topic sentence

II.B.4 4. What sentence introduces the subject presented in the paragraph?
   A. Concluding sentence
   B. Declarative sentence
   C. Supporting sentence
   D. Topic sentence

II.C.4 5. What sentence in a paragraph is (a) relevant to the topic, (b) appropriate in scope for the information that follows it, and (c) interesting to attract the reader's attention?
   A. Concluding sentence
   B. Declarative sentence
   C. Supporting sentence
   D. Topic sentence

II.D.1 *Directions:* Locate the topic sentences in the following paragraphs. Place the number before the topic sentence on your answer sheet for each question.

Question 6	Question 7
(1) In order to determine how heavy an object is, we can measure it in ounces, pounds, or tons. (2) There are 16 ounces in a pound and 2000 pounds in a ton. (3) Some measuring scales only measure in ounces, some in pounds and ounces, and others in tons and pounds. (4) Regardless of the size of an object, there is usually a scale that can be used to measure its weight.	(1) The state fair started Saturday. (2) This year there will be sewing contests, vegetable growing contests, cooking contests, art contests, animal contests, and much more. (3) There is lots of food for sale in the booths along the midway. (4) Besides all this, there are great rides to enjoy. (5) If you have time, you should come to the fair.

Note: The verbal information questions on the posttest (3–5) would be located with the verbal information questions from general paragraph, supporting sentence, and concluding sentence objectives. Placing items together from all the verbal information objectives will eliminate the problem of clueing terminology from other items related to topic sentences.

II.E.1   *Directions:* Read the following incomplete paragraphs carefully and then choose the best topic sentence for each one from among the sentences provided.

II.E.1   8.   _____ . My piano teacher says that I am really getting better. The recital is only a month away, and I plan to practice very hard each day. With lots of practice, I can be even better by the time the recital is here. Playing the piano and getting better all the time are very enjoyable to me.

Topic sentences:
A. Piano is fun.
B. I have been practicing the piano a lot lately.
C. Recitals make me nervous.
D. My piano teacher expects too much of me.

II.E.1   9.   _____ . Mother says that one way I can show others that I am responsible is always to be on time. She said I should be on time for school, and I should always be on time when I come home from school. She said I should arrive at a friend's house or a game at the time I said I would be there. She believes that I should also leave a friend's house at the designated time and not over-extend my welcome. I think I will get a watch and at least try to be on time.

Topic sentences:
A. There is never enough time.
B. Responsibility is important at home and school.
C. Dad said that I was irresponsible, but I really didn't mean to be.
D. I enjoy visiting at a friend's house as long as I don't stay too long.

Directions: Evaluate the topic sentences in the following paragraphs. After reading the topic sentence and the complete paragraph, select the one description from beneath the paragraph that you believe best fits the topic sentence.

II.E.1   10.   Many people in our neighborhood have garage sales. You should begin planning your sale a week or two in advance. First, scour your room, the family room, the attic, the basement, and the garage to find old toys and games that you have outgrown. Second, go over your sale items with your parents to see that they do not have other plans for the items you picked. Next plan a sale price for each item with your parents and tag the items. When you are ready, move your items outside, post signs, and begin the sale!

Topic sentence is:
A. Good the way it is written.
B. The topic sentence is not relevant.
C. The topic sentence is too broad.
D. The topic sentence is too specific.

II.E.4   11.   Tennis is a game that is very hard to play. With a lot of practice, some people can get pretty good, but most people never quite get the swing of it. No matter how hard I try, I just do not seem to get better. I think I will try golf instead!

Topic sentence is:
A. Good the way it is written.
B. The topic sentence is not relevant.
C. The topic sentence is too broad.
D. The topic sentence is too specific.

Directions: Write topic sentences for each of the following incomplete paragraphs. Use your own paper to write the topic sentences. Write your name in the upper left corner and today's date in the upper right corner of your paper. Put the question number (e.g., 12, 13) on your paper, and write the topic sentence for each paragraph beside the correct question number.

II.F.1 12. _____ . I can sleep in. I can help others who need it at home or in my neighborhood. I could come up with a scheme to earn some money. I could have a friend over or go to a friend's house. I could walk alone along a stream and watch the water go by. Oh, so much to do . . . so few Saturdays.

II.F.1 13. _____ . We can all play an important part in conserving energy at home and at school. We can turn lights off when we leave a room. We can take shorter showers and turn off the water while we brush our teeth. We can recycle paper, bottles, and plastic. If we all try, our natural resources will last longer.

Sample Rating Scale

TABLE 9.12

A Sample Rating Scale for Evaluating Students' Original Paragraphs

WRITING PROCEDURAL PARAGRAPHS (WASHING A DOG)					
Name _____		Date _____	Score _____ (44) _____%		
Criteria	No 0	Vaguely 1	Mostly 2	Well 3	**Comments**
I. Paragraph (7)					
A.1 Four to six sentences	0	1 (Yes)			
A.2 Indented	0	1 (Yes)			
B.1 Only one topic		1	2		
C.1 Describes procedure		1	2	3	
II. Topic Sentence (10)	0	1 (Included)			
A.1 Location (first)	0	1 (Yes)			
B.2 Introduces topic		1	2		
C.1 Relevant to paragraph		1	2		
C.2 Appropriate scope		1	2		
C.3 Interest for reader		1	2		
III. Supporting Sentences (14)	0	1 (Included)			
A.1 Location (middle)	0	1 (Yes)			
B.2 Elaborates topic		1	2	3	
C.1 Relevant to topic		1	2	3	
C.2 Sequence of ideas		1	2	3	
C.3 Transition		1	2	3	
IV. Concluding Sentence (13)	0	1 (Included)			
A.1 Location (last)	0	1 (Yes)			
B.1 Summarizes		1	2	3	
C.1 Transition		1	2	3	
C.2 Relevance		1	2	3	
C.3 Scope		1	2		
Totals	( )	+ ( )	+ ( )	= _____	

APPENDIX I

Sample Group Performance Measures

FIGURE 6.11

Group Performance Measures for the Paragraph Unit Posttest

X	f	fX	x	x^2	fx^2
43	5	215	5	25	125
42	2	84	4	16	32
41	1	41	3	9	9
40	1	40	2	4	4
39	1	39	1	1	1
38	1	38	0	0	0
37	2	74	−1	1	2
36	1	36	−2	4	4
35	2	70	−3	9	18
34	1	34	−4	16	16
33	1	33	−5	25	25
32	1	32	−6	36	36
24	1	24	−14	196	196
Sums	20	760			468

Central Tendency
Mean 760/20 = 38
Median 38.5
Mode 43

Variability
Range 19
Standard
Deviation 4.84

Distribution: Negatively Skewed

FIGURE 6.12

Paragraph Unit Posttest Data Recalculated after Eliminating Outlier Student's Raw Score

X	f	fX	x	x^2	fx^2
43	5	215	4.26	18.75	90.75
42	2	84	3.26	10.63	21.26
41	1	41	2.26	5.11	5.11
40	1	40	1.26	1.59	1.59
39	1	39	.26	.07	.07
38	1	38	−.74	.55	.55
37	2	74	−1.74	3.03	6.06
36	1	36	−2.74	7.51	7.51
35	2	70	−3.74	13.99	27.98
34	1	34	−4.74	22.47	22.47
33	1	33	−5.74	32.95	32.95
32	1	32	−6.74	45.43	45.43
Sums	19	736			261.73

Central Tendency
Mean 736/19 = 38.74
Median 39
Mode 43

Variability
Range 43 − 32 = 11
Standard
Deviation 3.71

Distribution: Negatively Skewed

Sample Item Analysis

TABLE 7.18
Item Analysis for the Topic Sentence Portion of the Paragraph Posttest (Objectives II.A.4 to II.F.1 in Tables 3.6 and 4.2)

	TOPIC SENTENCE OBJECTIVES						
Objective Codes	II.A.4	II.B.4	II.C.4	II.D.1	II.E.1	II.E.4	II.F.1
Items	3	4	5	6 7	8 9	10 11	12 13
Correct Answers	4	4	4	1 1	2 4	1 4	*Hand Scored*
Augustine	*	*	*	* *	* *	* *	* *
Prince	*	*	*	* *	* *	* *	* *
Deddens	*	*	*	* *	* *	* *	* *
Talbot	*	*	*	* *	* *	* *	* *
McComas	*	*	*	* *	* *	* *	* *
Rust	*	*	*	* *	* *	* *	* *
Carey	*	*	*	* *	* *	* *	* *
Cromer	*	*	*	* *	* *	* *	* *
Hager	*	*	*	* *	* *	* *	* *
McLaughlin	*	*	*	* *	* *	* *	* *
White	*	*	*	* *	* *	* *	* *
Otto	*	*	*	* *	* *	* *	* *
Lovejoy	*	*	*	* *	* *	* *	* *
Hill	*	*	*	* *	* *	* *	* *
Scragg	*	*	2	* *	* *	* *	* *
Gormley	*	*	3	* *	* 3	* *	* *
Bailey	*	*	2	* *	1 *	* *	* *
Deiters	*	*	2	* *	* 3	* *	* x

Objective Codes	II.A.4	II.B.4	II.C.4	II.D.1	II.E.1	II.E.4	II.F.1
Items	3	4	5	6 7	8 9	10 11	12 13
Correct Answers	*4*	*4*	*4*	*1 1*	*2 4*	*1 4*	*Hand Scored*
Stewart	*	*	3	* *	* *	2 *	* x
Smith	*	*	2	* *	* 3	2 2	x x
Total p	1.0	1.0	.70	1.0 1.0	.95 .85	.90 .95	.95 .85
p_{ul}	1.0	1.0	.50	1.0 1.0	.90 .70	.80 .90	.90 .70
d	.00	.00	1.00	.00 .00	.20 .60	.40 .20	.20 .60
r_{pbi}	.00	.00	.79	.00 .00	.19 .63	.69 .67	.67 .72

Sample Norm-Referenced Analysis and Mastery Analysis

TABLE 8.3

Norm-Referenced Analysis of Students' Achievement on the Objective Portion of the Paragraph Unit Posttest

N = 20 **Mean = 38**	**Standard** **Deviation = 4.84**					**N = 19** **Mean = 38.74**	**Standard** **Deviation = 3.71**	
	Total Class Group						**Recalculated without Outlier**	
X	Percentage Correct	f	z	T	Percentile	z	T	Percentile
43	100	5	1.03	60	88	1.15	61	87
42	98	2	.83	58	70	.88	59	68
41	95	1	.62	56	63	.61	56	61
40	93	1	.41	54	58	.34	53	55
39	91	1	.21	52	53	.07	51	50
38	88	1	.00	50	48	.20	48	45
37	86	2	−.21	48	40	−.47	45	37
36	84	1	−.41	46	33	−.74	43	29
35	81	2	−.62	44	25	−1.00	40	21
34	79	1	−.83	42	18	−1.28	37	13
33	77	1	−1.03	40	13	−1.55	35	8
32	74	1	−1.24	38	8	−1.82	32	3
24	56	1	−2.89	21	2			

Note: Using the total class group: A z score for the raw score 43 is calculated as follows: $(43 − 38)/4.84 = 1.03$. A T score for the raw score 43 is calculated as follows: $(1.03 \times 10) + 50 = 60$. A percentile score for the raw score 43 is calculated as follows: $(15 + 2.5)/20 \times 100 = 88$.

TABLE 8.6

Mastery Analysis of Students' Performance for Only the Topic Sentence Portion of the Paragraph Posttest (Objectives II.A.4 to II.F.1 in Tables 3.6 and 4.2)

	TOPIC SENTENCE OBJECTIVES							
Objective Codes	II.A.4	II.B.4	II.C.4	II.D.1	II.E.1	II.E.4	II.F.1	Total Objectives Mastered
Items:	3	4	5	6 7	8 9	10 11	12 13	7
Correct Answers:	4	4	4	1 1	2 4	1 4	Hand Scored	
Augustine	*	*	*	* *	* *	* *	* *	7
Prince	*	*	*	* *	* *	* *	* *	7
Deddens	*	*	*	* *	* *	* *	* *	7
Talbot	*	*	*	* *	* *	* *	* *	7
McComas	*	*	*	* *	* *	* *	* *	7
Rust	*	*	*	* *	* *	* *	* *	7
Carey	*	*	*	* *	* *	* *	* *	7
Cromer	*	*	*	* *	* *	* *	* *	7
Hager	*	*	*	* *	* *	* *	* *	7
McLaughlin	*	*	*	* *	* *	* *	* *	7
White	*	*	*	* *	* *	* *	* *	7
Otto	*	*	*	* *	* *	* *	* *	7
Lovejoy	*	*	*	* *	* *	* *	* *	7
Hill	*	*	*	* *	* *	* *	* *	7
Scragg	*	*	2	* *	* *	* *	* *	6
Gormley	*	3	*	* *	* 3	* *	* *	5
Bailey	*	*	2	* *	1 *	* *	* *	5
Deiters	*	*	2	* *	* 3	* *	* x	4
Stewart	*	*	3	* *	* *	2 *	* x	4
Smith	*	*	2	* *	* 3	2 1	x x	3
Number of Students Who Mastered	20	20	14	20	16	18	17	
Percentage of Students Who Mastered	100%	100%	70%	100%	80%	90%	85%	

521

TABLE 8.7
Prescribed Instructional Activities Based on Mastery Analysis

CONCEPTS/ CONTENT	A State/Recall Physical Characteristics of:	B State/Recall Functional Characteristics of:	C State/Recall Quality Characteristics of:	D Discriminate Between Examples & Nonexamples	E Evaluate Given Examples	F Produce Examples of:
I. Topic Sentence			Bailey Deiters Gormley Scragg Smith Stewart		Bailey Deiters Gormley Smith Stewart	Deiters Smith Stewart
III. Supporting Sentences						
IV. Concluding Sentence						

TABLE 8.8
A Partial Student Progress Chart for the Instructional Goal, "Write a Paragraph"

ENABLING SKILLS	PARAGRAPH			TOPIC SENTENCES							
	I A	I B	I D	II A	II B	II C	II D	II E	II F	II	Etc.
Augustine	x	x	x	x	x	x	x	x	x	M	
Bailey	x	x	x	x	x		x		x	PM	
Carey	x	x	x	x	x	x	x	x	x	M	
Cromer	x	x	x	x	x	x	x	x	x	M	
Deddens	x	x	x	x	x	x	x	x	x	M	
Deiters	x	x	x	x	x		x				
Gormley	x	x	x	x	x		x		x	PM	
Hager	x	x	x	x	x	x	x	x	x	M	
Hill		x	x	x	x	x	x	x	x	M	
Lovejoy	x	x	x	x	x	x	x	x	x	M	
McComas	x	x	x	x	x	x	x	x	x	M	
McLaughlin	x	x	x	x	x	x	x	x	x	M	
Otto	x	x	x	x	x	x	x	x	x	M	
Prince	x	x	x	x	x	x	x	x	x	M	
Rust	x	x	x	x	x	x	x	x	x	M	
Scragg	x	x	x	x	x		x	x	x	M	
Smith	x	x	x	x	x		x				
Stewart	x	x	x	x	x		x				
Talbot	x	x	x	x	x	x	x	x	x	M	
White	x	x	x	x	x	x	x	x	x	M	

Note: x = at least minimal mastery of enabling skill; **PM** = Partial Mastery of concept strand (e.g., topic sentences, supporting sentences, and concluding sentences); **M** = Mastery of concept strand.

INDEX